ESSAYS: THE PHILOSOPHY CLASSIC

Also available in the same series:

Beyond Good and Evil: The Philosophy Classic
by Friedrich Nietzsche (ISBN: 978-0-857-08848-2)

Meditations: The Philosophy Classic
by Marcus Aurelius (ISBN 978-0-857-08846-8)

On the Origin of Species: The Science Classic
by Charles Darwin (ISBN: 978-0-857-08847-5)

Tao Te Ching: The Ancient Classic
by Lao Tzu (ISBN: 978-0-857-08311-1)

The Art of War: The Ancient Classic
by Sun Tzu (ISBN: 978-0-857-08009-7)

The Game of Life and How to Play It: The Self-Help Classic
by Florence Scovel Shinn (ISBN: 978-0-857-08840-6)

The Interpretation of Dreams: The Psychology Classic
by Sigmund Freud (ISBN: 978-0-857-08844-4)

The Prince: The Original Classic
by Niccolò Machiavelli (ISBN: 978-0-857-08078-3)

The Republic: The Influential Classic
by Plato (ISBN: 978-0-857-08313-5)

The Science of Getting Rich: The Original Classic
by Wallace Wattles (ISBN: 978-0-857-08008-0)

The Wealth of Nations: The Economics Classic
by Adam Smith (ISBN: 978-0-857-08077-6)

Think and Grow Rich: The Original Classic
by Napoleon Hill (ISBN: 978-1-906-46559-9)

The Prophet: The Spiritual Classic
by Kahlil Gibran (ISBN: 978–0–857–08855-0)

Utopia: The Influential Classic
by Thomas More (ISBN: 978-1-119-75438-1)

The Communist Manifesto: The Political Classic
by Karl Marx and Friedrich Engels (ISBN: 978-0-857-08876-5)

Letters from a Stoic: The Ancient Classic
by Seneca (ISBN: 978-1-119-75135-9)

A Room of One's Own: The Feminist Classic
by Virginia Woolf (ISBN: 978-0-857-08882-6)

Twelve Years a Slave: The Black History Classic
by Solomon Northup (ISBN: 978-0-857-08906-9)

Narrative of the Life of Frederick Douglass: The Black History Classic
by Frederick Douglass (ISBN: 978-0-857-08910-6)

The Interesting Narrative of Olaudah Equiano: The Black History Classic
by Olaudah Equiano (ISBN: 978-0-857-08913-7)

Thus Spoke Zarathustra: The Philosophy Classic
by Friedrich Nietzsche (ISBN: 978-0-857-08930-4)

ESSAYS

The Philosophy Classic
A Selected Edition for the Modern
Reader

MICHEL DE MONTAIGNE

With an Introduction by
PHILIPPE DESAN

CAPSTONE
A Wiley Brand

This edition first published 2022
Introduction copyright © 2022 Philippe Desan

This edition of *Essays* is based on the English translation of 1685 by Charles Cotton, edited by William Carew Hazlitt in 1877, which is in the public domain.

Registered office
John Wiley & Sons Ltd, The Atrium, Southern Gate, Chichester, West Sussex, PO19 8SQ, United Kingdom

Editorial Office
John Wiley & Sons Ltd, The Atrium, Southern Gate, Chichester, West Sussex, PO19 8SQ, United Kingdom

For details of our global editorial offices, customer services, and more information about Wiley products visit us at www.wiley.com.

Wiley also publishes its books in a variety of electronic formats and by print-on-demand. Some content that appears in standard print versions of this book may not be available in other formats.

Designations used by companies to distinguish their products are often claimed as trademarks. All brand names and product names used in this book are trade names, service marks, trademarks or registered trademarks of their respective owners. The publisher is not associated with any product or vendor mentioned in this book.

Library of Congress Cataloging-in-Publication Data is Available:

ISBN 9780857089335 (hardback)
ISBN 9780857089342 (ePub)
ISBN 9780857089359 (ePDF)

Cover Design: Wiley

Set in 10/13 pt ITC New Baskerville Std by Straive

C089335_210222

CONTENTS

Michel de Montaigne, c. 1590, anonymous artist

AN INTRODUCTION

BY PHILIPPE DESAN

Michel de Montaigne was born in 1533.

His father had high ambitions for his son and made certain he received the best education possible at the College de Guyenne in Bordeaux. The young Michel excelled at Latin and was an avid reader of the ancients. His favorite readings were Plutarch and Seneca, with a particular interest in past historians. Later, his father bought him a public charge so that Michel could enter the Parlement of Bordeaux (judicial Court of Appeal) as a young magistrate. However, political and religious tensions were so extreme in the southwest of France of the 1560s that, unable to adjust to the intricacies of local politics, Montaigne eventually abandoned his public roles.

After the death of his father in 1569, Montaigne retired as a gentleman on his *seigneurie* (feudal lands) with the intention of living "nobly". His political patrons, the Foix family, arranged for him to be knighted in the highly coveted Order of Saint Michael (at the time the highest honor for a nobleman in France). This "proof" of his nobility represented quite an accomplishment for someone whose ancestors were merely rich merchants and had become *bourgeois* of the city of Bordeaux, thanks to the commerce of wine and salt fish.

Because of his new noble aspirations, Michel abandoned his patronymic name of Eyquem and adopted the name of the noble house – Montaigne – purchased by his grandfather, Ramon Eyquem, in 1477. He was henceforth known as "Lord Michel de Montaigne, Knight of the noble Order of St Michael, and one of the Gentlemen in Ordinary of the French King's Chamber".

THE ESSAYS

In 1580, Montaigne published in Bordeaux a book unique in its title: *Essays*. A literary genre was born. In a time when most books were about great people or events, or works of academic theology or philosophy, the author tells the reader that his only desire is to show himself "familiar and private". He denies any intention of glory for himself or benefit to his reader:

"Had my intention been to forestall and purchase the world's opinion and favor, I would surely have adorned myself more quaintly, or kept a more grave or solemn march."

In his opening message "To the Reader", he declares his will to paint himself "in my simple, natural, and ordinary garb, without study or artifice, for it was myself I had to paint." He ends the note by saying, "Thus, reader, I am myself the subject of my book; it is not worth your while to take up your time longer with such a frivolous matter."

We must take these declarations of humility with a grain of salt, and indeed they may simply have been a literary strategy for the author of a work categorized as a "novelty" by its publisher – an author who, after all, was not then famous, and who had apparently not accomplished anything worth writing about. It is telling that, after a few editions of the *Essays*, and after he had become much better known, Montaigne would never modify this modest-sounding Preface to the reader.

Montaigne started writing his first essays (all very short) in 1571, when he was in his late thirties. Over the next 20 years, until his death in 1592, he would rewrite and republish the *Essays* several times. However, it would be false to believe that Montaigne was only a writer. He had diplomatic and political aspirations, and the literary aspect of his career always came *after* his political and public life, at least until he became very sick (kidney stones) after 1590.

In 1581, Montaigne became mayor of Bordeaux, the fifth-largest city in France at this time. In 1582, his publisher took advantage of his new political visibility to publish a second edition of the *Essays*. In 1588, with his growing notoriety, Montaigne published a third edition with copious additions and even added a third book with 13 new chapters. He was now published in Paris by one of the most successful publishers and book dealers of his time: Abel L'Angelier. Until his death, Montaigne would continue adding text in the margins of his copy of this Parisian edition.

There is a habit among modern editors of the *Essays* to segment Montaigne's text in three layers, often signaled by A, B, and C. These correspond to three different editions (1580, 1588, and the posthumous edition of 1595). The text of the first edition (1580) represents approximately 44 percent of the complete *Essays*. The additions between 1580 and 1588 (with the third book added) amount to another 33 percent of the total text, and the marginal manuscript additions written between 1588 and his death (published in the first posthumous edition of 1595 by Marie de Gournay) make up another 23 percent of a complete modern edition of the *Essays*.

However, the book was never intended to be read with these layers in mind. Such editorial artifice might help the modern reader to identify contradictions over time and across editions, but it also creates the impression of an evolution of the text which was never intended by Montaigne. As he pointed out:

"I am grown older by a great many years since my first publications, which were in the year 1580; but I very much doubt whether I am grown an inch the wiser. I now, and I anon, are two several persons; but whether better, I cannot determine" (Book III, Chapter 9).

PERSONAL OVER ABSTRACT

The *Essays* resembles a patchwork of personal reflections which all tend toward a single goal: to live better in the present and to prepare for death. These considerations offer a point of departure for the modern reader's assessment of his or her own life. It is indeed a book in which the "competent reader" (Book I, Chapter 23) must invest themselves in order to benefit personally and, in turn, produce their own judgments. In brief, one does not read Montaigne, one practices Montaigne.

For modern readers, an important question endures while reading the *Essays*: how does one systematize and synthesize the thought of an author who did not claim to write anything other than *essays* – literally "attempts" – bound to never quite succeed? The very form of the essay presupposes its failure, for otherwise it would no longer be an essay. But in the case of Montaigne, the quest is always more interesting and beneficial than the end.

Thinkers and philosophers are meant to create *systems*, not essays! Yet Montaigne elaborated a philosophy of life without precepts, mottos, or systems. His thought claims to be amorphous, or better, multisided (which does not mean powerless). Whereas Descartes and all Western thought, from the seventeenth century on, sought to develop philosophies *of content*, Montaigne, on the contrary, endeavored to think in terms of *the form* itself, or rather many different forms of thought, knowledge, and human experience. For him, these forms can only be apprehended in their relation to other thoughts, other cultures, other possible worlds (Christopher Columbus had recently "discovered" a New World).

Montaigne's true originality is to think of form itself as an organizing principle of all knowledge. All is form – or rather *forms* – since diversity and variety are inherent to the human condition. For example, he argues that what matters is not what is said but how we say it. Things are a matter of opinion ruled by subjectivity. He concludes his first edition of the *Essays* with a statement that recaps what is essential in the book:

> "And there never were, in the world, two opinions alike, no more than two hairs, or two grains: their most universal quality is diversity" (Book II, Chapter 37).

For Montaigne, variety is the driving principle of humanity and its history. From the books of the ancients to the worldview of cannibals in the New World, we see the complexity of human thought and practice.

Essays, 1588 edition

MY WORLD, NOT *THE* WORLD

Montaigne makes the conscious decision to describe the world in its multifaceted representations rather than seek to show some prescriptive overlying order. The world is always *his* world, nothing more. Judgment cannot be generalized or imposed on others. For this reason, civilizations must be understood on their own terms and should not be judged according to their "advancements" in relation to other civilizations. On this point, Montaigne is very critical of the conquest of the New World and its accompanying moral discourse. He prefers to imagine himself on the other side of what he observes, so that he can understand fully what it feels like and means to be different.

The more he looks at customs around the world, the more he doubts that humans can be generalized into a single essence. He excels at describing his own existence (with its particular experiences) in relation to other existences and develops his method of *distingo*: understanding oneself first, one can begin to understand others. This interactionist principle of human existence defines Montaigne's writing – and it is an approach we should take seriously, today more than ever.

Starting from a materialist perspective (the existential conditions observable throughout the world and universe), Montaigne realizes that the body is the foundation for all knowledge, and that the mind itself is inseparable from the body:

"Is it not a ridiculous attempt for us to forge for those to whom, by our own confession, our knowledge is not able to attain, another body, and to lend a false form of our own invention; as is manifest in this motion of the planets; to which, seeing our wits cannot possibly arrive, nor conceive their natural conduct, we lend them material, heavy, and substantial springs of our own by which to move. . ." (Book II, Chapter 12).

Human experience has limits, which is where the mind comes in. In this crucial moment – one that defines "modernity" – knowledge thus depends on both the experiences of the body and the conceptualizations of the mind. They cannot be separated. However, epistemologically, this harmony between what Descartes will call "common sense" (reason) and the senses does not last long. In the seventeenth century they are separated to create modern philosophy, which in its abstractions relegates the senses and the body to "noise".

MONTAIGNE THE PHILOSOPHER

For Montaigne, reason and imagination are both equal in terms of producing new knowledge. Like the oscillations of the world and the universe, "the body and soul are in perpetual moving and action" (II, 37). This perpetual motion defines life itself. Montaigne's philosophy is movement since there can be no knowledge outside the human body. We could argue that Montaigne is a wanderer of writing: "my style and my wit wander at the same rate" (III, 9). The wandering body never allows itself to be imprisoned in common places; it constantly flees forward. Montaigne is always elsewhere; we rarely find him where he tells us he is going. From this understanding, all knowledge becomes relative insofar as it depends on bodily experiences that will sometimes adapt to the mind, and at other times dominate the mind.

Montaigne acknowledges that the mind and the body often assert their monstrosity in remarkable ways (the religious wars of his time, for example), but this is an evil that he deems worthy of consideration and reflection. Theory and action are for him inseparable. As he puts it, "my fancy does not go by itself, as when my legs move it" (III, 3). All ideas require action. The mind may explore the world in all its shapes and forms, but personal experiences validate the ideas that we form. This journey through the meanders of thought – a thought which can only be understood in its relation to different thoughts – leads Montaigne into an analysis of himself, a process we call introspection. While he lays himself open to the many contradictions of his experience, he chooses not to suppress them from his book.

Introspection and reflections about the self only work because Montaigne establishes "commerces" with others, principally his friend who passed away (Étienne de la Boétie), notable women in his circle such as Diane de Foix, and books (ancient philosophers, whom he copiously references and quotes). And yet, Montaigne would not really become the Montaigne we know and appreciate today, i.e. the observer of cultural differences and the founder of anthropology (a discipline that is not prescriptive, but simply tries to describe human variation), until he finally accepted (after 1585) to content himself with "reporting" human behaviors in all their contradictions – rather than looking for a common denominator in them.

"Others form man; I only report him: and represent a particular one, ill fashioned enough, and whom, if I had to model him anew, I should certainly make something else than what he is but that's past recalling" (III, 2).

Montaigne would soon abandon any attempt to find the "human condition" (his term), and therefore a possible unity or an essence of the human race, in order to concentrate on a descriptive anthropology. Descartes is often presented as the architect of modern philosophy (creating a blueprint of human essence). Montaigne remains an endless surveyor, observer and describer of human customs and mores.

MONTAIGNE THE SOCIAL THINKER

No grand theory, no system is present in the *Essays*. Over the centuries, critics have generally refused to consider Montaigne a social thinker; he's been pictured as a literary man and "accidental" philosopher, withdrawn in his tower, playing with his cat. And yet, although there is no project of a better society in the *Essays*, it is possible to identify several constitutive elements of a sociology and an anthropology that we could group under the heading of "social discourse" (one that is often critical of the social organization of his time) in Montaigne's often contradictory statements. This social discourse is manifested in his own political actions as a mayor of Bordeaux and governor of Guyenne. Indeed, Montaigne's two terms as mayor of Bordeaux from 1581 to 1585 allow us to form a more precise idea of his social commitments and his participation in the political debate of his time.

Let us give two examples. Re-elected with difficulty as mayor in 1583, Montaigne turned against the Parlement (his former employer) and denounced abuses such as tax evasion by those who enriched themselves on the backs of the poor. Too many judicial officers were exempt from taxes, and too many relatives of presidents and councilors were declared "noble" and therefore not subject to taxation. In a book of grievances (*cahier de doléances*) addressed to the king, Montaigne and six members of the Jurade (city council) complained about the fact that "the richest and opulent families of the said city would have been exempt" from these taxes "for the privilege claimed by all the officers of justice and their widowers". Thus, in the year 1583, Montaigne spoke firmly regarding social justice and openly criticized the ennoblement of members of Parlement and their families. He spoke as a noble himself and seems to have forgotten his own' family's rise in society. The author of the *Essays* reminded Henry III that the king's justice must be administered free of charge (court actions were expensive) and "to the smallest crowd of the people as possible". He also endorsed the following statement: "all levies might be imposed equally on everyone, the strong carrying the poor, and suggest that it is very reasonable that those who have greater resources feel the burden more than those who survive only by chance and the sweat of their brows".

MONTAIGNE THE POLITICAL ACTOR

Despite Montaigne's social declarations in favor of justice and equality, many of his contemporaries were quick to point out his failure as mayor of Bordeaux. He did not contradict his critics:

"They say also that my administration passed over without leaving any mark or trace. Good! They moreover accuse my cessation in a time when everybody almost was convicted of doing too much" (III, 10).

Indeed, Montaigne was perceived as a "centrist" at a time when extremes assumed power on both sides (Catholics and Protestants). He preferred negotiation and moderation in a time of *coups de force* and violence. But the result of a position perceived as indecisive and feeble-minded was isolation. Montaigne could have done more, but the political price would have been higher still.

His service in public life led him to make some negative judgments upon it in the *Essays*. If the *Essays* had first been conceived as a means to enter public life, it slowly became a means to remove himself from it. Politics is about winners and losers, and Montaigne never felt comfortable with decisions that would please one camp to the detriment of another. He was even accused of nonchalance and indolence by his detractors:

"All public actions are subject to uncertain and various interpretations; for too many heads judge of them. Some say of this civic employment of mine (and I am willing to say a word or two about it, not that it is worth so much, but to give an account of my manners in such things), that I have behaved myself in it as a man who is too supine and of a languid temperament; and they have some color for what they say. I endeavored to keep my mind and my thoughts in repose" (III, 10).

If Montaigne failed in politics, it was perhaps because he was "too human." At least that is the way he liked to represent his political career after his two terms as mayor of Bordeaux. His unconditional confidence in men would have led him to be deceived. After all, he valued nobiliary values (honor and keeping his word, for example) and deplored bourgeois values (efficiency and utility). Likewise, his difficulty in thinking of people as aggregates or groups sharing the same ideology (corporatism, or the "orders" – clergy, nobility, others – of the *Ancien Régime*) turned out to be a disadvantage for someone who only felt comfortable in individual relationships. Montaigne was never a party man, and his personal judgment did not accommodate political platforms or positions supported by what he perceived as unnatural alliances.

Montaigne was ultimately a lone wolf in his political behavior. The *Essays* enabled him to reflect upon his experiences in public life, and he ultimately chose to highlight the positive side. But he wanted to move on. After 1588 (i.e. in the manuscript additions of a copy of the 1588 edition of his *Essays*), Montaigne started to emphasize the private aspect of his book and distanced himself from his former public life.

ON TIME AND HISTORY

Montaigne wrote his *Essays* at a time of great social, religious, and political transformation. In the face of this turmoil, he preferred to focus his attention on the present moment, believing it impossible to predict future behaviors and actions. He considered it a waste of time to imagine a better tomorrow, and to focus on the now:

"I do not paint its being. I paint its passage; not a passing from one age to another, or, as the people say, from seven to seven years, but from day to day, from minute to minute, I must accommodate my history to the hour" (III, 2).

Montaigne made a famous declaration on the wars of religion: "It will be much if, a hundred years hence, it be remembered in general that in our times there were civil wars in France" (II, 16). He was obviously wrong, but that is not the gist of his point. He approached history on a very pragmatic level and could even be labelled a "conservative" when it came to social action. His position was always to avoid turmoil in the public sphere and to therefore make do with the social order in place. Liberty was for him a matter of free speech and freedom of conscience but was never followed by a call to arms. That meant peace at any price, even if the benefits fell to reactionaries. However, this conservatism only applied to public life. His book, on the contrary, represented a personal space to express compassion, respect, and appreciation of differences.

Montaigne theorizes his conception of "immediate history" in several places. For him, events might be given historical importance because they are ideologically invested at different times. The present does not yet have the capacity to "transform documents into monuments" (to cite the French historian and philosopher Michel Foucault in *The Archaeology of Knowledge*), and, for Montaigne, events of his time are purely anecdotal and therefore relegated to an exemplary status. In this sense, Montaigne always remains close to an atomist conception of society and history, rather than looking for great themes or laws that thread through it.

The people, for example, remain an unpredictable entity whose motivations and actions can never be explained in a reasoned way. What is the use of explaining events that respond to other logics, at other times? The social and religious fragmentation of the late Renaissance generated in Montaigne a form of relativism which did not allow any regrouping or organization into rules or laws. We do not learn from the past; it is in this way that the wars of religion can never be invoked in a didactic way. Memory does nothing to help reason.

Let us remind the reader, one last time, that the *Essays* were written over 20 years. It is therefore normal that political and ideological positions expressed in a specific social and political context would change over time. Montaigne, like many of his contemporaries (Machiavelli for example), is pragmatic when it comes to politics, and his sense of adaptation (not to mention evolution) is reflected in his ability to absorb contradictions within the same book, while claiming that his views do not contradict each other. Montaigne literally puts himself to the test:

"whether it be that I am then another self, or that I take sub-jects by other circumstances and considerations: so it is that I may peradventure contradict myself, but, as Demades said, I never contradict the truth. Could my soul once take foot-ing, I would not essay but resolve: but it is always learning and making trial" (III, 2).

Montaigne's position towards the Reformation, for example, changed over time, until it became compatible, in the early 1580s, with the current of politics which sought to guarantee civil peace and was therefore ready to grant more freedoms (of conscience and wor-ship) to Protestants. During times as tormented as the civil wars in France, we understand the difficulty of thinking about the social realm in a systematic fashion. Too many counter-examples weaken possible conclusions on political actions and modes of social organization. Moreover, the acceleration of events gives the feeling of a headlong rush. If we are to produce a theory of anything, it is at the daily level – and, in this sense, this is what Montaigne is doing.

Of course, his study of antiquity allowed Montaigne to find a cer-tain stability of example that contemporaneous events did not provide him. But he was fully aware that things were changing fast, and that his world would never be the same – like the world of the cannibals encountering the foreign invaders. Living through the savagery of the religious wars produced a form of skepticism that was far from aca-demic. It also shaped the form of the essay and produced a permanent questioning.

THE MONTAIGNE METHOD

It is true that Montaigne contradicts himself, which makes reading the *Essays* difficult, and sometimes problematic. The danger with Montaigne is to take him at his word and discover a few pages later that he says the opposite of what he had previously written. An analysis of his declarations organized in themes therefore has its limits. And yet, Montaigne offers personal and social considerations worth meditating on, not as a doctrine or a philosophy, but rather as attempts to seize a problem at a specific time. The *Essays* work as a laboratory that allows us to identify some essential principles of a model of individual and society that is almost always unrealizable, but nonetheless thinkable. For Montaigne, experimentation prevails over application, and the rules resulting from observation and experience never quite allow us to conceive of a social science, or to pass from theory to practice.

Rather than developing a grand analysis of humankind, Montaigne prefers to describe what he observes on the ground (for example, during his travels through Germany, Switzerland, and Italy) or what has been observed directly and without mediation by others (like the sailor who travelled to the New World and was employed by Montaigne). Thus, his reflections on mores and customs should not be seen as philosophical investigations on an abstract and unattainable human condition. For this reason, we cannot speak of a Montaignian ontology, or philosophy of being.

Montaigne strives to understand his own mores – always in their political, religious, and cultural context – in relation to other cultures, other schools, and other systems of thought. But should we only be amazed at otherness? Is it possible to take an inventory of people around the world and infer fundamental rules? These questions are always present in the *Essays*. Even a cursory reading makes it clear that Montaigne does not believe in human "essence". Humans are incredibly varied across cultures, and so the category of "humanity" is problematic. It is safer to just observe singular behaviors and actions.

Until the seventeenth century, resemblance as an organizing principle was enough to create the illusion of a theory of knowledge, of a hidden order which brought together everything that seemed, at first glance, different. The Spanish theologians of the *Conquista* looked at the Indians of the New World in this way, i.e. as a pretext for the domination of other cultures because they could not find in these societies what the West valued (writing, monuments, private property). This ideological bias is criticized by Montaigne in his essay "On Cannibals". On the contrary, valuing difference as an enhancement of his own self, Montaigne delights at seeing himself in the eyes of the cannibals.

Because Montaigne is always aware of his own cultural and social environment, he carefully avoids moral judgment; his interest in different cultures and customs is only illustrative of human complexity. He leaves it to others to find an order in the world and its peoples, and the "progress" of civilizations does not interest him very much. As a good observer, Montaigne turns his gaze towards the generic Other (neighbors, foreigners, cannibals) and tries to understand the irreducibility of cultural specificities: "Every nation has particular opinions touching their use, and particular rules and methods in using them" (II, 37). The "empire of custom" (I, 22) makes us confuse the universal qualities of humans with the importance in our own societies of these "qualities". Being French or German, according to Montaigne, is in fact nothing more than following the customs of these countries. The power of customs even tends to modify human physiology: "You make a German sick if you lay him upon a mattress, as you do an Italian if you lay him on a feather-bed, and a Frenchman, if without curtains or fire. A Spanish stomach cannot hold out to eat as we can, nor ours to drink like the Swiss" (III, 13).

BIRTH OF THE MODERN, SKEPTICAL SELF

Throughout the *Essays*, freedom of personal judgment is privileged over society and education; the subject can always understand the world by himself and for himself. This self-sufficiency of the individual, out of its historical reality, also represents a trap for many modern readers of the *Essays*. In fact, one finds few references to possible political actions in Montaigne's writings; the accent is almost always placed on commenting on the world rather than changing it. Montaigne's trademark is the moment of introspection, withdrawal, and self-sufficiency.

The possibility of a theoretical truth of the world unconsciously conforms with our own bourgeois mentality, precisely because it isolates the subject from its immediate social and political environment. It is true that Montaigne offers a foundation for the liberal ideology that will soon assert itself from the eighteenth century on. Montaigne's doubts and questions about authority (leading to independence of thought and eventually liberty), and the confidence in his own judgment, have been associated with the birth of modern liberalism. A modern self emerges that is distanced from the authorities of the past, enjoying the victory of private judgment over institutions that limit individual freedom. However, this type of ideological appropriation often ignores the biography of Montaigne. He was not a political thinker, and the *Essays* were conceived in a specific political, religious, and social context.

Other critics have seen in Montaigne an adept of skepticism, but they seem to forget that one is not born a sceptic, one becomes one. Skepticism is not a philosophical choice for Montaigne; it is anchored in the reality of his time and resulted from a slow deterioration in moral values during the second half of the sixteenth century. With Montaigne, it is difficult to speak of skepticism in the singular – as the mere expression of the philosophical doctrine of this name. One should rather speak of "skeptical moments" in the plural. These moments were produced by personal experiences which were first and foremost of a political nature before becoming, eventually, a *modus operandi*. Indeed, it is difficult not to link philosophy and political experiences in Montaigne's work.

We have thus often confused a philosophical system – Skepticism – with what, in Montaigne's *Essays*, is essentially an inclination or a posture of the mind in the face of specific negative or dangerous political situations. The *Essays* are strewn with skeptical conclusions and impressions that are the result of Montaigne and his estate being in the middle of an atmosphere of unrest and terror. Shocked by the events he lived through – from the Saint-Bartholomew's Day massacre in 1572 to the assassination of Henry III in 1588 – it is very difficult to regroup his conflicting reactions and attitudes into a doctrine. One thing is certain: the religious situation of France between 1563 (beginning of the religious wars) and 1592 profoundly influenced the writing of Montaigne's book and nourished his skepticism.

THE NECESSITY OF DOUBT

Resistant to models and systems, Montaigne takes pleasure in the fortuitous and contradictory aspect of the multitude of things encountered. He attempts to seize them in the fleeting moment of personal judgment that must be understood within its historical milieu. Judgment is never final, because it expresses a point in time and space, of this man in this world.

Montaigne's biography is filled with these "doubt moments" which, through their repetition, create in the author a skeptical reflex which in time becomes a natural reaction. Yet the reflex has the function of helping him rediscover a moral stability in a time of upheaval – a time when as he famously puts it, "the world eternally turns round" (III, 2).

The various political and religious crises that punctuated the second half of the sixteenth century called into question a morality that was now discredited and obsolete. In short, utility replaced honesty. Montaigne offers an excellent analysis of this moral crisis in "On Profit and Honesty" (III, 1). In this chapter written after 1585, he shows how bourgeois values gradually replaced noble values such as honor, frankness, loyalty, good faith, and moral transparency. Past behaviors no longer exemplified moral models, as personal profit was now established as the only rule of behavior. Montaigne is the witness of this ideological transformation – anchored in historical and economic developments – which sees honor and truth replaced by utility, success, and personal experience. It is perhaps a weaker path "which is a means much more weak and cheap; but truth is so great a thing that we ought not to disdain any mediation that will guide us to it" (III, 13).

The reappraisal of the notion of truth is obviously influenced by Montaigne's personal experiences. They leave him with a feeling of a permanent relativism which no longer allows him to judge anything in a lasting way. In a time when the vicissitudes of religious conflict seemed to govern everything, it makes sense to doubt what education has transmitted to you. In place of eternal values, a new truth has emerged: the truth of those who came out victorious.

Rather than commenting on the political, religious, and social situation of his country, Montaigne takes refuge in personal introspection. It replaces the rhetorical demonstrations of which he was always suspect. Morality is shaped by the military actions of clashing religious forces. Doubt then becomes a natural reflex at a time when all humanist benchmarks are systematically destabilized. The truths of yesterday crumble and the sandy soil upon which philosophy was built suddenly opens. The end of the Renaissance is a yawning abyss that engulfs past practices and knowledge, leaving only the necessity of doubt.

CONCLUSION

To summarize: The famous "the world eternally turns round" evoked by Montaigne no longer allows man to impose on others received knowledge or to claim possession of universal truths. The skeptical attitude which characterized the end of the Renaissance, and of which Montaigne is one of the best examples, was essentially due to an ideological and moral crisis linked to the experience of the wars of religion. In the second half of the sixteenth century, skepticism cannot be conceived of as a philosophical system; it rather a simple reaction to events – a response to a moral crisis which no longer allowed one to have ready-made answers.

The implication, which was clear to Montaigne, was that the truth could no longer be taught; it had to be discovered by the individual subject. In matters of authority, everything was now up for grabs. Far from being received, truth must now be conceived individually from unique and private experiences. Montaigne was for this reason outside any didactic scheme: "so many interpretations dissipate truth and break it" (III, 13). He further concedes that "example is a vague and universal mirror, and of various reflections" (III, 13) and therefore loses its exemplarity. This is why Montaigne systematically deconstructs models to reduce them to specific cases.

At this time of crisis in political, social, and religious authority, the best reasoning comes from seeing what is in front of our eyes, rather than looking for guidance from previously celebrated universal truths. As Montaigne writes in his chapter on Raimond Sebond:

"I always call reason that appearance or show of discourses which every man devised or forged in himself: that reason, of whose condition there may be a hundred, one contrary to another, about one self same subject: it is an instrument of lead and wax, stretching, pliable, and that may be fitted to all biases and squared to all measures" (II, 12).

Skepticism towards the religious and political situation relegates Montaigne to the role of a passive observer. He reports without judging, at least in a vindictive way. His approach of a "middle path" was aptly called *politique* (as the term was defined in the 1570s and 1580s), namely a compromise and *juste milieu* between extreme positions.

In the end, the *Essays* analyze what can be broadly defined as human nature, the endless process by which people attempt to impose themselves and their opinions upon others through the production of laws, policies, or philosophies. For Montaigne, this recurring battle for "truth" needs to be put into a historical perspective:

"The truth of these days is not that which really is, but what every man persuades another man to believe" (II, 18).

Montaigne's famous motto, "What do I know?" (inscribed above the fireplace in his study), is a question that always needs to be asked, even when others give us ready answers.

In summary, reading him today teaches us that the angle we have defines the world we see. Or, as he wrote: "it does not only import that we see the thing, but how and after what manner we see it" (I, 40).

NOTE ON THE TRANSLATION

For this edition we have used Charles Cotton's translation. Cotton (1630– 1687) was considered one of the "most charming" poets of the late seventeenth century. In 1667, he translated the *Moral Philosophy of the Stoics* by Guillaume Du Vair and, a few years later (1671), *Horace* by Corneille.

Published in 1685, Cotton's translation of the *Essays* is dedicated to George Savile, Marquis of Halifax. Almost a century after John Florio's first translation of the *Essays* in English, Cotton's language reflects the taste of his time. His prose is simple, clear, less flowery, and certainly more exact than that of Florio or other writers of the Renaissance. His translation enjoyed some popularity through the eighteenth century considering the large number of reissues (1693, 1700, 1711, 1738, 1743, 1759, 1760). Close to Montaigne's original language, this translation (which we have modernized slightly, removing some archaic words) remains very readable today. It includes some of Cotton's remarks and references, along with those of a later editor, William Carew Hazlitt. There are also remarks from the translator of a 1724 French edition, Peter Coste. All these notes are in square brackets, as distinct from the regular brackets used by Montaigne himself.

As a complete edition of the *Essays* would run to over 1200 pages, most modern editions are selected. We have chosen 11 out of 57 chapters from Book I, 8 out of 37 chapters from Book II, and 7 out of 13 chapters from Book III. Although the unavoidable and best known chapters such as "To Study Philosophy Is to Learn to Die", "On the Education of Children", "On Friendship", "On Cannibals", "On Books",

"On Repentance", "On Coaches", "On Vanity", and "On Experience" are present in this edition, we have also selected less known chapters which are often kept out of the Montaignian canon but nonetheless seem relevant for the twenty-first-century reader.

MICHEL DE MONTAIGNE – TIMELINE

- Born in 1533, the son of Dordogne landowner Pierre Eyquem, and Antoinette de Louppes. Her family is Christian but descended from Sephardic Jews.
- Receives excellent education at the College de Guyenne in Bordeaux. Well-versed in Latin by age 7. In his teens studies at the Universities of Bordeaux and Toulouse.
- At age 20, follows his father in becoming a councilor at the Bordeaux parliament, where he meets friend and mentor Étienne de la Boétie. Period working at the court of Charles IX.
- 1565: marries Françoise de La Chassaigne. The marriage is arranged; she is mentioned a handful of times in the *Essays*.
- 1568: father dies and he inherits family estate including chateau in Perigord. Works in a library in a circular tower above the estate buildings. Writes: "Miserable, to my mind, is the man who has no place in his house where he can be alone, where he can privately attend to his needs, where he can conceal himself!"
- 1569: publishes in Paris a French translation of Raymond Sebond's *Theologia Naturalis*.
- 1570: daughter Toinette is born. Dies three months later.
- 1571: daughter Léonor is born, the only one of several daughters to survive into adulthood.
- 1572–4: France is in civil war. Montaigne joins the royalist side and works on its behalf in Bordeaux.
- 1577: has his first attack of "the stone" – a hereditary kidney disease.
- 1580: the *Essays* are published. Montaigne presents a copy to Henry III.

- 1580–81: journeys around Europe, going from one spa to another seeking a cure. Has audience with Pope Gregory XIII. Recalled home when elected (against his will) mayor of Bordeaux, a position previously held by his father.
- 1582: second edition of the *Essays* published.
- 1583: heir to the throne Henry de Navarre visits Montaigne and stays in his chateau. Re-elected mayor of Bordeaux.
- 1588: third edition of the *Essays* published, including the new Book III. Arrested and taken to the Bastille as a hostage but released the same day.
- 1592: Montaigne dies. His wife and Marie de Gournay, a writer and translator who had become close to Montaigne, arrange for the publication of a final 1595 edition of the *Essays*.
- 1613: first English translation of the *Essays* published, by John Florio.

Château de Montaigne, by Jean-Jérôme Baugean, c. 1800, with Montaigne's tower in the foreground. It still exists as a Monument historique and can be visited.

GUIDE TO THE CHAPTERS

BOOK I

On Idleness

When Montaigne retired from public life to his famous tower study on his estate, it did not turn out as he expected. Time on his hands did not lead to clarity of thought; rather, it made him more self-obsessed, melancholic, and prone to undisciplined imaginings.

On Liars

To lie well you need a good memory, which Montaigne distinctly lacks. In fact, his poor memory was a blessing in that he quickly forgot slights and could enjoy books he had read many times before. As humans are a species of word and speech, lying is the greatest vice, Montaigne argues.

That the Way We See Good and Evil Depends Upon the Opinion We Have of Them

Events are not good or bad in their own right, but our experience depends on how we perceive them. Montaigne agrees in principle, but chronic pain from his kidney stones and colic make it hard to live by these principles.

To Study Philosophy Is to Learn How To Die

A key part of Stoic philosophy was the premeditation or practicing of death so that it would not take us unawares. One should have perfect equanimity in the face of death or misfortune. Montaigne considers the vanity of humans who busy themselves and take on great projects as if they would live forever.

On the Power of Imagination

Mental impressions, ideas, thoughts, and fears have a hold on us, and it is often only by "sorcery" or tricks that we can loosen their power. Montaigne's example is sexual performance; he reveals old wedding-night customs designed to make things go well. Other examples of the power of thought and images include a woman who, having birthed a hairy child, blamed it on having a portrait of John the Baptist above her bed. Montaigne discounts history as being largely the work of the imagination; he is better at observing the present.

On Custom, and That We Should Not Easily Change an Established Law

The discovery of new worlds and peoples in Montaigne's time, plus the constant turmoil of political events in France and Europe, made him err on the side of custom or "rules of thumb". What has been around for a long time has survived for good reason. "Novelty" is usually just some individual's idea of how things could change, often with negative social results.

On the Education of Children

In a chapter dedicated to his friend Diane de Foix (at the time, pregnant) Montaigne is full of quite modern ideas about how to bring up children, including teaching by inspiration rather than strong discipline. By analogy, kings and rulers should also act like a responsible and loving parent, instilling good values among their subjects.

On Friendship

"Friendship" here for Montaigne means bonds established in all kinds of relationships that are about the meeting of two souls (rather than just bodies). His model here is his deep friendship with Etienne de la Boétie, who had been accused of seditionary writings. Their loyalty to each other over time is analogous to a citizen who is loyal to the state.

On Moderation

Whatever pleasures humans find, they take things to excess, thereby making pleasure a vice. Even the study of philosophy, if engaged in too much, will make a person have contempt for religion and accepted laws and customs. "Everything in moderation", and having respect for others, are a good rule for life.

On Cannibals

Montaigne is unusually open-minded for his time on the matter of "natives". We only think them barbarous because they are so different to us in dress, beliefs, and customs. Western civilization has its own array of enterprises and customs which would look cruel and nonsensical to outsiders. Amid our hubris, we would do well to remember that the greatest "art" in the universe is nature itself.

On Solitude

Wherever we go, we take ourselves along. Montaigne sought freedom of mind and tranquility in his tower study, but found he was a prisoner of wandering, unhelpful thoughts. We do not need physical solitude as monks and nuns seek, but to be *in* the world and yet live with some level of detachment.

BOOK II

On the Inconstancy of Our Actions

Humans are full of contradictions, and mostly drift along with the flow of life without having a real plan. Our moods and affections change with the weather, and there's as much difference within *us*, as *between* individuals. Given that we allow chance to play such a part in our lives, it's no wonder that chance will dominate and take us places we'd rather not go.

Use Makes Perfect

Sometimes translated as "On Practice", the practice in question is not mastering of a skill but preparing for death. Montaigne, like most people, feared death. That was until he was thrown off his horse in an accident and was concussed; from that moment he had more equanimity. Relating the incident leads to a discussion of how much one should talk about oneself. Not too much, he thinks, but never talking of oneself also goes against human nature.

On Books

Montaigne reveals his reading habits, noting that he will only keep reading a book he really enjoys; he feels the ancient books are more solid than recent ones; and he follows Horace's division of books into those that merely delight, and those that delight and are useful (particularly ones that help him be a better person). Among the poets, he ranks Virgil highest. Among the useful writers, he likes Plutarch and Seneca; Cicero is too wordy. Among historians, he finds most weak because they put narrative over fact.

On Cruelty

The chapter begins by discussing virtue. Montaigne does not see himself as particularly virtuous. If he has good qualities, most were developed through education and good family – neither of which were his creation. He is not free of vice by any means, but one vice he would never engage in is cruelty. If someone is put to death, let it be quick. Torture for public enjoyment is disgusting. We should be kind to animals because they have feelings.

GUIDE TO THE CHAPTERS

On Giving the Lie

Montaigne's own age, in fact every age in history including the classical world, is one of lies and dissimulation. He despises lying for the bad effects it carries through time. It is both cowardly towards other people, and disrespects God. His *Essays* are, if nothing else, an attempt to convey the truth – even if messy or awkward, or lacking direction or resolution.

On a Monstrous Child

Montaigne relates seeing two curiosities: male conjoined twins; and a man born with no genitals who nevertheless was aroused by women. Though they may seem "monsters", in God's eyes they cannot be, because as God made everything in nature, it all must be perfect. The universe has a great multitude of life, which we can wonder at.

On Three Good Women

A further meditation on love and marriage. Montaigne takes three examples from antiquity of devotion of wives to their husbands. He also salutes the great suicide of Seneca, who stayed true to his Stoic principles, with equanimity shown until the end.

BOOK III

On Profit and Honesty

Sometimes, there appears to be a conflict between personal virtue and matters of politics or business. Cicero wrote that what is right and what is expedient can never be separate things, and Montaigne largely agrees. In a time of war (as he was), one has to take sides, but in all personal and public dealings one should act with justice and sympathy, never becoming so inflamed that one acts with vengeance or cruelty.

On Repentance

Montaigne's subject here is the question of whether one has acted honorably, given the facts and circumstances at the time of decision. He has largely trusted his own judgment on things, and therefore is fully responsible for this life. It is less worrisome anyway to appreciate that things turned out as they meant to, and that one's decisions matter little in the scheme of things. There is little that can agitate Montaigne, and his relative lack of ambition or intensity has worked well for him. If you are moderate, you will have peace.

On Some Verses of Virgil

The chapter title disguises the real subject: human sexuality. Montaigne begins by noting he is too old to engage in much sex now, but he enjoys himself with memories. He admits his marriage was arranged but respects the institution of marriage and has kept to his vows. Sex is so strong an impulse that the world revolves around it. Women have desires as strong as men, and he looks wryly on women who claim to have their mind only on higher things. It is only education and custom that make women and men seem so different.

On Coaches

Horse-drawn coaches were still a symbol of luxury in Montaigne's time, so he uses them as the means to criticize pomp and ostentation. When rulers have grand transports and caravans, it is a sign that they lack confidence in their power and judgment and make up for it with display. They spend on lavish festivals to make the people feel good about them, when the money would be better spent on ports, bridges, schools, hospitals. He contrasts this with the apparent nobility of the New World rulers, admiring the civilization they built before the Spanish conquest.

On the Art of Conversation

Montaigne loves conversation so much, that he would rather lose his sight than his speech or hearing. In contrast to the solitariness of reading, conversation builds our character and skills. He welcomes strange or shocking views, because from every chat you learn something and it gets you closer to truth. He prefers being contradicted to being praised, and loves light-hearted banter. Speaking reveals who you are. Many a ruler would have preserved the sense of awe around them by keeping silent.

On Vanity

Montaigne admits that the greatest vanity is writing about vanity. Yet here he is, with his self-indulgent scribblings. Each person contributes in some way to the decline of their era. Some through their vain actions foster more injustice or cruelty than there was before. Others (like he himself) simply add more silliness or laziness. He should be content with running his estate, like his father was, but he fancies himself as a man of state, travelling and meeting important people. The Delphic maxim is Know yourself, but when he has examined himself, all he has found is emptiness and foolishness.

On Experience

Montaigne's meditation on his life-long search for wisdom, paradoxically, comes down to being a point of consciousness within a body. For this reason he goes into some details on his diet, sleeping habits, illnesses, etc. Though he has done nothing of great distinction, he has had thousands of experiences – and so feels as qualified to comment on life as anyone. Using the analogy of his kidney disease, and his aversion to medicine, he argues that life is to be faced up to, not avoided. In doing so we might find some (very modest) self-knowledge or wisdom.

ABOUT PHILIPPE DESAN

Philippe Desan is the Howard L. Willett Professor Emeritus of History of Culture at the University of Chicago. He specializes in the history of ideas in the Renaissance and more particularly in Montaigne. Books include the definitive biography, *Montaigne. A Life* (Princeton University Press, 2018) as well as *Montaigne: penser le social* (Odile Jacob, 2018) and the *Oxford Handbook of Montaigne* (Oxford University Press, 2016). Editor-in-chief of *Montaigne Studies* since 1988, he received the Grand Prize from the French Academy in 2015 for his scientific work.

ABOUT TOM BUTLER-BOWDON

Tom Butler-Bowdon is the author of the bestselling 50 Classics series, which brings the ideas of important books to a wider audience. Titles include *50 Philosophy Classics, 50 Psychology Classics, 50 Politics Classics, 50 Self-Help Classics* and *50 Economics Classics*.

As series editor for the Capstone Classics series, Tom has written Introductions to Plato's *The Republic*, Machiavelli's *The Prince*, Adam Smith's *The Wealth of Nations*, Sun Tzu's *The Art of War*, Lao Tzu's *Tao TeChing*, and Napoleon Hill's *Think and Grow Rich*.

Tom is a graduate of the London School of Economics and the University of Sydney.

www.Butler-Bowdon.com

CONTENTS

TO THE READER

THIS, reader, is a book without guile. It tells you, at the very outset, that I had no other end in putting it together but what was domestic and private. I had no regard therein either to your service or my glory; my powers are equal to no such design. It was intended for the particular use of my relations and friends, in order that, when they have lost me, which they must soon do, they may here find some traces of my quality and humour, and may thereby nourish a more entire and lively recollection of me. Had I proposed to court the favour of the world, I had set myself out in borrowed beauties; but it was my wish to be seen in my simple, natural, and ordinary garb, without study or artifice, for it was myself I had to paint. My defects will appear to the life, in all their native form, as far as consists with respect to the public. Had I been born among those nations who, it is said, still live in the pleasant liberty of the Jaw of nature, I assure you I should readily have depicted myself at full length and quite naked. Thus, reader, I am myself the subject of my book; it is not worth your while to take up your time longer with such a frivolous matter; so fare thee well.

MONTAIGNE, 1st March, 1580

BOOK I

8

ON IDLENESS

As we see some grounds that have long lain idle and untilled, when grown rich and fertile by rest, to abound with and spend their virtue in the product of innumerable sorts of weeds and wild herbs that are unprofitable, and that to make them perform their true office, we are to cultivate and prepare them for such seeds as are proper for our service; and as we see women that, without knowledge of man, do sometimes of themselves bring forth inanimate and formless lumps of flesh, but that to cause a natural and perfect generation they are to be husbanded with another kind of seed: even so it is with minds, which if not applied to some certain study that may fix and restrain them, run into a thousand extravagances, eternally roving here and there in the vague expanse of the imagination:

> *Sicut aqua tremulum labris ubi lumen ahenis,*
> *Sole repercussum, aut radiantis imagine lunae,*
> *Omnia pervolitat late loca; jamque sub auras*
> *Erigitur, summique ferit laquearia tecti.*

> [As when in brazen vats of water the trembling beams of light, reflected from the sun, or from the image of the radiant moon, swiftly float over every place around, and now are darted up on high, and strike the ceilings of the upmost roof.
>
> —*Aeneid*, viii. 22.]

in which wild agitation there is no folly, nor idle fancy they do not light upon:

Velut aegri somnia, vanae
Finguntur species.

    [As a sick man's dreams, creating vain phantasms.
                       —Horace, *Ars Poetica*, 7.]

The soul that has no established aim loses itself, for, as it is said:

Quisquis ubique habitat, Maxime, nusquam habitat.

    [He who lives everywhere, lives nowhere.
                       —Martial, vii. 73.]

When I lately retired to my own house, with a resolution, as much as possibly I could, to avoid all manner of concern in affairs, and to spend in privacy and repose the little remainder of time I have to live, I fancied I could not more oblige my mind than to suffer it at full leisure to entertain and divert itself, which I now hoped it might henceforth do, as being by time become more settled and mature; but I find –

Variam semper dant otia mentem.

    [Leisure ever creates varied thought.
                       —Lucan, *Pharsalia*, iv. 704]

that, quite contrary, it is like a horse that has broke from his rider, who voluntarily runs into a much more violent career than any horseman would put him to, and creates me so many chimaeras and fantastic monsters, one upon another, without order or design, that, the better at leisure to contemplate their strangeness and absurdity, I have begun to commit them to writing, hoping in time to make it ashamed of itself.

4

ON LIARS

There is not a man living whom it would so little become to speak from memory as myself, for I have scarcely any at all, and do not think that the world has another so marvellously treacherous as mine. My other faculties are all sufficiently ordinary and mean; but in this I think myself very rare and singular, and deserving to be thought famous. Besides the natural inconvenience I suffer by it (for, certes, the necessary use of memory considered, Plato had reason when he called it a great and powerful goddess), in my country, when they would say a man has no sense, they say, such an one has no memory; and when I complain of the defect of mine, they do not believe me, and reprove me, as though I accused myself for a fool: not discerning the difference between memory and understanding, which is to make matters still worse for me. But they do me wrong; for experience, rather, daily shows us, on the contrary, that a strong memory is commonly coupled with infirm judgment. They do, me, moreover (who am so perfect in nothing as in friendship), a great wrong in this, that they make the same words which accuse my infirmity, represent me for an ungrateful person; they bring my affections into question upon the account of my memory, and from a natural imperfection, make out a defect of conscience. "He has forgot," says one, "this request, or that promise; he no more remembers his friends; he has forgot to say or do, or conceal such and such a thing, for my sake." And, truly, I am apt enough to forget many things, but to neglect anything my friend has given me in charge,

I never do it. And it should be enough, methinks, that I feel the misery and inconvenience of it, without branding me with malice, a vice so contrary to my humour.

However, I derive these comforts from my infirmity: first, that it is an evil from which principally I have found reason to correct a worse, that would easily enough have grown upon me, namely, ambition; the defect being intolerable in those who take upon them public affairs. That, like examples in the progress of nature demonstrate to us, she has fortified me in my other faculties proportionably as she has left me unfurnished in this; I should otherwise have been apt implicitly to have reposed my mind and judgment upon the bare report of other men, without ever setting them to work upon their own force, had the inventions and opinions of others been ever been present with me by the benefit of memory. That by this means I am not so talkative, for the magazine of the memory is ever better furnished with matter than that of the invention. Had mine been faithful to me, I had ere this deafened all my friends with my babble, the subjects themselves arousing and stirring up the little faculty I have of handling and employing them, heating and distending my discourse, which were a pity: as I have observed in several of my intimate friends, who, as their memories supply them with an entire and full view of things, begin their narrative so far back, and crowd it with so many impertinent circumstances, that though the story be good in itself, they make a shift to spoil it; and if otherwise, you are either to curse the strength of their memory or the weakness of their judgment: and it is a hard thing to close up a discourse, and to cut it short, when you have once started; there is nothing wherein the force of a horse is so much seen as in a round and sudden stop. I see even those who are pertinent enough, who would, but cannot stop short in their career; for whilst they are seeking out a handsome period to conclude with, they go on at random, straggling about upon impertinent trivialities, as men staggering upon weak legs. But, above all, old men who retain the memory of things past, and forget how often they have told them, are dangerous company; and I have known stories from the mouth of a man

6

of very great quality, otherwise very pleasant in themselves, become very wearisome by being repeated a hundred times over and over again to the same people.

Secondly, that, by this means, I the less remember the injuries I have received; insomuch that, as the ancient said [Cicero, *Pro Ligurio*, c. 12] I should have a register of injuries, or a prompter, as Darius, who, that he might not forget the offence he had received from those of Athens, so oft as he sat down to dinner, ordered one of his pages three times to repeat in his ear, "Sir, remember the Athenians" [Herodotus, *Histories* v. 105.] and then, again, the places which I revisit, and the books I read over again, still smile upon me with a fresh novelty.

It is not without good reason said "that he who has not a good memory should never take upon him the trade of lying." I know very well that the grammarians [Aulus Gellius, xi. ii; Nonius, v. 80] distinguish between an untruth and a lie, and say that to tell an untruth is to tell a thing that is false, but that we ourselves believe to be true; and that the definition of the word to lie in Latin, from which our French is taken, is to tell a thing which we know in our conscience to be untrue; and it is of this last sort of liars only that I now speak. Now, these do either wholly contrive and invent the untruths they utter, or so alter and disguise a true story that it ends in a lie. When they disguise and often alter the same story, according to their own fancy, it is very hard for them, at one time or another, to escape being trapped, by reason that the real truth of the thing, having first taken possession of the memory, and being there lodged impressed by the medium of knowledge and science, it will be difficult that it should not represent itself to the imagination, and shoulder out falsehood, which cannot there have so sure and settled footing as the other; and the circumstances of the first true knowledge evermore running in their minds, will be apt to make them forget those that are illegitimate, and only, forged by their own fancy. In what they, wholly invent, forasmuch as there is no contrary impression to jostle their invention there seems to be less danger of tripping; and yet even this by reason it is a vain body and without any hold, is very apt to escape the memory, if it be not well assured. Of which I had very pleasant experience, at the expense of such as profess only to form and accommodate their speech to the affair they have in hand, or to humour of the great folks to whom they are speaking; for the circumstances to which these men stick not to enslave their faith and conscience being subject to several changes, their language must vary accordingly: whence it happens that of the same thing they tell one man that it is this, and another that it is that, giving it several colours; which men, if they once come to confer notes, and find out the cheat, what becomes of this fine art? To which may be added, that they must of necessity very often ridiculously trap themselves; for what memory can be sufficient to retain so many different shapes as they have forged upon one and the same subject? I have known many in my time very ambitious of the repute of this fine wit; but they do not see that if they have the reputation of it, the effect can no longer be.

In plain truth, lying is an accursed vice. We are not men, nor have other tie upon one another, but by our word. If we did but discover the horror and gravity of it, we should pursue it with fire and sword, and more justly than other crimes. I see that parents commonly, and with indiscretion enough, correct their children for little innocent faults, and torment them for wanton tricks, that have neither impression nor consequence; whereas, in my opinion, lying only, and, which is of something a lower form, obstinacy, are the faults which are to be severely whipped out of them, both in their infancy and in their progress, otherwise they grow up and increase with them; and after a tongue has once got the knack of lying, it is not to be imagined how impossible it is to reclaim it whence it comes to pass that we see some, who are otherwise very honest men, so subject and enslaved to this vice. I have an honest lad to my tailor, whom I never knew guilty of one truth, no, not when it had been to his advantage. If falsehood had, like truth, but one face only, we should be upon better terms; for we should then take for certain the

8

contrary to what the liar says: but the reverse of truth has a hundred thousand forms, and a field indefinite, without bound or limit. The Pythagoreans make good to be certain and finite, and evil, infinite and uncertain. There are a thousand ways to miss the white, there is only one to hit it. For my own part, I have this vice in so great horror, that I am not sure I could prevail with my conscience to secure myself from the most manifest and extreme danger by an impudent and solemn lie. An ancient father says "that a dog we know is better company than a man whose language we do not understand."

Ut externus alienopene non sit hominis vice.

[As a foreigner cannot be said to supply us the place of a man.

—Pliny, *Natural History.* vii. I]

And how much less sociable is false speaking than silence?

King Francis I vaunted that he had by this means nonplussed Francesco Taverna, ambassador of Francesco Sforza, Duke of Milan, a man very famous for his science in talking in those days. This gentleman had been sent to excuse his master to his Majesty about a thing of very great consequence, which was this: the King, still to maintain some intelligence with Italy, out of which he had lately been driven, and particularly with the duchy of Milan, had thought it convenient to have a gentleman on his behalf to be with that Duke: an ambassador in effect, but in outward appearance a private person who pretended to reside there upon his own particular affairs; for the Duke, much more depending upon the Emperor, especially at a time when he was in a treaty of marriage with his niece, daughter to the King of Denmark, who is now dowager of Lorraine, could not manifest any practice and conference with us without his great interest. For this commission one Merveille, a Milanese gentleman, and an equerry to the King, being thought very fit, was accordingly despatched thither with private credentials, and instructions as ambassador, and with other letters of recommendation to the Duke about his own private concerns, the better to mask and colour the business; and was so long in that court, that the Emperor at last had some inkling of his real employment there; which was the occasion of what followed after, as we suppose; which was, that under pretence of some murder, his trial was in two days despatched, and his head in the night struck off in prison. Messire Francesco being come, and prepared with a long counterfeit history of the affair (for the King had applied himself to all the princes of Christendom, as well as to the Duke himself, to demand satisfaction), had his audience at the morning council; where, after he had for the support of his cause laid open several plausible justifications of the fact, that his master had never looked upon this Merveille for other than a private gentleman and his own subject, who was there only in order to his own business, neither had he ever lived under any other aspect; absolutely disowning that he had ever heard he was one of the King's household or that his Majesty so much as knew him, so far was he from taking him for an ambassador: the King, in his turn, pressing him with several objections and demands, and challenging him on all sides, tripped him up at last by asking, why, then, the execution was performed by night, and as it were by stealth? At which the poor confounded ambassador, the more handsomely to disengage himself, made answer, that the Duke would have been very loth, out of respect to his Majesty, that such an execution should have been performed by day. Any one may guess if he was not well rated when he came home, for having so grossly tripped in the presence of a prince of so delicate a nostril as King Francis.

Pope Julius II. having sent an ambassador to the King of England to animate him against King Francis, the ambassador having had his audience, and the King, before he would give an answer, insisting upon the difficulties he should find in setting on foot so great a preparation as would be necessary to attack so potent a King, and urging some reasons to that effect, the ambassador very unseasonably replied that he had also himself considered the same difficulties, and had represented them to the Pope. From which saying of his, so directly opposite to the thing propounded and the business he came about, which was immediately to incite him to war, the King of England first derived the argument (which he afterward found to be true), that this ambassador, in his own mind, was on the side of the French; of which having advertised his master, his estate at his return home was confiscated, and he himself very narrowly escaped the losing of his head. [Erasmus, *Opus Epistolarum* (1703), iv. col. 684.]

THAT THE WAY WE SEE GOOD AND EVIL DEPENDS ON THE OPINION WE HAVE OF THEM

Men, says Epictetus, are tormented with the opinions they have of things and not by the things themselves. It were a great victory obtained for the relief of our miserable human condition, could this proposition be established for certain and true throughout. For if evils have no admission into us but by the judgment we ourselves make of them, it should seem that it is, then, in our own power to despise them or to turn them to good. If things surrender themselves to our mercy, why do we not convert and accommodate them to our advantage? If what we call evil and torment is neither evil nor torment of itself, but only that our fancy gives it that quality, it is in us to change it, and it being in our own choice, if there be no constraint upon us, we must certainly be very strange fools to take arms for that side which is most offensive to us, and to give sickness, want, and contempt a bitter and nauseous taste, if it be in our power to give them a pleasant relish, and if, fortune simply providing the matter, it is for us to give it the form. Now, that what we call evil is not so of itself, or at least to that degree that we make it, and that it depends upon us to give it another taste and complexion (for all comes to one), let us examine how that can be maintained.

If the original being of those things we fear had power to lodge itself in us by its own authority, it would then lodge itself alike, and in like manner, in all; for men are all of the same kind, and saving in greater and less proportions, are all provided with the same utensils and instruments to conceive and to judge; but the diversity of opinions we have of those things clearly evidences that they only enter us by composition; one person, peradventure, admits them in their true being, but a thousand others give them a new and contrary being in them. We hold death, poverty, and pain for our principal enemies; now, this death, which some repute the most dreadful of all dreadful things, who does not know that others call it the only secure harbour from the storms and tempests of life, the sovereign good of nature, the sole support of liberty, and the common and prompt remedy of all evils? And as the one expect it with fear and trembling, the others support it with greater ease than life itself. That one complains of its facility:

> *Mors! Utinam pavidos vitae subducere nolles.*
> *Sed virtus to sola daret!*

[O death! wouldst that thou might spare the coward, but that valour alone should pay thee tribute.

—Lucan, *Pharsalia*, iv. 580.]

Now, let us leave these boastful courages. Theodorus answered Lysimachus, who threatened to kill him, "Thou wilt do a brave feat," said he, "to attain the force of a cantharides." The majority of philosophers are observed to have either purposely anticipated, or hastened and assisted their own death. How many ordinary people do we see led to execution, and that not to a simple death, but mixed with shame and sometimes with grievous torments, appear with such assurance, whether through firm courage or natural simplicity, that a man can discover no change from their ordinary condition; settling their domestic affairs, commending themselves to their friends, singing, preaching, and addressing the people, nay, sometimes sallying into jests, and drinking to their companions, quite as well as Socrates?

14

CHAPTER 14

One that they were leading to the gallows told them they must not take him through such a street, lest a merchant who lived there should arrest him by the way for an old debt. Another told the hangman he must not touch his neck for fear of making him laugh, he was so ticklish. Another answered his confessor, who promised him he should that day sup with our Lord, "Do you go then," said he, "in my room [place]; for I for my part keep fast to-day." Another having called for drink, and the hangman having drunk first, said he would not drink after him, for fear of catching some evil disease. Everybody has heard the tale of the Picard, to whom, being upon the hangman's ladder, they presented a common wench, telling him (as our law does sometimes permit) that if he would marry her they would save his life; he, having a while considered her and perceiving that she halted: "Come, tie up, tie up," said he, "she limps." And they tell another story of the same kind of a fellow in Denmark, who being condemned to lose his head, and the like condition being proposed to him upon the scaffold, refused it, by reason the girl they offered him had hollow cheeks and too sharp a nose. A servant at Toulouse being accused of heresy, for the sum of his belief referred himself to that of his master, a young student, prisoner with him, choosing rather to die than suffer himself to be persuaded that his master could err. We read that of the inhabitants of Arras, when Louis XI took that city, a great many let themselves be hanged rather than they would say, "God save the King." And amongst that mean-souled race of men, the buffoons, there have been some who would not leave their fooling at the very moment of death. One that the hangman was turning off the ladder cried: "Launch the galley," an ordinary saying of his. Another, whom at the point of death his friends had laid upon a bed of straw before the fire, the physician asking him where his pain lay: "Between the bench and the fire," said he, and the priest, to give him extreme unction, groping for his feet which his pain had made him pull up to him: "You will find them," said he, "at the end of my legs." To one who being present exhorted him to recommend himself to God: "Why, is someone

15

going to Him?" said he; and the other replying: "It will presently be yourself, if it be His good pleasure." "Shall I be sure to be there by to-morrow night?" said he. "Do, but recommend yourself to Him," said the other, "and you will soon be there." "I were best then," said he, "to wait and carry my recommendations myself."

In the kingdom of Narsingah to this day the wives of their priests are buried alive with the bodies of their husbands; all other wives are burnt at their husbands' funerals, which they not only firmly but cheerfully undergo. At the death of their king, his wives and concubines, his favourites, all his officers, and domestic servants, who make up a whole people, present themselves so gaily to the fire where his body is burnt, that they seem to take it for a singular honour to accompany their master in death. During our late wars of Milan, where there happened so many takings and retakings of towns, the people, impatient of so many changes of fortune, took such a resolution to die, that I have heard my father say he there saw a list taken of five-and-twenty masters of families who made themselves away in one week's time: an incident somewhat resembling that of the Xanthians, who being besieged by Brutus, fell – men, women, and children – into such a furious appetite of dying, that nothing can be done to evade death which they did not to avoid life; insomuch that Brutus had much difficulty in saving a very small number. ["Only fifty were saved." – Plutarch, *Life of Brutus*, c. 8.]

Every opinion is of force enough to cause itself to be espoused at the expense of life. The first article of that valiant oath that Greece took and observed in the Median war, was that everyone should sooner exchange life for death, than their own laws for those of Persia. What a world of people do we see in the wars between the Turks and the Greeks, who would rather embrace a cruel death than uncircumcise themselves to be baptised? An example of which no sort of religion is incapable.

The kings of Castile having banished the Jews out of their dominions, John, King of Portugal, in consideration of eight crowns a head, sold them a retreat into his for a certain limited time, upon condition that the time fixed coming to expire they should begone, and he to furnish them with shipping to transport them into Africa. The day comes, which once lapsed they were given to understand that such as were afterward found in the kingdom should remain slaves; vessels were very slenderly provided; and those who embarked in them were rudely and villainously used by the passengers, who, besides other indignities, kept them cruising upon the sea, one while forwards and another backwards, till they had spent all their provisions, and were constrained to buy of them at so dear a rate and so long withal, that they set them not on shore till they were all stripped to the very shirts. The news of this inhuman usage being brought to those who remained behind, the greater part of them resolved upon slavery and some made a show of changing religion. Emmanuel, the successor of John, being come to the crown, first set them at liberty, and afterwards altering his mind, ordered them to depart his country, assigning three ports for their passage. He hoped, says Bishop Osorius, no contemptible Latin historian of these later times, that the favour of the liberty he had given them having failed of converting them to Christianity, yet the difficulty of committing themselves to the mercy of the mariners and of abandoning a country they were now habituated to and were grown very rich in, to go and expose themselves in strange and unknown regions, would certainly do it. But finding himself deceived in his expectation, and that they were all resolved upon the voyage, he cut off two of the three ports he had promised them, to the end that the length and incommodity of the passage might reduce some, or that he might have opportunity, by crowding them all into one place, the more conveniently to execute what he had designed, which was to force all the children under fourteen years of age from the arms of their fathers and mothers, to transport them from their sight and conversation, into a place where they might be instructed and brought up in our religion. He says that this produced a most horrid spectacle the natural affection between the parents and their children, and moreover their zeal to their ancient belief, contending against this violent decree, fathers and mothers were commonly seen making themselves away, and by a yet much more rigorous example, precipitating out of love and compassion their young children into wells and pits, to avoid the severity of this law. As to the remainder of them, the time that had been prefixed being expired, for want of means to transport them they again returned into slavery. Some also turned Christians, upon whose faith, as also that of their posterity, even to this day, which is a hundred years since, few Portuguese can yet rely; though custom and length of time are much more powerful counsellors in such changes than all other constraints whatever. In the town of Castelnaudari, fifty heretic Albigeois at one time suffered themselves to be burned alive in one fire rather than they would renounce their opinions.

Quoties non modo ductores nostri, sed universi etiam exercitus,
ad non dubiam mortem concurrerunt?

[How often have not only our leaders, but whole armies, run to a certain and manifest death?"
— Cicero, *Tusculum Disputations*, i. 37.]

I have seen an intimate friend of mine run headlong upon death with a real affection, and that was rooted in his heart by divers plausible arguments which he would never permit me to dispossess him of, and upon the first honourable occasion that offered itself to him, precipitate himself into it, without any manner of visible reason, with an obstinate and ardent desire of dying. We have several examples in our own times of persons, even young children, who for fear of some little inconvenience have despatched themselves. And what shall we not fear, says one of the ancients [Seneca, *Letters*, 70.] to this purpose, if we dread that which cowardice itself has chosen for its refuge?

Should I here produce a long catalogue of those, of all sexes and conditions and sects, even in the most happy ages, who have either with great constancy looked death in the face, or voluntarily sought it, and sought it not only to avoid the evils of this life, but some purely to avoid the satiety of living, and others for the hope of a better condition elsewhere, I should never have done. The number is so infinite that in truth I should have a better bargain to reckon up those who have feared it. This one case therefore shall serve for all: Pyrrho the philosopher being one day in a boat in a very great tempest, showed to those around him who were terrified, the example of a hog that was not at all concerned at the storm. Shall we then dare to say that this advantage of reason, of which we so much boast, and upon the account of which we think ourselves masters and emperors over the rest of all creation, was given us for a torment? To what end serves the knowledge of things if it renders us more unmanly? If we thereby lose the tranquillity and repose we should enjoy without it? And if it put us into a worse condition than Pyrrho's hog? Shall we employ the understanding that was conferred upon us for our greatest good to our own ruin; setting ourselves against the design of nature and the universal order of things, which intend that everyone should make use of the faculties, members, and means he has to his own best advantage?

But it may be objected: Your rule is true enough as to what concerns death; but what will you say of indigence? What will you, moreover, say of pain, which Aristippus, Hieronymus, and most of the sages have reputed the worst of evils; and those who have denied it by word of mouth have, however, confessed it in effect? Posidonius being extremely tormented with a sharp and painful disease, Pompeius came to visit him, excusing himself that he had taken so unseasonable a time to come to hear him discourse of philosophy. "The gods forbid," said Posidonius to him, "that pain should ever have the power to hinder me from talking," and thereupon fell immediately upon a discourse of the contempt of pain: but, in the meantime, his own infirmity was playing his part, and plagued him to purpose; to which he cried out, "You may work your will, pain, and torment me with all your power, but you shall never make me say that you are evil." This story makes a fuss, but what has it to do with the contempt of pain? He only fights it with words, and in the meantime, if the shootings pains he felt did not move him, why did he interrupt his discourse? Why did he fancy he did so great a thing in forbearing to confess it an evil? All does not here consist in the imagination; our fancies may work upon other things: but here is the certain science that is playing its part, of which our senses themselves are judges:

Qui nisi sunt veri, ratio quoque falsa sit omnis.

[Which, if they be not true, all reasoning may also be false.
—Lucretius, iv. 486.]

Shall we persuade our skins that the jerks of a whip agreeably tickle us, or our taste that a potion of aloes is vin de Graves? Pyrrho's hog is here in the same predicament with us; he is not afraid of death, it is true, but if you beat him he will cry out to some purpose. Shall we force the general law of nature, which in every living creature under heaven is seen to tremble under pain? The very trees seem to groan under the blows they receive. Death is only felt by reason, forasmuch as it is the motion of an instant;

Aut fuit, aut veniet; nihil est praesentis in illa.

[Death has been, or will come: there is nothing of the present in it.
—Estienne de la Boétie, *Satires.*]

Morsque minus poenae, quam mora mortis, habet.

[The delay of death is more painful than death itself.
—Ovid, *Epistles.* Ariadne to Theseus, v. 42.]

CHAPTER 14

A thousand beasts, a thousand men, are sooner dead than threatened. That also which we principally pretend to fear in death is pain, its ordinary forerunner: yet, if we may believe a holy father:

Malam mortem non facit, nisi quod sequitur mortem.

[It is only which follows death what makes death bad.
——St. Augustine, *City of God*, i. ii.]

And I should yet say, more probably, that neither that which goes before nor that which follows after is at all of the appurtenances of death.

We excuse ourselves falsely: and I find by experience that it is rather the impatience of the imagination of death that makes us impatient of pain, and that we find it doubly grievous as it threatens us with death. But reason accusing our cowardice for fearing a thing so sudden, so inevitable, and so insensible, we take the other as the more excusable pretence. All ills that carry no other danger along with them but simply the evils themselves, we treat as things of no danger: the toothache or the gout, painful as they are, yet being not reputed mortal, who reckons them in the catalogue of diseases?

But let us presuppose that in death we principally regard the pain; as also there is nothing to be feared in poverty but the miseries it brings along with it of thirst, hunger, cold, heat, watching, and the other inconveniences it makes us suffer, still we have nothing to do with anything but pain. I will grant, and very willingly, that it is the worst incident of our being (for I am the man upon earth who the most hates and avoids it, considering that hitherto, I thank God, I have had so little traffic with it), but still it is in us, if not to annihilate, at least to lessen it by patience; and though the body and the reason should mutiny, to maintain the soul, nevertheless, in good condition. Were it not so, who had ever given reputation to virtue; valour, force, magnanimity, and resolution? where were their parts to be played if there were no pain to be defied?

Avida est periculi virtus.

[Courage is greedy of danger.

— Seneca, *De Providentia*, c. 4]

Were there no lying upon the hard ground, no enduring, armed at all points, the meridional heats, no feeding upon the flesh of horses and asses, no seeing a man's self hacked and hewed to pieces, no suffering a bullet to be pulled out from amongst the shattered bones, no sewing up, cauterising and searching of wounds, by what means were the advantage we covet to have over the vulgar to be acquired? It is not fleeting evil and pain, the sages say, that a man should most covet, but to perform acts which bring us the greater labour and pain.

Non est enim hilaritate, neclascivia, nec risu, aut joco
comite levitatis, sed saepe etiam tristes firmitate et
constantia sunt beati.

[For men are not only happy by mirth and wantonness, by laughter and jesting, the companion of levity, but ofttimes the serious sort reap felicity from their firmness and constancy.

—Cicero, *De Finibus*. ii. 10.]

And for this reason it has ever been impossible to persuade our forefathers but that the victories obtained by dint of force and the hazard of war were not more honourable than those performed in great security by stratagem or practice:

Laetius est, quoties magno sibi constat honestum.

[A good deed is all the more a satisfaction by how much the more it has cost us.

—Lucan, *Pharsalia*, ix. 404.]

Chapter 14

Besides, this ought to be our comfort, that naturally, if the pain be violent, it is but short; and if long, nothing violent:

Si gravis, brevis; Si longus, levis.

You will not feel it long if you feel it too much; it will either put an end to itself or to you; it comes to the same thing:

Remember that the greatest pains are terminated by death; that slighter pains have long intermissions of repose, and that we are masters of the more moderate sort: so that, if they be tolerable, we bear them; if not, we can go out of life, as from a theatre, when it does not please us.

—Cicero, *De Finibus*, i. 15.

That which makes us suffer pain with so much impatience is not being accustomed to find our chief contentment in the soul; that we do not enough rely upon her who is the sole and sovereign mistress of our condition. The body, saving in the greater or less proportion, has but one and the same bent and bias; whereas the soul is variable into all sorts of forms; and subject to herself and to her own empire, all things whatsoever, both the senses of the body and all other accidents: and therefore it is that we ought to study her, to inquire into her, and to rouse up all her powerful faculties. There is neither reason, force, nor prescription that can anything prevail against her inclination and choice. Of so many thousands of biases that she has at her disposal, let us give her one proper to our repose and conversation, and then we shall not only be sheltered and secured from all manner of injury and offence, but moreover gratified and obliged, if she will, with evils and offences. She makes her profit indifferently of all things; error, dreams, serve her to good use, as loyal matter to lodge us in safety and contentment. It is plain enough to be seen that it is the sharpness of our mind that gives the edge to our pains and pleasures: beasts that have no such thing, leave to their bodies their own free and natural sentiments, and consequently in every kind very near the same, as appears by the resembling application of their motions. If we would not disturb in our members the jurisdiction that appertains to them in this, it is to be believed it would be the better for us, and that nature has given them a just and moderate temper both to pleasure and pain; neither can it fail of being just, being equal and common. But seeing we have enfranchised ourselves from her rules to give ourselves up to the rambling liberty of our own fancies, let us at least help to incline them to the most agreeable side. Plato fears our too vehemently engaging ourselves with pain and pleasure, forasmuch as these too much knit and ally the soul to the body; whereas I rather, quite contrary, by reason it too much separates and disunites them. As an enemy is made more fierce by our flight, so pain grows proud to see us truckle under her. She will surrender upon much better terms to them who make head against her: a man must oppose and stoutly set himself against her. In retiring and giving ground, we invite and pull upon ourselves the ruin that threatens us. As the body is more firm in an encounter, the more stiffly and obstinately it applies itself to it, so is it with the soul.

But let us come to examples, which are the proper game of folks of such feeble force as myself; where we shall find that it is with pain as with stones, that receive a brighter or a duller lustre according to the foil they are set in, and that it has no more room in us than we are pleased to allow it:

Tantum doluerunt, quantum doloribus se inseruerunt.

[They suffered so much the more, by how much more they gave way to suffering.

—St. Augustine, *City of God*, i. 10.]

We are more sensible of one little touch of a surgeon's lancet than of twenty wounds with a sword in the heat of fight. The pains of childbearing, said by the physicians and by God himself to be

24

great, and which we pass through with so many ceremonies – there are whole nations that make nothing of them. I set aside the Lacedaemonian women, but what else do you find in the Swiss among our foot-soldiers, if not that, as they trot after their husbands, you see them to-day carry the child at their necks that they carried yesterday in their bellies? The counterfeit Egyptians we have amongst us go themselves to wash theirs, so soon as they come into the world, and bathe in the first river they meet. Besides so many wenches as daily drop their children by stealth, as they conceived them, that fair and noble wife of Sabinus, a patrician of Rome, for another's interest, endured alone, without help, without crying out, or so much as a groan, the bearing of twins. [Plutarch, *On Love*, c. 34.] A poor simple boy of Lacedaemon having stolen a fox (for they more fear the shame of stupidity in stealing than we do the punishment of the knavery), and having got it under his coat, rather endured the tearing out of his bowels than he would discover his theft. And another offering incense at a sacrifice, suffered himself to be burned to the bone by a coal that fell into his sleeve, rather than disturb the ceremony. And there have been a great number, for a sole trial of virtue, following their institutions, who have at seven years old endured to be whipped to death without changing their countenance. And Cicero has seen them fight in parties, with fists, feet, and teeth, till they have fainted and sunk down, rather than confess themselves overcome:

> Custom could never conquer nature; she is ever invincible; but we have infected the mind with shadows, delights, negligence, sloth; we have grown effeminate through opinions and corrupt morality.
> —Cicero, *Tusculum Disputations*, v. 27

Everyone knows the story of Scaevola, that having slipped into the enemy's camp to kill their general, and having missed his blow, to repair his fault, by a more strange invention and to deliver his country, he boldly confessed to Porsenna, who was the king he had a purpose to kill, not only his design, but moreover added that there were then in the camp a great number of Romans, his accomplices in the enterprise, as good men as he; and to show what a one he himself was, having caused a pan of burning coals to be brought, he saw and endured his arm to broil and roast, till the king himself, conceiving horror at the sight, commanded the pan to be taken away. What would you say of him that would not vouchsafe to respite his reading in a book whilst he was under incision? And of the other that persisted to mock and laugh in contempt of the pains inflicted upon him; so that the provoked cruelty of the executioners that had him in handling, and all the inventions of tortures redoubled upon him, one after another, spent in vain, gave him the bucklers? But he was a philosopher. But what! a gladiator of Caesar's endured, laughing all the while, his wounds to be searched, lanced, and laid open:

> What ordinary gladiator ever groaned? Which of them ever change countenance? Which of them not only stood or fell indecorously?
> Which, when he had fallen and was commanded to receive the stroke of the sword, contracted his neck.
>
> —Cicero, *Tusculum Disputations*, ii. 17.

Let us bring in the women too. Who has not heard at Paris of her that caused her face to be flayed only for the fresher complexion of a new skin? There are who have drawn good and sound teeth to make their voices more soft and sweet, or to place the other teeth in better order. How many examples of the contempt of pain have we in that sex? What can they not do, what do they fear to do, for never so little hope of an addition to their beauty?

Vallere queis cura est albos a stirpe capillos,
Et faciem, dempta pelle, referre novam.

Chapter 14

[Who carefully pluck out their grey hairs by the roots, and renew
their faces by peeling off the old skin.

—Tibullus, i. 8, 45.]

I have seen some of them swallow sand, ashes, and do their
utmost to destroy their stomachs to get pale complexions. To make
a fine Spanish body, what racks will they not endure of girding and
bracing, till they have notches in their sides cut into the very quick,
and sometimes to death?

It is an ordinary thing with several nations at this day to wound
themselves in good earnest to gain credit to what they profess; of
which our king relates notable examples of what he has seen in
Poland and done towards himself. [Henry III.] But besides this,
which I know to have been imitated by some in France, when I came
from that famous assembly of the Estates at Blois, I had a little before
seen a maid in Picardy, who to manifest the ardour of her promises,
as also her constancy, give herself, with a bodkin she wore in her hair,
four or five good lusty stabs in the arm, till the blood gushed out to
some purpose. The Turks give themselves great scars in honour of
their mistresses, and to the end they may the longer remain, they
presently clap fire to the wound, where they hold it an incredible
time to stop the blood and form the cicatrice; people that have been
eyewitnesses of it have both written and sworn it to me. But for ten
aspers [a Turkish coin worth about a penny] there are there every
day fellows to be found that will give themselves a good deep slash
in the arms or thighs. I am willing, however, to have the testimonies
nearest to us when we have most need of them; for Christendom
furnishes us with enough. After the example of our blessed Guide
there have been many who have crucified themselves. We learn by
testimony very worthy of belief, that King St. Louis wore a hair-shirt
till in his old age his confessor gave him a dispensation to leave it off;
and that every Friday he caused his shoulders to be drubbed by his
priest with five small chains of iron which were always carried about
amongst his night accoutrements for that purpose.

27

William, our last Duke of Guienne, the father of that Eleanor who transmitted that duchy to the houses of France and England, continually for the last ten or twelve years of his life wore a suit of armour under a religious habit by way of penance. Foulke, Count of Anjou, went as far as Jerusalem, there to cause himself to be whipped by two of his servants, with a rope about his neck, before the sepulchre of our Lord. But do we not, moreover, every Good Friday, in various places, see great numbers of men and women beat and whip themselves till they lacerate and cut the flesh to the very bones? I have often seen it, and it is without any enchantment; and it was said there were some amongst them (for they go disguised) who for money undertook by this means to save harmless the religion of others, by a contempt of pain, so much the greater, as the incentives of devotion are more effectual than those of avarice. Q. Maximus buried his son when he was a consul, and M. Cato his when praetor elect, and L. Paulus both his, within a few days one after another, with such a countenance as expressed no manner of grief. I said once merrily of a certain person, that he had disappointed the divine justice; for the violent death of three grown-up children of his being one day sent him, for a severe scourge, as it is to be supposed, he was so far from being afflicted at the accident, that he rather took it for a particular grace and favour of heaven. I do not follow these monstrous humours, though I lost two or three at nurse, if not without grief, at least without repining, and yet there is hardly any accident that pierces nearer to the quick. I see a great many other occasions of sorrow, that should they happen to me I should hardly feel; and have despised some, when they have befallen me, to which the world has given so terrible a figure that I should blush to boast of my constancy:

Ex quo intelligitur, non in natura, sed in opinione, esse aegritudinem.

[By which one may understand that grief is not in nature, but in opinion.

—Cicero, *Tusculum Disputations.*, iii. 28.]

CHAPTER 14

Opinion is a powerful party, bold, and without measure. Whoever so greedily hunted after security and repose as Alexander and Caesar did after disturbance and difficulties? Teres, the father of Sitalces, was wont to say that "when he had no wars, he fancied there was no difference between him and his groom". Cato the consul, to secure some cities of Spain from revolt, only interdicting the inhabitants from wearing arms, a great many killed themselves:

Ferox gens, nullam vitam rati sine armis esse.

[A fierce people, who thought there was no life without war.
—Livy, xxxiv. 17.]

How many do we know who have forsaken the calm and sweetness of a quiet life at home amongst their acquaintance, to seek out the horror of unhabitable deserts; and having precipitated themselves into so abject a condition as to become the scorn and contempt of the world, have hugged themselves with the conceit, even to affectation. Cardinal Borromeo, who died lately at Milan, amidst all the jollity that the air of Italy, his youth, birth, and great riches, invited him to, kept himself in so austere a way of living, that the same robe he wore in summer served him for winter too; he had only straw for his bed, and his hours of leisure from affairs he continually spent in study upon his knees, having a little bread and a glass of water set by his book, which was all the provision of his repast, and all the time he spent in eating.

I know some who consentingly have acquired both profit and advancement from cuckoldom, of which the bare name only affrights so many people.

If the sight be not the most necessary of all our senses, it is at least the most pleasant; but the most pleasant and most useful of all our members seem to be those of generation; and yet a great many have conceived a mortal hatred against them only for this, that they were too pleasant, and have deprived themselves of them only for their value: as much thought he of his eyes that put them out.

The generality and more solid sort of men look upon abundance of children as a great blessing; I, and some others, think it as great a benefit to be without them. And when you ask Thales why he does not marry, he tells you, because he has no mind to leave any posterity behind him.

That our opinion gives the value to things is very manifest in the great number of those which we do, not so much prizing them, as ourselves, and never considering either their virtues or their use, but only how dear they cost us, as though that were a part of their substance; and we only repute for value in them, not what they bring to us, but what we add to them. By which I understand that we are great economisers of our expense: as it weighs, it serves for so much as it weighs. Our opinion will never suffer it to want of its value: the price gives value to the diamond; difficulty to virtue; suffering to devotion; and griping to physic. A certain person, to be poor, threw his crowns into the same sea to which so many come, in all parts of the world, to fish for riches. Epicurus says that to be rich is no relief, but only an alteration, of affairs. In truth, it is not want, but rather abundance, that creates avarice. I will deliver my own experience concerning this affair.

I have since my emergence from childhood lived in three sorts of conditions. The first, which continued for some twenty years, I passed over without any other means but what were casual and depending upon the allowance and assistance of others, without stint, but without certain revenue. I then spent my money so much the more cheerfully, and with so much the less care how it went, as it wholly depended upon my overconfidence of fortune. I never lived more at my ease; I never had the repulse of finding the purse of any of my friends shut against me, having enjoined myself this necessity above all other necessities whatever, by no means to fail of payment at the appointed time, which also they have a thousand times respited, seeing how careful I was to satisfy them; so that I practised at once a thrifty, and withal a kind of alluring, honesty. I naturally feel a kind of pleasure in paying, as if I eased my shoulders of a troublesome weight and freed myself from an image of slavery; as also that I find a ravishing kind of satisfaction in pleasing another and doing a just action. I except payments where the trouble of bargaining and reckoning is required; and in such cases; where I can meet with nobody to ease me of that charge, I delay them, how scandalously and injuriously soever, all I possibly can, for fear of the wranglings for which both my humour and way of speaking are so totally improper and unfit. There is nothing I hate so much as driving a bargain; it is a mere traffic of cozenage and impudence, where, after an hour's cheapening and hesitating, both parties abandon their word and oath for five sols' abatement. Yet I always borrowed at great disadvantage; for, wanting the confidence to speak to the person myself, I committed my request to the persuasion of a letter, which usually is no very successful advocate, and is of very great advantage to him who has a mind to deny. I, in those days, more jocundly and freely referred the conduct of my affairs to the stars, than I have since done to my own providence and judgment. Most good managers look upon it as a horrible thing to live always thus in uncertainty, and do not consider, in the first place, that the greatest part of the world live so: how many worthy men have wholly abandoned their own certainties, and yet daily do it, to the winds, to trust to the inconstant favour of princes and of fortune? Caesar ran above a million of gold, more than he was worth, in debt to become Caesar; and how many merchants have begun their traffic by the sale of their farms, which they sent into the Indies:

Tot per impotentia freta.

[Through so many ungovernable seas.

—Catullus, iv. 18.]

In so great a siccity of devotion as we see in these days, we have a thousand and a thousand colleges that pass it over commodiously enough, expecting every day their dinner from the liberality of

Heaven. Secondly, they do not take notice that this certitude upon which they so much rely is not much less uncertain and hazardous than hazard itself. I see misery as near beyond two thousand crowns a year as if it stood close by me; for besides that it is in the power of chance to make a hundred breaches to poverty through the greatest strength of our riches – there being very often no mean between the highest and the lowest fortune:

Fortuna vitrea est: turn, quumsplendet, frangitur.

[Fortune is glass: in its greatest brightness it breaks.
—Ex Mim. Publilius Syrus.]

and to turn all our barricadoes and bulwarks topsy-turvy, I find that, by divers causes, indigence is as frequently seen to inhabit with those who have estates as with those that have none; and that, peradventure, it is then far less grievous when alone than when accompanied with riches. These flow more from good management than from revenue;

Faber est suae quisque fortunae.

[Everyone is the maker of his own fortune.
—Sallust, *De Repub. Ord., i. I.*]

and an uneasy, necessitous, busy, rich man seems to me more miserable than he that is simply poor.

In divitiis inopes, quod genus egestatis gravissimum est.

[Poor in the midst of riches, which is the sorest kind of poverty.
—Seneca, *Epistles*, 74.]

The greatest and most wealthy princes are by poverty and want driven to the most extreme necessity; for can there be any more

extreme than to become tyrants and unjust usurpers of their subjects' goods and estates?

My second condition of life was to have money of my own,
wherein I so ordered the matter that I had soon laid up a very notable sum out of a mean fortune, considering with myself that that
only was to be reputed having which a man reserves from his ordinary expense, and that a man cannot absolutely rely upon revenue
he hopes to receive, how clear soever the hope may be. For what,
said I, if I should be surprised by such or such an accident? And
after such-like vain and vicious imaginations, would very learnedly,
by this hoarding of money, provide against all inconveniences; and
could, moreover, answer such as objected to me that the number
of these was too infinite, that if I could not lay up for all, I could,
however, do it at least for some and for many. Yet was not this done
without a great deal of solicitude and anxiety of mind; I kept it very
close, and though I dare talk so boldly of myself, never spoke of my
money, but falsely, as others do, who being rich, pretend to be poor,
and being poor, pretend to be rich, dispensing their consciences
from ever telling sincerely what they have: a ridiculous and shameful prudence. Was I going a journey? Methought I was never enough
provided: and the more I loaded myself with money, the more also
was I loaded with fear, one while of the danger of the roads, another
of the fidelity of him who had the charge of my baggage, of whom,
as some others that I know, I was never sufficiently secure if I had
him not always in my eye. If I chanced to leave my cash-box behind
me, O, what strange suspicions and anxiety of mind did I enter into,
and, which was worse, without daring to acquaint anybody with it.
My mind was eternally taken up with such things as these, so that,
all things considered, there is more trouble in keeping money than
in getting it. And if I did not altogether so much as I say, or was
not really so scandalously solicitous of my money as I have made
myself out to be, yet it cost me something at least to restrain myself
from being so. I reaped little or no advantage by what I had, and
my expenses seemed nothing less to me for having the more to

33

spend; for, as Bion said, the hairy men are as angry as the bald to be pulled; and after you are once accustomed to it and have once set your heart upon your heap, it is no more at your service; you cannot find in your heart to break it: it is a building that you will fancy must of necessity all tumble down to ruin if you stir but the least pebble; necessity must first take you by the throat before you can prevail upon yourself to touch it; and I would sooner have pawned anything I had, or sold a horse, and with much less constraint upon myself, than have made the least breach in that beloved purse I had so carefully laid by. But the danger was that a man cannot easily prescribe certain limits to this desire (they are hard to find in things that a man conceives to be good), and to stint this good husbandry so that it may not degenerate into avarice: men still are intent upon adding to the heap and increasing the stock from sum to sum, till at last they vilely deprive themselves of the enjoyment of their own proper goods, and throw all into reserve, without making any use of them at all. According to this rule, they are the richest people in the world who are set to guard the walls and gates of a wealthy city. All moneyed men I conclude to be covetous. Plato places corporal or human goods in this order: health, beauty, strength, riches; and riches, says he, are not blind, but very clear-sighted, when illuminated by prudence. Dionysius the son did a very handsome act upon this subject; he was informed that one of the Syracusans had hid a treasure in the earth, and thereupon sent to the man to bring it to him, which he accordingly did, privately reserving a small part of it only to himself, with which he went to another city, where being cured of his appetite of hoarding, he began to live at a more liberal rate; which Dionysius hearing, caused the rest of his treasure to be restored to him, saying, that since he had learned to use it, he very willingly returned it back to him.

I continued some years in this hoarding humour, when I know not what good demon fortunately put me out of it, as he did the Syracusan, and made me throw abroad all my reserve at random, the pleasure of a certain journey I took at very great expense having made me spurn this fond love of money underfoot; by which means I am now fallen into a third way of living (I speak what I think of it), doubtless much more pleasant and regular, which is, that I live at the height of my revenue; sometimes the one, sometimes the other may perhaps exceed, but it is very little and but rarely that they differ. I live from hand to mouth, and content myself in having sufficient for my present and ordinary expense; for as to extraordinary occasions, all the laying up in the world would never suffice. And it is the greatest folly imaginable to expect that fortune should ever sufficiently arm us against herself; it is with our own arms that we are to fight her; accidental ones will betray us in the pinch of the business. If I lay up, it is for some near and contemplated purpose; not to purchase lands, of which I have no need, but to purchase pleasure:

Non esse cupidum, pecunia est; non esse emacem, vertigal est.

[Not to be covetous, is money; not to be acquisitive, is revenue.
—Cicero, *Paradoxa Stoicorum.*, vi. 3.]

I neither am in any great apprehension of wanting, nor in desire of any more:

Divinarum fructus est in copia; copiam declarant satietas.

[The fruit of riches is in abundance; satiety declares abundance.
—Idem, ibid., vi. 2.]

And I am very well pleased that this reformation in me has fallen out in an age naturally inclined to avarice, and that I see myself cleared of a folly so common to old men, and the most ridiculous of all human follies.

Feraulez, a man that had run through both fortunes, and found that the increase of substance was no increase of appetite either to eating or drinking, sleeping or the enjoyment of his wife, and who on the other side felt the care of his economics lie heavy upon his shoulders, as it does on mine, was resolved to please a poor young man, his faithful friend, who panted after riches, and made him a gift of all his, which were excessively great, and, moreover, of all he was in the daily way of getting by the liberality of Cyrus, his good master, and by the war; conditionally that he should take care handsomely to maintain and plentifully to entertain him as his guest and friend; which being accordingly done, they afterwards lived very happily together, both of them equally content with the change of their condition. It is an example that I could imitate with all my heart; and I very much approve the fortune of the aged prelate whom I see to have so absolutely stripped himself of his purse, his revenue, and care of his expense, committing them one while to one trusty servant, and another while to another, that he has spun out a long succession of years, as ignorant, by this means, of his domestic affairs as a mere stranger.

The confidence in another man's virtue is no light evidence of a man's own, and God willingly favours such a confidence. As to what concerns him of whom I am speaking, I see nowhere a better governed house, more nobly and constantly maintained than his. Happy to have regulated his affairs to so just a proportion that his estate is sufficient to do it without his care or trouble, and without any hindrance, either in the spending or laying it up, to his other more quiet employments, and more suitable both to his place and liking.

Plenty, then, and indigence depend upon the opinion everyone has of them; and riches no more than glory or health have other beauty or pleasure than he lends them by whom they are possessed.

Everyone is well or ill at ease, according as he so finds himself; not he whom the world believes, but he who believes himself to be so, is content; and in this alone belief gives itself being and reality. Fortune does us neither good nor hurt; she only presents us the matter and the seed, which our soul, more powerful than she, turns and applies as she best pleases; the sole cause and sovereign mistress of her own happy or unhappy condition. All external accessions receive taste and colour from the internal constitution, as clothes warm us, not with their heat, but our own, which they are fit to cover and nourish; he who would shield therewith a cold body, would do the same service for the cold, for so snow and ice are preserved. And, certes, after the same manner that study is a torment to an idle man, abstinence from wine to a drunkard, frugality to the spend-thrift, and exercise to a lazy, tender-bred fellow, so it is of all the rest. The things are not so painful and difficult of themselves, but our weakness or cowardice makes them so. To judge of great, and high matters requires a suitable soul; otherwise we attribute the vice to them which is really our own. A straight oar seems crooked in the water it does not only import that we see the thing, but how and after what manner we see it.

After all this, why, amongst so many discourses that by so many arguments persuade men to despise death and to endure pain, can we not find out one that helps us? And of so many sorts of imagina-tions as have so prevailed upon others as to persuade them to do so, why does not everyone apply someone to himself, the most suitable to his own humour? If he cannot digest a strong-working decoction to eradicate the evil, let him at least take a lenitive to ease it:

> *It is an effeminate and flimsy opinion, nor more so in pain than in pleasure, in which, while we are at our ease, we cannot bear without a cry the sting of a bee. The whole business is to commend thyself.*

—Cicero, *Tusculum Disputations*, ii. 22.

As to the rest, a man does not transgress philosophy by permit-ting the acrimony of pains and human frailty to prevail so much above measure; for they constrain her to go back to her unanswer-able replies: "If it be ill to live in necessity, at least there is no neces-sity upon a man to live in necessity": "No man continues ill long but by his own fault." He who has neither the courage to die nor the heart to live, who will neither resist nor fly, what can we do with him?

20

TO STUDY PHILOSOPHY
IS TO LEARN HOW TO DIE

Cicero says "that to study philosophy is nothing but to prepare one's self to die." The reason of which is, because study and contemplation do in some sort withdraw from us our soul, and employ it separately from the body, which is a kind of apprenticeship and a resemblance of death; or, else, because all the wisdom and reasoning in the world do in the end conclude in this point, to teach us not to fear to die. And to say the truth, either our reason mocks us, or it ought to have no other aim but our contentment only, nor to endeavour anything but, in sum, to make us live well, and, as the Holy Scripture says, at our ease. All the opinions of the world agree in this, that pleasure is our end, though we make use of divers means to attain it: they would, otherwise, be rejected at the first motion; for who would give ear to him that should propose affliction and misery for his end? The controversies and disputes of the philosophical sects upon this point are merely verbal:

> *Transcurramus solertissimas nugas.*

> [Let us skip over those subtle trifles.
> —Seneca, *Epistles*, 117.]

—there is more in them of opposition and obstinacy than is consistent with so sacred a profession; but whatsoever personage a man takes upon himself to perform, he ever mixes his own part with it.

Let the philosophers say what they will, the thing at which we all aim, even in virtue is pleasure. It amuses me to rattle in ears this word, which they so nauseate to and if it signify some supreme pleasure and contentment, it is more due to the assistance of virtue than to any other assistance whatever. This pleasure, for being more gay, more sinewy, more robust and more manly, is only the more seriously voluptuous, and we ought give it the name of pleasure, as that which is more favourable, gentle, and natural, and not that from which we have denominated it. The other and meaner pleasure, if it could deserve this fair name, it ought to be by way of competition, and not of privilege. I find it less exempt from traverses and inconveniences than virtue itself; and, besides that the enjoyment is more momentary, fluid, and frail, it has its watchings, fasts, and labours, its sweat and its blood; and, moreover, has particular to itself so many several sorts of sharp and wounding passions, and so dull a satiety attending it, as equal it to the severest penance. And we mistake if we think that these incommodities serve it for a spur and a seasoning to its sweetness (as in nature one contrary is quickened by another), or say, when we come to virtue, that like consequences and difficulties overwhelm and render it austere and inaccessible; whereas, much more aptly than in voluptuousness, they ennoble, sharpen, and heighten the perfect and divine pleasure they procure us. He renders himself unworthy of it who will counterpoise its cost with its fruit, and neither understands the blessing nor how to use it. Those who preach to us that the quest of it is craggy, difficult, and painful, but its fruition pleasant, what do they mean by that but to tell us that it is always unpleasing? For what human means will ever attain its enjoyment? The most perfect have been fain to content themselves to aspire unto it, and to approach it only, without ever possessing it. But they are deceived, seeing that of all the pleasures we know, the very pursuit is pleasant. The attempt ever relishes of the quality of the thing to which it is directed, for it is a good part of, and consubstantial with, the effect. The felicity and beatitude that glitters in Virtue, shines throughout all her appurtenances and avenues, even to the first entry and utmost limits.

CHAPTER 20

Now, of all the benefits that virtue confers upon us, the contempt of death is one of the greatest, as the means that accommodates human life with a soft and easy tranquillity, and gives us a pure and pleasant taste of living, without which all other pleasure would be extinct. Which is the reason why all the rules centre and concur in this one article. And although they all in like manner, with common accord, teach us also to despise pain, poverty, and the other accidents to which human life is subject, it is not, nevertheless, with the same solicitude, as well by reason these accidents are not of so great necessity, the greater part of mankind passing over their whole lives without ever knowing what poverty is, and some without sorrow or sickness, as Xenophilus the musician, who lived a hundred and six years in a perfect and continual health; as also because, at the worst, death can, whenever we please, cut short and put an end to all other inconveniences. But as to death, it is inevitable:

> *Omnes eodem cogimur; omnium*
> *Versatur urna serius ocius*
> *Sors exitura, et nos in aeternum*
> *Exilium impositura cymbae.*

[We are all bound one voyage; the lot of all, sooner or later, is to come out of the urn. All must to eternal exile sail away.
—Horace, *Odes*, ii. 3, 25.]

and, consequently, if it frights us, it is a perpetual torment, for which there is no sort of consolation. There is no way by which it may not reach us. We may continually turn our heads this way and that, as in a suspected country:

Quae, quasi saxum Tantalo, semper impendet.

[Ever, like Tantalus stone, hangs over us.
—Cicero, *De Finibus*, i. 18.]

41

Our courts of justice often send back condemned criminals to be executed upon the place where the crime was committed; but, carry them to fine houses by the way, prepare for them the best entertainment you can—

> *Non Siculae dapes*
> *Dulce melaborabunt saporem:*
> *Non avium cyatheaceae cantus*
> *Somnum reducent.*

[Sicilian dainties will not tickle their palates, nor the melody of birds and harps bring back sleep.

—Horace, *Odes*, iii. 1, 18.]

Do you think they can relish it? and that the fatal end of their journey being continually before their eyes, would not alter and deprave their palate from tasting these regalios?

> *Audit iter, numeratque dies, spatioque viarum*
> *Metitur vitam; torquetur peste futura.*

[He considers the route, computes the time of travelling, measuring his life by the length of the journey; and torments himself by thinking of the blow to come.

—Claudianus, *In Rufinum*, ii. 137.]

The end of our race is death; it is the necessary object of our aim, which, if it fright us, how is it possible to advance a step without a fit of ague? The remedy the vulgar use is not to think on it; but from what brutish stupidity can they derive so gross a blindness? They must bridle the ass by the tail:

> *Qui capite ipse suo instituit vestigia retro*

[Who in his folly seeks to advance backwards

—Lucretius, iv. 474.]

CHAPTER 20

It is no wonder if he be often trapped in the pitfall. They affright people with the very mention of death, and many cross themselves, as it were the name of the devil. And because the making a man's will is in reference to dying, not a man will be persuaded to take a pen in hand to that purpose, till the physician has passed sentence upon and totally given him over, and then between and terror, God knows in how fit a condition of understanding he is to do it.

The Romans, by reason that this poor syllable death sounded so harshly to their ears and seemed so ominous, found out a way to soften and spin it out by a periphrasis, and instead of pronouncing such a one is dead, said, "Such a one has lived," or "Such a one has ceased to live" [Plutarch, *Life of Cicero*, c. 22] for, provided there was any mention of life in the case, though past, it carried yet some sound of consolation. And from them it is that we have borrowed our expression, "The late Monsieur such and such a one." ["feu Monsieur un tel."] Peradventure, as the saying is, the term we have lived is worth our money. I was born between eleven and twelve o'clock in the forenoon the last day of February 1533, according to our computation, beginning the year the 1st of January [This was in virtue of an ordinance of Charles IX in 1563. Previously the year commenced at Easter, so that the 1st January 1563 became the first day of the year 1563.] and it is now but just fifteen days since I was complete nine-and-thirty years old; I make account to live, at least, as many more. In the meantime, to trouble a man's self with the thought of a thing so far off were folly. But what? Young and old die upon the same terms; no one departs out of life otherwise than if he had but just before entered into it; neither is any man so old and decrepit, who, having heard of Methuselah, does not think he has yet twenty good years to come. Fool that you are! who has assured unto you the term of life? Thou dependest upon physicians' tales: rather consult effects and experience. According to the common course of things, it is long since that thou hast lived by extraordinary favour; thou hast already outlived the ordinary term of life. And that it is so, reckon up thy acquaintance, how many more have died before they arrived

at thy age than have attained unto it; and of those who have enno-
bled their lives by their renown, take but an account, and I dare lay
a wager thou wilt find more who have died before than after five-
and-thirty years of age. It is full both of reason and piety, too, to take
example by the humanity of Jesus Christ Himself; now, He ended
His life at three-and-thirty years. The greatest man, that was no more
than a man, Alexander, died also at the same age. How many several
ways has death to surprise us?

Quid quisque, vitet, nunquam homini satis
Cautum est in horas.

[Be as cautious as he may, man can never foresee the danger that
may at any hour befall him.

—Horace, *Odes*, ii. 13, 13.]

To omit fevers and pleurisies, who would ever have imagined
that a duke of Brittany [Jean II, died 1305] should be pressed to
death in a crowd as that duke was at the entry of Pope Clement,
my neighbour, into Lyons? [Montaigne speaks of him as if he had
been a contemporary neighbour, perhaps because he was the Arch-
bishop of Bordeaux. Bertrand le Got was Pope under the title of
Clement V, 1305-14.] Hast thou not seen one of our kings [Henry
II, killed in a tournament, July 10, 1559] killed at a tilting, and did
not one of his ancestors die by jostle of a hog? [Philip, eldest son of
Louis le Gros] Aeschylus, threatened with the fall of a house, was to
much purpose circumspect to avoid that danger, seeing that he was
knocked on the head by a tortoise falling out of an eagle's talons
in the air. Another was choked with a grape-stone; [Val. Max., ix.
12, ext. 2.] an emperor killed with the scratch of a comb in combing his head. Aemilius Lepidus with a stumble at his own threshold, [Pliny, *Natural History*, vii. 33] and Aufidius with a jostle against
the door as he entered the council-chamber. And between the very
thighs of women, Cornelius Gallus the proctor; Tigillinus, captain

of the watch at Rome; Ludovico, son of Guido di Gonzaga, Marquis of Mantua; and (of worse example) Speusippus, a Platonic philosopher, and one of our Popes. The poor judge Bebius gave adjournment in a case for eight days; but he himself, meanwhile, was condemned by death, and his own stay of life expired. Whilst Caius Julius, the physician, was anointing the eyes of a patient, death closed his own; and, if I may bring in an example of my own blood, a brother of mine, Captain St. Martin, a young man, three-and-twenty years old, who had already given sufficient testimony of his valour, playing a match at tennis, received a blow of a ball a little above his right ear, which, as it gave no manner of sign of wound or contusion, he took no notice of it, nor so much as sat down to repose himself, but, nevertheless, died within five or six hours after of an apoplexy occasioned by that blow.

These so frequent and common examples passing every day before our eyes, how is it possible a man should disengage himself from the thought of death, or avoid fancying that it has us every moment by the throat? What matter is it, you will say, which way it comes to pass, provided a man does not terrify himself with the expectation? For my part, I am of this mind, and if a man could by any means avoid it, though by creeping under a calf's skin, I am one that should not be ashamed of the shift; all I aim at is, to pass my time at my ease, and the recreations that will most contribute to it, I take hold of, as little glorious and exemplary as you will:

> *Praetulerim . . . delirus inersque videri,*
> *Dum mea delectent mala me, vel Denique fallant,*
> *Quam sapere, et ringi.*

[I had rather seem mad and a sluggard, so that my defects are agreeable to myself, or that I am not painfully conscious of them, than be wise, and chaptious.

—Horace, *Epistles*, ii. 2, 126]

But it is folly to think of doing anything that way. They go, they come, they gallop and dance, and not a word of death. All this is very fine; but withal, when it comes either to themselves, their wives, their children, or friends, surprising them at unawares and unprepared, then, what torment, what outcries, what madness and despair! Did you ever see anything so subdued, so changed, and so confounded? A man must, therefore, make more early provision for it; and this brutish negligence, could it possibly lodge in the brain of any man of sense (which I think utterly impossible), sells us its merchandise too dear. Were it an enemy that could be avoided, I would then advise to borrow arms even of cowardice itself; but seeing it is not, and that it will catch you as well flying and playing the poltroon, as standing to it like an honest man:

> *Nempe et fugacem persequitur virum,*
> *Nec parcit imbellis juventae*
> *Poplitibus timidoque tergo.*

> [He pursues the flying poltroon, nor spares the hamstrings of the unwarlike youth who turns his back.
> —Horace, *Epistles*, iii. 2, 14]

And seeing that no temper of arms is of proof to secure us:

> *Ille licet ferro cautus, se condat et aere,*
> *Mors tamen inclusum protrahet inde caput*

> [Let him hide beneath iron or brass in his fear, death will pull his head out of his armour.
> —Propertius iii. 18]

—let us learn bravely to stand our ground, and fight him. And to begin to deprive him of the greatest advantage he has over us, let us take a way quite contrary to the common course. Let us disarm him

46

of his novelty and strangeness, let us converse and be familiar with him, and have nothing so frequent in our thoughts as death. Upon all occasions represent him to our imagination in his every shape; at the stumbling of a horse, at the falling of a tile, at the least prick with a pin, let us presently consider, and say to ourselves, "Well, and what if it had been death itself?" and, thereupon, let us encourage and fortify ourselves. Let us evermore, amidst our jollity and feasting, set the remembrance of our frail condition before our eyes, never suffering ourselves to be so far transported with our delights, but that we have some intervals of reflecting upon, and considering how many several ways this jollity of ours tends to death, and with how many dangers it threatens it. The Egyptians were wont to do after this manner, who in the height of their feasting and mirth, caused a dried skeleton of a man to be brought into the room to serve for a memento to their guests:

> *Omnem crede diem tibi diluxisse supremum*
> *Grata superveniet, quae non sperabitur, hora.*

[Think each day when past is thy last; the next day, as unexpected, will be the more welcome.

—Horace, *Epistles*, i. 4, 13]

Where death waits for us is uncertain; let us look for him everywhere. The premeditation of death is the premeditation of liberty; he who has learned to die has unlearned to serve. There is nothing evil in life for him who rightly comprehends that the privation of life is no evil: to know, how to die delivers us from all subjection and constraint. Paulus Emilius answered him whom the miserable King of Macedon, his prisoner, sent to entreat him that he would not lead him in his triumph, "Let him make that request to himself." [Plutarch, *Life of Paulus Aemilius*, c. 17; Cicero, *Tusculum Disputations*, v. 40.]

In truth, in all things, if nature do not help a little, it is very hard for art and industry to perform anything to purpose. I am in my own nature not melancholic, but meditative; and there is nothing I have more continually entertained myself withal than imaginations of death, even in the most wanton time of my age:

Jucundum quum aetas florida ver ageret.

[When my florid age rejoiced in pleasant spring.
—Catullus, lxviii.]

In the company of ladies, and at games, some have perhaps thought me possessed with some jealousy, or the uncertainty of some hope, whilst I was entertaining myself with the remembrance of someone, surprised, a few days before, with a burning fever of which he died, returning from an entertainment like this, with his head full of idle fancies of love and jollity, as mine was then, and that, for aught I knew, the same-destiny was attending me.

Jam fuerit, nec post unquam revocare licebit.

[Presently the present will have gone, never to be recalled.
—Lucretius, iii. 928.]

Yet did not this thought wrinkle my forehead any more than any other. It is impossible but we must feel a sting in such imaginations as these, at first; but with often turning and returning them in one's mind, they, at last, become so familiar as to be no trouble at all: otherwise, I, for my part, should be in a perpetual fright and frenzy; for never man was so distrustful of his life, never man so uncertain as to its duration. Neither health, which I have hitherto ever enjoyed very strong and vigorous, and very seldom interrupted, does prolong, nor sickness contract my hopes. Every minute, methinks, I am escaping, and it eternally runs in my mind, that what may be done to-morrow, may be done to-day. Hazards and dangers do, in truth, little or nothing hasten our end; and if we consider how many thousands more remain and hang over our heads, besides the accident that immediately threatens us, we shall find that the sound and the sick, those that are abroad at sea, and those that sit by the fire, those who are engaged in battle, and those who sit idle at home, are the one as near it as the other.

Nemo altero fragilior est; nemo in crastinum sui certior.

[No man is more fragile than another: no man more certain than another of tomorrow.

—Seneca, *Epistles*, 91.]

For anything I have to do before I die, the longest leisure would appear too short, were it but an hour's business I had to do.

A friend of mine the other day turning over my tablets, found therein a memorandum of something I would have done after my decease, whereupon I told him, as it was really true, that though I was no more than a league's distance only from my own house, and merry and well, yet when that thing came into my head, I made haste to write it down there, because I was not certain to live till I came home. As a man that am eternally brooding over my own thoughts, and confine them to my own particular concerns, I am at all hours as well prepared as I am ever like to be, and death, whenever he shall come, can bring nothing along with him I did not expect long before. We should always, as near as we can, be booted and spurred, and ready to go, and, above all things, take care, at that time, to have no business with anyone but one's self:

Quid brevi fortes jaculamur avo
Multa?

[Why for so short a life tease ourselves with so many projects?
—Horace, *Odes*, ii. 16, 17.]

for we shall there find work enough to do, without any need of
addition. One man complains, more than of death, that he is
thereby prevented of a glorious victory; another, that he must die
before he has married his daughter, or educated his children; a
third seems only troubled that he must lose the society of his wife;
a fourth, the conversation of his son, as the principal comfort and
concern of his being. For my part, I am, thanks be to God, at this
instant in such a condition, that I am ready to dislodge, whenever
it shall please Him, without regret for anything whatsoever. I disengage myself throughout from all worldly relations; my leave is soon
taken of all but myself. Never did any one prepare to bid adieu to
the world more absolutely and unreservedly, and to shake hands
with all manner of interest in it, than I expect to do. The deadest
deaths are the best:

'Miser, O miser,' aiunt, 'omnia ademit'
    Una dies infesta mihi tot praemia vitae.'

['Wretch that I am,' they cry, 'one fatal day has deprived me of
all joys of life.'

—Lucretius, iii. 911.]

And the builder,

Manuet opera interrupta, minaeque
Murorum ingentes.

[The works remain incomplete, the tall pinnacles of the walls
unmade.

—*Aeneid*, iv. 88.]

CHAPTER 20

A man must design nothing that will require so much time to the finishing, or, at least, with no such passionate desire to see it brought to perfection. We are born to action:

Quum moriar, medium solvar et inter opus.

[When I shall die, let it be doing that I had designed.
—Ovid, *Amores*, ii. 10, 36.]

I would always have a man to be doing, and, as much as in him lies, to extend and spin out the offices of life; and then let death take me planting my cabbages, indifferent to him, and still less of my gardens not being finished. I saw one die, who, at his last gasp, complained of nothing so much as that destiny was about to cut the thread of a chronicle he was then compiling, when he was gone no farther than the fifteenth or sixteenth of our kings:

Illud in his rebus non addunt: nec tibi earum
jam desiderium rerum super insidet una.

[They do not add, that dying, we have no longer a desire to possess things.
—Lucretius, iii. 913.]

We are to discharge ourselves from these vulgar and hurtful humours. To this purpose it was that men first appointed the places of sepulture adjoining the churches, and in the most frequented places of the city, to accustom, says Lycurgus, the common people, women, and children, that they should not be startled at the sight of a corpse, and to the end, that the continual spectacle of bones, graves, and funeral obsequies should put us in mind of our frail condition:

Quin etiam exhilarare viris convivia caede
Mos olim, et miscere epulis spectacular dira
Certantum ferro, saepe et super ipsa cadentum
Pocula, respersis non parco sanguine mensis.

51

[It was formerly the custom to enliven banquets with slaughter, and to combine with the repast the dire spectacle of men contending with the sword, the dying in many cases falling upon the cups, and covering the tables with blood.

—Silius Italicus, xi. 51.]

And as the Egyptians after their feasts were wont to present the company with a great image of death, by one that cried out to them, "Drink and be merry, for such shalt thou be when thou art dead"; so it is my custom to have death not only in my imagination, but continually in my mouth. Neither is there anything of which I am so inquisitive, and delight to inform myself, as the manner of men's deaths, their words, looks, and bearing; nor any places in history I am so intent upon; and it is manifest enough, by my crowding in examples of this kind, that I have a particular fancy for that subject. If I were a writer of books, I would compile a register, with a comment, of the various deaths of men: he who should teach men to die would at the same time teach them to live. Dicarchus made one, to which he gave that title; but it was designed for another and less profitable end.

Someone may object, that the pain and terror of dying so infinitely exceed all manner of imagination, that the best fencer will be quite out of his play when it comes to the push. Let them say what they will: to premeditate is doubtless a very great advantage; and besides, is it nothing to go so far, at least, without disturbance or alteration? Moreover, Nature herself assists and encourages us: if the death be sudden and violent, we have not leisure to fear; if otherwise, I perceive that as I engage further in my disease, I naturally enter into a certain loathing and disdain of life. I find I have much more ado to digest this resolution of dying, when I am well in health, than when languishing of a fever; and by how much I have less to do with the commodities of life, by reason that

I begin to lose the use and pleasure of them, by so much I look upon death with less terror. Which makes me hope, that the further I remove from the first, and the nearer I approach to the latter, I shall the more easily exchange the one for the other. And, as I have experienced in other occurrences, that, as Caesar says, things often appear greater to us at distance than near at hand, I have found, that being well, I have had maladies in much greater horror than when really afflicted with them. The vigour wherein I now am, the cheerfulness and delight wherein I now live, make the contrary estate appear in so great a disproportion to my present condition, that, by imagination, I magnify those inconveniences by one-half, and apprehend them to be much more troublesome, than I find them really to be, when they lie the most heavy upon me; I hope to find death the same.

Let us but observe in the ordinary changes and declinations we daily suffer, how nature deprives us of the light and sense of our bodily decay. What remains to an old man of the vigour of his youth and better days?

Heu! senibus vitae portio quanta manet.

[Alas, to old men what portion of life remains!
— Maximian, vel Pseudo-Gallus, i. 16.]

Caesar, to an old weather-beaten soldier of his guards, who came to ask him leave that he might kill himself, taking notice of his withered body and decrepit motion, pleasantly answered, "Thou fanciest, then, that thou art yet alive." [Seneca, *Epistles*, 77.] Should a man fall into this condition on the sudden, I do not think humanity capable of enduring such a change: but nature, leading us by the hand, an easy and, as it were, an insensible pace, step by step conducts us to that miserable state, and by that means makes it familiar to us, so that we are insensible of the stroke when our youth dies in us, though it be really a harder death than the final dissolution of a languishing body, than the death of old age; forasmuch as the fall is not so great from an uneasy being to none at all, as it is from a sprightly and flourishing being to one that is troublesome and painful. The body, bent and bowed, has less force to support a burden; and it is the same with the soul, and therefore it is, that we are to raise her up firm and erect against the power of this adversary. For, as it is impossible she should ever be at rest, whilst she stands in fear of it; so, if she once can assure herself, she may boast (which is a thing as it were surpassing human condition) that it is impossible that disquiet, anxiety, or fear, or any other disturbance, should inhabit or have any place in her:

> *Non vulnus instants Tyranni*
> *Mentha cadi solida, neque Auster*
> *Dux inquieti turbidus Adriae,*
> *Nec fulminantis magna Jovis manus.*

[Not the menacing look of a tyrant shakes her well-settled soul, nor turbulent Auster, the prince of the stormy Adriatic, nor yet the strong hand of thundering Jove, such a temper moves.
—Horace, *Odes*, iii. 3, 3.]

She is then become sovereign of all her lusts and passions, mistress of necessity, shame, poverty, and all the other injuries of fortune. Let us, therefore, as many of us as can, get this advantage; it is the true and sovereign liberty here on earth, that fortifies us wherewithal to defy violence and injustice, and to condemn prisons and chains:

> *In manicis et*
> *Compedibus saevo te sub custode tenebo.*
> *Ipse Deus, simul atque volam, me solvet. Opinor,*
> *Hoc sentit; moriar; mors ultima linea rerum est.*

CHAPTER 20

[I will keep thee in fetters and chains, in custody of a
savage keeper. A god will when I ask Him, set me free.
This god I think is death. Death is the term of all things.
—Horace, *Epistles*, i. 16, 76.]

Our very religion itself has no surer human foundation than
the contempt of life. Not only the argument of reason invites us to
it – for why should we fear to lose a thing, which being lost, cannot
be lamented? – but, also, seeing we are threatened by so many sorts
of death, is it not infinitely worse eternally to fear them all, than
once to undergo one of them? And what matters it, when it shall
happen, since it is inevitable? To him that told Socrates, "The thirty
tyrants have sentenced thee to death"; "And nature them," said he.
[Socrates was not condemned to death by the thirty tyrants, but by
the Athenians. Diogenes Laertius, ii.35.] What a ridiculous thing it
is to trouble ourselves about taking the only step that is to deliver
us from all trouble! As our birth brought us the birth of all things,
so in our death is the death of all things included. And therefore to
lament that we shall not be alive a hundred years hence, is the same
folly as to be sorry we were not alive a hundred years ago. Death is
the beginning of another life. So did we weep, and so much it cost
us to enter into this, and so did we put off our former veil in enter-
ing into it. Nothing can be a grievance that is but once. Is it reasonable so long to fear a thing that will so soon be despatched? Long
life, and short, are by death made all one; for there is no long, nor
short, to things that are no more. Aristotle tells us that there are
certain little beasts upon the banks of the river Hypanis, that never
live above a day: they which die at eight of the clock in the morning, die in their youth, and those that die at five in the evening, in
their decrepitude: which of us would not laugh to see this moment
of continuance put into the consideration of weal or woe? The most
and the least, of ours, in comparison with eternity, or yet with the
duration of mountains, rivers, stars, trees, and even of some animals,
is no less ridiculous. [Seneca, *Consolatione ad Marciam*, c. 20.]

But nature compels us to it. "Go out of this world," says she, "as you entered into it; the same pass you made from death to life, without passion or fear, the same, after the same manner, repeat from life to death. Your death is a part of the order of the universe, it is a part of the life of the world.

> *Inter se mortales mutua vivunt*
> *Et, quasi cursores, vitai lampada tradunt.*

[Mortals, amongst themselves, live by turns, and, like the runners in the games, give up the lamp, when they have won the race, to the next comer.

—Lucretius, ii. 75, 78.]

"Shall I exchange for you this beautiful contexture of things? It is the condition of your creation; death is a part of you, and whilst you endeavour to evade it, you evade yourselves. This very being of yours that you now enjoy is equally divided between life and death. The day of your birth is one day's advance towards the grave:

> *Prima, qux vitam dedit, hora carpsit.*

[The first hour that gave us life took away also an hour.
—Seneca, *Hercules Furens*, 3 Chor. 874.]

> *Nascentes morimur, finisque ab origine pendet.*

[As we are born we die, and the end commences with the beginning.

—Manilius, *Astronomica*, iv. 16.]

"All the whole time you live, you purloin from life and live at the expense of life itself. The perpetual work of your life is but to lay the foundation of death. You are in death, whilst you are in life, because you still are after death, when you are no more alive; or, if you had rather have it so, you are dead after life, but dying all the while you live; and death handles the dying much more rudely than the dead, and more sensibly and essentially. If you have made your profit of life, you have had enough of it; go your way satisfied.

> *Cur non ut plenus vita; conviva recedis?*

> [Why not depart from life as a sated guest from a feast?
> —Lucretius, iii. 951.]

"If you have not known how to make the best use of it, if it was unprofitable to you, what need you care to lose it, to what end would you desire longer to keep it?

> *Cur amplius addere quaeris,*
> *Rursum quod pereat male, et ingratum occidat omne?*

> [Why seek to add longer life, merely to renew ill-spent time, and be again tormented?
> —Lucretius, iii. 914.]

"Life in itself is neither good nor evil; it is the scene of good or evil as you make it. And, if you have lived a day, you have seen all: one day is equal and like to all other days. There is no other light, no other shade; this very sun, this moon, these very stars, this very order and disposition of things, is the same your ancestors enjoyed, and that shall also entertain your posterity:

> *Non alium videre patres, aliumve nepotes*
> *Aspicient.*

> [Your grandsires saw no other thing; nor will your posterity.
> —Manilius, i. 529.]

"And, come the worst that can come, the distribution and variety of all the acts of my comedy are performed in a year. If you have observed the revolution of my four seasons, they comprehend the infancy, the youth, the virility, and the old age of the world: the year has played his part, and knows no other art but to begin again; it will always be the same thing:

Versamur ibidem, atque insumus usque.

[We are turning in the same circle, ever therein confined.
—Lucretius, iii. 1093.]

Atque in se sua per vestigia volvitur annus.

[The year is ever turning around in the same footsteps.
—Virgil, *Georgics*, ii. 402.]

"I am not prepared to create for you any new recreations:

Nam tibi prxterea quod machiner, inveniamque
Quod placeat, nihil est; eadem sunt omnia semper'

[I can devise, nor find anything else to please you: it is the same thing over and over again.
—Lucretius iii. 957]

"Give place to others, as others have given place to you. Equality is the soul of equity. Who can complain of being comprehended in the same destiny, wherein all are involved? Besides, live as long as you can, you shall by that nothing shorten the space you are to be dead; it is all to no purpose; you shall be every whit as long in the condition you so much fear, as if you had died at nurse:

> *Licet quot vis vivendo vincere secla,*
> *Mors aeterna tamen nihilominus illa manebit.*

[Live triumphing over as many ages as you will, death still will remain eternal.

—Lucretius, iii. 1103]

"And yet I will place you in such a condition as you shall have no reason to be displeased.

> *In vera nescis nullum fore morte alium te,*
> *Qui possit vivus tibi to lugere peremptum,*
> *Stansque jacentem.*

[Know you not that, when dead, there can be no other living self to lament you dead, standing on your grave.

—Idem., ibid., 898.]

"Nor shall you so much as wish for the life you are so concerned about:

> *'Nec sibi enim quisquam tum se vitamque requirit.*
> *Nec desiderium nostril nos afficit ullum.*

"Death is less to be feared than nothing, if there could be anything less than nothing.

> *Multo . . . mortem minus ad nos esse putandium,*
> *Si minus esse potest, quam quod nihil esse videmus.*

"Neither can it any way concern you, whether you are living or dead: living, by reason that you are still in being; dead, because you are no more. Moreover, no one dies before his hour: the time you leave behind was no more yours than that was lapsed and gone before you came into the world; nor does it any more concern you.

> *Respice enim, quam nil ad nos anteacta vetustas*
> *Temporis aeterni fuerit.*

[Consider how as nothing to us is the old age of times past.
                                                              – Lucretius iii. 985]

Wherever your life ends, it is all there. The utility of living consists not in the length of days, but in the use of time; a man may have lived long, and yet lived but a little. Make use of time while it is present with you. It depends upon your will, and not upon the number of days, to have a sufficient length of life. Is it possible you can imagine never to arrive at the place towards which you are continually going? and yet there is no journey but hath its end. And, if company will make it more pleasant or more easy to you, does not all the world go the self-same way?

Omnia te, vita perfuncta, sequentur.

[All things, then, life over, must follow thee.

—Lucretius, iii. 981.]

"Does not all the world dance the same brawl that you do? Is there anything that does not grow old, as well as you? A thousand men, a thousand animals, a thousand other creatures, die at the same moment that you die:

> *Nam nox nulla diem, neque noctem aurora sequuta est,*
> *Quae non audierit mistos vagitibus aegris*
> *Ploratus, mortis comites et funeris atri.*

CHAPTER 20

[No night has followed day, no day has followed night, in which there has not been heard sobs and sorrowing cries, the companions of death and funerals.

—Lucretius, v. 579.]

"To what end should you endeavour to draw back, if there be no possibility to evade it? You have seen examples enough of those who have been well pleased to die, as thereby delivered from heavy miseries; but have you ever found any who have been dissatisfied with dying? It must, therefore, needs be very foolish to condemn a thing you have neither experimented in your own person, nor by that of any other. Why do you complain of me and of destiny? Do we do you any wrong? Is it for you to govern us, or for us to govern you? Though, peradventure, thy age may not be accomplished, yet thy life is: a man of low stature is as much a man as a giant; neither men nor their lives are measured by the ell. Chiron refused to be immortal, when he was acquainted with the conditions under which he was to enjoy it, by the god of time itself and its duration, his father Saturn. Do but seriously consider how much more insupportable and painful an immortal life would be to man than what I have already given him. If you had not death, you would eternally curse me for having deprived you of it; I have mixed a little bitterness with it, to the end, that seeing of what convenience it is, you might not too greedily and indiscreetly seek and embrace it: and that you might be so established in this moderation, as neither to nauseate life, nor have any antipathy for dying, which I have decreed you shall once do, I have tempered the one and the other between pleasure and pain. It was I that taught Thales, the most eminent of your sages, that to live and to die were indifferent; which made him, very wisely, answer him, "Why then he did not die?" "Because," said he, "it is indifferent." [Diogenes Laertius, i. 35.] Water, earth, air, and fire, and the other parts of this creation of mine, are no more instruments of thy life than they are of thy death. Why do you fear thy last

61

day? it contributes no more to thy dissolution, than everyone of the rest: the last step is not the cause of lassitude: it does not confess it. Every day travels towards death; the last only arrives at it." These are the good lessons our mother Nature teaches.

I have often considered with myself whence it should proceed, that in war the image of death, whether we look upon it in ourselves or in others, should, without comparison, appear less dreadful than at home in our own houses (for if it were not so, it would be an army of doctors and whining milksops), and that being still in all places the same, there should be, notwithstanding, much more assurance in peasants and the meaner sort of people, than in others of better quality. I believe, in truth, that it is those terrible ceremonies and preparations wherewith we set it out, that more terrify us than the thing itself; a new, quite contrary way of living; the cries of mothers, wives, and children; the visits of astounded and afflicted friends; the attendance of pale and blubbering servants; a dark room, set round with burning tapers; our beds environed with physicians and divines; in sum, nothing but ghostliness and horror round about us; we seem dead and buried already. Children are afraid even of those they are best acquainted with, when disguised in a visor; and so it is with us; the visor must be removed as well from things as from persons, that being taken away, we shall find nothing underneath but the very same death that a mean servant or a poor chambermaid died a day or two ago, without any manner of apprehension. Happy is the death that deprives us of leisure for preparing such ceremonials.

21

ON THE POWER
OF IMAGINATION

Fortis imaginatio generat casum
[A strong imagination begets the event itself.]

I am one of those who are most sensible of the power of imagination: everyone is jostled by it, but some are overthrown by it. It has a very piercing impression upon me; and I make it my business to avoid, wanting force to resist it. I could live by the sole help of healthful and jolly company: the very sight of another's pain materially pains me, and I often usurp the sensations of another person. A perpetual cough in another tickles my lungs and throat. I more unwillingly visit the sick in whom by love and duty I am interested, than those I care not for, to whom I less look. I take possession of the disease I am concerned at, and take it to myself. I do not at all wonder that fancy should give fevers and sometimes kill such as allow it too much scope, and are too willing to entertain it.

Simon Thomas was a great physician of his time: I remember, that happening one day at Toulouse to meet him at a rich old fellow's house, who was troubled with weak lungs, and discoursing with the patient about the method of his cure, he told him, that one thing which would be very conducive to it, was to give me such occasion to be pleased with his company, that I might come often to see him, by which means, and by fixing his eyes upon the freshness of my complexion, and his imagination upon the sprightliness and vigour that glowed in my youth, and possessing all his senses with the flourishing age wherein I then was, his habit of body might, peradventure, be amended; but he forgot to say that mine, at the same time, might be made worse.

Gallus Vibius so much bent his mind to find out the essence and motions of madness, that, in the end, he himself went out of his wits, and to such a degree, that he could never after recover his judgment, and might brag that he was become a fool by too much wisdom. Some there are who through fear anticipate the hangman; and there was the man, whose eyes being unbound to have his pardon read to him, was found stark dead upon the scaffold, by the stroke of imagination. We start, tremble, turn pale, and blush, as we are variously moved by imagination; and, being a-bed, feel our bodies agitated with its power to that degree, as even sometimes to expiring. And boiling youth, when fast asleep, grows so warm with fancy, as in a dream to satisfy amorous desires:

> *Ut, quasi transactis saepe omnibus rebu, profundant*
> *Fluminis ingentes, fluctus, vestemque cruentent.*

[So that, as though they had actually completed the act, they pour forth floods of semen and pollute their garments.]

Although it be no new thing to see horns grown in a night on the forehead of one that had none when he went to bed, notwithstanding, what befell Cippus, King of Italy, is memorable; who having one day been a very delighted spectator of a bullfight, and having all the night dreamed that he had horns on his head, did, by the force of imagination, really cause them to grow there. Passion gave to the son of Croesus the voice which nature had denied him. And Antiochus fell into a fever, inflamed with the beauty of Stratonice, too deeply imprinted in his soul. Pliny pretends to have seen Lucius Cossitius, who from a woman was turned into a man upon her very wedding-day. Pontanus and others report the like metamorphosis to have happened in these latter days in Italy. And, through the vehement desire of him and his mother:

Volta puer solvit, quae foemina voverat, Iphis.

[Iphus fulfilled as a boy vows made as a girl.]

Myself passing by Vitry le Francois, saw a man the Bishop of Soissons had, in confirmation, called Germain, whom all the inhabitants of the place had known to be a girl till two-and-twenty years of age, called Mary. He was, at the time of my being there, very full of beard, old, and not married. He told us, that by straining himself in a leap his male organs came out; and the girls of that place have, to this day, a song, wherein they advise one another not to take too great strides, for fear of being turned into men, as Mary Germain was. It is no wonder if this sort of accident frequently happen; for if imagination have any power in such things, it is so continually and vigorously bent upon this subject, that to the end it may not so often relapse into the same thought and violence of desire, it were better, once for all, to give these young wenches the things they long for.

Some attribute the scars of King Dagobert and of St. Francis to the force of imagination. It is said, that by it bodies will sometimes be removed from their places; and Celsus tells us of a priest whose soul would be ravished into such an ecstasy that the body would, for a long time, remain without sense or respiration. St. Augustine makes mention of another, who, upon the hearing of any lamentable or doleful cries, would presently fall into a swoon, and be so far out of himself, that it was in vain to call, bawl in his ears, pinch or burn him, till he voluntarily came to himself; and then he would say, that he had heard voices as it were afar off, and did feel when they pinched and burned him; and, to prove that this was no obstinate dissimulation in defiance of his sense of feeling, it was manifest, that all the while he had neither pulse nor breathing.

It is very probable, that visions, enchantments, and all extraordinary effects of that nature, derive their credit principally from the power of imagination, working and making its impression upon vulgar and more easy souls, whose belief is so strangely imposed upon, as to think they see what they do not see.

I am not satisfied whether those pleasant ligatures [Les nouements d'aiguillettes, as they were called, knots tied by someone, at a wedding, on a strip of leather, cotton, or silk, and which, especially when passed through the wedding-ring, were supposed to have the magical effect of preventing a consummation of the marriage until they were untied. See Louandre, *La Sorcellerie*, 1853, p. 73. The same superstition and appliance existed in England.] with which this age of ours is so occupied, that there is almost no other talk, are not mere voluntary impressions of apprehension and fear; for I know, by experience, in the case of a particular friend of mine, one for whom I can be as responsible as for myself, and a man that cannot possibly fall under any manner of suspicion of insufficiency, and as little of being enchanted, who having heard a companion of his make a relation of an unusual frigidity that surprised him at a very unseasonable time; being afterwards himself engaged upon the same account, the horror of the former story on a sudden so strangely possessed his imagination, that he ran the same fortune the other had done; and from that time forward, the scurvy remembrance of his disaster running in his mind and tyrannising over him, he was subject to relapse into the same misfortune. He found some remedy, however, for this fancy in another fancy, by himself frankly confessing and declaring beforehand to the party with whom he was to have to do, this subjection of his, by which means, the agitation of his soul was, in some sort, appeased; and knowing that, now, some such misbehaviour was expected from him, the restraint upon his faculties grew less. And afterwards, at such times as he was in no such apprehension, when setting about the act (his thoughts being then disengaged and free, and his body in its true and natural estate) he was at leisure to cause the part to be handled and communicated to the knowledge of the other party, he was totally freed from that vexatious infirmity. After a man has once done a woman right, he is never after in danger of misbehaving himself with that person, unless upon the account of some excusable weakness. Neither is this disaster to be feared, but in adventures, where the soul is overextended with desire or respect, and, especially, where the opportunity is of an unforeseen and pressing nature; in those cases, there is no means for a man to defend himself from such a surprise, as shall put him altogether out of sorts. I have known some, who have secured themselves from this mischance, by coming half sated elsewhere, purposely to abate the ardour of the fury, and others, who, being grown old, find themselves less impotent by being less able; and one, who found an advantage in being assured by a friend of his, that he had a counter-charm of enchantments that would secure him from this disgrace. The story itself is not, much amiss, and therefore you shall have it.

A Count of a very great family, and with whom I was very intimate, being married to a fair lady, who had formerly been courted by one who was at the wedding, all his friends were in very great fear; but especially an old lady his kinswoman, who had the ordering of the solemnity, and in whose house it was kept, suspecting his rival would offer foul play by these sorceries. Which fear she communicated to me. I bade her rely upon me: I had, by chance, about me a certain flat plate of gold, whereon were graven some celestial figures, supposed good against sunstroke or pains in the head, being applied to the suture: where, that it might the better remain firm, it was sewed to a ribbon to be tied under the chin; a foppery germaine to this of which I am speaking. Jacques Pelletier, who lived in my house, had presented this to me for a singular rarity. I had a fancy to make some use of this knack, and therefore privately told the Count, that he might possibly run the same fortune other bridegrooms had sometimes done, especially someone being in the house, who, no doubt, would be glad to do him such a courtesy: but let him boldly go to bed. For I would do him the office of a friend, and, if need were, would not spare a miracle it was in my power to do, provided he would engage to me, upon his honour, to keep it to himself; and only, when they came to bring him his caudle [it was a custom in France to bring the bridegroom a hot alcoholic/medicinal drink in the middle of the night on his wedding-night] if matters had not gone well with him, to give me such a sign, and leave the rest to me. Now he had had his ears so battered, and his mind so prepossessed with the eternal tattle of this business, that when he came to it, he did really find himself tied with the trouble of his imagination, and, accordingly, at the time appointed, gave me the sign. Whereupon, I whispered him in the ear, that he should rise, under pretence of putting us out of the room, and after a jesting manner pull my nightgown from my shoulders – we were of much about the same height – throw it over his own, and there keep it till he had performed what I had appointed him to do, which was, that when we were all gone out of the chamber, he should withdraw to make water, should three times repeat such and such words, and as often do such and such actions; that at every of the three times, he should tie the ribbon I put into his hand about his middle, and be sure to place the medal that was fastened to it, the figures in such a posture, exactly upon his reins, which being done, and having the last of the three times so well girt and fast tied the ribbon that it could neither untie nor slip from its place, let him confidently return to his business, and withal not forget to spread my gown upon the bed, so that it might be sure to cover them both. These ape's tricks are the main of the effect, our fancy being so far seduced as to believe that such strange means must, of necessity, proceed from some abstruse science: their very inanity gives them weight and reverence. And, certain it is, that my figures approved themselves more venereal than solar, more active than prohibitive. It was a sudden whimsey, mixed with a little curiosity, that made me do a thing so contrary to my nature; for I am an enemy to all subtle and counterfeit actions, and abominate all manner of trickery, though it be for sport, and to an advantage; for though the action may not be vicious in itself, its mode is vicious.

CHAPTER 21

Amasis, King of Egypt, having married Laodice, a very beautiful Greek virgin, though noted for his abilities elsewhere, found himself quite another man with his wife, and could by no means enjoy her; at which he was so enraged, that he threatened to kill her, suspecting her to be a witch. As it is usual in things that consist in fancy, she put him upon devotion and prayers, and having accordingly made his vows to Venus, he found himself divinely restored the very first night after his oblations and sacrifices.

Now women are to blame to entertain us with that disdainful, coy, and angry countenance, which extinguishes our vigour, as it kindles our desire; which made the daughter-in-law of Pythagorassay, "That the woman who goes to bed to a man, must put off her modesty with her petticoat, and put it on again with the same." The soul of the assailant, being disturbed with many several alarms, readily loses the power of performance; and whoever the imagination has once put this trick upon, and confounded with the shame of it (and she never does it but at the first acquaintance, by reason men are then more ardent and eager, and also, at this first account a man gives of himself, he is much more timorous of miscarrying), having made an ill beginning, he enters into such fever and despite at the accident, as are apt to remain and continue with him upon following occasions.

Married people, having all their time before them, ought never to compel or so much as to offer at the feat, if they do not find themselves quite ready: and it is less unseemly to fail on the nuptial sheets, when a man perceives himself full of agitation and trembling, and to await another opportunity at more private and more composed leisure, than to make himself perpetually miserable, for having misbehaved himself and been baffled at the first assault. Till possession be taken, a man that knows himself subject to this infirmity, should leisurely and by degrees make several little trials and light offers, without obstinately attempting at once, to force an absolute conquest over his own mutinous and indisposed faculties. Such as know their members to be naturally obedient, need take no other care but only to counterplot their apprehensions and fantasies.

The indocile liberty of this member is very remarkable, so importunately unruly in its swollenness and impatience, when we do not require it, and so unseasonably disobedient, when we stand most in need of it: so imperiously contesting in authority with the will, and with so much haughty obstinacy denying all solicitation, both of hand and mind. And yet, though his rebellion is so universally complained of, and that proof is thence deduced to condemn him, if he had, nevertheless, feed me to plead his cause, I should peradventure, bring the rest of his fellow-members into suspicion of complotting this mischief against him, out of pure envy at the importance and pleasure especial to his employment; and to have, by confederacy, armed the whole world against him, by malevolently charging him alone, with their common offence. For let anyone consider, whether there is any one part of our bodies that does not often refuse to perform its office at the precept of the will, and that does not often exercise its function in defiance of her command. They have everyone of them passions of their own, that rouse and awaken, stupefy and benumb them, without our leave or consent. How often do the involuntary motions of the countenance discover our inward thoughts, and betray our most private secrets to the bystanders. The same cause that animates this member, does also, without our knowledge, animate the lungs, pulse, and heart, the sight of a pleasing object imperceptibly diffusing a flame through all our parts, with a feverish motion. Is there nothing but these veins and muscles that swell and flag without the consent, not only of the will, but even of our knowledge also? We do not command our hairs to stand on end, nor our skin to shiver either with fear or desire; the hands often convey themselves to parts to which we do not direct them; the tongue will be interdict, and the voice congealed, when we know not how to help it. When we have nothing to eat, and would willingly forbid it, the appetite does not, for all that, forbear to stir up the parts that are subject to it, no more nor less than the other appetite we were speaking of, and in like manner, as unseasonably leaves us, when it thinks fit. The vessels that serve to discharge the belly have their

Chapter 21

own proper dilatations and compressions, without and beyond our concurrence, as well as those which are destined to purge the reins; and that which, to justify the prerogative of the will, St. Augustine urges, of having seen a man who could command his rear to discharge as often together as he pleased, Vives, his commentator, yet further fortifies with another example in his time – of one that could break wind in tune; but these cases do not suppose any more pure obedience in that part; for is anything commonly more tumultuary or indiscreet? To which let me add, that I myself knew one so rude and ungoverned, as for forty years together made his master vent with one continued and unintermitted outbursting, and it is like will do so till he die of it. And I could heartily wish, that I only knew by reading, how often a man's belly, by the denial of one single puff, brings him to the very door of an exceeding painful death; and that the emperor [The Emperor Claudius, who, however, according to Suetonius (Vita, c. 32), only intended to authorise this singular privilege by an edict] who gave liberty to let fly in all places, had, at the same time, given us power to do it. But for our will, in whose behalf we prefer this accusation, with how much greater probability may we reproach herself with mutiny and sedition, for her irregularity and disobedience? Does she always will what we would have her to do? Does she not often will what we forbid her to will, and that to our manifest prejudice? Does she suffer herself, more than any of the rest, to be governed and directed by the results of our reason? To conclude, I should move, in the behalf of the gentleman, my client, it might be considered, that in this fact, his cause being inseparably and indistinctly conjoined with an accessory, yet he only is called in question, and that by arguments and accusations, which cannot be charged upon the other; whose business, indeed, it is sometimes inopportunely to invite, but never to refuse, and invite, moreover, after a tacit and quiet manner; and therefore is the malice and injustice of his accusers most manifestly apparent. But be it how it will, protesting against the proceedings of the advocates and judges, nature will, in the meantime, proceed after her own way, who had done but well, had she endowed this member with some particular privilege; the author of the sole immortal work of mortals; a divine work, according to Socrates; and love, the desire of immortality, and himself an immortal demon.

Someone, perhaps, by such an effect of imagination may have had the good luck to leave behind him here, the scrofula, which his companion who has come after, has carried with him into Spain. And it is for this reason you may see why men in such cases require a mind prepared for the thing that is to be done. Why do the physicians possess, beforehand, their patients' credulity with so many false promises of cure, if not to the end, that the effect of imagination may supply the imposture of their decoctions? They know very well, that a great master of their trade has given it under his hand, that he has known some with whom the very sight of physic would work. All which conceits come now into my head, by the remembrance of a story was told me by a domestic apothecary of my father's, a blunt Swiss, a nation not much addicted to vanity and lying, of a merchant he had long known at Toulouse, who being a valetudinary, and much afflicted with the stone, had often occasion to take clysters, of which he caused several sorts to be prescribed him by the physicians, according to the accidents of his disease; which, being brought him, and none of the usual forms, as feeling if it were not too hot, and the like, being omitted, he lay down, the syringe advanced, and all ceremonies performed, injection alone excepted; after which, the apothecary being gone, and the patient accommodated as if he had really received a clyster, he found the same operation and effect that those do who have taken one indeed; and if at any time the physician did not find the operation sufficient, he would usually give him two or three more doses, after the same manner. And the fellow swore, that to save charges (for he paid as if he had really taken them) this sick man's wife, having sometimes made trial of warm water only, the effect discovered the cheat, and finding these would do no good, was fain to return to the old way.

CHAPTER 21

A woman fancying she had swallowed a pin in a piece of bread, cried and lamented as though she had an intolerable pain in her throat, where she thought she felt it stick; but an ingenious fellow that was brought to her, seeing no outward tumour nor alteration, supposing it to be only a conceit taken at some crust of bread that had hurt her as it went down, caused her to vomit, and, unseen, threw a crooked pin into the basin, which the woman no sooner saw, but believing she had cast it up, she presently found herself eased of her pain. I myself knew a gentleman, who having treated a large company at his house, three or four days after bragged in jest (for there was no such thing), that he had made them eat of a baked cat; at which, a young gentlewoman, who had been at the feast, took such a horror, that falling into a violent vomiting and fever, there was no possible means to save her. Even brute beasts are subject to the force of imagination as well as we; witness dogs, who die of grief for the loss of their masters; and bark and tremble and start in their sleep; so horses will kick and whinny in their sleep.

Now all this may be attributed to the close affinity and relation between the soul and the body intercommunicating their fortunes; but it is quite another thing when the imagination works not only upon one's own particular body, but upon that of others also. And as an infected body communicates its malady to those that approach or live near it, as we see in the plague, the smallpox, and sore eyes, that run through whole families and cities:

> *Dum spectant oculi laesos, laeduntur et ipsi;*
> *Multaque corporibus transitione nocent.*

[When we look at people with sore eyes, our own eyes become sore. Many things are hurtful to our bodies by transition.
—Ovid, *Remedia Amoris*, 615.]

—so the imagination, being vehemently agitated, darts out infection capable of offending the foreign object. The ancients had an opinion of certain women of Scythia, that being animated and enraged against any one, they killed him only with their looks. Tortoises and ostriches hatch their eggs with only looking on them, which infers that their eyes have in them some ejaculative virtue. And the eyes of witches are said to be assailant and hurtful:

Nescio quis teneros oculus mihi fascinate agnos.

[Some eye, I know not whose is bewitching my tender lambs.
—Virgil, *Eclogues.*, iii. 103.]

Magicians are no very good authority with me. But we experimentally see that women impart the marks of their fancy to the children they carry in the womb; witness her that was gave birth to a Moor; and there was presented to Charles the Emperor and King of Bohemia, a girl from about Pisa, all over rough and covered with hair, whom her mother said to be so conceived by reason of a picture of St. John the Baptist, that hung within the curtains of her bed.

It is the same with beasts; witness Jacob's sheep, and the hares and partridges that the snow turns white upon the mountains. There was at my house, a little while ago, a cat seen watching a bird upon the top of a tree: these, for some time, mutually fixing their eyes one upon another, the bird at last let herself fall dead into the cat's claws, either dazzled by the force of its own imagination, or drawn by some attractive power of the cat. Such as are addicted to the pleasures of the field, have, I make no question, heard the story of the falconer, who having earnestly fixed his eyes upon a kite in the air; laid a wager that he would bring her down with the sole power of his sight, and did so, as it was said; for the tales I borrow I charge upon the consciences of those from whom I have them. The discourses are my own, and found themselves upon the proofs of reason, not of experience; to which everyone has liberty to add

CHAPTER 21

his own examples; and who has none, let him not forbear, the number and varieties of accidents considered, to believe that there are plenty of them; if I do not apply them well, let some other do it for me. And, also, in the subject of which I treat, our manners and motions, testimonies and instances; how fabulous soever, provided they are possible, serve as well as the true; whether they have really happened or no, at Rome or Paris, to John or Peter, it is still within the verge of human capacity, which serves me to good use. I see, and make my advantage of it, as well in shadow as in substance; and amongst the various readings thereof in history, I cull out the most rare and memorable to fit my own turn. There are authors whose only end and design it is to give an account of things that have happened; mine, if I could arrive unto it, should be to deliver of what may happen. There is a just liberty allowed in the schools, of supposing similitudes, when they have none at hand. I do not, however, make any use of that privilege, and as to that matter, in superstitious religion, surpass all historical authority. In the examples which I here bring in, of what I have heard, read, done, or said, I have forbidden myself to dare to alter even the most light and indifferent circumstances; my conscience does not falsify one tittle; what my ignorance may do, I cannot say.

And this it is that makes me sometimes doubt in my own mind, whether a divine, or a philosopher, and such men of exact and tender prudence and conscience, are fit to write history: for how can they stake their reputation upon a popular faith? how be responsible for the opinions of men they do not know? and with what assurance deliver their conjectures for current pay? Of actions performed before their own eyes, wherein several persons were actors, they would be unwilling to give evidence upon oath before a judge; and there is no man, so familiarly known to them, for whose intentions they would become absolute caution. For my part, I think it less hazardous to write of things past, than present, by how much the writer is only to give an account of things everyone knows he must of necessity borrow upon trust.

I am solicited to write the affairs of my own time by some, who fancy I look upon them with an eye less blinded with passion than another, and have a clearer insight into them by reason of the free access fortune has given me to the heads of various factions; but they do not consider, that to purchase the glory of Sallust, I would not give myself the trouble, sworn enemy as I am to obligation, assiduity, or perseverance: that there is nothing so contrary to my style, as a continued narrative, I so often interrupt and cut myself short in my writing for want of breath; I have neither composition nor explanation worth anything, and am ignorant, beyond a child, of the phrases and even the very words proper to express the most common things; and for that reason it is, that I have undertaken to say only what I can say, and have accommodated my subject to my strength. Should I take one to be my guide, peradventure I should not be able to keep pace with him; and in the freedom of my liberty might deliver judgments, which upon better thoughts, and according to reason, would be illegitimate and punishable. Plutarch would say of what he has delivered to us, that it is the work of others: that his examples are all and everywhere exactly true: that they are useful to posterity, and are presented with a lustre that will light us the way to virtue, is his own work. It is not of so dangerous consequence, as in a medicinal drug, whether an old story be so or so.

ON CUSTOM, AND THAT WE SHOULD NOT EASILY CHANGE AN ESTABLISHED LAW

He seems to me to have had a right and true apprehension of the power of custom, who first invented the story of a country-woman who, having accustomed herself to play with and carry a young calf in her arms, and daily continuing to do so as it grew up, obtained this by custom, that, when grown to be a great ox, she was still able to bear it. For, in truth, custom is a violent and treacherous schoolmistress. She, by little and little, slily and unperceived, slips in the foot of her authority, but having by this gentle and humble beginning, with the benefit of time, fixed and established it, she then unmasks a furious and tyrannic countenance, against which we have no more the courage or the power so much as to lift up our eyes. We see her, at every turn, forcing and violating the rules of nature:

Usus efficacissimus rerum omnium magister.

[Custom is the best master of all things.
—Pliny, *Natural History*, xxvi. 2.]

I refer to her Plato's cave in his Republic, and the physicians, who so often submit the reasons of their art to her authority; as the story of that king, who by custom brought his stomach to that pass, as to live by poison, and the maid that Albertus reports to have lived upon spiders. In that new world of the Indies, there were found great nations, and in very differing climates, who were of the same diet, made provision of them, and fed them for their tables; as also, they did grasshoppers, mice, lizards, and bats; and in a time of scarcity of such delicacies, a toad was sold for six crowns, all which they cook, and dish up with several sauces. There were also others found, to whom our diet, and the flesh we eat, were venomous and mortal:

Consuetudinis magna vis est: pernoctant venatores in nive:
in montibus uri se patiuntur: pugiles, caestibus contusi,
ne ingemiscunt quidem.

[The power of custom is very great: huntsmen will lie out all night in the snow, or suffer themselves to be burned up by the sun on the mountains; boxers, hurt by the caestus, never utter a groan.

—Cicero, *Tusculum Disputations*, ii. 17]

These strange examples will not appear so strange if we consider what we have ordinary experience of, how much custom stupefies our senses. We need not go to what is reported of the people about the cataracts of the Nile; and what philosophers believe of the music of the spheres, that the bodies of those circles being solid and smooth, and coming to touch and rub upon one another, cannot fail of creating a marvellous harmony, the changes and cadences of which cause the revolutions and dances of the stars; but that the hearing sense of all creatures here below, being universally, like that of the Egyptians, deafened, and stupefied with the continual noise, cannot, how great soever, perceive it [This passage is taken from Cicero, "Dream of Scipio"; see his De Republica, vi. II. The Egyptians were said to be stunned by the noise of the Cataracts.] Smiths, millers, pewterers, forgemen, and armourers could never be able to live in the perpetual noise of their own trades, did it strike their ears with the same violence that it does ours.

My perfumed doublet gratifies my own scent at first; but after I have worn it three days together, it is only pleasing to the bystanders. This is yet more strange, that custom, notwithstanding long intermissions and intervals, should yet have the power to unite and establish the effect of its impressions upon our senses, as is manifest in such as live near unto steeples and the frequent noise of the bells. I myself lie at home in a tower, where every morning and evening a very great bell rings out the Ave Maria: the noise shakes my very tower, and at first seemed insupportable to me; but I am so used to it, that I hear it without any manner of offence, and often without awaking at it.

Plato [Diogenes Laertius, iii. 38. But he whom Plato censured was not a boy playing at nuts, but a man throwing dice.] reprehending a boy for playing at nuts, "Thou reprovest me," says the boy, "for a very little thing." "Custom," replied Plato, "is no little thing." I find that our greatest vices derive their first propensity from our most tender infancy, and that our principal education depends upon the nurse. Mothers are mightily pleased to see a child writhe off the neck of a chicken, or to please itself with hurting a dog or a cat; and such wise fathers there are in the world, who look upon it as a notable mark of a martial spirit, when they hear a son miscall, or see him domineer over a poor peasant, or a lackey, that dares not reply, nor turn again; and a great sign of wit, when they see him cheat and overreach his playfellow by some malicious treachery and deceit. Yet these are the true seeds and roots of cruelty, tyranny, and treason; they bud and put out there, and afterwards shoot up vigorously, and grow to prodigious bulk, cultivated by custom. And it is a very dangerous mistake to excuse these vile inclinations upon the tenderness of their age, and the triviality of the subject: first, it is nature that speaks, whose declaration is then more sincere, and inward thoughts more undisguised, as it is more weak and young; secondly, the deformity of cozenage does not consist nor depend upon the difference between crowns and pins; but I rather hold it more just to conclude thus: why should he not cozen in crowns since he does it in pins, than as they do, who say they only play for pins, they would not do it if it were for money? Children should carefully be instructed to abhor vices for their own contexture; and the natural deformity of those vices ought so to be represented to them, that they may not only avoid them in their actions, but especially so to abominate them in their hearts, that the very thought should be hateful to them, with what mask soever they may be disguised.

I know very well, for what concerns myself, that from having been brought up in my childhood to a plain and straightforward way of dealing, and from having had an aversion to all manner of juggling and foul play in my childish sports and recreations (and, indeed, it is to be noted, that the plays of children are not performed in play, but are to be judged in them as their most serious actions), there is no game so small wherein from my own bosom naturally, and without study or endeavour, I have not an extreme aversion from deceit. I shuffle and cut and make as much clatter with the cards, and keep as strict account for farthings, as it were for double pistoles; when winning or losing against my wife and daughter, it is indifferent to me, as when I play in good earnest with others, for round sums. At all times, and in all places, my own eyes are sufficient to look to my fingers; I am not so narrowly watched by any other, neither is there any I have more respect to.

I saw the other day, at my own house, a little fellow, a native of Nantes, born without arms, who has so well taught his feet to perform the services his hands should have done him, that truly these have half forgotten their natural office; and, indeed, the fellow calls them his hands; with them he cuts anything, charges and discharges a pistol, threads a needle, sews, writes, puts off his hat, combs his head, plays at cards and dice, and all this with as much dexterity as any other could do who had more, and more proper limbs to assist him. The money I gave him – for he gains his living by showing these feats – he took in his foot, as we do in our hand. I have seen another who, being yet a boy, flourished a two-handed sword, and, if I may so say, handled a halberd with the mere motions of his

80

neck and shoulders for want of hands; tossed them into the air, and caught them again, darted a dagger, and cracked a whip as well as any coachman in France.

But the effects of custom are much more manifest in the strange impressions she imprints in our minds, where she meets with less resistance. What has she not the power to impose upon our judgments and beliefs? Is there any so fantastic opinion (omitting the gross impostures of religions, with which we see so many great nations, and so many understanding men, so strangely besotted; for this being beyond the reach of human reason, any error is more excusable in such as are not endued, through the divine bounty, with an extraordinary illumination from above), but, of other opinions, are there any so extravagant, that she has not planted and established for laws in those parts of the world upon which she has been pleased to exercise her power? And therefore that ancient exclamation was exceeding just:

Non pudet physicum, id est speculatorem venatoremque naturae,
ab animis consuetudine imbutis petere testimonium veritatis?

[Is it not a shame for a natural philosopher, that is, for an observer and hunter of nature, to seek testimony of the truth from minds prepossessed by custom?

—Cicero, *De Natura Deorum*, i. 30.]

I do believe, that no so absurd or ridiculous fancy can enter into human imagination, that does not meet with some example of public practice, and that, consequently, our reason does not ground and back up. There are people, amongst whom it is the fashion to turn their backs upon him they salute, and never look upon the man they intend to honour. There is a place, where, whenever the king spits, the greatest ladies of his court put out their hands to receive it; and another nation, where the most eminent persons about him stoop to take up his ordure in a linen cloth. Let us here steal room to insert a story.

A French gentleman was always wont to blow his nose with his fingers (a thing very much against our fashion), and he justifying himself for so doing, and he was a man famous for pleasant repartees, he asked me, what privilege this filthy excrement had, that we must carry about us a fine handkerchief to receive it, and, which was more, afterwards to lap it carefully up, and carry it all day about in our pockets, which, he said, could not but be much more nauseous and offensive, than to see it thrown away, as we did all other evacuations. I found that what he said was not altogether without reason, and by being frequently in his company, that slovenly action of his was at last grown familiar to me; which nevertheless we make a face at, when we hear it reported of another country. Miracles appear to be so, according to our ignorance of nature, and not according to the essence of nature the continually being accustomed to anything, blinds the eye of our judgment. Barbarians are no more a wonder to us, than we are to them; nor with any more reason, as everyone would confess, if after having travelled over those remote examples, men could settle themselves to reflect upon, and rightly to confer them, with their own. Human reason is a tincture almost equally infused into all our opinions and manners, of what form soever they are; infinite in matter, infinite in diversity. But I return to my subject.

There are peoples, where, his wife and children excepted, no one speaks to the king but through a tube. In one and the same nation, the virgins discover those parts that modesty should persuade them to hide, and the married women carefully cover and conceal them. To which, this custom, in another place, has some relation, where chastity, but in marriage, is of no esteem, for unmarried women may prostitute themselves to as many as they please, and being got with child, may lawfully take physic, in the sight of everyone, to destroy their fruit. And, in another place, if a tradesman marry, all of the same condition, who are invited to the wedding, lie with the bride before him; and the greater number of

them there is, the greater is her honour, and the opinion of her
ability and strength: if an officer marry, it is the same, the same with
a labourer, or one of mean condition; but then it belongs to the
lord of the place to perform that office; and yet a severe loyalty during marriage is afterward strictly enjoined. There are places where
brothels of young men are kept for the pleasure of women; where
the wives go to war as well as the husbands, and not only share in
the dangers of battle, but, moreover, in the honours of command.
Others, where they wear rings not only through their noses, lips,
cheeks, and on their toes, but also weighty gimmals of gold thrust
through their paps and buttocks; where, in eating, they wipe their
fingers upon their thighs, genitories, and the soles of their feet:
where children are excluded, and brothers and nephews only
inherit; and elsewhere, nephews only, saving in the succession of
the prince: where, for the regulation of community in goods and
estates, observed in the country, certain sovereign magistrates have
committed to them the universal charge and overseeing of the agriculture, and distribution of the fruits, according to the necessity of
everyone where they lament the death of children, and feast at the
decease of old men: where they lie ten or twelve in a bed, men and
their wives together: where women, whose husbands come to violent ends, may marry again, and others not: where the condition of
women is looked upon with such contempt, that they kill all the
native females, and buy wives of their neighbours to supply their
use; where husbands may repudiate their wives, without showing
any cause, but wives cannot part from their husbands, for what
cause soever; where husbands may sell their wives in case of sterility;
where they boil the bodies of their dead, and afterward pound
them to a pulp, which they mix with their wine, and drink it; where
the most coveted sepulture is to be eaten by dogs, and elsewhere by
birds; where they believe the souls of the blessed live in all manner
of liberty, in delightful fields, furnished with all sorts of delicacies,
and that it is these souls, repeating the words we utter, which we call
Echo; where they fight in the water, and shoot their arrows with the

most mortal aim, swimming; where, for a sign of subjection, they lift up their shoulders, and hang down their heads; where they put off their shoes when they enter the king's palace; where the eunuchs, who take charge of the sacred women, have, moreover, their lips and noses cut off, that they may not be loved; where the priests put out their own eyes, to be better acquainted with their demons, and the better to receive their oracles; where everyone makes to himself a deity of what he likes best; the hunter of a lion or a fox, the fisher of some fish; idols of every human action or passion; in which place, the sun, the moon, and the earth are the 'principal deities, and the form of taking an oath is, to touch the earth, looking up to heaven; where both flesh and fish is eaten raw; where the greatest oath they take is, to swear by the name of some dead person of reputation, laying their hand upon his tomb; where the newyear's gift the king sends every year to the princes, his vassals, is fire, which being brought, all the old fire is put out, and the neighbouring people are bound to fetch of the new, everyone for themselves, upon pain of high treason; where, when the king, to betake himself wholly to devotion, retires from his administration (which often falls out), his next successor is obliged to do the same, and the right of the kingdom devolves to the third in succession: where they vary the form of government, according to the seeming necessity of affairs: depose the king when they think good, substituting certain elders to govern in his stead, and sometimes transferring it into the hands of the commonality: where men and women are both circumcised and also baptized: where the soldier, who in one or several engagements, has been so fortunate as to present seven of the enemies' heads to the king, is made noble: where they live in that rare and unsociable opinion of the mortality of the soul: where the women are delivered without pain or fear: where the women wear copper leggings upon both legs, and if a louse bite them, are bound in magnanimity to bite them again, and dare not marry, till first they have made their king a tender of their virginity, if he please to accept it: where the ordinary way of salutation is by putting a finger down to the earth, and then pointing it up toward heaven: where men carry burdens upon their heads, and women on their shoulders; where the women make water standing, and the men squatting: where they send their blood in token of friendship, and offer incense to the men they would honour, like gods: where, not only to the fourth, but in any other remote degree, kindred are not permitted to marry: where the children are four years at nurse, and often twelve; in which place, also, it is accounted mortal to give the child suck the first day after it is born: where the correction of the male children is peculiarly designed to the fathers, and to the mothers of the girls; the punishment being to hang them by the heels in the smoke: where they circumcise the women: where they eat all sorts of herbs, without other scruple than of the badness of the smell: where all things are open the finest houses, furnished in the richest manner, without doors, windows, trunks, or chests to lock, a thief being there punished double what they are in other places: where they crack lice with their teeth like monkeys, and abhor to see them killed with one's nails: where in all their lives they neither cut their hair nor pare their nails; and, in another place, pare those of the right hand only, letting the left grow for ornament and bravery: where they suffer the hair on the right side to grow as long as it will, and shave the other; and in the neighbouring provinces, some let their hair grow long before, and some behind, shaving close the rest: where parents let out their children, and husbands their wives, to their guests to hire: where a man may get his own mother with child, and fathers make use of their own daughters or sons, without scandal: where, at their solemn feasts, they interchangeably lend their children to one another, without any consideration of nearness of blood. In one place, men feed upon human flesh; in another, it is reputed a pious office for a man to kill his father at a certain age; elsewhere, the fathers dispose of their children, whilst yet in their mothers' wombs, some to be preserved and carefully brought up, and others to be abandoned or made away. Elsewhere the old husbands lend their wives to young men; and in another place they are in common without offence; in one place particularly, the women take it for a mark of honour to have as many gay fringed tassels at the bottom of their garment, as they have lain with several men. Moreover, has not custom made a republic of women separately by themselves? has it not put arms into their hands, and made them raise armies and fight battles? And does she not, by her own precept, instruct the most ignorant vulgar, and make them perfect in things which all the philosophy in the world could never beat into the heads of the wisest men? For we know entire nations, where death was not only despised, but entertained with the greatest triumph; where children of seven years old suffered themselves to be whipped to death, without changing countenance; where riches were in such contempt, that the meanest citizen would not have deigned to stoop to take up a purse of crowns. And we know regions, very fruitful in all manner of provisions, where, notwithstanding, the most ordinary diet, and that they are most pleased with, is only bread, cresses, and water. Did not custom, moreover, work that miracle in Chios that, in seven hundred years, it was never known that ever maid or wife committed any act to the prejudice of her honour?

To conclude; there is nothing, in my opinion, that she does not, or may not do; and therefore, with very good reason it is that Pindar calls her the ruler of the world. He that was seen to beat his father, and reproved for so doing, made answer, that it was the custom of their family; that, in like manner, his father had beaten his grandfather, his grandfather his great-grandfather, "And this," says he, pointing to his son, "when he comes to my age, shall beat me." And the father, whom the son dragged and hauled along the streets, commanded him to stop at a certain door, for he himself, he said, had dragged his father no farther, that being the utmost limit of the hereditary outrage the sons used to practise upon the fathers in their family. It is as much by custom as infirmity, says Aristotle, that women tear their hair, bite their nails, and eat coals and earth, and more by custom than nature that men abuse themselves with one another.

CHAPTER 23

The laws of conscience, which we pretend to be derived from nature, proceed from custom; everyone, having an inward veneration for the opinions and manners approved and received amongst his own people, cannot, without very great reluctance, depart from them, nor apply himself to them without applause. In times past, when those of Crete would curse any one, they prayed the gods to engage him in some ill custom. But the principal effect of its power is, so to seize and ensnare us, that it is hardly in us to disengage ourselves from its gripe, or so to come to ourselves, as to consider of and to weigh the things it enjoins. To say the truth, by reason that we suck it in with our milk, and that the face of the world presents itself in this posture to our first sight, it seems as if we were born upon condition to follow on this track; and the common fancies that we find in repute everywhere about us, and infused into our minds with the seed of our fathers, appear to be the most universal and genuine; from whence it comes to pass, that whatever is off the hinges of custom, is believed to be also off the hinges of reason; how unreasonably for the most part, God knows.

If, as we who study ourselves have learned to do, everyone who hears a good sentence, would immediately consider how it does in any way touch his own private concern, everyone would find, that it was not so much a good saying, as a severe lash to the ordinary stupidity of his own judgment: but men receive the precepts and admonitions of truth, as directed to the common sort, and never to themselves; and instead of applying them to their own manners, do only very ignorantly and unprofitably commit them to memory. But let us return to the empire of custom.

Such people as have been bred up to liberty, and subject to no other dominion but the authority of their own will, look upon all other form of government as monstrous and contrary to nature. Those who are inured to monarchy do the same; and what opportunity soever fortune presents them with to change, even then, when with the greatest difficulties they have disengaged themselves from one master, that was troublesome and grievous to them, they presently run, with the same difficulties, to create another; being unable to take into hatred subjection itself.

It is by the mediation of custom, that everyone is content with the place where he is planted by nature; and the Highlanders of Scotland no more pant after Touraine; than the Scythians after Thessaly. Darius asking certain Greeks what they would take to assume the custom of the Indians, of eating the dead bodies of their fathers (for that was their use, believing they could not give them a better nor more noble sepulture than to bury them in their own bodies), they made answer, that nothing in the world should hire them to do it; but having also tried to persuade the Indians to leave their custom, and, after the Greek manner, to burn the bodies of their fathers, they conceived a still greater horror at the motion. [Herodotus, iii. 38.] Everyone does the same, for use veils from us the true aspect of things.

> *Nil adeo magnum, nec tam mirabile quidquam*
> *Principio, quod non minuant mirarier omnes Paullatim.*

[There is nothing at first so grand, so admirable, which by degrees people do not regard with less admiration.

—Lucretius, ii. 1027]

Taking upon me once to justify something in use amongst us, and that was received with absolute authority for a great many leagues round about us, and not content, as men commonly do, to establish it only by force of law and example, but inquiring still further into its origin, I found the foundation so weak, that I who made it my business to confirm others, was very near being dissatisfied myself. It is by this receipt that Plato [Laws, viii. 6.] undertakes to cure the unnatural and preposterous loves of his time, as one which he esteems of sovereign virtue, namely, that the public opinion condemns them; that the poets, and all other sorts of writers, relate horrible stories of them; a recipe, by virtue of which the most beautiful daughters no more allure their fathers' lust; nor brothers, of the finest shape and fashion, their sisters' desire; the very fables of Thyestes, Oedipus, and Macareus, having with the harmony of their song, infused this wholesome opinion and belief into the tender brains of children. Chastity is, in truth, a great and shining virtue, and of which the utility is sufficiently known; but to treat of it, and to set it off in its true value, according to nature, is as hard as it is easy to do so according to custom, laws, and precepts. The fundamental and universal reasons are of very obscure and difficult research, and our masters either lightly pass them over, or not daring so much as to touch them, precipitate themselves into the liberty and protection of custom, there puffing themselves out and triumphing to their heart's content: such as will not suffer themselves to be withdrawn from this original source, do yet commit a greater error, and subject themselves to wild opinions; witness Chrysippus, [Sextus Empiricus, Pyyrhon. Hypotyp., i. 14.] who, in so many of his writings, has strewed the little account he made of incestuous conjunctions, committed with how near relations soever.

Whoever would disengage himself from this violent prejudice of custom, would find several things received with absolute and undoubting opinion, that have no other support than the hoary head and rivelled face of ancient usage. But the mask taken off, and things being referred to the decision of truth and reason, he will find his judgment as it were altogether overthrown, and yet restored to a much more sure estate. For example, I shall ask him, what can be more strange than to see a people obliged to obey laws they never understood; bound in all their domestic affairs, as marriages, donations, wills, sales, and purchases, to rules they cannot possibly know, being neither written nor published in their own language, and of which they are of necessity to purchase both the interpretation and the use? Not according to the ingenious opinion of Isocrates, [Discourse to Nicocles.] who counselled his king to make the traffics and negotiations of his subjects, free, frank, and of profit to them, and their quarrels and disputes burdensome, and laden with heavy impositions and penalties; but, by a prodigious opinion, to make sale of reason itself, and to give to laws a course of merchandise. I think myself obliged to fortune that, as our historians report, it was a Gascon gentleman, a countryman of mine, who first opposed Charlemagne, when he attempted to impose upon us Latin and imperial laws.

What can be more savage, than to see a nation where, by lawful custom, the office of a judge is bought and sold, where judgments are paid for with ready money, and where justice may legitimately be denied to him that has not wherewithal to pay; a merchandise in so great repute, as in a government to create a fourth estate of wrangling lawyers, to add to the three ancient ones of the church, nobility, and people; which fourth estate, having the laws in their own hands, and sovereign power over men's lives and fortunes, makes another body separate from nobility: whence it comes to pass, that there are double laws, those of honour and those of justice, in many things altogether opposite one to another; the nobles as rigorously condemning a lie taken, as the other do a lie revenged: by the law of arms, he shall be degraded from all nobility and honour who puts up with an affront; and by the civil law, he who vindicates his reputation by revenge incurs a capital punishment: he who applies himself to the law for reparation of an offence done to his honour, disgraces himself; and he who does not, is censured and punished by the law. Yet of these two so different things, both of them referring to one head, the one has the charge of peace, the other of war; those have the profit, these the honour; those the wisdom, these the virtue; those the word, these the action; those justice, these valour; those reason, these force; those the long robe, these the short; – divided between them.

For what concerns indifferent things, as clothes, who is there seeking to bring them back to their true use, which is the body's service and convenience, and upon which their original grace and fitness depend; for the most fantastic, in my opinion, that can be imagined, I will instance amongst others, our flat caps, that long tail of velvet that hangs down from our women's heads, with its party-coloured trappings; and that vain and futile model of a member we cannot in modesty so much as name, which, nevertheless, we make show and parade of in public. These considerations, notwithstanding, will not prevail upon any understanding man to decline the common mode; but, on the contrary, methinks, all singular and particular fashions are rather marks of folly and vain affectation than of sound reason, and that a wise man, within, ought to withdraw and retire his soul from the crowd, and there keep it at liberty and in power to judge freely of things; but as to externals, absolutely to follow and conform himself to the fashion of the time. Public society has nothing to do with our thoughts, but the rest, as our actions, our labours, our fortunes, and our lives, we are to lend and abandon them to its service and to the common opinion, as did that good and great Socrates who refused to preserve his life by a disobedience to the magistrate, though a very wicked and unjust one for it is the rule of rules, the general law of laws, that everyone observe those of the place wherein he lives.

[*It is good to obey the laws of one's country.*

—Excerpta ex Trag. Gyaecis, Grotio interp., 1626, p. 937.]

And now to another point. It is a very great doubt, whether any so manifest benefit can accrue from the alteration of a law received, let it be what it will, as there is danger and inconvenience in altering it; forasmuch as government is a structure composed of divers parts and members joined and united together, with so strict connection, that it is impossible to stir so much as one brick or stone, but the whole body will be sensible of it. The legislator of the Thurians [Charondas; Diod. Sic., xii. 24.] ordained, that whosoever would go about either to abolish an old law, or to establish a new, should present himself with a halter about his neck to the people, to the end, that if the innovation he would introduce should not be approved by everyone, he might immediately be hanged; and he of the Lacedaemonians employed his life to obtain from his citizens a faithful promise that none of his laws should be violated. [Lycurgus; Plutarch, in Vita, c. 22.] The Ephoros who so rudely cut the two strings that Phrynis had added to music never stood to examine whether that addition made better harmony, or that by its means the instrument was more full and complete; it was enough for him to condemn the invention, that it was a novelty, and an alteration of the old fashion. Which also is the meaning of the old rusty sword carried before the magistracy of Marseilles.

For my own part, I have a great aversion from a novelty, what face or what pretence soever it may carry along with it, and have reason, having been an eyewitness of the great evils it has produced. For those which for so many years have lain so heavy upon us, it is not wholly accountable; but one may say, with colour enough, that it has accidentally produced and begotten the mischiefs and ruin that have since happened, both without and against it; it, principally, we are to accuse for these disorders:

Heu! patior telis vulnera facta meis.

[Alas! The wounds were made by my own weapons.
—Ovid, *Epistles Phyllis Demophoonti*, vers. 48.]

They who give the first shock to a state, are almost naturally the first overwhelmed in its ruin the fruits of public commotion are seldom enjoyed by him who was the first motor; he beats and disturbs the water for another's net. The unity and contexture of this monarchy, of this grand edifice, having been ripped and torn in her old age, by this thing called innovation, has since laid open a rent, and given sufficient admittance to such injuries: the royal majesty with greater difficulty declines from the summit to the middle, then it falls and tumbles headlong from the middle to the bottom. But if the inventors do the greater mischief, the imitators are more vicious to follow examples of which they have felt and punished both the horror and the offence. And if there can be any degree of honour in ill-doing, these last must yield to the others the glory of contriving, and the courage of making the first attempt. All sorts of new disorders easily draw, from this primitive and ever-flowing fountain, examples and precedents to trouble and discompose our government: we read in our very laws, made for the remedy of this first evil, the beginning and pretences of all sorts of wicked enterprises; and that befalls us, which Thucydides said of the civil wars of his time, that, in favour of public vices, they gave them new and more plausible names for their excuse, sweetening and disguising their true titles; which must be done, forsooth, to reform our conscience and belief:

Honesta oratio est;

[Fine words truly.

—*Ter. And.,* i. I, 114.]

but the best pretence for innovation is of very dangerous consequence:

Aden nihil motum ex antique probabile est.

[We are ever wrong in changing ancient ways.

—Livy, xxxiv. 54]

And freely to speak my thoughts, it argues a strange self-love and great presumption to be so fond of one's own opinions, that a public peace must be overthrown to establish them, and to introduce so many inevitable mischiefs, and so dreadful a corruption of manners, as a civil war and the mutations of state consequent to it, always bring in their train, and to introduce them, in a thing of so high concern, into the bowels of one's own country. Can there be worse husbandry than to set up so many certain and knowing vices against errors that are only contested and disputable? And are there any worse sorts of vices than those committed against a man's own conscience, and the natural light of his own reason? The Senate, upon the dispute between it and the people about the administration of their religion, was bold enough to return this evasion for current pay:

> *Ad deos id magis, quam ad se, pertinere: ipsos visuros,*
> *ne sacra sua polluantur;*

[Those things belong to the gods to determine than to them; let the gods, therefore, take care that their sacred mysteries were not profaned.

—Livy, x. 6.]

according to what the oracle answered to those of Delphos who, fearing to be invaded by the Persians in the Median war, inquired of Apollo, how they should dispose of the holy treasure of his temple; whether they should hide, or remove it to some other place? He returned them answer, that they should stir nothing from thence, and only take care of themselves, for he was sufficient to look to what belonged to him. [Herodotus, viii. 36.].

The Christian religion has all the marks of the utmost utility and justice: but none more manifest than the severe injunction it lays indifferently upon all to yield absolute obedience to the civil magistrate, and to maintain and defend the laws. Of which, what a wonderful example has the divine wisdom left us, that, to establish the salvation of mankind, and to conduct His glorious victory over death and sin, would do it after no other way, but at the mercy of our ordinary forms of justice subjecting the progress and issue of so high and so salutiferous an effect, to the blindness and injustice of

Chapter 23

our customs and observances; sacrificing the innocent blood of so many of His elect, and so long a loss of so many years, to the maturing of this inestimable fruit? There is a vast difference between the case of one who follows the forms and laws of his country, and of another who will undertake to regulate and change them; of whom the first pleads simplicity, obedience, and example for his excuse, who, whatever he shall do, it cannot be imputed to malice; it is at the worst but misfortune:

> *Quisnest enim, quem non moveat clarissimis monumentis*
> *testata consignataque antiquitas?*

[For who is there that antiquity, attested and confirmed by the fairest monuments, cannot move?
—Cicero, *De Divinatione*, i. 40.]

besides what Isocrates says, that defect is nearer allied to moderation than excess: the other is a much more ruffling gamester; for whosoever shall take upon him to choose and alter, usurps the authority of judging, and should look well about him, and make it his business to discern clearly the defect of what he would abolish, and the virtue of what he is about to introduce.

This so vulgar consideration is that which settled me in my station, and kept even my most extravagant and ungoverned youth under the rein, so as not to burden my shoulders with so great a weight, as to render myself responsible for a science of that importance, and in this to dare, what in my better and more mature judgment, I durst not do in the most easy and indifferent things I had been instructed in, and wherein the temerity of judging is of no consequence at all; it seeming to me very unjust to go about to subject public and established customs and institutions, to the weakness and instability of a private and particular fancy (for private reason has but a private jurisdiction), and to attempt that upon the divine, which no government will endure a man should do, upon the civil laws; with which, though human reason has much more commerce than with the other, yet are they sovereignly judged by their own proper judges, and the extreme sufficiency serves only to expound and set forth the law and custom received, and neither to wrest it, nor to introduce anything, of innovation. If, sometimes, the divine providence has gone beyond the rules to which it has necessarily bound and obliged us men, it is not to give us any dispensation to do the same; those are masterstrokes of the divine hand, which we are not to imitate, but to admire, and extraordinary examples, marks of express and particular purposes, of the nature of miracles, presented before us for manifestations of its almightiness, equally above both our rules and force, which it would be folly and impiety to attempt to represent and imitate; and that we ought not to follow, but to contemplate with the greatest reverence: acts of His personage, and not for us. Cotta very opportunely declares:

> *Quum de religione agitur, Ti. Coruncanium, P. Scipionem,*
> *P. Scaevolam, pontifices maximos, non Zenonem, autCleanthem,*
> *Aut Chrysippum, sequor.*

[When matter of religion is in question, I follow the high priests T. Coruncanius, P. Scipio, P. Scaevola, and not Zeno, Cleanthes, or Chrysippus.

—Cicero, *De Natura Deorum*, iii. 2.]

God knows, in the present quarrel of our civil war, where there are a hundred articles to dash out and to put in, great and very considerable, how many there are who can truly boast, they have exactly and perfectly weighed and understood the grounds and reasons of the one and the other party; it is a number, if they make any number, that would be able to give us very little disturbance. But what becomes of all the rest, under what ensigns do they march, in what quarter do they lie? Theirs have the same effect with other weak and ill-applied medicines; they have only set the humours they would purge more violently in work, stirred and exasperated by the conflict, and left them still behind. The potion was too weak to purge, but strong enough to weaken us; so that it does not work, but we keep it still in our bodies, and reap nothing from the operation but intestine gripes and dolours.

So it is, nevertheless, that Fortune still reserving her authority in defiance of whatever we are able to do or say, sometimes presents us with a necessity so urgent, that it is requisite the laws should a little yield and give way; and when one opposes the increase of an innovation that thus intrudes itself by violence, to keep a man's self in so doing, in all places and in all things within bounds and rules against those who have the power, and to whom all things are lawful that may in any way serve to advance their design, who have no other law nor rule but what serves best to their own purpose, it is a dangerous obligation and an intolerable inequality:

Aditum nocendi perfido praestat fides,

[Putting faith in a treacherous person, opens the door to harm.
—Seneca, *Oedipus*, act iii., verse 686.]

forasmuch as the ordinary discipline of a healthful state does not provide against these extraordinary accidents; it presupposes a body that supports itself in its principal members and offices, and a common consent to its obedience and observation. A legitimate proceeding is cold, heavy, and constrained, and not fit to make head against a headstrong and unbridled proceeding. It is known to be to this day cast in the dish of those two great men, Octavius and Cato, in the two civil wars of Sylla and Caesar, that they would rather suffer their country to undergo the last extremities, than relieve their fellow-citizens at the expense of its laws, or be guilty of any innovation; for in truth, in these last necessities, where there is no other remedy, it would, peradventure, be more discreetly done, to stoop and yield a little to receive the blow, than, by opposing without possibility of doing good, to give occasion to violence to trample all under foot; and better to make the laws do what they can, when they cannot do what they would. After this manner did he [Agesilaus] who suspended them for four-and-twenty hours, and he who, for once shifted a day in the calendar, and that other [Alexander the Great] who of the month of June made a second of May. The Lacedaemonians themselves, who were so religious observers of the laws of their country, being straitened by one of their own edicts, by which it was expressly forbidden to choose the same man twice to be admiral; and on the other side, their affairs necessarily requiring, that Lysander should again take upon him that command, they made one Aratus admiral; it is true, but withal, Lysander went general of the navy; and, by the same subtlety, one of their ambassadors being sent to the Athenians to obtain the revocation of some decree, and Pericles remonstrating to him, that it was forbidden to take away the tablet wherein a law had once been engrossed, he advised him to turn it only, that being not forbidden; and Plutarch commends Philopoemen, that being born to command, he knew how to do it, not only according to the laws, but also to overrule even the laws themselves, when the public necessity so required.

ON THE EDUCATION OF CHILDREN

TO MADAME DIANE DE FOIX,
Comtesse de Gurson

I never yet saw that father, but let his son be never so decrepit or deformed, would not, notwithstanding, own him: not, nevertheless, if he were not totally besotted, and blinded with his paternal affection, that he did not well enough discern his defects; but that with all defaults he was still his. Just so, I see better than any other, that all I write here are but the idle reveries of a man that has only nibbled upon the outward crust of sciences in his early years, and only retained a general and formless image of them; who has got a little snatch of everything and nothing of the whole, 'a la Francoise'. For I know, in general, that there is such a thing as physic, as jurisprudence: four parts in mathematics, and, roughly, what all these aim and point at; and, peradventure, I yet know farther, what sciences in general pretend unto, in order to the service of our life: but to dive farther than that, and to have cudgelled my brains in the study of Aristotle, the monarch of all modern learning, or particularly addicted myself to any one science, I have never done it; neither is there any one art of which I am able to draw the first lineaments and dead colour; insomuch that there is not a boy of the lowest form in a school, that may not pretend to be wiser than I, who am not able to examine him in his first lesson, which, if I am at any time forced upon, I am necessitated in my own defence, to ask him, unaptly enough, some universal questions, such as may serve to try his natural understanding; a lesson as strange and unknown to him, as his is to me.

I never seriously settled myself to the reading any book of solid learning but Plutarch and Seneca; and there, like the Danaides, I eternally fill, and it as constantly runs out; something of which drops upon this paper, but little or nothing stays with me. History is my particular game as to matter of reading, or else poetry, for which I have particular kindness and esteem: for, as Cleanthes said, as the voice, forced through the narrow passage of a trumpet, comes out more forcible and shrill: so, methinks, a sentence pressed within the harmony of verse darts out more briskly upon the understanding, and strikes my ear and apprehension with a smarter and more pleasing effect. As to the natural parts I have, of which this is the essay, I find them to bow under the burden; my fancy and judgment do but grope in the dark, tripping and stumbling in the way; and when I have gone as far as I can, I am in no degree satisfied; I discover still a new and greater extent of land before me, with a troubled and imperfect sight and wrapped up in clouds, that I am not able to penetrate. And taking upon me to write indifferently of whatever comes into my head, and therein making use of nothing but my own proper and natural means, if it befall me, as oft-times it does, accidentally to meet in any good author, the same heads and commonplaces upon which I have attempted to write (as I did but just now in Plutarch's "Discourse of the Force of Imagination"), to see myself so weak and so forlorn, so heavy and so flat, in comparison of those better writers, I at once pity or despise myself. Yet do I please myself with this, that my opinions have often the honour and good fortune to jump with theirs, and that I go in the same path, though at a very great distance, and can say, "Ah, that is so." I am farther satisfied to find that I have a quality, which everyone is not blessed withal, which is, to discern the vast difference between them and me; and notwithstanding all that, suffer my own inventions, low and feeble as they are, to run on in their career, without mending or plastering up the defects that this comparison has laid open to my own view. And, in plain truth, a man had need of a good strong back to keep pace with these people. The indiscreet scribblers of our times, who, amongst their laborious nothings, insert whole sections and pages out of ancient authors, with a design, by that means, to illustrate their own writings, do quite contrary; for this infinite dissimilitude of ornaments renders the complexion of their own compositions so sallow and deformed, that they lose much more than they get.

The philosophers, Chrysippus and Epicurus, were in this of two quite contrary humours: the first not only in his books mixed passages and sayings of other authors, but entire pieces, and, in one, the whole Medea of Euripides; which gave Apollodorus occasion to say, that should a man pick out of his writings all that was none of his, he would leave him nothing but blank paper: whereas the latter, quite on the contrary, in three hundred volumes that he left behind him, has not so much as one quotation. [Diogenes Laertius, *Lives of Chyysippus*, vii. 181, and Epicurus, x. 26.]

I happened the other day upon this piece of fortune; I was reading a French book, where after I had a long time run dreaming over a great many words, so dull, so insipid, so void of all wit or common sense, that indeed they were only French words: after a long and tedious travel, I came at last to meet with a piece that was lofty, rich, and elevated to the very clouds; of which, had I found either the declivity easy or the ascent gradual, there had been some excuse; but it was so perpendicular a precipice, and so wholly cut off from the rest of the work, that by the first six words, I found myself flying into the other world, and thence discovered the vale whence I came so deep and low, that I have never had since the heart to descend into it any more. If I should set out one of my discourses with such rich spoils as these, it would but too evidently manifest the imperfection of my own writing. To reprehend the fault in others that I am guilty of myself, appears to me no more unreasonable, than to condemn, as I often do, those of others in myself: they are to be everywhere reproved, and ought to have no sanctuary allowed them. I know very well how audaciously I myself, at every turn, attempt to equal myself to my thefts, and to make my style go hand in hand with them, not without a temerarious hope of deceiving the eyes of my reader from discerning the difference; but withal it is as much by the benefit of my application, that I hope to do it, as by that of my invention or any force of my own. Besides, I do not offer to contend with the whole body of these champions, nor hand to hand with anyone of them: it is only by flights and little light attempts that I engage them; I do not grapple with them, but try their strength only, and never engage so far as I make a show to do. If I could hold them in play, I were a brave fellow; for I never attack them; but where they are most sinewy and strong. To cover a man's self (as I have seen some do) with another man's armour, so as not to discover so much as his fingers' ends; to carry on a design (as it is not hard for a man that has anything of a scholar in him, in an ordinary subject to do) under old inventions patched up here and there with his own trumpery, and then to endeavour to conceal the theft, and to make it pass for his own, is first injustice and meanness of spirit in those who do it, who having nothing in them of their own fit to procure them a reputation, endeavour to do it by attempting to impose things upon the world in their own name, which they have no manner of title to; and next, a ridiculous folly to content themselves with acquiring the ignorant approbation of the vulgar by such a pitiful cheat, at the price at the same time of degrading themselves in the eyes of men of understanding, who turn up their noses at all this borrowed incrustation, yet whose praise alone is worth the having. For my own part, there is nothing I would not sooner do than that, neither have I said so much of others, but to get a better opportunity to explain myself. Nor in this do I glance at the composers of centos, who declare themselves for such; of which sort of writers I have in my time known many very ingenious, and particularly one under the name of Capilupus, besides the ancients. These are really men of wit, and that make it appear they are so, both by that and other ways of writing; as for example, Lipsius, in that learned and laborious contexture of his Politics.

But, be it how it will, and how inconsiderable soever these ineptitudes may be, I will say I never intended to conceal them, no more than my old bald grizzled likeness before them, where the painter has presented you not with a perfect face, but with mine. For these are my own particular opinions and fancies, and I deliver them as only what I myself believe, and not for what is to be believed by others. I have no other end in this writing, but only to discover myself, who, also shall, peradventure, be another thing to-morrow, if I chance to meet any new instruction to change me. I have no authority to be believed, neither do I desire it, being too conscious of my own inerudition to be able to instruct others.

Someone, then, having seen the preceding chapter, the other day told me at my house, that I should a little farther have extended my discourse on the education of children.

Now, madam, if I had any sufficiency in this subject, I could not possibly better employ it, than to present my best instructions to the little man that threatens you shortly with a happy birth (for you are too generous to begin otherwise than with a male); for, having had so great a hand in the treaty of your marriage, I have a certain particular right and interest in the greatness and prosperity of the issue that shall spring from it; beside that, your having had the best of my services so long in possession, sufficiently obliges me to desire the honour and advantage of all wherein you shall be concerned. But, in truth, all I understand as to that particular is only this, that the greatest and most important difficulty of human science is the education of children. For as in agriculture, the husbandry that is to precede planting, as also planting itself, is certain, plain, and well known; but after that which is planted comes to life, there is a great deal more to be done, more art to be used, more care to be taken, and much more difficulty to cultivate and bring it to perfection so it is with men; it is no hard matter to get children; but after they are born, then begins the trouble, solicitude, and care rightly to train, principle, and bring them up. The symptoms of their inclinations in that tender age are so obscure, and the promises so uncertain and fallacious, that it is very hard to establish any solid judgment or conjecture upon them. Look at Cimon, for example, and Themistocles, and a thousand others, who very much deceived the expectation men had of them. Cubs of bears and puppies readily discover their natural inclination; but men, so soon as ever they are grownup, applying themselves to certain habits, engaging themselves in certain opinions, and conforming themselves to particular laws and customs, easily alter, or at least disguise, their true and real disposition; and yet it is hard to force the propension of nature. Whence it comes to pass, that for not having chosen the right course, we often take very great pains, and consume a good part of our time in training up children to things, for which, by their natural constitution, they are totally unfit. In this difficulty, nevertheless, I am clearly of opinion, that they ought to be elemented in the best and most advantageous studies, without taking too much notice of, or being too superstitious in those light prognostics they give of themselves in their tender years, and to which Plato, in his Republic, gives, methinks, too much authority.

Madam, science is a very great ornament, and a thing of marvellous use, especially in persons raised to that degree of fortune in which you are. And, in truth, in persons of mean and low condition, it cannot perform its true and genuine office, being naturally more prompt to assist in the conduct of war, in the government of peoples, in negotiating the leagues and friendships of princes and foreign nations, than in forming a syllogism in logic, in pleading a process in law, or in prescribing a dose of pills in physic. Wherefore, madam, believing you will not omit this so necessary feature in the education of your children, who yourself have tasted its sweetness, and are of a learned extraction (for we yet have the writings of the ancient Counts of Foix, from whom my lord, your husband, and yourself, are both of you descended, and Monsieur de Candale, your uncle, every day obliges the world with others, which will extend the knowledge of this quality in your family for so many succeeding ages), I will, upon this occasion, presume to acquaint your ladyship with one particular fancy of my own, contrary to the common method, which is all I am able to contribute to your service in this affair.

The charge of the tutor you shall provide for your son, upon the choice of whom depends the whole success of his education, has several other great and considerable parts and duties required in so important a trust, besides that of which I am about to speak: these, however, I shall not mention, as being unable to add anything of moment to the common rules: and in this, wherein I take upon me to advise, he may follow it so far only as it shall appear advisable.

For a, boy of quality then, who pretends to letters not upon the account of profit (for so mean an object is unworthy of the grace and favour of the Muses, and moreover, in it a man directs his service to and depends upon others), nor so much for outward ornament, as for his own proper and peculiar use, and to furnish and enrich himself within, having rather a desire to come out an accomplished cavalier than a mere scholar or learned man; for such a one, I say, I would, also, have his friends solicitous to find him out a tutor, who has rather a well-made than a well-filled head; ["'Tete bien faite', an expression created by Montaigne, and which has remained a part of our language." – Servan] seeking, indeed, both the one and the other, but rather of the two to prefer manners and judgment to mere learning, and that this man should exercise his charge after a new method.

It is the custom of pedagogues to be eternally thundering in their pupil's ears, as they were pouring into a funnel, whilst the business of the pupil is only to repeat what the others have said: now I would have a tutor to correct this error, and, that at the very first, he should according to the capacity he has to deal with, put it to the test, permitting his pupil himself to taste things, and of himself to discern and choose them, sometimes opening the way to him, and sometimes leaving him to open it for himself; that is, I would not have him alone to invent and speak, but that he should also hear his pupil speak in turn. Socrates, and since him Arcesilaus, made first their scholars speak, and then they spoke to them [Diogenes Laertius, iv. 36.]

> *Obest plerumque iis, qui discere volunt,*
> *Auctoritas eorum, qui docent.*

[The authority of those who teach, is very often an impediment to those who desire to learn.

—Cicero, *De Natura Deorum*, i. 5.]

It is good to make him, like a young horse, trot before him, that he may judge of his going, and how much he is to abate of his own speed, to accommodate himself to the vigour and capacity of the other. For want of which due proportion we spoil all; which also to know how to adjust, and to keep within an exact and due measure, is one of the hardest things I know, and it is the effect of a high and well-tempered soul, to know how to condescend to such puerile motions and to govern and direct them. I walk firmer and more secure up hill than down.

Such as, according to our common way of teaching, undertake, with one and the same lesson, and the same measure of direction, to instruct several boys of differing and unequal capacities, are infinitely mistaken; and it is no wonder, if in a whole multitude of scholars, there are not found above two or three who bring away any good account of their time and discipline. Let the master not only examine him about the grammatical construction of the bare words of his lesson, but about the sense and let him judge of the profit he has made, not by the testimony of his memory, but by that of his life. Let him make him put what he has learned into a hundred several forms, and accommodate it to so many several subjects, to see if he yet rightly comprehends it, and has made it his own, taking instruction of his progress by the pedagogic institutions of Plato. It is a sign of crudity and indigestion to disgorge what we eat in the same condition it was swallowed; the stomach has not performed its office unless it have altered the form and condition of what was committed to it to concoct. Our minds work only upon trust, when bound and compelled to follow the appetite of another's fancy, enslaved and captivated under the authority of another's instruction; we have been so subjected to the trammel, that we have no free, nor natural pace of our own; our own vigour and liberty are extinct and gone:

Nunquam tutelae suae fiunt.

[They are ever in wardship.

—Seneca, *Epistles,* 33.]

I was privately carried at Pisa to see a very honest man, but so great an Aristotelian, that his most usual thesis was: "That the touchstone and square of all solid imagination, and of all truth, was an absolute conformity to Aristotle's doctrine; and that all besides was nothing but inanity and chimera; for that he had seen all, and said all." A position, that for having been a little too injuriously and broadly interpreted, brought him once and long kept him in great danger of the Inquisition at Rome.

Let him make him examine and thoroughly sift everything he reads, and lodge nothing in his fancy upon simple authority and upon trust. Aristotle's principles will then be no more principles to him, than those of Epicurus and the Stoics: let this diversity of opinions be propounded to, and laid before him; he will himself choose, if he be able; if not, he will remain in doubt.

Che non men the saver, dubbiar m' aggrata.

[I love to doubt, as well as to know.

—Dante, *Inferno,* xi. 93.]

for, if he embrace the opinions of Xenophon and Plato, by his own reason, they will no more be theirs, but become his own. Who follows another, follows nothing, finds nothing, nay, is inquisitive after nothing.

Non sumus sub rege; sibi quisque se vindicet.

[We are under no king; let each vindicate himself.
—Seneca, *Epistles*, 33.]

Let him, at least, know that he knows. It will be necessary that he imbibe their knowledge, not that he be corrupted with their precepts; and no matter if he forget where he had his learning, provided he know how to apply it to his own use. Truth and reason are common to everyone, and are no more his who spake them first, than his who speaks them after: it is no more according to Plato, than according to me, since both he and I equally see and understand them. Bees cull their several sweets from this flower and that blossom, here and there where they find them, but themselves afterwards make the honey, which is all and purely their own, and no more thyme and marjoram: so the several fragments he borrows from others, he will transform and shuffle together to compile a work that shall be absolutely his own; that is to say, his judgment: his instruction, labour and study, tend to nothing else but to form that. He is not obliged to discover whence he got the materials that have assisted him, but only to produce what he has himself done with them. Men that live upon pillage and borrowing, expose their purchases and buildings to everyone's view: but do not proclaim how they came by the money. We do not see the fees and perquisites of a gentleman of the long robe; but we see the alliances wherewith he fortifies himself and his family, and the titles and honours he has obtained for him and his. No man divulges his revenue; or, at least, which way it comes in but everyone publishes his acquisitions. The advantages of our study are to become better and more wise.

It is, says Epicharmus, the understanding that sees and hears, it is the understanding that improves everything, that orders everything, and that acts, rules, and reigns: all other faculties are blind, and deaf, and without soul. And certainly we render it timorous and servile, in not allowing it the liberty and privilege to do anything of itself. Whoever asked his pupil what he thought of grammar and rhetoric, or of such and such a sentence of Cicero? Our masters stick them, full feathered, in our memories, and there establish them like oracles, of which the letters and syllables are of the substance of the thing. To know by rote, is no knowledge, and signifies no more but only to retain what one has intrusted to our memory. That which a man rightly knows and understands, he is the free disposer of at his own full liberty, without any regard to the author from whence he had it, or fumbling over the leaves of his book. A mere bookish learning is a poor, paltry learning; it may serve for ornament, but there is yet no foundation for any superstructure to be built upon it, according to the opinion of Plato, who says, that constancy, faith, and sincerity, are the true philosophy, and the other sciences, that are directed to other ends; mere adulterate paint. I could wish that Paluel or Pompey, those two noted dancers of my time, could have taught us to cut capers, by only seeing them do it, without stirring from our places, as these men pretend to inform the understanding without ever setting it to work, or that we could learn to ride, handle a pike, touch a lute, or sing without the trouble of practice, as these attempt to make us judge and speak well, without exercising us in judging or speaking. Now in this initiation of our studies in their progress, whatsoever presents itself before us is book sufficient; a roguish trick of a page, a sottish mistake of a servant, a jest at the table, are so many new subjects.

And for this reason, conversation with men is of very great use and travel into foreign countries; not to bring back (as most of our young monsieurs do) an account only of how many paces Santa Rotonda [The Pantheon of Agrippa] is in circuit; or of the richness of Signora Livia's petticoats; or, as some others, how much Nero's face, in a statue in such an old ruin, is longer and broader than that made for him on some medal; but to be able chiefly to give an account of the humours, manners, customs, and laws of those nations where he has been, and that we may whet and sharpen our wits by rubbing them against those of others. I would that a boy should be sent abroad very young, and first, so as to kill two birds with one stone, into those neighbouring nations whose language is most differing from our own, and to which, if it be not formed betimes, the tongue will grow too stiff to bend.

And also it is the general opinion of all, that a child should not be brought up in his mother's lap. Mothers are too tender, and their natural affection is apt to make the most discreet of them all so over-fond, that they can neither find in their hearts to give them due correction for the faults they may commit, nor suffer them to be inured to hardships and hazards, as they ought to be. They will not endure to see them return all dust and sweat from their exercise, to drink cold drink when they are hot, nor see them mount an unruly horse, nor take a foil in hand against a rude fencer, or so much as to discharge a carbine. And yet there is no remedy; whoever will breed a boy to be good for anything when he comes to be a man, must by no means spare him when young, and must very often transgress the rules of physic:

Vitamque sub dio, et trepidis agat
In rebus.

[Let him live in open air, and ever in movement about something.
—Horace, *Odes*, ii., 3, 5.]

It is not enough to fortify his soul; you are also to make his sinews strong; for the soul will be oppressed if not assisted by the members, and would have too hard a task to discharge two offices alone. I know very well to my cost, how much mine groans under the burden, from being accommodated with a body so tender and indisposed, as eternally leans and presses upon her; and often in my reading perceive that our masters, in their writings, make examples pass for magnanimity and fortitude of mind, which really are rather toughness of skin and hardness of bones; for I have seen men, women, and children, naturally born of so hard and insensible a constitution of body, that a sound cudgelling has been less to them than a flirt with a finger would have been to me, and that would neither cry out, wince, nor shrink, for a good swinging beating; and when wrestlers counterfeit the philosophers in patience, it is rather strength of nerves than stoutness of heart. Now to be inured to undergo labour, is to be accustomed to endure pain:

Labor callum obducit dolori.

[Labour hardens us against pain.
—Cicero, *Tusculum Disputations*, ii. 15.]

A boy is to be broken in to the toil and roughness of exercise, so as to be trained up to the pain and suffering of dislocations, cholics, cauteries, and even imprisonment and the rack itself; for he may come by misfortune to be reduced to the worst of these, which (as this world goes) is sometimes inflicted on the good as well as the bad. As for proof, in our present civil war whoever draws his sword against the laws, threatens the honestest men with the whip and the halter.

And, moreover, by living at home, the authority of this governor, which ought to be sovereign over the boy he has received into his charge, is often checked and hindered by the presence of parents; to which may also be added, that the respect the whole family pay him, as their master's son, and the knowledge he has of the estate and greatness he is heir to, are, in my opinion, no small inconveniences in these tender years.

And yet, even in this conversing with men I spoke of but now, I have observed this vice, that instead of gathering observations from others, we make it our whole business to lay ourselves open to them, and are more concerned how to expose and set out our own commodities, than how to increase our stock by acquiring new. Silence, therefore, and modesty are very advantageous qualities in conversation. One should, therefore, train up this boy to be sparing and an husband of his knowledge when he has acquired it; and to forbear taking exceptions at or reproving every idle saying or ridiculous story that is said or told in his presence; for it is a very unbecoming rudeness to carp at everything that is not agreeable to our own palate. Let him be satisfied with correcting himself, and not seem to condemn everything in another he would not do himself, nor dispute it as against common customs.

Licet sapere sine pompa, sine invidia.

[Let us be wise without ostentation, without envy.
—Seneca, *Epistles*, 103.]

Let him avoid these vain and uncivil images of authority, this childish ambition of coveting to appear better bred and more accomplished, than he really will, by such carriage, discover himself to be. And, as if opportunities of interrupting and reprehending were not to be omitted, to desire thence to derive the reputation of something more than ordinary. For as it becomes none but great poets to make use of the poetical licence, so it is intolerable for any but men of great and illustrious souls to assume privilege above the authority of custom:

Si quid Socrates ant Aristippus contra morem et consuetudinem fecerunt, idem sibi ne arbitretur licere: magnis enim illi et divinis bonis hanc licentiam assequebantur.

[If Socrates and Aristippus have committed any act against manners and custom, let him not think that he is allowed to do the same; for it was by great and divine benefits that they obtained this privilege.

—Cicero, *De Officius*, i. 41.]

Let him be instructed not to engage in discourse or dispute but with a champion worthy of him, and, even there, not to make use of all the little subtleties that may seem pat for his purpose, but only such arguments as may best serve him. Let him be taught to be curious in the election and choice of his reasons, to abominate impertinence, and consequently, to affect brevity; but, above all, let him be taught to acquiesce and submit to truth so soon as ever he shall discover it, whether in his opponent's argument, or upon better consideration of his own; for he shall never be preferred to the chair for a mere clatter of words and syllogisms, and is no further engaged to any argument whatever, than as he shall in his own judgment approve it: nor yet is arguing a trade, where the liberty of recantation and getting off upon better thoughts, are to be sold for ready money:

Neque, ut omnia, qux praescripta et imperata sint,
defendat, necessitate ulla cogitur.

[Neither is there any necessity upon him, that he should defend all things that are prescribed and enjoined him.

—Cicero, *Academica*, ii. 3.]

If his governor be of my humour, he will form his will to be a very good and loyal subject to his prince, very affectionate to his person, and very stout in his quarrel; but withal he will cool in him the desire of having any other tie to his service than public duty. Besides several other inconveniences that are inconsistent with the liberty every honest man ought to have, a man's judgment, being bribed and prepossessed by these particular obligations, is either blinded and less free to exercise its function, or is blemished with ingratitude and indiscretion. A man that is purely a courtier, can neither have power nor will to speak or think otherwise than favourably and well of a master, who, amongst so many millions of other subjects, has picked out him with his own hand to nourish and advance; this favour, and the profit flowing from it, must needs, and not without some show of reason, corrupt his freedom and dazzle him; and we commonly see these people speak in another kind of phrase than is ordinarily spoken by others of the same nation, though what they say in that courtly language is not much to be believed.

Let his conscience and virtue be eminently manifest in his speaking, and have only reason for their guide. Make him understand, that to acknowledge the error he shall discover in his own argument, though only found out by himself, is an effect of judgment and sincerity, which are the principal things he is to seek after; that obstinacy and contention are common qualities, most appearing in mean souls; that to revise and correct himself, to forsake an unjust argument in the height and heat of dispute, are rare, great, and philosophical qualities.

Let him be advised, being in company, to have his eye and ear in every corner; for I find that the places of greatest honour are commonly seized upon by men that have least in them, and that the greatest fortunes are seldom accompanied with the ablest parts. I have been present when, whilst they at the upper end of the chamber have been only commenting the beauty of the arras, or the flavour of the wine, many things that have been very finely said at the lower end of the table have been lost and thrown away. Let him examine every man's talent; a peasant, a bricklayer, a passenger: one may learn something from everyone of these in their several capacities, and something will be picked out of their discourse whereof some use may be made at one time or another; nay, even the folly and impertinence of others will contribute to his instruction. By observing the graces and manners of all he sees, he will create to himself an emulation of the good, and a contempt of the bad.

CHAPTER 26

Let an honest curiosity be suggested to his fancy of being inquisitive after everything; whatever there is singular and rare near the place where he is, let him go and see it; a fine house, a noble fountain, an eminent man, the place where a battle has been anciently fought, the passages of Caesar and Charlemagne:

> *Qux tellus sit lenta gelu, quae putris ab aestu,*
> *Ventus in Italiam quis bene vela ferat.*

[What country is bound in frost, what land is friable with heat, what wind serves fairest for Italy.

—Propertius, iv. 3, 39.]

Let him inquire into the manners, revenues, and alliances of princes, things in themselves very pleasant to learn, and very useful to know.

In this conversing with men, I mean also, and principally, those who only live in the records of history; he shall, by reading those books, converse with the great and heroic souls of the best ages. It is an idle and vain study to those who make it so by doing it after a negligent manner, but to those who do it with care and observation, it is a study of inestimable fruit and value; and the only study, as Plato reports, that the Lacedaemonians reserved to themselves. What profit shall he not reap as to the business of men, by reading the Lives of Plutarch? But, withal, let my governor remember to what end his instructions are principally directed, and that he do not so much imprint in his pupil's memory the date of the ruin of Carthage, as the manners of Hannibal and Scipio; nor so much where Marcellus died, as why it was unworthy of his duty that he died there. Let him not teach him so much the narrative parts of history as to judge them; the reading of them, in my opinion, is a thing that of all others we apply ourselves unto with the most differing measure. I have read a hundred things in Livy that another has not, or not taken notice of at least; and Plutarch has read a hundred more there than ever I could find, or than, peradventure, that author ever wrote; to some it is merely a grammar study, to others the very anatomy of philosophy, by which the most abstruse parts of our human nature penetrate. There are in Plutarch many long discourses very worthy to be carefully read and observed, for he is, in my opinion, of all others the greatest master in that kind of writing; but there are a thousand others which he has only touched and glanced upon, where he only points with his finger to direct us which way we may go if we will, and contents himself sometimes with giving only one brisk hit in the nicest article of the question, whence we are to grope out the rest. As, for example, where he says [In the Essay on False Shame] that the inhabitants of Asia came to be vassals to one only, for not having been able to pronounce one syllable, which is No. Which saying of his gave perhaps matter and occasion to La Boetie to write his "Voluntary Servitude." Only to see him pick out a light action in a man's life, or a mere word that does not seem to amount even to that, is itself a whole discourse. It is to our prejudice that men of understanding should so immoderately affect brevity; no doubt their reputation is the better by it, but in the meantime we are the worse. Plutarch had rather we should applaud his judgment than commend his knowledge, and had rather leave us with an appetite to read more, than glutted with that we have already read. He knew very well, that a man may say too much even upon the best subjects, and that Alexandridas justly reproached him who made very good. but too long speeches to the Ephori, when he said: "O stranger! thou speakest the things thou shouldst speak, but not as thou shouldst speak them." [Plutarch, Apothegms of the Lacedamonians.] Such as have lean and spare bodies stuff themselves out with clothes; so they who are defective in matter endeavour to make amends with words.

Human understanding is marvellously enlightened by daily conversation with men, for we are, otherwise, compressed and heaped up in ourselves, and have our sight limited to the length of our own noses. One asking Socrates of what country he was, he did not make answer, of Athens, but of the world; [Cicero, *Tusculum Disputations.*, v. 37; Plutarch, *On Exile*, c. 4.] he whose imagination was fuller and wider, embraced the whole world for his country, and extended his society and friendship to all mankind; not as we do, who look no further than our feet. When the vines of my village are nipped with the frost, my parish priest presently concludes, that the indignation of God has gone out against all the human race, and that the cannibals have already got the pip. Who is it that, seeing the havoc of these civil wars of ours, does not cry out, that the machine of the world is near dissolution, and that the day of judgment is at hand; without considering, that many worse things have been seen, and that in the meantime, people are very merry in a thousand other parts of the earth for all this? For my part, considering the licence and impunity that always attend such commotions, I wonder they are so moderate, and that there is no more mischief done. To him who feels the hailstones patter about his ears, the whole hemisphere appears to be in storm and tempest; like the ridiculous Savoyard, who said very gravely, that if that simple king of France could have managed his fortune as he should have done, he might in time have come to have been steward of the household to the duke his master: the fellow could not, in his shallow imagination, conceive that there could be anything greater than a Duke of Savoy. And, in truth, we are all of us, insensibly, in this error, an error of a very great weight and very pernicious consequence. But whoever shall represent to his fancy, as in a picture, that great image of our mother nature, in her full majesty and lustre, whoever in her face shall read so general and so constant a variety, whoever shall observe himself in that figure, and not himself but a whole kingdom, no bigger than the least touch or prick of a pencil in comparison of the whole, that man alone is able to value things according to their true estimate and grandeur.

This great world which some do yet multiply as several species under one genus, is the mirror wherein we are to behold ourselves, to be able to know ourselves as we ought to do in the true bias.

In short, I would have this to be the book my young gentleman should study with the most attention. So many humours, so many sects, so many judgments, opinions, laws, and customs, teach us to judge aright of our own, and inform our understanding to discover its imperfection and natural infirmity, which is no trivial speculation. So many mutations of states and kingdoms, and so many turns and revolutions of public fortune, will make us wise enough to make no great wonder of our own. So many great names, so many famous victories and conquests drowned and swallowed in oblivion, render our hopes ridiculous of eternising our names by the taking of half-a-score of light horse, or a henroost, which only derives its memory from its ruin. The pride and arrogance of so many foreign pomps, the inflated majesty of so many courts and grandeurs, accustom and fortify our sight without closing our eyes to behold the lustre of our own; so many trillions of men, buried before us, encourage us not to fear to go seek such good company in the other world: and so of the rest Pythagoras was want to say, [Cicero, *Tusculum Disputations*, v. 3.] that our life resembles the great and populous assembly of the Olympic games, wherein some exercise the body, that they may carry away the glory of the prize: others bring merchandise to sell for profit: there are also some (and those none of the worst sort) who pursue no other advantage than only to look on, and consider how and why everything is done, and to be spectators of the lives of other men, thereby the better to judge of and regulate their own.

To examples may fitly be applied all the profitable discourses of philosophy, to which all human actions, as to their best rule, ought to be especially directed: a scholar shall be taught to know –

> *Quid fas optare: quid asper*
> *Utile nummus habet: patrix carisque propinquis*
> *Quantum elargiri deceat: quern te Deus esse*
> *Jussit, et humana qua parte locatus es in re;*
> *Quid sumus, et quidnam victuri gignimur.*

CHAPTER 26

[Learn what it is right to wish; what is the true use of coined
money; how much it becomes us to give in liberality to our
country and our dear relations; whom and what the Deity commanded thee to be; and in what part of the human system thou
art placed; what we are ant to what purpose engendered.

—Persius, iii. 69]

what it is to know, and what to be ignorant; what ought to be the
end and design of study; what valour, temperance, and justice are;
the difference between ambition and avarice, servitude and subjection, licence and liberty; by what token a man may know true and
solid contentment; how far death, affliction, and disgrace are to be
apprehended;

Et quo quemque modo fugiatque feratque laborem.

[And how you may shun or sustain every hardship.

–Virgil, *Aeneid*, iii. 459.]

by what secret springs we move, and the reason of our various agitations and irresolutions: for, methinks the first doctrine
with which one should season his understanding, ought to be that
which regulates his manners and his sense; that teaches him to
know himself, and how both well to dig and well to live. Amongst
the liberal sciences, let us begin with that which makes us free;
not that they do not all serve in some measure to the instruction
and use of life, as all other things in some sort also do; but let
us make choice of that which directly and professedly serves to
that end. If we are once able to restrain the offices of human life
within their just and natural limits, we shall find that most of the
sciences in use are of no great use to us, and even in those that
are, that there are many very unnecessary cavities and dilatations
which we had better let alone, and, following Socrates' direction,

limit the course of our studies to those things only where is a true and real utility:

> *Sapere aude;*
> *Incipe; Qui recte vivendi prorogat horam,*
> *Rusticus exspectat, dum defluat amnis; at ille*
> *Labitur, et labetur in omne volubilis oevum.*

[Dare to be wise; begin! he who defers the hour of living well is like the clown, waiting till the river shall have flowed out: but the river still flows, and will run on, with constant course, to ages without end.

—Horace, *Epistles*, i. 2.]

It is a great foolery to teach our children:

> *Quid moveant Pisces, animosaque signa Leonis,*
> *Lotus et Hesperia quid Capricornus aqua,*

[What influence Pisces have, or the sign of angry Leo, or Capricorn, washed by the Hesperian wave.

—Propertius, iv. I, 89.]

the knowledge of the stars and the motion of the eighth sphere before their own:

[What care I about the Pleiades or the stars of Taurus?

–Anacreon, *Ode*, xvii. 10.]

Anaximenes writing to Pythagoras, "To what purpose," said he, "should I trouble myself in searching out the secrets of the stars, having death or slavery continually before my eyes?" for the kings of Persia were at that time preparing to invade his country. Everyone

CHAPTER 26

ought to say thus, "Being assaulted, as I am by ambition, avarice, temerity, superstition, and having within so many other enemies of life, shall I go ponder over the world's changes?"

After having taught him what will make him more wise and good, you may then entertain him with the elements of logic, physics, geometry, rhetoric, and the science which he shall then himself most incline to, his judgment being beforehand formed and fit to choose, he will quickly make his own. The way of instructing him ought to be sometimes by discourse, and sometimes by reading; sometimes his governor shall put the author himself, which he shall think most proper for him, into his hands, and sometimes only the marrow and substance of it; and if himself be not conversant enough in books to turn to all the fine discourses the books contain for his purpose, there may some man of learning be joined to him, that upon every occasion shall supply him with what he stands in need of, to furnish it to his pupil. And who can doubt but that this way of teaching is much more easy and natural than that of Gaza, [Theodore Gaza, rector of the Academy of Ferrara.] in which the precepts are so intricate, and so harsh, and the words so vain, lean; and insignificant, that there is no hold to be taken of them, nothing that quickens and elevates the wit and fancy, whereas here the mind has what to feed upon and to digest. This fruit, therefore, is not only without comparison, much more fair and beautiful; but will also be much more early ripe.

It is a thousand pities that matters should be at such a pass in this age of ours, that philosophy, even with men of understanding, should be, looked upon as a vain and fantastic name, a thing of no use, no value, either in opinion or effect, of which I think those ergotisms and petty sophistries, by prepossessing the avenues to it, are the cause. And people are much to blame to represent it to children for a thing of so difficult access, and with such a frowning, grim, and formidable aspect. Who is it that has disguised it thus, with this false, pale, and ghostly countenance? There is nothing more airy, more gay, more frolic, and I had like to have said, more wanton. She preaches nothing but feasting and jollity; a melancholic anxious look shows that she does not inhabit there. Demetrius the grammarian finding in the temple of Delphos a knot of philosophers set chatting together, said to them, [Plutarch, Treatise on Oracles which have ceased] "Either I am much deceived, or by your cheerful and pleasant countenances, you are engaged in no, very deep discourse." To which one of them, Heracleon the Megarean, replied: "Tis for such as are puzzled about inquiring whether the future tense of the verb —— is spelt with a double A, or that hunt after the derivation of the comparatives —— and ——, and the superlatives — and ——, to knit their brows whilst discoursing of their science: but as to philosophical discourses, they always divert and cheer up those that entertain them, and never deject them or make them sad."

> *Deprendas animi tormenta latentis in aegro*
> *Corpore; deprendas et gaudia; sumit utrumque*
> *Inde habitum facies.*

[You may discern the torments of mind lurking in a sick body; you may discern its joys: either expression the face assumes from the mind.

—Juvenal, ix. 18.]

The soul that lodges philosophy, ought to be of such a constitution of health, as to render the body in like manner healthful too; she ought to make her tranquillity and satisfaction shine so as to appear without, and her contentment ought to fashion the outward behaviour to her own mould, and consequently to fortify it with a graceful confidence, an active and joyous carriage, and a serene and contented countenance. The most manifest sign of wisdom is a continual cheerfulness; her state is like that of things in the regions above the moon, always clear and serene. It is Baroco and Baralipton [Two terms of the ancient scholastic logic] that render their disciples so dirty and ill-favoured, and not she; they do not so much as know her but by hearsay. What! It is she that calms and appeases the storms and tempests of the soul, and who teaches famine and fevers to laugh and sing; and that, not by certain imaginary epicycles, but by natural and manifest reasons. She has virtue for her end, which is not, as the schoolmen say, situate upon the summit of a perpendicular, rugged, inaccessible precipice: such as have approached her find her, quite on the contrary, to be seated in a fair, fruitful, and flourishing plain, whence she easily discovers all things below; to which place any one may, however, arrive, if he know but the way, through shady, green, and sweetly-flourishing avenues, by a pleasant, easy, and smooth descent, like that of the celestial vault. It is for not having frequented this supreme, this beautiful, triumphant, and amiable, this equally delicious and courageous virtue, this so professed and implacable enemy to anxiety, sorrow, fear, and constraint, who, having nature for her guide, has fortune and pleasure for her companions, that they have gone, according to their own weak imagination, and created this ridiculous, this sorrowful, querulous, despiteful, threatening, terrible image of it to themselves and others, and placed it upon a rock apart, amongst thorns and brambles, and made of it a hobgoblin to affright people.

But the governor that I would have, that is such a one as knows it to be his duty to possess his pupil with as much or more affection than reverence to virtue, will be able to inform him, that the poets have evermore accommodated themselves to the public humour, and make him sensible, that the gods have planted more toil and sweat in the avenues of the cabinets of Venus than in those of Minerva. And when he shall once find him begin to apprehend, and shall represent to him a Bradamante or an Angelica [Heroines of Ariosto] for a mistress, a natural, active, generous, and not a viragoish, but a manly beauty, in comparison of a soft, delicate, artificial simpering, and affected form; the one in the habit of a heroic youth, wearing a glittering helmet, the other tricked up in curls and ribbons like a wanton minx; he will then look upon his own affection as brave and masculine, when he shall choose quite contrary to that effeminate shepherd of Phrygia.

Such a tutor will make a pupil digest this new lesson, that the height and value of true virtue consists in the facility, utility, and pleasure of its exercise; so far from difficulty, that boys, as well as men, and the innocent as well as the subtle, may make it their own; it is by order, and not by force, that it is to be acquired. Socrates, her first minion, is so averse to all manner of violence, as totally to throw it aside, to slip into the more natural facility of her own progress; it is the nursing mother of all human pleasures, who in rendering them just, renders them also pure and permanent; in moderating them, keeps them in breath and appetite; in interdicting those which she herself refuses, whets our desire to those that she allows; and, like a kind and liberal mother, abundantly allows all that nature requires, even to satiety, if not to lassitude: unless we mean to say that the regimen which stops the toper before he has drunk himself drunk, the glutton before he has eaten to a surfeit, and the lecher before he has got the pox, is an enemy to pleasure. If the ordinary fortune fail, she does without it, and forms another, wholly her own, not so fickle and unsteady as the other. She can be rich, be potent and wise, and knows how to lie upon soft perfumed beds: she loves life, beauty, glory, and health; but her proper and peculiar office is to know how to regulate the use of all these good things, and how to lose them without concern: an office much more noble than troublesome, and without which the whole course of life is unnatural, turbulent, and deformed, and there it is indeed, that men may justly represent those monsters upon rocks and precipices.

If this pupil shall happen to be of so contrary a disposition, that he had rather hear a tale of a tub than the true narrative of some noble expedition or some wise and learned discourse; who at the beat of drum, that excites the youthful ardour of his companions, leaves that to follow another that calls to a morris or the bears; who would not wish, and find it more delightful and more excellent, to return all dust and sweat victorious from a battle, than from tennis or from a ball, with the prize of those exercises; I see no other remedy, but that he be bound prentice in some good town to learn to make minced pies, though he were the son of a duke; according to Plato's precept, that children are to be placed out and disposed of, not according to the wealth, qualities, or condition of the father, but according to the faculties and the capacity of their own souls.

Since philosophy is that which instructs us to live, and that infancy has there its lessons as well as other ages, why is it not communicated to children betimes?

> *Udum et mole lutum est; nunc, nunc properandus, et acri*
> *Fingendus sine fine rota.*

[The clay is moist and soft: now, now make haste, and form the pitcher on the rapid wheel.

—Persius, iii. 23.]

They begin to teach us to live when we have almost done living. A hundred students have got the pox before they have come to read Aristotle's lecture on temperance. Cicero said, that though he should live two men's ages, he should never find leisure to study the lyric poets; and I find these sophisters yet more deplorably unprofitable. The boy we would breed has a great deal less time to spare; he owes but the first fifteen or sixteen years of his life to education; the remainder is due to action. Let us, therefore, employ that short time in necessary instruction. Away with the thorny subtleties of dialectics; they are abuses, things by which our lives can never be amended: take the plain philosophical discourses, learn how rightly to choose, and then rightly to apply them; they are more easy to be understood than one of Boccaccio's novels; a child from nurse is much more capable of them, than of learning to read or to write. Philosophy has discourses proper for childhood, as well as for the decrepit age of men.

I am of Plutarch's mind, that Aristotle did not so much trouble his great disciple with the knack of forming syllogisms, or with the elements of geometry; as with infusing into him good precepts concerning valour, prowess, magnanimity, temperance, and the contempt of fear; and with this ammunition, sent him, whilst yet a boy, with no more than thirty thousand foot, four thousand horse, and but forty-two thousand crowns, to subjugate the empire of the whole earth. For the other acts and sciences, he says, Alexander highly indeed commended their excellence and charm, and had them in very great honour and esteem, but not ravished with them to that degree as to be tempted to affect the practice of them In his own person:

> *Petite hinc, juvenesque senesque,*
> *Finem ammo certum, miserisque viatical canis.*

[Young men and old men, derive hence a certain end to the mind, and stores for miserable grey hairs.

—Persius, v. 64.]

Epicurus, in the beginning of his letter to Meniceus, [Diogenes Laertius, x. 122] says, "That neither the youngest should refuse to philosophise, nor the oldest grow weary of it." Who does otherwise, seems tacitly to imply, that either the time of living happily is not yet come, or that it is already past. And yet, a for all that, I would not have this pupil of ours imprisoned and made a slave to his book; nor would I have him given up to the morosity and melancholic humour of a sour ill-natured pedant.

I would not have his spirit cowed and subdued, by applying him to the rack, and tormenting him, as some do, fourteen or fifteen hours a day, and so make a pack-horse of him. Neither should I think it good, when, by reason of a solitary and melancholic complexion, he is discovered to be overmuch addicted to his book, to

126

nourish that humour in him; for that renders him unfit for civil conversation, and diverts him from better employments. And how many have I seen in my time totally brutified by an immoderate thirst after knowledge? Carneades was so besotted with it, that he would not find time so much as to comb his head or to pare his nails. Neither would I have his generous manners spoiled and corrupted by the incivility and barbarism of those of another. The French wisdom was anciently turned into proverb: "Early, but of no continuance." And, in truth, we yet see, that nothing can be more ingenious and pleasing than the children of France; but they ordinarily deceive the hope and expectation that have been conceived of them; and grown up to be men, have nothing extraordinary or worth taking notice of: I have heard men of good understanding say, these colleges of ours to which we send our young people (and of which we have but too many) make them such animals as they are.

But to our little monsieur, a closet, a garden, the table, his bed, solitude, and company, morning and evening, all hours shall be the same, and all places to him a study; for philosophy, who, as the formatrix of judgment and manners, shall be his principal lesson, has that privilege to have a hand in everything. The orator Isocrates, being at a feast entreated to speak of his art, all the company were satisfied with and commended his answer: "It is not now a time," said he, "to do what I can do; and that which it is now time to do, I cannot do." [Plutarch, *Symposiacs*, i. I.] For to make orations and rhetorical disputes in a company met together to laugh and make good cheer, had been very unreasonable and improper, and as much might have been said of all the other sciences. But as to what concerns philosophy, that part of it at least that treats of man, and of his offices and duties, it has been the common opinion of all wise men, that, out of respect to the sweetness of her conversation, she is ever to be admitted in all sports and entertainments. And Plato, having invited her to his feast, we see after how gentle and obliging a manner, accommodated both to time and place, she entertained the company, though in a discourse of the highest and most important nature:

> *Aeque pauperibus prodest, locupletibus aeque;*
> *Et, neglecta, aeque pueris senibusque nocebit.*

[It profits poor and rich alike, but, neglected, equally hurts old and young.

—Horace, *Epistles*, i. 25.]

By this method of instruction, my young pupil will be much more and better employed than his fellows of the college are. But as the steps we take in walking to and fro in a gallery, though three times as many, do not tire a man so much as those we employ in a formal journey, so our lesson, as it were accidentally occurring, without any set obligation of time or place, and falling naturally into every action, will insensibly insinuate itself. By which means our very exercises and recreations, running, wrestling, music, dancing, hunting, riding, and fencing, will prove to be a good part of our study. I would have his outward fashion and mien, and the disposition of his limbs, formed at the same time with his mind. It is not a soul, it is not a body that we are training up, but a man, and we ought not to divide him. And, as Plato says, we are not to fashion one without the other, but make them draw together like two horses harnessed to a coach. By which saying of his, does he not seem to allow more time for, and to take more care of exercises for the body, and to hold that the mind, in a good proportion, does her business at the same time too?

As to the rest, this method of education ought to be carried on with a severe sweetness, quite contrary to the practice of our pedants, who, instead of tempting and alluring children to letters by apt and gentle ways, do in truth present nothing before them but rods and ferules, horror and cruelty. Away with this violence! away with this compulsion! than which, I certainly believe nothing more dulls and degenerates a well-descended nature. If you would have him apprehend shame and chastisement, do not harden him to them: inure him to heat and cold, to wind and sun, and to dangers that he ought to despise; wean him from all effeminacy and delicacy in clothes and lodging, eating and drinking; accustom him to everything, that he may not be a Sir Paris, a carpet-knight, but a sinewy, hardy, and vigorous young man. I have ever from a child to the age wherein I now am, been of this opinion, and am still constant to it. But amongst other things, the strict government of most of our colleges has evermore displeased me; peradventure, they might have erred less perniciously on the indulgent side. It is a real house of correction of imprisoned youth. They are made debauched by being punished before they are so. Do but come in when they are about their lesson, and you shall hear nothing but the outcries of boys under execution, with the thundering noise of their pedagogues drunk with fury. A very pretty way this, to tempt these tender and timorous souls to love their book, with a furious countenance, and a rod in hand! A cursed and pernicious way of proceeding! Besides what Quintilian has very well observed, that this imperious authority is often attended by very dangerous consequences, and particularly our way of chastising. How much more decent would it be to see their classes strewed with green leaves and fine flowers, than with the bloody stumps of birch and willows? Were it left to my ordering. I should paint the school with the pictures of joy and gladness; Flora and the Graces, as the philosopher Speusippus did his. Where their profit is, let them there have their pleasure too. Such viands as are proper and wholesome for children, should be sweetened with sugar, and such as are dangerous to them, embittered with gall. It is marvellous to see how solicitous Plato is in his Laws concerning the gaiety and diversion of the youth of his city, and how much and often he enlarges upon the races, sports, songs, leaps, and dances: of which, he says, that antiquity has given the ordering and patronage particularly to the gods themselves, to Apollo, Minerva, and the Muses. He insists long upon, and is very particular in, giving innumerable precepts for exercises; but as to the lettered sciences, says very little, and only seems particularly to recommend poetry upon the account of music.

All singularity in our manners and conditions is to be avoided, as inconsistent with civil society. Who would not be astonished at so strange a constitution as that of Demophoon, steward to Alexander the Great, who sweated in the shade and shivered in the sun? I have seen those who have run from the smell of a mellow apple with greater precipitation than from a harquebuss-shot; others afraid of a mouse; others vomit at the sight of cream; others ready to swoon at the making of a feather bed; Germanicus could neither endure the sight nor the crowing of a cock. I will not deny, but that there may, peradventure, be some occult cause and natural aversion in these cases; but, in my opinion, a man might conquer it, if he took it in time. Precept has in this wrought so effectually upon me, though not without some pains on my part, I confess, that beer excepted, my appetite accommodates itself indifferently to all sorts of diet. Young bodies are supple; one should, therefore, in that age bend and ply them to all fashions and customs: and provided a man can contain the appetite and the will within their due limits, let a young man, in God's name, be rendered fit for all nations and all companies, even to debauchery and excess, if need be; that is, where he shall do it out of complacency to the customs of the place. Let him be able to do everything, but love to do nothing but what is good. The philosophers themselves do not justify Callisthenes for forfeiting the favour of his master Alexander the Great, by refusing to pledge him a cup of wine. Let him laugh, play, wench with his prince: nay, I would have him, even in his debauches, too hard for the rest of the company, and to excel his companions in ability and vigour, and that he may not give over doing it, either through defect of power or knowledge how to do it, but for want of will.

Multum interest, utrum peccare ali quis nolit, an nesciat.

[There is a vast difference between forbearing to sin, and not
knowing how to sin.

—Seneca, *Epistles*, 90.]

I thought I passed a compliment upon a lord, as free from those
excesses as any man in France, by asking him before a great deal of
very good company, how many times in his life he had been drunk
in Germany, in the time of his being there about his Majesty's affairs;
which he also took as it was intended, and made answer, "Three
times"; and withal told us the whole story of his debauches. I know
some who, for want of this faculty, have found a great inconvenience in negotiating with that nation. I have often with great admiration reflected upon the wonderful constitution of Alcibiades, who
so easily could transform himself to so various fashions without any
prejudice to his health; one while outdoing the Persian pomp and
luxury, and another, the Lacedaemonian austerity and frugality; as
reformed in Sparta, as voluptuous in Ionia:

Omnis Aristippum decuit color, et status, et res.

[Every complexion of life, and station, and circumstance became
Aristippus.

—Horace, *Epistles*, xvii. 23.]

I would have my pupil to be such an one,

Quem duplici panno patentia velat,
Mirabor, vitae via si conversa decebit,
Personamque feret non inconcinnus utramque.

[I should admire him who with patience bearing a patched
garment,

bears well a changed fortune, acting both parts equally well.
—Horace *Epistles*, xvii. 25.]

These are my lessons, and he who puts them in practice shall reap more advantage than he who has had them read to him only, and so only knows them. If you see him, you hear him; if you hear him, you see him. God forbid, says one in Plato, that to philosophise were only to read a great many books, and to learn the arts.

> *Hanc amplissimam omnium artium bene vivendi disciplinam,*
> *vita magis quam literis, persequuti sunt.*

[They have proceeded to this discipline of living well, which of all arts is the greatest, by their lives, rather than by their reading.
—Cicero, *Tusculum Disputations*, iv. 3.]

Leo, prince of the Phliasians, asking Heraclides Ponticusof what art or science he made profession: "I know," said he, "neither art nor science, but I am a philosopher." One reproaching Diogenes that, being ignorant, he should pretend to philosophy; "I there-fore," answered he, "pretend to it with so much the more reason." Hegesias entreated that he would read a certain book to him: "You are pleasant," said he; "you choose those figs that are true and natural, and not those that are painted; why do you not also choose exercises which are naturally true, rather than those written?"

The lad will not so much get his lesson by heart as he will prac-tise it: he will repeat it in his actions. We shall discover if there be prudence in his exercises, if there be sincerity and justice in his deportment, if there be grace and judgment in his speaking; if there be constancy in his sickness; if there be modesty in his mirth, tem-perance in his pleasures, order in his domestic economy, indiffer-ence in palate, whether what he eats or drinks be flesh or fish, wine or water:

132

CHAPTER 26

Qui disciplinam suam non ostentationem scientiae, sed legem vitae
putet: quique obtemperet ipse sibi, et decretis pareat.

[Who considers his own discipline, not as a vain ostentation of
science, but as a law and rule of life; and who obeys his own
decrees, and the laws he has prescribed for himself.
— Cicero, *Tusculum Disputations*, ii. 4.]

The conduct of our lives is the true mirror of our doctrine.
Zeuxidamus, to one who asked him, why the Lacedaemonians did
not commit their constitutions of chivalry to writing, and deliver
them to their young men to read, made answer, that it was because
they would inure them to action, and not amuse them with words.
With such a one, after fifteen or sixteen years' study, compare one of
our college Latinists, who has thrown away so much time in nothing
but learning to speak. The world is nothing but babble; and I hardly
ever yet saw that man who did not rather prate too much, than speak
too little. And yet half of our age is embezzled this way: we are kept
four or five years to learn words only, and to tack them together into
clauses; as many more to form them into a long discourse, divided
into four or five parts; and other five years, at least, to learn suc-
cinctly to mix and interweave them after a subtle and intricate manner let us leave all this to those who make a profession of it.

Going one day to Orleans, I met in that plain on this side Clery,
two pedants who were travelling towards Bordeaux, about fifty paces
distant from one another; and, a good way further behind them, I
discovered a troop of horse, with a gentleman at the head of them,
who was the late Monsieur le Comte de la Rochefoucauld. One of
my people inquired of the foremost of these masters of arts, who
that gentleman was that came after him; he, having not seen the
train that followed after, and thinking his companion was meant,
pleasantly answered, "He is not a gentleman; he is a grammarian;
and I am a logician." Now we who, quite contrary, do not here pretend to breed a grammarian or a logician, but a gentleman, let us

leave them to abuse their leisure; our business lies elsewhere. Let but our pupil be well furnished with things, words will follow but too fast; he will pull them after him if they do not voluntarily follow. I have observed some to make excuses, that they cannot express themselves, and pretend to have their fancies full of a great many very fine things, which yet, for want of eloquence, they cannot utter; it is a mere shift, and nothing else. Will you know what I think of it? I think they are nothing but shadows of some imperfect images and conceptions that they know not what to make of within, nor consequently bring out; they do not yet themselves understand what they would be at, and if you but observe how they haggle and stammer upon the point of parturition, you will soon conclude, that their labour is not to delivery, but about conception, and that they are but licking their formless embryo. For my part, I hold, and Socrates commands it, that whoever has in his mind a sprightly and clear imagination, he will express it well enough in one kind of tongue or another, and, if he be dumb, by signs –

Verbaque praevisam rem non invita sequentur;

[Once a thing is conceived in the mind, the words to express it soon present themselves. (The words will not reluctantly follow the thing preconceived.)

—Horace, *De Arte Poetica.* v. 311.]

And as another as poetically says in his prose:

Quum res animum occupavere, verbs ambiunt,

[When things are once in the mind, the words offer themselves readily. (When things have taken possession of the mind, the words trip.)

—Seneca, *Controversiae,* iii. proem.]

134

and this other.

Ipsae res verbs rapiunt.

[The things themselves force the words to express them.
—Cicero, *De Finibus*, iii. 5.]

He knows nothing of ablative, conjunctive, substantive, or grammar, no more than his lackey, or a fishwife of the Petit Pont; and yet these will give you a bellyful of talk, if you will hear them, and peradventure shall trip as little in their language as the best masters of art in France. He knows no rhetoric, nor how in a preface to bribe the benevolence of the courteous reader; neither does he care to know it. Indeed all this fine decoration of painting is easily effaced by the lustre of a simple and blunt truth; these fine flourishes serve only to amuse the vulgar, of themselves incapable of more solid and nutritive diet, as Aper very evidently demonstrates in Tacitus. The ambassadors of Samos, prepared with a long and elegant oration, came to Cleomenes, king of Sparta, to incite him to a war against the tyrant Polycrates; who, after he had heard their harangue with great gravity and patience, gave them this answer: "As to the exordium, I remember it not, nor consequently the middle of your speech; and for what concerns your conclusion, I will not do what you desire:" [Plutarch, Apothegms of the Lacedaemonians] a very pretty answer this, methinks, and a pack of learned orators most sweetly gravelled. And what did the other man say? The Athenians were to choose one of two architects for a very great building they had designed; of these, the first, a pert affected fellow, offered his service in a long premeditated discourse upon the subject of the work in hand, and by his oratory inclined the voices of the people in his favour; but the other in three words: "O Athenians, what this man says, I will do." [Plutarch, Instructions to Statesmen, c. 4] When Cicero was in the height and heat of an eloquent harangue, many were struck with admiration; but Cato only laughed, saying, "We have a pleasant (mirth-making) consul." Let it go before, or come after, a good sentence or a thing well said, is always in season; if it neither suit well with what went before, nor has much coherence with what follows after, it is good in itself. I am none of those who think that good rhyme makes a good poem. Let him make short long, and long short if he will, it is no great matter; if there be invention, and that the wit and judgment have well performed their offices, I will say, here's a good poet, but an ill rhymer.

Emunctae naris, durus componere versus.

[Of delicate humour, but of rugged versification.
—Horace, *Satire*, iv. 8.]

Let a man, says Horace, divest his work of all method and measure,

Tempora certa modosque, et, quod prius ordine verbum est,
Posterius facias, praeponens ultima primis
Invenias etiam disjecti membra poetae.

[Take away certain rhythms and measures, and make the word which was first in order come later, putting that which should be last first, you will still find the scattered remains of the poet.
—Horace, *Satire*, i. 4, 58.]

he will never the more lose himself for that; the very pieces will be fine by themselves. Menander's answer had this meaning, who being reproved by a friend, the time drawing on at which he had promised a comedy, that he had not yet fallen in hand with it; "It is made, and ready," said he, "all but the verses." [Plutarch, Whether the Athenians more excelled in Arms or in Letters] Having contrived the subject, and disposed the scenes in his fancy, he took little care for the rest. Since Ronsard and Du Bellay have given reputation

136

to our French poesy, every little dabbler, for aught I see, swells his words as high, and makes his cadences very near as harmonious as they:

Plus sonat, quam valet.

[More sound than sense

—Seneca, *Epistles*, 40]

For the vulgar, there were never so many poetasters as now; but though they find it no hard matter to imitate their rhyme, they yet fall infinitely short of imitating the rich descriptions of the one, and the delicate invention of the other of these masters.

But what will become of our young gentleman, if he be attacked with the sophistic subtlety of some syllogism? "A Westfalia ham makes a man drink; drink quenches thirst: ergo a Westfalia ham quenches thirst." Why, let him laugh at it; it will be more discretion to do so, than to go about to answer it; or let him borrow this pleasant evasion from Aristippus: "Why should I trouble myself to untie that, which bound as it is, gives me so much trouble?" [Diogenes Laertius, ii. 70] One offering at this dialectic juggling against Cleanthes, Chrysippus took him short, saying, "Reserve these baubles to play with children, and do not by such fooleries divert the serious thoughts of a man of years." If these ridiculous subtleties,

Contorta et aculeata sophismata,

as Cicero calls them, are designed to possess him with an untruth, they are dangerous; but if they signify no more than only to make him laugh, I do not see why a man need to be fortified against them. There are some so ridiculous, as to go a mile out of their way to hook in a fine word:

Aut qui non verba rebus aptant, sed res extrinsecus
arcessunt, quibus verba conveniant.

[Who do not fit words to the subject, but seek out for things
quite from the purpose to fit the words.
—Quintilian, viii. 3.]

And as another says,

Qui, alicujus verbi decore placentis, vocentur ad id,
quod non proposuerant scribere.

[Who by their fondness of some fine sounding word, are
tempted to something they had no intention to treat of.
—Seneca, *Epistles,* 59.]

I for my part rather bring in a fine sentence by head and shoulders to fit my purpose, than divert my designs to hunt after a sentence. On the contrary, words are to serve, and to follow a man's
purpose; and let Gascon come in play where French will not do.
I would have things so excelling, and so wholly possessing the imagination of him that hears, that he should have something else to do,
than to think of words. The way of speaking that I love, is natural
and plain, the same in writing as in speaking, and a sinewy and mus-
cular way of expressing a man's self, short and pithy, not so elegant
and artificial as prompt and vehement;

Haec demum sapiet dictio, qux feriet;

[That has most weight and wisdom which pierces the ear. (That
utterance indeed will have a taste which shall strike the ear.)
—Epitaph on Lucan, in *Fabricius, Bibliotheca Latina,* ii. 10.]

rather hard than wearisome; free from affectation; irregular,
incontinuous, and bold; where every piece makes up an entire
body; not like a pedant, a preacher, or a pleader, but rather a
soldier-like style, as Suetonius calls that of Julius Caesar; and yet

I see no reason why he should call it so. I have ever been ready to imitate the negligent garb, which is yet observable amongst the young men of our time, to wear my cloak on one shoulder, my cap on one side, a stocking in disorder, which seems to express a kind of haughty disdain of these exotic ornaments, and a contempt of the artificial; but I find this negligence of much better use in the form of speaking. All affectation, particularly in the French gaiety and freedom, is ungraceful in a courtier, and in a monarchy every gentleman ought to be fashioned according to the court model; for which reason, an easy and natural negligence does well. I no more like a web where the knots and seams are to be seen, than a fine figure, so delicate, that a man may tell all the bones and veins:

Quae veritati operam dat oratio, incomposita sit et simplex.

[Let the language that is dedicated to truth be plain and unaffected.

—Seneca, *Epistles*, 40.]

Quis accurat loquitur, nisi qui vult putide loqui?

[For who studies to speak accurately, that does not at the same time wish to perplex his auditory?

—*Idem, Epistles*, 75.]

That eloquence prejudices the subject it would advance, that wholly attracts us to itself. And as in our outward habit, it is a ridiculous effeminacy to distinguish ourselves by a particular and unusual garb or fashion; so in language, to study new phrases, and to affect words that are not of current use, proceeds from a puerile and scholastic ambition. May I be bound to speak no other language than what is spoken in the market-places of Paris! Aristophanes the grammarian was quite out, when he reprehended Epicurus for his plain way of delivering himself, and the design of his oratory, which was only perspicuity of speech. The imitation of words, by its own facility, immediately disperses itself through a whole people; but the imitation of inventing and fitly applying those words is of a slower progress. The generality of readers, for having found a like robe, very mistakingly imagine they have the same body and inside too, whereas force and sinews are never to be borrowed; the gloss, and outward ornament, that is, words and elocution, may. Most of those I converse with, speak the same language I here write; but whether they think the same thoughts I cannot say. The Athenians, says Plato, study fulness and elegancy of speaking; the Lacedaemonians affect brevity, and those of Crete to aim more at the fecundity of conception than the fertility of speech; and these are the best. Zeno used to say that he had two sorts of disciples, one that he called cy—ous, curious to learn things, and these were his favourites; the other, aoy—ous, that cared for nothing but words. Not that fine speaking is not a very good and commendable quality; but not so excellent and so necessary as some would make it; and I am scandalised that our whole life should be spent in nothing else. I would first understand my own language, and that of my neighbours, with whom most of my business and conversation lies.

No doubt but Greek and Latin are very great ornaments, and of very great use, but we buy them too dear. I will here discover one way, which has been experimented in my own person, by which they are to be had better cheap, and such may make use of it as will. My late father having made the most precise inquiry that any man could possibly make amongst men of the greatest learning and judgment, of an exact method of education, was by them cautioned of this inconvenience then in use, and made to believe, that the tedious time we applied to the learning of the tongues of them who had them for nothing, was the sole cause we could not arrive to the grandeur of soul and perfection of knowledge, of the ancient Greeks and Romans. I do not, however, believe that to be the only cause. So it is, that the expedient my father found out for this was,

CHAPTER 26

that in my infancy, and before I began to speak, he committed me to the care of a German, who since died a famous physician in France, totally ignorant of our language, and very fluent and a great critic in Latin. This man, whom he had fetched out of his own country, and whom he entertained with a great salary for this only one end, had me continually with him; he had with him also joined two others, of inferior learning, to attend me, and to relieve him; these spoke to me in no other language but Latin. As to the rest of his household, it was an inviolable rule, that neither himself, nor my mother, nor valet, nor chambermaid, should speak anything in my company, but such Latin words as each one had learned to gabble with me. It is not to be imagined how great an advantage this proved to the whole family; my father and my mother by this means learned Latin enough to understand it perfectly well, and to speak it to such a degree as was sufficient for any necessary use; as also those of the servants did who were most frequently with me. In short, we Latined it at such a rate, that it overflowed to all the neighbouring villages, where there yet remain, that have established themselves by custom, several Latin appellations of artisans and their tools. As for what concerns myself, I was above six years of age before I understood either French or Perigordin, any more than Arabic; and without art, book, grammar, or precept, whipping, or the expense of a tear, I had, by that time, learned to speak as pure Latin as my master himself, for I had no means of mixing it up with any other. If, for example, they were to give me a theme after the college fashion, they gave it to others in French; but to me they were to give it in bad Latin, to turn it into that which was good. And Nicolas Grouchy, who wrote a book De Comitiis Romanorum; Guillaume Guerente, who wrote a comment upon Aristotle: George Buchanan, that great Scottish poet: and Marc Antoine Muret (whom both France and Italy have acknowledged for the best orator of his time), my domestic tutors, have all of them often told me that I had in my infancy that language so very fluent and ready, that they were afraid to enter into discourse with me. And particularly Buchanan, whom I since saw attending the late Mareschal de Brissac, then told me, that he was about to write a treatise of education, the example of which he intended to take from mine; for he was then tutor to that Comte de Brissac who afterward proved so valiant and so brave a gentleman.

As to Greek, of which I have but a mere smattering, my father also designed to have it taught me by a device, but a new one, and by way of sport; tossing our declensions to and fro, after the manner of those who, by certain games of tables, learn geometry and arithmetic. For he, amongst other rules, had been advised to make me relish science and duty by an unforced will, and of my own voluntary motion, and to educate my soul in all liberty and delight, without any severity or constraint; which he was an observer of to such a degree, even of superstition, if I may say so, that some being of opinion that it troubles and disturbs the brains of children suddenly to wake them in the morning, and to snatch them violently—and over-hastily from sleep (wherein they are much more profoundly involved than we), he caused me to be wakened by the sound of some musical instrument, and was never unprovided of a musician for that purpose. By this example you may judge of the rest, this alone being sufficient to recommend both the prudence and the affection of so good a father, who is not to be blamed if he did not reap fruits answerable to so exquisite a culture. Of this, two things were the cause: first, a sterile and improper soil; for, though I was of a strong and healthful constitution, and of a disposition tolerably sweet and tractable, yet I was, withal, so heavy, idle, and indisposed, that they could not rouse me from my sloth, not even to get me out to play. What I saw, I saw clearly enough, and under this heavy complexion nourished a bold imagination and opinions above my age. I had a slow wit that would go no faster than it was led; a tardy understanding, a languishing invention, and above all, incredible defect of memory; so that, it is no wonder, if from all these nothing considerable could be extracted. Secondly, like those who, impatient of a long and steady cure, submit to all sorts of prescriptions and recipes, the good man being extremely timorous of any way failing in a thing he had so wholly set his heart upon, suffered himself at last to be overruled by the common opinions, which always follow their leader as a flight of cranes, and complying with the method of the time, having no more those persons he had brought out of Italy, and who had given him the first model of education, about him, he sent me at six years of age to the College of Guienne, at that time the best and most flourishing in France. And there it was not possible to add anything to the care he had to provide me the most able tutors, with all other circumstances of education, reserving also several particular rules contrary to the college practice; but so it was, that with all these precautions, it was a college still. My Latin immediately grew corrupt, of which also by discontinuance I have since lost all manner of use; so that this new way of education served me to no other end, than only at my first coming to prefer me to the first forms; for at thirteen years old, that I came out of the college, I had run through my whole course (as they call it), and, in truth, without any manner of advantage, that I can honestly brag of, in all this time.

The first taste which I had for books came to me from the pleasure in reading the fables of Ovid's Metamorphoses; for, being about seven or eight years old, I gave up all other diversions to read them, both by reason that this was my own natural language, the easiest book that I was acquainted with, and for the subject, the most accommodated to the capacity of my age: for as for the Lancelot of the Lake, the Amadis of Gaul, the Huon of Bordeaux, and such farragos, by which children are most delighted with, I had never so much as heard their names, no more than I yet know what they contain; so exact was the discipline wherein I was brought up. But this was enough to make me neglect the other lessons that were prescribed me; and here it was infinitely to my advantage, to have to do with an understanding tutor, who very well knew discreetly to connive at this and other truantries of the same nature; for by this means I ran through Virgil's *Aeneid*, and then Terence, and then Plautus, and then some Italian comedies, allured by the sweetness of the subject; whereas had he been so foolish as to have taken me off this diversion, I do really believe, I had brought away nothing from the college but a hatred of books, as almost all our young gentlemen do. But he carried himself very discreetly in that business, seeming to take no notice, and allowing me only such time as I could steal from my other regular studies, which whetted my appetite to devour those books. For the chief things my father expected from their endeavours to whom he had delivered me for education, were affability and good-humour; and, to say the truth, my manners had no other vice but sloth and want of metal. The fear was not that I should do ill, but that I should do nothing; nobody prognosticated that I should be wicked, but only useless; they foresaw idleness, but no malice; and I find it falls out accordingly: The complaints I hear of myself are these: "He is idle, cold in the offices of friendship and relation, and in those of the public, too particular, too disdainful." But the most injurious do not say, "Why has he taken such a thing? Why has he not paid such an one?" but, "Why does he part with nothing? Why does he not give?" And I should take it for a favour that men would expect from me no greater effects of supererogation than these. But they are unjust to exact from me what I do not owe, far more rigorously than they require from others that which they do owe. In condemning me to it, they efface the gratification of the action, and deprive me of the gratitude that would be my due for it; whereas the active well-doing ought to be of so much the greater value from my hands, by how much I have never been passive that way at all. I can the more freely dispose of my fortune the more it is mine, and of myself the more I am my own. Nevertheless, if I were good at setting out my own actions, I could, peradventure, very well repel these reproaches, and could give some to understand, that they are not so much offended, that I do not enough, as that I am able to do a great deal more than I do.

Yet for all this heavy disposition of mine, my mind, when retired into itself, was not altogether without strong movements, solid and clear judgments about those objects it could comprehend, and could also, without any helps, digest them; but, amongst other things, I do

144

really believe, it had been totally impossible to have made it to submit by violence and force. Shall I here acquaint you with one faculty of my youth? I had great assurance of countenance, and flexibility of voice and gesture, in applying myself to any part I undertook to act: for before—

Alter ab undecimo tum me vix ceperat annus,

[I had just entered my twelfth year.

—Virgil, *Bucolicon*, 39.]

I played the chief parts in the Latin tragedies of Buchanan, Guerente, and Muret, that were presented in our College of Guienne with great dignity: now Andreas Goveanus, our principal, as in all other parts of his charge, was, without comparison, the best of that employment in France; and I was looked upon as one of the best actors. It is an exercise that I do not disapprove in young people of condition; and I have since seen our princes, after the example of some of the ancients, in person handsomely and commendably perform these exercises; it was even allowed to persons of quality to make a profession of it in Greece.

Aristoni tragico actori rem aperit: huic et genus et
fortuna honesta erant: nec ars, quia nihil tale apud
Graecos pudori est, ea deformabat.

[He imparted this matter to Aristo the tragedian; a man of good family and fortune, which neither of them receive any blemish by that profession; nothing of this kind being reputed a disparagement in Greece.

—Livy, xxiv. 24.]

Nay, I have always taxed those with impertinence who condemn these entertainments, and with injustice those who refuse to admit such comedians as are worth seeing into our good towns, and grudge the people that public diversion. Well-governed corporations take care to assemble their citizens, not only to the solemn duties of devotion, but also to sports and spectacles. They find society and friendship augmented by it; and besides, can there possibly be allowed a more orderly and regular diversion than what is performed m the sight of everyone, and very often in the presence of the supreme magistrate himself? And I, for my part, should think it reasonable, that the prince should sometimes gratify his people at his own expense, out of paternal goodness and affection; and that in populous cities there should be theatres erected for such entertainments, if but to divert them from worse and private actions.

To return to my subject, there is nothing like alluring the appetite and affections; otherwise you make nothing but so many asses laden with books; by dint of the lash, you give them their pocketful of learning to keep; whereas, to do well you should not only lodge it with them, but make them espouse it.

28

ON FRIENDSHIP

Having considered the proceedings of a painter on my staff, I had a mind to imitate his way. He chooses the fairest place and middle of any wall, or panel, wherein to draw a picture, which he finishes with his utmost care and art, and the vacuity about it he fills with grotesques, which are odd fantastic figures without any grace but what they derive from their variety, and the extravagance of their shapes. And in truth, what are these things I scribble, other than grotesques and monstrous bodies, made of various parts, without any certain figure, or any other than accidental order, coherence, or proportion?

Desinit in piscem mulier formosa superne.

[A fair woman in her upper form terminates in a fish.
—Horace, *De Arte Poetica*, v. 4.]

In this second part I go hand in hand with my painter; but fall very short of him in the first and the better, my power of handling not being such, that I dare to offer at a rich piece, finely polished, and set off according to art. I have therefore thought fit to borrow one of Estienne de la Boetie, and such a one as shall honour and adorn all the rest of my work – namely, a discourse that he called "Voluntary Servitude" but, since, those who did not know him have properly enough called it "Le contr Un." He wrote in his youth, ["Not being as yet eighteen years old." Edition of 1588.] by way of essay, in honour of liberty against tyrants; and it has since run through the hands of men of great learning and judgment, not without singular and merited commendation; for it is finely written, and as full as anything can possibly be. And yet one may confidently say it is far short of what he was able to do; and if in that more mature age, wherein I had the happiness to know him, he had taken a design like this of mine, to commit his thoughts to writing, we should have seen a great many rare things, and such as would have gone very near to have rivalled the best writings of antiquity: for in natural parts especially, I know no man comparable to him. But he has left nothing behind him, save this treatise only (and that too by chance, for I believe he never saw it after it first went out of his hands), and some observations upon that edict of January [1562, which granted to the Huguenots the public exercise of their religion.] made famous by our civil-wars, which also shall elsewhere, peradventure, find a place. These were all I could recover of his remains, I to whom with so affectionate a remembrance, upon his death-bed, he by his last will bequeathed his library and papers, the little book of his works only excepted, which I committed to the press. And this particular obligation I have to this treatise of his, that it was the occasion of my first coming acquainted with him; for it was showed to me long before I had the good fortune to know him; and the first knowledge of his name, proving the first cause and foundation of a friendship, which we afterwards improved and maintained, so long as God was pleased to continue us together, so perfect, inviolate, and entire, that certainly the like is hardly to be found in story, and amongst the men of this age, there is no sign nor trace of any such thing in use; so much concurrence is required to the building of such a one, that it is much, if fortune bring it but once to pass in three ages.

There is nothing to which nature seems so much to have inclined us, as to society; and Aristotle, says that the good legislators had more respect to friendship than to justice. Now the most supreme point of its perfection is this: for, generally, all those that pleasure, profit, public or private interest create and nourish, are so

much the less beautiful and generous, and so much the less friendships, by how much they mix another cause, and design, and fruit
in friendship, than itself. Neither do the four ancient kinds, natural,
social, hospitable, venereal, either separately or jointly, make up a
true and perfect friendship.

That of children to parents is rather respect: friendship is
nourished by communication, which cannot by reason of the great
disparity, be between these, but would rather perhaps offend the
duties of nature; for neither are all the secret thoughts of fathers
fit to be communicated to children, lest it beget an indecent familiarity between them; nor can the advices and reproofs, which is
one of the principal offices of friendship, be properly performed
by the son to the father. There are some countries where 'twas
the custom for children to kill their fathers; and others, where the
fathers killed their children, to avoid their being an impediment
one to another in life; and naturally the expectations of the one
depend upon the ruin of the other. There have been great philosophers who have made nothing of this tie of nature, as Aristippus
for one, who being pressed home about the affection he owed to
his children, as being come out of him, presently fell to spit, saying, that this also came out of him, and that we also breed worms
and lice; and that other, that Plutarch endeavoured to reconcile to
his brother: "I make never the more account of him," said he, "for
coming out of the same hole." This name of brother does indeed
carry with it a fine and delectable sound, and for that reason, he
and I called one another brothers but the complication of interests, the division of estates, and that the wealth of the one should
be the property of the other, strangely relax and weaken the fraternal tie: brothers pursuing their fortune and advancement by
the same path, it is hardly possible but they must of necessity often
jostle and hinder one another. Besides, why is it necessary that the
correspondence of manners, parts, and inclinations, which begets
the true and perfect friendships, should always meet in these relations? The father and the son may be of quite contrary humours,

and so of brothers: he is my son, he is my brother; but he is passionate, ill-natured, or a fool. And moreover, by how much these are friendships that the law and natural obligation impose upon us, so much less is there of our own choice and voluntary freedom; whereas that voluntary liberty of ours has no production more promptly and; properly its own than affection and friendship. Not that I have not in my own person experimented all that can possibly be expected of that kind, having had the best and most indulgent father, even to his extreme old age, that ever was, and who was himself descended from a family for many generations famous and exemplary for brotherly concord:

> *Et ipse*
> *Notus in fratres animi paterni.*

[And I myself, known for paternal love toward my brothers.
—Horace, *Ode*, ii. 2, 6.]

We are not here to bring the love we bear to women, though it be an act of our own choice, into comparison, nor rank it with the others. The fire of this, I confess,

> *Neque enim est dea nescia nostri*
> *Qux dulcem curis miscet amaritiem,*

[Nor is the goddess unknown to me who mixes a sweet bitterness with my love.
—*Catullus*, lxviii. 17.]

is more active, more eager, and more sharp: but withal, it is more precipitant, fickle, moving, and inconstant; a fever subject to intermissions and paroxysms, that has seized but on one part of us. Whereas in friendship, it is a general and universal fire, but temperate and equal, a constant established heat, all gentle and smooth, without poignancy or roughness. Moreover, in love, it is no other than frantic desire for that which flies from us:

> *Come segue la lepre il cacciatore*
> *Al freddo, al caldo, alla montagna, al lito;*
> *Ne piu l'estima poi the presa vede;*
> *E sol dietro a chi fugge affretta il piede*

[As the hunter pursues the hare, in cold and heat, to the mountain, to the shore, nor cares for it farther when he sees it taken, and only delights in chasing that which flees from him.

—Aristo, x. 7.]

so soon as it enters unto the terms of friendship, that is to say, into a concurrence of desires, it vanishes and is gone, fruition destroys it, as having only a fleshly end, and such a one as is subject to satiety. Friendship, on the contrary, is enjoyed proportionably as it is desired; and only grows up, is nourished and improved by enjoyment, as being of itself spiritual, and the soul growing still more refined by practice. Under this perfect friendship, the other fleeting affections have in my younger years found some place in me, to say nothing of him, who himself so confesses but too much in his verses; so that I had both these passions, but always so, that I could myself well enough distinguish them, and never in any degree of comparison with one another; the first maintaining its flight in so lofty and so brave a place, as with disdain to look down, and see the other flying at a far humbler pitch below.

As concerning marriage, besides that it is a covenant, the entrance into which only is free, but the continuance in it forced and compulsory, having another dependence than that of our own free will, and a bargain commonly contracted to other ends, there almost always happens a thousand intricacies in it to unravel, enough to break the thread and to divert the current of a lively affection: whereas friendship has no manner of business or traffic with aught but itself. Moreover, to say truth, the ordinary talent of women is not such as is sufficient to maintain the conference and communication required to the support of this sacred tie; nor do they appear to be endued with constancy of mind, to sustain the pinch of so hard and durable a knot. And doubtless, if without this, there could be such a free and voluntary familiarity contracted, where not only the souls might have this entire fruition, but the bodies also might share in the alliance, and a man be engaged throughout, the friendship would certainly be more full and perfect; but it is without example that this sex has ever yet arrived at such perfection; and, by the common consent of the ancient schools, it is wholly rejected from it.

That other Grecian licence [homosexuality] is justly abhorred by our manners, which also, from having, according to their practice, a so necessary disparity of age and difference of offices between the lovers, answered no more to the perfect union and harmony that we here require than the other:

> *Quis est enim iste amor amicitiae? cur neque deformem*
> *adolescentem quisquam amat, neque formosum senem?*

[For what is that friendly love? why does no one love a deformed youth or a comely old man?
—Cicero, *Tusculum Disputations*, iv. 33.]

Neither will that very picture that the Academy presents of it, as I conceive, contradict me, when I say, that this first fury inspired by the son of Venus into the heart of the lover, upon sight of the flower and prime of a springing and blossoming youth, to which they allow all the insolent and passionate efforts that an immoderate ardour can produce, was simply founded upon external beauty, the false image of corporal generation; for it could not ground this love upon the soul, the sight of which as yet lay concealed, was but now springing, and not of maturity to blossom; that this fury, if it seized upon a low spirit, the means by which it preferred its suit were rich presents, favour in advancement to dignities, and such trumpery, which they by no means approve; if on a more generous soul, the pursuit was suitably generous, by philosophical instructions, precepts to revere religion, to obey the laws, to die for the good of one's country; by examples of valour, prudence, and justice, the lover studying to render himself acceptable by the grace and beauty of the soul, that of his body being long since faded and decayed, hoping by this mental society to establish a more firm and lasting contract. When this courtship came to effect in due season (for that which they do not require in the lover, namely, leisure and discretion in his pursuit, they strictly require in the person loved, forasmuch as he is to judge of an internal beauty, of difficult knowledge and abstruse discovery), then there sprung in the person loved the desire of a spiritual conception; by the mediation of a spiritual beauty. This was the principal; the corporeal, an accidental and secondary matter; quite the contrary as to the lover. For this reason they prefer the person beloved, maintaining that the gods in like manner preferred him too, and very much blame the poet Aeschylus for having, in the loves of Achilles and Patroclus, given the lover's part to Achilles, who was in the first and beardless flower of his adolescence, and the handsomest of all the Greeks. After this general community, the sovereign, and most worthy part presiding and governing, and performing its proper offices, they say, that thence great utility was derived, both by private and public concerns; that it constituted the force and power of the countries where it prevailed, and the chiefest security of liberty and justice. Of which the healthy loves of Harmodius and Aristogiton are instances. And therefore it is that they called it sacred and divine, and conceive that nothing but the violence of tyrants and the baseness of the common people are inimical to it. Finally, all that can be said in favour of the Academy is, that it was a love which ended in friendship, which well enough agrees with the Stoical definition of love:

> *Amorem conatum esse amicitiae faciendae*
> *ex pulchritudinis specie.*

[Love is a desire of contracting friendship arising from the beauty of the object.
—Cicero, *Tusculum Disputations*, vi. 34.]

I return to my own more just and true description:

> *Omnino amicitiae, corroboratis jam confirmatisque,*
> *et ingeniis, et aetatibus, judicandae sunt.*

[Those are only to be reputed friendships that are fortified and confirmed by judgement and the length of time.
—Cicero, *De Amicitia*, c. 20.]

For the rest, what we commonly call friends and friendships, are nothing but acquaintance and familiarities, either occasionally contracted, or upon some design, by means of which there happens some little intercourse between our souls. But in the friendship I speak of, they mix and work themselves into one piece, with so universal a mixture, that there is no more sign of the seam by which they were first conjoined. If a man should importune me to give a reason why I loved him, I find it could no otherwise be expressed, than by making answer: because it was he, because it was I. There is, beyond all that I am able to say, I know not what inexplicable and fated power that brought on this union. We sought one another long before we met, and by the characters we heard of one another, which wrought upon our affections more than, in reason, mere reports should do; I think it was by some secret appointment of heaven. We embraced in our names; and at our first meeting, which

154

was accidentally at a great city entertainment, we found ourselves so mutually taken with one another, so acquainted, and so endeared between ourselves, that from thenceforward nothing was so near to us as one another. He wrote an excellent Latin satire, since printed, wherein he excuses the precipitation of our intelligence, so suddenly come to perfection, saying, that destined to have so short a continuance, as begun so late (for we were both full-grown men, and he some years the older), there was no time to lose, nor were we tied to conform to the example of those slow and regular friendships, that require so many precautions of long preliminary conversation: This has no other idea than that of itself, and can only refer to itself: this is no one special consideration, nor two, nor three, nor four, nor a thousand; it is I know not what quintessence of all this mixture, which, seizing my whole will, carried it to plunge and lose itself in his, and that having seized his whole will, brought it back with equal concurrence and appetite to plunge and lose itself in mine. I may truly say lose, reserving nothing to ourselves that was either his or mine. [All this relates to Estienne de la Boétie.]

When Laelius, [Cicero, *De Amicitia*, c. II.] in the presence of the Roman consuls, who after thay had sentenced Tiberius Gracchus, prosecuted all those who had had any familiarity with him also; came to ask Caius Blosius, who was his chiefest friend, how much he would have done for him, and that he made answer: "All things." – "How! All things!" said Laelius. "And what if he had commanded you to fire our temples?" –"He would never have commanded me that," replied Blosius. – "But what if he had?" said Laelius. – "I would have obeyed him," said the other. If he was so perfect a friend to Gracchus as the histories report him to have been, there was yet no necessity of offending the consuls by such a bold confession, though he might still have retained the assurance he had of Gracchus' disposition. However, those who accuse this answer as seditious, do not well understand the mystery; nor presuppose, as it was true, that he had Gracchus' will in his sleeve, both by the power of a friend, and the perfect knowledge he had of the man: they were more friends than citizens, more friends to one another than either enemies or friends to their country, or than friends to ambition and innovation; having absolutely given up themselves to one another, either held absolutely the reins of the other's inclination; and suppose all this guided by virtue, and all this by the conduct of reason, which also without these it had not been possible to do, Blosius' answer was such as it ought to be. If any of their actions flew out of the handle, they were neither (according to my measure of friendship) friends to one another, nor to themselves. As to the rest, this answer carries no worse sound, than mine would do to one that should ask me: "If your will should command you to kill your daughter, would you do it?" and that I should make answer, that I would; for this expresses no consent to such an act, forasmuch as I do not in the least suspect my own will, and as little that of such a friend. It is not in the power of all the eloquence in the world, to dispossess me of the certainty I have of the intentions and resolutions of my friend; nay, no one action of his, what face soever it might bear, could be presented to me, of which I could not presently, and at first sight, find out the moving cause. Our souls had drawn so unanimously together, they had considered each other with so ardent an affection, and with the like affection laid open the very bottom of our hearts to one another's view, that I not only knew his as well as my own; but should certainly in any concern of mine have trusted my interest much more willingly with him, than with myself.

Let no one, therefore, rank other common friendships with such a one as this. I have had as much experience of these as another, and of the most perfect of their kind: but I do not advise that any should confound the rules of the one and the other, for they would find themselves much deceived. In those other ordinary friendships, you are to walk with bridle in your hand, with prudence and circumspection, for in them the knot is not so sure that a man may not half suspect it will slip. "Love him," said Chilo, [Aulus Gellius, i. 3.] "so as if you were one day to hate him; and hate him so as you were one day to love him." This precept, though abominable in the sovereign and perfect friendship I speak of, is nevertheless very sound as to the practice of the ordinary and customary ones, and to which the saying that Aristotle had so frequent in his mouth, "O my friends, there is no friend," may very fitly be applied. In this noble commerce, good offices, presents, and benefits, by which other friendships are supported and maintained, do not deserve so much as to be mentioned; and the reason is the concurrence of our wills; for, as the kindness I have for myself receives no increase, for anything I relieve myself withal in time of need (whatever the Stoics say), and as I do not find myself obliged to myself for any service I do myself: so the union of such friends, being truly perfect, deprives them of all idea of such duties, and makes them loathe and banish from their conversation these words of division and distinction, benefits, obligation, acknowledgment, entreaty, thanks, and the like. All things, wills, thoughts, opinions, goods, wives, children, honours, and lives, being in effect common between them, and that absolute concurrence of affections being no other than one soul in two bodies (according to that very proper definition of Aristotle), they can neither lend nor give anything to one another. This is the reason why the lawgivers, to honour marriage with some resemblance of this divine alliance, interdict all gifts between man and wife; inferring by that, that all should belong to each of them, and that they have nothing to divide or to give to each other.

If, in the friendship of which I speak, one could give to the other, the receiver of the benefit would be the man that obliged his friend; for each of them contending and above all things studying how to be useful to the other, he that administers the occasion is the liberal man, in giving his friend the satisfaction of doing that towards him which above all things he most desires. When the philosopher Diogenes wanted money, he used to say, that he redemanded it of his friends, not that he demanded it. And to let you see the practical working of this, I will here produce an ancient and singular example. Eudamidas, a Corinthian, had two friends, Charixenus a Sicyonian and Areteus a Corinthian; this man coming to die, being poor, and his two friends rich, he made his will after this manner. "I bequeath to Areteus the maintenance of my mother, to support and provide for her in her old age; and to Charixenus I bequeath the care of marrying my daughter, and to give her as good a portion as he is able; and in case one of these chance to die, I hereby substitute the survivor in his place." They who first saw this will made themselves very merry at the contents: but the legatees, being made acquainted with it, accepted it with very great content; and one of them, Charixenus, dying within five days after, and by that means the charge of both duties devolving solely on him, Areteus nurtured the old woman with very great care and tenderness, and of five talents he had in estate, he gave two and a half in marriage with an only daughter he had of his own, and two and a half in marriage with the daughter of Eudamidas, and on one and the same day solemnised both their nuptials.

This example is very full, if one thing were not to be objected, namely the multitude of friends for the perfect friendship I speak of is indivisible; each one gives himself so entirely to his friend, that he has nothing left to distribute to others: on the contrary, is sorry that he is not double, treble, or quadruple, and that he has not many souls and many wills, to confer them all upon this one object. Common friendships will admit of division; one may love the beauty of this person, the good-humour of that, the liberality of a third, the paternal affection of a fourth, the fraternal love of a fifth, and so of the rest: but this friendship that possesses the whole soul, and there rules and sways with an absolute sovereignty, cannot possibly admit of a rival. If two at the same time should call to you for succour, to which of them would you run? Should they require of you contrary offices, how could you serve them both? Should one commit a thing to your silence that it were of importance to the other to know, how would you disengage yourself? A unique and particular friendship dissolves all other obligations whatsoever: the secret I have sworn not to reveal to any other, I may without perjury communicate to him who is not another, but myself. It is miracle enough certainly, for a man to double himself, and those that talk of tripling, talk they know not of what. Nothing is extreme, that has its like; and he who shall suppose, that of two, I love one as much as the other, that they mutually love one another too, and love me as much as I love them, multiplies into a confraternity the most single of units, and whereof, moreover, one alone is the hardest thing in the world to find. The rest of this story suits very well with what I was saying; for Eudamidas, as a bounty and favour, bequeaths to his friends a legacy of employing themselves in his necessity; he leaves them heirs to this liberality of his, which consists in giving them the opportunity of conferring a benefit upon him; and doubtless, the force of friendship is more eminently apparent in this act of his, than in that of Areteus. In short, these are effects not to be imagined nor comprehended by such as have not experience of them, and which make me infinitely honour and admire the answer of that young soldier to Cyrus, by whom being asked how much he would take for a horse, with which he had won the prize of a race, and whether he would exchange him for a kingdom? – "No, truly, sir," said he, "but I would give him with all my heart, to get thereby a true friend, could I find out any man worthy of that alliance." [Xenophon, *Cyropadia*, viii. 3.] He did not say ill in saying, "could I find": for though one may almost everywhere meet with men sufficiently qualified for a superficial acquaintance, yet in this, where a man is to deal from the very bottom of his heart, without any manner of reservation, it will be requisite that all the wards and springs be truly wrought and perfectly sure.

In confederations that hold but by one end, we are only to provide against the imperfections that particularly concern that end. It can be of no importance to me of what religion my physician or my lawyer is; this consideration has nothing in common with the offices of friendship which they owe me; and I am of the same indifference in the domestic acquaintance my servants must necessarily contract with me. I never inquire, when I am to take a footman, if he be chaste, but if he be diligent; and am not solicitous if my muleteer be given to gaming, as if he be strong and able; or if my cook be a swearer, if he be a good cook. I do not take upon me to direct what other men should do in the government of their families, there are plenty that meddle enough with that, but only give an account of my method in my own:

Mihi sic usus est: tibi, ut opus est facto, face.

[This has been my way; as for you, do as you find needful.
—Terence, *Heautontimorumenos*, i. I., 28.]

For table-talk, I prefer the pleasant and witty before the learned and the grave; in bed, beauty before goodness; in common discourse the ablest speaker, whether or not there be sincerity in the case. And, as he that was found astride upon a hobby-horse, playing with his children, entreated the person who had surprised him in that posture to say nothing of it till himself came to be a father, [Plutarch, *Life of Agesilaus*, c. 9.] supposing that the fondness that would then possess his own soul, would render him a fairer judge of such an action; so I, also, could wish to speak to such as have had experience of what I say: though, knowing how remote a thing such a friendship is from the common practice, and how rarely it is to be found, I despair of meeting with any such judge. For even these discourses left us by antiquity upon this subject, seem to me flat and poor, in comparison of the sense I have of it, and in this particular, the effects surpass even the precepts of philosophy.

Nil ego contulerim jucundo sanus amico.

[While I have sense left to me, there will never be anything more acceptable to me than an agreeable friend.
                                                    —Horace, *Satire*, i. 5, 44.]

Chapter 28

The ancient Menander declared him to be happy that had had the good fortune to meet with but the shadow of a friend: and doubtless he had good reason to say so, especially if he spoke by experience: for in good earnest, if I compare all the rest of my life, though, thanks be to God, I have passed my time pleasantly enough, and at my ease, and the loss of such a friend excepted, free from any grievous affliction, and in great tranquillity of mind, having been contented with my natural and original commodities, without being solicitous after others; if I should compare it all, I say, with the four years I had the happiness to enjoy the sweet society of this excellent man, it is nothing but smoke, an obscure and tedious night. From the day that I lost him:

> *Quem semper acerbum,*
> *Semper honoratum (sic, di, voluistis) habebo,*

[A day for me ever sad, for ever sacred, so have you willed ye gods.

—*Aeneid,* v. 49.]

I have only led a languishing life; and the very pleasures that present themselves to me, instead of administering anything of con-solation, double my affliction for his loss. We were halves through-out, and to that degree, that methinks, by outliving him, I defraud him of his part.

> *Nec fas esse ulla me voluptate hic frui*
> *Decrevi, tantisper dum ille abest meus particeps.*

[I have determined that it will never be right for me to enjoy any pleasure, so long as he, with whom I shared all pleasures is away.

—Terence, *Heautontimorumenos,* i. I. 97.]

161

I was so grown and accustomed to be always his double in all places and in all things, that methinks I am no more than half of myself:

> *Illam meae si partem anima tulit*
> *Maturior vis, quid moror altera?*
> *Nec carus aeque, nec superstes*
> *Integer? Ille dies utramque*
> *Duxit ruinam.*

[If that half of my soul were snatch away from me by an untimely stroke, why should the other stay? That which remains will not be equally dear, will not be whole: the same day will involve the destruction of both.]

or:

[If a superior force has taken that part of my soul, why do I, the remaining one, linger behind? What is left is not so dear, nor an entire thing: this day has wrought the destruction of both.

—Horace, *Odes*, ii. 17, 5.]

There is no action or imagination of mine wherein I do not miss him; as I know that he would have missed me: for as he surpassed me by infinite degrees in virtue and all other accomplishments, so he also did in the duties of friendship:

> *Qui sdesiderio sit pudor, aut modus*
> *Tam cari capitis?*

[What shame can there be, or measure, in lamenting so dear a friend?

—Horace, *Odes*, i. 24, I.]

O misero frater adempte mihi!
Omnia tecum una perierunt gaudia nostra,
Quae tuus in vita dulcis alebat amor.
Tu mea, tu moriens fregisti commoda, frater;
Tecum una tota est nostra sepulta anima
Cujus ego interitu tota de menthe fugavi
Haec studia, atque omnes delicias animi.
Alloquar? audiero nunquam tua verba loquentem?
Nunquam ego te, vita frater amabilior
Aspiciam posthac; at certe semper amabo;

[O brother, taken from me miserable! with thee, all our joys have vanished, those joys which, in thy life, thy dear love nourished. Dying, thou, my brother, hast destroyed all my happiness. My whole soul is buried with thee. Through whose death I have banished from my mind these studies, and all the delights of the mind. Shall I address thee? I shall never hear thy voice. Never shall I behold thee hereafter. O brother, dearer to me than life. Nought remains, but assuredly I shall ever love thee.

—Catullus, lxviii. 20; lxv.]

But let us hear a boy of sixteen [La Boétie] speak [Montaigne wanted to quote from de la Boétie's work here, but did not feel able to given the reasons that follow]:

Because I have found that that work has been since brought out, and with a mischievous design, by those who aim at disturbing and changing the condition of our government, without troubling themselves to think whether they are likely to improve it: and because they have mixed up his work with some of their own performance, I have refrained from inserting it here. But that the memory of the author may not be injured, nor suffer with such as could not come near-hand to be acquainted with his principles, I here give them to understand, that it was written by him in his boyhood, and that by way of exercise only, as a common theme that has been hackneyed by a thousand writers. I make no question but that he himself believed what he wrote, being so conscientious that he would not so much as lie in jest: and I moreover know, that could it have been in his own choice, he had rather have been born at Venice, than at Sarlac; and with reason. But he had another maxim sovereignty imprinted in his soul, very religiously to obey and submit to the laws under which he was born. There never was a better citizen, more affectionate to his country; nor a greater enemy to all the commotions and innovations of his time: so that he would much rather have employed his talent to the extinguishing of those civil flames, than have added any fuel to them; he had a mind fashioned to the model of better ages.

ON MODERATION

As if we had an infectious touch, we, by our manner of handling, corrupt things that in themselves are laudable and good: we may grasp virtue so that it becomes vicious, if we embrace it too stringently and with too violent a desire. Those who say, there is never any excess in virtue, forasmuch as it is not virtue when it once becomes excess, only play upon words:

> *Insani sapiens nomen ferat, aequus iniqui,*
> *Ultra quam satis est, virtutem si petat ipsam.*

[Let the wise man bear the name of a madman, the just one of an unjust, if he seek wisdom more than is sufficient.
—Horace, *Epistles*, i. 6, 15.]

[The wise man is no longer wise, the just man no longer just, if he seek to carry his love for wisdom or virtue beyond that which is necessary.]

This is a subtle consideration of philosophy. A man may both be too much in love with virtue, and be excessive in a just action. Holy Writ agrees with this, Be not wiser than you should, but be soberly wise. [St. Paul, Epistle to the Romans, xii. 3.] I have known a great man,

[It is likely that Montaigne meant Henry III., king of France. The Cardinal d'Ossat, writing to Louise, the queen-dowager, told her, in his frank manner, that he had lived as much or more like a monk than a monarch (Letter XXIII.) And Pope Sextus V., speaking of that prince one day to the Cardinal de Joyeuse, protector of the affairs of France, said to him pleasantly, 'There is nothing that your king hath not done, and does not do so still, to be a monk, nor anything that I have not done, not to be a monk.'

—Coste.]

prejudice the opinion men had of his devotion, by pretending to be devout beyond all examples of others of his condition. I love temperate and moderate natures. An immoderate zeal, even to that which is good, even though it does not offend, astonishes me, and puts me to study what name to give it. Neither the mother of Pausanias,

[Montaigne would here give us to understand, upon the authority of Diodorus Siculus, that Pausanias' mother gave the first hint of the punishment that was to be inflicted on her son. 'Pausanias,' says this historian, 'perceiving that the ephori, and some other Lacedoemonians, aimed at apprehending him, got the start of them, and went and took sanctuary in Minerva's temple: and the Lacedaemonians, being doubtful whether they ought to take him from thence in violation of the franchise there, it is said that his own mother came herself to the temple but spoke nothing nor did anything more than lay a piece of brick, which she brought with her, on the threshold of the temple, which, when she had done, she returned home. The Lacedaemonians, taking the hint from the mother, caused the gate of the temple to be walled up, and by this means starved Pausanias, so that he died with hunger, &c. (lib. xi. cap. 10., of Amyot's translation). The name of Pausanias' mother was

CHAPTER 30

Alcithea, as we are informed by Thucydides' scholiast, who only says that it was reported, that when they set about walling up the gates of the chapel in which Pausanias had taken refuge, his mother Alcithea laid the first stone.

—Coste.]

who was the first instructor of her son's process, and threw the first stone towards his death, nor Posthumius the dictator, who put his son to death, whom the ardour of youth had successfully pushed upon the enemy a little more advanced than the rest of his squadron, do appear to me so much just as strange; and I should neither advise nor like to follow so savage a virtue, and that costs so dear.

[Opinions differ as to the truth of this fact. Livy thinks he has good authority for rejecting it because it does not appear in history that Posthumious was branded with it, as Titus Manlius was, about 100 years after his time; for Manlius, having put his son to death for the like cause, obtained the odious name of Imperiosus, and since that time Manliana imperia has been used as a term to signify orders that are too severe; Manliana Imperia, says Livy, were not only horrible for the time present, but of a bad example to posterity. And this historian makes no doubt but such commands would have been actually styled Posthumiana Imperia, if Posthumius had been the first who set so barbarous an example (Livy, lib. iv. cap. 29, and lib. viii. cap. 7). But, however, Montaigne has Valer. Maximus on his side, who says expressly, that Posthumius caused his son to be put to death, and Diodorus of Sicily (lib. xii. cap. 19).

—Coste.]

The archer that shoots over, misses as much as he that falls short, and it is equally troublesome to my sight, to look up at a great light, and to look down into a dark abyss. Callicles in Plato says,

167

that the extremity of philosophy is hurtful, and advises not to dive into it beyond the limits of profit; that, taken moderately, it is pleasant and useful; but that in the end it renders a man brutish and vicious, a condemner of religion and the common laws, an enemy to civil conversation, and all human pleasures, incapable of all public administration, unfit either to assist others or to relieve himself, and a fit object for all sorts of injuries and affronts. He says true; for in its excess, it enslaves our natural freedom, and by an impertinent subtlety, leads us out of the fair and beaten way that nature has traced for us.

The love we bear to our wives is very lawful, and yet theology thinks fit to curb and restrain it. As I remember, I have read in one place of St. Thomas Aquinas, [Secunda Secundx, *Summa Theologicae* 154, art. 9.] where he condemns marriages within any of the forbidden degrees, for this reason, amongst others, that there is some danger, lest the friendship a man bears to such a woman, should be immoderate; for if the conjugal affection be full and perfect between them, as it ought to be, and that it be over and above surcharged with that of kindred too, there is no doubt, but such an addition will carry the husband beyond the bounds of reason.

Those sciences that regulate the manners of men, divinity and philosophy, will have their say in everything; there is no action so private and secret that can escape their inspection and jurisdiction. They are best taught who are best able to control and curb their own liberty; women expose their nudities as much as you will upon the account of pleasure, though in the necessities of physic they are altogether as shy. I will, therefore, in their behalf:

[Coste translates this: "on the part of philosophy and theology,"
observing that but few wives would think themselves obliged to
Montaigne for any such lesson to their husbands.]

CHAPTER 30

teach the husbands, that is, such as are too vehement in the exercise of the matrimonial duty – if such there still be – this lesson, that the very pleasures they enjoy in the society of their wives are reproachable if immoderate, and that a licentious and riotous abuse of them is a fault as reprovable here as in illicit connections. Those immodest and debauched tricks and postures, that the first ardour suggests to us in this affair, are not only indecently but detrimentally practised upon our wives. Let them at least learn impudence from another hand; they are ever ready enough for our business, and I for my part always went the plain way to work.

Marriage is a solemn and religious tie, and therefore the pleasure we extract from it should be a sober and serious delight, and mixed with a certain kind of gravity; it should be a sort of discreet and conscientious pleasure. And seeing that the chief end of it is generation, some make a question, whether when men are out of hopes as when they are superannuated or already with child, it be lawful to embrace our wives. It is homicide, according to Plato. [Laws, 8.] Certain nations (the Mohammedan, amongst others) abominate all conjunction with women with child, others also, with those who are in their courses. Zenobia would never admit her husband for more than one encounter, after which she left him to his own swing for the whole time of her conception, and not till after that would again receive him: [Trebellius Pollio, Thirty Tyrants., c. 30.] a brave and generous example of conjugal continence. It was doubtless from some lascivious poet, [The lascivious poet is Homer; see his *Iliad*, xiv. 294.] and one that himself was in great distress for a little of this sport, that Plato borrowed this story; that Jupiter was one day so hot upon his wife, that not having so much patience as till she could get to the couch, he threw her upon the floor, where the vehemence of pleasure made him forget the great and important resolutions he had but newly taken with the rest of the gods in his celestial council, and to brag that he had had as good a bout, as when he got her maidenhead, unknown to their parents.

The kings of Persia were wont to invite their wives to the beginning of their festivals; but when the wine began to work in good earnest, and that they were to give the reins to pleasure, they sent them back to their private apartments, that they might not participate in their immoderate lust, sending for other women in their stead, with whom they were not obliged to so great a decorum of respect. [Plutarch, Precepts of Marriage, c. 14.] All pleasures and all sorts of gratifications are not properly and fitly conferred upon all sorts of persons. Epaminondas had committed to prison a young man for certain debauches; for whom Pelopidas mediated, that at his request he might be set at liberty, which Epaminondas denied to him, but granted it at the first word to a wench of his, that made the same intercession; saying, that it was a gratification fit for such a one as she, but not for a captain. Sophocles being joint praetor with Pericles, seeing accidentally a fine boy pass by: "O what a charming boy is that!" said he. "That might be very well," answered Pericles, "for any other than a praetor, who ought not only to have his hands, but his eyes, too, chaste." [Cicero, *De Officiis*, i. 40.] Aelius Verus, the emperor, answered his wife, who reproached him with his love to other women, that he did it upon a conscientious account, forasmuch as marriage was a name of honour and dignity, not of wanton and lascivious desire; and our ecclesiastical history preserves the memory of that woman in great veneration, who parted from her husband because she would not comply with his indecent and inordinate desires. In fine, there is no pleasure so just and lawful, where intemperance and excess are not to be condemned.

But, to speak the truth, is not man a most miserable creature the while? It is scarce, by his natural condition, in his power to taste one pleasure pure and entire; and yet must he be contriving doctrines and precepts to curtail that little he has; he is not yet wretched enough, unless by art and study he augment his own misery:

Fortunae miseras auximus arte vias.

[We artificially augment the wretchedness of fortune.
—Properitius, liber iii. 7, 44.]

Human wisdom makes as ill use of her talent, when she exercises it in rescinding from the number and sweetness of those pleasures that are naturally our due, as she employs it favourably and well in artificially disguising and tricking out the ills of life, to alleviate the sense of them. Had I ruled the roast, I should have taken another and more natural course, which, to say the truth, is both commodious and holy, and should, peradventure, have been able to have limited it too; notwithstanding that both our spiritual and corporal physicians, as by compact between themselves, can find no other way to cure, nor other remedy for the infirmities of the body and the soul, than by misery and pain. To this end, watchings, fastings, hair-shirts, remote and solitary banishments, perpetual imprisonments, whips and other afflictions, have been introduced amongst men: but so, that they should carry a sting with them, and be real afflictions indeed; and not fall out as it once did to one Gallio, who having been sent an exile into the isle of Lesbos, news was not long after brought to Rome, that he there lived as merry as the day was long; and that what had been enjoined him for a penance, turned to his pleasure and satisfaction: whereupon the Senate thought fit to recall him home to his wife and family, and confine him to his own house, to accommodate their punishment to his feeling and apprehension. For to him whom fasting would make more healthful and more sprightly, and to him to whose palate fish were more acceptable than flesh, the prescription of these would have no curative effect; no more than in the other sort of physic, where drugs have no effect upon him who swallows them with appetite and pleasure: the bitterness of the potion and the abhorrence of the patient are necessary circumstances to the operation. The nature that would eat rhubarb like buttered turnips, would frustrate the use and virtue of it; it must be something to trouble and disturb the stomach, that must purge and cure it; and here the common rule, that things are cured by their contraries, fails; for in this one ill is cured by another.

This belief a little resembles that other so ancient one, of thinking to gratify the gods and nature by massacre and murder: an opinion universally once received in all religions. And still, in these later times wherein our fathers lived, Amurath at the taking of the Isthmus, immolated six hundred young Greeks to his father's soul, in the nature of a propitiatory sacrifice for his sins. And in those new countries discovered in this age of ours, which are pure and virgin yet, in comparison of ours, this practice is in some measure everywhere received: all their idols reek with human blood, not without various examples of horrid cruelty: some they burn alive, and take, half broiled, off the coals to tear out their hearts and entrails; some, even women, they flay alive, and with their bloody skins clothe and disguise others. Neither are we without great examples of constancy and resolution in this affair the poor souls that are to be sacrificed, old men, women, and children, themselves going about some days before to beg alms for the offering of their sacrifice, presenting themselves to the slaughter, singing and dancing with the spectators. The ambassadors of the king of Mexico, setting out to Fernando Cortez the power and greatness of their master, after having told him, that he had thirty vassals, of whom each was able to raise an hundred thousand fighting men, and that he kept his court in the fairest and best fortified city under the sun, added at last, that he was obliged yearly to offer to the gods fifty thousand men. And it is affirmed, that he maintained a continual war, with some potent neighbouring nations, not only to keep the young men in exercise, but principally to have wherewithal to furnish his sacrifices with his prisoners of war. At a certain town in another place, for the welcome of the said Cortez, they sacrificed fifty men at once. I will tell you this one tale more, and I have done; some of these people being beaten by him, sent to acknowledge him, and to treat with him of a peace, whose messengers carried him three sorts of gifts, which they presented in these terms: "Behold, lord, here are five slaves: if thou art a furious god that feedeth upon flesh and blood, eat these, and we will bring thee more; if thou art an affable god, behold here incense and feathers; but if thou art a man, take these fowls and these fruits that we have brought thee."

ON CANNIBALS

When King Pyrrhus invaded Italy, having viewed and considered the order of the army the Romans sent out to meet him; "I know not," said he, "what kind of barbarians" (for so the Greeks called all other nations) "these may be; but the disposition of this army that I see has nothing of barbarism in it." [Plutarch, *Life of Pyrrhus*, c. 8.] As much said the Greeks of that which Flaminius brought into their country; and Philip, beholding from an eminence the order and distribution of the Roman camp formed in his kingdom by Publius Sulpicius Galba, spake to the same effect. By which it appears how cautious men ought to be of taking things upon trust from vulgar opinion, and that we are to judge by the eye of reason, and not from common report.

I long had a man in my house that lived ten or twelve years in the New World, discovered in these latter days, and in that part of it where Villegaignon landed, [At Brazil, in 1557] which he called Antarctic France. This discovery of so vast a country seems to be of very great consideration. I cannot be sure, that hereafter there may not be another, so many wiser men than we having been deceived in this. I am afraid our eyes are bigger than our bellies, and that we have more curiosity than capacity; for we grasp at all, but catch nothing but wind.

Plato brings in Solon, [In Timaeus] telling a story that he had heard from the priests of Sais in Egypt, that of old, and before the Deluge, there was a great island called Atlantis, situate directly at the mouth of the straits of Gibraltar, which contained more countries than both Africa and Asia put together; and that the kings of that country, who not only possessed that Isle, but extended their dominion so far into the continent that they had a country of Africa as far as Egypt, and extending in Europe to Tuscany, attempted to encroach even upon Asia, and to subjugate all the nations that border upon the Mediterranean Sea, as far as the Black Sea; and to that effect overran all Spain, the Gauls, and Italy, so far as to penetrate into Greece, where the Athenians stopped them: but that some time after, both the Athenians, and they and their island, were swallowed by the Flood.

It is very likely that this extreme irruption and inundation of water made wonderful changes and alterations in the habitations of the earth, as it is said that the sea then divided Sicily from Italy –

> *Haec loca, vi quondam et vasta convulsa ruina,*
> *Dissiluisse ferunt, quum protenus utraque tellus*
> *Una foret*

[These lands, they say, formerly with violence and vast desolation convulsed, burst asunder, where erewhile were.
—*Aeneid,* iii. 414.]

Cyprus from Syria, the isle of Negropont from the continent of Beeotia, and elsewhere united lands that were separate before, by filling up the channel between them with sand and mud:

> *Sterilisque diu palus, aptaque remis,*
> *Vicinas urbes alit, et grave sentit aratrum.*

[That which was once a sterile marsh, and bore vessels on its bosom, now feeds neighbouring cities, and admits the plough.
—Horace, *De Arte Poetica,* v. 65.]

176

CHAPTER 31

But there is no great appearance that this isle was this New World so lately discovered: for that almost touched upon Spain, and it were an incredible effect of an inundation, to have tumbled back so prodigious a mass, above twelve hundred leagues: besides that our modern navigators have already almost discovered it to be no island, but terra firma, and continent with the East Indies on the one side, and with the lands under the two poles on the other side; or, if it be separate from them, it is by so narrow a strait and channel, that it none the more deserves the name of an island for that.

It should seem, that in this great body, there are two sorts of motions, the one natural and the other febrific, as there are in ours. When I consider the impression that our river of Dordogne has made in my time on the right bank of its descent, and that in twenty years it has gained so much, and undermined the foundations of so many houses, I perceive it to be an extraordinary agitation: for had it always followed this course, or were hereafter to do it, the aspect of the world would be totally changed. But rivers alter their course, sometimes beating against the one side, and sometimes the other, and sometimes quietly keeping the channel. I do not speak of sudden inundations, the causes of which everybody understands. In Medoc, by the seashore, the Sieur d'Arsac, my brother, sees an estate he had there, buried under the sands which the sea vomits before it: where the tops of some houses are yet to be seen, and where his rents and domains are converted into pitiful barren pasturage. The inhabitants of this place affirm, that of late years the sea has driven so vehemently upon them, that they have lost above four leagues of land. These sands are her harbingers: and we now see great heaps of moving sand, that march half a league before her, and occupy the land.

The other testimony from antiquity, to which some would apply this discovery of the New World, is in Aristotle; at least, if that little book of Unheard of Miracles be his. He there tells us, that certain Carthaginians, having crossed the Atlantic Sea without the Straits of Gibraltar, and sailed a very long time, discovered at last a great and fruitful island, all covered over with wood, and watered with several broad and deep rivers, far remote from all terra firma; and that they, and others after them, allured by the goodness and fertility of the soil, went thither with their wives and children, and began to plant a colony. But the senate of Carthage perceiving their people by little and little to diminish, issued out an express prohibition, that none, upon pain of death, should transport themselves thither; and also drove out these new inhabitants; fearing, it is said, lest in process of time they should so multiply as to supplant themselves and ruin their state. But this relation of Aristotle no more agrees with our new-found lands than the other.

This man that I had was a plain ignorant fellow, and therefore the more likely to tell truth: for your better-bred sort of men are much more curious in their observation, it is true, and discover a great deal more; but then they gloss upon it, and to give the greater weight to what they deliver, and allure your belief, they cannot forbear a little to alter the story; they never represent things to you simply as they are, but rather as they appeared to them, or as they would have them appear to you, and to gain the reputation of men of judgment, and the better to induce your faith, are willing to help out the business with something more than is really true, of their own invention. Now in this case, we should either have a man of irreproachable veracity, or so simple that he has not wherewithal to contrive, and to give a colour of truth to false relations, and who can have no ends in forging an untruth. Such a one was mine; and besides, he has at divers times brought to me several seamen and merchants who at the same time went the same voyage. I shall therefore content myself with his information, without inquiring what the cosmographers say to the business. We should have topographers to trace out to us the particular places where they have been; but for having had this advantage over us, to have seen the Holy Land, they would have the privilege, indeed, to tell us stories of all the other parts of the world beside. I would have everyone write what he knows, and as much as he knows, but no more; and that not in this only but in all other subjects; for such a person may have some particular knowledge and experience of the nature of such a river, or such a fountain, who, as to other things, knows no more than what everybody does, and yet to give a currency to his little pittance of learning, will undertake to write the whole body of physics: a vice from which great inconveniences derive their original.

Now, to return to my subject, I find that there is nothing barbarous and savage in this nation, by anything that I can gather, excepting, that everyone gives the title of barbarism to everything that is not in use in his own country. As, indeed, we have no other level of truth and reason than the example and idea of the opinions and customs of the place wherein we live: there is always the perfect religion, there the perfect government, there the most exact and accomplished usage of all things. They are savages at the same rate that we say fruits are wild, which nature produces of herself and by her own ordinary progress; whereas, in truth, we ought rather to call those wild whose natures we have changed by our artifice and diverted from the common order. In those, the genuine, most useful, and natural virtues and properties are vigorous and sprightly, which we have helped to degenerate in these, by accommodating them to the pleasure of our own corrupted palate. And yet for all this, our taste confesses a flavour and delicacy excellent even to emulation of the best of ours, in several fruits wherein those countries abound without art or culture. Neither is it reasonable that art should gain the pre-eminence of our great and powerful mother nature. We have so surcharged her with the additional ornaments and graces we have added to the beauty and riches of her own works by our inventions, that we have almost smothered her; yet in other places, where she shines in her own purity and proper lustre, she marvellously baffles and disgraces all our vain and frivolous attempts:

Et veniunt hederae sponte sua melius;
Surgit et in solis formosior arbutus antris;
Et volucres nulls dulcius arte canunt.

[The ivy grows best spontaneously, the arbutus best in shady caves; and the wild notes of birds are sweeter than art can teach.

—Propertius, i. 2, 10.]

Our utmost endeavours cannot arrive at so much as to imitate the nest of the least of birds, its contexture, beauty, and convenience: not so much as the web of a poor spider.

All things, says Plato, [Laws, 10.] are produced either by nature, by fortune, or by art; the greatest and most beautiful by the one or the other of the former, the least and the most imperfect by the last.

These nations then seem to me to be so far barbarous, as having received but very little form and fashion from art and human invention, and consequently to be not much remote from their original simplicity. The laws of nature, however, govern them still, not as yet much vitiated with any mixture of ours: but it is in such purity, that I am sometimes troubled we were not sooner acquainted with these people, and that they were not discovered in those better times, when there were men much more able to judge of them than we are. I am sorry that Lycurgus and Plato had no knowledge of them; for to my apprehension, what we now see in those nations, does not only surpass all the pictures with which the poets have adorned the golden age, and all their inventions in feigning a happy state of man, but, moreover, the fancy and even the wish and desire of philosophy itself; so native and so pure a simplicity, as we by experience see to be in them, could never enter into their imagination, nor could they ever believe that human society could have been maintained with so little artifice and human patchwork. I should tell Plato that it is a nation wherein there is no manner of traffic, no knowledge of letters, no science of numbers, no name of magistrate or political superiority; no use of service, riches or poverty, no contracts, no successions, no dividends, no properties, no employments, but those of leisure, no respect of kindred, but common, no clothing, no agriculture, no metal, no use of corn or wine; the very words that signify lying, treachery, dissimulation, avarice, envy, detraction, pardon, never heard of.

[This is the famous passage which Shakespeare, through Florio's version, 1603, or ed. 1613, p. 102, has employed in the "Tempest," ii. 1.]

How much would he find his imaginary Republic short of his perfection?

Viri a diis recentes.

[Men fresh from the gods. – Seneca, *Epistles*, 90.]

Hos natura modos primum dedit.

[These were the manners first taught by nature.
—Virgil, *Georgics*, ii. 20.]

As to the rest, they live in a country very pleasant and temperate, so that, as my witnesses inform me, it is rare to hear of a sick person, and they moreover assure me, that they never saw any of the natives, either paralytic, bleareyed, toothless, or crooked with age. The situation of their country is along the sea-shore, enclosed on the other side towards the land, with great and high mountains, having about a hundred leagues in breadth between. They have great store of fish and flesh, that have no resemblance to those of ours: which they eat without any other cookery, than plain boiling, roasting, and broiling. The first that rode a horse thither, though in several other voyages he had contracted an acquaintance and familiarity with them, put them into so terrible a fright, with his centaur appearance, that they killed him with their arrows before they could come to discover who he was. Their buildings are very long, and of capacity to hold two or three hundred people, made of the barks of tall trees, reared with one end upon the ground, and leaning to and supporting one another at the top, like some of our barns, of which the covering hangs down to the very ground, and serves for the side walls. They have wood so hard, that they cut with it, and make their swords of it, and their grills of it to broil their meat. Their beds are of cotton, hung swinging from the roof, like our seamen's hammocks, every man his own, for the wives lie apart from their husbands. They rise with the sun, and so soon as they are up, eat for all day, for they have no more meals but that; they do not then drink, as Suidas reports of some other people of the East that never drank at their meals; but drink very often all day after, and sometimes to a rousing pitch. Their drink is made of a certain root, and is of the colour of our claret, and they never drink it but lukewarm. It will not keep above two or three days; it has a somewhat sharp, brisk taste, is nothing heady, but very comfortable to the stomach; laxative to strangers, but a very pleasant beverage to such as are accustomed to it. They make use, instead of bread, of a certain white compound, like coriander seeds; I have tasted of it; the taste is sweet and a little flat. The whole day is spent in dancing. Their young men go a-hunting after wild beasts with bows and arrows; one part of their women are employed in preparing their drink the while, which is their chief employment. One of their old men, in the morning before they fall to eating, preaches to the whole family, walking from the one end of the house to the other, and several times repeating the same sentence, till he has finished the round, for their houses are at least a hundred yards long. Valour towards their enemies and love towards their wives, are the two heads of his discourse, never failing in the close, to put them in mind, that it is their wives who provide them their drink warm and well seasoned. The fashion of their beds, ropes, swords, and of the wooden bracelets they tie about their wrists, when they go to fight, and of the great canes, bored hollow at one end, by the sound of which they keep the cadence of their dances, are to be seen in several places, and amongst others, at my house. They shave all over, and much more neatly than we, without other razor than one of wood or stone. They believe in the immortality of the soul, and that those who have merited well of the gods are lodged in that part of heaven where the sun rises, and the accursed in the west.

They have I know not what kind of priests and prophets, who very rarely present themselves to the people, having their abode in the mountains. At their arrival, there is a great feast, and solemn assembly of many villages: each house, as I have described, makes a village, and they are about a French league distant from one another. This prophet declaims to them in public, exhorting them to virtue and their duty: but all their ethics are comprised in these two articles, resolution in war, and affection to their wives. He also prophesies to them events to come, and the issues they are to expect from their enterprises, and prompts them to or diverts them from war: but let him look to't; for if he fail in his divination, and anything happen otherwise than he has foretold, he is cut into a thousand pieces, if he be caught, and condemned for a false prophet: for that reason, if any of them has been mistaken, he is no more heard of.

Divination is a gift of God, and therefore to abuse it, ought to be a punishable imposture. Amongst the Scythians, where their diviners failed in the promised effect, they were laid, bound hand and foot, upon carts loaded with firs and bavins, and drawn by oxen, on which they were burned to death. [Herodotus, iv. 69.] Such as only meddle with things subject to the conduct of human capacity, are excusable in doing the best they can: but those other fellows that come to delude us with assurances of an extraordinary faculty, beyond our understanding, ought they not to be punished, when they do not make good the effect of their promise, and for the temerity of their imposture?

They have continual war with the nations that live further within the mainland, beyond their mountains, to which they go naked, and without other arms than their bows and wooden swords, fashioned at one end like the head of our javelins. The obstinacy of their battles is wonderful, and they never end without great effusion of blood: for as to running away, they know not what it is. Everyone for a trophy brings home the head of an enemy he has killed, which he fixes over the door of his house. After having a long time treated their prisoners very well, and given them all the regales they can think of, he to whom the prisoner belongs, invites a great assembly of his friends. They being come, he ties a rope to one of the arms of the prisoner, of which, at a distance, out of his reach, he holds the one end himself, and gives to the friend he loves best the other arm to hold after the same manner; which being. done, they two, in the presence of all the assembly, despatch him with their swords. After that, they roast him, eat him amongst them, and send some chops to their absent friends. They do not do this, as some think, for nourishment, as the Scythians anciently did, but as a representation of an extreme revenge; as will appear by this: that having observed the Portuguese, who were in league with their enemies, to inflict another sort of death upon any of them they took prisoners, which was to set them up to the girdle in the earth, to shoot at the remaining part till it was stuck full of arrows, and then to hang them, they thought those people of the other world (as being men who had sown the knowledge of a great many vices amongst their neighbours, and who were much greater masters in all sorts of mischief than they) did not exercise this sort of revenge without a meaning, and that it must needs be more painful than theirs, they began to leave their old way, and to follow this. I am not sorry that we should here take notice of the barbarous horror of so cruel an action, but that, seeing so clearly into their faults, we should be so blind to our own. I conceive there is more barbarity in eating a man alive, than when he is dead; in tearing a body limb from limb by racks and torments, that is yet in perfect sense; in roasting it by degrees; in causing it to be bitten and worried by dogs and swine (as we have not only read, but lately seen, not amongst inveterate and mortal enemies, but among neighbours and fellow-citizens, and, which is worse, under colour of piety and religion), than to roast and eat him after he is dead.

CHAPTER 31

Chrysippus and Zeno, the two heads of the Stoic sect, were of opinion that there was no hurt in making use of our dead carcasses, in what way soever for our necessity, and in feeding upon them too; [Diogenes Laertius, vii. 188.] as our own ancestors, who being besieged by Caesar in the city Alexia, resolved to sustain the famine of the siege with the bodies of their old men, women, and other persons who were incapable of bearing arms.

> *Vascones, ut fama est, alimentis talibus usi*
> *Produxere animas.*

[It is said the Gascons with such meats appeased their hunger.
—Juvenal, *Satires*, xv. 93.]

And the physicians make no bones of employing it to all sorts of use, either to apply it outwardly; or to give it inwardly for the health of the patient. But there never was any opinion so irregular, as to excuse treachery, disloyalty, tyranny, and cruelty, which are our familiar vices. We may then call these people barbarous, in respect to the rules of reason: but not in respect to ourselves, who in all sorts of barbarity exceed them. Their wars are throughout noble and generous, and carry as much excuse and fair pretence, as that human malady is capable of; having with them no other foundation than the sole jealousy of valour. Their disputes are not for the conquest of new lands, for these they already possess are so fruitful by nature, as to supply them without labour or concern, with all things necessary, in such abundance that they have no need to enlarge their borders. And they are, moreover, happy in this, that they only covet so much as their natural necessities require: all beyond that is superfluous to them: men of the same age call one another generally brothers, those who are younger, children; and the old men are fathers to all. These leave to their heirs in common the full possession of goods, without any manner of division, or other title than what nature bestows upon her creatures, in bringing them into the

185

world. If their neighbours pass over the mountains to assault them, and obtain a victory, all the victors gain by it is glory only, and the advantage of having proved themselves the better in valour and virtue: for they never meddle with the goods of the conquered, but presently return into their own country, where they have no want of anything necessary, nor of this greatest of all goods, to know happily how to enjoy their condition and to be content. And those in turn do the same; they demand of their prisoners no other ransom, than acknowledgment that they are overcome: but there is not one found in an age, who will not rather choose to die than make such a confession, or either by word or look recede from the entire grandeur of an invincible courage. There is not a man amongst them who had not rather be killed and eaten, than so much as to open his mouth to entreat he may not. They use them with all liberality and freedom, to the end their lives may be so much the dearer to them; but frequently entertain them with menaces of their approaching death, of the torments they are to suffer, of the preparations making in order to it, of the mangling their limbs, and of the feast that is to be made, where their carcass is to be the only dish. All which they do, to no other end, but only to extort some gentle or submissive word from them, or to frighten them so as to make them run away, to obtain this advantage that they were terrified, and that their constancy was shaken; and indeed, if rightly taken, it is in this point only that a true victory consists:

> *Victoria nulla est,*
> *Quam quae confessor animo quoque subjugate hostes.*

[No victory is complete, which the conquered do not admit to be so.
—Claudius, *De Sexto Consulatu Honorii*, v. 248.]

The Hungarians, a very warlike people, never pretend further than to reduce the enemy to their discretion; for having forced this confession from them, they let them go without injury or ransom, excepting, at the most, to make them engage their word never to bear arms against them again. We have sufficient advantages over our enemies that are borrowed and not truly our own; it is the quality of a porter, and no effect of virtue, to have stronger arms and legs; it is a dead and corporeal quality to set in array; it is a turn of fortune to make our enemy stumble, or to dazzle him with the light of the sun; it is a trick of science and art, and that may happen in a mean base fellow, to be a good fencer. The estimate and value of a man consist in the heart and in the will: there his true honour lies. Valour is stability, not of legs and arms, but of the courage and the soul; it does not lie in the goodness of our horse or our arms but in our own. He that falls obstinate in his courage—

Si succiderit, de genu pugnat

[If his legs fail him, he fights on his knees.
—Seneca, *De Providentia*, c. 2.]

– he who, for any danger of imminent death, abates nothing of his assurance; who, dying, yet darts at his enemy a fierce and disdainful look, is overcome not by us, but by fortune; he is killed, not conquered; the most valiant are sometimes the most unfortunate. There are defeats more triumphant than victories. Never could those four sister victories, the fairest the sun ever be held, of Salamis, Plataea, Mycale, and Sicily, venture to oppose all their united glories, to the single glory of the discomfiture of King Leonidas and his men, at the pass of Thermopylae. Whoever ran with a more glorious desire and greater ambition, to the winning, than Captain Iscolas to the certain loss of a battle? [Diodorus Siculus, xv. 64.] Who could have found out a more subtle invention to secure his safety, than he did to assure his destruction? He was set to defend a certain pass of Peloponnesus against the Arcadians, which, considering the nature of the place and the inequality of forces, finding it utterly

187

impossible for him to do, and seeing that all who were presented to the enemy, must certainly be left upon the place; and on the other side, reputing it unworthy of his own virtue and magnanimity and of the Lacedaemonian name to fail in any part of his duty, he chose a mean between these two extremes after this manner; the youngest and most active of his men, he preserved for the service and defence of their country, and sent them back; and with the rest, whose loss would be of less consideration, he resolved to make good the pass, and with the death of them, to make the enemy buy their entry as dear as possibly he could; as it fell out, for being presently environed on all sides by the Arcadians, after having made a great slaughter of the enemy, he and his were all cut in pieces. Is there any trophy dedicated to the conquerors which was not much more due to these who were overcome? The part that true conquering is to play, lies in the encounter, not in the coming off; and the honour of valour consists in fighting, not in subduing.

But to return to my story: these prisoners are so far from discovering the least weakness, for all the terrors that can be represented to them, that, on the contrary, during the two or three months they are kept, they always appear with a cheerful countenance; importune their masters to make haste to bring them to the test, defy, rail at them, and reproach them with cowardice, and the number of battles they have lost against those of their country. I have a song made by one of these prisoners, wherein he bids them "come all, and dine upon him, and welcome, for they shall withal eat their own fathers and grandfathers, whose flesh has served to feed and nourish him. These muscles," says he, "this flesh and these veins, are your own: poor silly souls as you are, you little think that the substance of your ancestors' limbs is here yet; notice what you eat, and you will find in it the taste of your own flesh:" in which song there is to be observed an invention that nothing relishes of the barbarian. Those that paint these people dying after this manner, represent the prisoner spitting in the faces of his executioners and making wry mouths at them. And it is most certain, that to the very last gasp, they never cease to brave and defy them both in word and gesture. In plain truth, these men are very savage in comparison of us; of necessity, they must either be absolutely so or else we are savages; for there is a vast difference between their manners and ours.

The men there have several wives, and so much the greater number, by how much they have the greater reputation for valour. And it is one very remarkable feature in their marriages, that the same jealousy our wives have to hinder and divert us from the friendship and familiarity of other women, those employ to promote their husbands' desires, and to procure them many spouses; for being above all things solicitous of their husbands' honour, it is their chiefest care to seek out, and to bring in the most companions they can, forasmuch as it is a testimony of the husband's virtue. Most of our ladies will cry out, that it is monstrous; whereas in truth it is not so, but a truly matrimonial virtue, and of the highest form. In the Bible, Sarah, with Leah and Rachel, the two wives of Jacob, gave the most beautiful of their handmaids to their husbands; Livia preferred the passions of Augustus to her own interest; [Suetonius, *Life of Augustus*, c. 71.] and the wife of King Deiotarus, Stratonice, did not only give up a fair young maid that served her to her husband's embraces, but moreover carefully brought up the children he had by her, and assisted them in the succession to their father's crown.

And that it may not be supposed, that all this is done by a simple and servile obligation to their common practice, or by any authoritative impression of their ancient custom, without judgment or reasoning, and from having a soul so stupid that it cannot contrive what else to do, I must here give you some touches of their sufficiency in point of understanding. Besides what I repeated to you before, which was one of their songs of war, I have another, a love-song, that begins thus:

Stay, adder, stay, that by thy pattern my sister may draw the fashion and work of a rich ribbon, that I may present to my beloved, by which means thy beauty and the excellent order of thy scales shall for ever be preferred before all other serpents.

Wherein the first couplet, "Stay, adder," &c., makes the burden of the song. Now I have conversed enough with poetry to judge thus much that not only there is nothing barbarous in this invention, but, moreover, that it is perfectly Anacreontic. To which it may be added, that their language is soft, of a pleasing accent, and something bordering upon the Greek termination.

Three of these people, not foreseeing how dear their knowledge of the corruptions of this part of the world will one day cost their happiness and repose, and that the effect of this commerce will be their ruin, as I presuppose it is in a very fair way (miserable men to suffer themselves to be deluded with desire of novelty and to have left the serenity of their own heaven to come so far to gaze at ours!), were at Rouen at the time that the late King Charles IX. was there. The king himself talked to them a good while, and they were made to see our fashions, our pomp, and the form of a great city. After which, someone asked their opinion, and would know of them, what of all the things they had seen, they found most to be admired? To which they made answer, three things, of which I have forgotten the third, and am troubled at it, but two I yet remember. They said, that in the first place they thought it very strange that so many tall men, wearing beards, strong, and well armed, who were about the king (it is like they meant the Swiss of the guard), should submit to obey a child, and that they did not rather choose out one amongst themselves to command. Secondly (they have a way of speaking in their language to call men the half of one another), that they had observed that there were amongst us men full and crammed with all manner of commodities, whilst, in the meantime, their halves were begging at their doors, lean and half-starved with hunger and poverty; and they thought it strange that these necessitous halves were able to suffer so great an inequality and injustice, and that they did not take the others by the throats, or set fire to their houses.

I talked to one of them a great while together, but I had so ill an interpreter, and one who was so perplexed by his own ignorance to apprehend my meaning, that I could get nothing out of him of any moment: Asking him what advantage he reaped from the superiority he had amongst his own people (for he was a captain, and our mariners called him king), he told me, to march at the head of them to war. Demanding of him further how many men he had to follow him, he showed me a space of ground, to signify as many as could march in such a compass, which might be four or five thousand men; and putting the question to him whether or no his authority expired with the war, he told me this remained: that when he went to visit the villages of his dependence, they planed him paths through the thick of their woods, by which he might pass at his ease. All this does not sound very ill, and the last was not at all amiss, for they wear no breeches.

39

ON SOLITUDE

Let us pretermit that long comparison betwween the active and the solitary life; and as for the fine sayings with which ambition and avarice palliate their vices, that we are not born for ourselves but for the public, [This is the eulogium passed by Lucan on Cato of Utica, ii. 383] let us boldly appeal to those who are in public affairs; let them lay their hands upon their hearts, and then say whether, on the contrary, they do not rather aspire to titles and offices and that tumult of the world to make their private advantage at the public expense. The corrupt ways by which in this our time they arrive at the height to which their ambitions aspire, manifestly enough declares that their ends cannot be very good. Let us tell ambition that it is she herself who gives us a taste of solitude; for what does she so much avoid as society? What does she so much seek as elbow-room? A man may do well or ill everywhere; but if what Bias says be true, that the greatest part is the worse part, or what the Preacher says: there is not one good of a thousand:

> Rari quippe boni: numero vix sunt totidem quot
> Thebarum portae, vel divitis ostia Nili,

[Good men indeed are scarce: there are hardly as many as there are gates of Thebes or mouths of the rich Nile.
—Juvenal, *Satires*, xiii. 26.]

the contagion is very dangerous in the crowd. A man must either imitate the vicious or hate them both are dangerous things, either to resemble them because they are many or to hate many because they are unresembling to ourselves. Merchants who go to sea are in the right when they are cautious that those who embark with them in the same bottom be neither dissolute blasphemers nor vicious other ways, looking upon such society as unfortunate. And therefore it was that Bias pleasantly said to some, who being with him in a dangerous storm implored the assistance of the gods: "Peace, speak softly," said he, "that they may not know you are here in my company." [Diogenes Laertius] And of more pressing example, Albuquerque, viceroy in the Indies for Emmanuel, king of Portugal, in an extreme peril of shipwreck, took a young boy upon his shoulders, for this only end that, in the society of their common danger his innocence might serve to protect him, and to recommend him to the divine favour, that they might get safe to shore. 'Tis not that a wise man may not live everywhere content, and be alone in the very crowd of a palace; but if it be left to his own choice, the schoolman will tell you that he should fly the very sight of the crowd: he will endure it if need be; but if it be referred to him, he will choose to be alone. He cannot think himself sufficiently rid of vice, if he must yet contend with it in other men. Charondas punished those as evil men who were convicted of keeping ill company. There is nothing so unsociable and sociable as man, the one by his vice, the other by his nature. And Antisthenes, in my opinion, did not give him a satisfactory answer, who reproached him with frequenting ill company, by saying that the physicians lived well enough amongst the sick, for if they contribute to the health of the sick, no doubt but by the contagion, continual sight of, and familiarity with diseases, they must of necessity impair their own.

Now the end, I take it, is all one, to live at more leisure and at one's ease: but men do not always take the right way. They often think they have totally taken leave of all business, when they have only exchanged one employment for another: there is little less

194

trouble in governing a private family than a whole kingdom. Wherever the mind is perplexed, it is in an entire disorder, and domestic employments are not less troublesome for being less important. Moreover, for having shaken off the court and the exchange, we have not taken leave of the principal vexations of life:

> *Ratio et prudential curas,*
> *Non locus effusi late maris arbiter, aufert;*

[Reason and prudence, not a place with a commanding view of the great ocean, banish care.

—Horace, *Epistles*, i. 2.]

ambition, avarice, irresolution, fear, and inordinate desires, do not leave us because we forsake our native country:

> *Et Post equitemsedetatracura;*

[Black care sits behind the horse man.

—Horace, *Odes*, iii. 1, 40].

they often follow us even to cloisters and philosophical schools; nor deserts, nor caves, hair-shirts, nor fasts, can disengage us from them:

> *Haeret lateri lethalis arundo.*

[The fatal shaft adheres to the side.

—*Aeneid*, iv. 73.]

One telling Socrates that such a one was nothing improved by his travels: "I very well believe it," said he, "for he took himself along with him"

Quid terras alio calentes
Sole mutamus? patriae quis exsul
Se quoque fugit?

[Why do we seek climates warmed by another sun? Who is the man that by fleeing from his country, can also flee from himself?
—Horace, *Odes*, ii. 16, 18.]

If a man do not first discharge both himself and his mind of the burden with which he finds himself oppressed, motion will but make it press the harder and sit the heavier, as the lading of a ship is of less encumbrance when fast and bestowed in a settled posture. You do a sick man more harm than good in removing him from place to place; you fix and establish the disease by motion, as stakes sink deeper and more firmly into the earth by being moved up and down in the place where they are designed to stand. Therefore, it is not enough to get remote from the public; 'tis not enough to shift the soil only; a man must flee from the popular conditions that have taken possession of his soul, he must sequester and come again to himself:

Rupi jam vincula, dicas
Nam luctata canis nodum arripit; attamen illi,
Quum fugit, a collo trahitur pars longa catenae.

[You say, perhaps, you have broken your chains: the dog who after long efforts has broken his chain, still in his flight drags a heavy portion of it after him.
—Persius, *Satire*, v. 158.]

We still carry our fetters along with us. It is not an absolute liberty; we yet cast back a look upon what we have left behind us; the fancy is still full of it:

Nisi purgatum est pectus, quae praelia nobis
Atque pericula tunc ingratis insinuandum?

CHAPTER 39

Quantae connscindunt hominem cupedinis acres
Sollicitum curae? Quantique perinde timores?
Quidve superbia, spurcitia, ac petulantia, quantas Efficiunt clades?
quid luxusdesidiesque?

[But unless the mind is purified, what internal combats and dangers must we incur in spite of all our efforts! How many bitter anxieties, how many terrors, follow upon unregulated passion! What destruction befalls us from pride, lust, petulant anger! What evils arise from luxury and sloth!

—Lucretius, v. 4.]

Our disease lies in the mind, which cannot escape from itself;

In culpa est animus, qui se non effugit unquam,
—Horace, Epistles, i. 14, 13.

and therefore is to be called home and confined within itself: that is the true solitude, and that may be enjoyed even in populous cities and the courts of kings, though more commodiously apart.

Now, since we will attempt to live alone, and to waive all manner of conversation amongst them, let us so order it that our content may depend wholly upon ourselves; let us dissolve all obligations that ally us to others; let us obtain this from ourselves, that we may live alone in good earnest, and live at our ease too.

Stilpo having escaped from the burning of his town, where he lost wife, children, and goods, Demetrius Poliorcetes seeing him, in so great a ruin of his country, appear with an undisturbed countenance, asked him if he had received no loss? To which he made answer, No; and that, thank God, nothing was lost of his. [Seneca, *Epistles,* 7.] This also was the meaning of the philosopher Antisthenes, when he pleasantly said, that "men should furnish themselves with such things as would float, and might with the owner escape the storm"; [Diogenes Laertius, vi. 6.] and certainly a wise man never loses anything if he have himself. When the city of Nola was ruined by the barbarians, Paulinus, who was bishop of that place, having there lost all he had, himself a prisoner, prayed after this manner: "O Lord, defend me from being sensible of this loss; for Thou knowest they have yet touched nothing of that which is mine." [St. Augustin, *City of God*, i. 10.] The riches that made him rich and the goods that made him good, were still kept entire. This it is to make choice of treasures that can secure themselves from plunder and violence, and to hide them in such a place into which no one can enter and that is not to be betrayed by any but ourselves. Wives, children, and goods must be had, and especially health, by him that can get it; but we are not so to set our hearts upon them that our happiness must have its dependence upon them; we must reserve a backshop, wholly our own and entirely free, wherein to settle our true liberty, our principal solitude and retreat. And in this we must for the most part entertain ourselves with ourselves, and so privately that no exotic knowledge or communication be admitted there; there to laugh and to talk, as if without wife, children, goods, train, or attendance, to the end that when it shall so fall out that we must lose any or all of these, it may be no new thing to be without them. We have a mind pliable in itself, that will be company; that has wherewithal to attack and to defend, to receive and to give: let us not then fear in this solitude to languish under an uncomfortable vacuity.

> *In solis sis tibi turba locis.*

> [In solitude, be company for thyself.
>
> —Tibullus, vi. 13. 12.]

Virtue is satisfied with herself, without discipline, without words, without effects. In our ordinary actions there is not one of a thousand that concerns ourselves. He that you see scrambling up the ruins of that wall, furious and transported, against whom so many harquebuss-shots are levelled; and that other all over scars, pale, and fainting with hunger, and yet resolved rather to die than to open the gates to him; do you think that these men are there upon their own account? No; peradventure in the behalf of one whom they never saw and who never concerns himself for their pains and danger, but lies wallowing the while in sloth and pleasure: this other slavering, blear-eyed, slovenly fellow, that you see come out of his study after midnight, do you think he has been tumbling over books to learn how to become a better man, wiser, and more content? No such matter; he will there end his days, but he will teach posterity the measure of Plautus' verses and the true orthography of a Latin word. Who is it that does not voluntarily exchange his health, his repose, and his very life for reputation and glory, the most useless, frivolous, and false coin that passes current amongst us? Our own death does not sufficiently terrify and trouble us; let us, moreover, charge ourselves with those of our wives, children, and family: our own affairs do not afford us anxiety enough; let us undertake those of our neighbours and friends, still more to break our brains and torment us:

Vah! quemquamne hominem in animum instituere, aut Parare, quod sit carius, quam ipse est sibi?

[Ah! can any man conceive in his mind or realise what is dearer than he is to himself?
—Terence, *Adelphoe* i. I, 13.]

Solitude seems to me to wear the best favour in such as have already employed their most active and flourishing age in the world's service, after the example of Thales. We have lived enough for others; let us at least live out the small remnant of life for ourselves; let us now call in our thoughts and intentions to ourselves, and to our own ease and repose. 'Tis no light thing to make a sure retreat; it will be enough for us to do without mixing other enterprises. Since God gives us leisure to order our removal, let us make ready, truss our baggage, take leave betimes of the company, and disentangle ourselves from those violent importunities that engage us elsewhere and separate us from ourselves.

We must break the knot of our obligations, how strong soever, and hereafter love this or that, but espouse nothing but ourselves: that is to say, let the remainder be our own, but not so joined and so close as not to be forced away without flaying us or tearing out part of our whole. The greatest thing in the world is for a man to know that he is his own. 'Tis time to wean ourselves from society when we can no longer add anything to it; he who is not in a condition to lend must forbid himself to borrow. Our forces begin to fail us; let us call them in and concentrate them in and for ourselves. He that can cast off within himself and resolve the offices of friendship and company, let him do it. In this decay of nature which renders him useless, burdensome, and importunate to others, let him take care not to be useless, burdensome, and importunate to himself. Let him soothe and caress himself, and above all things be sure to govern himself with reverence to his reason and conscience to that degree as to be ashamed to make a false step in their presence:

Rarum est enim, ut satis se quisque vereatur.

[For 'tis rarely seen that men have respect and reverence enough for themselves.

—Quintilian, x. 7.]

Socrates says that boys are to cause themselves to be instructed, men to exercise themselves in well-doing, and old men to retire from all civil and military employments, living at their own discretion, without the obligation to any office. There are some complexions more proper for these precepts of retirement than others. Such as are of a soft and dull apprehension, and of a tender will and affection, not readily to be subdued or employed, whereof I am one, both by natural condition and by reflection, will sooner incline to this advice than active and busy souls, which embrace: all, engage in all, are hot upon everything, which offer, present, and give themselves up to every occasion. We are to use these accidental and extraneous commodities, so far as they are pleasant to us, but by no means to lay our principal foundation there; 'tis no true one; neither nature nor reason allows it so to be. Why therefore should we, contrary to their laws, enslave our own contentment to the power of another? To anticipate also the accidents of fortune, to deprive ourselves of the conveniences we have in our own power, as several have done upon the account of devotion, and some philosophers by reasoning; to be one's own servant, to lie hard, to put out our own eyes, to throw our wealth into the river, to go in search of grief; these, by the misery of this life, aiming at bliss in another; those by laying themselves low to avoid the danger of falling: all such are acts of an excessive virtue. The stoutest and most resolute natures render even their seclusion glorious and exemplary:

> *Tuta et parvulalaudo,*
> *Quum res deficiunt, satis inter vilia fortis*
> *Verum, ubi quid Melius contingit et unctius, idem*
> *Hos sapere et solos aio bene vivere, quorum*
> *Conspicitur nitidis fundata pecunia villis.*

[When means are deficient, I laud a safe and humble condition, content with little: but when things grow better and more easy, I all the same say that you alone are wise and live well, whose invested money is visible in beautiful villas.

—Horace, *Epistles*, i. 15, 42.]

A great deal less would serve my turn well enough. It is enough for me, under fortune's favour, to prepare myself for her disgrace, and, being at my ease, to represent to myself, as far as my imagination can stretch, the ill to come; as we do at jousts and tiltings, where we counterfeit war in the greatest calm of peace. I do not think Arcesilaus the philosopher the less temperate and virtuous for knowing that he made use of gold and silver vessels, when the condition of his fortune allowed him so to do; I have indeed a better opinion of him than if he had denied himself what he used with liberality and moderation. I see the utmost limits of natural necessity: and considering a poor man begging at my door, ofttimes more jocund and more healthy than I myself am, I put myself into his place, and attempt to dress my mind after his mode; and running, in like manner, over other examples, though I fancy death, poverty, contempt, and sickness treading on my heels, I easily resolve not to be affrighted, forasmuch as a less than I takes them with so much patience; and am not willing to believe that a less understanding can do more than a greater, or that the effects of precept cannot arrive to as great a height as those of custom. And knowing of how uncertain duration these accidental conveniences are, I never forget, in the height of all my enjoyments, to make it my chiefest prayer to Almighty God, that He will please to render me content with myself and the condition wherein I am. I see young men very gay and frolic, who nevertheless keep a mass of pills in their trunk at home, to take when they've got a cold, which they fear so much the less, because they think they have remedy at hand. Everyone should do in like manner, and, moreover, if they find themselves subject to some more violent disease, should furnish themselves with such medicines as may numb and stupefy the part.

The employment a man should choose for such a life ought neither to be a laborious nor an unpleasing one; otherwise 'tis to no purpose at all to be retired. And this depends upon every one's liking and humour. Mine has no manner of complacency for husbandry, and such as love it ought to apply themselves to it with moderation:

[Endeavour to make circumstances subject to me, and not me subject to circumstances.

—Horace, *Epistles*, i. i, 19.]

Husbandry is otherwise a very servile employment, as Sallust calls it; though some parts of it are more excusable than the rest,

CHAPTER 39

as the care of gardens, which Xenophon attributes to Cyrus; and a mean may be found out betwixt the sordid and low application, so full of perpetual solicitude, which is seen in men who make it their entire business and study, and the stupid and extreme negligence, letting all things go at random which we see in others

> *Democriti pecus edit agellos*
> *Cultaque, dum peregre est animus sine corpore velox.*

[Democritus' cattle eat his corn and spoil his fields, whilst his soaring mind ranges abroad without the body.
—Horace, *Epistles*, i, 12, 12.]

But let us hear what advice the younger Pliny gives his friend Caninius Rufus upon the subject of solitude: "I advise thee, in the full and plentiful retirement wherein thou art, to leave to thy hinds the care of thy husbandry, and to addict thyself to the study of letters, to extract from thence something that may be entirely and absolutely thine own." By which he means reputation; like Cicero, who says that he would employ his solitude and retirement from public affairs to acquire by his writings an immortal life.

> *Usquea deone*
> *Scire tuum, nihil est, nisi to scire hoc, sciat alter?*

[Is all that thy learning nothing, unless another knows that thou knowest?
—Persius, *Satire*, i. 23.]

It appears to be reason, when a man talks of retiring from the world, that he should look quite out of [for] himself. These do it but by halves: they design well enough for themselves when they shall be no more in it; but still they pretend to extract the fruits of that design from the world, when absent from it, by a ridiculous contradiction.

The imagination of those who seek solitude upon the account of devotion, filling their hopes and courage with certainty of divine promises in the other life, is much more rationally founded. They propose to themselves God, an infinite object in goodness and power; the soul has there wherewithal, at full liberty, to satiate her desires: afflictions and sufferings turn to their advantage, being undergone for the acquisition of eternal health and joy; death is to be wished and longed for, where it is the passage to so perfect a condition; the asperity of the rules they impose upon themselves is immediately softened by custom, and all their carnal appetites baffled and subdued, by refusing to humour and feed them, these being only supported by use and exercise. This sole end of another happily immortal life is that which really merits that we should abandon the pleasures and conveniences of this; and he who can really and constantly inflame his soul with the ardour of this vivid faith and hope, erects for himself in solitude a more voluptuous and delicious life than any other sort of existence.

Neither the end, then, nor the means of this advice pleases me, for we often fall out of the frying-pan into the fire. [or: we always relapse ill from fever into fever.] This book-employment is as painful as any other, and as great an enemy to health, which ought to be the first thing considered; neither ought a man to be allured with the pleasure of it, which is the same that destroys the frugal, the avaricious, the voluptuous, and the ambitious man.

> [This plodding occupation of bookes is as painfull as any other, and as great an enemie unto health, which ought principally to be considered. And a man should not suffer him selfe to be inveigled by the pleasure he takes in them.
> —Florio, edit. 1613, p. 122.]

The sages give us caution enough to beware the treachery of our desires, and to distinguish true and entire pleasures from such as are mixed and complicated with greater pain. For the most of our pleasures, say they, wheedle and caress only to strangle us, like those thieves the Egyptians called Philistae; if the headache should come before drunkenness, we should have a care of drinking too much; but pleasure, to deceive us, marches before and conceals her train. Books are pleasant, but if, by being over-studious, we impair our health and spoil our good humour, the best pieces we have, let us give it over; I, for my part, am one of those who think, that no fruit derived from them can recompense so great a loss. As men who have long felt themselves weakened by indisposition, give themselves up at last to the mercy of medicine and submit to certain rules of living, which they are for the future never to transgress; so he who retires, weary of and disgusted with the common way of living, ought to model this new one he enters into by the rules of reason, and to institute and establish it by premeditation and reflection. He ought to have taken leave of all sorts of labour, what advantage soever it may promise, and generally to have shaken off all those passions which disturb the tranquillity of body and soul, and then choose the way that best suits with his own humour:

Unusquisque sua noverit ire via.

In husbandry, study, hunting, and all other exercises, men are to proceed to the utmost limits of pleasure, but must take heed of engaging further, where trouble begins to mix with it. We are to reserve so much employment only as is necessary to keep us in breath and to defend us from the inconveniences that the other extreme of a dull and stupid laziness brings along with it. There are sterile knotty sciences, chiefly hammered out for the crowd; let such be left to them who are engaged in the world's service. I for my part care for no other books, but either such as are pleasant and easy, to amuse me, or those that comfort and instruct me how to regulate my life and death:

Tacitum sylvas inter reptare salubres,
Curantem, quidquid dignum sapienti bonoque est.

[Silently meditating in the healthy groves, whatever is worthy of a wise and good man.

—Horace, *Epistles*, i. 4, 4.]

Wiser men, having great force and vigour of soul, may propose to themselves a rest wholly spiritual but for me, who have a very ordinary soul, it is very necessary to support myself with bodily conveniences; and age having of late deprived me of those pleasures that were more acceptable to me, I instruct and whet my appetite to those that remain, more suitable to this other reason. We ought to hold with all our force, both of hands and teeth, the use of the pleasures of life that our years, one after another, snatch away from us:

> *Carpamus dulcia; nostrum est,*
> *Quod vivis; cinis, et manes, et fabula fies.*

[Let us pluck life's sweets, 'tis for them we live: by and by we shall be ashes, a ghost, a mere subject of talk.

—Persius, *Satire*, v. 151.]

Now, as to the end that Pliny and Cicero propose to us of glory, 'tis infinitely wide of my account. Ambition is of all others the most contrary humour to solitude; glory and repose are things that cannot possibly inhabit in one and the same place. For so much as I understand, these have only their arms and legs disengaged from the crowd; their soul and intention remain confined behind more than ever:

> *Tun', vetule, auriculis alienis colligis escas?*

[Dost thou, then, old man, collect food for others' ears?
—Persius, *Satire*, i. 22.]

they have only retired to take a better leap, and by a stronger motion to give a brisker charge into the crowd. Will you see how they shoot short? Let us put into the counterpoise the advice of two philosophers, of two very different sects, writing, the one to Idomeneus, the other to Lucilius, their friends, to retire into solitude from worldly honours and affairs. "You have," say they, "hitherto lived swimming and floating; come now and die in the harbour: you have given the first part of your life to the light, give what remains to the shade. It is impossible to give over business, if you do not also quit the fruit; therefore disengage yourselves from all concern of name and glory; 'tis to be feared the lustre of your former actions will give you but too much light, and follow you into your most private retreat. Quit with other pleasures that which proceeds from the approbation of another man: and as to your knowledge and parts, never concern yourselves; they will not lose their effect if yourselves be the better for them. Remember him, who being asked why he took so much pains in an art that could come to the knowledge of but few persons? 'A few are enough for me,' replied he; 'I have enough with one; I have enough with never an one.' [Seneca, *Epistles*, 7.] He said true; you and a companion are theatre enough to one another, or you to yourself. Let the people be to you one, and be you one to the whole people. 'Tis an unworthy ambition to think to derive glory from a man's sloth and privacy: you are to do like the beasts of chase, who efface the track at the entrance into their den. You are no more to concern yourself how the world talks of you, but how you are to talk to yourself. Retire yourself into yourself, but first prepare yourself there to receive yourself: it were a folly to trust yourself in your own hands, if you cannot govern yourself. A man may miscarry alone as well as in company. Till you have rendered yourself one before whom you dare not trip, and till you have a bashfulness and respect for yourself,

Obversentur species honestae animo;

[Let honest things be ever present to the mind
——Cicero, *Tusculum Disputations*, ii. 22.]

present continually to your imagination Cato, Phocion, and Aristides, in whose presence the fools themselves will hide their faults, and make them controllers of all your intentions; should these deviate from virtue, your respect to those will set you right; they will keep you in this way to be contented with yourself; to borrow nothing of any other but yourself; to stay and fix your soul in certain and limited thoughts, wherein she may please herself, and having understood the true and real goods, which men the more enjoy the more they understand, to rest satisfied, without desire of prolongation of life or name." This is the precept of the true and natural philosophy, not of a boasting and prating philosophy, such as that of the two former.

BOOK II

1

ON THE INCONSTANCY
OF OUR ACTIONS

Such as make it their business to oversee human actions, do not find themselves in anything so much perplexed as to reconcile them and bring them into the world's eye with the same lustre and reputation; for they commonly so strangely contradict one another that it seems impossible they should proceed from one and the same person. We find the younger Marius one while a son of Mars and another a son of Venus. Pope Boniface VIII. entered, it is said, into his Papacy like a fox, behaved himself in it like a lion, and died like a dog; and who could believe it to be the same Nero, the perfect image of all cruelty, who, having the sentence of a condemned man brought to him to sign, as was the custom, cried out, "O that I had never been taught to write!" so much it went to his heart to condemn a man to death. All story is full of such examples, and every man is able to produce so many to himself, or out of his own practice or observation, that I sometimes wonder to see men of understanding give themselves the trouble of sorting these pieces, considering that irresolution appears to me to be the most common and manifest vice of our nature witness the famous verse of the player Publius:

Malum consilium est, quod mutari non potest.

[It is evil counsel that will admit no change.
—Pub. Mim., ex Aul. Gell., xvii. 14.]

211

There seems some reason in forming a judgment of a man from the most usual methods of his life; but, considering the natural instability of our manners and opinions, I have often thought even the best authors a little out in so obstinately endeavouring to make of us any constant and solid contexture; they choose a general air of a man, and according to that interpret all his actions, of which, if they cannot bend some to a uniformity with the rest, they are presently imputed to dissimulation. Augustus has escaped them, for there was in him so apparent, sudden, and continual variety of actions all the whole course of his life, that he has slipped away clear and undecided from the most daring critics. I can more hardly believe a man's constancy than any other virtue, and believe nothing sooner than the contrary. He that would judge of a man in detail and distinctly, bit by bit, would oftener be able to speak the truth. It is a hard matter, from all antiquity, to pick out a dozen men who have formed their lives to one certain and constant course, which is the principal design of wisdom; for to comprise it all in one word, says one of the ancients, and to contract all the rules of human life into one, "it is to will, and not to will, always one and the same thing: I will not vouchsafe," says he, "to add, provided the will be just, for if it be not just, it is impossible it should be always one." I have indeed formerly learned that vice is nothing but irregularity, and want of measure, and therefore it is impossible to fix constancy to it. It is a saying of Demosthenes, "that the beginning of all virtue is consultation and deliberation; the end and perfection, constancy." If we would resolve on any certain course by reason, we should pitch upon the best, but nobody has thought on it:

Quod petit, spernit; repetit, quod nuper omisit;
Aestuat, et vitae disconvenit ordine toto.

[That which he sought he despises; what he lately lost, he seeks again. He fluctuates, and is inconsistent in the whole order of life.

—Horace, *Epistles*, i. I, 98.]

CHAPTER 1

Our ordinary practice is to follow the inclinations of our appetite, be it to the left or right, upwards or downwards, according as we are wafted by the breath of occasion. We never meditate what we would have till the instant we have a mind to have it; and change like that little creature which receives its colour from what it is laid upon. What we but just now proposed to ourselves we immediately alter, and presently return again to it; it is nothing but shifting and inconsistency:

> *Ducimur, ut nervis alienis mobile lignum.*

[We are turned about like the top with the thong of others.
—Idem, *Satire*, ii. 7, 82.]

We do not go, we are driven; like things that float, now leisurely, then with violence, according to the gentleness or rapidity of the current:

> *Nonne videmus,*
> *Quid sibi quisque velit, nescire, et quaerere semper*
> *Commutare locum, quasi onus deponere possit?*

[Do we not see them, uncertain what they want, and always asking for something new, as if they could get rid of the burthen?
—Lucretius, iii. 1070.]

Every day a new whimsy, and our humours keep motion with the time.

> *Tales sunt hominum mentes, quali pater ipse*
> *Juppite rauctificas lustravit lumine terras.*

[Such are the minds of men, that they change as the light with which father Jupiter himself has illumined the increasing earth.
—Cicero, Poem Fragments, book x.]

213

We fluctuate between various inclinations; we will nothing freely, nothing absolutely, nothing constantly. In any one who had prescribed and established determinate laws and rules in his head for his own conduct, we should perceive an equality of manners, an order and an infallible relation of one thing or action to another, shine through his whole life; Empedocles observed this discrepancy in the Agrigentines, that they gave themselves up to delights, as if every day was their last, and built as if they had been to live for ever. The judgment would not be hard to make, as is very evident in the younger Cato; he who therein has found one step, it will lead him to all the rest; it is a harmony of very according sounds, that cannot jar. But with us 't is quite contrary; every particular action requires a particular judgment. The surest way to steer, in my opinion, would be to take our measures from the nearest allied circumstances, without engaging in a longer inquisition, or without concluding any other consequence. I was told, during the civil disorders of our poor kingdom, that a maid, hard by the place where I then was, had thrown herself out of a window to avoid being forced by a common soldier who was quartered in the house; she was not killed by the fall, and therefore, repeating her attempt would have cut her own throat, had she not been prevented; but having, nevertheless, wounded herself to some show of danger, she voluntarily confessed that the soldier had not as yet importuned her otherwise; than by courtship, earnest solicitation, and presents; but that she was afraid that in the end he would have proceeded to violence, all which she delivered with such a countenance and accent, and withal embrued in her own blood, the highest testimony of her virtue, that she appeared another Lucretia; and yet I have since been very well assured that both before and after she was not so difficult a piece. And, according to my host's tale in Ariosto, be as handsome a man and as worthy a gentleman as you will, do not conclude too much upon your mistress's inviolable chastity for having been repulsed; you do not know but she may have a better stomach to your muleteer.

CHAPTER 1

Antigonus, having taken one of his soldiers into a great degree of favour and esteem for his valour, gave his physicians strict charge to cure him of a long and inward disease under which he had a great while languished, and observing that, after his cure, he went much more coldly to work than before, he asked him what had so altered and cowed him: "Yourself, sir," replied the other, "by having eased me of the pains that made me weary of my life." Lucullus's soldier having been rifled by the enemy, performed upon them in revenge a brave exploit, by which having made himself a gainer, Lucullus, who had conceived a good opinion of him from that action, went about to engage him in some enterprise of very great danger, with all the plausible persuasions and promises he could think of;

Verbis, quae timido quoque possent addere mentem

[Words which might add courage to any timid man.
—Horace, *Epistles*, ii. 2, 1, 2.]

"Pray employ," answered he, "some miserable plundered soldier in that affair":

Quantumvis rusticus, ibit,
Ibit eo, quo vis, qui zonam perdidit, inquit;

[Some poor fellow, who has lost his purse, will go whither you wish, said he.
—Horace, *Epistles*, ii. 2, 39.]

and flatly refused to go. When we read that Mahomet having furiously rated Chasan, Bassa of the Janissaries, because he had seen the Hungarians break into his squadrons, and himself behave very ill in the business, and that Chasan, instead of any other answer, rushed furiously alone, scimitar in hand, into the first body of the enemy, where he was presently cut to pieces, we are not to look upon

215

that action, peradventure, so much as vindication as a turn of mind, not so much natural valour as a sudden despite. The man you saw yesterday so adventurous and brave, you must not think it strange to see him as great a poltroon the next: anger, necessity, company, wine, or the sound of the trumpet had roused his spirits; this is no valour formed and established by reason, but accidentally created by such circumstances, and therefore it is no wonder if by contrary circumstances it appear quite another thing.

These supple variations and contradictions so manifest in us, have given occasion to some to believe that man has two souls; other two distinct powers that always accompany and incline us, the one towards good and the other towards ill, according to their own nature and propension; so abrupt a variety not being imaginable to flow from one and the same source.

For my part, the puff of every accident not only carries me along with it according to its own proclivity, but moreover I dis-compose and trouble myself by the instability of my own posture; and whoever will look narrowly into his own bosom, will hardly find himself twice in the same condition. I give to my soul sometimes one face and sometimes another, according to the side I turn her to. If I speak variously of myself, it is because I consider myself vari-ously; all the contrarieties are there to be found in one corner or another; after one fashion or another: bashful, insolent; chaste, lustful; prating, silent; laborious, delicate; ingenious, heavy; mel-ancholic, pleasant; lying, true; knowing, ignorant; liberal, covetous, and prodigal: I find all this in myself, more or less, according as I turn myself about; and whoever will sift himself to the bottom, will find in himself, and even in his own judgment, this volubility and discordance. I have nothing to say of myself entirely, simply, and solidly without mixture and confusion. 'Distinguo' is the most universal member of my logic. Though I always intend to speak well of good things, and rather to interpret such things as fall out in the best sense than otherwise, yet such is the strangeness of our condition, that we are often pushed on to do well even by vice itself, if well-doing were not judged by the intention only. One gallant action, therefore, ought not to conclude a man valiant; if a man were brave indeed, he would be always so, and upon all occasions. If it were a habit of valour and not a sally, it would render a man equally resolute in all accidents; the same alone as in company; the same in lists as in a battle: for, let them say what they will, there is not one valour for the pavement and another for the field; he would bear a sickness in his bed as bravely as a wound in the field, and no more fear death in his own house than at an assault. We should not then see the same man charge into a breach with a brave assurance, and afterwards torment himself like a woman for the loss of a trial at law or the death of a child; when, being an infamous coward, he is firm in the necessities of poverty; when he shrinks at the sight of a barber's razor, and rushes fearless upon the swords of the enemy, the action is commendable, not the man.

Many of the Greeks, says Cicero, [Cicero, *Tusculum Disputations*, ii. 27.] cannot endure the sight of an enemy, and yet are courageous in sickness; the Cimbrians and Celtiberians quite contrary;

> *Nihil enim potest esse aequabile,*
> *quod non a certa ratione proficiscatur.*

[Nothing can be regular that does not proceed from a fixed ground of reason.

—Idem, ibid., c. 26.]

No valour can be more extreme in its kind than that of Alexander: but it is of but one kind, nor full enough throughout, nor universal. Incomparable as it is, it has yet some blemishes; of which his being so often at his wits' end upon every light suspicion of his captains conspiring against his life, and the carrying himself in that inquisition with so much vehemence and indiscreet injustice, and with a fear that subverted his natural reason, is one pregnant instance. The superstition, also, with which he was so much tainted, carries along with it some image of pusillanimity; and the excess of his penitence for the murder of Clytus is also a testimony of the unevenness of his courage. All we perform is no other than a cento, as a man may say, of several pieces, and we would acquire honour by a false title. Virtue cannot be followed but for herself, and if one sometimes borrows her mask to some other purpose, she presently pulls it away again. It is a vivid and strong tincture which, when the soul has once thoroughly imbibed it, will not out but with the piece. And, therefore, to make a right judgment of a man, we are long and very observingly to follow his trace: if constancy does not there stand firm upon her own proper base,

Cui vivendi via considerate atque proviso est,

[If the way of his life is thoroughly considered and traced out.
–Cicero, *Paradox*, v. 1.]

if the variety of occurrences makes him alter his pace (his path, I mean, for the pace may be faster or slower) let him go; such an one runs before the wind, "Avau le dent," as the motto of our Talebot has it.

It is no wonder, says one of the ancients, that chance has so great a dominion over us, since it is by chance we live. It is not possible for anyone who has not designed his life for some certain end, it is impossible for anyone to arrange the pieces, who has not the whole form already contrived in his imagination. Of what use are colours to him that knows not what he is to paint? No one lays down a certain design for his life, and we only deliberate thereof by pieces. The archer ought first to know at what he is to aim, and then accommodate his arm, bow, string, shaft, and motion to it; our counsels deviate and wander, because not levelled to any determinate end. No wind serves him who addresses his voyage to no certain, port. I cannot acquiesce in the judgment given by one in the behalf of

CHAPTER 1

Sophocles, who concluded him capable of the management of domestic affairs, against the accusation of his son, from having read one of his tragedies.

Neither do I allow of the conjecture of the Parians, sent to regulate the Milesians sufficient for such a consequence as they from thence derived coming to visit the island, they took notice of such grounds as were best husbanded, and such country-houses as were best governed; and having taken the names of the owners, when they had assembled the citizens, they appointed these farmers for new governors and magistrates; concluding that they, who had been so provident in their own private concerns, would be so of the public too. We are all lumps, and of so various and inform a contexture, that every piece plays, every moment, its own game, and there is as much difference between us and ourselves as between us and others:

> *Magnam rem puta, unum hominem agere.*

> [Esteem it a great thing always to act as one and the same
> man.
>
> —Seneca, *Epistles*, 150.]

Since ambition can teach man valour, temperance, and liberality, and even justice too; seeing that avarice can inspire the courage of a shop-boy, bred and nursed up in obscurity and ease, with the assurance to expose himself so far from the fireside to the mercy of the waves and angry Neptune in a frail boat; that she further teaches discretion and prudence; and that even Venus can inflate boys under the discipline of the rod with boldness and resolution, and infuse masculine courage into the heart of tender virgins in their mothers' arms:

> *Hac duce, custodes furtim transgressa jacentes,*
> *Ad juvenem tenebris sola puella venit:*

[She leading, the maiden, furtively passing by the recumbent guards, goes alone in the darkness to the youth.

—Tibullus, ii. 2, 75.]

it is not all the understanding has to do, simply to judge us by our outward actions; it must penetrate the very soul, and there discover by what springs the motion is guided. But that being a high and hazardous undertaking, I could wish that fewer would attempt it.

6

USE MAKES PERFECT

It is not to be expected that argument and instruction, though we never so voluntarily surrender our belief to what is read to us, should be of force to lead us on so far as to action, if we do not, over and above, exercise and form the soul by experience to the course for which we design it; it will, otherwise, doubtless find itself at a loss when it comes to the pinch of the business. This is the reason why those amongst the philosophers who were ambitious to attain to a greater excellence, were not contented to await the severities of fortune in the retirement and repose of their own habitations, lest he should have surprised them raw and inexpert in the combat, but sallied out to meet her, and purposely threw themselves into the proof of difficulties. Some of them abandoned riches to exercise themselves in a voluntary poverty; others sought out labour and an austerity of life, to inure them to hardships and inconveniences; others have deprived themselves of their dearest members, as of sight, and of the instruments of generation, lest their too delightful and effeminate service should soften and debauch the stability of their souls.

But in dying, which is the greatest work we have to do, practice can give us no assistance at all. A man may by custom fortify himself against pain, shame, necessity, and such-like accidents, but as to death, we can experiment it but once, and are all apprentices when we come to it. There have, anciently, been men so excellent managers of their time that they have tried even in death itself to relish and taste it, and who have bent their utmost faculties of mind to discover what this passage is, but they are none of them come back to tell us the news:

> *Nemo expergitus exstat,*
> *Frigida quern semel est vitai pausa sequuta.*

[No one wakes who has once fallen into the cold sleep of death.
—Lucretius, iii. 942]

Julius Canus, a noble Roman, of singular constancy and virtue, having been condemned to die by that worthless fellow Caligula, besides many marvellous testimonies that he gave of his resolution, as he was just going to receive the stroke of the executioner, was asked by a philosopher, a friend of his: "Well, Canus, whereabout is your soul now? what is she doing? What are you thinking of?" – "I was thinking," replied the other, "to keep myself ready, and the faculties of my mind full settled and fixed, to try if in this short and quick instant of death, I could perceive the motion of the soul when she parts from the body, and whether she has any sentiment at the separation, that I may after come again if I can, to acquaint my friends with it." This man philosophises not unto death only, but in death itself. What a strange assurance was this, and what bravery of courage, to desire his death should be a lesson to him, and to have leisure to think of other things in so great an affair:

> *Jus hoc animi morientis habebat.*

[This mighty power of mind he had dying.
—Lucan, viii. 636.]

And yet I fancy, there is a certain way of making it familiar to us, and in some sort of making trial what it is. We may gain experience, if not entire and perfect, yet such, at least, as shall not be totally useless to us, and that may render us more confident and more assured. If we cannot overtake it, we may approach it and view it, and if we do not advance so far as the fort, we may at least discover and make ourselves acquainted with the avenues. It is not without reason that we are taught to consider sleep as a resemblance of death: with how great facility do we pass from waking to sleeping, and with how little concern do we lose the knowledge of light and of ourselves. Peradventure, the faculty of sleeping would seem useless and contrary to nature, since it deprives us of all action and sentiment, were it not that by it nature instructs us that she has equally made us to die as to live; and in life presents to us the eternal state she reserves for us after it, to accustom us to it and to take from us the fear of it. But such as have by violent accident fallen into a swoon, and in it have lost all sense, these, methinks, have been very near seeing the true and natural face of death; for as to the moment of the passage, it is not to be feared that it brings with it any pain or displeasure, forasmuch as we can have no feeling without leisure; our sufferings require time, which in death is so short, and so precipitous, that it must necessarily be insensible. They are the approaches that we are to fear, and these may fall within the limits of experience.

Many things seem greater by imagination than they are in effect; I have passed a good part of my life in a perfect and entire health; I say, not only entire, but, moreover, sprightly and wanton. This state, so full of verdure, jollity, and vigour, made the consideration of sickness so formidable to me, that when I came to experience it, I found the attacks faint and easy in comparison with what I had apprehended. Of this I have daily experience; if I am under the shelter of a warm room, in a stormy and tempestuous night, I wonder how people can live abroad, and am afflicted for those who are out in the fields: if I am there myself, I do not wish to be anywhere else. This one thing of being always shut up in a chamber I fancied insupportable: but I was presently inured to be so imprisoned a week, nay a month together, in a very weak, disordered, and sad condition; and I have found that, in the time of my health, I much more pitied the sick, than I think myself to be pitied when I am so, and that the force of my imagination enhances near one-half of the essence and reality of the thing.

I hope that when I come to die I shall find it the same, and that, after all, it is not worth the pains I take, so much preparation and so much assistance as I call in, to undergo the stroke. But, at all events, we cannot give ourselves too much advantage.

In the time of our third or second troubles (I do not well remember which), going one day abroad to take the air, about a league from my own house, which is seated in the very centre of all the bustle and mischief of the late civil wars in France; thinking myself in all security and so near to my retreat that I stood in need of no better equipage, I had taken a horse that went very easy upon his pace, but was not very strong. Being upon my return home, a sudden occasion falling out to make use of this horse in a kind of service that he was not accustomed to, one of my train, a lusty, tall fellow, mounted upon a strong German horse, that had a very ill mouth, fresh and vigorous, to play the brave and set on ahead of his fellows, comes thundering full speed in the very track where I was, rushing like a Colossus upon the little man and the little horse, with such a career of strength and weight, that he turned us both over and over, topsy-turvy with our heels in the air: so that there lay the horse overthrown and stunned with the fall, and I ten or twelve paces from him stretched out at length, with my face all battered and broken, my sword which I had had in my hand, above ten paces beyond that, and my belt broken all to pieces, without motion or sense any more than a stock. It was the only swoon I was ever in till that hour in my life. Those who were with me, after having used all the means they could to bring me to myself, concluding me dead, took me up in their arms, and carried me with very much difficulty home to my house, which was about half a French league from thence. On the way, having been for more than two hours given over for a dead man, I began to move and to fetch my breath; for so great abundance of blood was fallen into my stomach, that nature had need to rouse her forces to discharge it. They then raised me upon my feet, where I threw off a whole bucket of clots of blood, as this I did also several times by the way. This gave me so much ease, that I began to

recover a little life, but so leisurely and by so small advances, that my
first sentiments were much nearer the approaches of death than life:

> *Perche, dubbiosa ancor del suo ritorno,*
> *Non s'assicura attonita la mente.*

[For the soul, doubtful as to its return, could not compose itself
—Tasso, *Gierus. Lib.*, xii. 74.]

The remembrance of this accident, which is very well imprinted
in my memory, so naturally representing to me the image and idea
of death, has in some sort reconciled me to that untoward adventure. When I first began to open my eyes, it was with so perplexed,
so weak and dead a sight, that I could yet distinguish nothing but
only discern the light:

> *Come quel ch'or apre, or'chiude*
> *Gli occhi, mezzo tra'l sonno e l'esser desto.*

[As a man that now opens, now shuts his eyes, between sleep
and waking.
—Tasso, *Gierus. Libra* viii., 26.]

As to the functions of the soul, they advanced with the same
pace and measure with those of the body. I saw myself all bloody, my
doublet being stained all over with the blood I had vomited. The first
thought that came into my mind was that I had a harquebuss shot in
my head, and indeed, at the time there were a great many fired round
about us. Methought my life but just hung upon my, lips: and I shut
my eyes, to help, methought, to thrust it out, and took a pleasure
in languishing and letting myself go. It was an imagination that only
superficially floated upon my soul, as tender and weak as all the rest,
but really, not only exempt from anything displeasing, but mixed with
that sweetness that people feel when they glide into a slumber.

225

I believe it is the very same condition those people are in, whom we see swoon with weakness in the agony of death we pity them without cause, supposing them agitated with grievous dolours, or that their souls suffer under painful thoughts. It has ever been my belief, contrary to the opinion of many, and particularly of La Boétie, that those whom we see so subdued and stupefied at the approaches of their end, or oppressed with the length of the disease, or by accident of an apoplexy or falling sickness,

> *Vi morbi saepe coactus*
> *Ante oculos aliquis nostros, ut fulminis ictu,*
> *Concidit, et spumas agit; ingemit, et tremit artus;*
> *Desipit, extentat nervos, torquetur, anhelat,*
> *Inconstanter, et in jactando membra fatigat;*

[Often, compelled by the force of disease, someone as thunderstruck falls under our eyes, and foams, groans, and trembles, stretches, twists, breathes irregularly, and in paroxysms wears out his strength.

—Lucretius, iii. 485.]

or hurt in the head, whom we hear to mutter, and by fits to utter grievous groans; though we gather from these signs by which it seems as if they had some remains of consciousness, and that there are movements of the body; I have always believed, I say, both the body and the soul benumbed and asleep,

> *Vivit, et est vitae nescius ipse suae,*

[He lives, and does not know that he is alive.
—Ovid, *Tristia*, i. 3, 12.]

and could not believe that in so great a stupefaction of the members and so great a defection of the senses, the soul could maintain any force within to take cognisance of herself, and that, therefore, they had no tormenting reflections to make them consider and be sensible of the misery of their condition, and consequently were not much to be pitied.

I can, for my part, think of no state so insupportable and dreadful, as to have the soul vivid and afflicted, without means to declare itself; as one should say of such as are sent to execution with their tongues first cut out (were it not that in this kind of dying, the most silent seems to me the most graceful, if accompanied with a grave and constant countenance); or if those miserable prisoners, who fall into the hands of the base hangman soldiers of this age, by whom they are tormented with all sorts of inhuman usage to compel them to some excessive and impossible ransom; kept, in the meantime, in such condition and place, where they have no means of expressing or signifying their thoughts and their misery. The poets have feigned some gods who favour the deliverance of such as suffer under a languishing death:

> *Hunc ego Diti*
> *Sacrum jussa fero, teque isto corpore solvo.*

[I bidden offer this sacred thing to Pluto, and from that body dismiss thee.

—*Aeneid*, iv. 782.]

both the interrupted words, and the short and irregular answers one gets from them sometimes, by bawling and keeping a clutter about them; or the motions which seem to yield some consent to what we would have them do, are no testimony, nevertheless, that they live, an entire life at least. So it happens to us in the yawning of sleep, before it has fully possessed us, to perceive, as in a dream, what is done about us, and to follow the last things that are said with a perplexed and uncertain hearing which seems but to touch upon the borders of the soul; and to make answers to the last words that have been spoken to us, which have more in them of chance than sense.

Now seeing I have in effect tried it, I have no doubt but I have hitherto made a right judgment; for first, being in a swoon, I laboured to rip open the buttons of my doublet with my nails, for my sword was gone; and yet I felt nothing in my imagination that hurt me; for we have many motions in us that do not proceed from our direction;

Semianimesque micant digiti, ferrumque retractant;

[Half-dead fingers grope about, and grasp again the sword.
—*Aeneid*, x. 396.]

so falling people extend their arms before them by a natural impulse, which prompts our limbs to offices and motions without any commission from our reason.

Falciferos memorant currus abscindere membra . . .
Ut tremere in terra videatur ab artubus id quod
Decidit abscissum; cum mens tamen atque hominis vis
Mobilitate mali, non quit sentire dolorem.

[They relate that scythe-bearing chariots mow off limbs, so that they quiver on the ground; and yet the mind of him from whom the limb is taken by the swiftness of the blow feels no pain.
—Lucretius, iii. 642.]

My stomach was so oppressed with the coagulated blood, that my hands moved to that part, of their own voluntary motion, as they frequently do to the part that itches, without being directed by our will. There are several animals, and even men, in whom one may perceive the muscles to stir and tremble after they are dead.

Chapter 6

Everyone experimentally knows that there are some members which grow stiff and flag without his leave. Now, those passions which only touch the outward bark of us, cannot be said to be ours: to make them so, there must be a concurrence of the whole man; and the pains which are felt by the hand or the foot while we are sleeping, are none of ours.

As I drew near my own house, where the alarm of my fall was already got before me, and my family were come out to meet me, with the hubbub usual in such cases, not only did I make some little answer to some questions which were asked me; but they moreover tell me, that I was sufficiently collected to order them to bring a horse to my wife whom on the road, I saw struggling and tiring herself which is hilly and rugged. This should seem to proceed from a soul its functions; but it was nothing so with me. I knew not what I said or did, and they were nothing but idle thoughts in the clouds, that were stirred up by the senses of the eyes and ears, and proceeded not from me. I knew not for all that, whence I came or whither I went, neither was I capable to weigh and consider what was said to me: these were light effects, that the senses produced of themselves as of custom; what the soul contributed was in a dream, lightly touched, licked and bedewed by the soft impression of the senses. Notwithstanding, my condition was, in truth, very easy and quiet; I had no affliction upon me, either for others or myself; it was an extreme languor and weakness, without any manner of pain. I saw my own house, but knew it not. When they had put me to bed I found an inexpressible sweetness in that repose; for I had been desperately tugged and lugged by those poor people who had taken the pains to carry me upon their arms a very great and a very rough way, and had in so doing all quite tired out themselves, twice or thrice one after another. They offered me several remedies, but I would take none, certainly believing that I was mortally wounded in the head. And, in earnest, it had been a very happy death, for the weakness of my understanding deprived me of the faculty of discerning, and that of my body of the sense of feeling; I was suffering myself

229

to glide away so sweetly and after so soft and easy a manner, that I scarce find any other action less troublesome than that was. But when I came again to myself and to resume my faculties:

Ut tandem sensus convaluere mei,

[When at length my lost senses again returned.
—Ovid, *Tristia,* i. 3, 14.]

which was two or three hours after, I felt myself on a sudden involved in terrible pain, having my limbs battered and ground with my fall, and was. so ill for two or three nights after, that I thought I was once more dying again, but a more painful death, having concluded myself as good as dead before, and to this hour am sensible of the bruises of that terrible shock. I will not here omit, that the last thing I could make them beat into my head, was the memory of this accident, and I had it over and over again repeated to me, whither I was going, from whence I came, and at what time of the day this mischance befell me, before I could comprehend it. As to the manner of my fall, that was concealed from me in favour to him who had been the occasion, and other flim-flams were invented. But a long time after, and the very next day that my memory began to return and to represent to me the state wherein I was, at the instant that I perceived this horse coming full drive upon me (for I had seen him at my heels, and gave myself for gone, but this thought had been so sudden, that fear had had no leisure to introduce itself) it seemed to me like a flash of lightning that had pierced my soul, and that I came from the other world.

This long story of so light an accident would appear vain enough, were it not for the knowledge I have gained by it for my own use; for I do really find, that to get acquainted with death, needs no more but nearly to approach it. Everyone, as Pliny says, is a good doctrine to himself, provided he be capable of discovering himself near at hand.

CHAPTER 6

Here, this is not my doctrine, it is my study; and is not the lesson of another, but my own; and if I communicate it, it ought not to be ill taken, for that which is of use to me, may also, peradventure, be useful to another. As to the rest, I spoil nothing, I make use of nothing but my own; and if I play the fool, it is at my own expense, and nobody else is concerned in it; for it is a folly that will die with me, and that no one is to inherit. We hear but of two or three of the ancients, who have beaten this path, and yet I cannot say if it was after this manner, knowing no more of them but their names. No one since has followed the track: it is a rugged road, more so than it seems, to follow a pace so rambling and uncertain, as that of the soul; to penetrate the dark profundities of its intricate internal windings; to choose and lay hold of so many little nimble motions; it is a new and extraordinary undertaking, and that withdraws us from the common and most recommended employments of the world. It is now many years since that my thoughts have had no other aim and level than myself, and that I have only pried into and studied myself: or, if I study any other thing, it is to apply it to or rather in myself. And yet I do not think it a fault, if, as others do by other much less profitable sciences, I communicate what I have learned in this, though I am not very well pleased with my own progress. There is no description so difficult, nor doubtless of so great utility, as that of a man's self: and withal, a man must curl his hair and set out and adjust himself, to appear in public: now I am perpetually tricking myself out, for I am eternally upon my own description. Custom has made all speaking of a man's self vicious, and positively interdicts it, in hatred to the boasting that seems inseparable from the testimony men give of themselves:

In vitium ducit culpae fuga.

[The avoiding a mere fault often leads us into a greater.
Or: The escape from a fault leads into a vice
—Horace, *De Arte Poetics*, verse 31.]

Instead of blowing the child's nose, this is to take his nose off altogether. I think the remedy worse than the disease. But, allowing it to be true that it must of necessity be presumption to entertain people with discourses of one's self, I ought not, pursuing my general design, to forbear an action that publishes this infirmity of mine, nor conceal the fault which I not only practise but profess. Notwithstanding, to speak my thought freely, I think that the custom of condemning wine, because some people will be drunk, is itself to be condemned; a man cannot abuse anything but what is good in itself; and I believe that this rule has only regard to the popular vice. They are bits for calves, with which neither the saints whom we hear speak so highly of themselves, nor the philosophers, nor the divines will be curbed; neither will I, who am as little the one as the other, If they do not write of it expressly, at all events, when the occasions arise, they don't hesitate to put themselves on the public highway. Of what does Socrates treat more largely than of himself? To what does he more direct and address the discourses of his disciples, than to speak of themselves, not of the lesson in their book, but of the essence and motion of their souls? We confess ourselves religiously to God and our confessor; as our neighbours, do to all the people. But some will answer that we there speak nothing but accusation against ourselves; why then, we say all; for our very virtue itself is faulty and penetrable. My trade and art is to live; he that forbids me to speak according to my own sense, experience, and practice, may as well enjoin an architect not to speak of building according to his own knowledge, but according to that of his neighbour; according to the knowledge of another, and not according to his own. If it be vainglory for a man to publish his own virtues, why does not Cicero prefer the eloquence of Hortensius, and Hortensius that of Cicero? Peradventure they mean that I should give testimony of myself by works and effects, not barely by words. I chiefly paint my thoughts, a subject void of form and incapable of operative production; it is all that I can do to couch it in this airy body of the voice; the wisest and devoutest men have lived in the greatest care to avoid all apparent effects. Effects would more speak of fortune than of me; they manifest their own office and not mine, but uncertainly and by conjecture; patterns of someone particular virtue. I expose myself entire; it is a body where, at one view, the veins, muscles, and tendons are apparent, every of them in its proper place; here the effects of a cold; there of the heart beating, very dubiously. I do not write my own acts, but myself and my essence.

I am of opinion that a man must be very cautious how he values himself, and equally conscientious to give a true report, be it better or worse, impartially. If I thought myself perfectly good and wise, I would rattle it out to some purpose. To speak less of one's self than what one really is is folly, not modesty; and to take that for current pay which is under a man's value is pusillanimity and cowardice, according to, Aristotle. No virtue assists itself with falsehood; truth is never matter of error. To speak more of one's self than is really true is not always mere presumption; it is, moreover, very often folly; to, be immeasurably pleased with what one is, and to fall into an indiscreet self-love, is in my opinion the substance of this vice. The most sovereign remedy to cure it, is to do quite contrary to what these people direct who, in forbidding men to speak of themselves, consequently, at the same time, interdict thinking of themselves too. Pride dwells in the thought; the tongue can have but a very little share in it.

They fancy that to think of one's self is to be delighted with one's self; to frequent and converse with one's self, to be overindulgent; but this excess springs only in those who take but a superficial view of themselves, and dedicate their main inspection to their affairs; who call it mere reverie and idleness to occupy one's self with one's self, and the building one's self up a mere building of castles in the air; who look upon themselves as a third person only, a stranger. If any one be in rapture with his own knowledge, looking only on those below him, let him but turn his eye upward towards past ages, and his pride will be abated, when he shall there find so many thousand wits that trample him under foot. If he enter into a flattering presumption of his personal valour, let him but recollect the lives of Scipio, Epaminondas; so many armies, so many nations, that leave him so far behind them. No particular quality can make any man proud, that will at the same time put the many other weak and imperfect ones he has in the other scale, and the nothingness of human condition to make up the weight. Because Socrates had alone digested to purpose the precept of his god, "to know himself," and by that study arrived at the perfection of setting himself at nought, he only was reputed worthy the title of a sage. Whosoever shall so know himself, let him boldly speak it out.

10

ON BOOKS

I make no doubt but that I often happen to speak of things that are much better and more truly handled by those who are masters of the trade. You have here purely an essay of my natural parts, and not of those acquired: and whoever shall catch me tripping in ignorance, will not in any sort get the better of me; for I should be very unwilling to become responsible to another for my writings, who am not so to myself, nor satisfied with them. Whoever goes in quest of knowledge, let him fish for it where it is to be found; there is nothing I so little profess. These are fancies of my own, by which I do not pretend to discover things but to lay open myself; they may, peradventure, one day be known to me, or have formerly been, according as fortune has been able to bring me in place where they have been explained; but I have utterly forgotten it; and if I am a man of some reading, I am a man of no retention; so that I can promise no certainty, more than to make known to what point the knowledge I now have has risen. Therefore, let none lay stress upon the matter I write, but upon my method in writing it. Let them observe, in what I borrow, if I have known how to choose what is proper to raise or help the invention, which is always my own. For I make others say for me, not before but after me, what, either for want of language or want of sense, I cannot myself so well express. I do not number my borrowings, I weigh them; and had I designed to raise their value by number, I had made them twice as many; they are all, or within a very few, so famed and ancient authors, that they seem, methinks, themselves sufficiently to tell who they are, without giving me the trouble. In reasons, comparisons, and arguments, if I transplant any into my own soil, and confound them amongst my own, I purposely conceal the author, to awe the temerity of those precipitate censors who fall upon all sorts of writings, particularly the late ones, of men yet living; and in the vulgar tongue which puts everyone into a capacity of criticising and which seem to convict the conception and design as vulgar also. I will have them give Plutarch a fillip on my nose, and rail against Seneca when they think they rail at me. I must shelter my own weakness under these great reputations. I shall love any one that can unplume me, that is, by clearness of understanding and judgment, and by the sole distinction of the force and beauty of the discourse. For I who, for want of memory, am at every turn at a loss to, pick them out of their national livery, am yet wise enough to know, by the measure of my own abilities, that my soil is incapable of producing any of those rich flowers that I there find growing; and that all the fruits of my own growth are not worth any one of them. For this, indeed, I hold myself responsible; if I get in my own way; if there be any vanity and defect in my writings which I do not of myself perceive nor can discern, when pointed out to me by another; for many faults escape our eye, but the infirmity of judgment consists in not being able to discern them, when by another laid open to us. Knowledge and truth may be in us without judgment, and judgment also without them; but the confession of ignorance is one of the finest and surest testimonies of judgment that I know. I have no other officer to put my writings in rank and file, but only fortune. As things come into my head, I heap them one upon another; sometimes they advance in whole bodies, sometimes in single file. I would that everyone should see my natural and ordinary pace, irregular as it is; I suffer myself to jog on at my own rate. Neither are these subjects which a man is not permitted to be ignorant in, or casually and at a venture, to discourse of. I could wish to have a more perfect knowledge of things, but I will not buy it so dear as it costs. My design is to pass over easily, and not laboriously, the remainder of my life; there is nothing that I will cudgel my brains about; no, not even knowledge, of what value soever.

I seek, in the reading of books, only to please myself by an honest diversion; or, if I study, it is for no other science than what treats of the knowledge of myself, and instructs me how to die and how to live well.

Has meus ad metas sudet oportete quus.

[My horse must work according to my step.

—Propertius, iv.]

I do not bite my nails about the difficulties I meet with in my reading; after a charge or two, I give them over. Should I insist upon them, I should both lose myself and time; for I have an impatient understanding, that must be satisfied at first: what I do not discern at once is by persistence rendered more obscure. I do nothing without gaiety; continuation and a too obstinate endeavour, darkens, stupefies, and tires my judgment. My sight is confounded and dissipated with poring; I must withdraw it, and refer my discovery to new attempts; just as, to judge rightly of the lustre of scarlet, we are taught to pass the eye lightly over it, and again to run it over at several sudden and reiterated glances. If one book do not please me, I take another; and I never meddle with any, but at such times as I am weary of doing nothing. I care not much for new ones, because the old seem fuller and stronger; neither do I converse much with Greek authors, because my judgment cannot do its work with imperfect intelligence of the material.

Amongst books that are simply pleasant, of the moderns, Boccaccio's Decameron, Rabelais, and the Basia of Johannes Secundus (if those may be ranged under the title) are worth reading for amusement. As to the Amadis, and such kind of stuff, they had not the credit of arresting even my childhood. And I will, moreover, say, whether boldly or rashly, that this old, heavy soul of mine is now no longer tickled with Ariosto, no, nor with the worthy Ovid; his facility and inventions, with which I was formerly so ravished, are now of no more relish, and I can hardly have the patience to read them. I speak my opinion freely of all things, even of those that, perhaps, exceed my capacity, and that I do not conceive to be, in any wise, under my jurisdiction. And, accordingly, the judgment I deliver, is to show the measure of my own sight, and not of the things I make so bold to criticise. When I find myself disgusted with Plato's 'Axiochus', as with a work, with due respect to such an author be it spoken, without force, my judgment does not believe itself: it is not so arrogant as to oppose the authority of so many other famous judgments of antiquity, which it considers as its tutors and masters, and with whom it is rather content to err; in such a case, it condemns itself either to stop at the outward bark, not being able to penetrate to the heart, or to consider it by sortie false light. It is content with only securing itself from trouble and disorder; as to its own weakness, it frankly acknowledges and confesses it. It thinks it gives a just interpretation to the appearances by its conceptions presented to it; but they are weak and imperfect. Most of the fables of Aesop have diverse senses and meanings, of which the mythologists chose someone that quadrates well to the fable; but, for the most part, it is but the first face that presents itself and is superficial only; there yet remain others more vivid, essential, and profound, into which they have not been able to penetrate; and just so it is with me.

But, to pursue the business of this essay, I have always thought that, in poesy, Virgil, Lucretius, Catullus, and Horace by many degrees excel the rest; and signally, Virgil in his Georgics, which I look upon as the most accomplished piece in poetry; and in comparison of which a man may easily discern that there are some places in his Aeneids, to which the author would have given a little more of the file, had he had leisure: and the fifth book of his Aeneids seems to me the most perfect. I also love Lucan, and willingly read him, not so much for his style, as for his own worth, and the truth and solidity of his opinions and judgments. As for good Terence, the refined elegance and grace of the Latin tongue, I find him admirable in his vivid representation of our manners and the movements of the soul; our actions throw me at every turn upon him; and I cannot read him so often that I do not still discover some new grace and beauty. Such as lived near Virgil's time complained that some should compare Lucretius to him. I am of opinion that the comparison is, in truth, very unequal: a belief that, nevertheless, I have much ado to assure myself in, when I come upon some excellent passage in Lucretius. But if they were so angry at this comparison, what would they say to the brutish and barbarous stupidity of those who, nowadays, compare him with Ariosto? Would not Ariosto himself say?

O seclum insipiens et inficetum!

[O stupid and tasteless age.

—Catullus, xliii. 8.]

I think the ancients had more reason to be angry with those who compared Plautus with Terence, though much nearer the mark, than Lucretius with Virgil. It makes much for the estimation and preference of Terence, that the father of Roman eloquence has him so often, and alone of his class, in his mouth; and the opinion that the best judge of Roman poets [Horace, De Art. Poetica, 279.] has passed upon his companion. I have often observed that those of our times, who take upon them to write comedies (in imitation of the Italians, who are happy enough in that way of writing), take three or four plots of those of Plautus or Terence to make one of their own, and, crowd five or six of Boccaccio's novels into one single comedy. That which makes them so load themselves with matter is the diffidence they have of being able to support themselves with their own strength. They must find out something to lean to; and not having of their own stuff wherewith to entertain us, they bring in the story to supply the defect of language. It is quite otherwise with my author; the elegance and perfection of his way of speaking make us lose the appetite of his plot; his refined grace and elegance of diction everywhere occupy us: he is so pleasant throughout,

Liquidus, puroque simillimus amni,

[Liquid, and likest the pure river.
—Horace, *Epistles*, ii. s, 120.]

and so possesses the soul with his graces that we forget those of his fable. This same consideration carries me further: I observe that the best of the ancient poets have avoided affectation and the hunting after, not only fantastic Spanish and Petrarchic elevations, but even the softer and more gentle touches, which are the ornament of all succeeding poesy. And yet there is no good judgment that will condemn this in the ancients, and that does not incomparably more admire the equal polish, and that perpetual sweetness and flourishing beauty of Catullus's epigrams, than all the stings with which Martial arms the tails of his. This is by the same reason that I gave before, and as Martial says of himself:

Minus illi ingenio laborandum fuit,
in cujus locum materia successerat:

[He had the less for his wit to do that the subject itself supplied what was necessary.
—Martial, Preface before Book xiii.]

The first, without being moved, or without getting angry, make themselves sufficiently felt; they have matter enough of laughter throughout, they need not tickle themselves; the others have need of foreign assistance; as they have the less wit they must have the more body; they mount on horseback, because they are not able to stand on their own legs. As in our balls, those mean fellows who teach to dance, not being able to represent the presence and dignity of our noblesse, are fain to put themselves forward with dangerous jumping, and other strange motions and tumblers tricks; and the ladies are less put to it in dance; where there are various coupees, changes, and quick motions of body, than in some other of a more sedate kind, where they are only to move a natural pace, and to represent their ordinary grace and presence. And so I have seen good drolls, when in their own everyday clothes, and with the same face they always wear, give us all the pleasure of their art, when their apprentices, not yet arrived at such a pitch of perfection, are fain to meal their faces, put themselves into ridiculous disguises, and make a hundred grotesque faces to give us whereat to laugh. This conception of mine is nowhere more demonstrable than in comparing the *Aeneid* with Orlando Furioso; of which we see the first, by dint of wing, flying in a brave and lofty place, and always following his point: the latter, fluttering and hopping from tale to tale, as from branch to branch, not daring to trust his wings but in very short flights, and perching at every turn, lest his breath and strength should fail.

Excursusque breves tentat.

[And he attempts short excursions.

—Virgil, *Georgics*, iv. 194.]

These, then, as to this sort of subjects, are the authors that best please me.

As to what concerns my other reading, that mixes a little more profit with the pleasure, and whence I learn how to marshal my opinions and conditions, the books that serve me to this purpose are Plutarch, since he has been translated into French, and Seneca. Both of these have this notable convenience suited to my humour, that the knowledge I there seek is discoursed in loose pieces, that do not require from me any trouble of reading long, of which I am incapable. Such are the minor works of the first and the epistles of the latter, which are the best and most profiting of all their writings. It is no great attempt to take one of them in hand, and I give over at pleasure; for they have no sequence or dependence upon one another. These authors, for the most part, concur in useful and true opinions; and there is this parallel between them, that fortune brought them into the world about the same century: they were both tutors to two Roman emperors: both sought out from foreign countries: both rich and both great men. Their instruction is the cream of philosophy, and delivered after a plain and pertinent manner. Plutarch is more uniform and constant; Seneca more various and waving: the last toiled and bent his whole strength to fortify virtue against weakness, fear, and vicious appetites; the other seems more to slight their power, and to disdain to alter his pace and to stand upon his guard. Plutarch's opinions are Platonic, gentle, and accommodated to civil society; those of the other are Stoical and Epicurean, more remote from the common use, but, in my opinion, more individually commodious and more firm. Seneca seems to lean a little to the tyranny of the emperors of his time, and only seems; for I take it for certain that he speaks against his judgment when he condemns the action of the generous murderers of Caesar. Plutarch is frank throughout: Seneca abounds with brisk touches and sallies; Plutarch with things that warm and move you more; this contents and pays you better: he guides us, the other pushes us on.

As to Cicero, his works that are most useful to my design are they that treat of manners and rules of our life. But boldly to confess the truth (for since one has passed the barriers of impudence, there is no bridle), his way of writing appears to me negligent and uninviting: for his prefaces, definitions, divisions, and etymologies take up the greatest part of his work: whatever there is of life and marrow is smothered and lost in the long preparation. When I have spent an hour in reading him, which is a great deal for me, and try to recollect what I have thence extracted of juice and substance, for the most part I find nothing but wind; for he is not yet come to the arguments that serve to his purpose, and to the reasons that properly help to form the knot I seek. For me, who only desire to become more wise, not more learned or eloquent, these logical and Aristotelian dispositions of parts are of no use. I would have a man begin with the main proposition. I know well enough what death and pleasure are; let no man give himself the trouble to anatomise them to me. I look for good and solid reasons, at the first dash, to instruct me how to stand their shock, for which purpose neither grammatical subtleties nor the quaint contexture of words and argumentations are of any use at all. I am for discourses that give the first charge into the heart of the redoubt; his languish about the subject; they are proper for the schools, for the bar, and for the pulpit, where we have leisure to nod, and may awake, a quarter of an hour after, time enough to find again the thread of the discourse. It is necessary to speak after this manner to judges, whom a man has a design to gain over, right or wrong, to children and common people, to whom a man must say all, and see what will come of it. I would not have an author make it his business to render me attentive: or that he should cry out fifty times Oyez! as the heralds do. The Romans, in their religious exercises, began with 'Hoc age' as we in ours do with 'Sursum corda'; these are so many words lost to me: I come already fully prepared from my chamber. I need no allurement, no invitation, no sauce; I eat the meat raw, so that, instead of whetting my appetite by these preparatives, they tire and pall it. Will the licence of the time excuse my sacrilegious boldness if I censure the dialogism of Plato himself as also dull and heavy, too much stifling the matter, and lament so much time lost by a man, who had so many better things to say, in so many long and needless preliminary interlocutions? My ignorance will better excuse me in that I understand not Greek so well as to discern the beauty of his language. I generally choose books that use sciences, not such as only lead to them. The two first, and Pliny, and their like, have nothing of this Hoc age; they will have to do with men already instructed; or if they have, it is a substantial Hoc age; and that has a body by itself. I also delight in reading the Epistles to Atticus, not only because they contain a great deal of the history and affairs of his time, but much more because I therein discover much of his own private humours; for I have a singular curiosity, as I have said elsewhere, to pry into the souls and the natural and true opinions of the authors, with whom I converse. A man may indeed judge of their parts, but not of their manners nor of themselves, by the writings they exhibit upon the theatre of the world. I have a thousand times lamented the loss of the treatise Brutus wrote upon Virtue, for it is well to learn the theory from those who best know the practice.

But seeing the matter preached and the preacher are different things, I would as willingly see Brutus in Plutarch, as in a book of his own. I would rather choose to be certainly informed of the conference he had in his tent with some particular friends of his the night before a battle, than of the harangue he made the next day to his army; and of what he did in his closet and his chamber, than what he did in the public square and in the senate. As to Cicero, I am of the common opinion that, learning excepted, he had no great natural excellence. He was a good citizen, of an affable nature, as all fat, heavy men, such as he was, usually are; but given to ease, and had, in truth, a mighty share of vanity and ambition. Neither do I know how to excuse him for thinking his poetry fit to be published; it is no great imperfection to make ill verses, but it is an imperfection not to be able to judge how unworthy his verses were of the glory of his name. For what concerns his eloquence, that is totally out of all comparison, and I believe it will never be equalled. The younger Cicero, who resembled his father in nothing but in name, whilst commanding in Asia, had several strangers one day at his table, and, amongst the rest, Cestius seated at the lower end, as men often intrude to the open tables of the great. Cicero asked one of his people who that man was, who presently told him his name; but he, as one who had his thoughts taken up with something else, and who had forgotten the answer made him, asking three or four times, over and over again; the same question, the fellow, to deliver himself from so many answers and to make him know him by some particular circumstance; "it is that Cestius," said he, "of whom it was told you, that he makes no great account of your father's eloquence in comparison of his own." At which Cicero, being suddenly nettled, commanded poor Cestius presently to be seized, and caused him to be very well whipped in his own presence; a very discourteous entertainer! Yet even amongst those, who, all things considered, have reputed his, eloquence incomparable, there have been some, who have not stuck to observe some faults in it: as that great Brutus his friend, for example, who said 'twas a broken and feeble eloquence, 'fyactam et elumbem'. The orators also, nearest to the age wherein he lived, reprehended in him the care he had of a certain long cadence in his periods, and particularly took notice of these words, 'essevideatur', which he there so often makes use of. For my part, I more approve of a shorter style, and that comes more roundly off. He does, though, sometimes shuffle his parts more briskly together, but it is very seldom. I have myself taken notice of this one passage:

> *Ego vero me minus diu senem mallem,*
> *Quam esse senem, antequam essem.*

[I had rather be old a brief time, than be old before old age.
—Cicero, *De Senectute*, c. 10.]

The historians are my right ball, for they are pleasant and easy, and where man, in general, the knowledge of whom I hunt after, appears more vividly and entire than anywhere else:

[The easiest of my amusements, the right ball at tennis being that which coming to the player from the right hand, is much easier played with.—Coste.]

the variety and truth of his internal qualities, in gross and piecemeal, the diversity of means by which he is united and knit, and the accidents that threaten him. Now those that write lives, by reason they insist more upon counsels than events, more upon what sallies from within, than upon what happens without, are the most proper for my reading; and, therefore, above all others, Plutarch is the man for me. I am very sorry we have not a dozen Laertii, [Diogenes Laertius, who wrote the Lives of the Philosophers] or that he was not further extended; for I am equally curious to know the lives and fortunes of these great instructors of the world, as to know the diversities of their doctrines and opinions. In this kind of study of histories, a man must tumble over, without distinction, all sorts of authors, old and new, French or foreign, there to know the things of which they variously treat. But Caesar, in my opinion, particularly deserves to be studied, not for the knowledge of the history only, but for himself, so great an excellence and perfection he has above all the rest, though Sallust be one of the number. In earnest, I read this author with more reverence and respect than is usually allowed to human writings; one while considering him in his person, by his actions and miraculous greatness, and another in the purity and inimitable polish of his language, wherein he not only excels all other historians, as Cicero confesses, but, peradventure, even Cicero himself; speaking of his enemies with so much sincerity in his judgment, that, the false colours with which he strives to palliate his evil cause, and the ordure of his pestilent ambition excepted, I think there is no fault to be objected against him, saving this, that he speaks too sparingly of himself, seeing so many great things could not have been performed under his conduct, but that his own personal acts must necessarily have had a greater share in them than he attributes to them.

I love historians, whether of the simple sort, or of the higher order. The simple, who have nothing of their own to mix with it, and who only make it their business to collect all that comes to their knowledge, and faithfully to record all things, without choice or discrimination, leave to us the entire judgment of discerning the truth. Such, for example, amongst others, is honest Froissart, who has proceeded in his undertaking with so frank a plainness that, having committed an error, he is not ashamed to confess and correct it in the place where the finger has been laid, and who represents to

246

us even the variety of rumours that were then spread abroad, and the different reports that were made to him; it is the naked and inform matter of history, and of which everyone may make his profit, according to his understanding. The more excellent sort of historians have judgment to pick out what is most worthy to be known; and, of two reports, to examine which is the most likely to be true: from the condition of princes and their humours, they conclude their counsels, and attribute to them words proper for the occasion; such have title to assume the authority of regulating our belief to what they themselves believe; but certainly, this privilege belongs to very few. For the middle sort of historians, of which the most part are, they spoil all; they will chew our meat for us; they take upon them to judge of, and consequently, to incline the history to their own fancy; for if the judgment lean to one side, a man cannot avoid wresting and writhing his narrative to that bias; they undertake to select things worthy to be known, and yet often conceal from us such a word, such a private action, as would much better instruct us; omit, as incredible, such things as they do not understand, and peradventure some, because they cannot express good French or Latin. Let them display their eloquence and intelligence, and judge according to their own fancy: but let them, withal, leave us something to judge of after them, and neither alter nor disguise, by their abridgments and at their own choice, anything of the substance of the matter, but deliver it to us pure and entire in all its dimensions.

For the most part, and especially in these latter ages, persons are culled out for this work from amongst the common people, upon the sole consideration of well-speaking, as if we were to learn grammar from them; and the men so chosen have fair reason, being hired for no other end and pretending to nothing but babble, not to be very solicitous of any part but that, and so, with a fine jingle of words, prepare us a pretty contexture of reports they pick up in the streets. The only good histories are those that have been written themselves who held command in the affairs whereof they write, or who participated in the conduct of them, or, at least, who have had the conduct of others of the same nature. Such are almost all the Greek and Roman histories: for, several eye-witnesses having written of the same subject, in the time when grandeur and learning commonly met in the same person, if there happen to be an error, it must of necessity be a very slight one, and upon a very doubtful incident. What can a man expect from a physician who writes of war, or from a mere scholar, treating of the designs of princes? If we could take notice how scrupulous the Romans were in this, there would need but this example: Asinius Pollio found in the histories of Caesar himself something misreported, a mistake occasioned; either by reason he could not have his eye in all parts of his army at once and had given credit to some individual persons who had not delivered him a very true account; or else, for not having had too perfect notice given him by his lieutenants of what they had done in his absence. [Suetonius, *Life of Caesar*, c. 56.] By which we may see, whether the inquisition after truth be not very delicate, when a man cannot believe the report of a battle from the knowledge of him who there commanded, nor from the soldiers who were engaged in it, unless, after the method of a judicial inquiry, the witnesses be confronted and objections considered upon the proof of the least detail of every incident. In good earnest the knowledge we have of our own affairs, is much more obscure: but that has been sufficiently handled by Bodin, and according to my own sentiment [In the work by Jean Bodin, entitled "Methodus ad facilem historianum cognitionem." 1566.] A little to aid the weakness of my memory (so extreme that it has happened to me more than once, to take books again into my hand as new and unseen, that I had carefully read over a few years before, and scribbled with my notes) I have adopted a custom of late, to note at the end of every book (that is, of those I never intend to read again) the time when I made an end on't, and the judgment I had made of it, to the end that this might, at least, represent to me the character and general idea I had conceived of the author in reading it; and I will here transcribe some of those annotations.

CHAPTER 10

I wrote this, some ten years ago, in my Guicciardini (of what language soever my books speak to me in, I always speak to them in my own): "He is a diligent historiographer, from whom, in my opinion, a man may learn the truth of the affairs of his time, as exactly as from any other; in the most of which he was himself also a personal actor, and in honourable command. There is no appearance that he disguised anything, either upon the account of hatred, favour, or vanity; of which the free censures he passes upon the great ones, and particularly those by whom he was advanced and employed in commands of great trust and honour, as Pope Clement VII., give ample testimony. As to that part which he thinks himself the best at, namely, his digressions and discourses, he has indeed some very good, and enriched with fine features; but he is too fond of them: for, to leave nothing unsaid, having a subject so full, ample, almost infinite, he degenerates into pedantry and smacks a little of scholastic prattle. I have also observed this in him, that of so many souls and so many effects, so many motives and so many counsels as he judges, he never attributes any one to virtue, religion, or conscience, as if all these were utterly extinct in the world: and of all the actions, how brave soever in outward show they appear in themselves, he always refers the cause and motive to some vicious occasion or some prospect of profit. It is impossible to imagine but that, amongst such an infinite number of actions as he makes mention of, there must be someone produced by the way of honest reason. No corruption could so universally have infected men that someone would not escape the contagion which makes me suspect that his own taste was vicious, whence it might happen that he judged other men by himself."

In my Philip de Commines there is this written: "You will here find the language sweet and delightful, of a natural simplicity, the narration pure, with the good faith of the author conspicuous therein; free from vanity, when speaking of himself, and from affection or envy, when speaking of others: his discourses and exhortations rather accompanied with zeal and truth, than with any exquisite sufficiency; and, throughout, authority and gravity, which bespeak him a man of good extraction, and brought up in great affairs."

Upon the Memoirs of Monsieur du Bellay I find this: "It is always pleasant to read things written by those that have experienced how they ought to be carried on; but withal, it cannot be denied but there is a manifest decadence in these two lords [Martin du Bellay and Guillaume de Langey, brothers, who jointly wrote the Memoirs.] from the freedom and liberty of writing that shine in the elder historians, such as the Sire de Joinville, the familiar companion of St. Louis; Eginhard, chancellor to Charlemagne; and of later date, Philip de Commines. What we have here is rather an apology for King Francis, against the Emperor Charles V., than history. I will not believe that they have falsified anything, as to matter of fact; but they make a common practice of twisting the judgment of events, very often contrary to reason, to our advantage, and of omitting whatsoever is ticklish to be handled in the life of their master; witness the proceedings of Messieurs de Montmorency and de Biron, which are here omitted: nay, so much as the very name of Madame d'Estampes is not here to be found. Secret actions an historian may conceal; but to pass over in silence what all the world knows and things that have drawn after them public and such high consequences, is an inexcusable defect. In fine, whoever has a mind to have a perfect knowledge of King Francis and the events of his reign, let him seek it elsewhere, if my advice may prevail. The only profit a man can reap from these Memoirs is in the special narrative of battles and other exploits of war wherein these gentlemen were personally engaged; in some words and private actions of the princes of their time, and in the treaties and negotiations carried on by the Seigneur de Langey, where there are everywhere things worthy to be known, and discourses above the vulgar strain."

11

ON CRUELTY

I fancy virtue to be something else, and something more noble, than good nature, and the mere propension to goodness, that we are born into the world withal. Well-disposed and well-descended souls pursue, indeed, the same methods, and represent in their actions the same face that virtue itself does: but the word virtue imports, I know not what, more great and active than merely for a man to suffer himself, by a happy disposition, to be gently and quietly drawn to the rule of reason. He who, by a natural sweetness and facility, should despise injuries received, would doubtless do a very fine and laudable thing; but he who, provoked and nettled to the quick by an offence, should fortify himself with the arms of reason against the furious appetite of revenge, and after a great conflict, master his own passion, would certainly do a great deal more. The first would do well; the latter virtuously: one action might be called goodness, and the other virtue; for methinks, the very name of virtue presupposes difficulty and contention, and cannot be exercised without an opponent. It is for this reason, perhaps, that we call God good, mighty, liberal and just; but we do not call Him virtuous, being that all His operations are natural and without endeavour. [Rousseau, in his *Emile*, book v., adopts this passage almost in the same words.] It has been the opinion of many philosophers, not only Stoics, but Epicureans.

I borrow from the vulgar opinion, which is false, notwithstanding the witty conceit of Arcesilaus in answer to one, who, being reproached that many scholars went from his school to the Epicurean, but never any from thence to his school, said in answer, "I believe it indeed; numbers of capons being made out of cocks, but never any cocks out of capons." [Diogenes Laertius, Life of Archesilaus, lib. iv., 43.] For, in truth, the Epicurean sect is not at all inferior to the Stoic in steadiness, and the rigour of opinions and precepts. And a certain Stoic, showing more honesty than those disputants, who, in order to quarrel with Epicurus, and to throw the game into their hands, make him say what he never thought, putting a wrong construction upon his words, clothing his sentences, by the strict rules of grammar, with another meaning, and a different opinion from that which they knew he entertained in his mind and in his morals, the Stoic, I say, declared that he abandoned the Epicurean sect, upon this among other considerations, that he thought their road too lofty and inaccessible;

> *[And those are called lovers of pleasure, being in effect*
> *lovers of honour and justice, who cultivate and observe all*
> *the virtues.*
>
> —Cicero, *Epistulae ad Familiares,* xv. i, 19.]

These philosophers say that it is not enough to have the soul seated in a good place, of a good temper, and well disposed to virtue; it is not enough to have our resolutions and our reasoning fixed above all the power of fortune, but that we are, moreover, to seek occasions wherein to put them to the proof: they would seek pain, necessity, and contempt to contend with them and to keep the soul in breath:

> *Multum sibi adjicit virtus lacessita.*

> [Virtue is much strengthened by combats. or: Virtue attacked adds to its own force.
>
> –Seneca, *Epistles,* 13.]

Chapter 11

It is one of the reasons why Epaminondas, who was yet of a third sect, [The Pythagorean] refused the riches fortune presented to him by very lawful means; because, said he, I am to contend with poverty, in which extreme he maintained himself to the last. Socrates put himself, methinks, upon a ruder trial, keeping for his exercise a confounded scolding wife, which was fighting at sharps. Metellus having, of all the Roman senators, alone attempted, by the power of virtue, to withstand the violence of Saturninus, tribune of the people at Rome, who would, by all means, cause an unjust law to pass in favour of the commons, and, by so doing, having incurred the capital penalties that Saturninus had established against the dissentient, entertained those who, in this extremity, led him to execution with words to this effect: That it was a thing too easy and too base to do ill; and that to do well where there was no danger was a common thing; but that to do well where there was danger was the proper office of a man of virtue. These words of Metellus very clearly represent to us what I would make out, viz., that virtue refuses facility for a companion; and that the easy, smooth, and descending way by which the regular steps of a sweet disposition of nature are conducted is not that of a true virtue; she requires a rough and stormy passage; she will have either exotic difficulties to wrestle with, like that of Metellus, by means whereof fortune delights to interrupt the speed of her career, or internal difficulties, that the inordinate appetites and imperfections of our condition introduce to disturb her.

I am come thus far at my ease; but here it comes into my head that the soul of Socrates, the most perfect that ever came to my knowledge, should by this rule be of very little recommendation; for I cannot conceive in that person any the least motion of a vicious inclination: I cannot imagine there could be any difficulty or constraint in the course of his virtue: I know his reason to be so powerful and sovereign over him that she would never have suffered a vicious appetite so much as to spring in him. To a virtue so elevated as his, I have nothing to oppose. Methinks I see him march, with a victorious and triumphant pace, in pomp and at his ease, without opposition or disturbance. If virtue cannot shine bright, but by the conflict of contrary appetites, shall we then say that she cannot subsist without the assistance of vice, and that it is from her that she derives her reputation and honour? What then, also, would become of that brave and generous Epicurean pleasure, which makes account that it nourishes virtue tenderly in her lap, and there makes it play and wanton, giving it for toys to play withal, shame, fevers, poverty, death, and torments? If I presuppose that a perfect virtue manifests itself in contending, in patient enduring of pain, and undergoing the uttermost extremity of the gout; without being moved in her seat; if I give her troubles and difficulty for her necessary objects: what will become of a virtue elevated to such a degree, as not only to despise pain, but, moreover, to rejoice in it, and to be tickled with the throes of a sharp colic, such as the Epicureans have established, and of which many of them, by their actions, have given most manifest proofs? As have several others, who I find to have surpassed in effects even the very rules of their discipline. Witness the younger Cato: When I see him die, and tearing out his own bowels, I am not satisfied simply to believe that he had then his soul totally exempt from all trouble and horror: I cannot think that he only maintained himself in the steadiness that the Stoical rules prescribed him; temperate, without emotion, and imperturbed. There was, methinks, something in the virtue of this man too sprightly and fresh to stop there; I believe that, without doubt, he felt a pleasure and delight in so noble an action, and was more pleased in it than in any other of his life:

Sic abiit a vita, ut causam moriendi nactum se esse gauderet.

[He quitted life rejoicing that a reason for dying had arisen.
——Cicero, *Tusculum Disputations*, i. 30.]

I believe it so thoroughly that I question whether he would have been content to have been deprived of the occasion of so

CHAPTER 11

brave an exploit; and if the goodness that made him embrace the public concern more than his own, withheld me not, I should easily fall into an opinion that he thought himself obliged to fortune for having put his virtue upon so brave a trial, and for having favoured that theif [Caesar] in treading underfoot the ancient liberty of his country. Methinks I read in this action I know not what exaltation in his soul, and an extraordinary and manly emotion of pleasure, when he looked upon the generosity and height of his enterprise:

> *Deliberate morte ferocior,*

[The more courageous from the deliberation to die.
—Horace, *Odes*, i. 37, 29.]

not stimulated with any hope of glory, as the popular and effeminate judgments of some have concluded (for that consideration was too mean and low to possess so generous, so haughty, and so determined a heart as his), but for the very beauty of the thing in itself, which he who had the handling of the springs discerned more clearly and in its perfection than we are able to do. Philosophy has obliged me in determining that so brave an action had been indecently placed in any other life than that of Cato; and that it only appertained to his to end so; notwithstanding, and according to reason, he commanded his son and the senators who accompanied him to take another course in their affairs:

> *Catoni, quum incredibilem natura tribuisset gravitatem,*
> *eamque ipse perpetue constantia roboravisset, semperque*
> *in proposito consilio permansisset, moriendum potius,*
> *quam tyranni vultus aspiciendus, erat.*

[Cato, whom nature had given incredible dignity, which he had fortified by perpetual constancy, ever remaining of his predetermined opinion, preferred to die rather than to look on the countenance of a tyrant.

—Cicero, *De Officius*, i. 31.]

Every death ought to hold proportion with the life before it; we do not become others for dying. I always interpret the death by the life preceding; and if anyone tell me of a death strong and constant in appearance, annexed to a feeble life, I conclude it produced by some feeble cause, and suitable to the life before. The easiness then of his death and the facility of dying he had acquired by the vigour of his soul; shall we say that it ought to abate anything of the lustre of his virtue? And who, that has his brain never so little tinctured with the true philosophy, can be content to imagine Socrates only free from fear and passion in the accident of his prison, fetters, and condemnation? and that will not discover in him not only firmness and constancy (which was his ordinary condition), but, moreover, I know not what new satisfaction, and a frolic cheerfulness in his last words and actions? In the start he gave with the pleasure of scratching his leg when his irons were taken off, does he not discover an equal serenity and joy in his soul for being freed from past inconveniences, and at the same time to enter into the knowledge of the things to come? Cato shall pardon me, if he please; his death indeed is more tragical and more lingering; but yet this is, I know not how, methinks, finer. Aristippus, to one that was lamenting this death: "The gods grant me such an one," said he. A man discerns in the soul of these two great men and their imitators (for I very much doubt whether there were ever their equals) so perfect a habitude to virtue, that it was turned to a complexion. It is no longer a laborious virtue, nor the precepts of reason, to maintain which the soul is so racked, but the very essence of their soul, its natural and ordinary habit; they have rendered it such by a long practice of philosophical precepts having lit upon a rich and fine nature; the vicious passions that spring in us can find no entrance into them; the force and vigour of their soul stifle and extinguish irregular desires, so soon as they begin to move.

CHAPTER 11

Now, that it is not more noble, by a high and divine resolution, to hinder the birth of temptations, and to be so formed to virtue, that the very seeds of vice are rooted out, than to hinder by main force their progress; and, having suffered ourselves to be surprised with the first motions of the passions, to arm ourselves and to stand firm to oppose their progress, and overcome them; and that this second effect is not also much more generous than to be simply endowed with a facile and affable nature, of itself disaffected to debauchery and vice, I do not think can be doubted; for this third and last sort of virtue seems to render a man innocent, but not virtuous; free from doing ill, but not apt enough to do well: considering also, that this condition is so near neighbour to imperfection and cowardice, that I know not very well how to separate the confines and distinguish them: the very names of goodness and innocence are, for this reason, in some sort grown into contempt. I very well know that several virtues, as chastity, sobriety, and temperance, may come to a man through personal defects. Constancy in danger, if it must be so called, the contempt of death, and patience in misfortunes, may ofttimes be found in men for want of well judging of such accidents, and not apprehending them for such as they are. Want of apprehension and stupidity sometimes counterfeit virtuous effects as I have often seen it happen, that men have been commended for what really merited blame. An Italian lord once said this, in my presence, to the disadvantage of his own nation: that the subtlety of the Italians, and the vivacity of their conceptions were so great, and they foresaw the dangers and accidents that might befall them so far off, that it was not to be thought strange, if they were often, in war, observed to provide for their safety, even before they had discovered the peril; that we French and the Spaniards, who were not so cunning, went on further, and that we must be made to see and feel the danger before we would take the alarm; but that even then we could not stick to it. But the Germans and Swiss, more gross and heavy, had not the sense to look about them, even when the blows were falling about their ears. Peradventure, he only talked so for mirth's sake;

and yet it is most certain that in war raw soldiers rush into dangers with more precipitancy than after they have been cudgelled:

> *Haud ignarus . . . . quantum nova gloria in armis,*
> *Et praedulce decus, primo certamine possit.*

[Not ignorant how much power the fresh glory of arms and sweetest honour possess in the first contest.

—*Aeneid*, xi. 154.]

For this reason it is that, when we judge of a particular action, we are to consider the circumstances, and the whole man by whom it is performed, before we give it a name.

To instance in myself: I have sometimes known my friends call that prudence in me, which was merely fortune; and repute that courage and patience, which was judgment and opinion; and attribute to me one title for another, sometimes to my advantage and sometimes otherwise. As to the rest, I am so far from being arrived at the first and most perfect degree of excellence, where virtue is turned into habit, that even of the second I have made no great proofs. I have not been very solicitous to curb the desires by which I have been importuned. My virtue is a virtue, or rather an innocence, casual and accidental. If I had been born of a more irregular complexion, I am afraid I should have made scurvy work; for I never observed any great stability in my soul to resist passions, if they were never so little vehement: I know not how to nourish quarrels and debates in my own bosom, and, consequently, owe myself no great thanks that I am free from several vices:

> *Si vitiis mediocribus et mea paucis*
> *Mendosa est natura, alioqui recta, velut si*
> *Egregio inspersos reprehendas corpore naevos:*

CHAPTER 11

[If my nature be disfigured only with slight and few vices, and is
otherwise just, it is as if you should blame moles on a fair body.
—Horatius, *Satire*, i. 6, 65.]

I owe it rather to my fortune than my reason. She has caused me
to be descended of a race famous for integrity and of a very good
father; I know not whether or no he has infused into me part of his
humours, or whether domestic examples and the good education
of my infancy have insensibly assisted in the work, or, if I was otherwise born so:

> *Seu Libra, seu me Scorpius adspicit*
> *Formidolosus, pars violentior*
> *Natalis hors, seutyrannus*
> *Hesperive Capricornus undae:*

[Whether the Balance or dread Scorpio, more potent over my
natal hour, aspects me, or Capricorn, supreme over the
Hesperian sea.
—Horace, *Odes*, ii. 117.]

but so it is, that I have naturally a horror for most vices. The answer
of Antisthenes to him who asked him, which was the best apprenticeship "to unlearn evil," seems to point at this. I have them in horror,
I say, with a detestation so natural, and so much my own, that the
same instinct and impression I brought of them with me from my
nurse, I yet retain, and no temptation whatever has had the power
to make me alter it. Not so much as my own discourses, which in
some things lashing out of the common road might seem easily to
license me to actions that my natural inclination makes me hate.
I will say a prodigious thing, but I will say it, however: I find myself
in many things more under reputation by my manners than by my
opinion, and my concupiscence less debauched than my reason.
Aristippus instituted opinions so bold in favour of pleasure and

riches as set all the philosophers against him: but as to his manners, Dionysius the tyrant, having presented three beautiful women before him, to take his choice; he made answer, that he would choose them all, and that Paris got himself into trouble for having preferred one before the other two: but, having taken them home to his house, he sent them back untouched. His servant finding himself overladen upon the way, with the money he carried after him, he ordered him to pour out and throw away that which troubled him. And Epicurus, whose doctrines were so irreligious and effeminate, was in his life very laborious and devout; he wrote to a friend of his that he lived only upon biscuit and water, entreating him to send him a little cheese, to lie by him against he had a mind to make a feast. Must it be true, that to be a perfect good man, we must be so by an occult, natural, and universal propriety, without law, reason, or example? The debauches wherein I have been engaged, have not been, I thank God, of the worst sort, and I have condemned them in myself, for my judgment was never infected by them; on the contrary, I accuse them more severely in myself than in any other; but that is all, for, as to the rest. I oppose too little resistance and suffer myself to incline too much to the other side of the balance, excepting that I moderate them, and prevent them from mixing with other vices, which for the most part will cling together, if a man have not a care. I have contracted and curtailed mine, to make them as single and as simple as I can:

> *Nec ultra*
> *Erroremfoveo.*

[Nor do I cherish error further. or: Nor carry wrong further.
—Juvenal, viii. 164.]

For as to the opinion of the Stoics, who say, "That the wise man when he works, works by all the virtues together, though one be most apparent, according to the nature of the action"; and herein the similitude of a human body might serve them somewhat, for the action of anger cannot work, unless all the humours assist it, though choler predominate; – if they will thence draw a like consequence, that when the wicked man does wickedly, he does it by all the vices together, I do not believe it to be so, or else I understand them not, for I by effect find the contrary. These are sharp, unsubstantial subleties, with which philosophy sometimes amuses itself. I follow some vices, but I fly others as much as a saint would do. The Peripatetics also disown this indissoluble connection; and Aristotle is of opinion that a prudent and just man may be intemperate and inconsistent. Socrates confessed to some who had discovered a certain inclination to vice in his physiognomy, that it was, in truth, his natural propension, but that he had by discipline corrected it. And such as were familiar with the philosopher Stilpo said, that being born with addiction to wine and women, he had by study rendered himself very abstinent both from the one and the other.

What I have in me of good, I have, quite contrary, by the chance of my birth; and hold it not either by law, precept, or any other instruction; the innocence that is in me is a simple one; little vigour and no art. Amongst other vices, I mortally hate cruelty, both by nature and judgment, as the very extreme of all vices: nay, with so much tenderness that I cannot see a chicken's neck pulled off without trouble, and cannot without impatience endure the cry of a hare in my dog's teeth, though the chase be a violent pleasure. Such as have sensuality to encounter, freely make use of this argument, to show that it is altogether "vicious and unreasonable; that when it is at the height, it masters us to that degree that a man's reason can have no access," and instance our own experience in the act of love,

> *Quum jam praesagit gaudia corpus,*
> *Atque in eo est Venus,*
> *ut muliebria conserat arva.*

wherein they conceive that the pleasure so transports us, that our reason cannot perform its office, whilst we are in such ecstasy and rapture. I know very well it may be otherwise, and that a man may sometimes, if he will, gain this point over himself to sway his soul, even in the critical moment, to think of something else; but then he must ply it to that bent. I know that a man may triumph over the utmost effort of this pleasure: I have experienced it in myself, and have not found Venus so imperious a goddess, as many, and much more virtuous men than I, declare. I do not consider it a miracle, as the Queen of Navarre does in one of the Tales of her Heptameron ["Vu gentil liure pour son estoffe."] (which is a very pretty book of its kind), nor for a thing of extreme difficulty, to pass whole nights, where a man has all the convenience and liberty he can desire, with a long-coveted mistress, and yet be true to the pledge first given to satisfy himself with kisses and suchlike endearments, without pressing any further. I conceive that the example of the pleasure of the chase would be more proper; wherein though the pleasure be less, there is the higher excitement of unexpected joy, giving no time for the reason, taken by surprise, to prepare itself for the encounter, when after a long quest the beast starts up on a sudden in a place where, peradventure, we least expected it; the shock and the ardour of the shouts and cries of the hunters so strike us, that it would be hard for those who love this lesser chase, to turn their thoughts upon the instant another way; and the poets make Diana triumph over the torch and shafts of Cupid:

> *Quis non malarum, quas amor curas habet,*
> *Haec inter obliviscitur?*

[Who, amongst such delights would not remove out of his thoughts the anxious cares of love?

—Horace, *Epodes*, ii. 37.]

To return to what I was saying before, I am tenderly compassion-ate of others' afflictions, and should readily cry for company, if, upon any occasion whatever, I could cry at all. Nothing tempts my tears but tears, and not only those that are real and true, but whatever they are, feigned or painted. I do not much lament the dead, and should envy them rather; but I very much lament the dying. The savages do not so much offend me, in roasting and eating the bodies of the dead, as they do who torment and persecute the living. Nay, I cannot look so much as upon the ordinary executions of justice, how reasonable soever, with a steady eye. Someone having to give testimony of Julius Caesar's clemency; "he was," says he, "mild in his revenges. Having compelled the pirates to yield by whom he had before been taken prisoner and put to ransom; forasmuch as he had threatened them with the cross, he indeed condemned them to it, but it was after they had been first strangled. He punished his secretary Philemon, who had attempted to poison him, with no greater severity than mere death." Without naming that Latin author, [Suetonius, *Life of Casay*, c. 74.] who thus dares to allege as a testimony of mercy the killing only of those by whom we have been offended; it is easy to guess that he was struck with the horrid and inhuman examples of cruelty practised by the Roman tyrants.

For my part, even in justice itself, all that exceeds a simple death appears to me pure cruelty; especially in us who ought, having regard to their souls, to dismiss them in a good and calm condition; which cannot be, when we have agitated them by insufferable torments. Not long since, a soldier who was a prisoner, perceiving from a tower where he was shut up, that the people began to assemble to the place of execution, and that the carpenters were busy erecting a scaffold, he presently concluded that the preparation was for him, and therefore entered into a resolution to kill himself, but could find no instrument to assist him in his design except an old rusty cart-nail that fortune presented to him; with this he first gave himself two great wounds about his throat, but finding these would not do, he presently after-wards gave himself a third in the belly, where he left the nail sticking up to the head. The first of his keepers who came in found him in this condition: yet alive, but sunk down and exhausted by his wounds. To make use of time, therefore, before he should die, they made haste to read his sentence; which having done, and he hearing that he was only condemned to be beheaded, he seemed to take new courage, accepted wine which he had before refused, and thanked his judges for the unhoped-for mildness of their sentence; saying, that he had taken a resolution to despatch himself for fear of a more severe and insupportable death, having entertained an opinion, by the prepara-tions he had seen in the place, that they were resolved to torment him with some horrible execution, and seemed to be delivered from death in having it changed from what he apprehended.

I should advise that those examples of severity by which it is designed to retain the people in their duty, might be exercised upon the dead bodies of criminals; for to see them deprived of sepulture, to see them boiled and divided into quarters, would almost work as much upon the vulgar, as the pain they make the living endure; though that in effect be little or nothing, as God himself says, "Who kill the body, and after that have no more that they can do;" [Luke, xii. 4.] and the poets singularly dwell upon the horrors of this pic-ture, as something worse than death:

> *Heu! reliquias semiustas regis, denudates ossibus,*
> *Per terram sanie delibutas foede divexarier.*

[Alas! that the half-burnt remains of the king, exposing his bones, should be foully dragged along the ground besmeared with gore.
—Cicero, *Tusculum Disputations*, i. 44.]

I happened to come by one day accidentally at Rome, just as they were upon executing Catena, a notorious robber: he was strangled without any emotion of the spectators, but when they came to cut him in quarters, the hangman gave not a blow that the people did not follow with a doleful cry and exclamation, as if everyone had lent his sense of feeling to the miserable carcase. Those inhuman excesses ought to be exercised upon the bark, and not upon the quick. Artaxerxes, in almost a like case, moderated the severity of the ancient laws of Persia, ordaining that the nobility who had committed a fault, instead of being whipped, as they were used to be, should be stripped only and their clothes whipped for them; and that whereas they were wont to tear off their hair, they should only take off their high-crowned tiara.' [Plutarch, Notable Sayings of the Ancient King.] The so devout Egyptians thought they sufficiently satisfied the divine justice by sacrificing hogs in effigy and representation; a bold invention to pay God so essential a substance in picture only and in show.

I live in a time wherein we abound in incredible examples of this vice, through the licence of our civil wars; and we see nothing in ancient histories more extreme than what we have proof of every day, but I cannot, any the more, get used to it. I could hardly persuade myself, before I saw it with my eyes, that there could be found souls so cruel and fell, who, for the sole pleasure of murder, would commit it; would hack and lop off the limbs of others; sharpen their wits to invent unusual torments and new kinds of death, without hatred, without profit, and for no other end but only to enjoy the pleasant spectacle of the gestures and motions, the lamentable groans and cries of a man dying in anguish. For this is the utmost point to which cruelty can arrive:

> *Ut homo hominem, non iratus, non timens,*
> *tantum spectaturus, occidat.*

[That a man should kill a man, not being angry, not in fear, only for the sake of the spectacle.

—Seneca, *Epistles*, 90.]

For my own part, I cannot without grief see so much as an innocent beast pursued and killed that has no defence, and from which we have received no offence at all; and that which frequently happens, that the stag we hunt, finding himself weak and out of breath, and seeing no other remedy, surrenders himself to us who pursue him, imploring mercy by his tears:

> *Questuque cruentus,*
> *Atque imploranti similis,*

[Who, bleeding, by his tears seems to crave mercy.
>   —*Aeneid*, vii. 501.]

has ever been to me a very unpleasing sight; and I hardly ever take a beast alive that I do not presently turn out again. Pythagoras bought them of fishermen and fowlers to do the same:

> *Primoque a caede ferarum,*
> *Incaluisse puto maculatum sanguine ferrum.*

[I think 'twas slaughter of wild beasts that first stained the steel of man with blood.
>   —Ovid, *Metamorphoses*, xv. 106.]

Those natures that are sanguinary towards beasts discover a natural proneness to cruelty. After they had accustomed themselves at Rome to spectacles of the slaughter of animals, they proceeded to those of the slaughter of men, of gladiators. Nature has herself, I fear, imprinted in man a kind of instinct to inhumanity; nobody takes pleasure in seeing beasts play with and caress one another, but everyone is delighted with seeing them dismember, and tear one another to pieces. And that I may not be laughed at for the sympathy I have with them, theology itself enjoins us some favour in their behalf; and considering that one and the same master has lodged us together in this palace for his service, and that they, as well as we, are of his family, it has reason to enjoin us some affection and regard to them. Pythagoras borrowed the metempsychosis from the Egyptians; but it has since been received by several nations, and particularly by our Druids:

> *Morte carent animae; semperque, priore relicts*
> *Sede, novis domibus vivunt, habitantque receptae.*

[Souls never die, but, having left their former seat, live
  and are received into new homes.
  —Ovid, *Metamorphoses*, xv. 158.]

The religion of our ancient Gauls maintained that souls, being eternal, never ceased to remove and shift their places from one body to another; mixing moreover with this fancy some consideration of divine justice; for according to the deportments of the soul, whilst it had been in Alexander, they said that God assigned it another body to inhabit, more or less painful, and proper for its condition:

> *Muta ferarum*
> *Cogit vincla pati; truculentos ingerit ursis,*
> *Praedonesque lupis; fallaces vulpibus addit:*
> *Atque ubi per varios annos, per mille figuras*
>
> *Egit, Lethaeo purgatos flumine, tandem*
> *Rursus ad humanae revocat primordia formae:*

[He makes them wear the silent chains of brutes, the bloodthirsty souls he encloses in bears, the thieves in wolves, the deceivers in foxes; where, after successive years and a thousand forms, man had spent his life, and after purgation in Lethe's flood, at last he restores them to the primordial human shapes.
  —Claudian, *In Rufinum*, ii. 482.]

If it had been valiant, he lodged it in the body of a lion; if voluptuous, in that of a hog; if timorous, in that of a hart or hare; if malicious, in that of a fox, and so of the rest, till having purified it by this chastisement, it again entered into the body of some other man:

> *Ipse ego nam memini, Trojani, tempore belli*
> *Panthoides Euphorbus eram.*

[For I myself remember that, in the days of the Trojan war, I was Euphorbus, son of Pantheus.

—Ovid, *Metamorphoses*, xv. 160; and see
Diogenes Laertius, *Life of Pythagoras*.]

As to the relationship between us and beasts, I do not much admit of it; nor of that which several nations, and those among the most ancient and most noble, have practised, who have not only received brutes into their society and companionship, but have given them a rank infinitely above themselves, esteeming them one while familiars and favourites of the gods, and having them in more than human reverence and respect; others acknowledged no other god or divinity than they:

> *Bellux a barbaris propter beneficium consecratae.*

[Beasts, out of opinion of some benefit received by them, were consecrated by barbarians

—Cicero, *De Natura Deorum*, i. 36.]

> *Crocodilon adorat*
> *Pars haec; illa pavet saturam serpentibus ibin:*
> *Effigies sacri hic nitet aurea cercopitheci;*
> *Hic piscem flumints, illic*
> *Oppida tota canem venerantur.*

CHAPTER 11

[This place adores the crocodile; another dreads the ibis, feeder on serpents; here shines the golden image of the sacred ape; here men venerate the fish of the river; there whole towns worship a dog.

—Juvenal, xv. 2.]

And the very interpretation that Plutarch, gives to this error, which is very well conceived, is advantageous to them: for he says that it was not the cat or the ox, for example, that the Egyptians adored: but that they, in those beasts, adored some image of the divine faculties; in this, patience and utility: in that, vivacity, or, as with our neighbours the Burgundians and all the Germans, impatience to see themselves shut up; by which they represented liberty, which they loved and adored above all other godlike attributes, and so of the rest. But when, amongst the more moderate opinions, I meet with arguments that endeavour to demonstrate the near resemblance between us and animals, how large a share they have in our greatest privileges, and with how much probability they compare us together, truly I abate a great deal of our presumption, and willingly resign that imaginary sovereignty that is attributed to us over other creatures.

But supposing all this were not true, there is nevertheless a certain respect, a general duty of humanity, not only to beasts that have life and sense, but even to trees, and plants. We owe justice to men, and graciousness and benignity to other creatures that are capable of it; there is a certain commerce and mutual obligation between them and us. Nor shall I be afraid to confess the tenderness of my nature so childish, that I cannot well refuse to play with my dog, when he the most unseasonably importunes me to do so. The Turks have alms and hospitals for beasts. The Romans had public care to the nourishment of geese, by whose vigilance their Capitol had been preserved. The Athenians made a decree that the mules and moyls which had served at the building of the temple called Hecatompedon should be free and suffered to pasture at their own choice, without hindrance. The Agrigentines had a common use solemnly to inter the beasts they had a kindness for, as horses of some rare quality, dogs, and useful birds, and even those that had only been kept to divert their children; and the magnificence that was ordinary with them in all other things, also particularly appeared in the sumptuosity and numbers of monuments erected to this end, and which remained in their beauty several ages after. The Egyptians buried wolves, bears, crocodiles, dogs, and cats in sacred places, embalmed their bodies, and put on mourning at their death. Cimon gave an honourable sepulture to the mares with which he had three times gained the prize of the course at the Olympic Games. The ancient Xantippus caused his dog to be interred on an eminence near the sea, which has ever since retained the name, and Plutarch says, that he had a scruple about selling for a small profit to the slaughterer an ox that had been long in his service.

18

ON GIVING THE LIE

Well, but someone will say to me, this design of making a man's self the subject of his writing, were indeed excusable in rare and famous men, who by their reputation had given others a curiosity to be fully informed of them. It is most true, I confess and know very well, that a mechanic will scarce lift his eyes from his work to look at an ordinary man, whereas a man will forsake his business and his shop to stare at an eminent person when he comes into a town. It misbecomes any other to give his own character, but him who has qualities worthy of imitation, and whose life and opinions may serve for example: Caesar and Xenophon had a just and solid foundation whereon to found their narrations, the greatness of their own performances; and were to be wished that we had the journals of Alexander the Great, the commentaries that Augustus, Cato, Sylla, Brutus, and others left of their actions; of such persons men love and contemplate the very statues even in copper and marble. This remonstrance is very true; but it very little concerns me:

Non recito cuiquam, nisi amicis, idque coactus;
Non ubivis, coramve quibuslibet, in medio qui
Scripta foro recitant, sunt multi, quique lavantes.

[I repeat my poems only to my friends, and when bound to do so; not before everyone and everywhere; there are plenty of reciters in the open market-place and at the baths.

—Horace, *Satire.* i. 4, 73.]

I do not here form a statue to erect in the great square of a city, in a church, or any public place:

Non equidem hoc studeo, bullatisut mihi nugis,
Pagina turgescat......
Secreti loquimur:

[I study not to make my pages swell with empty trifles; you and I are talking in private.

—Persius, *Satire*, v. 19.]

it is for some corner of a library, or to entertain a neighbour, a kinsman, a friend, who has a mind to renew his acquaintance and familiarity with me in this image of myself. Others have been encouraged to speak of themselves, because they found the subject worthy and rich; I, on the contrary, am the bolder, by reason the subject is so poor and sterile that I cannot be suspected of ostentation. I judge freely of the actions of others; I give little of my own to judge of, because they are nothing: I do not find so much good in myself, that I cannot tell it without blushing.

What contentment would it not be to me to hear any one thus relate to me the manners, faces, countenances, the ordinary words and fortunes of my ancestors? how attentively should I listen to it! In earnest, it would be evil nature to despise so much as the pictures of our friends and predecessors, the fashion of their clothes and arms. I preserve their writing, seal, and a particular sword they wore, and have not thrown the long staves my father used to carry in his hand, out of my closet.

Paterna vestis, et annulus, tanto charior est
posteris, quanto erga parentes major affectus.

Chapter 18

[A father's garment and ring is by so much dearer to his posterity, as there is the greater affection towards parents.
—St. Augustine, *De Civitat Dei*, i. 13.]

If my posterity, nevertheless, shall be of another mind, I shall be avenged on them; for they cannot care less for me than I shall then do for them. All the traffic that I have in this with the public is, that I borrow their utensils of writing, which are more easy and most at hand; and in recompense shall, peradventure, keep a pound of butter in the market from melting in the sun: [Montaigne semi-seriously speculates on the possibility of his MS. being used to wrap up butter.]

> *Ne toga cordyllis, ne penula desit olivis;*
> *Et laxas scombris saepe dabo tunicas;*

[Let not wrappers be wanting to tunny-fish, nor olives; and I shall supply loose coverings to mackerel.
—Martial, xiii. I, I.]

And though nobody should read me, have I wasted time in entertaining myself so many idle hours in so pleasing and useful thoughts? In moulding this figure upon myself, I have been so often constrained to temper and compose myself in a right posture, that the copy is truly taken, and has in some sort formed itself; painting myself for others, I represent myself in a better colouring than my own natural complexion. I have no more made my book than my book has made me: it is a book consubstantial with the author, of a peculiar design, a parcel of my life, and whose business is not designed for others, as that of all other books is. In giving myself so continual and so exact an account of myself, have I lost my time? For they who sometimes cursorily survey themselves only, do not so strictly examine themselves, nor penetrate so deep, as he who makes it his business, his study, and his employment, who intends a lasting record, with all his fidelity, and with all his force: The most delicious

273

pleasures digested within, avoid leaving any trace of themselves, and avoid the sight not only of the people, but of any other person. How often has this work diverted me from troublesome thoughts? and all that are frivolous should be reputed so. Nature has presented us with a large faculty of entertaining ourselves alone; and often calls us to it, to teach us that we owe ourselves in part to society, but chiefly and mostly to ourselves. That I may habituate my fancy even to meditate in some method and to some end, and to keep it from losing itself and roving at random, it is but to give to body and to record all the little thoughts that present themselves to it. I give ear to my whimsies, because I am to record them. It often falls out, that being displeased at some action that civility and reason will not permit me openly to reprove, I here disgorge myself, not without design of public instruction: and also these poetical lashes,

> *Zon zur l'oeil, ion sur le groin,*
> *Zon zur le dos du Sagoin,*

[A slap on his eye, a slap on his snout, a slap on Sagoin's back.

—Marot. Fripelippes, Valet de Marot a Sagoin]

imprint themselves better upon paper than upon the flesh. What if I listen to books a little more attentively than ordinary, since I watch if I can purloin anything that may adorn or support my own? I have not at all studied to make a book; but I have in some sort studied because I had made it; if it be studying to scratch and pinch now one author, and then another, either by the head or foot, not with any design to form opinions from them, but to assist, second, and fortify those I already have embraced. But whom shall we believe in the report he makes of himself in so corrupt an age? considering there are so few, if, any at all, whom we can believe when speaking of others, where there is less interest to lie. The first thing done in the corruption of manners is banishing truth; for, as Pindar says, to be true is the beginning of a great virtue, and the first article that Plato requires in the governor of his Republic. The truth of these days is not that which really is, but what every man persuades another man to believe; as we generally give the name of money not only to pieces of the dust alloy, but even to the false also, if they will pass. Our nation has long been reproached with this vice; for Salvianus of Marseilles, who lived in the time of the Emperor Valentinian, says that lying and forswearing themselves is with the French not a vice, but a way of speaking. He who would enhance this testimony, might say that it is now a virtue in them; men form and fashion themselves to it as to an exercise of honour; for dissimulation is one of the most notable qualities of this age.

I have often considered whence this custom that we so religiously observe should spring, of being more highly offended with the reproach of a vice so familiar to us than with any other, and that it should be the highest insult that can in words be done us to reproach us with a lie. Upon examination, I find that it is natural most to defend the defects with which we are most tainted. It seems as if by resenting and being moved at the accusation, we in some sort acquit ourselves of the fault; though we have it in effect, we condemn it in outward appearance. May it not also be that this reproach seems to imply cowardice and feebleness of heart? of which can there be a more manifest sign than to eat a man's own words – nay, to lie against a man's own knowledge? Lying is a base vice; a vice that one of the ancients portrays in the most odious colours when he says, "that it is to manifest a contempt of God, and withal a fear of men." It is not possible more fully to represent the horror, baseness, and irregularity of it; for what can a man imagine more hateful and contemptible than to be a coward towards men, and valiant against his Maker? Our intelligence being by no other way communicable to one another but by a particular word, he who falsifies that betrays public society. It is the only way by which we communicate our thoughts and wills; it is the interpreter of the soul, and if it deceive us, we no longer know nor have further tie upon one another; if that deceive us, it breaks all our correspondence, and dissolves all the ties of government. Certain nations of the newly discovered Indies (I need not give them names, seeing they are no more; for, by wonderful and unheardof example, the desolation of that conquest has extended to the utter abolition of names and the ancient knowledge of places) offered to their gods human blood, but only such as was drawn from the tongue and ears, to expiate for the sin of lying, as well heard as pronounced. That good fellow of Greece [Plutarch, *Life of Lysander*, c. 4.] said that children are amused with toys and men with words.

As to our diverse usages of giving the lie, and the laws of honour in that case, and the alteration they have received, I defer saying what I know of them to another time, and shall learn, if I can, in the meanwhile, at what time the custom took beginning of so exactly weighing and measuring words, and of making our honour interested in them; for it is easy to judge that it was not anciently amongst the Romans and Greeks. And it has often seemed to me strange to see them rail at and give one another the lie without any quarrel. Their laws of duty steered some other course than ours. Caesar is sometimes called thief, and sometimes drunkard, to his teeth. We see the liberty of invective they practised upon one another, I mean the greatest chiefs of war of both nations, where words are only revenged with words, and do not proceed any farther.

ON A MONSTROUS CHILD

This story shall go by itself; for I will leave it to physicians to discourse of. Two days ago I saw a child that two men and a nurse, who said they were the father, the uncle, and the aunt of it, carried about to get money by showing it, by reason it was so strange a creature. It was, as to all the rest, of a common form, and could stand upon its feet; could go and gabble much like other children of the same age; it had never as yet taken any other nourishment but from the nurse's breasts, and what, in my presence, they tried to put into the mouth of it, it only chewed a little and spat it out again without swallowing; the cry of it seemed indeed a little odd and particular, and it was just fourteen months old. Under the breast it was joined to another child, but without a head, and which had the spine of the back without motion, the rest entire; for though it had one arm shorter than the other, it had been broken by accident at their birth; they were joined breast to breast, and as if a lesser child sought to throw its arms about the neck of one something bigger. The juncture and thickness of the place where they were conjoined was not above four fingers, or thereabouts, so that if you thrust up the imperfect child you might see the navel of the other below it, and the joining was between the paps and the navel. The navel of the imperfect child could not be seen, but all the rest of the belly, so that all that was not joined of the imperfect one, as arms, buttocks, thighs, and legs, hung dangling upon the other, and might reach to the mid-leg. The nurse, moreover, told us that it urinated out of both bodies, and that the members of the other were nourished, sensible, and in the same plight with that she gave suck to, excepting that they were shorter and less. This double body and several limbs relating to one head might be interpreted a favourable prognostic to the king, [Henry III.] of maintaining these various parts of our state under the union of his laws; but lest the event should prove otherwise, it is better to let it alone, for in things already past there needs no divination,

> *Ut quum facts sunt, tum ad conjecturam*
> *Aliqui interpretation revocentur;*

[So as when they are come to pass, they may then by some interpretation be recalled to conjecture
>>> —Cicero, *De Divinatione*, ii. 31.]

as it is said of Epimenides, that he always prophesied backward.

I have just seen a herdsman in Medoc, of about thirty years of age, who has no sign of any genital parts; he has three holes by which he incessantly voids his water; he is bearded, has desire, and seeks contact with women.

Those that we call monsters are not so to God, who sees in the immensity of His work the infinite forms that He has comprehended therein; and it is to be believed that this figure which astonishes us has relation to some other figure of the same kind unknown to man. From His all wisdom nothing but good, common; and regular proceeds; but we do not discern the disposition and relation:

> *Quod crebro videt, non miratur, etiamsi,*
> *cur fiat, nescit. Quod ante non vidit, id,*
> *si evenerit, ostentum esse censet.*

Chapter 30

[What he often sees he does not admire, though he be ignorant how it comes to pass. When a thing happens he never saw before, he thinks that it is a portent.

—Cicero, *De Divinatione*, ii. 22.]

Whatever falls out contrary to custom we say is contrary to nature, but nothing, whatever it be, is contrary to her. Let, therefore, this universal and natural reason expel the error and astonishment that novelty brings along with it.

35

ON THREE GOOD WOMEN

They are not by the dozen, as everyone knows, and especially in the duties of marriage, for that is a bargain full of so many nice circumstances that it is hard a woman's will should long endure such a restraint; men, though their condition be something better under that tie, have yet enough to do. The true touch and test of a happy marriage have respect to the time of the companionship, if it has been constantly gentle, loyal, and agreeable. In our age, women commonly reserve the publication of their good offices, and their vehement affection towards their husbands, until they have lost them, or at least, till then defer the testimonies of their good will; a too slow testimony and unseasonable. By it they rather manifest that they never loved them till dead: their life is nothing but trouble; their death full of love and courtesy. As fathers conceal their affection from their children, women, likewise, conceal theirs from their husbands, to maintain a modest respect. This mystery is not for my palate; it isto much purpose that they scratch themselves and tear their hair. I whisper in a waiting-woman's or secretary's ear: "How were they, how did they live together?" I always have that good saying m my head:

Jactantius moerent, quae minus dolent.

[They make the most ado who are least concerned. Or: They mourn the more ostentatiously, the less they grieve.
—Tacitus, *Annals*, ii. 77, writing of Germanicus.]

Their whimpering is offensive to the living and vain to the dead. We should willingly give them leave to laugh after we are dead, provided they will smile upon us whilst we are alive. Is it not enough to make a man revive in pure spite, that she, who spat in my face whilst I was in being, shall come to kiss my feet when I am no more? If there be any honour in lamenting a husband, it only appertains to those who smiled upon them whilst they had them; let those who wept during their lives laugh at their deaths, as well outwardly as within. Therefore, never regard those blubbered eyes and that pitiful voice; consider her deportment, her complexion, the plumpness of her cheeks under all those formal veils; it is there she talks plain French. There are few who do not mend upon't, and health is a quality that cannot lie. That starched and ceremonious countenance looks not so much back as forward, and is rather intended to get a new husband than to lament the old. When I was a boy, a very beautiful and virtuous lady, who is yet living, the widow of a prince, wore somewhat more ornament in her dress than our laws of widowhood allow, and being reproached with it, she made answer that it was because she was resolved to have no more love affairs, and would never marry again.

I have here, not at all dissenting from our customs, made choice of three women, who have also expressed the utmost of their goodness and affection about their husbands' deaths; yet are they examples of another kind than are now m use, and so austere that they will hardly be drawn into imitation.

The younger Pliny had near a house of his in Italy a neighbour who was exceedingly tormented with certain ulcers in his private parts. His wife seeing him so long to languish, entreated that he would give her leave to see and at leisure to consider of the condition of his disease, and that she would freely tell him what she thought. This permission being obtained, and she having curiously examined the business, found it impossible he could ever be cured, and that all he had to hope for or expect was a great while to linger out a painful and miserable life, and therefore, as the most sure and sovereign remedy, resolutely advised him to kill himself. But finding him a little tender and backward in so rude an attempt: "Do not think, my friend," said she, "that the torments I see thee endure are not as sensible to me as to thyself, and that to deliver myself from them, I will not myself make use of the same remedy I have prescribed to thee. I will accompany thee in the cure as I have done in the disease; fear nothing, but believe that we shall have pleasure in this passage that is to free us from so many miseries, and we will go happily together." Which having said, and roused up her husband's courage, she resolved that they should throw themselves headlong into the sea out of a window that overlooked it, and that she might maintain to the last the loyal and vehement affection wherewith she had embraced him during his life, she would also have him die in her arms; but lest they should fail, and should quit their hold in the fall through fear, she tied herself fast to him by the waist, and so gave up her own life to procure her husband's repose. This was a woman of mean condition; and, amongst that class of people, it is no very new thing to see some examples of rare virtue:

> *Extrema per illos*
> *Justitia excedens terries vestigial fecit.*

[Justice, when she left the earth, took her last steps among them.
—Virgil, *Georgics*, ii. 473.]

The other two were noble and rich, where examples of virtue are rarely lodged.

Arria, the wife of Caecina Paetus, a consular person, was the mother of another Arria, the wife of Thrasea Paetus, he whose virtue was so renowned in the time of Nero, and by this son-in-law, the grandmother of Fannia: for the resemblance of the names of these men and women, and their fortunes, have led to several mistakes. This first Arria, her husband Caecina Paetus, having been taken prisoner by some of the Emperor Claudius' people, after Scribonianus' defeat, whose party he had embraced in the war, begged of those who were to carry him prisoner to Rome, that they would take her into their ship, where she would be of much less charge and trouble to them than a great many persons they must otherwise have to attend her husband, and that she alone would undertake to serve him in his chamber, his kitchen, and all other offices. They refused, whereupon she put herself into a fisher-boat she hired on the spot, and in that manner followed him from Sclavonia. When she had come to Rome, Junia, the widow of Scribonianus, having one day, from the resemblance of their fortune, accosted her in the Emperor's presence; she rudely repulsed her with these words, "I," said she, "speak to thee, or give ear to anything thou sayest! to thee in whose lap Scribonianus was slain, and thou art yet alive!" These words, with several other signs, gave her friends to understand that she would undoubtedly despatch herself, impatient of supporting her husband's misfortune. And Thrasea, her son-in-law, beseeching her not to throw away herself, and saying to her, "What! if I should run the same fortune that Caecina has done, would you that your daughter, my wife, should do the same?" – "Would I?" replied she, "yes, yes, I would: if she had lived as long, and in as good understanding with thee as I have done, with my husband." These answers made them more careful of her, and to have a more watchful eye to her proceedings. One day, having said to those who looked to her: "Tis to much purpose that you take all this pains to prevent me; you may indeed make me die an ill death, but to keep me from dying is not in your power"; she in a sudden phrenzy started from a chair whereon she sat, and with all her force dashed her head against the wall, by which blow being laid flat in a swoon, and very much wounded, after they had again with great ado brought her to herself: "I told you," said she, "that if you refused me some easy way of dying, I should find out another, how painful soever." The conclusion of so admirable a virtue was this: her husband Paetus, not having resolution enough of his own to despatch himself, as he was by the emperor's cruelty enjoined, one day, amongst others, after having first employed all the reasons and exhortations which she thought most prevalent to persuade him to it, she snatched the poignard he wore from his side, and holding it ready in her hand, for the conclusion of her admonitions; "Do thus, Paetus," said she, and in the same instant giving herself a mortal stab in the breast, and then drawing it out of the wound, presented it to him, ending her life with this noble, generous, and immortal saying, "Paete, non dolet" – having time to pronounce no more but those three never-to-be-forgotten words: "Paetus, it is not painful."

> *Casta suo gladium cum trader Arria Paeto,*
> *Quem de visceribus traxerat ipsa suis*
> *Si qua fides, vulnus quod feci non dolet, inquit,*
> *Sed quod to facies, id mihi, Paete, dolet.*

[When the chaste Arria gave to Poetus the reeking sword she had drawn from her breast, 'If you believe me,' she said, 'Paetus, the wound I have made hurts not, but it is that which thou wilt make that hurts me.'

—Martial, i. 14.]

The action was much more noble in itself, and of a braver sense than the poet expressed it: for she was so far from being deterred by the thought of her husband's wound and death and her own, that she had been their promotress and adviser: but having performed this high and courageous enterprise for her husband's only convenience, she had even in the last gasp of her life no other concern but for him, and of dispossessing him of the fear of dying with her. Paetus presently struck himself to the heart with the same weapon, ashamed, I suppose, to have stood in need of so dear and precious an example.

Pompeia Paulina, a young and very noble Roman lady, had married Seneca in his extreme old age. Nero, his fine pupil, sent his guards to him to denounce the sentence of death, which was performed after this manner: When the Roman emperors of those times had condemned any man of quality, they sent to him by their officers to choose what death he would, and to execute it within such or such a time, which was limited, according to the degree of their indignation, to a shorter or a longer respite, that they might therein have better leisure to dispose their affairs, and sometimes depriving them of the means of doing it by the shortness of the time; and if the condemned seemed unwilling to submit to the order, they had people ready at hand to execute it either by cutting the veins of the arms and legs, or by compelling them by force to swallow a draught of poison. But persons of honour would not abide this necessity, but made use of their own physicians and surgeons for this purpose. Seneca, with a calm and steady countenance, heard their charge, and presently called for paper to write his will, which being by the captain refused, he turned himself towards his friends, saying to them, "Since I cannot leave you any other acknowledgment of the obligation I have to you, I leave you at least the best thing I have, namely, the image of my life and manners, which I entreat you to keep in memory of me, that by so doing you may acquire the glory of sincere and real friends." And there withal, one while appeasing the sorrow he saw in them with gentle words, and presently raising his voice to reprove them: "What," said he, "are become of all our brave philosophical precepts? What are become of all the provisions we have so many years laid up against the accidents of fortune? Is Nero's cruelty unknown to us? What could we expect from him who had murdered his mother and his brother, but that he should put his tutor to death who had brought him up?" After having spoken these words in general, he turned himself towards his wife, and embracing her fast in his arms, as, her heart and strength failing her, she was ready to sink down with grief, he begged of her, for his sake, to bear this accident with a little more patience, telling her, that now the hour was come wherein he was to show, not by argument and discourse, but effect, the fruit he had acquired by his studies, and that he really embraced his death, not only without grief, but moreover with joy. "Wherefore, my dearest," said he, "do not dishonour it with thy tears, that it may not seem as if thou lovest thyself more than my reputation. Moderate thy grief, and comfort thyself in the knowledge thou hast had of me and my actions, leading the remainder of thy life in the same virtuous manner thou hast hitherto done." To which Paulina, having a little recovered her spirits, and warmed the magnanimity of her courage with a most generous affection, replied,"No, Seneca," said she, "I am not a woman to suffer you to go alone in such a necessity: I will not have you think that the virtuous examples of your life have not taught me how to die; and when can I ever better or more fittingly do it, or more to my own desire, than with you? and therefore assure yourself I will go along with you."

Then Seneca, taking this noble and generous resolution of his wife in good part, and also willing to free himself from the fear of leaving her exposed to the cruelty of his enemies after his death: "I have, Paulina," said he, "instructed thee in what would serve thee happily to live; but thou more covetest, I see, the honour of dying: in truth, I will not grudge it thee; the constancy and resolution in our common end are the same, but the beauty and glory of thy part are much greater." Which being said, the surgeons, at the same time, opened the veins of both their arms, but as those of Seneca were more shrunk up, as well with age as abstinence, made his blood flow too slowly, he moreover commanded them to open the veins of his thighs; and lest the torments he endured might pierce his wife's heart, and also to free himself from the affliction of seeing her in so sad a condition, after having taken a very affectionate leave of her, he entreated she would suffer them to carry her into her chamber, which they accordingly did. But all these incisions being not yet enough to make him die, he commanded Statius Anneus, his physician, to give him a draught of poison, which had not much better effect; for by reason of the weakness and coldness of his limbs, it could not arrive at his heart. Wherefore they were forced to superadd a very hot bath, and then, feeling his end approach, whilst he had breath he continued excellent discourses upon the subject of his present condition, which the secretaries wrote down so long as they could hear his voice, and his last words were long after in high honour and esteem amongst men, and it is a great loss to us that they have not come down to our times. Then, feeling the last pangs of death, with the bloody water of the bath he bathed his head, saying: "This water I dedicate to Jupiter the deliverer." Nero, being presently informed of all this, fearing lest the death of Paulina, who was one of the best-born ladies of Rome, and against whom he had no particular unkindness, should turn to his reproach, sent orders in all haste to bind up her wounds, which her attendants did without her knowledge, she being already half dead, and without all manner of sense. Thus, though she lived contrary to her own design, it was very honourably, and befitting her own virtue, her pale complexion ever after manifesting how much life had run from her veins.

These are my three very true stories, which I find as entertaining and as tragic as any of those we make out of our own heads wherewith to amuse the common people; and I wonder that they who are addicted to such relations, do not rather cull out ten thousand very fine stories, which are to be found in books, that would save them the trouble of invention, and be more useful and diverting; and he who would make a whole and connected body of them would need to add nothing of his own, but the connection only, as it were the solder of another metal; and might by this means embody a great many true events of all sorts, disposing and diversifying them according as the beauty of the work should require, after the same manner, almost, as Ovid has made up his Metamorphoses of the infinite number of various fables.

In the last couple, this is, moreover, worthy of consideration, that Paulina voluntarily offered to lose her life for the love of her husband, and that her husband had formerly also forborne to die for the love of her. We may think there is no just counterpoise in this exchange; but, according to his stoical humour, I fancy he thought he had done as much for her, in prolonging his life upon her account, as if he had died for her. In one of his letters to Lucilius, after he has given him to understand that, being seized with an ague in Rome, he presently took coach to go to a house he had in the country, contrary to his wife's opinion, who would have him stay, and that he had told her that the ague he was seized with was not a fever of the body but of the place, it follows thus: "She let me go," says he, "giving me a strict charge of my health. Now I, who know that her life is involved in mine, begin to make much of myself, that I may preserve her. And I lose the privilege my age has given me, of being more constant and resolute in many things, when I call to mind that in this old fellow there is a young girl who is interested in his health. And since I cannot persuade her to love me more courageously, she makes me more solicitously love myself: for we must allow something to honest affections, and, sometimes, though occasions importune us to the contrary, we must call back life, even though it be with torment: we must hold the soul fast in our teeth, since the rule of living, amongst good men, is not so long as they please, but as long as they ought. He that loves not his wife nor his friend so well as to prolong his life for them, but will obstinately die, is too delicate and too effeminate: the soul must impose this upon itself, when the utility of our friends so requires; we must sometimes lend ourselves to our friends, and when we would die for ourselves must break that resolution for them. It is a testimony of grandeur of courage to return to life for the consideration of another, as many excellent persons have done: and it is a mark of singular good nature to preserve old age (of which the greatest convenience is the indifference as to its duration, and a more stout and disdainful use of life), when a man perceives that this office is pleasing, agreeable, and useful to some person by whom he is very much beloved. And a man reaps by it a very pleasing reward; for what can be more delightful than to be so dear to his wife, as upon her account he shall become dearer to himself? Thus has my

Paulina loaded me not only with her fears, but my own; it has not been sufficient to consider how resolutely I could die, but I have also considered how irresolutely she would bear my death. I am enforced to live, and sometimes to live in magnanimity." These are his own words, as excellent as they everywhere are.

BOOK III

1

ON PROFIT AND HONESTY

No man is free from speaking foolish things; but the worst on it is, when a man labours to play the fool:

Nae iste magno conatu magnas nugas dixerit.

[Truly he, with a great effort will shortly say a mighty trifle.
—Terence, *Heautontimorumenos*, act iii., s. 4.]

This does not concern me; mine slip from me with as little care as they are of little value, and it is the better for them. I would presently part with them for what they are worth, and neither buy nor sell them, but as they weigh. I speak on paper, as I do to the first person I meet; and that this is true, observe what follows.

To whom ought not treachery to be hateful, when Tiberius refused it in a thing of so great importance to him? He had word sent him from Germany that if he thought fit, they would rid him of Arminius by poison: this was the most potent enemy the Romans had, who had defeated them so ignominiously under Varus, and who alone prevented their aggrandisement in those parts.

He returned answer, "that the people of Rome were wont to revenge themselves of their enemies by open ways, and with their swords in their hands, and not clandestinely and by fraud": wherein he quitted the profitable for the honest. You will tell me that he was a braggadocio; I believe so too: and it is no great miracle in men of his profession. But the acknowledgment of virtue is not less valid in the mouth of him who hates it, forasmuch as truth forces it from him, and if he will not inwardly receive it, he at least puts it on for a decoration.

Our outward and inward structure is full of imperfection; but there is nothing useless in nature, not even inutility itself; nothing has insinuated itself into this universe that has not therein some fit and proper place. Our being is cemented with sickly qualities: ambition, jealousy, envy, revenge, superstition, and despair have so natural a possession in us, that its image is discerned in beasts; nay, and cruelty, so unnatural a vice; for even in the midst of compassion we feel within, I know not what tart-sweet titillation of ill-natured pleasure in seeing others suffer; and the children feel it:

> *Suave mari magno, turbantibus aequora ventis,*
> *E terra magnum alterius spectare laborem:*

[It is sweet, when the winds disturb the waters of the vast sea, to witness from land the peril of other persons.

—Lucretius, ii. I.]

of the seeds of which qualities, whoever should divest man, would destroy the fundamental conditions of human life. Likewise, in all governments there are necessary offices, not only abject, but vicious also. Vices there help to make up the seam in our piecing, as poisons are useful for the conservation of health. If they become excusable because they are of use to us, and that the common necessity covers their true qualities, we are to resign this part to the strongest and boldest citizens, who sacrifice their honour and conscience, as others of old sacrificed their lives, for the good of their country: we, who are weaker, take upon us parts both that are more easy and less hazardous. The public weal requires that men should betray, and lie, and massacre; let us leave this commission to men who are more obedient and more supple.

Chapter 1

In earnest, I have often been troubled to see judges, by fraud and false hopes of favour or pardon, allure a criminal to confess his fact, and therein to make use of cozenage and impudence. It would become justice, and Plato himself, who countenances this manner of proceeding, to furnish me with other means more suitable to my own liking: this is a malicious kind of justice, and I look upon it as no less wounded by itself than by others. I said not long since to some company in discourse, that I should hardly be drawn to betray my prince for a particular man, who should be much ashamed to betray any particular man for my prince; and I do not only hate deceiving myself, but that any one should deceive through me; I will neither afford matter nor occasion to any such thing.

In the little I have had to mediate between our princes [Between the King of Navarre, afterwards Henry IV., and the Duc de Guise. See De Thou, De Vita Sua, iii. 9.] in the divisions and subdivisions by which we are at this time torn to pieces, I have been very careful that they should neither be deceived in me nor deceive others by me. People of that kind of trading are very reserved, and pretend to be the most moderate imaginable and nearest to the opinions of those with whom they have to do; I expose myself in my stiff opinion, and after a method the most my own; a tender negotiator, a novice, who had rather fail in the affair than be wanting to myself. And yet it has been hitherto with so good luck (for fortune has doubtless the best share in it), that few things have passed from hand to hand with less suspicion or more favour and privacy. I have a free and open way that easily insinuates itself and obtains belief with those with whom I am to deal at the first meeting. Sincerity and pure truth, in what age soever, pass for current; and besides, the liberty and freedom of a man who treats without any interest of his own is never hateful or suspected, and he may very well make use of the answer of Hyperides to the Athenians, who complained of his blunt way of speaking: "Messieurs, do not consider whether or no I am free, but whether I am so without a bribe, or without any advantage to my own affairs." My liberty of speaking has also easily cleared me from all suspicion of dissembling by its vehemency, leaving nothing unsaid, so that I could have said no worse behind their backs, and in that it carried along with it a manifest show of simplicity and indifference. I pretend to no other fruit by acting than to act, and add to it no long arguments or propositions; every action plays its own game, win if it can.

As to the rest, I am not swayed by any passion, either of love or hatred, towards the great, nor has my will captivated either by particular injury or obligation. I look upon our kings with an affection simply loyal and respectful, neither prompted nor restrained by any private interest, and I love myself for it. Nor does the general and just cause attract me otherwise than with moderation, and without heat. I am not subject to those penetrating and close compacts and engagements. Anger and hatred are beyond the duty of justice; and are passions only useful to those who do not keep themselves strictly to their duty by simple reason:

Utatur motu animi, qui uti ratione non potest.

[He may employ his passion, who can make no use of his reason.
—Cicero, *Tusculum Disputations*, iv. 25.]

All legitimate intentions are temperate and equable of themselves; if otherwise, they degenerate into seditious and unlawful. This is it which makes me walk everywhere with my head erect, my face and my heart open. In truth, and I am not afraid to confess it, I should easily, in case of need, hold up one candle to St. Michael and another to his dragon, like the old woman; I will follow the right side even to the fire, but exclusively, if I can. Let Montaigne be overwhelmed in the public ruin if need be; but if there be no need, I should think myself obliged to fortune to save me, and I will make use of all the length of line my duty allows for his preservation. Was it not Atticus who, being of the just but losing side, preserved himself by his moderation in that universal shipwreck of the world, amongst

CHAPTER 1

so many mutations and diversities? For private man, as he was, it is more easy; and in such kind of work, I think a man may justly not be ambitious to offer and insinuate himself. For a man, indeed, to be wavering and irresolute, to keep his affection unmoved and without inclination in the troubles of his country and public divisions, I neither think it handsome nor honest:

> *Ea non media, sed nulla via est, velut eventum*
> *exspectantium, quo fortunae consilia sua applicent.*

[That is not a middle way, but no way, to await events, by which they refer their resolutions to fortune.
— Livy, xxxii. 21.]

This may be allowed in our neighbours' affairs; and thus Gelo, the tyrant of Syracuse, suspended his inclination in the war between the Greeks and barbarians, keeping a resident ambassador with presents at Delphos, to watch and see which way fortune would incline, and then take fit occasion to fall in with the victors. It would be a kind of treason to proceed after this manner in our own domestic affairs, wherein a man must of necessity be of the one side or the other; though for a man who has no office or express command to call him out, to sit still I hold it more excusable (and yet I do not excuse myself upon these terms) than in foreign expeditions, to which, however, according to our laws, no man is pressed against his will. And yet even those who wholly engage themselves in such a war may behave themselves with such temper and moderation, that the storm may fly over their heads without doing them any harm. Had we not reason to hope such an issue in the person of the late Bishop of Orleans, the Sieur de Morvilliers? [An able negotiator, who, though protected by the Guises, and strongly supporting them, was yet very far from persecuting the Reformists. He died in 1577.]

And I know, amongst those who behave themselves most bravely in the present war, some whose manners are so gentle, obliging, and

297

just, that they will certainly stand firm, whatever event Heaven is preparing for us. I am of opinion that it properly belongs to kings only to quarrel with kings; and I laugh at those spirits who, out of lightness of heart, lend themselves to so disproportioned disputes; for a man has never the more particular quarrel with a prince, by marching openly and boldly against him for his own honour and according to his duty; if he does not love such a person, he does better, he esteems him. And notably the cause of the laws and of the ancient government of a kingdom, has this always annexed to it, that even those who, for their own private interest, invade them, excuse, if they do not honour, the defenders.

But we are not, as we nowadays do, to call peevishness and inward discontent, that spring from private interest and passion, duty, nor a treacherous and malicious conduct, courage; they call their proneness to mischief and violence zeal; it is not the cause, but their interest, that inflames them; they kindle and begin a war, not because it is just, but because it is war.

A man may very well behave himself commodiously and loyally too amongst those of the adverse party; carry yourself, if not with the same equal affection (for that is capable of different measure), at least with an affection moderate, well tempered, and such as shall not so engage you to one party, that it may demand all you are able to do for that side, content yourself with a moderate proportion of their, favour and goodwill; and to swim in troubled waters without fishing in them.

The other way, of offering a man's self and the utmost service he is able to do, both to one party and the other, has still less of prudence in it than conscience. Does not he to whom you betray another, to whom you were as welcome as to himself, know that you will at another time do as much for him? He holds you for a villain; and in the meantime hears what you will say, gathers intelligence from you, and works his own ends out of your disloyalty; double-dealing men are useful for bringing in, but we must have a care they carry out as little as is possible.

CHAPTER 1

I say nothing to one party that I may not, upon occasion, say to the other, with a little alteration of accent; and report nothing but things either indifferent or known, or what is of common consequence. I cannot permit myself, for any consideration, to tell them a lie. What is intrusted to my secrecy, I religiously conceal; but I take as few trusts of that nature upon me as I can. The secrets of princes are a troublesome burthen to such as are not interested in them. I very willingly bargain that they trust me with little, but confidently rely upon what I tell them. I have ever known more than I desired. One open way of speaking introduces another open way of speaking, and draws out discoveries, like wine and love. Philippides, in my opinion, answered King Lysimachus very discreetly, who, asking him what of his estate he should bestow upon him? "What you will," said he, "provided it be none of your secrets." I see everyone is displeased if the bottom of the affair be concealed from him wherein he is employed, or that there be any reservation in the thing; for my part, I am content to know no more of the business than what they would have me employ myself in, nor desire that my knowledge should exceed or restrict what I have to say. If I must serve for an instrument of deceit, let it be at least with a safe conscience: I will not be reputed a servant either so affectionate or so loyal as to be fit to betray any one: he who is unfaithful to himself, is excusably so to his master. But they are princes who do not accept men by halves, and despise limited and conditional services: I cannot help it: I frankly tell them how far I can go; for a slave I should not be, but to reason, and I can hardly submit even to that. And they also are to blame to exact from a freeman the same subjection and obligation to their service that they do from him they have made and bought, or whose fortune particularly and expressly depends upon theirs. The laws have delivered me from a great anxiety; they have chosen a side for me, and given me a master; all other superiority and obligation ought to be relative to that, and cut, off from all other. Yet this is not to say, that if my affection should otherwise incline me, my hand should presently obey it; the will and desire are a law to themselves; but actions must receive commission from the public appointment.

All this proceeding of mine is a little dissonant from the ordinary forms; it would produce no great effects, nor be of any long duration; innocence itself could not, in this age of ours, either negotiate without dissimulation, or traffic without lying; and, indeed, public employments are by no means for my palate: what my profession requires, I perform after the most private manner that I can. Being young, I was engaged up to the ears in business, and it succeeded well; but I disengaged myself in good time. I have often since avoided meddling in it, rarely accepted, and never asked it; keeping my back still turned to ambition; but if not like rowers who so advance backward, yet so, at the same time, that I am less obliged to my resolution than to my good fortune, that I was not wholly embarked in it. For there are ways less displeasing to my taste, and more suitable to my ability, by which, if she had formerly called me to the public service, and my own advancement towards the world's opinion, I know I should, in spite of all my own arguments to the contrary, have pursued them. Such as commonly say, in opposition to what I profess, that what I call freedom, simplicity, and plainness in my manners, is art and subtlety, and rather prudence than goodness, industry than nature, good sense than good luck, do me more honour than disgrace: but, certainly, they make my subtlety too subtle; and whoever has followed me close, and pryed narrowly into me, I will give him the victory, if he does not confess that there is no rule in their school that could match this natural motion, and maintain an appearance of liberty and licence, so equal and inflexible, through so many various and crooked paths, and that all their wit and endeavour could never have led them through. The way of truth is one and simple; that of particular profit, and the commodity of affairs a man is entrusted with, is double, unequal, and casual. I have often seen these counterfeit and artificial liberties practised, but, for the most part, without success; they relish of Aesop's ass who, in emulation of the dog, obligingly clapped his two fore-feet upon his master's shoulders; but as many caresses as the dog had for such an expression of kindness, twice so many blows with a cudgel had the poor ass for his compliment:

Id maxime quemque decet, quod est cujusque suum maxime.

[That best becomes every man which belongs most to him;
—Cicero, *De Officius*, i. 31.]

I will not deprive deceit of its due; that were but ill to understand the world: I know it has often been of great use, and that it maintains and supplies most men's employment. There are vices that are lawful, as there are many actions, either good or excusable, that are not lawful in themselves.

The justice which in itself is natural and universal is otherwise and more nobly ordered than that other justice which is special, national, and constrained to the ends of government,

Veri juris germanaeque justitiae solidam et expressam
effigiem nullam tenemus; umbra et imaginibu sutimur;

[We retain no solid and express portraiture of true right and germane justice; we have only the shadow and image of it.
—Cicero, *De Officius*, iii. 17.]

insomuch that the sage Dandamis, hearing the lives of Socrates, Pythagoras, and Diogenes read, judged them to be great men every way, excepting that they were too much subjected to the reverence of the laws, which, to second and authorise, true virtue must abate very much of its original vigour; many vicious actions are introduced, not only by their permission, but by their advice:

Ex senatus consultis plebisquescitis scelera exercentur.

[Crimes are committed by the decrees of the Senate and the popular assembly.

—Seneca, *Epistles*, 95.]

I follow the common phrase that distinguishes between profitable and honest things, so as to call some natural actions, that are not only profitable but necessary, dishonest and foul.

But let us proceed in our examples of treachery two pretenders to the kingdom of Thrace [Rhescuporis and Cotys. Tacitus, *Annals*, ii. 65] were fallen into dispute about their title; the emperor hindered them from proceeding to blows: but one of them, under colour of bringing things to a friendly issue by an interview, having invited his competitor to an entertainment in his own house, imprisoned and killed him. Justice required that the Romans should have satisfaction for this offence; but there was a difficulty in obtaining it by ordinary ways; what, therefore, they could not do legitimately, without war and without danger, they resolved to do by treachery; and what they could not honestly do, they did profitably. For which end, one Pomponius Flaccus was found to be a fit instrument. This man, by dissembled words and assurances, having drawn the other into his toils, instead of the honour and favour he had promised him, sent him bound hand and foot to Rome. Here one traitor betrayed another, contrary to common custom: for they are full of mistrust, and it is hard to overreach them in their own art: witness the sad experience we have lately had. [Montaigne here probably refers to the feigned reconciliation between Catherine de Medici and Henri, Duc de Guise, in 1588.]

Let who will be Pomponius Flaccus, and there are enough who would: for my part, both my word and my faith are, like all the rest, parts of this common body: their best effect is the public service; this I take for presupposed. But should one command me to take charge of the courts of law and lawsuits, I should make answer, that I understood it not; or the place of a leader of pioneers, I would say, that I was called to a more honourable employment; so likewise, he that would employ me to lie, betray, and forswear myself, though not to assassinate or to poison, for some notable service, I should say, "If I have robbed or stolen anything from any man, send me rather to the galleys." For it is permissible in a man of honour to say, as the Lacedaemonians did, [Plutarch, Difference between a Flatterer and a Friend, c. 21.] having been defeated by Antipater, when just upon concluding an agreement: "You may impose as heavy and ruinous taxes upon us as you please, but to command us to do shameful and dishonest things, you will lose your time, for it is to no purpose." Everyone ought to make the same vow to himself that the kings of Egypt made their judges solemnly swear, that they would not do anything contrary to their consciences, though never so much commanded to it by themselves. In such commissions there is evident mark of ignominy and condemnation; and he who gives it at the same time accuses you, and gives it, if you understand it right, for a burden and a punishment. As much as the public affairs are bettered by your exploit, so much are your own the worse, and the better you behave yourself in it, it is so much the worse for yourself; and it will be no new thing, nor, peradventure, without some colour of justice, if the same person ruin you who set you on work.

If treachery can be in any case excusable, it must be only so when it is practised to chastise and betray treachery. There are examples enough of treacheries, not only rejected, but chastised and punished by those in favour of whom they were undertaken. Who is ignorant of Fabricius, sentence against the physician of Pyrrhus?

But this we also find recorded, that some persons have commanded a thing, who afterward have severely avenged the execution of it upon him they had employed, rejecting the reputation of so unbridled an authority, and disowning so abandoned and base a servitude and obedience. Jaropelk, Duke of Russia, tampered with a gentleman of Hungary to betray Boleslaus, king of Poland, either by killing him, or by giving the Russians opportunity to do him some notable mischief. This worthy went ably to work: he was more assiduous than before in the service of that king, so that he obtained the honour to be of his council, and one of the chiefest in his trust. With these advantages, and taking an opportune occasion of his master's absence, he betrayed Vislicza, a great and rich city, to the Russians, which was entirely sacked and burned, and not only all the inhabitants of both sexes, young and old, put to the sword, but moreover a great number of neighbouring gentry, whom he had drawn thither to that end. Jaropelk, his revenge being thus satisfied and his anger appeased, which was not, indeed, without pretence (for Boleslaus had highly offended him, and after the same manner), and sated with the fruit of this treachery, coming to consider the fulness of it, with a sound judgment and clear from passion, looked upon what had been done with so much horror and remorse that he caused the eyes to be bored out and the tongue and shameful parts to be cut off of him who had performed it.

Antigonus persuaded the Argyraspides to betray Eumenes, their general, his adversary, into his hands; but after he had caused him, so delivered, to be slain, he would himself be the commissioner of the divine justice for the punishment of so detestable a crime, and committed them into the hands of the governor of the province, with express command, by whatever means, to destroy and bring them all to an evil end, so that of that great number of men, not so much as one ever returned again into Macedonia: the better he had been served, the more wickedly he judged it to be, and meriting greater punishment.

The slave who betrayed the place where his master, P. Sulpicius, lay concealed, was, according to the promise of Sylla's proscription, manumitted for his pains; but according to the promise of the public justice, which was free from any such engagement, he was thrown headlong from the Tarpeian rock.

Chapter 1

Our King Clovis, instead of the arms of gold he had promised them, caused three of Cararie's servants to be hanged after they had betrayed their master to him, though he had debauched them to it: he hanged them with the purse of their reward about their necks; after having satisfied his second and special faith, he satisfied the general and first.

Mohammed II having resolved to rid himself of his brother, out of jealousy of state, according to the practice of the Ottoman family, he employed one of his officers in the execution, who, pouring a quantity of water too fast into him, choked him. This being done, to expiate the murder, he delivered the murderer into the hands of the mother of him he had so caused to be put to death, for they were only brothers by the father's side; she, in his presence, ripped up the murderer's bosom, and with her own hands rifled his breast for his heart, tore it out, and threw it to the dogs. And even to the worst people it is the sweetest thing imaginable, having once gained their end by a vicious action, to foist, in all security, into it some show of virtue and justice, as by way of compensation and conscientious correction; to which may be added, that they look upon the ministers of such horrid crimes as upon men who reproach them with them, and think by their deaths to erase the memory and testimony of such proceedings.

Or if, perhaps, you are rewarded, not to frustrate the public necessity for that extreme and desperate remedy, he who does it cannot for all that, if he be not such himself, but look upon you as an accursed and execrable fellow, and conclude you a greater traitor than he does, against whom you are so: for he tries the malignity of your disposition by your own hands, where he cannot possibly be deceived, you having no object of preceding hatred to move you to such an act; but he employs you as they do condemned malefactors in executions of justice, an office as necessary as dishonourable. Besides the baseness of such commissions, there is, moreover, a prostitution of conscience. Seeing that the daughter of Sejanus could not be put to death by the law of Rome, because she was a virgin, she was, to make it lawful, first ravished by the hangman and then strangled: not only his hand but his soul is slave to the public convenience.

When Amurath I., more grievously to punish his subjects who had taken part in the parricide rebellion of his son, ordained that their nearest kindred should assist in the execution, I find it very handsome in some of them to have rather chosen to be unjustly thought guilty of the parricide of another than to serve justice by a parricide of their own. And where I have seen, at the taking of some little fort by assault in my time, some rascals who, to save their own lives, would consent to hang their friends and companions, I have looked upon them to be of worse condition than those who were hanged. It is said, that Witold, Prince of Lithuania, introduced into the nation the practice that the criminal condemned to death should with his own hand execute the sentence, thinking it strange that a third person, innocent of the fault, should be made guilty of homicide.

A prince, when by some urgent circumstance or some impetuous and unforeseen accident that very much concerns his state, compelled to forfeit his word and break his faith, or otherwise forced from his ordinary duty, ought to attribute this necessity to a lash of the divine rod: vice it is not, for he has given up his own reason to a more universal and more powerful reason; but certainly it is a misfortune: so that if anyone should ask me what remedy? "None," say I, "if he were really racked between these two extremes: 'sed videat, ne quoeratur latebya perjurio', he must do it: but if he did it without regret, if it did not weigh on him to do it, it is a sign his conscience is in a sorry condition." If there be a person to be found of so tender a conscience as to think no cure whatever worth so important a remedy, I shall like him never the worse; he could not more excusably or more decently perish. We cannot do all we would, so that we must often, as the last anchorage, commit the protection of our vessels to the simple conduct of heaven. To what more just necessity does he reserve himself? What is less possible for him to do than what he cannot do but at the expense of his faith and honour,

CHAPTER 1

things that, perhaps, ought to be dearer to him than his own safety, or even the safety of his people. Though he should, with folded arms, only call God to his assistance, has he not reason to hope that the divine goodness will not refuse the favour of an extraordinary arm to just and pure hands? These are dangerous examples, rare and sickly exceptions to our natural rules: we must yield to them, but with great moderation and circumspection: no private utility is of such importance that we should upon that account strain our consciences to such a degree: the public may be, when very manifest and of very great concern.

Timoleon made a timely expiation for his strange exploit by the tears he shed, calling to mind that it was with a fraternal hand that he had slain the tyrant; and it justly pricked his conscience that he had been necessitated to purchase the public utility at so great a price as the violation of his private morality. Even the Senate itself, by his means delivered from slavery, durst not positively determine of so high a fact, and divided into two so important and contrary aspects; but the Syracusans, sending at the same time to the Corinthians to solicit their protection, and to require of them a captain fit to re-establish their city in its former dignity and to clear Sicily of several little tyrants by whom it was oppressed, they deputed Timoleon for that service, with this cunning declaration; "that according as he should behave himself well or ill in his employment, their sentence should incline either to favour the deliverer of his country, or to disfavour the murderer of his brother." This fantastic conclusion carries along with it some excuse, by reason of the danger of the example, and the importance of so strange an action: and they did well to discharge their own judgment of it, and to refer it to others who were not so much concerned. But Timoleon's comportment in this expedition soon made his cause more clear, so worthily and virtuously he demeaned himself upon all occasions; and the good fortune that accompanied him in the difficulties he had to overcome in this noble employment, seemed to be strewed in his way by the gods, favourably conspiring for his justification.

307

The end of this matter is excusable, if any can be so; but the profit of the augmentation of the public revenue, that served the Roman Senate for a pretence to the foul conclusion I am going to relate, is not sufficient to warrant any such injustice.

Certain cities had redeemed themselves and their liberty by money, by the order and consent of the Senate, out of the hands of L. Sylla: the business coming again in question, the Senate condemned them to be taxable as they were before, and that the money they had disbursed for their redemption should be lost to them. Civil war often produces such villainous examples; that we punish private men for confiding in us when we were public ministers: and the self-same magistrate makes another man pay the penalty of his change that has nothing to do with it; the pedagogue whips his scholar for his docility; and the guide beats the blind man whom he leads by the hand; a horrid image of justice.

There are rules in philosophy that are both false and weak. The example that is proposed to us for preferring private utility before faith given, has not weight enough by the circumstances they put to it; robbers have seized you, and after having made you swear to pay them a certain sum of money, dismiss you. It is not well done to say, that an honest man can be quit of his oath without payment, being out of their hands. It is no such thing: what fear has once made me willing to do, I am obliged to do it when I am no longer in fear; and though that fear only prevailed with my tongue without forcing my will, yet am I bound to keep my word. For my part, when my tongue has sometimes inconsiderately said something that I did not think, I have made a conscience of disowning it: otherwise, by degrees, we shall abolish all the right another derives from our promises and oaths:

Quasi vero forti viro vis possit adhiberi.

[As though a man of true courage could be compelled.
—Cicero, *De Officius*, iii. 30.]

308

Chapter 1

And it is only lawful, upon the account of private interest, to excuse breach of promise, when we have promised something that is unlawful and wicked in itself; for the right of virtue ought to take place of the right of any obligation of ours.

I have formerly placed Epaminondas in the first rank of excellent men, and do not repent it. How high did he stretch the consideration of his own particular duty? he who never killed a man whom he had overcome; who, for the inestimable benefit of restoring the liberty of his country, made conscience of killing a tyrant or his accomplices without due form of justice: and who concluded him to be a wicked man, how good a citizen soever otherwise, who amongst his enemies in battle spared not his friend and his guest. This was a soul of a rich composition: he married goodness and humanity, nay, even the tenderest and most delicate in the whole school of philosophy, to the roughest and most violent human actions. Was it nature or art that had intenerated that great courage of his, so full, so obstinate against pain and death and poverty, to such an extreme degree of sweetness and compassion? Dreadful in arms and blood, he overran and subdued a nation invincible by all others but by him alone; and yet in the heat of an encounter, could turn aside from his friend and guest. Certainly he was fit to command in war who could so rein himself with the curb of good nature, in the height and heat of his fury, a fury inflamed and foaming with blood and slaughter. It is a miracle to be able to mix any image of justice with such violent actions: and it was only possible for such a steadfastness of mind as that of Epaminondas therein to mix sweetness and the facility of the gentlest manners and purest innocence. And whereas one told the Mamertini that statutes were of no efficacy against armed men; and another told the tribune of the people that the time of justice and of war were distinct things; and a third said that the noise of arms deafened the voice of laws, this man was not precluded from listening to the laws of civility and pure courtesy. Had he not borrowed from his enemies the custom of sacrificing to the Muses when he went to war, that they might by their sweetness and gaiety soften his martial and rigorous fury? Let us not fear, by the example of so great a master, to believe that there is something unlawful, even against an enemy, and that the common concern ought not to require all things of all men, against private interest:

> *Manente memoria, etiam in dissidio publicorum*
> *foederum, privati juris:*

[The memory of private right remaining even amid public dissensions.

—Livy, xxv. 18.]

> *Et nulla potentia vires*
> *Praestandi, ne quid peccet amicus, habet;*

[No power on earth can sanction treachery against a friend.
—Ovid, *De Ponto*, i. 7, 37.]

and that all things are not lawful to an honest man for the service of his prince, the laws, or the general quarrel:

> *Non enim patria praestat omnibus officiis...*
> *et ipsi conducit pios habere cives in parentes.*

[The duty to one's country does not supersede all other duties. The country itself requires that its citizens should act piously toward their parents.

—Cicero, *De Officius*, iii. 23.]

Tis an instruction proper for the time wherein we live: we need not harden our courage with these arms of steel; it is enough that our shoulders are inured to them: it is enough to dip our pens in ink without dipping them in blood. If it be grandeur of courage, and the effect of a rare and singular virtue, to condemn friendship, private obligations, a man's word and relationship, for the common good and obedience to the magistrate, it is certainly sufficient to excuse us, that it is a grandeur that can have no place in the grandeur of Epaminondas' courage.

I abominate those mad exhortations of this other discomposed soul,

> *Dum tela micant, non vos pietatis imago*
> *Ulla, nec adversa conspecti fronte parentes*
> *Commoveant; vultus gladio turbate verendos.*

[While swords glitter, let no idea of piety, nor the face even of a father presented to you, move you: mutilate with your sword those venerable features

—Lucan, vii. 320.]

Let us deprive wicked, bloody, and treacherous natures of such a pretence of reason: let us set aside this guilty and extravagant justice, and stick to more human imitations. How great things can time and example do! In an encounter of the civil war against Cinna, one of Pompey's soldiers having unawares killed his brother, who was of the contrary party, he immediately for shame and sorrow killed himself: and some years after, in another civil war of the same people, a soldier demanded a reward of his officer for having killed his brother.

A man but ill proves the honour and beauty of an action by its utility: and very erroneously concludes that everyone is obliged to it, and that it becomes everyone to do it, if it be of utility:

Omnia non pariter rerum sunt omnibus apta.

[All things are not equally fit for all men.

—Propertius, iii. 9, 7.]

311

Let us take that which is most necessary and profitable for human society; it will be marriage; and yet the council of the saints find the contrary much better, excluding from it the most venerable vocation of man: as we design those horses for stallions of which we have the least esteem.

2

ON REPENTANCE

Others form man; I only report him: and represent a particular one, ill fashioned enough, and whom, if I had to model him anew, I should certainly make something else than what he is but that's past recalling. Now, though the features of my picture alter and change, it is not, however, unlike: the world eternally turns round; all things therein are incessantly moving, the earth, the rocks of Caucasus, and the pyramids of Egypt, both by the public motion and their own. Even constancy itself is no other but a slower and more languishing motion. I cannot fix my object; it is always tottering and reeling by a natural giddiness; I take it as it is at the instant I consider it; I do not paint its being, I paint its passage; not a passing from one age to another, or, as the people say, from seven to seven years, but from day to day, from minute to minute, I must accommodate my history to the hour: I may presently change, not only by fortune, but also by intention. It is a counterpart of various and changeable accidents, and of irresolute imaginations, and, as it falls out, sometimes contrary: whether it be that I am then another self, or that I take subjects by other circumstances and considerations: so it is that I may peradventure contradict myself, but, as Demades said, I never contradict the truth. Could my soul once take footing, I would not essay but resolve: but it is always learning and making trial.

I propose a life ordinary and without lustre: it is all one; all moral philosophy may as well be applied to a common and private life, as to one of richer composition: every man carries the entire form of human condition. Authors communicate themselves to the people by some especial and extrinsic mark; I, the first of any, by my universal being; as Michel de Montaigne, not as a grammarian, a poet, or a lawyer. If the world find fault that I speak too much of myself, I find fault that they do not so much as think of themselves. But is it reason that, being so particular in my way of living, I should pretend to recommend myself to the public knowledge? And is it also reason that I should produce to the world, where art and handling have so much credit and authority, crude and simple effects of nature, and of a weak nature to boot? Is it not to build a wall without stone or brick, or some such thing, to write books without learning and without art? The fancies of music are carried on by art; mine by chance. I have this, at least, according to discipline, that never any man treated of a subject he better understood and knew than I what I have undertaken, and that in this I am the most understanding man alive: secondly, that never any man penetrated farther into his matter, nor better and more distinctly sifted the parts and sequences of it, nor ever more exactly and fully arrived at the end he proposed to himself. To perfect it, I need bring nothing but fidelity to the work; and that is there, and the most pure and sincere that is anywhere to be found. I speak truth, not so much as I would, but as much as I dare; and I dare a little the more, as I grow older; for, methinks, custom allows to age more liberty of prating, and more indiscretion of talking of a man's self. That cannot fall out here, which I often see elsewhere, that the work and the artificer contradict one another: "Can a man of such sober conversation have written so foolish a book?" Or "Do so learned writings proceed from a man of so weak conversation?" He who talks at a very ordinary rate, and writes rare matter, it is to say that his capacity is borrowed and not his own. A learned man is not learned in all things: but a sufficient man is sufficient throughout, even to ignorance itself; here my book and I go hand in hand together. Elsewhere men may commend or censure the work, without reference to the workman; here they cannot: who touches the one, touches the other. He who shall judge of it without

Chapter 2

knowing him, will more wrong himself than me; he who does know him, gives me all the satisfaction I desire. I shall be happy beyond my desert, if I can obtain only thus much from the public approbation, as to make men of understanding perceive that I was capable of profiting by knowledge, had I had it; and that I deserved to have been assisted by a better memory.

Be pleased here to excuse what I often repeat, that I very rarely repent, and that my conscience is satisfied with itself, not as the conscience of an angel, or that of a horse, but as the conscience of a man; always adding this clause, not one of ceremony, but a true and real submission, that I speak inquiring and doubting, purely and simply referring myself to the common and accepted beliefs for the resolution. I do not teach; I only relate.

There is no vice that is absolutely a vice which does not offend, and that a sound judgment does not accuse; for there is in it so manifest a deformity and inconvenience, that peradventure they are in the right who say that it is chiefly begotten by stupidity and ignorance: so hard is it to imagine that a man can know without abhorring it. Malice sucks up the greatest part of its own venom, and poisons itself. Vice leaves repentance in the soul, like an ulcer in the flesh, which is always scratching and lacerating itself: for reason effaces all other grief and sorrows, but it begets that of repentance, which is so much the more grievous, by reason it springs within, as the cold and heat of fevers are more sharp than those that only strike upon the outward skin. I hold for vices (but everyone according to its proportion), not only those which reason and nature condemn, but those also which the opinion of men, though false and erroneous, have made such, if authorised by law and custom.

There is likewise no virtue which does not rejoice a well-descended nature: there is a kind of, I know not what, congratulation in well-doing that gives us an inward satisfaction, and a generous boldness that accompanies a good conscience: a soul daringly vicious may, peradventure, arm itself with security, but it cannot supply itself with this complacency and satisfaction. It is no little satisfaction to feel a man's self preserved from the contagion of so depraved an age, and to say to himself: "Whoever could penetrate into my soul would not there find me guilty either of the affliction or ruin of any one, or of revenge or envy, or any offence against the public laws, or of innovation or disturbance, or failure of my word; and though the licence of the time permits and teaches everyone so to do, yet have I not plundered any Frenchman's goods, or taken his money, and have lived upon what is my own, in war as well as in peace; neither have I set any man to work without paying him his hire." These testimonies of a good conscience please, and this natural rejoicing is very beneficial to us, and the only reward that we can never fail of.

To ground the recompense of virtuous actions upon the approbation of others is too uncertain and unsafe a foundation, especially in so corrupt and ignorant an age as this, wherein the good opinion of the vulgar is injurious: upon whom do you rely to show you what is recommendable? God defend me from being an honest man, according to the descriptions of honour I daily see everyone make of himself:

Quae fuerant vitia, mores sunt.

[What before had been vices are now manners.
—Seneca, *Epistles*, 39.]

Some of my friends have at times schooled and scolded me with great sincerity and plainness, either of their own voluntary motion, or by me entreated to it as to an office, which to a well-composed soul surpasses not only in utility, but in kindness, all other offices of friendship: I have always received them with the most open arms, both of courtesy and acknowledgment; but to say the truth, I have often found so much false measure, both in their reproaches and praises, that I had not done much amiss, rather to have done ill, than to have done well according to their notions. We, who live private lives, not exposed to any other view than our own, ought chiefly to have settled a pattern within ourselves by which to try our

316

actions: and according to that, sometimes to encourage and sometimes to correct ourselves. I have my laws and my judicature to judge of myself, and apply myself more to these than to any other rules: I do, indeed, restrain my actions according to others; but extend them not by any other rule than my own. You yourself only know if you are cowardly and cruel, loyal and devout: others see you not, and only guess at you by uncertain conjectures, and do not so much see your nature as your art; rely not therefore upon their opinions, but stick to your own:

> *Tuo tibi judicio est utendum.... Virtutis et vitiorum grave ipsius conscientiae pondus est: qua sublata, jacent omnia.*

[You must employ your own judgment upon yourself, great is the weight of your own conscience in the discovery of virtues and vices: which taken away, all things are lost.

—Cicero, *De Natura Deorum,* iii. 35;
Tusculum Disputations, i. 25.]

But the saying that repentance immediately follows the sin seems not to have respect to sin in its high estate, which is lodged in us as in its own proper habitation. One may disown and retract the vices that surprise us, and to which we are hurried by passions; but those which by a long habit are rooted in a strong and vigorous will are not subject to contradiction. Repentance is no other but a recanting of the will and an opposition to our fancies, which lead us which way they please. It makes this person disown his former virtue and continency:

> *Quae mens est hodie, cur eadem non puero fait?*
> *Vel cur his animis incolumes non redeunt genae?*

[What my mind is, why was it not the same, when I was a boy? or why do not the cheeks return to these feelings?

—Horace, *Odes,* v. 10, 7.]

It is an exact life that maintains itself in due order in private. Everyone may juggle his part, and represent an honest man upon the stage: but within, and in his own bosom, where all may do as they list, where all is concealed, to be regular, there's the point. The next degree is to be so in his house, and in his ordinary actions, for which we are accountable to none, and where there is no study nor artifice. And therefore Bias, setting forth the excellent state of a private family, says: "of which a the master is the same within, by his own virtue and temper, that he is abroad, for fear of the laws and report of men." And it was a worthy saying of Julius Drusus, to the masons who offered him, for three thousand crowns, to put his house in such a posture that his neighbours should no longer have the same inspection into it as before; "I will give you," said he, "six thousand to make it so that everybody may see into every room." It is honourably recorded of Agesilaus, that he used in his journeys always to take up his lodgings in temples, to the end that the people and the gods themselves might pry into his most private actions. Such a one has been a miracle to the world, in whom neither his wife nor servant has ever seen anything so much as remarkable; few men have been admired by their own domestics; no one was ever a prophet, not merely in his own house, but in his own country, says the experience of histories: [No man is a hero to his valet-de-chambre, said Marshal Catinat] it is the same in things of nought, and in this low example the image of a greater is to be seen. In my country of Gascony, they look upon it as a drollery to see me in print; the further off I am read from my own home, the better I am esteemed. I purchase printers in Guienne; elsewhere they purchase me. Upon this it is that they lay their foundation who conceal themselves present and living, to obtain a name when they are dead and absent. I had rather have a great deal less in hand, and do not expose myself to the world upon any other account than my present share; when I leave it I quit the rest. See this functionary whom the people escort in state, with wonder and applause, to his very door; he puts off the pageant with his robe, and falls so much the lower by how much he was higher exalted: in himself within, all is tumult and degraded. And though all should be regular there, it will require a vivid and well-chosen judgment to perceive it in these low and private actions; to which may be added, that order is a dull, sombre virtue. To enter a breach, conduct an embassy, govern a people, are actions of renown; to reprehend, laugh, sell, pay, love, hate, and gently and justly converse with a man's own family and with himself; not to relax, not to give a man's self the lie, is more rare and hard, and less remarkable. By which means, retired lives, whatever is said to the contrary, undergo duties of as great or greater difficulty than the others do; and private men, says Aristotle,' serve virtue more painfully and highly than those in authority do: we prepare ourselves for eminent occasions, more out of glory than conscience. The shortest way to arrive at glory, would be to do that for conscience which we do for glory: and the virtue of Alexander appears to me of much less vigour in his great theatre, than that of Socrates in his mean and obscure employment. I can easily conceive Socrates in the place of Alexander, but Alexander in that of Socrates, I cannot. Who shall ask the one what he can do, he will answer, "Subdue the world": and who shall put the same question to the other, he will say, "Carry on human life conformably with its natural condition"; a much more general, weighty, and legitimate science than the other.

The virtue of the soul does not consist in flying high, but in walking orderly; its grandeur does not exercise itself in grandeur, but in mediocrity. As they who judge and try us within, make no great account of the lustre of our public actions, and see they are only streaks and rays of clear water springing from a slimy and muddy bottom so, likewise, they who judge of us by this gallant outward appearance, in like manner conclude of our internal constitution; and cannot couple common faculties, and like their own, with the other faculties that astonish them, and are so far out of their sight. Therefore it is that we give such savage forms to demons: and who does not give Tamerlane great eyebrows, wide nostrils, a dreadful visage, and a prodigious stature, according to the imagination he has conceived by the report of his name? Had any one formerly brought me to Erasmus, I should hardly have believed but that all was adage and apothegm he spoke to his man or his hostess. We much more aptly imagine an artisan upon his close-stool, or upon his wife, than a great president venerable by his port and sufficiency: we fancy that they, from their high tribunals, will not abase themselves so much as to live. As vicious souls are often incited by some foreign impulse to do well, so are virtuous souls to do ill; they are therefore to be judged by their settled state, when they are at home, whenever that may be; and, at all events, when they are nearer repose, and in their native station.

Natural inclinations are much assisted and fortified by education; but they seldom alter and overcome their institution: a thousand natures of my time have escaped towards virtue or vice, through a quite contrary discipline:

> *Sic ubi, desuetae silvis, in carcere clausae*
> *Mansuevere ferx, et vultus posuere minaces,*
> *Atque hominem didicere pati, si torrida parvus*
> *Venit in ora cruor, redeunt rabiesque fororque,*
> *Admonitaeque tument gustato sanguine fauces*
> *Fervet, et a trepido vix abstinet ira magistro;*

[So savage beasts, when shut up in cages and grown unaccustomed to the woods, have become tame, and have laid aside their fierce looks, and submit to the rule of man; if again a slight taste of blood comes into their mouths, their rage and fury return, their jaws are erected by thirst of blood, and their anger scarcely abstains from their trembling masters.

—Lucan, iv. 237.]

CHAPTER 2

these original qualities are not to be rooted out; they may be covered and concealed. The Latin tongue is as it were natural to me; I understand it better than French; but I have not been used to speak it, nor hardly to write it, these forty years. Unless upon extreme and sudden emotions which I have fallen into twice or thrice in my life, and once seeing my father in perfect health fall upon me in a swoon, I have always uttered from the bottom of my heart my first words in Latin; nature deafened, and forcibly expressing itself, in spite of so long a discontinuation; and this example is said of many others.

They who in my time have attempted to correct the manners of the world by new opinions, reform seeming vices; but the essential vices they leave as they were, if indeed they do not augment them, and augmentation is therein to be feared; we defer all other well doing upon the account of these external reformations, of less cost and greater show, and thereby expiate good cheap, for the other natural, consubstantial, and intestine vices. Look a little into our experience: there is no man, if he listen to himself, who does not in himself discover a particular and governing form of his own, that jostles his education, and wrestles with the tempest of passions that are contrary to it. For my part, I seldom find myself agitated with surprises; I always find myself in my place, as heavy and unwieldy bodies do; if I am not at home, I am always near at hand; my dissipations do not transport me very far; there is nothing strange or extreme in the case; and yet I have sound and vigorous turns.

The true condemnation, and which touches the common practice of men, is that their very retirement itself is full of filth and corruption; the idea of their reformation composed, their repentance sick and faulty, very nearly as much as their sin. Some, either from having been linked to vice by a natural propension or long practice, cannot see its deformity. Others (of which constitution I am) do indeed feel the weight of vice, but they counterbalance it with pleasure, or some other occasion; and suffer and lend themselves to it for a certain price, but viciously and basely. Yet there might, haply, be imagined so vast a disproportion of measure, where with justice the pleasure might excuse the sin, as we say of utility; not only if accidental and out of sin, as in thefts, but in the very exercise of sin, or in the enjoyment of women, where the temptation is violent, and, it is said, sometimes not to be overcome.

Being the other day at Armaignac, on the estate of a kinsman of mine, I there saw a peasant who was by everyone nicknamed the thief. He thus related the story of his life: that, being born a beggar, and finding that he should not be able, so as to be clear of indigence, to get his living by the sweat of his brow, he resolved to turn thief, and by means of his strength of body had exercised this trade all the time of his youth in great security; for he ever made his harvest and vintage in other men's grounds, but a great way off, and in so great quantities, that it was not to be imagined one man could have carried away so much in one night upon his shoulders; and, moreover, he was careful equally to divide and distribute the mischief he did, that the loss was of less importance to every particular man. He is now grown old, and rich for a man of his condition, thanks to his trade, which he openly confesses to everyone. And to make his peace with God, he says, that he is daily ready by good offices to make satisfaction to the successors of those he has robbed, and if he do not finish (for to do it all at once he is not able), he will then leave it in charge to his heirs to perform the rest, proportionably to the wrong he himself only knows he has done to each. By this description, true or false, this man looks upon theft as a dishonest action, and hates it, but less than poverty, and simply repents; but to the extent he has thus recompensed he repents not. This is not that habit which incorporates us into vice, and conforms even our understanding itself to it; nor is it that impetuous whirlwind that by gusts troubles and blinds our souls, and for the time precipitates us, judgment and all, into the power of vice.

I customarily do what I do thoroughly and make but one step on it; I have rarely any movement that hides itself and steals away from my reason, and that does not proceed in the matter by the consent of all my faculties, without division or intestine sedition; my judgment is to have all the blame or all the praise; and the blame it once has, it has always; for almost from my infancy it has ever been one: the same inclination, the same turn, the same force; and as to universal opinions, I fixed myself from my childhood in the place where I resolved to stick. There are some sins that are impetuous, prompt, and sudden; let us set them aside: but in these other sins so often repeated, deliberated, and contrived, whether sins of complexion or sins of profession and vocation, I cannot conceive that they should have so long been settled in the same resolution, unless the reason and conscience of him who has them, be constant to have them; and the repentance he boasts to be inspired with on a sudden, is very hard for me to imagine or form. I follow not the opinion of the Pythagorean sect, "that men take up a new soul when they repair to the images of the gods to receive their oracles," unless he mean that it must needs be extrinsic, new, and lent for the time; our own showing so little sign of purification and cleanness, fit for such an office.

They act quite contrary to the stoical precepts, who do indeed command us to correct the imperfections and vices we know ourselves guilty of, but forbid us therefore to disturb the repose of our souls: these make us believe that they have great grief and remorse within: but of amendment, correction, or interruption, they make nothing appear. It cannot be a cure if the malady be not wholly discharged; if repentance were laid upon the scale of the balance, it would weigh down sin. I find no quality so easy to counterfeit as devotion, if men do not conform their manners and life to the profession; its essence is abstruse and occult; the appearance easy and ostentatious.

For my own part, I may desire in general to be other than I am; I may condemn and dislike my whole form, and beg of Almighty God for an entire reformation, and that He will please to pardon my natural infirmity: but I ought not to call this repentance, methinks, no more than the being dissatisfied that I am not an angel or Cato. My actions are regular, and conformable to what I am and to my condition; I can do no better; and repentance does not properly touch things that are not in our power; sorrow does. I imagine an infinite number of natures more elevated and regular than mine; and yet I do not for all that improve my faculties, no more than my arm or will grow more strong and vigorous for conceiving those of another to be so. If to conceive and wish a nobler way of acting than that we have should produce a repentance of our own, we must then repent us of our most innocent actions, forasmuch as we may well suppose that in a more excellent nature they would have been carried on with greater dignity and perfection; and we would that ours were so. When I reflect upon the deportment of my youth, with that of my old age, I find that I have commonly behaved myself with equal order in both according to what I understand: this is all that my resistance can do. I do not flatter myself; in the same circumstances I should do the same things. It is not a patch, but rather an universal tincture, with which I am stained. I know no repentance, superficial, half-way, and ceremonious; it must sting me all over before I can call it so, and must prick my bowels as deeply and universally as God sees into me.

As to business, many excellent opportunities have escaped me for want of good management; and yet my deliberations were sound enough, according to the occurrences presented to me: it is their way to choose always the easiest and safest course. I find that, in my former resolves, I have proceeded with discretion, according to my own rule, and according to the state of the subject proposed, and should do the same a thousand years hence in like occasions; I do not consider what it is now, but what it was then, when I deliberated on it: the force of all counsel consists in the time; occasions and things eternally shift and change. I have in my life committed some important errors, not for want of good understanding, but for want of good luck. There are secret, and not to be foreseen, parts in matters we have in hand, especially in the nature of men; mute conditions, that make no show, unknown sometimes even to the possessors themselves, that spring and start up by incidental occasions; if my prudence could not penetrate into nor foresee them, I blame it not: it is commissioned no further than its own limits; if the event be too hard for me, and take the side I have refused, there is no remedy; I do not blame myself, I accuse my fortune, and not my work; this cannot be called repentance.

Phocion, having given the Athenians an advice that was not followed, and the affair nevertheless succeeding contrary to his opinion, someone said to him, "Well, Phocion, art thou content that matters go so well?"—"I am very well content," replied he, "that this has happened so well, but I do not repent that I counselled the other." When any of my friends address themselves to me for advice, I give it candidly and clearly, without sticking, as almost all other men do, at the hazard of the thing's falling out contrary to my opinion, and that I may be reproached for my counsel; I am very indifferent as to that, for the fault will be theirs for having consulted me, and I could not refuse them that office.

I, for my own part, can rarely blame any one but myself for my oversights and misfortunes, for indeed I seldom solicit the advice of another, if not by honour of ceremony, or excepting where I stand in need of information, special science, or as to matter of fact. But in things wherein I stand in need of nothing but judgment, other men's reasons may serve to fortify my own, but have little power to dissuade me; I hear them all with civility and patience; but, to my recollection, I never made use of any but my own. With me, they are but flies and atoms, that confound and distract my will; I lay no great stress upon my opinions; but I lay as little upon those of others, and fortune rewards me accordingly: if I receive but little advice, I also give but little. I am seldom consulted, and still more seldom believed, and know no concern, either public or private, that has been mended or bettered by my advice. Even they whom fortune had in some sort tied to my direction, have more willingly suffered themselves to be governed by any other counsels than mine. And as a man who am as jealous of my repose as of my authority, I am better pleased that it should be so; in leaving me there, they humour what I profess, which is to settle and wholly contain myself within myself. I take a pleasure in being uninterested in other men's affairs, and disengaged from being their warranty, and responsible for what they do.

In all affairs that are past, be it how it will, I have very little regret; for this imagination puts me out of my pain, that they were so to fall out they are in the great revolution of the world, and in the chain of stoical 'causes: your fancy cannot, by wish and imagination, move one tittle, but that the great current of things will not reverse both the past and the future.

As to the rest, I abominate that incidental repentance which old age brings along with it. He, who said of old, that he was obliged to his age for having weaned him from pleasure, was of another opinion than I am; I can never think myself beholden to impotency for any good it can do to me:

> *Nec tam aversa unquam videbitur ab opera suo providentia,*
> *ut debilitas inter optima inventa sit.*

[Nor can Providence ever seem so averse to her own work, that debility should be found to be amongst the best things.
—Quintilian, *Instituto Oratoria*, v. 12.]

Our appetites are rare in old age; a profound satiety seizes us after the act; in this I see nothing of conscience; chagrin and weakness imprint in us a drowsy and rheumatic virtue. We must not suffer ourselves to be so wholly carried away by natural alterations as to suffer our judgments to be imposed upon by them. Youth and pleasure have not formerly so far prevailed with me, that I did not well enough discern the face of vice in pleasure; neither does the distaste that years have brought me, so far prevail with me now, that I cannot discern pleasure in vice. Now that I am no more in my flourishing age, I judge as well of these things as if I were.

Chapter 2

Old though I am, for ladies' love unfit,
The power of beauty I remember yet. — Chaucer.

I, who narrowly and strictly examine it, find my reason the very same it was in my most licentious age, except, perhaps, that it is weaker and more decayed by being grown older; and I find that the pleasure it refuses me upon the account of my bodily health, it would no more refuse now, in consideration of the health of my soul, than at any time heretofore. I do not repute it the more valiant for not being able to combat; my temptations are so broken and mortified, that they are not worth its opposition; holding but out my hands, I repel them. Should one present the old concupiscence before it, I fear it would have less power to resist it than heretofore; I do not discern that in itself it judges anything otherwise now than it formerly did, nor that it has acquired any new light: wherefore, if there be convalescence, it is an enchanted one. Miserable kind of remedy, to owe one's health to one's disease! Tis not that our misfortune should perform this office, but the good fortune of our judgment. I am not to be made to do anything by persecutions and afflictions, but to curse them: that is, for people who cannot be roused but by a whip. My reason is much more free in prosperity, and much more distracted, and put to it to digest pains than pleasures: I see best in a clear sky; health admonishes me more cheerfully, and to better purpose, than sickness. I did all that in me lay to reform and regulate myself from pleasures, at a time when I had health and vigour to enjoy them; I should be ashamed and envious that the misery and misfortune of my old age should have credit over my good healthful, sprightly, and vigorous years, and that men should estimate me, not by what I have been, but by what I have ceased to be.

In my opinion, it is the happy living, and not (as Antisthenes' said) the happy dying, in which human felicity consists. I have not made it my business to make a monstrous addition of a philosopher's tail to the head and body of a libertine; nor would I have this wretched remainder give the lie to the pleasant, sound, and long part of my life: I would present myself uniformly throughout. Were I to live my life over again, I should live it just as I have lived it; I neither complain of the past, nor do I fear the future; and if I am not much deceived, I am the same within that I am without. It is one main obligation I have to my fortune, that the succession of my bodily estate has been carried on according to the natural seasons; I have seen the grass, the blossom, and the fruit, and now see the withering; happily, however, because naturally. I bear the infirmities I have the better, because they came not till I had reason to expect them, and because also they make me with greater pleasure remember that long felicity of my past life. My wisdom may have been just the same in both ages, but it was more active, and of better grace whilst young and sprightly, than now it is when broken, peevish, and uneasy. I repudiate, then, these casual and painful reformations. God must touch our hearts; our consciences must amend of themselves, by the aid of our reason, and not by the decay of our appetites; pleasure is, in itself, neither pale nor discoloured, to be discerned by dim and decayed eyes.

We ought to love temperance for itself, and because God has commanded that and chastity; but that which we are reduced to by catarrhs, and for which I am indebted to the stone, is neither chastity nor temperance; a man cannot boast that he despises and resists pleasure if he cannot see it, if he knows not what it is, and cannot discern its graces, its force, and most alluring beauties; I know both the one and the other, and may therefore the better say it. But; methinks, our souls in old age are subject to more troublesome maladies and imperfections than in youth; I said the same when young and when I was reproached with the want of a beard; and I say so now that my grey hairs give me some authority. We call the difficulty of our humours and the disrelish of present things wisdom; but, in truth, we do not so much forsake vices as we change them, and in my opinion, for worse. Besides a foolish and feeble pride, an impertinent prating, froward and insociable humours, superstition, and a ridiculous desire of riches when we have lost the use of them,

Chapter 2

I find there more envy, injustice, and malice. Age imprints more wrinkles in the mind than it does on the face; and souls are never, or very rarely seen, that, in growing old, do not smell sour and musty. Man moves all together, both towards his perfection and decay. In observing the wisdom of Socrates, and many circumstances of his condemnation, I should dare to believe that he in some sort himself purposely, by collusion, contributed to it, seeing that, at the age of seventy years, he might fear to suffer the lofty motions of his mind to be cramped and his wonted lustre obscured. What strange metamorphoses do I see age every day make in many of my acquaintance! It is a potent malady, and that naturally and imperceptibly steals into us; a vast provision of study and great precaution are required to evade the imperfections it loads us with, or at least to weaken their progress. I find that, notwithstanding all my entrenchments, it gets foot by foot upon me: I make the best resistance I can, but I do not know to what at last it will reduce me. But fall out what will, I am content the world may know, when I am fallen, from what I fell.

5

ON SOME VERSES OF VIRGIL

By how much profitable thoughts are more full and solid, by so much are they also more cumbersome and heavy: vice, death, poverty, diseases, are grave and grievous subjects. A man should have his soul instructed in the means to sustain and to contend with evils, and in the rules of living and believing well: and often rouse it up, and exercise it in this noble study; but in an ordinary soul it must be by intervals and with moderation; it will otherwise grow besotted if continually intent upon it. I found it necessary, when I was young, to put myself in mind and solicit myself to keep me to my duty; gaiety and health do not, they say, so well agree with those grave and serious meditations: I am at present in another state: the conditions of age but too much put me in mind, urge me to wisdom, and preach to me. From the excess of sprightliness I am fallen into that of severity, which is much more troublesome; and for that reason I now and then suffer myself purposely a little to run into disorder, and occupy my mind in wanton and youthful thoughts, wherewith it diverts itself. I am of late but too reserved, too heavy, and too ripe; years every day read to me lectures of coldness and temperance. This body of mine avoids disorder and dreads it; it is now my body's turn to guide my mind towards reformation; it governs, in turn, and more rudely and imperiously than the other; it lets me not an hour alone, sleeping or waking, but is always preaching to me death, patience, and repentance. I now defend myself from temperance, as I have formerly done from pleasure; it draws me too much

331

back, and even to stupidity. Now I will be master of myself, to all intents and purposes; wisdom has its excesses, and has no less need of moderation than folly. Therefore, lest I should wither, dry up, and overcharge myself with prudence, in the intervals and truces my infirmities allow me:

Mens intenta suis ne seit usque malis.

[That my mind may not eternally be intent upon my ills.

—Ovid, *Tristia,* iv. i, 4.]

I gently turn aside, and avert my eyes from the stormy and cloudy sky I have before me, which, thanks be to God, I regard without fear, but not without meditation and study, and amuse myself in the remembrance of my better years:

Animus quo perdidit, optat,
Atque in praeterita se totus imagine versat.

[The mind wishes to have what it has lost, and throws itself wholly into memories of the past.

—Petronius, c. 128.]

Let childhood look forward and age backward; was not this the signification of Janus' double face? Let years draw me along if they will, but it shall be backward; as long as my eyes can discern the pleasant season expired, I shall now and then turn them that way; though it escape from my blood and veins, I shall not, however, root the image of it out of my memory:

Hoc est
Vivere bis, vita posse priore frui.

[It is to live twice to be able to enjoy one's former life again.

—Martial, x. 23, 7.]

CHAPTER 5

Plato ordains that old men should be present at the exercises, dances, and sports of young people, that they may rejoice in others for the activity and beauty of body which is no more in themselves, and call to mind the grace and comeliness of that flourishing age; and wills that in these recreations the honour of the prize should be given to that young man who has most diverted the company. I was formerly wont to mark cloudy and gloomy days as extraordinary; these are now my ordinary days; the extraordinary are the clear and bright; I am ready to leap for joy, as for an unwonted favour, when nothing happens me. Let me tickle myself, I cannot force a poor smile from this wretched body of mine; I am only merry in conceit and in dreaming, by artifice to divert the melancholy of age; but, in faith, it requires another remedy than a dream. A weak contest of art against nature. "It is great folly to lengthen and anticipate human incommodities, as everyone does; I had rather be a less while old than be old before I am really so." I seize on even the least occasions of pleasure I can meet. I know very well, by hearsay, several sorts of prudent pleasures, effectually so, and glorious to boot; but opinion has not power enough over me to give me an appetite to them. I covet not so much to have them magnanimous, magnificent, and pompous, as I do to have them sweet, facile, and ready:

> *A natura discedimus; populo nos damus,*
> *nullius rei bono auctori.*

[We depart from nature and give ourselves to the people, who understand nothing.
> —Seneca, *Epistles*, 99.]

My philosophy is in action, in natural and present practice, very little in fancy: what if I should take pleasure in playing at cob-nut or to whip a top!

Non ponebat enim rumores ante salutem.

[He did not sacrifice his health even to rumours.
—Ennius, from Cicero, *De Officius*, i. 24.]

Pleasure is a quality of very little ambition; it thinks itself rich enough of itself without any addition of repute; and is best pleased where most retired. A young man should be whipped who pretends to a taste in wine and sauces; there was nothing which, at that age, I less valued or knew: now I begin to learn; I am very much ashamed on it; but what should I do? I am more ashamed and vexed at the occasions that put me upon it. It is for us to dote and trifle away the time, and for young men to stand upon their reputation and nice punctilios; they are going towards the world and the world's opinion; we are retiring from it:

Sibi arma, sibi equos, sibi hastas, sibi clavam, sibi pilam,
sibi natationes, et cursus habeant: nobis senibus, ex lusionibus
multis, talos relinquant et tesseras;

[Let them reserve to themselves arms, horses, spears, clubs, tennis, swimming, and races; and of all the sports leave to us old men cards and dice.

—Cicero, *De Senectute*, c. 16.]

the laws themselves send us home. I can do no less in favour of this wretched condition into which my age has thrown me than furnish it with toys to play withal, as they do children; and, in truth, we become such. Both wisdom and folly will have enough to do to support and relieve me by alternate services in this calamity of age:

Misce stultitiam consiliis brevem.

[Mingle with counsels a brief interval of folly.

—Horace, *Odes*, iv. 12, 27.]

Chapter 5

I accordingly avoid the lightest punctures; and those that formerly would not have rippled the skin, now pierce me through and through: my habit of body is now so naturally declining to ill:

In fragili corpore odiosa omnis offensio est;

[In a fragile body every shock is obnoxious.
     —Cicero, *De Senectute*, c. 18.]

Mensque pati durum sustinet aegra nihil.

[And the infirm mind can bear no difficult exertion.
     —Ovid, *Epistulae ex Ponto*, i. 5, 18.]

I have ever been very susceptibly tender as to offences: I am much more tender now, and open throughout.

Et minimae vires frangere quassa valent.

[And little force suffices to break what was cracked before.
     —Ovid, *De Tristia*, iii. 11, 22.]

My judgment restrains me from kicking against and murmuring at the inconveniences that nature orders me to endure, but it does not take away my feeling them: I, who have no other thing in my aim but to live and be merry, would run from one end of the world to the other to seek out one good year of pleasant and jocund tranquillity. A melancholic and dull tranquillity may be enough for me, but it benumbs and stupefies me; I am not contented with it. If there be any person, any knot of good company in country or city, in France or elsewhere, resident or in motion, who can like my humour, and whose humours I can like, let them but whistle and I will run and furnish them with essays in flesh and bone:

Seeing it is the privilege of the mind to rescue itself from old age, I advise mine to it with all the power I have; let it meanwhile continue green, and flourish if it can, like mistletoe upon a dead tree. But I fear it is a traitor; it has contracted so strict a fraternity with the body that it leaves me at every turn, to follow that in its need. I wheedle and deal with it apart in vain; I try in vain to wean it from this correspondence, to no effect; quote to it Seneca and Catullus, and ladies and royal masques; if its companion have the stone, it seems to have it too; even the faculties that are most peculiarly and properly its own cannot then perform their functions, but manifestly appear stupefied and asleep; there is no sprightliness in its productions, if there be not at the same time an equal proportion in the body too.

Our masters are to blame, that in searching out the causes of the extraordinary emotions of the soul, besides attributing it to a divine ecstasy, love, martial fierceness, poesy, wine, they have not also attributed a part to health: a boiling, vigorous, full, and lazy health, such as formerly the verdure of youth and security, by fits, supplied me withal; that fire of sprightliness and gaiety darts into the mind flashes that are lively and bright beyond our natural light, and of all enthusiasms the most jovial, if not the most extravagant.

It is, then, no wonder if a contrary state stupefy and clog my spirit, and produce a contrary effect:

Ad nullum consurgit opus, cum corpore languet;

[When the mind is languishing, the body is good for nothing.
Or: It rises to no effort; it languishes with the body.
—Pseudo Gallus, i. 125.]

and yet would have me obliged to it for giving, as it wants to make out, much less consent to this stupidity than is the ordinary case with men of my age. Let us, at least, whilst we have truce, drive away incommodities and difficulties from our commerce:

Dum licet, obducta solvatur fronte senectus:

[Whilst we can, let us banish old age from the brow.
—Herod., *Epistles*, xiii. 7.]

Tetrica sunt amcenanda jocularibus.

[Sour things are to be sweetened with those that are pleasant.
—Sidonius Apollin., *Epistles*, i. 9.]

I love a gay and civil wisdom, and fly from all sourness and austerity of manners, all repellent, mien being suspected by me:

Tristemque vultus tetrici arrogantiam:

[The arrogant sadness of a crabbed face.
—Auctor Incert.]

Et habet tristis quoque turba cinaedos.

[And the dull crowd also has its voluptuaries. Or:
An austere countenance sometimes covers a debauched mind.
—Idem.]

I am very much of Plato's opinion, who says that facile or harsh humours are great indications of the good or ill disposition of the mind. Socrates had a constant countenance, but serene and smiling, not sourly austere, like the elder Crassus, whom no one ever saw laugh. Virtue is a pleasant and gay quality.

337

I know very well that few will quarrel with the licence of my writings, who have not more to quarrel with in the licence of their own thoughts: I conform myself well enough to their inclinations, but I offend their eyes. It is a fine humour to strain the writings of Plato, to wrest his pretended intercourses with Phaedo, Dion, Stella, and Archeanassa:

Non pudeat dicere, quod non pudet sentire.

[Let us not be ashamed to speak what we are not ashamed to think.]

I hate a froward and dismal spirit, that slips over all the pleasures of life and seizes and feeds upon misfortunes; like flies, that cannot stick to a smooth and polished body, but fix and repose themselves upon craggy and rough places, and like cupping-glasses, that only suck and attract bad blood.

As to the rest, I have enjoined myself to dare to say all that I dare to do; even thoughts that are not to be published, displease me; the worst of my actions and qualities do not appear to me so evil as I find it evil and base not to dare to own them. Everyone is wary and discreet in confession, but men ought to be so in action; the boldness of doing ill is in some sort compensated and restrained by the boldness of confessing it. Whoever will oblige himself to tell all, should oblige himself to do nothing that he must be forced to conceal. I wish that this excessive licence of mine may draw men to freedom, above these timorous and mincing virtues sprung from our imperfections, and that at the expense of my immoderation I may reduce them to reason. A man must see and study his vice to correct it; they who conceal it from others, commonly conceal it from themselves; and do not think it close enough, if they themselves see it: they withdraw and disguise it from their own consciences:

Quare vitia sua nemo confitetur? Quia etiam nunc in
ilia est; somnium narrare vigilantis est.

338

CHAPTER 5

[Why does no man confess his vices? Because he is yet in them; it is for a waking man to tell his dream.

—Seneca, *Epistles*, 53.]

The diseases of the body explain themselves by their increase; we find that to be the gout which we called a rheum or a strain; the diseases of the soul, the greater they are, keep, themselves the most obscure; the most sick are the least sensible; therefore it is that with an unrelenting hand they most often, in full day, be taken to task, opened, and torn from the hollow of the heart. As in doing well, so in doing ill, the mere confession is sometimes satisfaction. Is there any deformity in doing amiss, that can excuse us from confessing ourselves? It is so great a pain to me to dissemble, that I evade the trust of another's secrets, wanting the courage to disavow my knowledge. I can keep silent, but deny I cannot without the greatest trouble and violence to myself imaginable to be very secret, a man must be so by nature, not by obligation. It is little worth, in the service of a prince, to be secret, if a man be not a liar to boot. If he who asked Thales the Milesian whether he ought solemnly to deny that he had committed adultery, had applied himself to me, I should have told him that he ought not to do it; for I look upon lying as a worse fault than the other. Thales advised him quite contrary, bidding him swear to shield the greater fault by the less; nevertheless, this counsel was not so much an election as a multiplication of vice. Upon which let us say this in passing, that we deal liberally with a man of conscience when we propose to him some difficulty in counterpoise of vice; but when we shut him up between two vices, he is put to a hard choice as Origen was either to idolatrise or to suffer himself to be carnally abused by a great Ethiopian slave they brought to him. He submitted to the first condition, and wrongly, people say. Yet those women of our times are not much out, according to their error, who protest they had rather burden their consciences with ten men than one mass.

If it be indiscretion so to publish one's errors, yet there is no great danger that it pass into example and custom; for Ariston said, that the winds men most fear are those that lay them open. We must tuck up this ridiculous rag that hides our manners: they send their consciences to the stews, and keep a starched countenance: even traitors and assassins espouse the laws of ceremony, and there fix their duty. So that neither can injustice complain of incivility, nor malice of indiscretion. It is pity but a bad man should be a fool to boot, and that outward decency should palliate his vice: this rough-cast only appertains to a good and sound wall, that deserves to be preserved and whited.

In favour of the Huguenots, who condemn our auricular and private confession, I confess myself in public, religiously and purely: St. Augustin, Origeti, and Hippocrates have published the errors of their opinions; I, moreover, of my manners. I am greedy of making myself known, and I care not to how many, provided it be truly; or to say better, I hunger for nothing; but I mortally hate to be mistaken by those who happen to learn my name. He who does all things for honour and glory, what can he think to gain by showing himself to the world in a vizor, and by concealing his true being from the people? Praise a humpback for his stature, he has reason to take it for an affront: if you are a coward, and men commend you for your valour, is it of you they speak? They take you for another. I should like him as well who glorifies himself in the compliments and congees that are made him as if he were master of the company, when he is one of the least of the train. Archelaus, king of Macedon, walking along the street, somebody threw water on his head, which they who were with him said he ought to punish: "Aye, but," said he, "whoever it was, he did not throw the water upon me, but upon him whom he took me to be." Socrates being told that people spoke ill of him, "Not at all," said he, "there is nothing, in me of what they say."

For my part, if any one should recommend me as a good pilot, as being very modest or very chaste, I should owe him no thanks; and so, whoever should call me traitor, robber, or drunkard, I should be as little concerned. They who do not rightly know themselves, may feed themselves with false approbations; not I, who see myself, and who examine myself even to my very bowels, and who very well know what is my due. I am content to be less commended, provided I am better known. I may be reputed a wise man in such a sort of wisdom as I take to be folly. I am vexed that my Essays only serve the ladies for a common piece of furniture, and a piece for the hall; this chapter will make me part of the water-closet. I love to traffic with them a little in private; public conversation is without favour and without savour. In farewells, we oftener than not heat our affections towards the things we take leave of; I take my last leave of the pleasures of this world: these are our last embraces.

But let us come to my subject: what has the act of generation, so natural, so necessary, and so just, done to men, to be a thing not to be spoken of without blushing, and to be excluded from all serious and moderate discourse? We boldly pronounce kill, rob, betray, and that we dare only to do between the teeth. Is it to say, the less we expend in words, we may pay so much the more in thinking? For it is certain that the words least in use, most seldom written, and best kept in, are the best and most generally known: no age, no manners, are ignorant of them, no more than the word bread they imprint themselves in everyone without being, expressed, without voice, and without figure; and the sex that most practises it is bound to say least of it. It is an act that we have placed in the franchise of silence, from which to take it is a crime even to accuse and judge it; neither dare we reprehend it but by periphrasis and picture. A great favour to a criminal to be so execrable that justice thinks it unjust to touch and see him; free, and safe by the benefit of the severity of his condemnation. Is it not here as in matter of books, that sell better and become more public for being suppressed? For my part, I will take Aristotle at his word, who says, that "bashfulness is an ornament to youth, but a reproach to old age." These verses are preached in the ancient school, a school that I much more adhere to than the modern: its virtues appear to me to be greater, and the vices less:

> *Ceux qui par trop fuyant Venus estrivent,*
> *Faillent autant que ceulx qui trop la suyvent.*

[They err as much who too much forbear Venus, as they who are too frequent in her rites. – A translation by Amyot from Plutarch, "A philosopher should converse with princes".]

Tu, dea, rerum naturam sola gubernas,
Nec sine to quicquam dias in luminis oras
Exoritur, neque fit laetum, nec amabile quidquam.

[Goddess, still thou alone governest nature, nor without thee anything comes into light; nothing is pleasant, nothing joyful.
—Lucretius, i. 22.]

I know not who could set Pallas and the Muses at variance with Venus, and make them cold towards Love; but I see no deities so well met, or that are more indebted to one another. Who will deprive the Muses of amorous imaginations, will rob them of the best entertainment they have, and of the noblest matter of their work: and who will make Love lose the communication and service of poesy, will disarm him of his best weapons: by this means they charge the god of familiarity and good will, and the protecting goddesses of humanity and justice, with the vice of ingratitude and unthankfulness. I have not been so long cashiered from the state and service of this god, that my memory is not still perfect in his force and value:

Agnosco veteris vestigia flammae;

[I recognise vestiges of my old flame.
—*Aeneid*, iv. 23.]

There are yet some remains of heat and emotion after the fever:

Nec mihi deficiat calor hic, hiemantibus annis!

[Nor let this heat of youth fail me in my winter years.]

CHAPTER 5

Withered and drooping as I am, I feel yet some remains of the past ardour:

> *Qual l'alto Egeo, per the Aquilone o Noto*
> *Cessi, the tutto prima il volse et scosse,*
> *Non s'accheta ei pero; ma'l suono e'l moto*
> *Ritien del l'onde anco agitate e grosse:*

[As Aegean seas, when storms be calmed again,
That rolled their tumbling waves with troublous blasts,
Do yet of tempests passed some show retain,
And here and there their swelling billows cast.

—Fairfax.]

but from what I understand of it, the force and power of this god are more lively and animated in the picture of poesy than in their own essence:

> *Et versus digitos habet:*

[Verse has fingers.

—Altered from Juvenal, iv. 196.]

it has I know not what kind of air, more amorous than love itself. Venus is not so beautiful, naked, alive, and panting, as she is here in Virgil:

> *Dixerat; et niveis hinc atque hinc Diva lacertis*
> *Cunctantem amplexus molli fovet. Ille repente*
> *Accepit solitam flammam; notusque medullas*
> *Intravit calor, et labefacta per ossa cucurrit*
> *Non secus atque olim tonitru, cum rupta corusco*
> *Ignea rima micans percurrit lumine nimbos.*
> *. . . . . . Ea verba loquutus,*

343

Optatos dedit amplexus; placidumque petivit
Conjugis infusus gremio per membra soporem.

[The goddess spoke, and throwing round him her snowy arms
in soft embraces, caresses him hesitating. Suddenly he caught
the wonted flame, and the well-known warmth pierced his marrow, and ran thrilling through his shaken bones: just as when
at times, with thunder, a stream of fire in lightning flashes
shoots across the skies. Having spoken these words, he gave her
the wished embrace, and in the bosom of his spouse sought
placid sleep.

—*Aeneid*, viii. 387 and 392.]

All that I find fault with in considering it is, that he has represented her a little too passionate for a married Venus; in this discreet
kind of coupling, the appetite is not usually so wanton, but more
grave and dull. Love hates that people should hold of any but itself,
and goes but faintly to work in familiarities derived from any other
title, as marriage is: alliance, dowry, therein sway by reason, as much
or more than grace and beauty. Men do not marry for themselves,
let them say what they will; they marry as much or more for their
posterity and family; the custom and interest of marriage concern
our race much more than us; and therefore it is, that I like to have
a match carried on by a third hand rather than a man's own, and by
another man's liking than that of the party himself; and how much
is all this opposite to the conventions of love? And also it is a kind of
incest to employ in this venerable and sacred alliance the heat and
extravagance of amorous licence, as I think I have said elsewhere.
A man, says Aristotle, must approach his wife with prudence and
temperance, lest in dealing too lasciviously with her, the extreme
pleasure make her exceed the bounds of reason. What he says upon
the account of conscience, the physicians say upon the account
of health: "that a pleasure excessively lascivious, voluptuous, and

frequent, makes the seed too hot, and hinders conception": it is said, elsewhere, that to a languishing intercourse, as this naturally is, to supply it with a due and fruitful heat, a man must do it but seldom and at appreciable intervals:

Quo rapiat sitiens Venerem, interiusque recondat.

[But let him thirstily snatch the joys of love and enclose them in his bosom.

—Virgil, *Georgics*, iii. 137.]

I see no marriages where the conjugal compatibility sooner fails than those that we contract upon the account of beauty and amorous desires; there should be more solid and constant foundation, and they should proceed with greater circumspection; this furious ardour is worth nothing.

They who think they honour marriage by joining love to it, do, methinks, like those who, to favour virtue, hold that nobility is nothing else but virtue. They are indeed things that have some relation to one another, but there is a great deal of difference; we should not so mix their names and titles; it is a wrong to them both so to confound them. Nobility is a brave quality, and with good reason introduced; but forasmuch as it is a quality depending upon others, and may happen in a vicious person, in himself nothing, it is in estimate infinitely below "virtue"; it is a virtue, if it be one, that is artificial and apparent, depending upon time and fortune: various in form, according to the country; living and mortal; without birth, as the river Nile; genealogical and common; of succession and similitude; drawn by consequence, and a very weak one. Knowledge, strength, goodness, beauty, riches, and all other qualities, fall into communication and commerce, but this is consummated in itself, and of no use to the service of others. There was proposed to one of our kings the choice of two candidates for the same command, of whom one was a gentleman, the other not; he ordered that, without respect to quality, they should choose him who had the most merit; but where the worth of the competitors should appear to be entirely equal, they should have respect to birth: this was justly to give it its rank. A young man unknown, coming to Antigonus to make suit for his father's command, a valiant man lately dead: "Friend," said he, "in such preferments as these, I have not so much regard to the nobility of my soldiers as to their prowess." And, indeed, it ought not to go as it did with the officers of the kings of Sparta, trumpeters, fiddlers, cooks, the children of whom always succeeded to their places, how ignorant soever, and were preferred before the most experienced in the trade. They of Calicut make of nobles a sort of superhuman persons: they are interdicted marriage and all but warlike employments: they may have of concubines their fill, and the women as many lovers, without being jealous of one another; but it is a capital and irremissible crime to couple with a person of meaner conditions than themselves; and they think themselves polluted, if they have but touched one in walking along; and supposing their nobility to be marvellously interested and injured in it, kill such as only approach a little too near them: insomuch that the ignoble are obliged to cry out as they walk, like the gondoliers of Venice, at the turnings of streets for fear of jostling; and the nobles command them to step aside to what part they please: by that means these avoid what they repute a perpetual ignominy, those certain death. No time, no favour of the prince, no office, or virtue, or riches, can ever prevail to make a plebeian become noble: to which this custom contributes, that marriages are interdicted between different trades; the daughter of one of the cordwainers' gild is not permitted to marry a carpenter; and parents are obliged to train up their children precisely in their own callings, and not put them to any other trade; by which means the distinction and continuance of their fortunes are maintained.

A good marriage, if there be any such, rejects the company and conditions of love, and tries to represent those of friendship. It is a sweet society of life, full of constancy, trust, and an infinite number of useful and solid services and mutual obligations; which any woman who has a right taste:

Optato quam junxit lumine taeda

[Whom the marriage torch has joined with the desired light.
—Catullus, lxiv. 79.]

would be loathe to serve her husband in quality of a mistress. If she be lodged in his affection as a wife, she is more honourably and securely placed. When he purports to be in love with another, and works all he can to obtain his desire, let anyone but ask him, on which he had rather a disgrace should fall, his wife or his mistress, which of their misfortunes would most afflict him, and to which of them he wishes the most grandeur, the answer to these questions is out of dispute in a sound marriage.

And that so few are observed to be happy, is a token of its price and value. If well formed and rightly taken, it is the best of all human societies; we cannot live without it, and yet we do nothing but decry it. It happens, as with cages, the birds without despair to get in, and those within despair of getting out. Socrates being asked, whether it was more commodious to take a wife or not, "Let a man take which course he will," said he; "he will repent." It is a contract to which the common saying:

Homo homini aut deus aut lupus,

[Man to man is either a god or a wolf.

—Erasmus, *Adag.*]

may very fitly be applied; there must be a concurrence of many qualities in the construction. It is found nowadays more convenient for simple and plebeian souls, where delights, curiosity, and idleness do not so much disturb it; but extravagant humours, such as mine, that hate all sorts of obligation and restraint, are not so proper for it:

Et mihi dulce magis resoluto vivere collo.

[And it is sweet to me to live with a loosened neck.
—Pseudo Gallus, i. 61.]

Might I have had my own will, I would not have married Wisdom herself, if she would have had me. But it is to much purpose to evade it; the common custom and usance of life will have it so. The most of my actions are guided by example, not by choice, and yet I did not go to it of my own voluntary motion; I was led and drawn to it by extrinsic occasions; for not only things that are incommodious in themselves, but also things however ugly, vicious, and to be avoided, may be rendered acceptable by some condition or accident; so unsteady and vain is all human resolution! and I was persuaded to it, when worse prepared and less tractable than I am at present, that I have tried what it is: and as great a libertine as I am taken to be, I have in truth more strictly observed the laws of marriage, than I either promised or expected. It is in vain to kick, when a man has once put on his fetters: a man must prudently manage his liberty; but having once submitted to obligation, he must confine himself within the laws of common duty, at least, do what he can towards it. They who engage in this contract, with a design to carry themselves in it with hatred and contempt, do an unjust and inconvenient thing; and the fine rule that I hear pass from hand to hand amongst the women, as a sacred oracle:

Serve thy husband as thy master, but guard thyself against him as from a traitor.

which is to say, comport thyself towards him with a dissembled, inimical, and distrustful reverence (a cry of war and defiance), is equally injurious and hard. I am too mild for such rugged designs: to say the truth, I am not arrived to that perfection of ability and refinement of wit, to confound reason with injustice, and to laugh at all rule and order that does not please my palate; because I hate superstition, I do not presently run into the contrary extreme of irreligion.

If a man does not always perform his duty, he ought at least to love and acknowledge it; it is treachery to marry without espousing.

Let us proceed.

Our poet represents a marriage happy in a good accord wherein nevertheless there is not much loyalty. Does he mean, that it is not impossible but a woman may give the reins to her own passion, and yield to the importunities of love, and yet reserve some duty toward marriage, and that it may be hurt, without being totally broken? A serving man may cheat his master, whom nevertheless he does not hate. Beauty, opportunity, and destiny (for destiny has also a hand in it),

> *Fatum est in partibus illis*
> *Quas sinus abscondit; nam, si tibi sidera cessent,*
> *Nil faciet longi mensura incognita nervi;*

[There is a fatality about the hidden parts: let nature have
endowed you however liberally, it is of no use, if your good star
fails you in the nick of time.

—Juvenal, ix. 32.]

have attached her to a stranger; though not so wholly, peradventure, but that she may have some remains of kindness for her husband. They are two designs, that have several paths leading to them, without being confounded with one another; a woman may yield to a man she would by no means have married, not only for the condition of his fortune, but for those also of his person. Few men have made a wife of a mistress, who have not repented it.

349

And even in the other world, what an unhappy life does Jupiter lead with his, whom he had first enjoyed as a mistress! It is, as the proverb runs, to befoul a basket and then put it upon one's head. I have in my time, in a good family, seen love shamefully and dishonestly cured by marriage: the considerations are widely different. We love at once, without any tie, two things contrary in themselves.

Socrates was wont to say, that the city of Athens pleased, as ladies do whom men court for love; everyone loved to come thither to take a turn, and pass away his time; but no one liked it so well as to espouse it, that is, to inhabit there, and to make it his constant residence. I have been vexed to see husbands hate their wives only because they themselves do them wrong; we should not, at all events, methinks, love them the less for our own faults; they should at least, upon the account of repentance and compassion, be dearer to us.

They are different ends, he says, and yet in some sort compatible; marriage has utility, justice, honour, and constancy for its share; a flat, but more universal pleasure: love founds itself wholly upon pleasure, and, indeed, has it more full, lively, and sharp; a pleasure inflamed by difficulty; there must be in it sting and smart: it is no longer love, if without darts and fire. The bounty of ladies is too profuse in marriage, and dulls the point of affection and desire: to evade which inconvenience, do but observe what pains Lycurgus and Plato take in their laws.

Women are not to blame at all, when they refuse the rules of life that are introduced into the world, forasmuch as the men make them without their help. There is naturally contention and brawling between them and us; and the strictest friendship we have with them is yet mixed with tumult and tempest. In the opinion of our author, we deal inconsiderately with them in this: after we have discovered that they are, without comparison, more able and ardent

Chapter 5

in the practice of love than we, and that the old priest testified as much, who had been one while a man, and then a woman:

Venus huic erat utraque nota:

[Both aspects of love were known to him,
        —Tiresias. Ovid, *Metamorphoses*, iii. 323.]

and moreover, that we have learned from their own mouths the proof that, in several ages, was made by an Emperor and Empress of Rome, [Proclus.] both famous for ability in that affair! For he in one night deflowered ten Sarmatian virgins who were his captives: but she had five-and-twenty bouts in one night, changing her man according to her need and liking;

Adhuc ardens rigidae tentigine vulvae
Et lassata viris, nondum satiata, recessit:

[Ardent still, she retired, fatigued, but not satisfied.
        —Juvenal, vi. 128.]

and that upon the dispute which happened in Cataluna, wherein a wife complaining of her husband's too frequent addresses to her, not so much, as I conceive, that she was incommodated by it (for I believe no miracles out of religion) as under this pretence, to curtail and curb in this, which is the fundamental act of marriage, the authority of husbands over their wives, and to show that their frowardness and malignity go beyond the nuptial bed, and spurn under foot even the graces and sweets of Venus; the husband, a man truly brutish and unnatural, replied, that even on fasting days he could not subsist with less than ten courses: whereupon came out that notable sentence of the Queen of Arragon, by which, after mature deliberation of her council, this good queen, to give a rule and example to all succeeding ages of the

351

moderation required in a just marriage, set down six times a day as a legitimate and necessary stint; surrendering and quitting a great deal of the needs and desires of her sex, that she might, she said, establish an easy, and consequently, a permanent and immutable rule. Hereupon the doctors cry out: what must the female appetite and concupiscence be, when their reason, their reformation and virtue, are taxed at such a rate, considering the divers judgments of our appetites? for Solon, master of the law school, taxes us but at three a month, that men may not fail in point of conjugal frequentation: after having, I say, believed and preached all this, we go and enjoin them continency for their particular share, and upon the last and extreme penalties.

There is no passion so hard to contend with as this, which we would have them only resist, not simply as an ordinary vice, but as an execrable abomination, worse than irreligion and parricide; whilst we, at the same time, go to't without offence or reproach. Even those amongst us who have tried the experiment have sufficiently confessed what difficulty, or rather impossibility, they have found by material remedies to subdue, weaken, and cool the body. We, on the contrary, would have them at once sound, vigorous plump, high-fed, and chaste; that is to say, both hot and cold; for the marriage, which we tell them is to keep them from burning, is but small refreshment to them, as we order the matter. If they take one whose vigorous age is yet boiling, he will be proud to make it known elsewhere;

> *Sit tandem pudor; aut eamus in jus;*
> *Multis mentula millibus redempta,*
> *Non est haec tua, Basse; vendidisti;*

[Let there be some shame, or we shall go to law: your vigour, bought by your wife with many thousands, is no longer yours: thou hast sold it.

—Martial, xii. 90.]

Polemon the philosopher was justly by his wife brought before the judge for sowing in a barren field the seed that was due to one that was fruitful: if, on the other hand, they take a decayed fellow, they are in a worse condition in marriage than either maids or widows. We think them well provided for, because they have a man to lie with, as the Romans concluded Clodia Laeta, a vestal nun, violated, because Caligula had approached her, though it was declared he did no more but approach her: but, on the contrary, we by that increase their necessity, forasmuch as the touch and company of any man whatever rouses their desires, that in solitude would be more quiet. And to the end, it is likely, that they might render their chastity more meritorious by this circumstance and consideration, Boleslas and Kinge his wife, kings of Poland, vowed it by mutual consent, being in bed together, on their very wedding day, and kept their vow in spite of all matrimonial conveniences.

We train them up from their infancy to the traffic of love; their grace, dressing, knowledge, language, and whole instruction tend that way: their governesses imprint nothing in them but the idea of love, if for nothing else but by continually representing it to them, to give them a distaste for it. My daughter, the only child I have, is now of an age that forward young women are allowed to be married at; she is of a slow, thin, and tender complexion, and has accordingly been brought up by her mother after a retired and particular manner, so that she but now begins to be weaned from her childish simplicity. She was reading before me in a French book where the word "fouteau", the name of a tree very well known, occurred; [The beech-tree; the name resembles in sound an obscene French word.] the woman, to whose conduct she is committed, stopped her short a little roughly, and made her skip over that dangerous step. I let her alone, not to trouble their rules, for I never concern myself in that sort of government; feminine polity has a mysterious procedure; we must leave it to them; but if I am not mistaken the commerce of twenty lacquies could not, in six months' time, have so imprinted in her memory the meaning, usage, and all the consequence of the sound of these wicked syllables, as this good old woman did by reprimand and interdiction.

Motus doceri Gaudet Ionicos
Matura virgo, et frangitur artibus;
Jam nunc et incestos amores
De tenero, meditatur ungui.

[The maid ripe for marriage delights to learn Ionic dances, and to imitate those lascivious movements. Nay, already from her infancy she meditates criminal amours.

—Horace, *Odes*, iii. 6, 21., the text has "fingitur".]

Let them but give themselves the rein a little, let them but enter into liberty of discourse, we are but children to them in this science. Hear them but describe our pursuits and conversation, they will very well make you understand that we bring them nothing they have not known before, and digested without our help.

Is it, perhaps, as Plato says, that they have formerly been debauched young fellows? I happened one day to be in a place where I could hear some of their talk without suspicion; I am sorry I cannot repeat it. By your lady, said I, we had need go study the phrases of Amadis, and the tales of Boccaccio and Aretin, to be able to discourse with them: we employ our time to much purpose indeed. There is neither word, example, nor step they are not more perfect in than our books; it is a discipline that springs with their blood,

Et mentem ipsa Venus dedit,

[Venus herself made them what they are,
—Virgil, *Georgics*, iii. 267.]

which these good instructors, nature, youth, and health, are continually inspiring them with; they need not learn, they breed it:

Nec tantum niveo gavisa estulla columbo,
Compar, velsi quid dicitur improbius,
Oscula mordenti semper decerpere rostro,

CHAPTER 5

Quantum praecipue multivola est mulier.

[No milk-white dove, or if there be a thing more lascivious,
takes so much delight in kissing as woman, wishful for every man
she sees.

—Catullus, lxvi. 125.]

So that if the natural violence of their desire were not a little
restrained by fear and honour, which were wisely contrived for them,
we should be all shamed. All the motions in the world resolve into
and tend to this conjunction; it is a matter infused throughout: it is
a centre to which all things are directed. We yet see the edicts of the
old and wise Rome made for the service of love, and the precepts of
Socrates for the instruction of courtesans:

> *Noncon libelli Stoici inter sericos*
> *Jacere pulvillos amant:*

[There are writings of the Stoics which we find lying upon
silken cushions.

—Horace, *Epodes*, viii. 15.]

Zeno, amongst his laws, also regulated the motions to be
observed in getting a maidenhead. What was the philosopher
Strato's book Of Carnal Conjunction? [Diogenes Laertius, v. 59]
And what did Theophrastus treat of in those he intituled, the one
"The Lover", and the other "Of Love?" Of what Aristippus in his
"Of Former Delights"? What do the so long and lively descriptions
in Plato of the loves of his time pretend to? and the book called
"The Lover", of Demetrius Phalereus? and "Clinias", or the "Rav-
ished Lover", of Heraclides; and that of Antisthenes, "Of Getting
Children", or, "Of Weddings", and the other, "Of the Master or the
Lover"? And that of Aristo: "Of Amorous Exercises"? What those
of Cleanthes: one, "Of Love", the other, "Of the Art of Loving"?

The amorous dialogues of Sphaereus? and the fable of Jupiter and Juno, of Chrysippus, impudent beyond all toleration? And his fifty so lascivious epistles? I will let alone the writings of the philosophers of the Epicurean sect, protectress of voluptuousness. Fifty deities were, in time past, assigned to this office; and there have been nations where, to assuage the lust of those who came to their devotion, they kept men and women in their temples for the worshippers to lie with; and it was an act of ceremony to do this before they went to prayers:

Nimirum propter continentiam incontinentia necessaria est;
Incendium ignibus extinguitur.

[Indeed incontinency is necessary for continency's sake; a conflagration is extinguished by fire.]

In the greatest part of the world, that member of our body was deified; in the same province, some flayed off the skin to offer and consecrate a piece; others offered and consecrated their seed. In another, the young men publicly cut through between the skin and the flesh of that part in several places, and thrust pieces of wood into the openings as long and thick as they would receive, and of these pieces of wood afterwards made a fire as an offering to their gods; and were reputed neither vigorous nor chaste, if by the force of that cruel pain they seemed to be at all dismayed. Elsewhere the most sacred magistrate was reverenced and acknowledged by that member and in several ceremonies the effigy of it was carried in pomp to the honour of various divinities. The Egyptian ladies, in their Bacchanalia, each carried one finely-carved of wood about their necks, as large and heavy as she could so carry it; besides which, the statue of their god presented one, which in greatness surpassed all the rest of his body. [Herodotus, ii. 48, says "nearly as large as the body itself."] The married women, near the place where I live, make of their kerchiefs the figure of one upon their foreheads, to glorify themselves in the enjoyment they have of it; and coming to be widows, they throw it behind, and cover it with their headcloths. The most modest matrons of Rome thought it an honour to offer flowers and garlands to the god Priapus; and they made the virgins, at the time of their espousals, sit upon his shameful parts. And I know not whether I have not in my time seen some air of like devotion. What was the meaning of that ridiculous piece of the chaussuye of our forefathers, and that is still worn by our Swiss? [Cod-pieces worn]. To what end do we make a show of our implements in figure under our breeches, and often, which is worse, above their natural size, by falsehood and imposture? I have half a mind to believe that this sort of vestment was invented in the better and more conscientious ages, that the world might not be deceived, and that everyone should give a public account of his proportions: the simple nations wear them yet, and near about the real size. In those days, the tailor took measure of it, as the shoemaker does now of a man's foot. That good man, who, when I was young, gelded so many noble and ancient statues in his great city, that they might not corrupt the sight of the ladies, according to the advice of this other ancient worthy:

Flagitii principium est, nudare inter gives corpora,

[It is the beginning of wickedness to expose their persons among the Citizens

—Ennius, ap. Cicero, *Tusculum Disputations*, iv. 33.]

should have called to mind, that, as in the mysteries of the Bona Dea, all masculine appearance was excluded, he did nothing, if he did not geld horses and asses, in short, all nature:

Omne adeo genus in terris, hominumque, ferarumque,
Et genus aequoreum, pecudes, pictaeque volucres,
In furias ignemque ruunt.

[So that all living things, men and animals, wild or tame,
and fish and gaudy fowl, rush to this flame of love.

–Virgil, *Georgics*, iii. 244.]

The gods, says Plato, have given us one disobedient and unruly
member that, like a furious animal, attempts, by the violence of its
appetite, to subject all things to it; and so they have given to women
one like a greedy and ravenous animal, which, if it be refused food
in season, grows wild, impatient of delay, and infusing its rage into
their bodies, stops the passages, and hinders respiration, causing a
thousand ills, till, having imbibed the fruit of the common thirst, it
has plentifully bedewed the bottom of their matrix. Now my legislator [The Pope who, as Montaigne has told us, took it into his head
to geld the statues.] should also have considered that, peradventure, it were a chaster and more fruitful usage to let them know
the fact as it is betimes, than permit them to guess according to the
liberty and heat of their own fancy; instead of the real parts they
substitute, through hope and desire, others that are three times
more extravagant; and a certain friend of mine lost himself by producing his in place and time when the opportunity was not present
to put them to their more serious use. What mischief do not those
pictures of prodigious dimension do that the boys make upon the
staircases and galleries of the royal houses? They give the ladies
a cruel contempt of our natural furniture. And what do we know
but that Plato, after other well-instituted republics, ordered that the
men and women, old and young, should expose themselves naked
to the view of one another, in his gymnastic exercises, upon that
very account? The Indian women who see the men in their natural
state, have at least cooled the sense of seeing. And let the women of
the kingdom of Pegu say what they will, who below the waist have
nothing to cover them but a cloth slit before, and so strait, that
what decency and modesty soever they pretend by it, at every step
all is to be seen, that it is an invention to allure the men to them,
and to divert them from boys, to whom that nation is generally

inclined; yet, peradventure they lose more by it than they get, and one may venture to say, that an entire appetite is more sharp than one already half-glutted by the eyes. Livia was wont to say, that to a virtuous woman a naked man was but a statue. The Lacedaemonian women, more virgins when wives than our daughters are, saw every day the young men of their city stripped naked in their exercises, themselves little heeding to cover their thighs in walking, believing themselves, says Plato, sufficiently covered by their virtue without any other robe. But those, of whom St. Augustin speaks, have given nudity a wonderful power of temptation, who have made it a doubt, whether women at the day of judgment shall rise again in their own sex, and not rather in ours, for fear of tempting us again in that holy state. In brief, we allure and flesh them by all sorts of ways: we incessantly heat and stir up their imagination, and then we find fault. Let us confess the truth; there is scarce one of us who does not more apprehend the shame that accrues to him by the vices of his wife than by his own, and that is not more solicitous (a wonderful charity) of the conscience of his virtuous wife than of his own; who had not rather commit theft and sacrilege, and that his wife was a murderess and a heretic, than that she should not be more chaste than her husband: an unjust estimate of vices. Both we and they are capable of a thousand corruptions more prejudicial and unnatural than lust: but we weigh vices, not according to nature, but according to our interest; by which means they take so many unequal forms.

The austerity of our decrees renders the application of women to this vice more violent and vicious than its own condition needs, and engages it in consequences worse than their cause: they will readily offer to go to the law courts to seek for gain, and to the wars to get reputation, rather than in the midst of ease and delights, to have to keep so difficult a guard. Do not they very well see that there is neither merchant nor soldier who will not leave his business to run after this sport, or the porter or cobbler, toiled and tired out as they are with labour and hunger?

Num tu, qux tenuit dives Achaemenes,
Aut pinguis Phrygiae Mygdonias opes,
Permutare velis crine Licymnim?
Plenas aut Arabum domos,
Dum fragrantia detorquet ad oscula
Cervicem, aut facili sxvitia negat,
Quae poscente magis gaudeat eripi,
Interdum rapere occupet?

[Would thou not exchange all that the wealthy Arhaemenes had, or the Mygdonian riches of fertile Phrygia, for one ringlet of Licymnia's hair? or the treasures of the Arabians, when she turns her head to you for fragrant kisses, or with easily assuaged anger denies them, which she would rather by far you took by force, and sometimes herself snatches one!

—Horace, *Odes*, ii. 12, 21.]

I do not know whether the exploits of Alexander and Caesar really surpass the resolution of a beautiful young woman, bred up after our fashion, in the light and commerce of the world, assailed by so many contrary examples, and yet keeping herself entire in the midst of a thousand continual and powerful solicitations. There is no doing more difficult than that not doing, nor more active:

I hold it more easy to carry a suit of armour all the days of one's life than a maidenhead; and the vow of virginity of all others is the most noble, as being the hardest to keep:

Diaboli virtus in lumbisest,

says St. Jerome. We have, doubtless, resigned to the ladies the most difficult and most vigorous of all human endeavours, and let us resign to them the glory too. This ought to encourage them to be obstinate in it; it is a brave thing for them to defy us, and to spurn under foot that vain pre-eminence of valour and virtue that we pretend to have over them; they will find if they do but observe it, that they will not only be much more esteemed for it, but also much more beloved. A gallant man does not give over his pursuit for being refused, provided it be a refusal of chastity, and not of choice; we may swear, threaten, and complain to much purpose; we therein do but lie, for we love them all the better: there is no allurement like modesty, if it be not rude and crabbed. It is stupidity and meanness to be obstinate against hatred and disdain; but against a virtuous and constant resolution, mixed with goodwill, it is the exercise of a noble and generous soul. They may acknowledge our service to a certain degree, and give us civilly to understand that they disdain us not; for the law that enjoins them to abominate us because we adore them, and to hate us because we love them, is certainly very cruel, if but for the difficulty of it. Why should they not give ear to our offers and requests, so long as they are kept within the bounds of modesty? wherefore should we fancy them to have other thoughts within, and to be worse than they seem? A queen of our time said with spirit, "that to refuse these courtesies is a testimony of weakness in women and a self-accusation of facility, and that a lady could not boast of her chastity who was never tempted."

The limits of honour are not cut so short; they may give themselves a little rein, and relax a little without being faulty: there lies on the frontier some space free, indifferent, and neuter. He that has beaten and pursued her into her fort is a strange fellow if he be not satisfied with his fortune: the price of the conquest is considered by the difficulty. Would you know what impression your service and merit have made in her heart? Judge of it by her behaviour. Such an one may grant more, who does not grant so much. The obligation of a benefit wholly relates to the good will of those who confer it: the other coincident circumstances are dumb, dead, and casual; it costs her dearer to grant you that little, than it would do her companion to grant all. If in anything rarity give estimation, it ought especially in this: do not consider how little it is that is given, but how few have it to give; the value of money alters according to the coinage and stamp of the place. Whatever the spite and indiscretion of some may make them say in the excess of their discontent, virtue and truth will in time recover all the advantage. I have known some whose reputation has for a great while suffered under slander, who have afterwards been restored to the world's universal approbation by their mere constancy without care or artifice; everyone repents, and gives himself the lie for what he has believed and said; and from girls a little suspected they have been afterward advanced to the first rank amongst the ladies of honour. Somebody told Plato that all the world spoke ill of him. "Let them talk," said he; "I will live so as to make them change their note." Besides the fear of God, and the value of so rare a glory, which ought to make them look to themselves, the corruption of the age we live in compels them to it; and if I were they, there is nothing I would not rather do than intrust my reputation in so dangerous hands. In my time the pleasure of telling (a pleasure little inferior to that of doing) was not permitted but to those who had some faithful and only friend; but now the ordinary discourse and common table-talk is nothing but boasts of favours received and the secret liberality of ladies. In earnest, it is too abject, too much meanness of spirit, in men to suffer such ungrateful, indiscreet, and giddy-headed people so to persecute, forage, and rifle those tender and charming favours.

This our immoderate and illegitimate exasperation against this vice springs from the most vain and turbulent disease that afflicts human minds, which is jealousy:

> *Quis vetat apposito lumen de lumine sumi?*
> *Dent licet assidue, nil tamen inde perit;*

[Who says that one light should not be lighted from another light? Let them give ever so much, as much ever remains to lose.
—Ovid, *De Arte Amandi*, iii. 93.]

she, and envy, her sister, seem to me to be the most foolish of the whole troop. As to the last, I can say little about it; it is a passion that, though said to be so mighty and powerful, had never to do with me. As to the other, I know it by sight, and that's all. Beasts feel it; the shepherd Cratis, having fallen in love with a she-goat, the he-goat, out of jealousy, came, as he lay asleep, to butt the head of the female, and crushed it. We have raised this fever to a greater excess by the examples of some barbarous nations; the best disciplined have been touched with it, and it is reason, but not transported:

Ense maritali nemo confossus adulter
Purpureo Stygias sanguine tinxit aquas.

[Never did adulterer slain by a husband
stain with purple blood the Stygian waters.]

Lucullus, Caesar, Pompey, Antony, Cato, and other brave men were cuckolds, and knew it, without making any bustle about it; there was in those days but one coxcomb, Lepidus, that died for grief that his wife had used him so.

Ah! tum temiserum Malique fati,
Quem attractis pedibus, patente porta,
Percurrent raphanique mugilesque:

[Wretched man! when, taken in the fact, you will be dragged out of doors by the heels, and suffer the punishment of your adultery.

—Catullus, xv. 17.]

and the god of our poet, when he surprised one of his companions with his wife, satisfied himself by putting them to shame only,

Atque aliquis de dis non tristibus optat
Sic fieri turpis:

[And one of the merry gods wishes that he should himself like to be so disgraced.

—Ovid, *Metamorphoses*, iv. 187.]

363

and nevertheless took anger at the lukewarm embraces she gave him; complaining that upon that account she was grown jealous of his affection:

> *Quid causas petis ex alto? fiducia cessit*
> *Quo tibi, diva, mei?*

[Do you seek causes from above? Why, goddess, has your confidence in me ceased?

—Virgil, *Aeneid*, viii. 395.]

nay, she entreats arms for a bastard of hers,

> *Arena rogo genitrix nato.*

[I, a mother, ask armour for a son.

—Idem, ibid., 383.]

which are freely granted; and Vulcan speaks honourably of Aeneas,

> *Arma acri facienda viro,*

[Arms are to be made for a valiant hero.

—*Aeneid*, viii. 441.]

with, in truth, a more than human humanity. And I am willing to leave this excess of kindness to the gods:

> *Nec divis homines componier aequum est.*

[Nor is it fit to compare men with gods.

—Catullus, lxviii. 141.]

CHAPTER 5

As to the confusion of children, besides that the gravest legislators ordain and affect it in their republics, it touches not the women, where this passion is, I know not how, much better seated:

Saepe etiam Juno, maxima coelicolam,
Conjugis in culpa flagravit quotidiana.

[Often was Juno, greatest of the heaven-dwellers, enraged by her husband's daily infidelities.
—Idem, ibid.]

When jealousy seizes these poor souls, weak and incapable of resistance, it is pity to see how miserably it torments and tyrannises over them; it insinuates itself into them under the title of friendship, but after it has once possessed them, the same causes that served for a foundation of good-will serve them for a foundation of mortal hatred. It is, of all the diseases of the mind, that which the most things serve for aliment and the fewest for remedy: the virtue, health, merit, reputation of the husband are incendiaries of their fury and ill-will:

Nullae sunt inimicitiae, nisi amoris, acerbae.

[No enmities are bitter, save that of love.
Or: No hate is implacable except the hatred of love.
—Propertius, ii. 8, 3.]

This fever defaces and corrupts all they have of beautiful and good besides; and there is no action of a jealous woman, let her be how chaste and how good a housewife soever, that does not relish of anger and wrangling; it is a furious agitation, that rebounds them to an extremity quite contrary to its cause. This held good with one

Octavius at Rome. Having lain with Pontia Posthumia, he augmented love with fruition, and solicited with all importunity to marry her; unable to persuade her, this excessive affection precipitated him to the effects of the most cruel and mortal hatred: he killed her. In like manner, the ordinary symptoms of this other amorous disease are civil wars, private conspiracies, and cabals:

Notumque furens quid faemina possit,

[And it is known what an angry woman is capable of doing.
—*Aeneid*, V. 21.]

and a rage which so much the more frets itself, as it is compelled to excuse itself by a pretence of good-will.

Now, the duty of chastity is of a vast extent; is it the will that we would have them restrain? This is a very supple and active thing; a thing very nimble, to be stayed. How? if dreams sometimes engage them so far that they cannot deny them: it is not in them, nor, peradventure, in chastity itself, seeing that is a female, to defend itself from lust and desire. If we are only to trust to their will, what a case are we in, then? Do but imagine what crowding there would be amongst men in pursuance of the privilege to run full speed, without tongue or eyes, into every woman's arms who would accept them. The Scythian women put out the eyes of all their slaves and prisoners of war, that they might have their pleasure of them, and they never the wiser. O, the furious advantage of opportunity! Should any one ask me, what was the first thing to be considered in love matters, I should answer that it was how to take a fitting time; and so the second; and so the third – it is a point that can do everything. I have sometimes wanted fortune, but I have also sometimes been wanting to myself in matters of attempt. God help him, who yet makes light of this! There is greater temerity required in this age of ours, which our young men excuse under the name of heat; but should women examine it more strictly, they would find that it rather proceeds from contempt. I was always superstitiously afraid of giving offence, and have ever had a great respect for her I loved: besides, he who in this traffic takes away the reverence, defaces at the same time the lustre. I would in this affair have a man a little play the child, the timorous, and the servant. If not this, I have in other bashfulness whereof altogether in things some air of the foolish Plutarch makes mention; and the course of my life has been divers ways hurt and blemished with it; a quality very ill suiting my universal form: and, indeed, what are we but sedition and discrepancy? I am as much out of countenance to be denied as I am to deny; and it so much troubles me to be troublesome to others that on occasion when duty compels me to try the good-will of any one in a thing that is doubtful and that will be chargeable to him, I do it very faintly, and very much against my will: but if it be for my own particular (whatever Homer truly says, that modesty is a foolish virtue in an indigent person), I commonly commit it to a third person to blush for me, and deny those who employ me with the same difficulty: so that it has sometimes befallen me to have had a mind to deny, when I had not the power to do it.

It is folly, then, to attempt to bridle in women a desire that is so powerful in them, and so natural to them. And when I hear them brag of having so maidenly and so temperate a will, I laugh at them: they retire too far back. If it be an old toothless trot, or a young dry consumptive thing, though it be not altogether to be believed, at least they say it with more similitude of truth. But they who still move and breathe, talk at that ridiculous rate to their own prejudice, by reason that inconsiderate excuses are a kind of self-accusation; like a gentleman, a neighbour of mine, suspected to be insufficient:

Languidior tenera cui pendens sicula beta,
Numquam se mediam sustulit ad tunicam,

[Catullus, lxvii. 2, i. – The sense is in the context.]

367

who three or four days after he was married, to justify himself, went about boldly swearing that he had ridden twenty stages the night before: an oath that was afterwards made use of to convict him of his ignorance in that affair, and to divorce him from his wife. Besides, it signifies nothing, for there is neither continency nor virtue where there are no opposing desires. It is true, they may say, but we will not yield; saints themselves speak after that manner. I mean those who boast in good gravity of their coldness and insensibility, and who expect to be believed with a serious countenance; for when it is spoken with an affected look, when their eyes give the lie to their tongue, and when they talk in the cant of their profession, which always goes against the hair, it is good sport. I am a great servant of liberty and plainness; but there is no remedy; if it be not wholly simple or childish, it is silly, and unbecoming ladies in this commerce, and presently runs into impudence. Their disguises and figures only serve to cosen fools; lying is there in its seat of honour; it is a by-way, that by a back-door leads us to truth. If we cannot curb their imagination, what would we have from them. Effects? There are enough of them that evade all foreign communication, by which chastity may be corrupted:

Illud saepe facit, quod sine teste facit;

[He often does that which he does without a witness.

—Martial, vii. 62, 6.]

and those which we fear the least are, peradventure, most to be feared; their sins that make the least noise are the worst:

Offendor maecha simpliciore minus.

[I am less offended with a more professed strumpet.

—Idem, vi. 7, 6.]

Chapter 5

There are ways by which they may lose their virginity without prostitution, and, which is more, without their knowledge:

Obsterix, virginis cujusdam integritatem manu velut explorans, sive malevolentia, sive inscitia, sive casu, dum inspicit, perdidit.

[By malevolence, or unskilfulness, or accident, the midwife, seeking with the hand to test some maiden's virginity, has sometimes destroyed it.

—St. Augustine, *De Civitate Dei*, i. 18.]

Such a one, by seeking her maidenhead, has lost it; another by playing with it has destroyed it. We cannot precisely circumscribe the actions, we interdict them; they must guess at our meaning under general and doubtful terms; the very idea we invent for their chastity is ridiculous: for, amongst the greatest patterns that I have is Fatua, the wife of Faunus: who never, after her marriage, suffered herself to be seen by any man whatever; and the wife of Hiero, who never perceived her husband's stinking breath, imagining that it was common to all men. They must become insensible and invisible to satisfy us.

Now let us confess that the knot of this judgment of duty principally lies in the will; there have been husbands who have suffered cuckoldom, not only without reproach or taking offence at their wives, but with singular obligation to them and great commendation of their virtue. Such a woman has been, who prized her honour above her life, and yet has prostituted it to the furious lust of a mortal enemy, to save her husband's life, and who, in so doing, did that for him she would not have done for herself! This is not the place wherein we are to multiply these examples; they are too high and rich to be set off with so poor a foil as I can give them here; let us reserve them for a nobler place; but for examples of ordinary lustre, do we not every day see women amongst us who surrender themselves for their husbands' sole benefit, and by their express order and mediation? and, of old, Phaulius the Argian, who offered his to King Philip out of ambition; as Galba did it out of civility, who, having entertained Maecenas at supper, and observing that his wife and he began to cast glances at one another and to make eyes and signs, let himself sink down upon his cushion, like one in a profound sleep, to give opportunity to their desires: which he handsomely confessed, for thereupon a servant having made bold to lay hands on the plate upon the table, he frankly cried, "What, you rogue? do you not see that I only sleep for Maecenas?" Such there may be, whose manners may be lewd enough, whose will may be more reformed than another, who outwardly carries herself after a more regular manner. As we see some who complain of having vowed chastity before they knew what they did; and I have also known others really, complain of having been given up to debauchery before they were of the years of discretion. The vice of the parents or the impulse of nature, which is a rough counsellor, may be the cause.

In the East Indies, though chastity is of singular reputation, yet custom permitted a married woman to prostitute herself to any one who presented her with an elephant, and that with glory, to have been valued at so high a rate. Phaedo the philosopher, a man of birth, after the taking of his country Elis, made it his trade to prostitute the beauty of his youth, so long as it lasted, to any one that would, for money thereby to gain his living: and Solon was the first in Greece, it is said, who by his laws gave liberty to women, at the expense of their chastity, to provide for the necessities of life; a custom that Herodotus says had been received in many governments before his time. And besides, what fruit is there of this painful solicitude? For what justice soever there is in this passion, we are yet to consider whether it turns to account or no: does any one think to curb them, with all his industry?

Pone seram; cohibe: sed quis custodiet ipsos
Custodes? cauta est, et ab illis incipit uxor.

CHAPTER 5

[Put on a lock; shut them up under a guard; but who shall guard the guard? she knows what she is about, and begins with them.
—Juvenal, vi. 346.]

What commodity will not serve their turn, in so knowing an age?

Curiosity is vicious throughout; but it is pernicious here. It is folly to examine into a disease for which there is no physic that does not inflame and make it worse; of which the shame grows still greater and more public by jealousy, and of which the revenge more wounds our children than it heals us. You wither and die in the search of so obscure a proof. How miserably have they of my time arrived at that knowledge who have been so unhappy as to have found it out? If the informer does not at the same time apply a remedy and bring relief, it is an injurious information, and that better deserves a stab than the lie. We no less laugh at him who takes pains to prevent it, than at him who is a cuckold and knows it not. The character of cuckold is indelible: who once has it carries it to his grave; the punishment proclaims it more than the fault. It is to much purpose to drag out of obscurity and doubt our private misfortunes, thence to expose them on tragic scaffolds; and misfortunes that only hurt us by being known; for we say a good wife or a happy marriage, not that they are really so, but because no one says to the contrary. Men should be so discreet as to evade this tormenting and unprofitable knowledge: and the Romans had a custom, when returning from any expedition, to send home before to acquaint their wives with their coming, that they might not surprise them; and to this purpose it is that a certain nation has introduced a custom, that the priest shall on the wedding-day open the way to the bride, to free the husband from the doubt and curiosity of examining in the first assault, whether she comes a virgin to his bed, or has been at the trade before.

But the world will be talking. I know, a hundred honest men cuckolds, honestly and not unbeseemingly; a worthy man is pitied, not disesteemed for it. Order it so that your virtue may conquer your misfortune; that good men may curse the occasion, and that he who wrongs you may tremble but to think on it. And, moreover, who escapes being talked of at the same rate, from the least even to the greatest?

> *Tot qui legionibus imperitivit*
> *Et meliorquam to multis fuit, improbe, rebus.*

[Many who have commanded legions, many a man much better far than you, you rascal.

—Lucretius, iii. 1039, 1041.]

Seest thou how many honest men are reproached with this in thy presence; believe that thou art no more spared elsewhere. But, the very ladies will be laughing too; and what are they so apt to laugh at in this virtuous age of ours as at a peaceable and well-composed marriage? Each amongst you has made somebody cuckold; and nature runs much in parallel, in compensation, and turn for turn. The frequency of this accident ought long since to have made it more easy; it is now passed into custom.

Miserable passion! which has this also, that it is incommunicable,

> *Fors etiam nostris invidit questibus aures;*

[Fortune also refuses ear to our complaints.

—Catullus, lxvii.]

for to what friend dare you intrust your griefs, who, if he does not laugh at them, will not make use of the occasion to get a share of the quarry? The sharps, as well as the sweets of marriage, are kept secret by the wise; and amongst its other troublesome conditions this to a prating fellow, as I am, is one of the chief, that custom has rendered it indecent and prejudicial to communicate to any one all that a man knows and all that a man feels. To give women the same counsel against jealousy would be so much time lost; their very being is so made up of suspicion, vanity, and curiosity, that to cure them by any legitimate way is not to be hoped. They often recover of this infirmity by a form of health much more to be feared than the disease itself; for as there are enchantments that cannot take away the evil but by throwing it upon another, they also willingly transfer this ever to their husbands, when they shake it off themselves. And yet I know not, to speak truth, whether a man can suffer worse from them than their jealousy; it is the most dangerous of all their conditions, as the head is of all their members. Pittacus used to say, [Plutarch, On Contentment, c. II.] that everyone had his trouble, and that his was the jealous head of his wife; but for which he should think himself perfectly happy. A mighty inconvenience, sure, which could poison the whole life of so just, so wise, and so valiant a man; what must we other little fellows do? The senate of Marseilles had reason to grant him his request who begged leave to kill himself that he might be delivered from the clamour of his wife; for it is a mischief that is never removed but by removing the whole piece; and that has no remedy but flight or patience, though both of them very hard. He was, methinks, an understanding fellow who said, 'twas a happy marriage between a blind wife and a deaf husband.

Let us also consider whether the great and violent severity of obligation we enjoin them does not produce two effects contrary to our design namely, whether it does not render the pursuants more eager to attack, and the women more easy to yield. For as to the first, by raising the value of the place, we raise the value and the desire of the conquest. Might it not be Venus herself, who so cunningly enhanced the price of her merchandise, by making the laws her bawds; knowing how insipid a delight it would be that was not heightened by fancy and hardness to achieve? In short, it is all swine's flesh, varied by sauces, as Flaminius' host said. Cupid is a roguish god, who makes it his sport to contend with devotion and justice: it is his glory that his power mates all powers, and that all other rules give place to his:

Materiam culpae prosequiturque suae.

[And seeks out a matter (motive) for his crimes.

—Ovid, *Tristia*, iv. I. 34.]

As to the second point; should we not be less cuckolds, if we less feared to be so? according to the humour of women whom interdiction incites, and who are more eager, being forbidden:

Ubi velis, nolunt; ubi nolis, volunt ultro;
Concessa pudet ire via.

[Where thou wilt, they won't; where thou wilt not, they spontaneously agree; they are ashamed to go in the permitted path.

—Terence, *Eunuchus,* act iv., sc. 8, v 43]

What better interpretation can we make of Messalina's behaviour? She, at first, made her husband a cuckold in private, as is the common use; but, bringing her business about with too much ease, by reason of her husband's stupidity, she soon scorned that way, and presently fell to making open love, to own her lovers, and to favour and entertain them in the sight of all: she would make him know and see how she used him. This animal, not to be roused with all this, and rendering her pleasures dull and flat by his too stupid facility, by which he seemed to authorise and make them lawful; what does she? Being the wife of a living and healthful emperor, and at Rome, the theatre of the world, in the face of the sun, and with solemn ceremony, and to Silius, who had long before enjoyed her, she publicly marries herself one day that her husband was gone out

374

of the city. Does it not seem as if she was going to become chaste by her husband's negligence? or that she sought another husband who might sharpen her appetite by his jealousy, and who by watching should incite her? But the first difficulty she met with was also the last: this beast suddenly roused these sleepy, sluggish sort of men are often the most dangerous: I have found by experience that this extreme toleration, when it comes to dissolve, produces the most severe revenge; for taking fire on a sudden, anger and fury being combined in one, discharge their utmost force at the first onset,

Irarumque omnes effundit habenas:

[He let loose his whole fury.

—*Aeneid*, xii. 499.]

he put her to death, and with her a great number of those with whom she had intelligence, and even one of them who could not help it, and whom she had caused to be forced to her bed with scourges.

What Virgil says of Venus and Vulcan, Lucretius had better expressed of a stolen enjoyment between her and Mars:

Belli feramoenera Mavors
Armipotens regit, ingremium qui saepe tuum se
Rejictt, aeterno devinctus vulnere amoris

....

Pascit amore avidos inhians in te, Dea, visus,
Eque tuo pendet resupini spiritus ore
Hunc tu, Diva, tuo recubantem corpore sancto
Circumfusa super, suaveis ex ore loquelas
Funde.

[Mars, the god of wars, who controls the cruel tasks of war, often reclines on thy bosom, and greedily drinks love at both his eyes, vanquished by the eternal wound of love: and his breath, as he reclines, hangs on thy lips; bending thy head over him as he lies upon thy sacred person, pour forth sweet and persuasive words.

—Lucretius, i. 23.]

When I consider this rejicit, fiascit, inhians, ynolli, fovet, medullas, labefacta, pendet, percurrit, and that noble circumfusa, mother of the pretty infuses; I disdain those little quibbles and verbal allusions that have since sprung up. Those worthy people stood in need of no subtlety to disguise their meaning; their language is downright, and full of natural and continued vigour; they are all epigram; not only the tail, but the head, body, and feet. There is nothing forced, nothing languishing, but everything keeps the same pace:

Contextus totes virilis est; non sunt circa flosculos occupati.

[The whole contexture is manly; they don't occupy themselves with little flowers of rhetoric.

—Seneca, *Epistles*, 33.]

It is not a soft eloquence, and without offence only; it is nervous and solid, that does not so much please, as it fills and ravishes the greatest minds. When I see these brave forms of expression, so lively, so profound, I do not say that it is well said, but well thought. It is the sprightliness of the imagination that swells and elevates the words:

Pectus est quod disertum Tacit.

[The heart makes the man eloquent.

—Quintilian, x. 7.]

Our people call language, judgment, and fine words, full conceptions. This painting is not so much carried on by dexterity of hand as by having the object more vividly imprinted in the soul.

376

CHAPTER 5

Gallus speaks simply because he conceives simply: Horace does not content himself with a superficial expression; that would betray him; he sees farther and more clearly into things; his mind breaks into and rummages all the magazine of words and figures wherewith to express himself, and he must have them more than ordinary, because his conception is so. Plutarch says' that he sees the Latin tongue by the things: it is here the same: the sense illuminates and produces the words, no more words of air, but of flesh and bone; they signify more than they say. Moreover, those who are not well skilled in a language present some image of this; for in Italy I said whatever I had a mind to in common discourse, but in more serious talk, I durst not have trusted myself with an idiom that I could not wind and turn out of its ordinary pace; I would have a power of introducing something of my own.

The handling and utterance of fine wits is that which sets off language; not so much by innovating it, as by putting it to more vigorous and various services, and by straining, bending, and adapting it to them. They do not create words, but they enrich their own, and give them weight and signification by the uses they put them to, and teach them unwonted motions, but withal ingeniously and discreetly. And how little this talent is given to all is manifest by the many French scribblers of this age: they are bold and proud enough not to follow the common road, but want of invention and discretion ruins them; there is nothing seen in their writings but a wretched affectation of a strange new style, with cold and absurd disguises, which, instead of elevating, depress the matter: provided they can but trick themselves out with new words, they care not what they signify; and to bring in a new word by the head and shoulders, they leave the old one, very often more sinewy and significant than the other.

There is stuff enough in our language, but there is a defect in cutting out: for there is nothing that might not be made out of our terms of hunting and war, which is a fruitful soil to borrow from; and forms of speaking, like herbs, improve and grow stronger by being

377

transplanted. I find it sufficiently abundant, but not sufficiently pliable and vigorous; it commonly quails under a powerful conception; if you would maintain the dignity of your style, you will often perceive it to flag and languish under you, and there Latin steps in to its relief, as Greek does to others. Of some of these words I have just picked out we do not so easily discern the energy, by reason that the frequent use of them has in some sort abased their beauty, and rendered it common; as in our ordinary language there are many excellent phrases and metaphors to be met with, of which the beauty is withered by age, and the colour is sullied by too common handling; but that nothing lessens the relish to an understanding man, nor does it derogate from the glory of those ancient authors who, it is likely, first brought those words into that lustre.

The sciences treat of things too refinedly, after an artificial, very different from the common and natural, way. My page makes love, and understands it; but read to him Leo Hebraeus [Leo the Jew, Ficinus, Cardinal Bembo, and Mario Equicola all wrote Treatises on Love.] and Ficinus, where they speak of love, its thoughts and actions, he understands it not. I do not find in Aristotle most of my ordinary motions; they are there covered and disguised in another robe for the use of the schools. Good speed them! were I of the trade, I would as much naturalise art as they artificialise nature. Let us let Bembo and Equicola alone.

When I write, I can very well spare both the company and the remembrance of books, lest they should interrupt my progress; and also, in truth, the best authors too much humble and discourage me: I am very much of the painter's mind, who, having represented cocks most wretchedly ill, charged all his boys not to suffer any natural cock to come into his shop; and had rather need to give myself a little lustre, of the invention of Antigenides the musician, who, when he was asked to sing or play, took care beforehand that the auditory should, either before or after, be satiated with some other ill musicians. But I can hardly be without Plutarch; he is so universal and so full, that upon all occasions, and what extravagant subject soever you take in hand, he will still be at your elbow, and hold out to you a liberal and not to be exhausted hand of riches and embellishments. It vexes me that he is so exposed to be the spoil of those who are conversant with him: I can scarce cast an eye upon him but I purloin either a leg or a wing.

And also for this design of mine it is convenient for me for me to write at home, in a wild country, where I have nobody to assist or relieve me; where I hardly see a man who understands the Latin of his Paternoster, and of French a little less. I might have made it better elsewhere, but then the work would have been less my own; and its principal end and perfection is to be exactly mine. I readily correct an accidental error, of which I am full, as I run carelessly on; but for my ordinary and constant imperfections, it were a kind of treason to put them out. When another tells me, or that I say to myself, "Thou art too thick of figures: this is a word of rough Gascon: that is a dangerous phrase (I do not reject any of those that are used in the common streets of France; they who would fight custom with grammar are triflers): this is an ignorant discourse: this is a paradoxical discourse: that is going too far: thou makest thyself too merry at times: men will think thou sayest a thing in good earnest which thou only speakest in jest." – "Yes, I know, but I correct the faults of inadvertence, not those of custom. Do I not talk at the same rate throughout? Do I not represent myself to the life? It is enough that I have done what I designed; all the world knows me in my book, and my book in me."

Now I have an apish, imitative quality: when I used to write verses (and I never made any but Latin), they evidently discovered the poet I had last read, and some of my first essays have a little exotic taste: I speak something another kind of language at Paris than I do at Montaigne. Whoever I steadfastly look upon easily leaves some impression of his upon me; whatever I consider I usurp, whether a foolish countenance, a disagreeable look, or a ridiculous way of speaking; and vices most of all, because they seize and stick to me, and will not leave hold without shaking. I swear more by imitation than by complexion: a murderous imitation, like that of the apes so terrible both in stature and strength, that Alexander met with in a certain country of the Indies, and which he would have had much ado any other way to have subdued; but they afforded him the means by that inclination of theirs to imitate whatever they saw done; for by that the hunters were taught to put on shoes in their sight, and to tie them fast with many knots, and to muffle up their heads in caps all composed of running nooses, and to seem to anoint their eyes with glue; so did those poor beasts employ their imitation to their own ruin they glued up their own eyes, haltered and bound themselves. The other faculty of playing the mimic, and ingeniously acting the words and gestures of another, purposely to make people merry and to raise their admiration, is no more in me than in a stock. When I swear my own oath, it is only, by God! of all oaths the most direct. They say that Socrates swore by the dog; Zeno had for his oath the same interjection at this time in use amongst the Italians, Cappari! Pythagoras swore By water and air. I am so apt, without thinking of it, to receive these superficial impressions, that if I have Majesty or Highness in my mouth three days together, they come out instead of Excellency and Lordship eight days after; and what I say to-day in sport and fooling I shall say the same to-morrow seriously. Wherefore, in writing, I more unwillingly undertake beaten arguments, lest I should handle them at another's expense. Every subject is equally fertile to me: a fly will serve the purpose, and it is well if this I have in hand has not been undertaken at the recommendation of as flighty a will. I may begin, with that which pleases me best, for the subjects are all linked to one another.

But my soul displeases me, in that it ordinarily produces its deepest and most airy conceits and which please me best, when I least expect or study for them, and which suddenly vanish, having at the instant, nothing to apply them to; on horseback, at table, and in bed: but most on horseback, where I am most given to think. My speaking is a little nicely jealous of silence and attention: if I am talking my best, whoever interrupts me, stops me. In travelling, the necessity of the way will often put a stop to discourse; besides which I, for the most part, travel without company fit for regular discourses, by which means I have all the leisure I would to entertain myself. It falls out as it does in my dreams; whilst dreaming I recommend them to my memory (for I am apt to dream that I dream), but, the next morning, I may represent to myself of what complexion they were, whether gay, or sad, or strange, but what they were, as to the rest, the more I endeavour to retrieve them, the deeper I plunge them in oblivion. So of thoughts that come accidentally into my head, I have no more but a vain image remaining in my memory; only enough to make me torment myself in their quest to no purpose.

Well, then, laying books aside, and more simply and materially speaking, I find, after all, that Love is nothing else but the thirst of enjoying the object desired, or Venus any other thing than the pleasure of discharging one's vessels, just as the pleasure nature gives in discharging other parts, that either by immoderation or indiscretion become vicious. According to Socrates, love is the appetite of generation by the mediation of beauty. And when I consider the ridiculous titillation of this pleasure, the absurd, crack-brained, wild motions with which it inspires Zeno and Cratippus, the indiscreet rage, the countenance inflamed with fury and cruelty in the sweetest effects of love, and then that austere air, so grave, severe, ecstatic, in so wanton an action; that our delights and our excrements are promiscuously shuffled together; and that the supreme pleasure brings along with it, as in pain, fainting and complaining; I believe it to be true, as Plato says, that the gods made man for their sport:

> *Quaenam ista jocandi*
> *Saevitia!*

[With a sportive cruelty. Or: What an unkindness there is in jesting!

—Claudian, *In Eutropium.* i. 24.]

381

and that it was in mockery that nature has ordered the most agitative of actions and the most common, to make us equal, and to put fools and wise men, beasts and us, on a level. Even the most contemplative and prudent man, when I imagine him in this posture, I hold him an impudent fellow to pretend to be prudent and contemplative; they are the peacocks' feet that abate his pride:

> *Ridentem dicere verum*
> *Quid vetat?*

[What prevents us from speaking truth with a smile?
—Horace, *Satire*, i. I, 24.]

They who banish serious imaginations from their sports, do, says one, like him who dares not adore the statue of a saint, if not covered with a veil. We eat and drink, indeed, as beasts do; but these are not actions that obstruct the functions of the soul, in these we maintain our advantage over them; this other action subjects all other thought, and by its imperious authority makes an ass of all Plato's divinity and philosophy; and yet there is no complaint of it. In everything else a man may keep some decorum, all other operations submit to the rules of decency; this cannot so much as in imagination appear other than vicious or ridiculous: find out, if you can, therein any serious and discreet procedure. Alexander said, that he chiefly knew himself to be mortal by this act and sleeping; sleep suffocates and suppresses the faculties of the soul; the familiarity with women likewise dissipates and exhausts them: doubtless it is a mark, not only of our original corruption, but also of our vanity and deformity.

On the one side, nature pushes us on to it, having fixed the most noble, useful, and pleasant of all her functions to this desire: and, on the other side, leaves us to accuse and avoid it, as insolent and indecent, to blush at it, and to recommend abstinence. Are we not brutes to call that work brutish which begets us? People of so many differing religions have concurred in several proprieties, as sacrifices, lamps, burning incense, fasts, and offerings; and amongst others, in the condemning this act: all opinions tend that way, besides the widespread custom of circumcision, which may be regarded as a punishment. We have, peradventure, reason to blame ourselves for being guilty of so foolish a production as man, and to call the act, and the parts that are employed in the act, shameful (mine, truly, are now shameful and pitiful). The Essenians, of whom Pliny speaks, kept up their country for several ages without either nurse or baby-clouts, by the arrival of strangers who, following this pretty humour, came continually to them: a whole nation being resolute, rather to hazard a total extermination, than to engage themselves in female embraces, and rather to lose the succession of men, than to beget one. It is said, that Zeno never had to do with a woman but once in his life, and then out of civility, that he might not seem too obstinately to disdain the sex. [Diogenes Laertius, vii. 13. – What is there said, however, is that Zeno seldom had commerce with boys, lest he should be deemed a very misogynist.]

Everyone avoids seeing a man born, everyone runs to see him die; to destroy him a spacious field is sought out in the face of the sun, but, to make him, we creep into as dark and private a corner as we can: it is a man's duty to withdraw himself bashfully from the light to create; but it is glory and the fountain of many virtues to know how to destroy what we have made: the one is injury, the other favour: for Aristotle says that to do any one a kindness, in a certain phrase of his country, is to kill him. The Athenians, to couple the disgrace of these two actions, having to purge the Isle of Delos, and to justify themselves to Apollo, interdicted at once all births and burials in the precincts thereof:

Nostri nosmet paenitet.

[We are ashamed of ourselves.
—Terence, *Phoymio*, i. 3, 20.]

There are some nations that will not be seen to eat. I know a lady, and of the best quality, who has the same opinion, that chewing disfigures the face, and takes away much from the ladies' grace and beauty; and therefore unwillingly appears at a public table with an appetite; and I know a man also, who cannot endure to see another eat, nor himself to be seen eating, and who is more shy of company when putting in than when putting out. In the Turkish empire, there are a great number of men who, to excel others, never suffer themselves to be seen when they make their repast: who never have any more than one a week; who cut and mangle their faces and limbs; who never speak to any one: fanatic people who think to honour their nature by disnaturing themselves; who value themselves upon their contempt of themselves, and purport to grow better by being worse. What monstrous animal is this, that is a horror to himself, to whom his delights are grievous, and who weds himself to misfortune? There are people who conceal their life:

Exilioque domos et dulcia limina mutant,

[And change for exile their homes and pleasant abodes.
—Virgil, *Georgics*, ii. 511.]

and withdraw them from the sight of other men; who avoid health and cheerfulness, as dangerous and prejudicial qualities. Not only many sects, but many peoples, curse their birth, and bless their death; and there is a place where the sun is abominated and darkness adored. We are only ingenious in using ourselves ill: it is the real quarry our intellects fly at; and intellect, when misapplied, is a dangerous tool!

O miseri! quorum gaudia crimen habent!

[O wretched men, whose pleasures are a crime!
—Pseudo Gallus, i. 180.]

Alas, poor man! thou hast enough inconveniences that are inevitable, without increasing them by throe own invention; and art miserable enough by nature, without being so by art; thou hast real and essential deformities enough, without forging those that are imaginary. Do thou think thou art too much at ease unless half thy ease is uneasy? do thou find that thou hast not performed all the necessary offices that nature has enjoined thee, and that she is idle in thee, if thou do not oblige thyself to other and new offices? Thou do not stick to infringe her universal and undoubted laws; but stickest to thy own special and fantastic rules, and by how much more particular, uncertain, and contradictory they are, by so much thou employest thy whole endeavour in them: the laws of thy parish occupy and bind thee: those of God and the world concern thee not. Run but a little over the examples of this kind; thy life is full of them.

Whilst the verses of these two poets, treat so reservedly and discreetly of wantonness as they do, methinks they discover it much more openly. Ladies cover their necks with network, priests cover several sacred things, and painters shadow their pictures to give them greater lustre: and it is said that the sun and wind strike more violently by reflection than in a direct line. The Egyptian wisely answered him who asked him what he had under his cloak, "It is hid under my cloak," said he, "that thou mayest not know what it is:" but there are certain other things that people hide only to show them. Hear that one, who speaks plainer,

Et nudum pressi corpus ad usque meum:

[And pressed her naked body to mine. Or: My body I applied even to her naked side.

—Ovid, *Amores*, i. 5, 24.]

methinks that he emasculates me. Let Martial turn up Venus as high as he may, he cannot show her so naked: he who says all that is to be said gluts and disgusts us. He who is afraid to express himself, draws us on to guess at more than is meant; there is treachery in this sort of modesty, and specially when they half open, as these do, so fair a path to imagination. Both the action and description should relish of theft.

The more respectful, more timorous, more coy, and secret love of the Spaniards and Italians pleases me. I know not who of old wished his throat as long as that of a crane, that he might the longer taste what he swallowed; it had been better wished as to this quick and precipitous pleasure, especially in such natures as mine that have the fault of being too prompt. To stay its flight and delay it with preambles: all things – a glance, a bow, a word, a sign, stand for favour and recompense between them. Were it not an excellent piece of thrift in him who could dine on the steam of the roast? It is a passion that mixes with very little solid essence, far more vanity and feverish raving; and we should serve and pay it accordingly. Let us teach the ladies to set a better value and esteem upon themselves, to amuse and fool us: we give the last charge at the first onset; the French impetuosity will still show itself; by spinning out their favours, and exposing them in small parcels, even miserable old age itself will find some little share of reward, according to its worth and merit. He who has no fruition but in fruition, who wins nothing unless he sweeps the stakes, who takes no pleasure in the chase but in the quarry, ought not to introduce himself in our school: the more steps and degrees there are, so much higher and more honourable is the uppermost seat: we should take a pleasure in being conducted to it, as in magnificent palaces, by various porticoes and passages, long and pleasant galleries, and many windings. This disposition of things would turn to our advantage; we should there longer stay and longer love; without hope and without desire we proceed not worth a pin. Our conquest and entire possession is what they ought infinitely to dread: when they wholly surrender themselves up to the mercy of our fidelity and constancy they run a mighty hazard; they are virtues very rare and hard to be found; the ladies are no sooner ours, than we are no more theirs:

> *Postquam cupidae mentis satiata libido est,*
> *Verba nihil metuere, nihil perjuria curant;*

[When our desires are once satisfied, we care little for oaths and promises.

—Catullus, lxiv. 147.]

And Thrasonides, a young man of Greece, was so in love with his passion that having gained a mistress's consent, he refused to enjoy her, that he might not by fruition quench and stupefy the unquiet ardour of which he was so proud, and with which he so fed himself. Dearness is a good sauce to meat: do but observe how much the manner of salutation, particular to our nation, has, by its facilities, made kisses, which Socrates says are so powerful and dangerous for the stealing of hearts, of no esteem. It is a displeasing custom and injurious for the ladies, that they must be obliged to lend their lips to every fellow who has three footmen at his heels, however ill-favoured he may be in himself:

> *Cujus livida naribus caninis*
> *Dependet glacies, rigetque barba . . .*
> *Centum occurrere malo culilingis:*

—Martial, vii. 94.

and we ourselves barely gain by it; for as the world is divided, for three beautiful women we must kiss fifty ugly ones; and to a tender stomach, like those of my age, an ill kiss overpays a good one.

In Italy they passionately court even their common women who sell themselves for money, and justify the doing so by saying, "that there are degrees of fruition, and that by such service they would procure for themselves that which is most entire; the women sell nothing but their bodies; the will is too free and too much of its own to be exposed to sale." So that these say, it is the will they undertake and they have reason. It is indeed the will that we are to serve and gain by wooing. I abhor to imagine mine, a body without affection: and this madness is, methinks, cousin-german to that of the boy who would needs pollute the beautiful statue of Venus made by Praxiteles; or that of the furious Egyptian, who violated the dead carcase of a woman he was embalming: which was the occasion of the law then made in Egypt, that the corpses of beautiful young women, of those of good quality, should be kept three days before they should be delivered to those whose office it was to take care for the interment. Periander did more wonderfully, who extended his conjugal affection (more regular and legitimate) to the enjoyment of his wife Melissa after she was dead. Does it not seem a lunatic humour in the Moon, seeing she could no otherwise enjoy her darling Endymion, to lay-him for several months asleep, and to please herself with the fruition of a boy who stirred not but in his sleep? I likewise say that we love a body without a soul or sentiment when we love a body without its consent and desire. All enjoyments are not alike: there are some that are hectic and languishing: a thousand other causes besides good-will may procure us this favour from the ladies; this is not a sufficient testimony of affection: treachery may lurk there, as well as elsewhere: they sometimes go to it by halves:

> *Tanquam thura merumque parent*
> *Absentem marmoreamve putes:*

[As if they are preparing frankincense and wine... you might think her absent or marble.

—Martial, xi. 103, 12, and 59, 8.]

I know some who had rather lend that than their coach, and who only impart themselves that way. You are to examine whether your company pleases them upon any other account, or, as some strong-chinned groom, for that only; in what degree of favour and esteem you are with them:

> *Tibi si datur uni,*
> *Quem lapide illa diem candidiore notat.*

[Wherefore that is enough, if that day alone is given us which she marks with a whiter stone.

—Catullus, lxviii. 147.]

What if they eat your bread with the sauce of a more pleasing imagination.

> *Te tenet, absentes alios suspirat amores.*

[She has you in her arms; her thoughts are with other absent lovers.

—Tibullus, i. 6, 35.]

What? have we not seen one in these days of ours who made use of this act for the purpose of a most horrid revenge, by that means to kill and poison, as he did, a worthy lady?

Such as know Italy will not think it strange if, for this subject, I seek not elsewhere for examples; for that nation may be called the regent of the world in this. They have more generally handsome and fewer ugly women than we; but for rare and excellent beauties we have as many as they. I think the same of their intellects: of those of the common sort, they have evidently far more brutishness is immeasurably rarer there; but in individual characters of the highest form, we are nothing indebted to them. If I should carry on the comparison, I might say, as touching valour, that, on the contrary, it is, to what it is with them, common and natural with us; but sometimes we see them possessed of it to such a degree as surpasses the greatest examples we can produce: The marriages of that country are defective in this; their custom commonly imposes so rude and so slavish a law upon the women, that the most distant acquaintance with a stranger is as capital an offence as the most intimate; so that all approaches being rendered necessarily substantial, and seeing that all comes to one account, they have no hard choice to make; and when they have broken down the fence, we may safely presume they get on fire:

> *Luxuria ipsis vinculis, sicut fera bestia,*
> *irritata, deinde emissa.*

[Lust, like a wild beast, being more excited by being bound, breaks from his chains with greater wildness.

—Livy, xxxiv. 4.]

They must give them a little more rein:

> *Vidi ego nuper equum, contra sua frena tenacem,*
> *Ore reluctanti fulminis ire modo:*

[I saw, the other day, a horse struggling against his bit, rush like a thunderbolt.

—Ovid, *Amores*, iii. 4, 13.]

the desire of company is allayed by giving it a little liberty. We are pretty much in the same case they are extreme in constraint, we in licence. It is a good custom we have in France that our sons are received into the best families, there to be entertained and bred up pages, as in a school of nobility; and it is looked upon as a discourtesy and an affront to refuse this to a gentleman. I have taken notice (for, so many families, so many differing forms) that the ladies who have been strictest with their maids have had no better luck than those who allowed them a greater liberty. There should be moderation in these things; one must leave a great deal of their conduct to their own discretion; for, when all comes to all, no discipline can curb them throughout. But it is true withal that she who comes off with flying colours from a school of liberty, brings with her whereon to repose more confidence than she who comes away sound from a severe and strict school.

Our fathers dressed up their daughters' looks in bashfulness and fear (their courage and desires being the same); we ours in confidence and assurance; we understand nothing of the matter; we must leave it to the Sarmatian women, who may not lie with a man till with their own hands they have first killed another in battle. For me, who have no other title left me to these things but by the ears, it is sufficient if, according to the privilege of my age, they retain me for one of their counsel. I advise them then, and us men too, to abstinence; but if the age we live in will not endure it, at least modesty and discretion. For, as in the story of Aristippus, who, speaking to some young men who blushed to see him go into a scandalous house, said "the vice is in not coming out, not in going in," let her who has no care of her conscience have yet some regard to her reputation; and though she be rotten within, let her carry a fair outside at least.

I commend a gradation and delay in bestowing their favours: Plato declares that, in all sorts of love, facility and promptness are forbidden to the defendant. It is a sign of eagerness which they ought to disguise with all the art they have, so rashly, wholly, and hand-over-hand to surrender themselves. In carrying themselves orderly and measuredly in the granting their last favours, they much more allure our desires and hide their own. Let them still fly before us, even those who have most mind to be overtaken: they better conquer us by flying, as the Scythians did. To say the truth, according to the law that nature has imposed upon them, it is not properly for them either to will or desire; their part is to suffer, obey, and consent and for this it is that nature has given them a perpetual capacity, which in us is but at times and uncertain; they are always fit for the encounter, that they may be always ready when we are so "Pati natee." ["Born to suffer." Seneca, *Epistles*, 95.] And whereas she has ordered that our appetites shall be manifest by a prominent demon-stration, she would have theirs to be hidden and concealed within, and has furnished them with parts improper for ostentation, and simply defensive. Such proceedings as this that follows must be left to the Amazonian licence: Alexander marching his army through Hyrcania, Thalestris, Queen of the Amazons, came with three hun-dred light horse of her own-sex, well mounted, and armed, having left the remainder of a very great, army that followed her behind the neighbouring mountains to give him a visit; where she publicly and in plain terms told him that the fame of his valour and victories had brought her thither to see him, and to make him an offer of her forces to assist him in the pursuit of his enterprises; and that, finding him so handsome, young, and vigorous, she, who was also perfect in all those qualities, advised that they might lie together, to the end that from the most valiant woman of the world and the bravest man then living, there might spring some great and wonderful issue for the time to come. Alexander returned her thanks for all the rest; but, to give leisure for the accomplishment of her last demand, he detained her thirteen days in that place, which were spent in royal feasting and jollity, for the welcome of so courageous a princess.

We are, almost throughout, unjust judges of their actions, as they are of ours. I confess the truth when it makes against me, as well as when it is on my side. It is an abominable intemperance that pushes them on so often to change, and that will not let them limit their affection to any one person whatever; as is evident in that god-dess to whom are attributed so many changes and so many lovers. But it is true withal that it is contrary to the nature of love if it be, not violent; and contrary to the nature of violence if it be constant. And they who wonder, exclaim, and keep such a clutter to find out the causes of this frailty of theirs, as unnatural and not to be believed, how comes it to pass they do not discern how often they are them-selves guilty of the same, without any astonishment or miracle at all? It would, peradventure, be more strange to see the passion fixed; it is not a simply corporeal passion. If there be no end to avarice and ambition, there is doubtless no more in desire; it still lives after

CHAPTER 5

satiety; and it is impossible to prescribe either constant satisfaction or end; it ever goes beyond its possession. And by that means inconstancy, peradventure, is in some sort more pardonable in them than in us: they may plead, as well as we, the inclination to variety and novelty common to us both; and secondly, without us, that they buy a cat in a sack: Joanna, queen of Naples, caused her first husband, Andrews, to be hanged at the bars of her window in a halter of gold and silk woven with her own hand, because in matrimonial performances she neither found his parts nor abilities answer the expectation she had conceived from his stature, beauty, youth, and activity, by which she had been caught and deceived. They may say there is more pains required in doing than in suffering; and so they are on their part always at least provided for necessity, whereas on our part it may fall out otherwise. For this reason it was, that Plato wisely made a law that before marriage, to determine of the fitness of persons, the judges should see the young men who pretended to it stripped stark naked, and the women but to the girdle only. When they come to try us they do not, perhaps, find us worthy of their choice:

> *Experta latus, madidoque simillima loro*
> *Inguina, nec lassa stare coact amanu,*
> *Deserit imbelles thalamos.*

[After using every endeavour to arouse him to action, she quits the barren couch.
—Martial, vii. 58.]

it is not enough that a man's will be good; weakness and insufficiency lawfully break a marriage,

> *Et quaerendum aliunde foret nervosiu sillud,*
> *Quod posset zonam solver virgineam:*

[And seeks a more vigorous lover to undo her virgin zone.
—Catullus, lxvii. 27.]

393

why not? and according to her own standard, an amorous intelligence, more licentious and active,

Si blando nequeat superesse labori.

[If his strength be unequal to the pleasant task.
—Virgil, *Georgics*, iii. 127.]

But is it not great impudence to offer our imperfections and imbecilities, where we desire to please and leave a good opinion and esteem of ourselves? For the little that I am able to do now:

Ad unum
Mollis opus.

[Fit but for once.

—Horace, *Epodes*, xii. 15.]

I would not trouble a woman, that I am to reverence and fear:

Fuge suspicari,
Cujus undenum trepidavit aetas
Claude3re lustrum.

[Fear not him whose eleventh lustrum is closed.
—Horace, *Odes*, ii. 4, 12, limits it to the eighth.]

Nature should satisfy herself in having rendered this age miserable, without rendering it ridiculous too. I hate to see it, for one poor inch of pitiful vigour which comes upon it but thrice a week, to strut and set itself out with as much eagerness as if it could do mighty feats; a true flame of flax; and laugh to see it so boil and bubble and then in a moment so congealed and extinguished. This appetite ought to appertain only to the flower of beautiful youth: trust not to its seconding that indefatigable, full, constant, magnanimous ardour you think in you, for it will certainly leave you in a pretty corner; but rather transfer it to some tender, bashful, and ignorant boy, who yet trembles at the rod, and blushes:

> *Indum sanguineo veluti violaverit ostro*
> *Si quis ebur, vel mista rubent ubi lilia multa*
> *Alba rosa.*

[As Indian ivory streaked with crimson, or white lilies mixed with the damask rose.

—Aeneid, xii. 67.]

Who can stay till the morning without dying for shame to behold the disdain of the fair eyes of her who knows so well his fumbling impertinence,

> *Et taciti fecere tamen convicia vultus,*

[Though she nothing say, her looks betray her anger.

—Ovid, Amores, i. 7, 21.]

has never had the satisfaction and the glory of having cudgelled them till they were weary, with the vigorous performance of one heroic night. When I have observed any one to be vexed with me, I have not presently accused her levity, but have been in doubt, if I had not reason rather to complain of nature; she has doubtless used me very uncivilly and unkindly:

> *Si non longa satis, si non bene mentula crassa*
> *Nimirum sapiunt, videntque parvam*
> *Matronae quoque mentulam illibenter:*

[The first of these verses is the commencement of an epigram of the Veterum Poetayurra Catalecta, and the two others are from an epigram in the same collection (Ad Matrones). They describe untranslatably Montaigne's charge against nature, indicated in the previous passage.]

and done me a most enormous injury. Every member I have, as much one as another, is equally my own, and no other more properly makes me a man than this.

I universally owe my entire picture to the public. The wisdom of my instruction consists in liberty, in truth, in essence: disdaining to introduce those little, feigned, common, and provincial rules into the catalogue of its real duties; all natural, general, and constant, of which civility and ceremony are daughters indeed, but illegitimate. We are sure to have the vices of appearance, when we shall have had those of essence: when we have done with these, we run full drive upon the others, if we find it must be so; for there is danger that we shall fancy new offices, to excuse our negligence towards the natural ones, and to confound them: and to manifest this, is it not seen that in places where faults are crimes, crimes are but faults; that in nations where the laws of decency are most rare and most remiss, the primitive laws of common reason are better observed: the innumerable multitude of so many duties stifling and dissipating our care. The application of ourselves to light and trivial things diverts us from those that are necessary and just. Oh, how these superficial men take an easy and plausible way in comparison of ours! These are shadows wherewith we palliate and pay one another; but we do not pay, but inflame the reckoning towards that great judge, who tucks up our rags and tatters above our shameful parts, and suckles not to view us all over, even to our inmost and most secret ordures: it were a useful decency of our maidenly modesty, could it keep him from this discovery. In fine, whoever could reclaim man from so scrupulous a verbal superstition, would do the world no great disservice. Our life is divided between folly and prudence: whoever will write of it but what is reverend and canonical, will leave above the one-half behind. I do not excuse myself to myself; and if I did, it should rather be for my excuses that I would excuse myself than for any other fault; I excuse myself of certain humours, which I think more strong in number than those that are on my side. In consideration of which, I will further say this (for I desire to please everyone, though it will be hard to do):

> *Esse unum hominem accommodatum ad tantam morum*
> *ac sermonum et voluntatum varietatem,*

> [For a man to conform to such a variety of manners,
> discourses, and will.
> —Q. Cicero, *De Petitione Consulatus*, c. 14.]

that they ought not to condemn me for what I make authorities, received and approved by so many ages, to utter: and that there is no reason that for want of rhyme they should refuse me the liberty they allow even to churchmen of our nation and time, and these amongst the most notable, of which here are two of their brisk verses:

> *Rimula, dispeream, ni monogramma tua est.*
> *Un vit d'amy la contente et bien traicte:*

> [St. Gelais, (*Euvres Poetiques*), p. 99, ed. of Lyons, 1574.]

besides how many others. I love modesty; and it is not out of judgment that I have chosen this scandalous way of speaking; it is nature that has chosen it for me. I commend it not, no more than other forms that are contrary to common use: but I excuse it, and by circumstances both general and particular, alleviate its accusation.

But to proceed. Whence, too, can proceed that usurpation of sovereign authority you take upon you over the women, who favour you at their own expense,

Si furtiva dedit mira munuscula nocte,

[If, in the stealthy night, she has made strange gifts.
—Catullus, lxviii. 145.]

so that you presently assume the interest, coldness, and authority of a husband? it is a free contract why do you not then keep to it, as you would have them do? there is no prescription upon voluntary things. it is against the form, but it is true withal, that I in my time have conducted this bargain as much as the nature of it would permit, as conscientiously and with as much colour of justice, as any other contract; and that I never pretended other affection than what I really had, and have truly acquainted them with its birth, vigour, and declination, its fits and intermissions: a man does not always hold on at the same rate. I have been so sparing of my promises, that I think I have been better than my word. They have found me faithful even to service of their inconstancy, a confessed and sometimes multiplied inconstancy. I never broke with them, whilst I had any hold at all, and what occasion soever they have given me, never broke with them to hatred or contempt; for such privacies, though obtained upon never so scandalous terms, do yet oblige to some good will: I have some-times, upon their tricks and evasions, discovered a little indiscreet anger and impatience; for I am naturally subject to rash emotions, which, though light and short, often spoil my market. At any time they have consulted my judgment, I never stuck to give them sharp and paternal counsels, and to pinch them to the quick. If I have left them any cause to complain of me, it is rather to have found in me, in comparison of the modern use, a love foolishly conscientious than anything else. I have kept my, word in things wherein I might easily have been dispensed; they sometimes surrendered themselves

Chapter 5

with reputation, and upon articles that they were willing enough should be broken by the conqueror: I have, more than once, made pleasure in its greatest effort strike to the interest of their honour; and where reason importuned me, have armed them against myself; so that they ordered themselves more decorously and securely by my rules, when they frankly referred themselves to them, than they would have done by their own. I have ever, as much as I could, wholly taken upon myself alone the hazard of our assignations, to acquit them; and have always contrived our meetings after the hardest and most unusual manner, as less suspected, and, moreover, in my opinion, more accessible. They are chiefly more open, where they think they are most securely shut; things least feared are least interdicted and observed; one may more boldly dare what nobody thinks you dare, which by its difficulty becomes easy. Never had any man his approaches more impertinently generative; this way of loving is more according to discipline but how ridiculous it is to our people, and how ineffectual, who better knows than I? yet I shall not repent me of it; I have nothing there more to lose:

> *Me tabula sacer*
> *Votiva paries, indicat uvida*
> *Suspendisse potenti*
> *Vestimenta maris deo:*

[The holy wall, by my votive table, shows that I have hanged up my wet clothes in honour of the powerful god of the sea.
—Horace, *Odes*, i. 5, 13.]

it is now time to speak out. But as I might, per adventure, say to another, "Thou talkest idly, my friend; the love of thy time has little commerce with faith and integrity;"

> *Haec si tu postules*
> *Ratione certa facere, nihilo plus agas,*

399

Quam si des operam, ut cum ratione insanias:

[If you seek to make these things certain by reason, you will do no more than if you should seek to be mad in your senses.

—Terence, *Eunuchus*, act i., sc. i, v. 16.]

on the contrary, also, if it were for me to begin again, certainly it should be by the same method and the same progress, how fruitless soever it might be to me; folly and insufficiency are commendable in an incommendable action: the farther I go from their humour in this, I approach so much nearer to my own. As to the rest, in this traffic, I did not suffer myself to be totally carried away; I pleased myself in it, but did not forget myself. I retained the little sense and discretion that nature has given me, entire for their service and my own: a little emotion, but no dotage. My conscience, also, was engaged in it, even to debauch and licentiousness; but, as to ingratitude, treachery, malice, and cruelty, never. I would not purchase the pleasure of this vice at any price, but content myself with its proper and simple cost:

Nullum intra se vitium est.

[Nothing is a vice in itself.

—Seneca, *Epistles*, 95.]

I almost equally hate a stupid and slothful laziness, as I do a toilsome and painful employment; this pinches, the other lays me asleep. I like wounds as well as bruises, and cuts as well as dry blows. I found in this commerce, when I was the most able for it, a just moderation between these extremes. Love is a sprightly, lively, and gay agitation; I was neither troubled nor afflicted with it, but heated, and moreover, disordered; a man must stop there; it hurts nobody but fools. A young man asked the philosopher Panetius if it were becoming a wise man to be in love? "Let the wise man look to that,"

CHAPTER 5

answered he, "but let not thou and I, who are not so, engage ourselves in so stirring and violent an affair, that enslaves us to others, and renders us contemptible to ourselves." He said true that we are not to intrust a thing so precipitous in itself to a soul that has not wherewithal to withstand its assaults and disprove practically the saying of Agesilaus, that prudence and love cannot live together. it is a vain employment, it is true, unbecoming, shameful, and illegitimate; but carried on after this manner, I look upon it as wholesome, and proper to enliven a drowsy soul and to rouse up a heavy body; and, as an experienced physician, I would prescribe it to a man of my form and condition, as soon as any other recipe whatever, to rouse and keep him in vigour till well advanced in years, and to defer the approaches of age. Whilst we are but in the suburbs, and that the pulse yet beats:

> *Dum nova canities, dum prima et recta senectus,*
> *Dum superset lachesi quod torqueat, et pedibus me*
> *Porto meis, nullo dextram subeunte bacillo,*

> [Whilst the white hair is new, whilst old age is still straight
> shouldered, whilst there still remains something for Lachesis to
> spin, whilst I walk on my own legs, and need no staff to lean upon.
> —Juvenal, iii. 26.]

we have need to be solicited and tickled by some such nipping incitation as this. Do but observe what youth, vigour, and gaiety it inspired the good Anacreon withal: and Socrates, who was then older than I, speaking of an amorous object:

"Leaning," said he, "my shoulder to her shoulder, and my head to hers, as we were reading together in a book, I felt, without dissembling, a sudden sting in my shoulder like the biting of an insect, which I still felt above five days after, and a continual itching crept into my heart." So that merely the accidental touch, and of a shoulder, heated and altered a soul cooled and enerved by age, and the

401

strictest liver of all mankind. And, pray, why not? Socrates was a man, and would neither be, nor seem, any other thing. Philosophy does not contend against natural pleasures, provided they be moderate, and only preaches moderation, not a total abstinence; the power of its resistance is employed against those that are adulterate and strange. Philosophy says that the appetites of the body ought not to be augmented by the mind, and ingeniously warns us not to stir up hunger by saturity; not to stuff, instead of merely filling, the belly; to avoid all enjoyments that may bring us to want; and all meats and drinks that bring thirst and hunger: as, in the service of love, she prescribes us to take such an object as may simply satisfy the body's need, and does not stir the soul, which ought only barely to follow and assist the body, without mixing in the affair. But have I not reason to hold that these precepts, which, indeed, in my opinion, are somewhat over strict, only concern a body in its best plight; and that in a body broken with age, as in a weak stomach, it is excusable to warm and support it by art, and by the mediation of the fancy to restore the appetite and cheerfulness it has lost of itself.

May we not say that there is nothing in us, during this earthly prison, that is purely either corporeal or spiritual; and that we injuriously break up a man alive; and that it seems but reasonable that we should carry ourselves as favourably, at least, towards the use of pleasure as we do towards that of pain! Pain was (for example) vehement even to perfection in the souls of the saints by penitence: the body had there naturally a sham by the right of union, and yet might have but little part in the cause; and yet are they not contented that it should barely follow and assist the afflicted soul: they have afflicted itself with grievous and special torments, to the end that by emulation of one another the soul and body might plunge man into misery by so much more salutiferous as it is more severe. In like manner, is it not injustice, in bodily pleasures, to subdue and keep under the soul, and say that it must therein be dragged along as to some enforced and servile obligation and necessity? It is rather

her part to hatch and cherish them, there to present herself, and to invite them, the authority of ruling belonging to her; as it is also her part, in my opinion, in pleasures that are proper to her, to inspire and infuse into the body all the sentiment it is capable of, and to study how to make them sweet and useful to it. For it is good reason, as they say, that the body should not pursue its appetites to the prejudice of the mind; but why is it not also the reason that the mind should not pursue hers to the prejudice of the body?

I have no other passion to keep me in breath. What avarice, ambition, quarrels, lawsuits do for others who, like me, have no particular vocation, love would much more commodiously do; it would restore to me vigilance, sobriety, grace, and the care of my person; it would reassure my countenance, so that the grimaces of old age, those deformed and dismal looks, might not come to disgrace it; would again put me upon sound and wise studies, by which I might render myself more loved and esteemed, clearing my mind of the despair of itself and of its use, and redintegrating it to itself; would divert me from a thousand troublesome thoughts, a thousand melancholic humours that idleness and the ill posture of our health loads us withal at such an age; would warm again, in dreams at least, the blood that nature is abandoning; would hold up the chin, and a little stretch out the nerves, the vigour and gaiety of life of that poor man who is going full drive towards his ruin. But I very well understand that it is a commodity hard to recover: by weakness and long experience our taste is become more delicate and nice; we ask most when we bring least, and are harder to choose when we least deserve to be accepted: and knowing ourselves for what we are, we are less confident and more distrustful; nothing can assure us of being beloved, considering our condition and theirs. I am out of countenance to see myself in company with those young wanton creatures:

> *Cujus in indomito constantior inguine nervus,*
> *Quam nova collibus arbor inhaeret.*

[In whose unbridled reins the vigour is more inherent than in the young tree on the hills.

—Horace, *Epodes*, xii. 19.]

To what end should we go insinuate our misery amid their gay and sprightly humour?

Possint ut juvenes visere fervidi.
Multo non sine risu,
Dilapsam in cineres facem.

[As the fervid youths may behold, not without laughter, a burning torch worn to ashes.

—Horace, *Odes*, iv. 13, 21.]

They have strength and reason on their side; let us give way; we have nothing to do there: and these blossoms of springing beauty suffer not themselves to be handled by such benumbed hands nor dealt with by mere material means, for, as the old philosopher answered one who jeered him because he could not gain the favour of a young girl he made love to: "Friend, the hook will not stick in such soft cheese." It is a commerce that requires relation and correspondence: the other pleasures we receive may be acknowledged by recompenses of another nature, but this is not to be paid but with the same kind of coin. In earnest, in this sport, the pleasure I give more tickles my imagination than that they give me; now, he has nothing of generosity in him who can receive pleasure where he confers none—it must needs be a mean soul that will owe all, and can be content to maintain relations with persons to whom he is a continual charge; there is no beauty, grace, nor privacy so exquisite that a gentleman ought to desire at this rate. If they can only be kind to us out of pity, I had much rather die than live upon charity. I would have right to ask, in the style wherein I heard them beg in Italy: "Fate ben per voi," ["Do good for yourself."] or after

Chapter 5

the manner that Cyrus exhorted his soldiers, "Who loves himself let him follow me." – "Consort yourself," someone will say to me, "with women of your own condition, whom like fortune will render more easy to your desire." O ridiculous and insipid composition!

> *Nolo*
> *Barbam vellere mortuo leoni.*

[I would not pluck the beard from a dead lion.

—Martial]

Xenophon lays it for an objection and an accusation against Menon, that he never made love to any but old women. For my part, I take more pleasure in but seeing the just and sweet mixture of two young beauties, or only in meditating on it in my fancy, than myself in acting second in a pitiful and imperfect conjunction;

I leave that fantastic appetite to the Emperor Galba, who was only for old curried flesh: and to this poor wretch:

> *O ego Di faciant talem to cernere possim,*
> *Caraque mutatis oscula ferre comis,*
> *Amplectique meis corpus non pingue lacertis!*

[Ovid, who (Ex. Ponto, i. 4, 49) writes to his wife, "O would the gods arrange that such I might see you, and bring dear kisses to your changed locks, and embrace your withered body with my arms"]

Amongst chief deformities I reckon forced and artificial beauties: Hemon, a young boy of Chios, thinking by fine dressing to acquire the beauty that nature had denied him, came to the philosopher Arcesilaus and asked him if it was possible for a wise man to be in love – "Yes," replied he, "provided it be not with a heavily made up and adulterated beauty like thine."

405

Ugliness of a confessed antiquity is to me less old and less ugly than another that is polished and plastered up. Shall I speak it, without the danger of having my throat cut? love, in my opinion, is not properly and naturally in its season, but in the age next to childhood,

> *Quem si puellarum insereres choro,*
> *Mille sagaces falleret hospites,*
> *Discrimen obscurum, solutis*
> *Crinibus ambiguoque vultu:*

[Who if you should place in a company of girls, it would require a thousand experts to distinguish him, with his loose locks and ambiguous countenance.

—Horace, *Odes*, ii. 5, 21.]

nor beauty neither; for whereas Homer extends it so far as to the budding of the beard, Plato himself has remarked this as rare: and the reason why the sophist Bion so pleasantly called the first appearing hairs of adolescence "Aristogitons" and "Harmodiuses" [Plutarch, On Love, c.34.] is sufficiently known. I find it in virility already in some sort a little out of date, though not so much as in old age;

> *Importunus enim transvolat aridas*
> *Quercus.*

[For it uncivilly passes over withered oaks.

—Horace, *Odes*, iv. 13, 9.]

and Marguerite, Queen of Navarre, like a woman, very far extends the advantage of women, ordaining that it is time, at thirty years old, to convert the title of fair into that of good. The shorter authority we give to love over our lives, it is so much the better for us. Do but

Chapter 5

observe his port; it is a beardless boy. Who knows not how, in his school they proceed contrary to all order; study, exercise, and usage are their ways for insufficiency there novices rule:

Amor ordinem nescit.

[Love ignores rules. Or: Love knows no rule.
                         —St. Jerome, *Letter to Chyomatius.*]

Doubtless his conduct is much more graceful when mixed with inadvertency and trouble; miscarriages and ill successes give him point and grace; provided it be sharp and eager, it is no great matter whether it be prudent or no: do but observe how he goes reeling, tripping, and playing: you put him in the stocks when you guide him by art and wisdom; and he is restrained of his divine liberty when put into those hairy and callous clutches.

As to the rest, I often hear the women set out this intelligence as entirely spiritual, and disdain to put the interest the senses there have into consideration; everything there serves; but I can say that I have often seen that we have excused the weakness of their understandings in favour of their outward beauty, but have never yet seen that in favour of mind, how mature and full soever, any of them would hold out a hand to a body that was never so little in decadence. Why does not someone of them take it into her head to make that noble Socratical bargain between body and soul, purchasing a philosophical and spiritual intelligence and generation at the price of her thighs, which is the highest price she can get for them? Plato ordains in his Laws that he who has performed any signal and advantageous exploit in war may not be refused during the whole expedition, his age or ugliness notwithstanding, a kiss or any other amorous favour from any woman whatever. What he thinks to be so just in recommendation of military valour, why may it not be the same in recommendation of any other good quality? and why does

407

not some woman take a fancy to possess over her companions the glory of this chaste love? I may well say chaste;

> *Nam si quando ad praelia ventum est,*
> *Ut quondam in stipulis magnus sine viribus ignis,*
> *Incassum furit:*

[For when they sometimes engage in love's battle,
his sterile ardour lights up but as the flame of a straw.
—Virgil, *Georgics*, iii. 98.]

the vices that are stifled in the thought are not the worst.

To conclude this notable commentary, which has escaped from me in a torrent of babble, a torrent sometimes impetuous and hurtful,

> *Ut missum sponsi furtive munere malum*
> *Procurrit casto virginis a gremio,*
> *Quod miserae oblitae molli sub veste locatuat,*
> *Dum adventu matris prosilit, excutitur,*
> *Atque illud prono praeceps agitur decursu*
> *Huic manat tristi conscius ore rubor.*

[As when an apple, sent by a lover secretly to his mistress, falls
from the chaste virgin's bosom, where she had quite forgotten it;
when, starting at her mother's coming in, it is shaken out and rolls
over the floor before her eyes, a conscious blush covers her face.
—Catullus, lxv. 19.]

I say that males and females are cast in the same mould, and that, education and usage excepted, the difference is not great. Plato indifferently invites both the one and the other to the society of all studies, exercises, and vocations, both military and civil, in his Commonwealth; and the philosopher Antisthenes rejected all

408

distinction between their virtue and ours. It is much more easy to accuse one sex than to excuse the other; it is according to the saying,

Le fourgon se moque de la paele.

[The Pot and the Kettle.]

6

ON COACHES

It is very easy to verify, that great authors, when they write of causes, not only make use of those they think to be the true causes, but also of those they believe not to be so, provided they have in them some beauty and invention: they speak true and usefully enough, if it be ingeniously. We cannot make ourselves sure of the supreme cause, and therefore crowd a great many together, to see if it may not accidentally be amongst them:

> *Namque unam dicere causam*
> *Non satis est, verum plures, unde una tamen sit.*

[Lucretius, vi. 704. – The sense is in the preceding passage.]

Do you ask me, whence comes the custom of blessing those who sneeze? We break wind three several ways; that which sallies from below is too filthy; that which breaks out from the mouth carries with it some reproach of gluttony; the third is sneezing, which, because it proceeds from the head and is without offence, we give it this civil reception: do not laugh at this distinction; they say it is Aristotle's.

I think I have seen in Plutarch (who of all the authors I know, is he who has best mixed art with nature, and judgment with knowledge), his giving as a reason for the rising of the stomach in those who are at sea, that it is occasioned by fear; having first found out some reason by which he proves that fear may produce such an effect. I, who am very subject to it, know well that this cause concerns not me; and I know it, not by argument, but by necessary experience. Without instancing what has been told me, that the same thing often happens in beasts, especially hogs, who are out of all apprehension of danger; and what an acquaintance of mine told me of himself, that though very subject to it, the disposition to vomit has three or four times gone off him, being very afraid in a violent storm, as it happened to that ancient:

Pejus vexabar, quam ut periculum mihi succurreret;

[I was too ill to think of danger. Or the reverse: I was too frightened to be ill.

—Seneca, *Epistles*, 53. 2]

I was never afraid upon the water, nor indeed in any other peril (and I have had enough before my eyes that would have sufficed, if death be one), so as to be astounded to lose my judgment. Fear springs sometimes as much from want of judgment as from want of courage. All the dangers I have been in I have looked upon without winking, with an open, sound, and entire sight; and, indeed, a man must have courage to fear. It formerly served me better than other help, so to order and regulate my retreat, that it was, if not without fear, nevertheless without affright and astonishment; it was agitated, indeed, but not amazed or stupefied. Great souls go yet much farther, and present to us flights, not only steady and temperate, but moreover lofty. Let us make a relation of that which Alcibiades reports of Socrates, his fellow in arms: "I found him," says he, "after the rout of our army, him and Lachez, last among those who fled, and considered him at my leisure and in security, for I was mounted on a good horse, and he on foot, as he had fought. I took notice, in the first place, how much judgment and resolution he showed, in comparison of Lachez, and then the bravery of his march, nothing different from his ordinary gait; his sight firm and regular, considering and judging what passed about him, looking one while upon those, and then upon others, friends and enemies, after such a manner as encouraged those, and signified to the others that he would sell his life dear to any one who should attempt to take it from him, and so they came off; for people are not willing to attack such kind of men, but pursue those they see are in a fright." That is the testimony of this great captain, which teaches us, what we every day experience, that nothing so much throws us into dangers as an inconsiderate eagerness of getting ourselves clear of them:

Quo timoris minus est, eo minus ferme periculi est.

[When there is least fear, there is for the most part least danger.

—Livy, xxii. 5.]

Our people are to blame who say that such an one is afraid of death, when they would express that he thinks of it and foresees it: foresight is equally convenient in what concerns us, whether good or ill. To consider and judge of danger is, in some sort, the reverse to being astounded. I do not find myself strong enough to sustain the force and impetuosity of this passion of fear, nor of any other vehement passion whatever: if I was once conquered and beaten down by it, I should never rise again very sound. Whoever should once make my soul lose her footing, would never set her upright again: she retastes and researches herself too profoundly, and too much to the quick, and therefore would never let the wound she had received heal and cicatrise. It has been well for me that no sickness has yet discomposed her: at every charge made upon me, I preserve my utmost opposition and defence; by which means the first that should rout me would keep me from ever rallying again. I have no after-game to play: on which side soever the inundation breaks my banks, I lie open, and am drowned without remedy. Epicurus says, that a wise man can never become a fool; I have an opinion reverse to this sentence, which is, that he who has once been a very fool, will never after be very wise. God grants me cold according to my cloth, and passions proportionable to the means I have to withstand them: nature having laid me open on the one side, has covered me on the other; having disarmed me of strength, she has armed me with insensibility and an apprehension that is regular, or, if you will, dull.

I cannot now long endure (and when I was young could much less) either coach, litter, or boat, and hate all other riding but on horseback, both in town and country. But I can bear a litter worse than a coach; and, by the same reason, a rough agitation upon the water, whence fear is produced, better than the motions of a calm. At the little jerks of oars, stealing the vessel from under us, I find, I know not how, both my head and my stomach disordered; neither-can I endure to sit upon a tottering chair. When the sail or the current carries us equally, or that we are towed, the equal agitation does not disturb me at all; it is an interrupted motion that offends me, and most of all when most slow: I cannot otherwise express it. The physicians have ordered me to squeeze and gird myself about the bottom of the belly with a napkin to remedy this evil; which however I have not tried, being accustomed to wrestle with my own defects, and overcome them myself.

Would my memory serve me, I should not think my time ill spent in setting down here the infinite variety that history presents us of the use of chariots in the service of war: various, according to the nations and according to the age; in my opinion, of great necessity and effect; so that it is a wonder that we have lost all knowledge of them. I will only say this, that very lately, in our fathers' time, the Hungarians made very advantageous use of them against the Turks; having in everyone of them a targetter and a musketeer, and a number of harquebuses piled ready and loaded, and all covered with a pavesade like a galliot [Canvas spread along the side of a ship of war, in action to screen the movements of those on board.] They formed the front of their battle with three thousand such coaches, and after the cannon had played, made them all pour in their shot upon the enemy, who had to swallow that volley before they tasted of the rest, which was no little advance; and that done, these chariots charged into their squadrons to break them and open a way for the rest; besides the use they might make of them to flank the soldiers in a place of danger when marching to the field, or to cover a post, and fortify it in haste. In my time, a gentleman on one of our frontiers, unwieldy of body, and finding no horse able to carry his weight, having a quarrel, rode through the country in a chariot of this fashion, and found great convenience in it. But let us leave these chariots of war.

As if their effeminacy had not been sufficiently known by better proofs, the last kings of our first race travelled in a chariot drawn by four oxen. Marc Antony was the first at Rome who caused himself to be drawn in a coach by lions, and a singing wench with him. [Cytheris, the Roman courtezan. – Plutarch's Life of Antony, c. 3.]

Heliogabalus did since as much, calling himself Cybele, the mother of the gods; and also drawn by tigers, taking upon him the person of the god Bacchus; he also sometimes harnessed two stags to his coach, another time four dogs, and another four naked wenches, causing himself to be drawn by them in pomp, stark naked too. The Emperor Firmus caused his chariot to be drawn by ostriches of a prodigious size, so that it seemed rather to fly than roll.

The strangeness of these inventions puts this other fancy in my head: that it is a kind of pusillanimity in monarchs, and a testimony that they do not sufficiently understand themselves what they are, when they study to make themselves honoured and to appear great by excessive expense: it were indeed excusable in a foreign country, but amongst their own subjects, where they are in sovereign command, and may do what they please, it derogates from their dignity the most supreme degree of honour to which they can arrive: just as, methinks, it is superfluous in a private gentleman to go finely dressed at home; his house, his attendants, and his kitchen sufficiently answer for him. The advice that Isocrates gives his king seems to be grounded upon reason: that he should be splendid in plate and furniture; forasmuch as it is an expense of duration that devolves on his successors; and that he should avoid all magnificences that will in a short time be forgotten. I loved to go fine when I was a younger brother, for want of other ornament; and it became me well: there are some upon whom their rich clothes weep: We have strange stories of the frugality of our kings about their own persons and in their gifts: kings who were great in reputation, valour, and fortune. Demosthenes vehemently opposes the law of his city that assigned the public money for the pomp of their public plays and festivals: he would that their greatness should be seen in numbers of ships well equipped, and good armies well provided for; and there is good reason to condemn Theophrastus, who, in his Book on Riches, establishes a contrary opinion, and maintains that sort of expense to be the true fruit of abundance. They are delights, says Aristotle, that a only please the baser sort of the people, and that vanish from the memory as soon as the people are sated with them, and for which no serious and judicious man can have any esteem. This money would, in my opinion, be much more royally, as more profitably, justly, and durably, laid out in ports, havens, walls, and fortifications; in sumptuous buildings, churches, hospitals, colleges, the reforming of streets and highways: wherein Pope Gregory XIII will leave a laudable memory to future times: and wherein our Queen Catherine would to long posterity manifest her natural liberality and munificence, did her means supply her affection. Fortune has done me a great despite in interrupting the noble structure of the Pont-Neuf of our great city, and depriving me of the hope of seeing it finished before I die.

Moreover, it seems to subjects, who are spectators of these triumphs, that their own riches are exposed before them, and that they are entertained at their own expense: for the people are apt to presume of kings, as we do of our servants, that they are to take care to provide us all things necessary in abundance, but not touch it themselves; and therefore the Emperor Galba, being pleased with a musician who played to him at supper, called for his money-box, and gave him a handful of crowns that he took out of it, with these words: "This is not the public money, but my own." Yet it so falls out that the people, for the most part, have reason on their side, and that the princes feed their eyes with what they have need of to fill their bellies.

Liberality itself is not in its true lustre in a sovereign hand: private men have therein the most right; for, to take it exactly, a king has nothing properly his own; he owes himself to others: authority is not given in favour of the magistrate, but of the people; a superior is never made so for his own profit, but for the profit of the inferior, and a physician for the sick person, and not for himself: all magistracy, as well as all art, has its end out of itself wherefore the tutors of young princes, who make it their business to imprint in them this virtue of liberality, and preach to them to deny nothing and to think nothing so well spent as what they give (a doctrine that I have known in great credit in my time), either have more particular regard to their own profit than to that of their master, or ill understand to whom they speak. It is too easy a thing to inculcate liberality on him who has as much as he will to practise it with at the expense of others; and, the estimate not being proportioned to the measure of the gift but to the measure of the means of him who gives it, it comes to nothing in so mighty hands; they find themselves prodigal before they can be reputed liberal. And it is but a little recommendation, in comparison with other royal virtues: and the only one, as the tyrant Dionysius said, that suits well with tyranny itself. I should rather teach him this verse of the ancient labourer:

That whoever will have a good crop must sow with his hand, and not pour out of the sack.

[Plutarch, *Apothegms*. "Whether the Ancients were more excellent in Arms than in Learning".]

he must scatter it abroad, and not lay it on a heap in one place: and that, seeing he is to give, or, to say better, to pay and restore to so many people according as they have deserved, he ought to be a loyal and discreet disposer. If the liberality of a prince be without measure or discretion, I had rather he were covetous.

Royal virtue seems most to consist in justice; and of all the parts of justice that best denotes a king which accompanies liberality, for this they have particularly reserved to be performed by themselves, whereas all other sorts of justice they remit to the administration of others. An immoderate bounty is a very weak means to acquire for them good will; it checks more people than it allures:

> *Quo in plures usus sis, minus in multos uti possis....*
> *Quid autem est stultius, quam, quod libenter facias,*
> *curare ut id diutius facere non possis;*

[By how much more you use it to many, by so much less will you be in a capacity to use it to many more. And what greater folly can there be than to order it so that what you would willingly do, you cannot do longer.

—Cicero, *De Officiis*, ii. 15.]

and if it be conferred without due respect of merit, it puts him out of countenance who receives it, and is received ungraciously. Tyrants have been sacrificed to the hatred of the people by the hands of those very men they have unjustly advanced; such kind of men as buffoons, panders, fiddlers, and such ragamuffins, thinking to assure to themselves the possession of benefits unduly received, if they manifest to have him in hatred and disdain of whom they hold them, and in this associate themselves to the common judgment and opinion.

The subjects of a prince excessive in gifts grow excessive in asking, and regulate their demands, not by reason, but by example. We have, seriously, very often reason to blush at our own impudence:

we are over-paid, according to justice, when the recompense equals our service; for do we owe nothing of natural obligation to our princes? If he bear our charges, he does too much; it is enough that he contribute to them: the overplus is called benefit, which cannot be exacted: for the very name Liberality sounds of Liberty.

In our fashion it is never done; we never reckon what we have received; we are only for the future liberality; wherefore, the more a prince exhausts himself in giving, the poorer he grows in friends. How should he satisfy immoderate desires, that still increase as they are fulfilled? He who has his thoughts upon taking, never thinks of what he has taken; covetousness has nothing so properly and so much its own as ingratitude.

The example of Cyrus will not do amiss in this place, to serve the kings of these times for a touchstone to know whether their gifts are well or ill bestowed, and to see how much better that emperor conferred them than they do, by which means they are reduced to borrow of unknown subjects, and rather of them whom they have wronged than of them on whom they have conferred their benefits, and so receive aids wherein there is nothing of gratuitous but the name. Croesus reproached him with his bounty, and cast up to how much his treasure would amount if he had been a little closer-handed. He had a mind to justify his liberality, and therefore sent despatches into all parts to the grandees of his dominions whom he had particularly advanced, entreating everyone of them to supply him with as much money as they could, for a pressing occasion, and to send him particulars of what each could advance. When all these answers were brought to him, everyone of his friends, not thinking it enough barely to offer him so much as he had received from his bounty, and adding to it a great deal of his own, it appeared that the sum amounted to a great deal more than Croesus' reckoning. Whereupon Cyrus: "I am not," said he, "less in love with riches than other princes, but rather a better husband; you see with how small a venture I have acquired the inestimable treasure of so many friends, and how much more faithful treasurers they are to me

419

than mercenary men without obligation, without affection; and my money better laid up than in chests, bringing upon me the hatred, envy, and contempt of other princes."

The emperors excused the superfluity of their plays and public spectacles by reason that their authority in some sort (at least in outward appearance) depended upon the will of the people of Rome, who, time out of mind, had been accustomed to be entertained and caressed with such shows and excesses. But they were private citizens, who had nourished this custom to gratify their fellow-citizens and companions (and chiefly out of their own purses) by such profusion and magnificence it had quite another taste when the masters came to imitate it:

> *Pecuniarum translatio a justis dominis ad alienos*
> *non debet liberalis videri.*

[The transferring of money from the right owners to strangers ought not to have the title of liberality.
—Cicero, *De Officius*, i. 14.]

Philip, seeing that his son went about by presents to gain the affection of the Macedonians, reprimanded him in a letter after this manner: "What! hast thou a mind that thy subjects shall look upon thee as their cash-keeper and not as their king? Wilt thou tamper with them to win their affections? Do it, then, by the benefits of thy virtue, and not by those of thy chest." And yet it was, doubtless, a fine thing to bring and plant within the amphitheatre a great number of vast trees, with all their branches in their full verdure, representing a great shady forest, disposed in excellent order; and, the first day, to throw into it a thousand ostriches and a thousand stags, a thousand boars, and a thousand fallow-deer, to be killed and disposed of by the people: the next day, to cause a hundred great lions, a hundred leopards, and three hundred bears to be killed in his presence; and for the third day, to make three hundred pair of gladiators fight it out to the last, as the Emperor Probus did. It was also very fine to see those vast amphitheatres, all faced with marble without, curiously wrought with figures and statues, and within glittering with rare enrichments:

Baltheus en! gemmis, enillita porticus auro:

[A belt glittering with jewels, and a portico overlaid with gold. —Calpurnius, *Eclogues*, vii. 47. A baltheus was a shoulder-belt or baldric.]

all the sides of this vast space filled and environed, from the bottom to the top, with three or four score rows of seats, all of marble also, and covered with cushions:

Exeat, inquit,
Si pudor est, et de pulvino surgat equestri,
Cujus res legi non sufficit;

[Let him go out, he said, if he has any sense of shame, and rise from the equestrian cushion, whose estate does not satisfy the law. —Juvenal, iii. 153. The Equites were required to possess a fortune of 400 sestertia, and they sat on the first fourteen rows behind the orchestra.]

where a hundred thousand men might sit at their ease: and, the place below, where the games were played, to make it, by art, first open and cleave in chasms, representing caves that vomited out the beasts designed for the spectacle; and then, secondly, to be overflowed by a deep sea, full of sea monsters, and laden with ships of war, to represent a naval battle; and, thirdly, to make it dry and even again for the combat of the gladiators; and, for the fourth scene, to have it strown with vermilion grain and storax [A resinous gum]

421

instead of sand, there to make a solemn feast for all that infinite number of people: the last act of one only day:

> *Quoties nos descendentis arenae*
> *Vidimus in partes, ruptaque voragine terrae*
> *Emersisse feras, et eisdem saepe latebris*
> *Aurea cum croceo creverunt arbuta libro!....*
> *Nec solum nobis silvestria cernere monstra*
> *Contigit; aequoreos ego cum certantibus ursis*
> *Spectavi vitulos, et equorum nominee dignum,*
> *Sen deforme pecus, quod in illo nascitur amni....*

[How often have we seen the stage of the theatre descend and part asunder, and from a chasm in the earth wild beasts emerge, and then presently give birth to a grove of gilded trees, that put forth blossoms of enamelled flowers. Nor yet of sylvan marvels alone had we sight: I saw sea-calves fight with bears, and a deformed sort of cattle, we might call sea-horses.

—Calpurnius, *Eclogues*, vii. 64.]

Sometimes they made a high mountain advance itself, covered with fruit-trees and other leafy trees, sending down rivulets of water from the top, as from the mouth of a fountain: otherwhiles, a great ship was seen to come rolling in, which opened and divided of itself, and after having disgorged from the hold four or five hundred beasts for fight, closed again, and vanished without help. At other times, from the floor of this place, they made spouts of perfumed water dart their streams upward, and so high as to sprinkle all that infinite multitude. To defend themselves from the injuries of the weather, they had that vast place one while covered over with purple curtains of needlework, and by-and-by with silk of one or another colour, which they drew off or on in a moment, as they had a mind:

Quamvis non modico caleant spectacula sole,
Vela reducuntur, cum venit Hermogenes.

[The curtains, though the sun should scorch the spectators, are drawn in, when Hermogenes appears. – Martial, xii. 29, 15. M. Tigellius Hermogenes, whom Horace and others have satirized as a thief.]

The network also that was set before the people to defend them from the violence of these turned-out beasts was woven of gold:

> *Auro quoque torts refulgent*
> *Retia.*

[The woven nets are refulgent with gold.
—Calpurnius, ubi supra.]

If there be anything excusable in such excesses as these, it is where the novelty and invention create more wonder than the expense; even in these vanities we discover how fertile those ages were in other kind of wits than these of ours. It is with this sort of fertility, as with all other products of nature: not that she there and then employed her utmost force: we do not go; we rather run up and down, and whirl this way and that; we turn back the way we came. I am afraid our knowledge is weak in all senses; we neither see far forward nor far backward; our understanding comprehends little, and lives but a little while; it is short both in extent of time and extent of matter:

> *Vixere fortes ante Agamemnona*
> *Mufti, sed omnes illacrymabiles*

Urgentur, ignotique longs
Nocte.

[Many brave men lived before Agamemnon, but all are pressed by the long night unmourned and unknown. – Horace, *Odes*, iv. 9, 25.]

Et supra bellum Thebanum et funera Trojae
Non alias alii quoque res cecinere poetae?

[Why before the Theban war and the destruction of Troy, have not other poets sung other events?

—Lucretius, v. 327.

And the narrative of Solon, of what he had learned from the Egyptian priests, touching the long life of their state, and their manner of learning and preserving foreign histories, is not, methinks, a testimony to be refused in this consideration:

Si interminatam in omnes partes magnitudinem regionum videremus
et temporum, in quam se injiciens animus et intendens, ita late
longeque peregrinatur, ut nullam oram ultimi videat, in qua possit
insistere: in haec immensitate . . . infinita vis innumerabilium
appareret fomorum.

[Could we see on all parts the unlimited magnitude of regions and of times, upon which the mind being intent, could wander so far and wide, that no limit is to be seen, in which it can bound its eye, we should, in that infinite immensity, discover an infinite force of innumerable atoms.]

CHAPTER 6

Though all that has arrived, by report, of our knowledge of times past should be true, and known by someone person, it would be less than nothing in comparison of what is unknown. And of this same image of the world, which glides away whilst we live upon it, how wretched and limited is the knowledge of the most curious; not only of particular events, which fortune often renders exemplary and of great concern, but of the state of great governments and nations, a hundred more escape us than ever come to our knowledge. We make a mighty business of the invention of artillery and printing, which other men at the other end of the world, in China, had a thousand years ago. Did we but see as much of the world as we do not see, we should perceive, we may well believe, a perpetual multiplication and vicissitude of forms. There is nothing single and rare in respect of nature, but in respect of our knowledge, which is a wretched foundation whereon to ground our rules, and that represents to us a very false image of things. As we nowadays vainly conclude the declension and decrepitude of the world, by the arguments we extract from our own weakness and decay:

Jamque adeo est affecta aetas effoet aque tellus;

[Our age is feeble, and the earth less fertile.
—Lucretius, ii. 1151.]

so did he vainly conclude as to its birth and youth, by the vigour he observed in the wits of his time, abounding in novelties and the invention of divers arts:

Verum, ut opinor, habet novitatem summa, recensque
Natura est mundi, neque pridem exordia coepit
Quare etiam quaedam nunc artes expoliuntur,
Nunc etiam augescunt; nunc addita navigiis sunt
Multa.

425

[But, as I am of opinion, the whole of the world is of recent origin, nor had its commencement in remote times; wherefore it is that some arts are still being refined, and some just on the increase; at present many additions are being made to shipping.

—Lucretius, v. 331.]

Our world has lately discovered another (and who will assure us that it is the last of its brothers, since the Daemons, the Sybils, and we ourselves have been ignorant of this till now?), as large, well-peopled, and fruitful as this whereon we live and yet so raw and childish, that we are still teaching it its A B C: it is not above fifty years since it knew neither letters, weights, measures, vestments, corn, nor vines: it was then quite naked in the mother's lap, and only lived upon what she gave it. If we rightly conclude of our end, and this poet of the youthfulness of that age of his, that other world will only enter into the light when this of ours shall make its exit; the universe will fall into paralysis; one member will be useless, the other in vigour. I am very much afraid that we have greatly precipitated its declension and ruin by our contagion; and that we have sold it opinions and our arts at a very dear rate. It was an infant world, and yet we have not whipped and subjected it to our discipline by the advantage of our natural worth and force, neither have we won it by our justice and goodness, nor subdued it by our magnanimity. Most of their answers, and the negotiations we have had with them, witness that they were nothing behind us in pertinency and clearness of natural understanding. The astonishing magnificence of the cities of Cusco and Mexico, and, amongst many other things, the garden of the king, where all the trees, fruits, and plants, according to the order and stature they have in a garden, were excellently formed in gold; as, in his cabinet, were all the animals bred upon his territory and in its seas; and the beauty of their manufactures, in jewels, feathers, cotton, and painting, gave ample proof that they were as little inferior to us in industry. But as to what concerns devotion,

426

CHAPTER 6

observance of the laws, goodness, liberality, loyalty, and plain dealing, it was of use to us that we had not so much as they; for they have
lost, sold, and betrayed themselves by this advantage over us.

As to boldness and courage, stability, constancy against pain,
hunger, and death, I should not fear to oppose the examples I find
amongst them to the most famous examples of elder times that we
find in our records on this side of the world. Far as to those who subdued them, take but away the tricks and artifices they practised to
gull them, and the just astonishment it was to those nations to see so
sudden and unexpected an arrival of men with beards, differing in
language, religion, shape, and countenance, from so remote a part
of the world, and where they had never heard there was any habitation, mounted upon great unknown monsters, against those who
had not only never seen a horse, but had never seen any other beast
trained up to carry a man or any other loading; shelled in a hard
and shining skin, with a cutting and glittering weapon in his hand,
against them, who, out of wonder at the brightness of a looking
glass or a knife, would exchange great treasures of gold and pearl;
and who had neither knowledge, nor matter with which, at leisure,
they could penetrate our steel: to which may be added the lightning
and thunder of our cannon and harquebuses, enough to frighten
Caesar himself, if surprised, with so little experience, against people
naked, except where the invention of a little quilted cotton was in
use, without other arms, at the most, than bows, stones, staves, and
bucklers of wood; people surprised under colour of friendship and
good faith, by the curiosity of seeing strange and unknown things;
take but away, I say, this disparity from the conquerors, and you take
away all the occasion of so many victories. When I look upon that in
vincible ardour wherewith so many thousands of men, women, and
children so often presented and threw themselves into inevitable
dangers for the defence of their gods and liberties; that generous
obstinacy to suffer all extremities and difficulties, and death itself,
rather than submit to the dominion of those by whom they had been
so shamefully abused; and some of them choosing to die of hunger

and fasting, being prisoners, rather than to accept of nourishment from the hands of their so basely victorious enemies: I see, that whoever would have attacked them upon equal terms of arms, experience, and number, would have had a hard, and, peradventure, a harder game to play than in any other war we have seen.

Why did not so noble a conquest fall under Alexander, or the ancient Greeks and Romans; and so great a revolution and mutation of so many empires and nations, fall into hands that would have gently levelled, rooted up, and made plain and smooth whatever was rough and savage amongst them, and that would have cherished and propagated the good seeds that nature had there produced; mixing not only with the culture of land and the ornament of cities, the arts of this part of the world, in what was necessary, but also the Greek and Roman virtues, with those that were original of the country? What a reparation had it been to them, and what a general good to the whole world, had our first examples and deportments in those parts allured those people to the admiration and imitation of virtue, and had begotten between them and us a fraternal society and intelligence? How easy had it been to have made advantage of souls so innocent, and so eager to learn, leaving, for the most part, naturally so good inclinations before? Whereas, on the contrary, we have taken advantage of their ignorance and inexperience, with greater ease to incline them to treachery, luxury, avarice, and towards all sorts of inhumanity and cruelty, by the pattern and example of our manners. Whoever enhanced the price of merchandise at such a rate? So many cities levelled with the ground, so many nations exterminated, so many millions of people fallen by the edge of the sword, and the richest and most beautiful part of the world turned upside down, for the traffic of pearl and pepper? Mechanic victories! Never did ambition, never did public animosities, engage men against one another in such miserable hostilities, in such miserable calamities.

Certain Spaniards, coasting the sea in quest of their mines, landed in a fruitful and pleasant and very well peopled country, and there made to the inhabitants their accustomed professions: "that they were peaceable men, who were come from a very remote country, and sent on the behalf of the King of Castile, the greatest prince of the habitable world, to whom the Pope, God's vicegerent upon earth, had given the principality of all the Indies; that if they would become tributaries to him, they should be very gently and courteously used"; at the same time requiring of them victuals for their nourishment, and gold whereof to make some pretended medicine; setting forth, moreover, the belief in one only God, and the truth of our religion, which they advised them to embrace, whereunto they also added some threats. To which they received this answer: "That as to their being peaceable, they did not seem to be such, if they were so. As to their king, since he was fain to beg, he must be necessitous and poor; and he who had made him this gift, must be a man who loved dissension, to give that to another which was none of his own, to bring it into dispute against the ancient possessors. As to victuals, they would supply them; that of gold they had little; it being a thing they had in very small esteem, as of no use to the service of life, whereas their only care was to pass it over happily and pleasantly: but that what they could find excepting what was employed in the service of their gods, they might freely take. As to one only God, the proposition had pleased them well; but that they would not change their religion, both because they had so long and happily lived in it, and that they were not wont to take advice of any but their friends, and those they knew: as to their menaces, it was a sign of want of judgment to threaten those whose nature and power were to them unknown; that, therefore, they were to make haste to quit their coast, for they were not used to take the civilities and professions of armed men and strangers in good part; otherwise they should do by them as they had done by those others," showing them the heads of several executed men round the walls of their city. A fair example of the babble of these children. But so it is, that the Spaniards did not, either in this or in several other places, where they did not find the merchandise they sought, make any stay or attempt, whatever other conveniences were there to be had; witness my "On Cannibals". [Montaigne's chapter from Book I]

Of the two most puissant monarchs of that world, and, peradventure, of this, kings of so many kings, and the last they turned out, he of Peru, having been taken in a battle, and put to so excessive a ransom as exceeds all belief, and it being faithfully paid, and he having, by his conversation, given manifest signs of a frank, liberal, and constant spirit, and of a clear and settled understanding, the conquerors had a mind, after having exacted one million three hundred and twenty-five thousand and five hundred weight of gold, besides silver, and other things which amounted to no less (so that their horses were shod with massy gold), still to see, at the price of what disloyalty and injustice whatever, what the remainder of the treasures of this king might be, and to possess themselves of that also. To this end a false accusation was preferred against him, and false witnesses brought to prove that he went about to raise an insurrection in his provinces, to procure his own liberty; whereupon, by the virtuous sentence of those very men who had by this treachery conspired his ruin, he was condemned to be publicly hanged and strangled, after having made him buy off the torment of being burnt alive, by the baptism they gave him immediately before execution; a horrid and unheard of barbarity, which, nevertheless, he underwent without giving way either in word or look, with a truly grave and royal behaviour. After which, to calm and appease the people, aroused and astounded at so strange a thing, they counterfeited great sorrow for his death, and appointed most sumptuous funerals.

The other king of Mexico, [Guatimosin] having for a long time defended his beleaguered city, and having in this siege manifested the utmost of what suffering and perseverance can do, if ever prince and people did, and his misfortune having delivered him alive into his enemies' hands, upon articles of being treated like a king, neither did he in his captivity discover anything unworthy of that title. His enemies, after their victory, not finding so much gold as they expected, when they had searched and rifled with their utmost

Chapter 6

diligence, they went about to procure discoveries by the most cruel torments they could invent upon the prisoners they had taken: but having profited nothing by these, their courage being greater than their torments, they arrived at last to such a degree of fury, as, contrary to their faith and the law of nations, to condemn the king himself, and one of the principal noblemen of his court, to the rack, in the presence of one another. This lord, finding himself overcome with pain, being environed with burning coals, pitifully turned his dying eyes towards his master, as it were to ask him pardon that he was able to endure no more; whereupon the king, darting at him a fierce and severe look, as reproaching his cowardice and pusillanimity, with a harsh and constant voice said to him thus only: "And what do thou think I suffer? am I in a bath? am I more at ease than thou?" Whereupon the other immediately quailed under the torment and died upon the spot. The king, half roasted, was carried thence; not so much out of pity (for what compassion ever touched so barbarous souls, who, upon the doubtful information of some vessel of gold to be made a prey of, caused not only a man, but a king, so great in fortune and desert, to be broiled before their eyes), but because his constancy rendered their cruelty still more shameful. They afterwards hanged him for having nobly attempted to deliver himself by arms from so long a captivity and subjection, and he died with a courage becoming so magnanimous a prince.

Another time, they burnt in the same fire four hundred and sixty men alive at once, the four hundred of the common people, the sixty the principal lords of a province, simply prisoners of war. We have these narratives from themselves for they not only own it, but boast of it and publish it. Could it be for a testimony of their justice or their zeal to religion? Doubtless these are ways too differing and contrary to so holy an end. Had they proposed to themselves to extend our faith, they would have considered that it does not amplify in the possession of territories, but in the gaining of men; and would have more than satisfied themselves with the slaughters occasioned by the necessity of war, without indifferently mixing a massacre, as upon wild beasts, as universal as fire and sword could make it; having only, by intention, saved so many as they meant to make miserable slaves of, for the work and service of their mines; so that many of the captains were put to death upon the place of conquest, by order of the kings of Castile, justly offended with the horror of their deportment, and almost all of them hated and disesteemed. God meritoriously permitted that all this great plunder should be swallowed up by the sea in transportation, or in the civil wars wherewith they devoured one another; and most of the men themselves were buried in a foreign land without any fruit of their victory.

That the revenue from these countries, though in the hands of so parsimonious and so prudent a prince [Phillip II] so little answers the expectation given of it to his predecessors, and to that original abundance of riches which was found at the first landing in those new discovered countries (for though a great deal be fetched thence, yet we see it is nothing in comparison of that which might be expected), is that the use of coin was there utterly unknown, and that consequently their gold was found all hoarded together, being of no other use but for ornament and show, as a furniture reserved from father to son by many puissant kings, who were ever draining their mines to make this vast heap of vessels and statues for the decoration of their palaces and temples; whereas our gold is always in motion and traffic; we cut it into a thousand small pieces, and cast it into a thousand forms, and scatter and disperse it in a thousand ways. But suppose our kings should thus hoard up all the gold they could get in several ages and let it lie idle by them.

Those of the kingdom of Mexico were in some sort more civilised and more advanced in arts than the other nations about them. Therefore did they judge, as we do, that the world was near its period, and looked upon the desolation we brought amongst them as a certain sign of it. They believed that the existence of the world was divided into five ages, and in the life of five successive suns, of which four had already ended their time, and that this which gave them light was the fifth. The first perished, with all other creatures,

432

Chapter 6

by an universal inundation of water; the second by the heavens falling upon us and suffocating every living thing to which age they assigned the giants, and showed bones to the Spaniards, according to the proportion of which the stature of men amounted to twenty feet; the third by fire, which burned and consumed all; the fourth by an emotion of the air and wind, which came with such violence as to beat down even many mountains, wherein the men died not, but were turned into baboons. What impressions will not the weakness of human belief admit? After the death of this fourth sun, the world was twenty-five years in perpetual darkness: in the fifteenth of which a man and a woman were created, who restored the human race: ten years after, upon a certain day, the sun appeared newly created, and since the account of their year takes beginning from that day: the third day after its creation the ancient gods died, and the new ones were since born daily. After what manner they think this last sun shall perish, my author knows not; but their number of this fourth change agrees with the great conjunction of stars which eight hundred and odd years ago, as astrologers suppose, produced great alterations and novelties in the world.

As to pomp and magnificence, upon the account of which I engaged in this discourse, neither Greece, Rome, nor Egypt, whether for utility, difficulty, or state, can compare any of their works with the highway to be seen in Peru, made by the kings of the country, from the city of Quito to that of Cusco (three hundred leagues), straight, even, five-and-twenty paces wide, paved, and provided on both sides with high and beautiful walls; and close by them, and all along on the inside, two perennial streams, bordered with beautiful plants, which they call moly. In this work, where they met with rocks and mountains, they cut them through, and made them even, and filled up pits and valleys with lime and stone to make them level. At the end of every day's journey are beautiful palaces, furnished with provisions, vestments, and arms, as well for travellers as for the armies that are to pass that way. In the estimate of this work I have reckoned the difficulty which is especially considerable in that

433

place; they did not build with any stones less than ten feet square, and had no other conveniency of carriage but by drawing their load themselves by force of arm, and knew not so much as the art of scaffolding, nor any other way of standing to their work, but by throwing up earth against the building as it rose higher, taking it away again when they had done.

Let us here return to our coaches. Instead of these, and of all other sorts of carriages, they caused themselves to be carried upon men's shoulders. This last king of Peru, the day that he was taken, was thus carried between two upon staves of gold, and set in a chair of gold in the middle of his army. As many of these sedan-men as were killed to make him fall (for they would take him alive), so many others (and they contended for it) took the place of those who were slain, so that they could never beat him down, what slaughter soever they made of these people, till a horseman, seizing upon him, brought him to the ground.

8

ON THE ART
OF CONVERSATION

It is a custom of our justice to condemn some for a warning to others. To condemn them for having done amiss, were folly, as Plato says, for what is done can never be undone; but it is to the end they may offend no more, and that others may avoid the example of their offence: we do not correct the man we hang; we correct others by him. I do the same; my errors are sometimes natural, incorrigible, and irremediable: but the good which virtuous men do to the public, in making themselves imitated, I, peradventure, may do in making my manners avoided:

> *Nonne vides, Albi ut male vivat filius? utque*
> *Barrus inops? magnum documentum, ne patriam rein*
> *Perdere guis velit;*

> [Do thou not see how ill the son of Albus lives? and how the indigent Barrus? a great warning lest any one should incline to dissipate his patrimony.
>
> —Horace, *Satire*, i. 4, 109.]

publishing and accusing my own imperfections, someone will learn to be afraid of them. The parts that I most esteem in myself, derive more honour from decrying, than for commending myself which is the reason why I so often fall into, and so much insist upon that strain. But, when all is summed up, a man never speaks of himself without loss; a man's accusations of himself are always believed; his praises never: There may, peradventure, be some of my own complexion who better instruct myself by contrariety than by similitude, and by avoiding than by imitation. The elder Cato was regarding this sort of discipline, when he said, "that the wise may learn more of fools, than fools can of the wise"; and Pausanias tells us of an ancient player upon the harp, who was wont to make his scholars go to hear one who played very ill, who lived over against him, that they might learn to hate his discords and false measures. The horror of cruelty more inclines me to clemency, than any example of clemency could possibly do. A good rider does not so much mend my seat, as an awkward attorney or a Venetian, on horseback; and a clownish way of speaking more reforms mine than the most correct. The ridiculous and simple look of another always warns and advises me; that which pricks, rouses and incites much better than that which tickles. The time is now proper for us to reform backward; more by dissenting than by agreeing; by differing more than by consent. Profiting little by good examples, I make use of those that are ill, which are everywhere to be found: I endeavour to render myself as agreeable as I see others offensive; as constant as I see others fickle; as affable as I see others rough; as good as I see others evil: but I propose to myself impracticable measures.

The most fruitful and natural exercise of the mind, in my opinion, is conversation; I find the use of it more sweet than of any other action of life; and for that reason it is that, if I were now compelled to choose, I should sooner, I think, consent to lose my sight, than my hearing and speech. The Athenians, and also the Romans, kept this exercise in great honour in their academies; the Italians retain some traces of it to this day, to their great advantage, as is manifest by the comparison of our understandings with theirs. The study of books is a languishing and feeble motion that heats not, whereas conversation teaches and exercises at once. If I converse with a strong mind

Chapter 8

and a rough disputant, he presses upon my flanks, and pricks me right and left; his imaginations stir up mine; jealousy, glory, and contention, stimulate and raise me up to something above myself; and acquiescence is a quality altogether tedious in discourse. But, as our mind fortifies itself by the communication of vigorous and regular understandings, it is not to be expressed how much it loses and degenerates by the continual commerce and familiarity we have with mean and weak spirits; there is no contagion that spreads like that; I know sufficiently by experience what it is worth a yard. I love to discourse and dispute, but it is with but few men, and for myself; for to do it as a spectacle and entertainment to great persons, and to make of a man's wit and words competitive parade is, in my opinion, very unbecoming a man of honour.

Folly is a bad quality; but not to be able to endure it, to fret and vex at it, as I do, is another sort of disease little less troublesome than folly itself; and is the thing that I will now accuse in myself. I enter into conference, and dispute with great liberty and facility, forasmuch as opinion meets in me with a soil very unfit for penetration, and wherein to take any deep root; no propositions astonish me, no belief offends me, though never so contrary to my own; there is no so frivolous and extravagant fancy that does not seem to me suitable to the production of human wit. We, who deprive our judgment of the right of determining, look indifferently upon the diverse opinions, and if we incline not our judgment to them, yet we easily give them the hearing: Where one scale is totally empty, I let the other waver under an old wife's dreams; and I think myself excusable, if I prefer the odd number; Thursday rather than Friday; if I had rather be the twelfth or fourteenth than the thirteenth at table; if I had rather, on a journey, see a hare run by me than cross my way, and rather give my man my left foot than my right, when he comes to put on my stockings. All such reveries as are in credit around us, deserve at least a hearing: for my part, they only with me import inanity, but they import that. Moreover, vulgar and casual opinions are something more than nothing in nature; and he who will not suffer himself to proceed so far, falls, peradventure, into the vice of obstinacy, to avoid that of superstition.

The contradictions of judgments, then, neither offend nor alter, they only rouse and exercise, me. We evade correction, whereas we ought to offer and present ourselves to it, especially when it appears in the form of conference, and not of authority. At every opposition, we do not consider whether or no it be dust, but, right or wrong, how to disengage ourselves: instead of extending the arms, we thrust out our claws. I could suffer myself to be rudely handled by my friend, so much as to tell me that I am a fool, and talk I know not of what. I love stout expressions amongst gentle men, and to have them speak as they think; we must fortify and harden our hearing against this tenderness of the ceremonious sound of words. I love a strong and manly familiarity and conversation: a friendship that pleases itself in the sharpness and vigour of its communication, like love in biting and scratching: it is not vigorous and generous enough, if it be not quarrelsome, if it be civilised and artificial, if it treads nicely and fears the shock:

Neque enim disputari sine reprehensione potest.

[Neither can a man dispute, but he must contradict. Or: Nor can people dispute without reprehension.
—Cicero, *De Finibus*, i. 8.]

When any one contradicts me, he raises my attention, not my anger: I advance towards him who controverts, who instructs me; the cause of truth ought to be the common cause both of the one and the other. What will the angry man answer? Passion has already confounded his judgment; agitation has usurped the place of reason. It were not amiss that the decision of our disputes should pass by wager: that there might be a material mark of our losses, to the end we might the better remember them; and that my man might tell me: "Your ignorance and obstinacy cost you last year, at several times, a hundred crowns." I hail and caress truth in what quarter soever I find it, and cheerfully surrender myself, and open my conquered arms as far off as I can discover it; and, provided it be not too imperiously, take a pleasure in being reproved, and accommodate myself to my accusers, very often more by reason of civility than amendment, loving to gratify and nourish the liberty of admonition by my facility of submitting to it, and this even at my own expense.

Nevertheless, it is hard to bring the men of my time to it: they have not the courage to correct, because they have not the courage to suffer themselves to be corrected; and speak always with dissimulation in the presence of one another: I take so great a pleasure in being judged and known, that it is almost indifferent to me in which of the two forms I am so: my imagination so often contradicts and condemns itself, that it is all one to me if another do it, especially considering that I give his reprehension no greater authority than I choose; but I break with him, who carries himself so high, as I know of one who repents his advice, if not believed, and takes it for an affront if it be not immediately followed. That Socrates always received smilingly the contradictions offered to his arguments, a man may say arose from his strength of reason; and that, the advantage being certain to fall on his side, he accepted them as a matter of new victory. But we see, on the contrary, that nothing in argument renders our sentiment so delicate, as the opinion of pre-eminence, and disdain of the adversary; and that, in reason, it is rather for the weaker to take in good part the oppositions that correct him and set him right. In earnest, I rather choose the company of those who ruffle me than of those who fear me; it is a dull and hurtful pleasure to have to do with people who admire us and approve of all we say. Antisthenes commanded his children never to take it kindly or for a favour, when any man commended them. I find I am much prouder of the victory I obtain over myself, when, in the very ardour of dispute, I make myself submit to my adversary's force of reason, than I am pleased with the victory I obtain over him through his weakness. In fine, I receive and admit of all manner of attacks that are direct, how weak soever; but I am too impatient of those that are made out of form. I care not what the subject is, the opinions are to me all one, and I am almost indifferent whether I get the better or the worse. I can peaceably argue a whole day together, if the argument be carried on with method; I do not so much require force and subtlety as order; I mean the order which we every day observe in the wranglings of shepherds and shop-boys, but never amongst us: if they start from their subject, it is out of incivility, and so it is with us; but their tumult and impatience never put them out of their theme; their argument still continues its course; if they interrupt, and do not stay for one another, they at least understand one another. Any one answers too well for me, if he answers what I say: when the dispute is irregular and disordered, I leave the thing itself, and insist upon the form with anger and indiscretion; falling into wilful, malicious, and imperious way of disputation, of which I am afterwards ashamed. It is impossible to deal fairly with a fool: my judgment is not only corrupted under the hand of so impetuous a master, but my conscience also.

Our disputes ought to be interdicted and punished as well as other verbal crimes: what vice do they not raise and heap up, being always governed and commanded by passion? We first quarrel with their reasons, and then with the men. We only learn to dispute that we may contradict; and so, everyone contradicting and being contradicted, it falls out that the fruit of disputation is to lose and annihilate truth. Therefore it is that Plato in his Republic prohibits this exercise to fools and ill-bred people. To what end do you go about to inquire of him, who knows nothing to the purpose? A man does no injury to the subject, when he leaves it to seek how he may treat it; I do not mean by an artificial and scholastic way, but by a natural one, with a sound understanding. What will it be in the end? One flies to the east, the other to the west; they lose the principal, dispersing it in the crowd of incidents after an hour of tempest, they know not what they seek: one is low, the other high, and a third wide. One catches at a word and a simile; another is no longer sensible of what is said in opposition to him, and thinks only of going on at his own rate, not of answering you: another, finding himself too weak to make good his rest, fears all, refuses all, at the very beginning, confounds the subject; or, in the very height of the dispute, stops short and is silent, by a peevish ignorance affecting a proud contempt or a foolishly modest avoidance of further debate: provided this man strikes, he cares not how much he lays himself open; the other counts his words, and weighs them for reasons; another only brawls, and uses the advantage of his lungs. Here's one who learnedly concludes against himself, and another who deafens you with prefaces and senseless digressions: an other falls into downright railing, and seeks a quarrel after the German fashion, to disengage himself from a wit that presses too hard upon him: and a last man sees nothing into the reason of the thing, but draws a line of circumvallation about you of dialectic clauses, and the formulas of his art.

Now, who would not enter into distrust of sciences, and doubt whether he can reap from them any solid fruit for the service of life, considering the use we put them to?

Nihil sanantibus litteris.

[Letters which cure nothing.

—Seneca, *Epistles*, 59.]

Who has got understanding by his logic? Where are all her fair promises?

Nec ad melius vivendum, nec ad commodius disserendum.

[It neither makes a man live better nor talk better.
—Cicero, *De Finibus*, i. 19.]

Is there more noise or confusion in the scolding of herring-wives than in the public disputes of men of this profession? I had rather my son should learn in a tap-house to speak, than in the schools to prate. Take a master of arts, and confer with him: why does he not make us sensible of this artificial excellence? and why does he not captivate women and ignoramuses, as we are, with admiration at the steadiness of his reasons and the beauty of his order? why does he not sway and persuade us to what he will? why does a man, who has so much advantage in matter and treatment, mix railing, indiscretion, and fury in his disputations? Strip him of his gown, his hood, and his Latin, let him not batter our ears with Aristotle, pure and simple, you will take him for one of us, or worse. Whilst they torment us with this complication and confusion of words, it fares with them, methinks, as with jugglers; their dexterity imposes upon our senses, but does not at all work upon our belief this legerdemain excepted, they perform nothing that is not very ordinary and mean: for being the more learned, they are none the less fools.

I love and honour knowledge as much as they that have it, and in its true use it is the most noble and the greatest acquisition of men; but in such as I speak of (and the number of them is infinite), who build their fundamental sufficiency and value upon it, who appeal from their understanding to their memory:

Sub aliena umbra latentes,

[Sheltering under the shadow of others.

—Seneca, *Epistles*, 33.]

and who can do nothing but by book, I hate it, if I dare to say so, worse than stupidity. In my country, and in my time, learning improves fortunes enough, but not minds; if it meet with those that are dull and heavy, it overcharges and suffocates them, leaving them a crude and undigested mass; if airy and fine, it purifies, clarifies, and subtilises them, even to extinction. It is a thing of almost indifferent quality; a very useful accession to a well-born soul, but hurtful and pernicious to others; or rather a thing of very precious use, that will not suffer itself to be purchased at an under rate; in the hand of some it is a sceptre, in that of others a fool's bauble.

But let us proceed. What greater victory do you expect than to make your enemy see and know that he is not able to encounter you? When you get the better of your argument; it is truth that wins; when you get the advantage of form and method, it is then you who win. I am of opinion that in, Plato and Xenophon Socrates disputes more in favour of the disputants than in favour of the dispute, and more to instruct Euthydemus and Protagoras in the, knowledge of their impertinence, than in the impertinence of their art. He takes hold of the first subject like one who has a more profitable end than to explain it – namely, to clear the understandings that he takes upon him to instruct and exercise. To hunt after truth is properly our business, and we are inexcusable if we carry on the chase impertinently and ill; to fail of seizing it is another thing, for we are born to inquire after truth: it belongs to a greater power to possess it. It is not, as Democritus said, hid in the bottom of the deeps, but rather elevated to an infinite height in the divine knowledge. The world is but a school of inquisition: it is not who shall enter the ring, but who shall run the best courses. He may as well play the fool who speaks true, as he who speaks false, for we are upon the manner, not the matter, of speaking. It is my humour as much to regard the form as the substance, and the advocate as much as the cause, as Alcibiades ordered we should: and every day pass away my time in reading authors without any consideration of their learning; their manner is what I look after, not their subject: And just so do I hunt after the conversation of any eminent wit, not that he may teach me, but that I may know him, and that knowing him, if I think him worthy of imitation, I may imitate him. Every man may speak truly, but to speak methodically, prudently, and fully, is a talent that few men have. The falsity that proceeds from ignorance does not offend me, but the foppery of it. I have broken off several treaties that would have been of advantage to me, by reason of the impertinent contestations of those with whom I treated. I am not moved once in a year at the faults of those over whom I have authority, but upon the account of the ridiculous obstinacy of their allegations, denials, excuses, we are every day going together by the ears; they neither understand what is said, nor why, and answer accordingly; it is enough to drive a man mad. I never feel any hurt upon my head but when it is knocked against another, and more easily forgive the vices of my servants than their boldness, importunity, and folly; let them do less, provided they understand what they do: you live in hope to warm their affection to your service, but there is nothing to be had or to be expected from a stock.

But what, if I take things otherwise than they are? Perhaps I do; and therefore it is that I accuse my own impatience, and hold, in the first place, that it is equally vicious both in him that is in the right, and in him that is in the wrong; for it is always a tyrannic sourness not to endure a form contrary to one's own: and, besides, there cannot, in truth, be a greater, more constant, nor more irregular folly than to be moved and angry at the follies of the world, for it principally makes us quarrel with ourselves; and the old philosopher never wanted an occasion for his tears whilst he considered himself. Miso, one of the seven sages, of a Timonian and Democritic humour, being asked, "what he laughed at, being alone?" – "That I do laugh alone," answered he. How many ridiculous things, in my own opinion, do I say and answer every day that comes over my head? and then how many more, according to the opinion of others? If I bite my own lips, what ought others to do? In fine, we must live amongst the living, and let the river run under the bridge without our care, or, at least, without our interference. In truth, why do we meet a man with a hunch-back, or any other deformity, without being moved, and cannot endure the encounter of a deformed mind without being angry? this vicious sourness sticks more to the judge than to the crime. Let us always have this saying of Plato in our mouths: "Do not I think things unsound, because I am not sound in myself? Am I not myself in fault? may not my observations reflect upon myself?" – a wise and divine saying, that lashes the most universal and common error of mankind. Not only the reproaches that we throw in the face of one another, but our reasons also, our arguments and controversies, are reboundable upon us, and we wound ourselves with our own weapons: of which antiquity has left me enough grave examples. It was ingeniously and home-said by him, who was the inventor of this sentence:

Stercus cuique suum bene olet.

[To every man his own excrements smell well.

—Erasmus]

We see nothing behind us; we mock ourselves an hundred times a day; when we deride our neighbours; and we detest in others the defects which are more manifest in us, and which we admire with marvellous inadvertency and impudence. It was but yesterday that I heard a man of understanding and of good rank, as pleasantly as justly scoffing at the folly of another, who did nothing but torment everybody with the catalogue of his genealogy and alliances, above half of them false (for they are most apt to fall into such ridiculous discourses, whose qualities are most dubious and least sure), and yet, would he have looked into himself, he would have discerned himself to be no less intemperate and wearisome in extolling his wife's pedigree. O importunate presumption, with which the wife sees herself armed by the hands of her own husband. Did he understand Latin, we should say to him:

Age, si hic non insanit satis sua sponte, instiga.

[Come! if of himself he is not mad enough, urge him on.
—Terence, *And.*, iv. 2, 9.]

I do not say that no man should accuse another, who is not clean himself, – for then no one would ever accuse, – clean from

445

the same sort of spot; but I mean that our judgment, falling upon another who is then in question, should not, at the same time, spare ourselves, but sentence us with an inward and severe authority. It is an office of charity, that he who cannot reclaim himself from a vice, should, nevertheless, endeavour to remove it from another, in whom, peradventure, it may not have so deep and so malignant a root; neither do him who reproves me for my fault that he himself is guilty of the same. What of that? The reproof is, notwithstanding, true and of very good use. Had we a good nose, our own ordure would stink worse to us, forasmuch as it is our own: and Socrates is of opinion that whoever should find himself, his son, and a stranger guilty of any violence and wrong, ought to begin with himself, present himself first to the sentence of justice, and implore, to purge himself, the assistance of the hand of the executioner; in the next place, he should proceed to his son, and lastly, to the stranger. If this precept seem too severe, he ought at least to present himself the first, to the punishment of his own conscience.

The senses are our first and proper judges, which perceive not things but by external accidents; and it is no wonder, if in all the parts of the service of our society, there is so perpetual and universal a mixture of ceremonies and superficial appearances; insomuch that the best and most effectual part of our polities therein consist. It is still man with whom we have to do, of whom the condition is wonderfully corporal. Let those who, of these late years, would erect for us such a contemplative and immaterial an exercise of religion, not wonder if there be some who think it had vanished and melted through their fingers had it not more upheld itself among us as a mark, title, and instrument of division and faction, than by itself. As in conference, the gravity, robe, and fortune of him who speaks, ofttimes gives reputation to vain arguments and idle words, it is not to be presumed but that a man, so attended and feared, has not in him more than ordinary sufficiency; and that he to whom the king has given so many offices and commissions and charges, he so supercilious and proud, has not a great deal more in him, than another who salutes him at so great a distance, and who has no employment at all. Not only the words, but the grimaces also of these people, are considered and put into the account; everyone making it his business to give them some fine and solid interpretation. If they stoop to the common conference, and that you offer anything but approbation and reverence, they then knock you down with the authority of their experience: they have heard, they have seen, they have done so and so: you are crushed with examples. I should willingly tell them, that the fruit of a surgeon's experience, is not the history of his practice and his remembering that he has cured four people of the plague and three of the gout, unless he knows how thence to extract something whereon to form his judgment, and to make us sensible that he has thence become more skillful in his art. As in a concert of instruments, we do not hear a lute, a harpsichord, or a flute alone, but one entire harmony, the result of all together. If travel and offices have improved them, it is a product of their understanding to make it appear. It is not enough to reckon experiences, they must weigh, sort and distil them, to extract the reasons and conclusions they carry along with them. There were never so many historians: it is, indeed, good and of use to read them, for they furnish us everywhere with excellent and laudable instructions from the magazine of their memory, which, doubtless, is of great concern to the help of life; but it is not that we seek for now: we examine whether these relaters and collectors of things are commendable themselves.

I hate all sorts of tyranny, both in word and deed. I am very ready to oppose myself against those vain circumstances that delude our judgments by the senses; and keeping my eye close upon those extraordinary greatnesses, I find that at best they are men, as others are:

Rarus enim ferme sensus communis in illa
Fortuna.

[For in those high fortunes, common sense is generally rare.
—Juvenal, viii. 73.]

447

Peradventure, we esteem and look upon them for less than they are, by reason they undertake more, and more expose themselves; they do not answer to the charge they have undertaken. There must be more vigour and strength in the bearer than in the burden; he who has not lifted as much as he can, leaves you to guess that he has still a strength beyond that, and that he has not been tried to the utmost of what he is able to do; he who sinks under his load, makes a discovery of his best, and the weakness of his shoulders. This is the reason that we see so many silly souls amongst the learned, and more than those of the better sort: they would have made good husbandmen, good merchants, and good artisans: their natural vigour was cut out to that proportion. Knowledge is a thing of great weight, they faint under it: their understanding has neither vigour nor dexterity enough to set forth and distribute, to employ or make use of this rich and powerful matter; it has no prevailing virtue but in a strong nature; and such natures are very rare – and the weak ones, says Socrates, corrupt the dignity of philosophy in the handling, it appears useless and vicious, when lodged in an ill-contrived mind. They spoil and make fools of themselves:

> *Humani qualis simulator simius oris,*
> *Quern puer arridens pretioso stamine serum*
> *Velavit, nudasque nates ac terga reliquit,*
> *Ludibrium mensis.*

[Just like an ape, simulator of the human face, whom a wanton boy has dizened up in rich silks above, but left the lower parts bare, for a laughing-stock for the tables.

—Claudian, *In Eutropium*, i 303.]

Neither is it enough for those who govern and command us, and have all the world in their hands, to have a common understanding, and to be able to do the same that we can; they are very much below us, if they be not infinitely above us: as they promise more, so they are to perform more.

And yet silence is to them, not only a countenance of respect and gravity, but very often of good advantage too: for Megabyzus, going to see Apelles in his painting-room, stood a great while without speaking a word, and at last began to talk of his paintings, for which he received this rude reproof: "Whilst thou wast silent, thou seemedst to be some great thing, by reason of thy chains and rich habit; but now that we have heard thee speak, there is not the meanest boy in my workshop that does not despise thee." Those princely ornaments, that mighty state, did not permit him to be ignorant with a common ignorance, and to speak impertinently of painting; he ought to have kept this external and presumptive knowledge by silence. To how many foolish fellows of my time has a sullen and silent mien procured the credit of prudence and capacity!

Dignities and offices are of necessity conferred more by fortune than upon the account of merit; and we are often to blame, to condemn kings when these are misplaced: on the contrary, it is a wonder they should have so good luck, where there is so little skill:

Principis est virtus maxima nosse suos;

[It is the chief virtue of a prince to know his people.
—Martial, viii. 15.]

for nature has not given them a sight that can extend to so many people, to discern which excels the rest, nor to penetrate into our bosoms, where the knowledge of our wills and best value lies they must choose us by conjecture and by groping; by the family, wealth, learning, and the voice of the people, which are all very feeble arguments. Whoever could find out a way by which they might judge by justice, and choose men by reason, would, in this one thing, establish a perfect form of government.

"Ay, but he brought that great affair to a very good pass." This is, indeed, to say something, but not to say enough: for this sentence is justly received, "That we are not to judge of counsels by events." The Carthaginians punished the ill counsels of their captains, though they were rectified by a successful issue; and the Roman people often denied a triumph for great and very advantageous victories because the conduct of their general was not answerable to his good fortune. We ordinarily see, in the actions of the world, that Fortune, to show us her power in all things, and who takes a pride in abating our presumption, seeing she could not make fools wise, has made them fortunate in emulation of virtue; and most favours those operations the web of which is most purely her own; whence it is that the simplest amongst us bring to pass great business, both public and private; and, as Seiramnes, the Persian, answered those who wondered that his affairs succeeded so ill, considering that his deliberations were so wise, "that he was sole master of his designs, but that success was wholly in the power of fortune"; these may answer the same, but with a contrary turn. Most worldly affairs are performed by themselves

Fata viam inveniunt;

[The destinies find the way.

—*Aeneid*, iii. 395]

the event often justifies a very foolish conduct; our interposition is little more than as it were a running on by rote, and more commonly a consideration of custom and example, than of reason. Being formerly astonished at the greatness of some affair, I have been made acquainted with their motives and address by those who had performed it, and have found nothing in it but very ordinary counsels; and the most common and usual are indeed, perhaps, the most sure and convenient for practice, if not for show. What if the plainest reasons are the best seated? the meanest, lowest, and most beaten more adapted to affairs? To maintain the authority of the

counsels of kings, it needs not that profane persons should participate of them, or see further into them than the outmost barrier; he
who will husband its reputation must be reverenced upon credit and
taken altogether. My consultation somewhat rough-hews the matter,
and considers it lightly by the first face it presents: the stress and
main of the business I have been wont to refer to heaven;

> *Permitte divis caetera.*

> [Leave the rest to the gods.
>
> —Horace, *Odes*, i. 9, 9.]

Good and ill fortune are, in my opinion, two sovereign powers;
it is folly to think that human prudence can play the part of Fortune; and vain is his attempt who presumes to comprehend both
causes and consequences, and by the hand to conduct the progress
of his design; and most especially vain in the deliberations of war.
There was never greater circumspection and military prudence than
sometimes is seen amongst us: can it be that men are afraid to lose
themselves by the way, that they reserve themselves to the end of the
game? I moreover affirm that our wisdom itself and consultation, for
the most part commit themselves to the conduct of chance; my will
and my reason are sometimes moved by one breath, and sometimes
by another; and many of these movements there are that govern
themselves without me: my reason has uncertain and casual agitations and impulsions:

> *Vertuntur species animorum, et pectora motus*
> *Nunc alios, alios, dum nubile ventus agebat,*
> *Concipiunt.*

> [The aspects of their minds change; and they conceive now such
> ideas, now such, just so long as the wind agitated the clouds.
>
> —Virgil, *Georgics*, i. 42.]

Let a man but observe who are of greatest authority in cities, and who best do their own business; we shall find that they are commonly men of the least parts: women, children, and madmen have had the fortune to govern great kingdoms equally well with the wisest princes, and Thucydides says, that the stupid more ordinarily do it than those of better understandings; we attribute the effects of their good fortune to their prudence:

Ut quisque Fortuna utitur,
Ita praecellet; atque exinde sapere illum omnes dicimus;

[He makes his way who knows how to use Fortune, and thereupon all call him wise.

—Plautus, *Pseudolus*, ii. 3, 13.]

wherefore I say unreservedly, events are a very poor testimony of our worth and parts.

Now, I was upon this point, that there needs no more but to see a man promoted to dignity; though we knew him but three days before a man of little regard, yet an image of grandeur of sufficiency insensibly steals into our opinion, and we persuade ourselves that, being augmented in reputation and train, he is also increased in merit; we judge of him, not according to his worth, but as we do by counters, according to the prerogative of his place. If it happen so that he fall again, and be mixed with the common crowd, everyone inquires with amazement into the cause of his having been raised so high. "Is this he," say they, "was he no wiser when he was there? Do princes satisfy themselves with so little? Truly, we were in good hands." This is a thing that I have often seen in my time. Nay, even the very disguise of grandeur represented in our comedies in some sort moves and gulls us. That which I myself adore in kings is the crowd of their adorers; all reverence and submission are due to them, except that of the understanding: my reason is not obliged to bow and bend; my knees are. Melanthius being asked what he thought of the tragedy of Dionysius,

CHAPTER 8

"I could not see it," said he, "it was so clouded with language"; so most of those who judge of the discourses of great men ought to say, "I did not understand his words, they were so clouded with gravity, grandeur, and majesty." Antisthenes one day tried to persuade the Athenians to give order that their asses might be employed in tilling the ground as well as the horses were; to which it was answered that that animal was not destined for such a service: "That's all one," replied he, "you have only to order it: for the most ignorant and incapable men you employ in the commands of your wars incontinently become worthy enough, because you employ them"; to which the custom of so many people, who canonise the king they have chosen out of their own body, and are not content only to honour, but must adore them, comes very near. Those of Mexico, after the ceremonies of their king's coronation are over, dare no more look him in the face; but, as if they had deified him by his royalty. Amongst the oaths they make him take to maintain their religion, their laws, and liberties, to be valiant, just, and mild, he moreover swears to make the sun run his course in his wonted light, to drain the clouds at fit seasons, to make rivers run their course, and to cause the earth to bear all things necessary for his people.

I differ from this common fashion, and am more apt to suspect the capacity when I see it accompanied with that grandeur of fortune and public applause; we are to consider of what advantage it is to speak when a man pleases, to choose his subject, to interrupt or change it, with a magisterial authority; to protect himself from the oppositions of others by a nod, a smile, or silence, in the presence of an assembly that trembles with reverence and respect. A man of a prodigious fortune coming to give his judgment upon some slight dispute that was foolishly set on foot at his table, began in these words: "It can be no other but a liar or a fool that will say otherwise than so and so." Pursue this philosophical point with a dagger in your hand.

There is another observation I have made, from which I draw great advantage; which is, that in conferences and disputes, every

453

word that seems to be good, is not immediately to be accepted. Most men are rich in borrowed sufficiency: a man may say a good thing, give a good answer, cite a good sentence, without at all seeing the force of either the one or the other. That a man may not understand all he borrows, may perhaps be verified in myself. A man must not always presently yield, what truth or beauty soever may seem to be in the opposite argument; either he must stoutly meet it, or retire, under colour of not understanding it, to try, on all parts, how it is lodged in the author. It may happen that we entangle ourselves, and help to strengthen the point itself. I have sometimes, in the necessity and heat of the combat, made answers that have gone through and through, beyond my expectation or hope; I only gave them in number, they were received in weight. As, when I contend with a vigorous man, I please myself with anticipating his conclusions, I ease him of the trouble of explaining himself, I strive to forestall his imagination whilst it is yet springing and imperfect; the order and pertinency of his understanding warn and threaten me afar off: I deal quite contrary with the others; I must understand, and presuppose nothing but by them. If they determine in general words, "this is good, that is naught," and that they happen to be in the right, see if it be not fortune that hits it off for them: let them a little circumscribe and limit their judgment; why, or how, it is so. These universal judgments that I see so common, signify nothing; these are men who salute a whole people in a crowd together; they, who have a real acquaintance, take notice of and salute them individually and by name. But it is a hazardous attempt; and from which I have, more than every day, seen it fall out, that weak understandings, having a mind to appear ingenious, in taking notice, as they read a book, of what is best and most to be admired, fix their admiration upon some thing so very ill chosen, that instead of making us discern the excellence of the author; they make us very well see their own ignorance. This exclamation is safe, "That is fine," after having heard a whole page of Virgil; by that the cunning sort save themselves; but to undertake to follow him line by line, and, with an expert and tried judgment,

Chapter 8

to observe where a good author excels himself, weighing the words, phrases, inventions, and his various excellences, one after another; keep aloof from that:

Videndum est, non modo quid quisque loquatur, sed etiam quid quisque sentiat, atque etiam qua de causa quisque sentiat.

[A man is not only to examine what everyone says, but also what everyone thinks, and from what reason everyone thinks.
—Cicero, *De Officiis*, i. 41.]

I every day hear fools say things that are not foolish: they say a good thing; let us examine how far they understand it, whence they have it, and what they mean by it. We help them to make use of this fine expression, of this fine sentence, which is none of theirs; they only have it in keeping; they have bolted it out at a venture; we place it for them in credit and esteem. You lend them your hand. To what purpose? they do not think themselves obliged to you for it, and become more inept still. Don't help them; let them alone; they will handle the matter like people who are afraid of burning their fingers; they dare change neither its seat nor light, nor break into it; shake it never so little, it slips through their fingers; they give it up, be it never so strong or fair they are fine weapons, but ill hafted: How many times have I seen the experience of this? Now, if you come to explain anything to them, and to confirm them, they catch at it, and presently rob you of the advantage of your interpretation; "It was what I was about to say; it was just my idea; if I did not express it so, it was for want of language." Mere wind! Malice itself must be employed to correct this arrogant ignorance. The dogma of Hegesias, "that we are neither to hate nor accuse, but instruct," is correct elsewhere; but here it is injustice and inhumanity to relieve and set him right who stands in no need on it, and is the worse for't. I love to let them step deeper into the mire; and so deep, that, if it be possible, they may at last discern their error.

455

Folly and absurdity are not to be cured by bare admonition; and what Cyrus answered to him, who importuned him to harangue his army, upon the point of battle, "that men do not become valiant and warlike upon a sudden, by a fine oration, no more than a man becomes a good musician by hearing a fine song," may properly be said of such an admonition as this. These are apprenticeships that are to be served beforehand, by a long and continued education. We owe this care and this assiduity of correction and instruction to our own people; but to go preach to the first passer-by, and to become tutor to the ignorance and folly of the first we meet, is a thing that I abhor. I rarely do it, even in private conversation, and rather give up the whole thing than proceed to these initiatory and school instructions; my humour is unfit either to speak or write for beginners; but for things that are said in common discourse, or amongst other things, I never oppose them either by word or sign, how false or absurd soever.

As to the rest, nothing vexes me so much in folly as that it is more satisfied with itself than any reason can reasonably be. It is unfortunate that prudence forbids us to satisfy and trust ourselves, and always dismisses us timorous and discontented; whereas obstinacy and temerity fill those who are possessed with them with joy and assurance. It is for the most ignorant to look at other men over the shoulder, always returning from the combat full of joy and triumph. And moreover, for the most part, this arrogance of speech and gaiety of countenance gives them the better of it in the opinion of the audience, which is commonly weak and incapable of well judging and discerning the real advantage. Obstinacy of opinion and heat in argument are the surest proofs of folly; is there anything so assured, resolute, disdainful, contemplative, serious and grave as the ass?

May we not include under the title of conference and communication the quick and sharp repartees which mirth and familiarity introduce amongst friends, pleasantly and wittily jesting and rallying with one another? It is an exercise for which my natural gaiety renders me fit enough, and which, if it be not so tense and serious as

Chapter 8

he other I spoke of but now, is, as Lycurgus thought, no less smart
and ingenious, nor of less utility. For my part, I contribute to it more
liberty than wit, and have therein more of luck than invention; but
I am perfect in suffering, for I endure a retaliation that is not only
tart, but indiscreet to boot, without being moved at all; and whoever
attacks me, if I have not a brisk answer immediately ready, I do not
study to pursue the point with a tedious and impertinent contest,
bordering upon obstinacy, but let it pass, and hanging down cheerfully my ears, defer my revenge to another and better time: there is
no merchant that always gains: Most men change their countenance
and their voice where their wits fail, and by an unseasonable anger,
instead of revenging themselves, accuse at once their own folly and
impatience. In this jollity, we sometimes pinch the secret strings of
our imperfections which, at another and graver time, we cannot
touch without offence, and so profitably give one another a hint of
our defects. There are other jeux de main, [practical jokes] rude
and indiscreet, after the French manner, that I mortally hate; my
skin is very tender and sensible: I have in my time seen two princes
of the blood buried upon that very account. It is unhandsome to
fight in play. As to the rest, when I have a mind to judge of any one,
I ask him how far he is contented with himself; to what degree his
speaking or his work pleases him. I will none of these fine excuses,
"I did it only in sport,

Ablatum mediis opus est incudibus istud.

[That work was taken from the anvil half finished.
—Ovid, *Tristia*, i. 6, 29.]

I was not an hour about it: I have never looked at it since." Well,
then, say I, lay these aside, and give me a perfect one, such as you
would be measured by. And then, what do you think is the best thing
in your work? is it this part or that? is it grace or the matter, the
invention, the judgment, or the learning? For I find that men are,

457

commonly, as wide of the mark in judging of their own works, as of those of others; not only by reason of the kindness they have for them, but for want of capacity to know and distinguish them: the work, by its own force and fortune, may second the workman, and sometimes outstrip him, beyond his invention and knowledge. For my part, I judge of the value of other men's works more obscurely than of my own; and place the Essays, now high, or low, with great doubt and inconstancy. There are several books that are useful upon the account of their subjects, from which the author derives no praise; and good books, as well as good works, that shame the workman. I may write the manner of our feasts, and the fashion of our clothes, and may write them ill; I may publish the edicts of my time, and the letters of princes that pass from hand to hand; I may make an abridgment of a good book (and every abridgment of a good book is a foolish abridgment), which book shall come to be lost; and so on: posterity will derive a singular utility from such compositions: but what honour shall I have unless by great good fortune? Most part of the famous books are of this condition.

When I read Philip de Commines, doubtless a very good author, several years ago, I there took notice of this for no vulgar saying, "That a man must have a care not to do his master so great service, that at last he will not know how to give him his just reward"; but I ought to commend the invention, not him, because I met with it in Tacitus, not long since:

> *Beneficia ea usque lxta sunt, dum videntur exsolvi posse;*
> *ubi multum antevenere, pro gratis odium redditur;*

[Benefits are so far acceptable as they appear to be capable of recompense; where they much exceed that point, hatred is returned instead of thanks.

—Tacitus, *Annals*, iv. 18.]

and Seneca vigorously says:

> *Nam qui putat esse turpe non reddere,*
> *non vult esse cui reddat:*

[For he who thinks it a shame not to requite, does not wish to have the man live to whom he owes return.

—Seneca, *Epistles*, 81.]

Q. Cicero says with less directness.:

> *Qui se non putat satisfacere,*
> *amicus essenullo modo potest.*

[Who thinks himself behind in obligation, can by no means be a friend.

—Q. Cicero, *De Petitione Consulatus*, c. 9.]

The subject, according to what it is, may make a man looked upon as learned and of good memory; but to judge in him the parts that are most his own and the most worthy, the vigour and beauty of his soul, one must first know what is his own and what is not; and in that which is not his own, how much we are obliged to him for the choice, disposition, ornament, and language he has there presented us with. What if he has borrowed the matter and spoiled the form, as it often falls out? We, who are little read in books, are in this strait, that when we meet with a high fancy in some new poet, or some strong argument in a preacher, we dare not, nevertheless, commend it till we have first informed ourselves, through some learned man, if it be the writer's wit or borrowed from some other; until that I always stand upon my guard.

I have lately been reading the history of Tacitus quite through, without interrupting it with anything else (which but seldom happens with me, it being twenty years since I have kept to any one book an hour together), and I did it at the instance of a gentleman for whom France has a great esteem, as well for his own particular worth, as upon the account of a constant form of capacity and virtue which runs through a great many brothers of them. I do not know any author in a public narrative who mixes so much consideration of manners and particular inclinations: and I am of a quite contrary opinion to him, holding that, having especially to follow the lives of the emperors of his time, so various and extreme in all sorts of forms, so many notable actions as their cruelty especially produced in their subjects, he had a stronger and more attractive matter to treat of than if he had had to describe battles and universal commotions; so that I often find him sterile, running over those brave deaths as if he feared to trouble us with their multitude and length. This form of history is by much the most useful; public movements depend most upon the conduct of fortune, private ones upon our own. It is rather a judgment than a narration of history; there are in it more precepts than stories: it is not a book to read, it is a book to study and learn; it is full of sententious opinions, right or wrong; it is a nursery of ethic and politic discourses, for the use and ornament of those who have any place in the government of the world. He always argues by strong and solid reasons, after a pointed and subtle manner, according to the affected style of that age, which was so in love with an inflated manner, that where point and subtlety were wanting in things it supplied these with lofty and swelling words. It is not much unlike the style of Seneca: I look upon Tacitus as more sinewy, and Seneca as more sharp. His pen seems most proper for a troubled and sick state, as ours at present is; you would often say that he paints and pinches us.

They who doubt his good faith sufficiently accuse themselves of being his enemy upon some other account. His opinions are sound, and lean to the right side in the Roman affairs. And yet I am angry at him for judging more severely of Pompey than consists with the opinion of those worthy men who lived in the same time, and had dealings with him; and to have reputed him on a par with Marius and Sylla, excepting that he was more close. Other writers have not acquitted his intention in the government of affairs from ambition and revenge; and even his friends were afraid that victory would have transported him beyond the bounds of reason, but not to so immeasurable a degree as theirs; nothing in his life threatened such express cruelty and tyranny. Neither ought we to set suspicion against evidence; and therefore I do not believe Plutarch in this matter. That his narrations were genuine and straightforward may, perhaps, be argued from this very thing, that they do not always apply to the conclusions of his judgments, which he follows according to the bias he has taken, very often beyond the matter he presents us withal, which he has not deigned to alter in the least degree. He needs no excuse for having approved the religion of his time, according as the laws enjoined, and to have been ignorant of the true; this was his misfortune, not his fault.

I have principally considered his judgment, and am not very well satisfied therewith throughout; as these words in the letter that Tiberius, old and sick, sent to the senate. "What shall I write to you, sirs, or how should I write to you, or what should I not write to you at this time? May the gods and goddesses lay a worse punishment upon me than I am every day tormented with, if I know!" I do not see why he should so positively apply them to a sharp remorse that tormented the conscience of Tiberius; at least, when I was in the same condition, I perceived no such thing.

And this also seemed to me a little mean in him that, having to say that he had borne an honourable office in Rome, he excuses himself that he does not say it out of ostentation; this seems, I say, mean for such a soul as his; for not to speak roundly of a man's self implies some want of courage; a man of solid and lofty judgment, who judges soundly and surely, makes use of his own example upon all occasions, as well as those of others; and gives evidence as freely of himself as of a third person. We are to pass by these common rules of civility, in favour of truth and liberty. I dare not only speak of myself, but to speak only of myself: when I write of anything else, I miss my way and wander from my subject. I am not so indiscreetly enamoured of myself, so wholly mixed up with, and bound to myself, that I cannot distinguish and consider myself apart, as I do a neighbour or a tree: it is equally a fault not to discern how far a man's worth extends, and to say more than a man discovers in himself. We owe more love to God than to ourselves, and know Him less; and yet speak of Him as much as we will.

If the writings of Tacitus indicate anything true of his qualities, he was a great personage, upright and bold, not of a superstitious but of a philosophical and generous virtue. One may think him bold in his relations; as where he tells us, that a soldier carrying a burden of wood, his hands were so frozen and so stuck to the load that they there remained closed and dead, being severed from his arms. I always in such things bow to the authority of so great witnesses.

What also he says, that Vespasian, "by the favour of the god Serapis, cured a blind woman at Alexandria by anointing her eyes with his spittle, and I know not what other miracle," he says by the example and duty of all his good historians. They record all events of importance; and amongst public incidents are the popular rumours and opinions. It is their part to relate common beliefs, not to regulate them: that part concerns divines and philosophers, directors of consciences; and therefore it was that this companion of his, and a great man like himself, very wisely said:

Equidem plura transcribo, quam credo: nam nec affirmare
sustineo, de quibus dubito, nec subducere quae accepi;

[Truly, I set down more things than I believe, for I can neither affirm things whereof I doubt, nor suppress what I have heard.

—Quintus Curtius, ix.]

CHAPTER 8

and this other:

Haec neque affirmare neque refellere operae
pretium est; famae rerum standum est.

[It is neither worth the while to affirm or to refute these things;
we must stand to report

—Livy, i., Preface, and viii. 6.]

And writing in an age wherein the belief of prodigies began to
decline, he says he would not, nevertheless, forbear to insert in his
Annals, and to give a relation of things received by so many worthy
men, and with so great reverence of antiquity; it is very well said.
Let them deliver to us history, more as they receive it than as they
believe it. I, who am monarch of the matter whereof I treat, and who
am accountable to none, do not, nevertheless, always believe myself;
I often hazard sallies of my own wit, wherein I very much suspect
myself, and certain verbal quibbles, at which I shake my ears; but
I let them go at a venture. I see that others get reputation by such
things: it is not for me alone to judge. I present myself standing and
lying, before and behind, my right side and my left, and, in all my
natural postures. Wits, though equal in force, are not always equal
in taste and application.

This is what my memory presents to me in gross, and with uncertainty enough; all judgments in gross are weak and imperfect.

ON VANITY

There is, peradventure, no more manifest vanity than to write of it so vainly. That which divinity has so divinely expressed to us ["Vanity of vanities: all is vanity." Ecclesiastes, i. 2.] ought to be carefully and continually meditated by men of understanding. Who does not see that I have taken a road, in which, incessantly and without labour, I shall proceed so long as there shall be ink and paper in the world? I can give no account of my life by my actions; fortune has placed them too low: I must do it by my fancies. And yet I have seen a gentleman who only communicated his life by the workings of his belly: you might see on his premises a show of a row of basins of seven or eight days' standing; it was his study, his discourse; all other talk stank in his nostrils. Here, but not so nauseous, are the excrements of an old mind, sometimes thick, sometimes thin, and always indigested. And when shall I have done representing the continual agitation and mutation of my thoughts, as they come into my head, seeing that Diomedes wrote six thousand books upon the sole subject of grammar?

What, then, ought prating to produce, since prattling and the first beginning to speak, stuffed the world with such a horrible load of volumes? So many words for words only. O Pythagoras, why didst not thou allay this tempest? They accused one Galba of old for living idly; he made answer, "That everyone ought to give account of his actions, but not of his home." He was mistaken, for justice also takes cognisance of those who glean after the reaper.

But there should be some restraint of law against foolish and impertinent scribblers, as well as against vagabonds and idle persons; which if there were, both I and a hundred others would be banished from the reach of our people. I do not speak this in jest: scribbling seems to be a symptom of a disordered and licentious age. When did we write so much as since our troubles? when the Romans so much, as upon the point of ruin? Besides that, the refining of wits does not make people wiser in a government: this idle employment springs from this, that everyone applies himself negligently to the duty of his vocation, and is easily debauched from it. The corruption of the age is made up by the particular contribution of every individual man; some contribute treachery, others injustice, irreligion, tyranny, avarice, cruelty, according to their power; the weaker sort contribute folly, vanity, and idleness; of these I am one. It seems as if it were the season for vain things, when the hurtful oppress us; in a time when doing ill is common, to do but what signifies nothing is a kind of commendation. It is my comfort, that I shall be one of the last who shall be called in question; and whilst the greater offenders are being brought to account, I shall have leisure to amend: for it would, methinks, be against reason to punish little inconveniences, whilst we are infested with the greater. As the physician Philotimus said to one who presented him his finger to dress, and who he perceived, both by his complexion and his breath, had an ulcer in his lungs: "Friend, it is not now time to play with your nails." [Plutarch, How we may distinguish a Flatterer from a Friend.]

And yet I saw, some years ago, a person, whose name and memory I have in very great esteem, in the very height of our great disorders, when there was neither law nor justice, nor magistrate who performed his office, no more than there is now, publish I know not what pitiful reformations about cloths, cookery, and law chicanery. Those are amusements wherewith to feed a people that are ill-used, to show that they are not totally forgotten. Those others do the same, who insist upon prohibiting particular ways of speaking, dances, and games, to a people totally abandoned to all sorts of execrable vices. It is no time to bathe and cleanse one's self, when one is seized by a violent fever; it was for the Spartans alone to fall to combing and curling themselves, when they were just upon the point of running headlong into some extreme danger of their life.

For my part, I have that worse custom, that if my slipper go awry, I let my shirt and my cloak do so too; I scorn to mend myself by halves.

When I am in a bad plight, I fasten upon the mischief; I abandon myself through despair; I let myself go towards the precipice, and, as they say, "throw the helve after the hatchet"; I am obstinate in growing worse, and think myself no longer worth my own care; I am either well or ill throughout. It is a favour to me, that the desolation of this kingdom falls out in the desolation of my age: I better suffer that my ill be multiplied, than if my well had been disturbed. [That, being ill, I should grow worse, than that, being well, I should grow ill.] The words I utter in mishap are words of anger: my courage sets up its bristles, instead of letting them down; and, contrary to others, I am more devout in good than in evil fortune, according to the precept of Xenophon, if not according to his reason; and am more ready to turn up my eyes to heaven to return thanks, than to crave. I am more solicitous to improve my health, when I am well, than to restore it when I am sick; prosperities are the same discipline and instruction to me that adversities and rods are to others. As if good fortune were a thing inconsistent with good conscience, men never grow good but in evil fortune. Good fortune is to me a singular spur to modesty and moderation: an entreaty wins, a threat checks me; favour makes me bend, fear stiffens me.

Amongst human conditions this is common enough: to be better pleased with foreign things than with our own, and to love innovation and change:

> *Ipsa dies ideo nos grato perluit haustu,*
> *Quod permutatis hora recurrit equis:*

[The light of day itself shines more pleasantly upon us because it changes its horses every hour.]

I have my share. Those who follow the other extreme, of being quite satisfied and pleased with and in themselves, of valuing what they have above all the rest, and of concluding no beauty can be greater than what they see, if they are not wiser than we, are really more happy; I do not envy their wisdom, but their good fortune.

This greedy humour of new and unknown things helps to nourish in me the desire of travel; but a great many more circumstances contribute to it; I am very willing to quit the government of my house. There is, I confess, a kind of convenience in commanding, though it were but in a barn, and in being obeyed by one's people; but it is too uniform and languid a pleasure, and is, moreover, of necessity mixed with a thousand vexatious thoughts: one while the poverty and the oppression of your tenants: another, quarrels amongst neighbours: another, the trespasses they make upon you afflict you;

> *Aut verberatae grandine vineae,*
> *Fundusque mendax, arbore nunc aquas*
> *Culpante, nunc torrentia agros*
> *Sidera, nunc hyemes iniquas.*

[Or hail-smitten vines and the deceptive farm; now trees damaged by the rains, or years of dearth, now summer's heat burning up the petals, now destructive winters.

—Horatius, *Odes*, iii. I, 29.]

and that God scarce in six months sends a season wherein your bailiff can do his business as he should; but that if it serves the vines, it spoils the meadows:

> *Aut nimiis torret fervoribus aetherius sol,*
> *Aut subiti perimunt imbres, gelidoeque pruinae,*
> *Flabraque ventorum violento turbine vexant;*

468

CHAPTER 9

[Either the scorching sun burns up your fields, or sudden rains or frosts destroy your harvests, or a violent wind carries away all before it.

—Lucretius, V. 216.]

to which may be added the new and neat-made shoe of the man of old, that hurts your foot, and that a stranger does not understand how much it costs you, and what you contribute to maintain that show of order that is seen in your family, and that peradventure you buy too dear.

I came late to the government of a house: they whom nature sent into the world before me long eased me of that trouble; so that I had already taken another bent more suitable to my humour. Yet, for so much as I have seen, it is an employment more troublesome than hard; whoever is capable of anything else, will easily do this. Had I a mind to be rich, that way would seem too long; I had served my kings, a more profitable traffic than any other. Since I pretend to nothing but the reputation of having got nothing or dissipated nothing, conformably to the rest of my life, improper either to do good or ill of any moment, and that I only desire to pass on, I can do it, thanks be to God, without any great endeavour. At the worst, evermore prevent poverty by lessening your expense; it is that which I make my great concern, and doubt not but to do it before I shall be compelled. As to the rest, I have sufficiently settled my thoughts to live upon less than I have, and live contentedly:

Non aestimatione census, verum victu atque cultu,
terminantur pecuniæ modus.

[It is not by the value of possessions, but by our daily subsistence and tillage, that our riches are truly estimated.

—Cicero, *Paradox,* vi. 3.]

My real need does not so wholly take up all I have, that Fortune has not whereon to fasten her teeth without biting to the quick. My presence, heedless and ignorant as it is, does me great service in my domestic affairs; I employ myself in them, but it goes against the hair, finding that I have this in my house, that though I burn my candle at one end by myself, the other is not spared.

Journeys do me no harm but only by their expense, which is great, and more than I am well able to bear, being always wont to travel with not only a necessary, but a handsome equipage; I must make them so much shorter and fewer; I spend therein but the froth, and what I have reserved for such uses, delaying and deferring my motion till that be ready. I will not that the pleasure of going abroad spoil the pleasure of being retired at home; on the contrary, I intend they shall nourish and favour one another. Fortune has assisted me in this, that since my principal profession in this life was to live at ease, and rather idly than busily, she has deprived me of the necessity of growing rich to provide for the multitude of my heirs. If there be not enough for one, of that whereof I had so plentifully enough, at his peril be it: his imprudence will not deserve that I should wish him any more. And everyone, according to the example of Phocion, provides sufficiently for his children who so provides for them as to leave them as much as was left him. I should by no means like Crates' way. He left his money in the hands of a banker with this condition – that if his children were fools, he should then give it to them; if wise, he should then distribute it to the most foolish of the people; as if fools, for being less capable of living without riches, were more capable of using them.

At all events, the damage occasioned by my absence seems not to deserve, so long as I am able to support it, that I should waive the occasions of diverting myself by that troublesome assistance.

There is always something that goes amiss. The affairs, one while of one house, and then of another, tear you to pieces; you

CHAPTER 9

pry into everything too near; your perspicacity hurts you here, as well as in other things. I steal away from occasions of vexing myself, and turn from the knowledge of things that go amiss; and yet I cannot so order it, but that every hour I jostle against something or other that displeases me; and the tricks that they most conceal from me, are those that I the soonest come to know; some there are that, not to make matters worse, a man must himself help to conceal. Vain vexations; vain sometimes, but always vexations. The smallest and slightest impediments are the most piercing: and as little letters most tire the eyes, so do little affairs most disturb us. The rout of little ills more offend than one, how great soever. By how much domestic thorns are numerous and slight, by so much they prick deeper and without warning, easily surprising us when least we suspect them. (Now Homer shows us clearly enough how surprise gives the advantage; who represents Ulysses weeping at the death of his dog; and not weeping at the tears of his mother; the first accident, trivial as it was, got the better of him, coming upon him quite unexpectedly;he sustained the second, though more potent, because he was prepared for it. It is light occasions that humble our lives.)

I am no philosopher; evils oppress me according to their weight, and they weigh as much according to the form as the matter, and very often more. If I have therein more perspicacity than the vulgar, I have also more patience; in short, they weigh with me, if they do not hurt me. Life is a tender thing, and easily molested. Since my age has made me grow more pensive and morose,

Nemo enim resistit sibi, cum caeperit impelli,

[For no man resists himself when he has begun to be driven forward.

—Seneca, *Epistles*, 13.]

471

for the most trivial cause imaginable, I irritate that humour, which afterwards nourishes and exasperates itself of its own motion; attracting and heaping up matter upon matter whereon to feed:

Stillicidi casus lapidem cavat:

[The ever falling drop hollows out a stone.

—Lucretius, i. 314.]

these continual tricklings consume and ulcerate me. Ordinary inconveniences are never light; they are continual and inseparable, especially when they spring from the members of a family, continual and inseparable. When I consider my affairs at distance and in gross, I find, because perhaps my memory is none of the best, that they have gone on hitherto improving beyond my reason or expectation; my revenue seems greater than it is; its prosperity betrays me: but when I pry more narrowly into the business, and see how all things go:

Tum vero in curas animum diducimus omnes;

[Indeed we lead the mind into all sorts of cares.

—*Aeneid*, v. 720.]

I have a thousand things to desire and to fear. To give them quite over, is very easy for me to do: but to look after them without trouble, is very hard. It is a miserable thing to be in a place where everything you see employs and concerns you; and I fancy that I more cheerfully enjoy the pleasures of another man's house, and with greater and a purer relish, than those of my own. Diogenes answered according to my humour him who asked him what sort of wine he liked the best: "That of another," said he. [Diogenes Laertius, vi. 54.]

My father took a delight in building at Montaigne, where he was born; and in all the government of domestic affairs I love to follow his example and rules, and I shall engage those who are to succeed me, as much as in me lies, to do the same. Could I do better for him, I would; and am proud that his will is still performing and acting by me. God forbid that in my hands I should ever suffer any image of life, that I am able to render to so good a father, to fail. And wherever I have taken in hand to strengthen some old foundations of walls, and to repair some ruinous buildings, in earnest I have done it more out of respect to his design, than my own satisfaction; and am angry at myself that I have not proceeded further to finish the beginnings he left in his house, and so much the more because I am very likely to be the last possessor of my race, and to give the last hand to it. For, as to my own particular application, neither the pleasure of building, which they say is so bewitching, nor hunting, nor gardens, nor the other pleasures of a retired life, can much amuse me. And it is what I am angry at myself for, as I am for all other opinions that are incommodious to me; which I would not so much care to have vigorous and learned, as I would have them easy and convenient for life, they are true and sound enough, if they are useful and pleasing. Such as hear me declare my ignorance in husbandry, whisper in my ear that it is disdain, and that I neglect to know its instruments, its seasons, its order, how they dress my vines, how they graft, and to know the names and forms of herbs and fruits, and the preparing the meat on which I live, the names and prices of the stuffs I wear, because, say they; I have set my heart upon some higher knowledge; they kill me in saying so. It is not disdain; it is folly, and rather stupidity than glory; I had rather be a good horseman than a good logician:

> *Quin to aliquid saltem potius, quorum indiget usus,*
> *Viminibus mollique paras detexere junco.*

[Do you not rather do something which is required, and make osier and reed basket.

—Virgil, *Eclogues*, ii. 71.]

We occupy our thoughts about the general, and about universal causes and conducts, which will very well carry on themselves without our care; and leave our own business at random, and Michael much more our concern than man. Now I am, indeed, for the most part at home; but I would be there better pleased than anywhere else:

> *Sit meae sedes utinam senectae,*
> *Sit modus lasso maris, et viarum,*
> *Militiaeque.*

[Let my old age have a fixed seat; let there be a limit to fatigues from the sea, journeys, warfare.

—Horace, *Odes*, ii. 6, 6.]

I know not whether or not I shall bring it about. I could wish that, instead of some other member of his succession, my father had resigned to me the passionate affection he had in his old age to his household affairs; he was happy in that he could accommodate his desires to his fortune, and satisfy himself with what he had; political philosophy may to much purpose condemn the meanness and sterility of my employment, if I can once come to relish it, as he did. I am of opinion that the most honourable calling is to serve the public, and to be useful to many,

> *Fructus enim ingenii et virtutis, omnisque praestantiae,*
> *tum maximus capitur, quum in proximum quemque confertur:*

[For the greatest enjoyment of evil and virtue, and of all excellence, is experienced when they are conferred on someone nearest.

—Cicero, *De Amicitia,* c.]

for myself, I disclaim it; partly out of conscience (for where I see the weight that lies upon such employments, I perceive also the little means I have to supply it; and Plato, a master in all political government himself, nevertheless took care to abstain from it), and partly out of cowardice. I content myself with enjoying the world without bustle; only-to live an excusable life, and such as may neither be a burden to myself nor to any other.

Never did any man more fully and feebly suffer himself to be governed by a third person than I should do, had I any one to whom to entrust myself. One of my wishes at this time should be, to have a son-in-law that knew handsomely how to cherish my old age, and to rock it asleep; into whose hands I might deposit, in full sovereignty, the management and use of all my goods, that he might dispose of them as I do, and get by them what I get, provided that he on his part were truly acknowledging, and a friend. But we live in a world where loyalty of one's own children is unknown.

He who has the charge of my purse in his travels, has it purely and without control; he could cheat me thoroughly, if he came to reckoning; and, if he is not a devil, I oblige him to deal faithfully with me by so entire a trust:

> *Multi fallere do cuerunt, dum timent falli;*
> *et aliis jus peccandi suspicando fecerunt.*

[Many have taught others to deceive, while they fear to be deceived, and, by suspecting them, have given them a title to do ill.

—Seneca, *Epistles*, 3.]

The most common security I take of my people is ignorance; I never presume any to be vicious till I have first found them so; and repose the most confidence in the younger sort, that I think are least spoiled by ill example. I had rather be told at two months' end that I have spent four hundred crowns, than to have my ears battered every night with three, five, seven: and I have been, in this way, as little robbed as another. It is true, I am willing enough not to see it; I, in some sort, purposely, harbour a kind of perplexed, uncertain knowledge of my money: up to a certain point, I am content to doubt. One must leave a little room for the infidelity or indiscretion of a servant; if you have left enough, in gross, to do your business, let the overplus of Fortune's liberality run a little more freely at her mercy; it is the gleaner's portion. After all, I do not so much value the fidelity of my people as I condemn their injury. What a mean and ridiculous thing it is for a man to study his money, to delight in handling and telling it over and over again! It is by this avarice makes its approaches.

In eighteen years that I have had my estate in my, own hands, I could never prevail with myself either to read over my deeds or examine my principal affairs, which ought, of necessity, to pass under my knowledge and inspection. It is not a philosophical disdain of worldly and transitory things; my taste is not purified to that degree, and I value them at as great a rate, at least, as they are worth; but it is, in truth, an inexcusable and childish laziness and negligence. What would I not rather do than read a contract? or than, as a slave to my own business, tumble over those dusty writings? or, which is worse, those of another man, as so many do nowadays, to get money? I grudge nothing but care and trouble, and endeavour nothing so much, as to be careless and at ease. I had been much fitter, I believe, could it have been without obligation and servitude, to have lived upon another man's fortune than my own: and, indeed, I do not know, when I examine it nearer, whether, according to my humour, what I have to suffer from my affairs and servants, has not in it something more abject, troublesome, and tormenting than there would be in serving a man better born than myself, who would govern me with a gentle rein, and a little at my own case:

> *Servitus obediential est fracti animi et abjecti,*
> *arbitrio carentis suo.*

[Servitude is the obedience of a subdued and abject mind, wanting its own free will.

—Cicero, *Paradox*, V. I.]

CHAPTER 9

Crates did worse, who threw himself into the liberty of poverty, only to rid himself of the inconveniences and cares of his house. This is what I would not do; I hate poverty equally with pain; but I could be content to change the kind of life I live for another that was humbler and less chargeable.

When absent from home, I divest myself of all these thoughts, and should be less concerned for the ruin of a tower, than I am, when present, at the fall of a tile. My mind is easily composed at distance, but suffers as much as that of the meanest peasant when I am at home; the reins of my bridle being wrongly put on, or a strap flapping against my leg, will keep me out of humour a day together. I raise my courage, well enough against inconveniences: lift up my eyes I can. *Sensus, o superi, sensus.* [The senses, O ye gods, the senses.]

I am at home responsible for whatever goes amiss. Few masters (I speak of those of medium condition such as mine), and if there be any such, they are more happy, can rely so much upon another, but that the greatest part of the burden will lie upon their own shoulders. This takes much from my grace in entertaining visitors, so that I have, peradventure, detained some rather out of expectation of a good dinner, than by my own behaviour; and lose much of the pleasure I ought to reap at my own house from the visitation and assembling of my friends. The most ridiculous carriage of a gentleman in his own house, is to see him bustling about the business of the place, whispering one servant, and looking an angry look at another: it ought insensibly to slide along, and to represent an ordinary current; and I think it unhandsome to talk much to our guests of their entertainment, whether by way of bragging or excuse. I love order and cleanliness –

> *Et cantharus et lanx*
> *Ostendunt mihi me –*

[The dishes and the glasses show me my own reflection.
—Horace, *Epistles*, i. 5, 23]

more than abundance; and at home have an exact regard to necessity, little to outward show. If a footman falls to cuffs at another man's house, or stumble and throw a dish before him as he is carrying it up, you only laugh and make a jest on it; you sleep whilst the master of the house is arranging a bill of fare with his steward for your morrow's entertainment. I speak according as I do myself; quite appreciating, nevertheless, good husbandry in general, and how pleasant quiet and prosperous household management, carried regularly on, is to some natures; and not wishing to fasten my own errors and inconveniences to the thing; nor to give Plato the lie, who looks upon it as the most pleasant employment to everyone to do his particular affairs without wrong to another.

When I travel I have nothing to care for but myself, and the laying out my money; which is disposed of by one single precept; too many things are required to the raking it together; in that I understand nothing; in spending, I understand a little, and how to give some show to my expense, which is indeed its principal use; but I rely too ambitiously upon it, which renders it unequal and difform, and, moreover, immoderate in both the one and the other aspect; if it makes a show, if it serve the turn, I indiscreetly let it run; and as indiscreetly tie up my purse-strings, if it does not shine, and does not please me. Whatever it be, whether art or nature, that imprints in us the condition of living by reference to others, it does us much more harm than good; we deprive ourselves of our own utilities, to accommodate appearances to the common opinion: we care not so much what our being is, as to us and in reality, as what it is to the public observation. Even the properties of the mind, and wisdom itself, seem fruitless to us, if only enjoyed by ourselves, and if it produce not itself to the view and approbation of others. There is a sort of men whose gold runs in streams underground imperceptibly; others expose it all in plates and branches; so that to the one a liard is worth a crown, and to the others the inverse: the world esteeming its use and value, according to the show. All over-nice solicitude about riches smells of avarice: even the very disposing of it, with a too systematic and artificial liberality, is not worth a painful super-intendence and solicitude: he, that will order his expense to just so much, makes it too pinched and narrow. The keeping or spending are, of themselves, indifferent things, and receive no colour of good or ill, but according to the application of the will.

The other cause that tempts me out to these journeys is, inaptitude for the present manners in our state. I could easily console myself for this corruption in regard to the public interest:

> *Pejoraque saecula ferri*
> *Temporibus, quorum sceleri non invenit ipsa*
> *Nomen, et a nullo posuit natura metallo;*

[And, worse than the iron ages, for whose crimes there is no similitude in any of Nature's metals.

—Juvenal, xiii. 28.]

but not to my own. I am, in particular, too much oppressed by them: for, in my neighbourhood, we are, of late, by the long licence of our civil wars, grown old in so riotous a form of state,

> *Quippe ubi fas versum atque nefas,*

[Where wrong and right have changed places.

—Virgil, *Georgics*, i. 504.]

that in earnest, it is a wonder how it can subsist:

> *Armati terram exercent, semperque recentes*
> *Convectare juvat praedas; et vivere rapto.*

[Men plough, girt with arms; ever delighting in fresh robberies, and living by rapine.

—*Aeneid*, vii. 748.]

In fine, I see by our example, that the society of men is maintained and held together, at what price soever; in what condition soever they are placed, they still close and stick together, both moving and in heaps; as ill united bodies, that, shuffled together without order, find of themselves a means to unite and settle, often better than they could have been disposed by art. King Philip mustered up a rabble of the most wicked and incorrigible rascals he could pick out, and put them all together into a city he had caused to be built for that purpose, which bore their name: I believe that they, even from vices themselves, erected a government amongst them, and a commodious and just society. I see, not one action, or three, or a hundred, but manners, in common and received use, so ferocious, especially in inhumanity and treachery, which are to me the worst of all vices, that I have not the heart to think of them without horror; and almost as much admire as I detest them: the exercise of these signal villainies carries with it as great signs of vigour and force of soul, as of error and disorder. Necessity reconciles and brings men together; and this accidental connection afterwards forms itself into laws: for there have been such, as savage as any human opinion could conceive, who, nevertheless, have maintained their body with as much health and length of life as any Plato or Aristotle could invent. And certainly, all these descriptions of polities, feigned by art, are found to be ridiculous and unfit to be put in practice.

These great and tedious debates about the best form of society, and the most commodious rules to bind us, are debates only proper for the exercise of our wits; as in the arts there are several subjects which have their being in agitation and controversy, and have no life but there. Such an idea of government might be of some value in a new world; but we take a world already made, and formed to certain customs; we do not beget it, as Pyrrha or Cadmus did. By what means soever we may have the privilege to redress and reform it anew, we can hardly writhe it from its wonted bent, but we shall break all. Solon being asked whether he had established the best laws he could for the Athenians; "Yes," said he, "of those they would have received." Varro excuses himself after the same manner: "that if he were to begin to write of religion, he would say what he believed; but seeing it was already received, he would write rather according to use than nature."

Not according to opinion, but in truth and reality, the best and most excellent government for every nation is that under which it is maintained: its form and essential convenience depend upon custom. We are apt to be displeased at the present condition; but I, nevertheless, maintain that to desire command in a few [an oligarchy] in a republic, or another sort of government in monarchy than that already established, is both vice and folly:

> Ayme l'estat, tel que to le veois estre
> S'il est royal ayme la royaute;
> S'il est de peu, ou biers communaute,
> Ayme l'aussi; car Dieu t'y a faict naistre.

[Love the government, such as you see it to be. If it be royal, love royalty; if it is a republic of any sort, still love it; for God himself created thee therein.]

So wrote the good Monsieur de Pibrac, whom we have lately lost, a man of so excellent a wit, such sound opinions, and such gentle manners. This loss, and that at the same time we have had of Monsieur de Foix, are of so great importance to the crown, that I do not know whether there is another couple in France worthy to supply the places of these two Gascons in sincerity and wisdom in the council of our kings. They were both variously great men, and certainly, according to the age, rare and great, each of them in his kind: but what destiny was it that placed them in these times, men so remote from and so disproportioned to our corruption and intestine tumults?

Nothing presses so hard upon a state as innovation: change only gives form to injustice and tyranny. When any piece is loosened, it may be proper to stay it; one may take care that the alteration and corruption natural to all things do not carry us too far from our beginnings and principles: but to undertake to found so great a mass anew, and to change the foundations of so vast a building, is for them to do, who to make clean, efface; who reform particular defects by an universal confusion, and cure diseases by death:

Non tam commutandarum quam evertendarum rerum cupidi.

[Not so desirous of changing as of overthrowing things.
—Cicero, *De Officiis*, ii. i.]

The world is unapt to be cured; and so impatient of anything that presses it, that it thinks of nothing but disengaging itself at what price soever. We see by a thousand examples, that it ordinarily cures itself to its cost. The discharge of a present evil is no cure, if there be not a general amendment of condition. The surgeon's end is not only to cut away the dead flesh; that is but the progress of his cure; he has a care, over and above, to fill up the wound with better and more natural flesh, and to restore the member to its due state. Whoever only proposes to himself to remove that which offends him, falls short: for good does not necessarily succeed evil; another evil may succeed, and a worse, as it happened to Caesar's murderers, who brought the republic to such a pass, that they had reason to repent the meddling with the matter. The same has since happened to several others, even down to our own times: the French, my contemporaries, know it well enough. All great mutations shake and disorder a state.

Whoever would look direct at a cure, and well consider of it before he began, would be very willing to withdraw his hands from meddling in it. Pacuvius Calavius corrected the vice of this proceeding by a notable example. His fellow-citizens were in mutiny against their magistrates; he being a man of great authority in the city of Capua, found means one day to shut up the Senators in the palace;

and calling the people together in the market-place, there told them that the day was now come wherein at full liberty they might revenge themselves on the tyrants by whom they had been so long oppressed, and whom he had now, all alone and unarmed, at his mercy. He then advised that they should call these out, one by one, by lot, and should individually determine as to each, causing whatever should be decreed to be immediately executed; with this proviso, that they should, at the same time, depute some honest man in the place of him who was condemned, to the end there might be no vacancy in the Senate. They had no sooner heard the name of one senator but a great cry of universal dislike was raised up against him. "I see," says Pacuvius, "that we must put him out; he is a wicked fellow; let us look out a good one in his room." Immediately there was a profound silence, everyone being at a stand whom to choose. But one, more impudent than the rest, having named his man, there arose yet a greater consent of voices against him, an hundred imperfections being laid to his charge, and as many just reasons why he should not stand. These contradictory humours growing hot, it fared worse with the second senator and the third, there being as much disagreement in the election of the new, as consent in the putting out of the old. In the end, growing weary of this bustle to no purpose, they began, someone way and some another, to steal out of the assembly: everyone carrying back this resolution in his mind, that the oldest and best known evil was ever more supportable than one that was, new and untried.

Seeing how miserably we are agitated (for what have we not done!)

> *Eheu! cicatricum, et sceleris pudet,*
> *Fratrumque: quid nos dura refugimus*
> *Aetas? quid intactum nefasti*
> *Liquimus? Unde manus inventus*
> *Metu Deorum continuit? quibus*
> *Pepercit aris.*

[Alas! our crimes and our fratricides are a shame to us! What crime does this bad age shrink from? What wickedness have we left undone? What youth is restrained from evil by the fear of the gods? What altar is spared?

—Horace, *Odes*, i. 33, 35]

I do not presently conclude,

> *Ipsa si velit Salus,*
> *Servare prorsus non potest hanc familiam;*

[If the goddess Salus herself wish to save this family, she absolutely cannot

—Terence, *Adelphoe*, iv. 7, 43.]

we are not, peradventure, at our last gasp. The conservation of states is a thing that, in all likelihood, surpasses our understanding; a civil government is, as Plato says, a mighty and puissant thing, and hard to be dissolved; it often continues against mortal and intestine diseases, against the injury of unjust laws, against tyranny, the corruption and ignorance of magistrates, the licence and sedition of the people. In all our fortunes, we compare ourselves to what is above us, and still look towards those who are better: but let us measure ourselves with what is below us: there is no condition so miserable wherein a man may not find a thousand examples that will administer consolation. It is our vice that we more unwillingly look upon what is above, than willingly upon what is below; and Solon was used to say, that "whoever would make a heap of all the ills together, there is no one who would not rather choose to bear away the ills he has than to come to an equal division with all other men from that heap, and take his share." Our government is, indeed, very sick, but there have been others more sick without dying. The gods play at ball with us and bandy us every way:

Enimvero Dii nos homines quasi pilas habent.

The stars fatally destined the state of Rome for an example of what they could do in this kind: in it are comprised all the forms and adventures that concern a state: all that order or disorder, good or evil fortune, can do. Who, then, can despair of his condition, seeing the shocks and commotions wherewith Rome was tumbled and tossed, and yet withstood them all? If the extent of dominion be the health of a state (which I by no means think it is, and Isocrates pleases me when he instructs Nicocles not to envy princes who have large dominions, but those who know how to preserve those which have fallen into their hands), that of Rome was never so sound, as when it was most sick. The worst of her forms was the most fortunate; one can hardly discern any image of government under the first emperors; it is the most horrible and tumultuous confusion that can be imagined; it endured it, notwithstanding, and therein continued, preserving not a monarchy limited within its own bounds, but so many nations so differing, so remote, so disaffected, so confusedly commanded, and so unjustly conquered:

> *Nec gentibus ullis*
> *Commodat in populum, terra pelagique potentem,*
> *Invidiam fortuna suam.*

[Fortune never gave it to any nation to satisfy its hatred against the people, masters of the seas and of the earth.

—Lucan, i. 32.]

Everything that totters does not fall. The contexture of so great a body holds by more nails than one; it holds even by its antiquity, like old buildings, from which the foundations are worn away by

485

time, without rough-cast or mortar, which yet live and support themselves by their own weight:

> *Nec jam validis radicibus haerens,*
> *Pondere tuta suo est.*

Moreover, it is not rightly to go to work, to examine only the flank and the foss, to judge of the security of a place; we must observe which way approaches can be made to it, and in what condition the assailant is: few vessels sink with their own weight, and without some exterior violence. Now, let us everyway cast our eyes; everything about us totters; in all the great states, both of Christendom and elsewhere, that are known to us, if you will but look, you will there see evident menace of alteration and ruin:

> *Et sua sunt illis incommoda; parque per omnes*
> *Tempestas.*

[They all share in the mischief; the tempest rages everywhere.
—*Aeneid,* ii.]

Astrologers may very well, as they do, warn us of great revolutions and imminent mutations: their prophecies are present and palpable, they need not go to heaven to foretell this. There is not only consolation to be extracted from this universal combination of ills and menaces, but, moreover, some hopes of the continuation of our state, forasmuch as, naturally, nothing falls where all falls: universal sickness is particular health: conformity is antagonistic to dissolution. For my part, I despair not, and fancy that I discover ways to save us:

> *Deus haec fortasse benigna*
> *Reducet in sedem vice.*

[The deity will perchance by a favourable turn restore us to our
former position.

—Horace, *Epodes*, xiii. 7.]

Who knows but that God will have it happen, as in human bodies that purge and restore themselves to a better state by long and
grievous maladies, which render them more entire and perfect
health than that they took from them? That which weighs the most
with me is, that in reckoning the symptoms of our ill, I see as many
natural ones, and that Heaven sends us, and properly its own, as of
those that our disorder and human imprudence contribute to it.
The very stars seem to declare that we have already continued long
enough, and beyond the ordinary term. This also afflicts me, that
the mischief which nearest threatens us, is not an alteration in the
entire and solid mass, but its dissipation and divulsion, which is the
most extreme of our fears.

I, moreover, fear, in these fantasies of mine, the treachery of my
memory, lest, by inadvertence, it should make me write the same
thing twice. I hate to examine myself, and never review, but very
unwillingly, what has once escaped my pen. I here set down nothing new. These are common thoughts, and having, peradventure,
conceived them an hundred times, I am afraid I have set them down
somewhere else already. Repetition is everywhere troublesome,
though it were in Homer; but it is ruinous in things that have only a
superficial and transitory show. I do not love over-insisting, even in
the most profitable things, as in Seneca; and the usage of his stoical
school displeases me, to repeat, upon every subject, at full length
and width the principles and presuppositions that serve in general,
and always to reallege anew common and universal reasons.

My memory grows cruelly worse every day:

Pocula Lethaeos ut si ducentia somnos,
Arente fauce traxerim;

487

[As if my dry throat had drunk seducing cups of Lethaean oblivion.

—Horace, *Epodes*, xiv. 3.]

I must be fain for the time to come (for hitherto, thanks be to God, nothing has happened much amiss), whereas others seek time and opportunity to think of what they have to say, to avoid all preparation, for fear of tying myself to some obligation upon which I must insist. To be tied and bound to a thing puts me quite out, and to depend upon so weak an instrument as my memory. I never read this following story that I am not offended at it with a personal and natural resentment: Lyncestes, accused of conspiracy against Alexander, the day that he was brought out before the army, according to the custom, to be heard as to what he could say for himself, had learned a studied speech, of which, hesitating and stammering, he pronounced some words. Whilst growing more and more perplexed, whilst struggling with his memory, and trying to recollect what he had to say, the soldiers nearest to him charged their pikes against him and killed him, looking upon him as convict; his confusion and silence served them for a confession; for having had so much leisure to prepare himself in prison, they concluded that it was not his memory that failed him, but that his conscience tied up his tongue and stopped his mouth. And, truly, well said; the place, the assembly, the expectation, astound a man, even when he has but the ambition to speak well; what can a man do when it is an harangue upon which his life depends?

For my part, the very being tied to what I am to say is enough to loose me from it. When I wholly commit and refer myself to my memory, I lay so much stress upon it that it sinks under me: it grows dismayed with the burden. So much as I trust to it, so much do I put myself out of my own power, even to the finding it difficult to keep my own countenance; and have been sometimes very much put to it to conceal the slavery wherein I was engaged; whereas my design is to manifest, in speaking, a perfect calmness both of face and accent, and casual and unpremeditated motions, as rising from present occasions, choosing rather to say nothing to purpose than to show that I came prepared to speak well, a thing especially unbecoming a man of my profession, and of too great obligation on him who cannot retain much. The preparation begets a great deal more expectation than it will satisfy. A man often strips himself to his doublet to leap no farther than he would have done in his gown:

> *Nihil est his, qui placer volunt, turn adversarium,*
> *quam expectatio.*

[Nothing is so adverse to those who make it their business to please as expectation
> —Cicero, *Academica,* ii. 4]

It is recorded of the orator Curio, that when he proposed the division of his oration into three or four parts, or three or four arguments or reasons, it often happened either that he forgot someone, or added one or two more. I have always avoided falling into this inconvenience, having ever hated these promises and prescriptions, not only out of distrust of my memory, but also because this method relishes too much of the artist:

> *Simpliciora militares decent.*

[Simplicity becomes warriors.
> —Quintilian, *Instituto Oratoria,* xi. I.]

It is enough that I have promised to myself never again to take upon me to speak in a place of respect, for as to speaking, when a man reads his speech, besides that it is very absurd, it is a mighty disadvantage to those who naturally could give it a grace by action; and to rely upon the mercy of my present invention, I would much less do it; it is heavy and perplexed, and such as would never furnish me in sudden and important necessities.

Permit, reader, this essay its course also, and this third sitting to finish the rest of my picture: I add, but I correct not. First, because I conceive that a man having once parted with his labours to the world, he has no further right to them; let him do better if he can, in some new undertaking, but not adulterate what he has already sold. Of such dealers nothing should be bought till after they are dead. Let them well consider what they do before they, produce it to the light who hastens them? My book is always the same, saving that upon every new edition (that the buyer may not go away quite empty) I take the liberty to add (as it is but an ill jointed marque-terie) some supernumerary emblem; it is but overweight, that does not disfigure the primitive form of the essays, but, by a little artful subtlety, gives a kind of particular value to everyone of those that follow. Thence, however, will easily happen some transposition of chronology, my stories taking place according to their opportune-ness, not always according to their age.

Secondly, because as to what concerns myself, I fear to lose by change: my understanding does not always go forward, it goes back-ward too. I do not much less suspect my fancies for being the second or the third, than for being the first, or present, or past; we often correct ourselves as foolishly as we do others. I am grown older by a great many years since my first publications, which were in the year 1580; but I very much doubt whether I am grown an inch the wiser. I now, and I anon, are two several persons; but whether better, I cannot determine. It were a fine thing to be old, if we only travelled towards improvement; but it is a drunken, stumbling, reeling, infirm motion: like that of reeds, which the air casually waves to and fro at pleasure. Antiochus had in his youth strongly written in favour of the Academy; in his old age he wrote as much against it; would not, which of these two soever I should follow, be still Antiochus? After having established the uncertainty, to go about to establish the certainty of human opinions, was it not to establish doubt, and not

CHAPTER 9

certainty, and to promise, that had he had yet another age to live, he would be always upon terms of altering his judgment, not so much for the better, as for something else?

The public favour has given me a little more confidence than I expected; but what I 'most fear is, lest I should glut the world with my writings; I had rather, of the two, pique my reader than tire him, as a learned man of my time has done. Praise is always pleasing, let it come from whom, or upon what account it will; yet ought a man to understand why he is commended, that he may know how to keep up the same reputation still: imperfections themselves may get commendation. The vulgar and common estimation is seldom happy in hitting; and I am much mistaken if, amongst the writings of my time, the worst are not those which have most gained the popular applause. For my part, I return my thanks to those good-natured men who are pleased to take my weak endeavours in good part; the faults of the workmanship are nowhere so apparent as in a matter which of itself has no recommendation. Blame not me, reader, for those that slip in here by the fancy or inadvertency of others; every hand, every artisan, contribute their own materials; I neither concern myself with orthography (and only care to have it after the old way) nor pointing, being very inexpert both in the one and the other. Where they wholly break the sense, I am very little concerned, for they at least discharge me; but where they substitute a false one, as they so often do, and wrest me to their conception, they ruin me. When the sentence, nevertheless, is not strong enough for my proportion, a civil person ought to reject it as spurious, and none of mine. Whoever shall know how lazy I am, and how indulgent to my own humour, will easily believe that I had rather write as many more essays, than be tied to revise these over again for so childish a correction.

I said elsewhere, that being planted in the very centre of this new religion, I am not only deprived of any great familiarity with men of other kind of manners than my own, and of other opinions, by which they hold together, as by a tie that supersedes all other obligations;

but moreover I do not live without danger, amongst men to whom all things are equally lawful, and of whom the most part cannot offend the laws more than they have already done; from which the extremist degree of licence proceeds. All the particular being summed up together, I do not find one man of my country, who pays so dear for the defence of our laws both in loss and damages (as the lawyers say) as myself; and some there are who vapour and brag of their zeal and constancy, that if things were justly weighed, do much less than I. My house, as one that has ever been open and free to all comers, and civil to all (for I could never persuade myself to make it a garrison of war, war being a thing that I prefer to see as remote as may be), has sufficiently merited popular kindness, and so that it would be a hard matter justly to insult over me upon my own dunghill; and I look upon it as a wonderful and exemplary thing that it yet continues a virgin from blood and plunder during so long a storm, and so many neighbouring revolutions and tumults. For to confess the truth, it had been possible enough for a man of my complexion to have shaken hands with any one constant and continued form whatever; but the contrary invasions and incursions, alternations and vicissitudes of fortune round about me, have hitherto more exasperated than calmed and mollified the temper of the country, and involved me, over and over again, with invincible difficulties and dangers.

I escape, it is true, but am troubled that it is more by chance, and something of my own prudence, than by justice; and am not satisfied to be out of the protection of the laws, and under any other safeguard than theirs. As matters stand, I live, above one half, by the favour of others, which is an untoward obligation. I do not like to owe my safety either to the generosity or affection of great persons, who allow me my legality and my liberty, or to the obliging manners of my predecessors, or my own: for what if I were another kind of man? If my deportment, and the frankness of my conversation or relationship, oblige my neighbours, it is that that they should acquit themselves of obligation in only permitting me to live, and they may say, "We allow him the free liberty of having divine service read in his own private chapel, when it is interdicted in all churches round about, and allow him the use of his goods and his life, as one who protects our wives and cattle in time of need." For my house has for many descents shared in the reputation of Lycurgus the Athenian, who was the general depository and guardian of the purses of his fellow-citizens. Now I am clearly of opinion that a man should live by right and by authority, and not either by recompense or favour. How many gallant men have rather chosen to lose their lives than to be debtors for them? I hate to subject myself to any sort of obligation, but above all, to that which binds me by the duty of honour. I think nothing so dear as what has been given me, and this because my will lies at pawn under the title of gratitude, and more willingly accept of services that are to be sold; I feel that for the last I give nothing but money, but for the other I give myself.

The knot that binds me by the laws of courtesy binds me more than that of civil constraint; I am much more at ease when bound by a scrivener, than by myself. Is it not reason that my conscience should be much more engaged when men simply rely upon it? In a bond, my faith owes nothing, because it has nothing lent it; let them trust to the security they have taken without me. I had much rather break the wall of a prison and the laws themselves than my own word. I am nice, even to superstition, in keeping my promises, and, therefore, upon all occasions have a care to make them uncertain and conditional. To those of no great moment, I add the jealousy of my own rule, to make them weight; it wracks and oppresses me with its own interest. Even in actions wholly my own and free, if I once say a thing, I conceive that I have bound myself, and that delivering it to the knowledge of another, I have positively enjoined it my own performance. Methinks I promise it, if I but say it: and therefore am not apt to say much of that kind. The sentence that I pass upon myself is more severe than that of a judge, who only considers the common obligation; but my conscience looks upon it with a more severe and penetrating eye. I lag in those duties to which I should be compelled if I did not go:

Hoc ipsum ita justum est, quod recte fit, si est voluntarium.

[This itself is so far just, that it is rightly done, if it is voluntary.
—Cicero, *De Officiis*, i. 9.]

If the action has not some splendour of liberty, it has neither grace nor honour:

Quod vos jus cogit, vix voluntate impetrent:

[That which the laws compel us to do, we scarcely do with a will.
—Terence, *Adelphoe*, iii. 3, 44.]

where necessity draws me, I love to let my will take its own course:

Quia quicquid imperio cogitur, exigenti magis,
quam praestanti, acceptum refertur.

[For whatever is compelled by power, is more imputed to him that exacts than to him that performs.
—Valerius Maximus, ii. 2, 6.]

I know some who follow this rule, even to injustice; who will sooner give than restore, sooner lend than pay, and will do them the least good to whom they are most obliged. I don't go so far as that, but I'm not far off.

I so much love to disengage and disobligate myself, that I have sometimes looked upon ingratitudes, affronts, and indignities which I have received from those to whom either by nature or accident I was bound in some way of friendship, as an advantage to me; taking this occasion of their ill-usage, for an acquaintance and discharge of so much of my debt. And though I still continue to pay them all the external offices of public reason, I, notwithstanding, find a great saving in doing that upon the account of justice which I did upon the score of affection, and am a little eased of the attention and solicitude of my inward will:

Est prudentis sustinere, ut currum, sic impetum benevolentia;

[It is the part of a wise man to keep a curbing hand upon the impetus of friendship, as upon that of his horse.
—Cicero, *De Amicitia*, c. 17.]

it is in me, too urging and pressing where I take; at least, for a man who loves not to be strained at all. And this husbanding my friendship serves me for a sort of consolation in the imperfections of those in whom I am concerned. I am very sorry they are not such as I could wish they were, but then I also am spared somewhat of my application and engagement towards them. I approve of a man who is the less fond of his child for having a scald head, or for being crooked; and not only when he is ill-conditioned, but also when he is of unhappy disposition, and imperfect in his limbs (God himself has abated so much from his value and natural estimation), provided he carry himself in this coldness of affection with moderation and exact justice: proximity, with me, lessens not defects, but rather aggravates them.

After all, according to what I understand in the science of benefit and acknowledgment, which is a subtle science, and of great use, I know no person whatever more free and less indebted than I am at this hour. What I do owe is simply to foreign obligations and benefits; as to anything else, no man is more absolutely clear:

Nec sunt mihi nota potentum
Munera.

[The gifts of great men are unknown to me.

—*Aeneid*, xii. 529.]

Princes give me a great deal if they take nothing from me; and do me good enough if they do me no harm; that's all I ask from them. O how am I obliged to God, that he has been pleased I should immediately receive from his bounty all I have, and specially reserved all my obligation to himself. How earnestly do I beg of his holy compassion that I may never owe essential thanks to anyone. O happy liberty wherein I have thus far lived. May it continue with me to the last. I endeavour to have no express need of any one:

In me omnis spec est mihi.

[All my hope is in myself.

—Terence, *Adelphoe*, iii. 5, 9.]

It is what everyone may do in himself, but more easily they whom God has placed in a condition exempt from natural and urgent necessities. It is a wretched and dangerous thing to depend upon others; we ourselves, in whom is ever the most just and safest dependence, are not sufficiently sure.

I have nothing mine but myself, and yet the possession is, in part, defective and borrowed. I fortify myself both in courage, which is the strongest assistant, and also in fortune, therein wherewith to satisfy myself, though everything else should forsake me. Hippias of Elis not only furnished himself with knowledge, that he might, at need, cheerfully retire from all other company to enjoy the Muses: nor only with the knowledge of philosophy, to teach his soul to be contented with itself, and bravely to subsist without outward conveniences, when fate would have it so; he was, moreover, so careful as to learn to cook, to shave himself, to make his own clothes, his own shoes and drawers, to provide for all his necessities in himself, and

496

CHAPTER 9

to wean himself from the assistance of others. A man more freely and cheerfully enjoys borrowed conveniences, when it is not an enjoyment forced and constrained by need; and when he has, in his own will and fortune, the means to live without them. I know myself very well; but it is hard for me to imagine any so pure liberality of any one towards me, any so frank and free hospitality, that would not appear to me discreditable, tyrannical, and tainted with reproach, if necessity had reduced me to it. As giving is an ambitious and author-itative quality, so is accepting a quality of submission; witness the insulting and quarrelsome refusal that Bajazet made of the presents that Tamerlane sent him; and those that were offered on the part of the Emperor Solyman to the Emperor of Calicut, so angered him, that he not only rudely rejected them, saying that neither he nor any of his predecessors had ever been wont to take, and that it was their office to give; but, moreover, caused the ambassadors sent with the gifts to be put into a dungeon. When Thetis, says Aristotle, flat-ters Jupiter, when the Lacedaemonians flatter the Athenians, they do not put them in mind of the good they have done them, which is always odious, but of the benefits they have received from them. Such as I see so frequently employ every in their affairs, and thrust themselves into so much obligation, would never do it, did they but relish as I do the sweetness of a pure liberty, and did they but weigh, as wise: men should, the burden of obligation: it is sometimes, peradventure, fully paid, but it is never dissolved. It is a miserable slavery to a man who loves to be at full liberty in all respects. Such as know me, both above and below me in station, are able to say whether they have ever known a man less importuning, soliciting, entreating, and pressing upon others than I. If I am so, and a degree beyond all modern example, it is no great wonder, so many parts of my manners contributing to it: a little natural pride, an impa-tience at being refused, the moderation of my desires and designs, my incapacity for business, and my most beloved qualities, idleness and freedom; by all these together I have conceived a mortal hatred

497

to being obliged to any other, or by any other than myself. I leave no stone unturned, to do without it, rather than employ the bounty of another in any light or important occasion or necessity whatever. My friends strangely trouble me when they ask me to ask a third person; and I think it costs me little less to disengage him who is indebted to me, by making use of him, than to engage myself to him who owes me nothing. These conditions being removed, and provided they require of me nothing if any great trouble or care (for I have declared mortal war against all care), I am very ready to do everyone the best service I can. I have been very willing to seek occasion to do people a good turn, and to attach them to me; and methinks there is no more agreeable employment for our means. But I have yet more avoided receiving than sought occasions of giving, and moreover, according to Aristotle, it is more easy., My fortune has allowed me but little to do others good withal, and the little it can afford, is put into a pretty close hand. Had I been born a great person, I should have been ambitious to have made myself beloved, not to make myself feared or admired: shall I more plainly express it? I should more have endeavoured to please than to profit others. Cyrus very wisely, and by the mouth of a great captain, and still greater philosopher, prefers his bounty and benefits much before his valour and warlike conquests; and the elder Scipio, wherever he would raise himself in esteem, sets a higher value upon his affability and humanity, than on his prowess and victories, and has always this glorious saying in his mouth: "That he has given his enemies as much occasion to love him as his friends." I will then say, that if a man must, of necessity, owe something, it ought to be by a more legitimate title than that whereof I am speaking, to which the necessity of this miserable war compels me; and not in so great a debt as that of my total preservation both of life and fortune: it overwhelms me.

I have a thousand times gone to bed in my own house with an apprehension that I should be betrayed and murdered that very night; compounding with fortune, that it might be without terror and with quick despatch; and, after my Paternoster, I have cried out,

Chapter 9

Impius haec tam culta novalia miles habebit!

[Shall impious soldiers have these new-ploughed grounds?
—Virgil, *Eclogues*, i. 71.]

What remedy? it is the place of my birth, and that of most of my ancestors; they have here fixed their affection and name. We inure ourselves to whatever we are accustomed to; and in so miserable a condition as ours is, custom is a great bounty of nature, which benumbs out senses to the sufferance of many evils. A civil war has this with it worse than other wars have, to make us stand sentinels in our own houses.

> *Quam miserum, porta vitam muroque tueri,*
> *Vixque suae tutum viribus esse domus!*

[It is miserable to protect one's life by doors and walls, and to be scarcely safe in one's own house.
—Ovid, *Tristia*, iv. I, 69.]

It is a grievous extremity for a man to be jostled even in his own house and domestic repose. The country where I live is always the first in arms and the last that lays them down, and where there is never an absolute peace:

> *Tunc quoque, cum pax est, trepidant formidine belli....*
> *Quoties Romam fortuna lacessit;*
> *Hac iter est bellis.... Melius, Fortuna, dedisses*
> *Orbe sub Eco sedem, gelidaque sub Arcto,*
> *Errantesque domos.*

[Even when there's peace, there is here still the fear of war when Fortune troubles peace, this is ever the way by which war passes.
—Ovid, *Tristia*, iii. 10, 67.]

[We might have lived happier in the remote East or in the icy
North, or among the wandering tribes.

—Lucan, i. 255.]

I sometimes extract the means to fortify myself against these considerations from indifference and indolence, which, in some sort,
bring us on to resolution. It often befalls me to imagine and expect
mortal dangers with a kind of delight: I stupidly plunge myself headlong into death, without considering or taking a view of it, as into
a deep and obscure abyss which swallows me up at one leap, and
involves me in an instant in a profound sleep, without any sense of
pain. And in these short and violent deaths, the consequence that
I foresee administers more consolation to me than the effect does
fear. They say, that as life is not better for being long, so death is
better for being not long. I do not so much evade being dead, as I
enter into confidence with dying. I wrap and shroud myself into the
storm that is to blind and carry me away with the fury of a sudden
and insensible attack. Moreover, if it should fall out that, as some
gardeners say, roses and violets spring more odoriferous near garlic
and onions, by reason that the last suck and imbibe all the ill odour
of the earth; so, if these depraved natures should also attract all the
malignity of my air and climate, and render it so much better and
purer by their vicinity, I should not lose all. That cannot be: but
there may be something in this, that goodness is more beautiful and
attractive when it is rare; and that contrariety and diversity fortify
and consolidate well-doing within itself, and inflame it by the jealousy of opposition and by glory. Thieves and robbers, of their special
favour, have no particular spite at me; no more have I to them: I
should have my hands too full. Like consciences are lodged under
several sorts of robes; like cruelty, disloyalty, rapine; and so much the
worse, and more falsely, when the more secure and concealed under
colour of the laws. I less hate an open professed injury than one that
is treacherous; an enemy in arms, than an enemy in a gown. Our
fever has seized upon a body that is not much the worse for it; there

was fire before, and now it is broken out into a flame; the noise is greater, not the evil. I ordinarily answer such as ask me the reason of my travels, "That I know very well what I fly from, but not what I seek." If they tell me that there may be as little soundness amongst foreigners, and that their manners are no better than ours: I first reply, that it is hard to be believed;

Tam multa: scelerum facies!

[There are so many forms of crime.

—Virgil, *Georgics*, i. 506.]

secondly, that it is always gain to change an ill condition for one that is uncertain; and that the ills of others ought not to afflict us so much as our own.

I will not here omit, that I never mutiny so much against France, that I am not perfectly friends with Paris; that city has ever had my heart from my infancy, and it has fallen out, as of excellent things, that the more beautiful cities I have seen since, the more the beauty of this still wins upon my affection. I love her for herself, and more in her own native being, than in all the pomp of foreign and acquired embellishments. I love her tenderly, even to her warts and blemishes. I am a Frenchman only through this great city, great in people, great in the felicity of her situation; but, above all, great and incomparable in variety and diversity of commodities: the glory of France, and one of the most noble ornaments of the world. May God drive our divisions far from her. Entire and united, I think her sufficiently defended from all other violences. I give her caution that, of all sorts of people, those will be the worst that shall set her in discord; I have no fear for her, but of herself, and, certainly, I have as much fear for her as for any other part of the kingdom. Whilst she shall continue, I shall never want a retreat, where I may stand at bay, sufficient to make me amends for parting with any other retreat.

Not because Socrates has said so, but because it is in truth my own humour, and peradventure not without some excess, I look upon all men as my compatriots, and embrace a Polander as a Frenchman, preferring the universal and common tie to all national ties whatever. I am not much taken with the sweetness of a native air: acquaintance wholly new and wholly my own appear to me full as good as the other common and fortuitous ones with Four neighbours: friendships that are purely of our own acquiring ordinarily carry it above those to which the communication of climate or of blood oblige us. Nature has placed us in the world free and unbound; we imprison ourselves in certain straits, like the kings of Persia, who obliged themselves to drink no other water but that of the river Choaspes, foolishly quitted claim to their right in all other streams, and, so far as concerned themselves, dried up all the other rivers of the world. What Socrates did towards his end, to look upon a sentence of banishment as worse than a sentence of death against him, I shall, I think, never be either so decrepit or so strictly habituated to my own country to be of that opinion. These celestial lives have images enough that I embrace more by esteem than affection; and they have some also so elevated and extraordinary that I cannot embrace them so much as by esteem, forasmuch as I cannot conceive them. That fancy was singular in a man who thought the whole world his city; it is true that he disdained travel, and had hardly ever set his foot out of the Attic territories. What say you to his complaint of the money his friends offered to save his life, and that he refused to come out of prison by the mediation of others, in order not to disobey the laws in a time when they were otherwise so corrupt? These examples are of the first kind for me; of the second, there are others that I could find out in the same person: many of these rare examples surpass the force of my action, but some of them, moreover, surpass the force of my judgment.

Besides these reasons, travel is in my opinion a very profitable exercise; the soul is there continually employed in observing new and unknown things, and I do not know, as I have often said a better school wherein to model life than by incessantly exposing to it the diversity of so many other lives, fancies, and usances, and by making it relish a perpetual variety of forms of human nature. The body is, therein, neither idle nor overwrought; and that moderate agitation puts it in breath. I can keep on horseback, tormented with the stone as I am, without alighting or being weary, eight or ten hours together:

Vires ultra sorternque senectae.

[Beyond the strength and lot of age.

—*Aeneid*, vi. 114.]

No season is enemy to me but the parching heat of a scorching sun; for the umbrellas made use of in Italy, ever since the time of the ancient Romans, more burden a man's arm than they relieve his head. I would fain know how it was that the Persians, so long ago and in the infancy of luxury, made ventilators where they wanted them, and planted shades, as Xenophon reports they did. I love rain, and to dabble in the dirt, as well as ducks do. The change of air and climate never touches me; every sky is alike; I am only troubled with inward alterations which I breed within myself, and those are not so frequent in travel. I am hard to be got out, but being once upon the road, I hold out as well as the best. I take as much pains in little as in great attempts, and am as solicitous to equip myself for a short journey, if but to visit a neighbour, as for the longest voyage. I have learned to travel after the Spanish fashion, and to make but one stage of a great many miles; and in excessive heats I always travel by night, from sun set to sunrise. The other method of baiting by the way, in haste and hurry to gobble up a dinner, is, especially in short days, very inconvenient. My horses perform the better; never any horse tired under me that was able to hold out the first day's journey. I water them at every brook I meet, and have only a care they have so much way to go before I come to my inn, as will digest the water in their bellies. My unwillingness to rise in a morning gives my servants leisure to dine at their ease before they set out; for my own part, I never eat too late; my appetite comes to me in eating, and not else; I am never hungry but at table.

Some of my friends blame me for continuing this travelling humour, being married and old. But they are out in't; it is the best time to leave a man's house, when he has put it into a way of continuing without him, and settled such order as corresponds with its former government. It is much greater imprudence to abandon it to a less faithful housekeeper, and who will be less solicitous to look after your affairs.

The most useful and honourable knowledge and employment for the mother of a family is the science of good housewifery. I see some that are covetous indeed, but very few that are good managers. It is the supreme quality of a woman, which a man ought to seek before any other, as the only dowry that must ruin or preserve our houses. Let men say what they will, according to the experience I have learned, I require in married women the economical virtue above all other virtues; I put my wife to't, as a concern of her own, leaving her, by my absence, the whole government of my affairs. I see, and am vexed to see, in several families I know, Monsieur about noon come home all jaded and ruffled about his affairs, when Madame is still dressing her hair and tricking up herself, indeed, in her closet: this is for queens to do, and that's a question, too: it is ridiculous and unjust that the laziness of our wives should be maintained with our sweat and labour. No man, so far as in me lie, shall have a clearer, a more quiet and free fruition of his estate than I. If the husband bring matter, nature herself will that the wife find the form.

As to the duties of conjugal friendship, that some think to be impaired by these absences, I am quite of another opinion. It is, on the contrary, an intelligence that easily cools by a too frequent and assiduous companionship. Every strange woman appears charming, and we all find by experience that being continually together is not so pleasing as to part for a time and meet again. These interruptions fill me with fresh affection towards my family, and render my house more pleasant to me. Change warms my appetite to the one and then to the other. I know that the arms of friendship are long enough to reach from the one end of the world to the other, and especially this, where there is a continual communication of offices that rouse the obligation and remembrance. The Stoics say that there is so great connection and relation amongst the sages, that he who dines in France nourishes his companion in Egypt; and that whoever does but hold out his finger, in what part of the world soever, all the sages upon the habitable earth feel themselves assisted by it. Fruition and possession principally appertain to the imagination; it more fervently and constantly embraces what it is in quest of, than what we hold in our arms. Cast up your daily amusements; you will find that you are most absent from your friend when he is present with you; his presence relaxes your attention, and gives you liberty to absent yourself at every turn and upon every occasion. When I am away at Rome, I keep and govern my house, and the conveniences I there left; see my walls rise, my trees shoot, and my revenue increase or decrease, very near as well as when I am there:

Ante oculos errat domus, errat forma locorum.

[My house and the forms of places float before my eyes
—Ovid, *Tristia*, iii. 4, 57.]

If we enjoy nothing but what we touch, we may say farewell to the money in our chests, and to our sons when they are gone a hunting. We will have them nearer to us: is the garden, or half a day's journey from home, far? What is ten leagues: far or near? If near, what is eleven, twelve, or thirteen, and so by degrees. In earnest, if there be a woman who can tell her husband what step ends the near and what step begins the remote, I would advise her to stop between;

> *Excludat jurgia finis … .*
> *Utor permisso; caudaeque pilos ut equinae*
> *Paulatim vello, et demo unum, demo etiam unum*
> *Dum cadat elusus ratione ruentis acervi:*

[Let the end shut out all disputes … . I use what is permitted; I pluck out the hairs of the horse's tail one by one; while I thus outwit my opponent.

—Horace, *Epistles*, ii, I, 38, 45]

and let them boldly call philosophy to their assistance; in whose teeth it may be cast that, seeing it neither discerns the one nor the other end of the joint, between the too much and the little, the long and the short, the light and the heavy, the near and the remote; that seeing it discovers neither the beginning nor the end, it must needs judge very uncertainly of the middle:

> *Rerum natura nullam nobis dedit cognitionem finium.*

[Nature has given to us no knowledge of the end of things.
—Cicero, *Academica*, ii. 29.]

Are they not still wives and friends to the dead who are not at the end of this but in the other world? We embrace not only the absent, but those who have been, and those who are not yet. We do not promise in marriage to be continually twisted and linked together, like some little animals that we see, or, like the bewitched folks of Karenty, [Karantia, a town in the isle of Rugen. See Saxo-Grammaticus, Hist. of Denmark, book xiv.] tied together like dogs; and a wife ought not to be so greedily enamoured of her husband's foreparts, that she cannot endure to see him turn his back, if occasion be. But may not this saying of that excellent painter of woman's humours be here introduced, to show the reason of their complaints?

> *Uxor, si cesses, aut to amare cogitat,*
> *Aut tete amari, aut potare, aut animo obsequi;*
> *Et tibi bene esse soli, cum sibi sit male;*

[Your wife, if you loiter, thinks that you love or are beloved; or that you are drinking or following your inclination; and that it is well for you when it is ill for her (all the pleasure is yours and hers all the care).

—Terence, *Adelphoe,* act i., sc. I, v. 7.]

or may it not be, that of itself opposition and contradiction entertain and nourish them, and that they sufficiently accommodate themselves, provided they incommodate you?

In true friendship, wherein I am perfect, I more give myself to my friend, than I endeavour to attract him to me. I am not only better pleased in doing him service than if he conferred a benefit upon me, but, moreover, had rather he should do himself good than me, and he most obliges me when he does so; and if absence be either more pleasant or convenient for him, it is also more acceptable to me than his presence; neither is it properly absence, when we can write to one another: I have sometimes made good use of our separation from one another: we better filled and further extended the possession of life in being parted. He [La Boétie.] lived, enjoyed, and saw for me, and I for him, as fully as if he had himself been there; one part of us remained idle, and we were too much blended in one another when we were together; the distance of place rendered the conjunction of our wills more rich. This insatiable desire of personal presence a little implies weakness in the fruition of souls.

As to what concerns age, which is alleged against me, it is quite contrary; it is for youth to subject itself to common opinions, and to curb itself to please others; it has wherewithal to please both the people and itself; we have but too much ado to please ourselves alone. As natural conveniences fail, let us supply them with those that are artificial. It is injustice to excuse youth for pursuing its pleasures, and to forbid old men to seek them. When young, I concealed my wanton passions with prudence; now I am old, I chase away melancholy by debauch. And thus do the platonic laws forbid men to travel till forty or fifty years old, so that travel might be more useful and instructive in so mature an age. I should sooner subscribe to the second article of the same Laws, which forbids it after threescore.

"But, at such an age, you will never return from so long a journey." What care I for that? I neither undertake it to return, nor to finish it my business is only to keep myself in motion, whilst motion pleases me; I only walk for the walk's sake. They who run after a benefit or a hare, run not; they only run who run at base, and to exercise their running. My design is divisible throughout: it is not grounded upon any great hopes: every day concludes my expectation: and the journey of my life is carried on after the same manner. And yet I have seen places enough a great way off, where I could have wished to have stayed. And why not, if Chrysippus, Cleanthes, Diogenes, Zeno, Antipater, so many sages of the sourest sect, readily abandoned their country, without occasion of complaint, and only for the enjoyment of another air. In earnest, that which most displeases me in all my travels is, that I cannot resolve to settle my abode where I should best like, but that I must always propose to myself to return, to accommodate myself to the common humour.

If I feared to die in any other place than that of my birth; if I thought I should die more uneasily remote from my own family, I should hardly go out of France; I should not, without fear, step out of my parish; I feel death always pinching me by the throat or by the back. But I am otherwise constituted; it is in all places alike to me. Yet, might I have my choice, I think I should rather choose to die on horseback than in bed; out of my own house, and far from my own people. There is more heartbreaking than consolation in tak-

Chapter 9

ing leave of one's friends; I am willing to omit that civility, for that, of all the offices of friendship, is the only one that is unpleasant; and I could, with all my heart, dispense with that great and eternal farewell. If there be any convenience in so many standers-by, it brings an hundred inconveniences along with it. I have seen many dying miserably surrounded with all this train: it is a crowd that chokes them. It is against duty, and is a testimony of little kindness and little care, to permit you to die in repose; one torments your eyes, another your ears, another your tongue; you have neither sense nor member that is not worried by them. Your heart is wounded with compassion to hear the mourning of friends, and, perhaps with anger, to hear the counterfeit condolings of pretenders. Whoever has been delicate and sensitive, when well, is much more so when ill. In such a necessity, a gentle hand is required, accommodated to his sentiment, to scratch him just in the place where he itches, otherwise scratch him not at all. If we stand in need of a wise woman [midwife, Fr. "sage femme".] to bring us into the world, we have much more need of a still wiser man to help us out of it. Such a one, and a friend to boot, a man ought to purchase at any cost for such an occasion. I am not yet arrived to that pitch of disdainful vigour that is fortified in itself, that nothing can assist or disturb; I am of a lower form; I endeavour to hide myself, and to escape from this passage, not by fear, but by art. I do not intend in this act of dying to make proof and show of my constancy. For whom should I do it? all the right and interest I have in reputation will then cease. I content myself with a death involved within itself, quiet, solitary, and all my own, suitable to my retired and private life; quite contrary to the Roman superstition, where a man was looked upon as unhappy who died without speaking, and who had not his nearest relations to close his eyes. I have enough to do to comfort myself, without having to console others; thoughts enough in my head, not to need that circumstances should possess me with new; and matter enough to occupy me without borrowing. This affair is out of the part of society; it is the act of one single person. Let us live and be merry amongst our friends; let us go repine and die amongst strangers; a man may find those, for his money, who will shift his pillow and rub his feet, and will trouble him no more than he would have them; who will present to him an indifferent countenance, and suffer him to govern himself, and to complain according to his own method.

I wean myself daily by my reason from this childish and inhuman humour, of desiring by our sufferings to move the compassion and mourning of our friends: we stretch our own incommodities beyond their just extent when we extract tears from others; and the constancy which we commend in everyone in supporting his adverse fortune, we accuse and reproach in our friends when the evil is our own; we are not satisfied that they should be sensible of our condition only, unless they be, moreover, afflicted. A man should diffuse joy, but, as much as he can, smother grief. He who makes himself lamented without reason is a man not to be lamented when there shall be real cause: to be always complaining is the way never to be lamented; by making himself always in so pitiful a taking, he is never commiserated by any. He who makes himself out dead when he is alive, is subject to be thought living when he is dying. I have seen some who have taken it ill when they have been told that they looked well, and that their pulse was good; restrain their smiles, because they betrayed a recovery, and be angry, at their health because it was not to be lamented: and, which is a great deal more, these were not women. I describe my infirmities, such as they really are, at most, and avoid all expressions of evil prognostic and composed exclamations. If not mirth, at least a temperate countenance in the standersby, is proper in the presence of a wise sick man: he does not quarrel with health, for, seeing himself in a contrary condition, he is pleased to contemplate it sound and entire in others, and at least to enjoy it for company: he does not, for feeling himself melt away, abandon all living thoughts, nor avoid ordinary discourse. I would study sickness whilst I am well; when it has seized me, it will make its impression real enough, without the help of my imagination. We prepare ourselves beforehand for the journeys we undertake, and resolve upon them; we leave the appointment of the hour when to take horse to the company, and in their favour defer it.

I find this unexpected advantage in the publication of my manners, that it in some sort serves me for a rule. I have, at times, some consideration of not betraying the history of my life: this public declaration obliges me to keep my way, and not to give the lie to the image I have drawn of my qualities, commonly less deformed and contradictory than consists with the malignity and infirmity of the judgments of this age. The uniformity and simplicity of my manners produce a face of easy interpretation; but because the fashion is a little new and not in use, it gives too great opportunity to slander. Yet so it is, that whoever would fairly assail me, I think I so sufficiently assist his purpose in my known and avowed imperfections, that he may that way satisfy his ill-nature without fighting with the wind. If I myself, to anticipate accusation and discovery, confess enough to frustrate his malice, as he conceives, it is but reason that he make use of his right of amplification, and to wire-draw my vices as far as he can; attack has its rights beyond justice; and let him make the roots of those errors I have laid open to him shoot up into trees: let him make his use, not only of those I am really affected with, but also of those that only threaten me; injurious vices, both in quality and number; let him cudgel me that way. I should willingly follow the example of the philosopher Bion: Antigonus being about to reproach him with the meanness of his birth, he presently cut him short with this declaration: "I am," said he, "the son of a slave, a butcher, and branded, and of a strumpet my father married in the lowest of his fortune; both of them were whipped for offences they had committed. An orator bought me, when a child, and finding me a pretty and hopeful boy, bred me up, and when he died left me all his estate, which I have transported into this city of Athens, and here settled myself to the study of philosophy. Let the historians never trouble themselves with inquiring about me: I will tell them about it." A free and generous confession enervates reproach and disarms slander. So it is that, one thing with another, I fancy men as often commend as undervalue me beyond reason; as, methinks also, from my childhood, in rank and degree of honour, they have given me a place rather above than below my right. I should find myself more at ease in a country where these degrees were either regulated or not regarded. Amongst men, when an altercation about the precedence either of walking or sitting exceeds three replies, it is reputed uncivil. I never stick at giving or taking place out of rule, to avoid the trouble of such ceremony; and never any man had a mind to go before me, but I permitted him to do it.

Besides this profit I make of writing of myself, I have also hoped for this other advantage, that if it should fall out that my humour should please or jump with those of some honest man before I die, he would then desire and seek to be acquainted with me. I have given him a great deal of made-way; for all that he could have, in many years, acquired by close familiarity, he has seen in three days in this memorial, and more surely and exactly. A pleasant fancy: many things that I would not confess to any one in particular, I deliver to the public, and send my best friends to a bookseller's shop, there to inform themselves concerning my most secret thoughts;

Excutienda damus praecordia.

[We give our hearts to be examined.

—Persius, V. 22.]

Did I, by good direction, know where to seek any one proper for my conversation, I should certainly go a great way to find him out: for the sweetness of suitable and agreeable company cannot; in my opinion, be bought too dear. O what a thing is a true friend! how true is that old saying, that the use of a friend is more pleasing and necessary than the elements of water and fire!

To return to my subject: there is, then, no great harm in dying privately and far from home; we conceive ourselves obliged to retire for natural actions less unseemly and less terrible than this. But, moreover, such as are reduced to spin out a long languishing life, ought not, perhaps, to wish to trouble a great family with their continual miseries; therefore the Indians, in a certain province, thought it just to knock a man on the head when reduced to such a necessity; and in another of their provinces, they all forsook him to shift for himself as well as he could. To whom do they not, at last, become tedious and insupportable? the ordinary offices of fife do not go that length. You teach your best friends to be cruel perforce; hardening wife and children by long use neither to regard nor to lament your sufferings. The groans of the stone are grown so familiar to my people, that nobody takes any notice of them. And though we should extract some pleasure from their conversation (which does not always happen, by reason of the disparity of conditions, which easily begets contempt or envy toward any one whatever), is it not too much to make abuse of this half a lifetime? The more I should see them constrain themselves out of affection to be serviceable to me, the more I should be sorry for their pains. We have liberty to lean, but not to lay our whole weight upon others, so as to prop ourselves by their ruin; like him who caused little children's throats to be cut to make use of their blood for the cure of a disease he had, or that other, who was continually supplied with tender young girls to keep his old limbs warm in the night, and to mix the sweetness of their breath with his, sour and stinking. I should readily advise Venice as a retreat in this decline of life. Decrepitude is a solitary quality. I am sociable even to excess, yet I think it reasonable that I should now withdraw my troubles from the sight of the world and keep them to myself. Let me shrink and draw up myself in my own shell, like a tortoise, and learn to see men without hanging upon them. I should endanger them in so slippery a passage: it is time to turn my back to company.

"But, in these travels, you will be taken ill in some wretched place, where nothing can be had to relieve you." I always carry most things necessary about me; and besides, we cannot evade Fortune if she once resolves to attack us. I need nothing extraordinary when I am sick. I will not be beholden to my bolus to do that for me which nature cannot. At the very beginning of my fevers and sicknesses that cast me down, whilst still entire, and but little, disordered in health, I reconcile myself to Almighty God by the last Christian, offices, and find myself by so doing less oppressed and more easy, and have got, methinks, so much the better of my disease. And I have yet less need of a notary or counsellor than of a physician. What I have not settled of my affairs when I was in health, let no one expect I should do it when I am sick. What I will do for the service of death is always done; I durst not so much as one day defer it; and if nothing be done, it is as much as to say either that doubt hindered my choice (and some-times it is well chosen not to choose), or that I was positively resolved not to do anything at all.

I write my book for few men and for few years. Had it been matter of duration, I should have put it into firmer language. According to the continual variation that ours has been subject to, up to this day, who can expect that its present form should be in use fifty years hence? It slips every day through our fingers, and since I was born, it is altered above one-half. We say that it is now perfect; and every age says the same of its own. I shall hardly trust to that, so long as it varies and changes as it does. It is for good and useful writings to rivet it to them, and its reputation will go according to the fortune of our state. For which reason I am not afraid to insert in it several private articles, which will spend their use amongst the men that are now living, and that concern the particular knowledge of some who will see further into them than every common reader. I will not, after all, as I often hear dead men spoken of, that men should say of me: "He judged, he lived so and so; he would have done this or that; could he have spoken when he was dying, he would have said so or so, and have given this thing or the other; I knew him better than any." Now, as much as decency permits, I here discover my inclinations and affections; but I do more willingly and freely by word of mouth to any one who desires to be informed. So it is that in these memoirs, if any one observe, he will find that I have either told or designed to tell all; what I cannot express, I point out with my finger:

> *Verum animo satis haec vestigia parva sagaci*
> *Sunt, per quae possis cognoscere caetera tute*

[By these footsteps a sagacious mind many easily find all other matters (are sufficient to enable one to learn the rest well.)
—Lucretius, i. 403.]

I leave nothing to be desired or to be guessed at concerning me. If people must be talking of me, I would have it to be justly and truly; I would come again, with all my heart, from the other world to give any one the lie who should report me other than I was, though he did it to honour me. I perceive that people represent, even living men, quite another thing than what they really are; and had I not stoutly defended a friend whom I have lost, [De la Boétie.] they would have torn him into a thousand contrary pieces.

To conclude the account of my poor humours, I confess that in my travels I seldom reach my inn but that it comes into my mind to consider whether I could there be sick and dying at my ease. I desire to be lodged in some private part of the house, remote from all noise, ill scents, and smoke. I endeavour to flatter death by these frivolous circumstances; or, to say better, to discharge myself from all other incumbrances, that I may have nothing to do, nor be troubled with anything but that which will lie heavy enough upon me without any other load. I would have my death share in the ease and conveniences of my life; it is a great part of it, and of great importance, and I hope it will not in the future contradict the past. Death has some forms that are more easy than others, and receives divers qualities, according to everyone's fancy. Amongst the natural deaths, that which proceeds from weakness and stupor

I think the most favourable; amongst those that are violent, I can worse endure to think of a precipice than of the fall of a house that will crush me in a moment, and of a wound with a sword than of a harquebus shot; I should rather have chosen to poison myself with Socrates, than stab myself with Cato. And, though it, be all one, yet my imagination makes as great a difference as between death and life, between throwing myself into a burning furnace and plunging into the channel of a river: so idly does our fear more concern itself in the means than the effect. It is but an instant, it is true, but withal an instant of such weight, that I would willingly give a great many days of my life to pass it over after my own fashion. Since everyone's imagination renders it more or less terrible, and since everyone has some choice amongst the several forms of dying, let us try a little further to find someone that is wholly clear from all offence. Might not one render it even voluptuous, like the Commoyientes of Antony and Cleopatra? I set aside the brave and exemplary efforts produced by philosophy and religion; but, amongst men of little mark there have been found some, such as Petronius and Tigellinus at Rome, condemned to despatch themselves, who have, as it were, rocked death asleep with the delicacy of their preparations; they have made it slip and steal away in the height of their accustomed diversions amongst girls and good fellows; not a word of consolation, no mention of making a will, no ambitious affectation of constancy, no talk of their future condition; amongst sports, feastings, wit, and mirth, common and indifferent discourses, music, and amorous verses. Were it not possible for us to imitate this resolution after a more decent manner? Since there are deaths that are good for fools, deaths good for the wise, let us find out such as are fit for those who are between both. My imagination suggests to me one that is easy, and, since we must die, to be desired. The Roman tyrants thought they did, in a manner, give a criminal life when they gave him the choice of his death. But was not Theophrastus, that so delicate, so modest, and so wise a philosopher, compelled by reason, when he does say this verse, translated by Cicero:

Vitam regit fortuna, non sapientia?

[Fortune, not wisdom, sways human life.
—Cicero, *Tusculum Disputations*, V. 31.]

Fortune assists the facility of the bargain of my life, having placed it in such a condition that for the future it can be neither advantage nor hindrance to those who are concerned in me; it is a condition that I would have accepted at any time of my life; but in this occasion of trussing up my baggage, I am particularly pleased that in dying I shall neither do them good nor harm. She has so ordered it, by a cunning compensation, that they who may pretend to any considerable advantage by my death will, at the same time, sustain a material inconvenience. Death sometimes is more grievous to us, in that it is grievous to others, and interests us in their interest as much as in our own, and sometimes more.

In this conveniency of lodging that I desire, I mix nothing of pomp and amplitude – I hate it rather; but a certain plain neatness, which is oftenest found in places where there is less of art, and that Nature has adorned with some grace that is all her own:

Non ampliter, sea munditer convivium.

[To eat not largely, but cleanly.
—Nepos, *Life of Atticus*, c. 13]

Plus salis quam sumptus.

[Rather enough than costly (More wit than cost)
—Nonius, xi. 19.]

And besides, it is for those whose affairs compel them to travel in the depth of winter through the Grisons country to be surprised upon the way with great inconveniences. I, who, for the most part, travel for my pleasure, do not order my affairs so ill. If the way be foul on my right hand, I turn on my left; if I find myself unfit to ride, I stay where I am; and, so doing, in earnest I see nothing that is not as pleasant and commodious as my own house. It is true that I always find superfluity superfluous, and observe a kind of trouble even in abundance itself. Have I left anything behind me unseen, I go back to see it; it is still on my way; I trace no certain line, either straight or crooked. [Rousseau has translated this passage in his *Emile*, book v.] Do I not find in the place to which I go what was reported to me – as it often falls out that the judgments of others do not jump with mine, and that I have found their reports for the most part false – I never complain of losing my labour: I have, at least, informed myself that what was told me was not true.

I have a constitution of body as free, and a palate as indifferent, as any man living: the diversity of manners of several nations only affects me in the pleasure of variety: every usage has its reason. Let the plate and dishes be pewter, wood, or earth; my meat be boiled or roasted; let them give me butter or oil, of nuts or olives, hot or cold, it is all one to me; and so indifferent, that growing old, I accuse this generous faculty, and would wish that delicacy and choice should correct the indiscretion of my appetite, and sometimes soothe my stomach. When I have been abroad out of France and that people, out of courtesy, have asked me if I would be served after the French manner, I laughed at the question, and always frequented tables the most filled with foreigners. I am ashamed to see our countrymen besotted with this foolish humour of quarrelling with forms contrary to their own; they seem to be out of their element when out of their own village: wherever they go, they keep to their own fashions and abominate those of strangers. Do they meet with a compatriot in Hungary? O the happy chance! They are henceforward inseparable;

Chapter 9

they cling together, and their whole discourse is to condemn the barbarous manners they see about them. Why barbarous, because they are not French? And those have made the best use of their travels who have observed most to speak against. Most of them go for no other end but to come back again; they proceed in their travel with vast gravity and circumspection, with a silent and incommunicable prudence, preserving themselves from the contagion of an unknown air. What I am saying of them puts me in mind of something like it I have at times observed in some of our young courtiers; they will not mix with any but men of their own sort, and look upon us as men of another world, with disdain or pity. Put them upon any discourse but the intrigues of the court, and they are utterly at a loss; as very owls and novices to us as we are to them. It is truly said that a well-bred man is a compound man. I, on the contrary, travel very much sated with our own fashions; I do not look for Gascons in Sicily; I have left enough of them at home; I rather seek for Greeks and Persians; they are the men I endeavour to be acquainted with and the men I study; it is there that I bestow and employ myself. And which is more, I fancy that I have met but with few customs that are not as good as our own; I have not, I confess, travelled very far; scarce out of the sight of the vanes of my own house.

As to the rest, most of the accidental company a man falls into upon the road beget him more trouble than pleasure; I waive them as much as I civilly can, especially now that age seems in some sort to privilege and sequester me from the common forms. You suffer for others or others suffer for you; both of them inconveniences of importance enough, but the latter appears to me the greater. It is a rare fortune, but of inestimable solace; to have a worthy man, one of a sound judgment and of manners conformable to your own, who takes a delight to bear you company. I have been at an infinite loss for such upon my travels. But such a companion should be chosen and acquired from your first setting out. There can be no pleasure to me without communication: there is not so much as a sprightly thought comes into my mind, that it does not grieve me to have produced alone, and that I have no one to communicate it to:

> *Si cum hac exceptione detur sapientia,*
> *ut illam inclusam teneam, nec enuntiem, rejiciam.*

[If wisdom be conferred with this reservation, that I must keep it to myself, and not communicate it to others, I would none of it.
—Seneca, *Epistles*, 6.]

This other has strained it one note higher:

> *Si contigerit ea vita sapienti, ut ommum rerum afliuentibus copiis,*
> *quamvis omnia, quae cognitione digna sunt, summo otio secum ipse*
> *consideret et contempletur, tamen, si solitude tanta sit, ut hominem*
> *videre non possit, excedat a vita.*

[If such a condition of life should happen to a wise man, that in the greatest plenty of all conveniences he might, at the most undisturbed leisure, consider and contemplate all things worth the knowing, yet if his solitude be such that he must not see a man, let him depart from life.
—Cicero, *De Officius*, i. 43.]

Architas pleases me when he says, "that it would be unpleasant, even in heaven itself, to wander in those great and divine celestial bodies without a companion. But yet it is much better to be alone than in foolish and troublesome company. Aristippus loved to live as a stranger in all places:

> *Me si fata meis paterentur ducere vitam*
> *Auspiciis,*

CHAPTER 9

[If the fates would let me live in my own way.
                              —*Aeneid*, iv. 340.]

I should choose to pass away the greatest part of my life on horseback:

> *Viseregestiens,*
> *Qua pane debacchentur ignes,*
> *Qua nebula, pluviique rores.*

[Visit the regions where the sun burns, where are the thick rain-clouds and the frosts.
                              —Horace, *Odes*, iii. 3, 54.]

"Have you not more easy diversions at home? What do you there want? Is not your house situated in a sweet and healthful air, sufficiently furnished, and more than sufficiently large? Has not the royal majesty been more than once there entertained with all its train? Are there not more below your family in good ease than there are above it in eminence? Is there any local, extraordinary, indigestible thought that afflicts you?"

> *Qua to nunc coquat, et vexet sub pectore fixa.*

[That may now worry you, and vex, fixed in your breast.
                              —Cicero, *De Senectute*, c. 1, Ex Ennio.]

"Where do you think to live without disturbance?"

> *Nunquam simpliciter Fortuna indulget.*

[Fortune is never simply complaisant (unmixed).
                              —Quintus Curtius, iv. 14]

521

You see, then, it is only you that trouble yourself; you will everywhere follow yourself, and everywhere complain; for there is no satisfaction here below, but either for brutish or for divine souls. He who, on so just an occasion, has no contentment, where will he think to find it? How many thousands of men terminate their wishes in such a condition as yours? Do but reform yourself; for that is wholly in your own power! whereas you have no other right but patience towards fortune:

Nulla placida quies est, nisi quam ratio composuit.

[There is no tranquillity but that which reason has conferred.
—Seneca, *Epistles*, 56.]

I see the reason of this advice, and see it perfectly well; but he might sooner have done, and more pertinently, in bidding me in one word be wise; that resolution is beyond wisdom; it is her precise work and product. Thus the physician keeps preaching to a poor languishing patient to "be cheerful"; but he would advise him a little more discreetly in bidding him "be well." For my part, I am but a man of the common sort. It is a wholesome precept, certain and easy to be understood, "Be content with what you have," that is to say, with reason: and yet to follow this advice is no more in the power of the wise men of the world than in me. It is a common saying, but of a terrible extent: what does it not comprehend? All things fall under discretion and qualification. I know very well that, to take it by the letter, this pleasure of travelling is a testimony of uneasiness and irresolution, and, in sooth, these two are our governing and predominating qualities. Yes, I confess, I see nothing, not so much as in a dream, in a wish, whereon I could set up my rest: variety only, and the possession of diversity, can satisfy me; that is, if anything can. In travelling, it pleases me that I may stay where I like, without inconvenience, and that I have a place wherein commodiously to divert myself. I love a private life, because it is my own choice that

522

Chapter 9

I love it, not by any dissenting from or dislike of public life, which, peradventure, is as much according to my complexion. I serve my prince more cheerfully because it is by the free election of my own judgment and reason, without any particular obligation; and that I am not reduced and constrained so to do for being rejected or disliked by the other party; and so of all the rest. I hate the morsels that necessity carves me; any commodity upon which I had only to depend would have me by the throat;

Alter remus aquas, alter mihi radat arenas;

[Let me have one oar in the water, and with the other rake the shore.
—Propertius, iii. 3, 23.]

one cord will never hold me fast enough. You will say, there is vanity in this way of living. But where is there not? All these fine precepts are vanity, and all wisdom is vanity:

Dominus novit cogitations sapientum, quoniam vanae sunt.

[The Lord knows the thoughts of the wise, that they are vain.
—Ps. xciii. II; or I Cor. iii. 20.]

These exquisite subtleties are only fit for sermons; they are discourses that will send us all saddled into the other world. Life is a material and corporal motion, an action imperfect and irregular of its own proper essence; I make it my business to serve it according to itself:

Quisque suos patimur manes.

[We each of us suffer our own particular demon.
—*Aeneid*, vi. 743.]

Sic est faciendum, ut contra naturam universam nihil contendamus;
Ea tamen conservata propriam sequamur.

[We must so order it as by no means to contend against universal
nature; but yet, that rule being observed, to follow our own.
—Cicero, *De Officiis*, i. 31.]

To what end are these elevated points of philosophy, upon
which no human being can rely? and those rules that exceed both
our use and force?

I see often that we have theories of life set before us which neither
the proposer nor those who hear him have any hope, nor, which is
more, any inclination to follow. Of the same sheet of paper whereon
the judge has but just written a sentence against an adulterer, he
steals a piece whereon to write a love-letter to his companion's wife.
She whom you have but just now illicitly embraced will presently, even
in your hearing, more loudly inveigh against the same fault in her
companion than a Portia would do; [The chaste daughter of Cato
of Utica] and men there are who will condemn others to death for
crimes that they themselves do not repute so much as faults. I have,
in my youth, seen a man of good rank with one hand present to the
people verses that excelled both in wit and debauchery, and with the
other, at the same time, the most ripe and pugnacious theological
reformation that the world has been treated withal these many years.
And so men proceed; we let the laws and precepts follow their way;
ourselves keep another course, not only from debauchery of manners, but ofttimes by judgment and contrary opinion. Do but hear a
philosophical lecture; the invention, eloquence, pertinency immediately strike upon your mind and move you; there is nothing that
touches or stings your conscience; it is not to this they address themselves. Is not this true? It made Aristo say, that neither a bath nor a
lecture did aught unless it scoured and made men clean. One may
stop at the skin; but it is after the marrow is picked out as, after we
have swallowed good wine out of a fine cup, we examine the designs

and workmanship. In all the courts of ancient philosophy, this is to be found, that the same teacher publishes rules of temperance and at the same time lessons in love and wantonness; Xenophon, in the very bosom of Clinias, wrote against the Aristippic virtue. It is not that there is any miraculous conversion in it that makes them thus wavering; it is that Solon represents himself, sometimes in his own person, and sometimes in that of a legislator; one while he speaks for the crowd, and another for himself; taking the free and natural rules for his own share, feeling assured of a firm and entire health:

Curentur dubii medicis majoribus aegri.

[Desperate maladies require the best doctors.
– Juvenal, xiii. 124.]

Antisthenes allows a sage to love, and to do whatever he thinks convenient, without regard to the laws, forasmuch as he is better advised than they, and has a greater knowledge of virtue. His disciple Diogenes said, that "men to perturbations were to oppose reason: to fortune, courage: to the laws, nature." For tender stomachs, constrained and artificial recipes must be prescribed: good and strong stomachs serve themselves simply with the prescriptions of their own natural appetite; after this manner do our physicians proceed, who eat melons and drink iced wines, whilst they confine their patients to syrups and sops. "I know not," said the courtezanLais, "what they may talk of books, wisdom, and philosophy; but these men knock as often at my door as any others." At the same rate that our licence carries us beyond what is lawful and allowed, men have, often beyond universal reason, stretched the precepts and rules of our life:

Nemo satis credit tantum delinquere, quantum
Permittas.

[No one thinks he has done ill to the full extent of what he may.
—Juvenal, xiv. 233.]

It were to be wished that there was more proportion between the command and the obedience; and the mark seems to be unjust to which one cannot attain. There is no so good man, who so squares all his thoughts and actions to the laws, that he is not faulty enough to deserve hanging ten times in his life; and he may well be such a one, as it were great injustice and great harm to punish and ruin:

> *Ole, quid ad te*
> *De cute quid faciat ille vel ille sua?*

[Olus, what is it to thee what he or she does with their skin?
—Martial, vii. 9, I.]

and such an one there may be, who has no way offended the laws, who, nevertheless, would not deserve the character of a virtuous man, and whom philosophy would justly condemn to be whipped; so unequal and perplexed is this relation. We are so far from being good men, according to the laws of God, that we cannot be so according to our own human wisdom never yet arrived at the duties it had itself prescribed; and could it arrive there, it would still prescribe to itself others beyond, to which it would ever aspire and pretend; so great an enemy to consistency is our human condition. Man enjoins himself to be necessarily in fault: he is not very discreet to cut out his own duty by the measure of another being than his own. To whom does he prescribe that which he does not expect any one should perform? is he unjust in not doing what it is impossible for him to do? The laws which condemn us not to be able, condemn us for not being able.

At the worst, this difform liberty of presenting ourselves two several ways, the actions after one manner and the reasoning after another, may be allowed to those who only speak of things; but it cannot be allowed to those who speak of themselves, as I do: I must march my pen as I do my feet. Common life ought to have relation to the other lives: the virtue of Cato was vigorous beyond the reason of the age he lived in; and for a man who made it his business to govern others, a man dedicated to the public service, it might be called a justice, if not unjust, at least vain and out of season. Even my own manners, which differ not above an inch from those current amongst us, render me, nevertheless, a little rough and unsociable at my age. I know not whether it be without reason that I am disgusted with the world I frequent; but I know very well that it would be without reason, should I complain of its being disgusted with me, seeing I am so with it. The virtue that is assigned to the affairs of the world is a virtue of many wavings, corners, and elbows, to join and adapt itself to human frailty, mixed and artificial, not straight, clear, constant, nor purely innocent. Our annals to this very day reproach one of our kings for suffering himself too simply to be carried away by the conscientious persuasions of his confessor: affairs of state have bolder precepts;

> *Exeat aula,*
> *Qui vult esse pius.*

[Let him who will be pious retire from the court.
—Lucan, viii. 493]

I formerly tried to employ in the service of public affairs opinions and rules of living, as rough, new, unpolished or unpolluted, as they were either born with me, or brought away from my education, and wherewith I serve my own turn, if not so commodiously, at least securely, in my own particular concerns: a scholastic and novice virtue; but I have found them unapt and dangerous. He who goes into a crowd must now go one way and then another, keep his elbows close, retire or advance, and quit the straight way, according to what he encounters; and must live not so much according to his own method as to that of others; not according to what he proposes to himself, but according to what is proposed to him, according to the time, according to the men, according to the occasions. Plato says, that whoever escapes from the world's handling with clean breeches, escapes by miracle: and says withal, that when he appoints his philosopher the head of a government, he does not mean a corrupt one like that of Athens, and much less such a one as this of ours, wherein wisdom itself would be to seek. A good herb, transplanted into a soil contrary to its own nature, much sooner conforms itself to the soil than it reforms the soil to it. I found that if I had wholly to apply myself to such employments, it would require a great deal of change and new modelling in me before I could be any way fit for it: And though I could so far prevail upon myself (and why might I not with time and diligence work such a feat), I would not do it. The little trial I have had of public employment has been so much disgust to me; I feel at times temptations toward ambition rising in my soul, but I obstinately oppose them:

At tu, Catulle, obstinatus obdura.

[But thou, Catullus, be obstinately firm.

—Catullus, viii. 19.]

I am seldom called to it, and as seldom offer myself uncalled; liberty and laziness, the qualities most predominant in me, are qualities diametrically contrary to that trade. We cannot well distinguish the faculties of men; they have divisions and limits hard and delicate to choose; to conclude from the discreet conduct of a private life a capacity for the management of public affairs is to conclude ill; a man may govern himself well who cannot govern others so, and compose Essays who could not work effects: men there may be who can order a siege well, who would ill marshal a battle; who can speak well in private, who would ill harangue a people or a prince; nay, it is peradventure rather a testimony in him who can do the one that he cannot do the other, than otherwise. I find that elevated souls are not much more proper for mean things than mean souls are for high ones. Could it be imagined that Socrates should have administered occasion of laughter, at the expense of his own reputation, to the Athenians for: having never been able to sum up the votes of his tribe, to deliver it to the council? Truly, the veneration I have for the perfections of this great man deserves that his fortune should furnish, for the excuse of my principal imperfections, so magnificent an example. Our sufficiency is cut out into small parcels; mine has no latitude, and is also very contemptible in number. Saturninus, to those who had conferred upon him the command in chief: "Companions," said he, "you have lost a good captain, to make of him a bad general."

Whoever boasts, in so sick a time as this, to employ a true and sincere virtue in the world's service, either knows not what it is, opinions growing corrupt with manners (and, in truth, to hear them describe it, to hear the most of them glorify themselves in their deportments, and lay down their rules; instead of painting virtue, they paint pure vice and injustice, and so represent it false in the education of princes); or if he does know it, boasts unjustly and let him say what he will, does a thousand things of which his own conscience must necessarily accuse him. I should willingly take Seneca's word on the experience he made upon the like occasion, provided he would deal sincerely with me. The most honourable mark of goodness in such a necessity is freely to confess both one's own faults and those of others; with the power of its virtue to stay one's inclination towards evil; unwillingly to follow this propension; to hope better, to desire better. I perceive that in these divisions wherein we are involved in France, everyone labours to defend his cause; but even the very best of them with dissimulation and disguise: he who would write roundly of the true state of the quarrel, would write rashly and wrongly. The most just party is at best but a member of a decayed and worm-eaten body; but of such a body, the member that is least affected calls itself sound, and with good reason, forasmuch as our qualities have no title but in comparison; civil innocence is measured according to times and places. Imagine this in Xenophon, related as a fine commendation of Agesilaus: that, being entreated by a neighbouring prince with whom he had formerly had war, to permit him to pass through his country, he granted his request, giving him free passage through Peloponnesus; and not only did not imprison or poison him, being at his mercy, but courteously received him according to the obligation of his promise, without doing him the least injury or offence. To such ideas as theirs this were an act of no especial note; elsewhere and in another age, the frankness and unanimity of such an action would be thought wonderful; our monkeyish capets [Capets, so called from their short capes, were the students of Montaigne College at Paris, and were held in great contempt.] would have laughed at it, so little does the Spartan innocence resemble that of France. We are not without virtuous men, but it is according to our notions of virtue. Whoever has his manners established in regularity above the standard of the age he lives in, let him either wrest or blunt his rules, or, which I would rather advise him to, let him retire, and not meddle with us at all. What will he get by it?

> *Egregium sanctumque virum si cerno, bimembri*
> *Hoc monstrum puero, et miranti jam sub aratro*
> *Piscibus inventis, et foetae comparo mulae.*

[If I see an exemplary and good man, I liken it to a two-headed boy, or a fish turned up by the plough, or a teeming mule.
—Juvenal, xiii. 64.]

One may regret better times, but cannot fly from the present; we may wish for other magistrates, but we must, notwithstanding, obey those we have; and, peradventure, it is more laudable to obey the bad than the good. So long as the image of the ancient and received laws of this monarchy shall shine in any corner of the kingdom, there will I be. If they unfortunately happen to thwart and

CHAPTER 9

contradict one another, so as to produce two parts, of doubtful and difficult choice, I will willingly choose to withdraw and escape the tempest; in the meantime nature or the hazards of war may lend me a helping hand. Between Caesar and Pompey, I should frankly have declared myself; but, as amongst the three robbers who came after, [Octavius, Mark Antony, and Lepidus.] a man must have been necessitated either to hide himself, or have gone along with the current of the time, which I think one may fairly do when reason no longer guides:

Quo diversus abis?

[Whither do thou run wandering?
—*Aeneid*, v. 166.]

This medley is a little from my theme; I go out of my way; but it is rather by licence than oversight; my fancies follow one another, but sometimes at a great distance, and look towards one another, but it is with an oblique glance. I have read a dialogue of Plato, [The Phaedrus] of the like motley and fantastic composition, the beginning about love, and all the rest to the end about rhetoric; they fear not these variations, and have a marvellous grace in letting themselves be carried away at the pleasure of the wind, or at least to seem as if they were. The titles of my chapters do not always comprehend the whole matter; they often denote it by some mark only, as these others, Andria, Eunuchus; or these, Sylla, Cicero, Toyquatus. I love a poetic progress, by leaps and skips; it is an art, as Plato says, light, nimble, demoniac. There are pieces in Plutarch where he forgets his theme; where the proposition of his argument is only found by incidence, stuffed and half stifled in foreign matter. Observe his footsteps in the Daemon of Socrates. O God! how beautiful are these frolicsome sallies, those variations and digressions, and all the more when they seem most fortuitous and careless. It is the indiligent reader who loses my subject, and not I; there will always be found some word or other in a corner that is to the purpose, though it lie very close. I ramble indiscreetly and tumultuously; my style and my wit wander at the same rate. He must fool it a little who would not be deemed wholly a fool, say both the precepts, and, still more, the examples of our masters. A thousand poets flag and languish after a prosaic manner; but the best old prose (and I strew it here up and down indifferently for verse) shines throughout with the lustre, vigour, and boldness of poetry, and not without some air of its fury. And certainly prose ought to have the pre-eminence in speaking. The poet, says Plato, seated upon the muses tripod, pours out with fury whatever comes into his mouth, like the pipe of a fountain, without considering and weighing it; and things escape him of various colours, of contrary substance, and with an irregular torrent. Plato himself is throughout poetical; and the old theology, as the learned tell us, is all poetry; and the first philosophy is the original language of the gods. I would have my matter distinguish itself; it sufficiently shows where it changes, where it concludes, where it begins, and where it rejoins, without interlacing it with words of connection introduced for the relief of weak or negligent ears, and without explaining myself. Who is he that had not rather not be read at all than after a drowsy or cursory manner?

Nihil est tam utile, quod intransitu prosit.

[Nothing is so useful as that which is cursorily so.
—Seneca, *Epistles*, 2.]

If to take books in hand were to learn them: to look upon them were to consider them: and to run these slightly over were to grasp them, I were then to blame to make myself out so ignorant as I say I am. Seeing I cannot fix the attention of my reader by the weight of what I write, "manco male", if I should chance to do it by my intricacies. "Nay, but he will afterwards repent that he ever perplexed himself about it." It is very true, but he will yet be there perplexed.

CHAPTER 9

And, besides, there are some humours in which comprehension produces disdain; who will think better of me for not understanding what I say, and will conclude the depth of my sense by its obscurity; which, to speak in good sooth, I mortally hate, and would avoid it if I could. Aristotle boasts somewhere in his writings that he affected it: a vicious affectation. The frequent breaks into chapters that I made my method in the beginning of my book, having since seemed to me to dissolve the attention before it was raised, as making it disdain to settle itself to so little, I, upon that account, have made them longer, such as require proposition and assigned leisure. In such an employment, to whom you will not give an hour you give nothing; and you do nothing for him for whom you only do it whilst you are doing something else. To which may be added that I have, peradventure, some particular obligation to speak only by halves, to speak confusedly and discordantly. I am therefore angry at this trouble-feast reason, and its extravagant projects that worry one's life, and its opinions, so fine and subtle, though they be all true, I think too dear bought and too inconvenient. On the contrary, I make it my business to bring vanity itself in repute, and folly too, if it produce me any pleasure; and let myself follow my own natural inclinations, without carrying too strict a hand upon them.

I have seen elsewhere houses in ruins, and statues both of gods and men: these are men still. It is all true; and yet, for all that, I cannot so often revisit the tomb of that so great and so puissant city, [Rome] that I do not admire and reverence it. The care of the dead is recommended to us; now, I have been bred up from my infancy with these dead; I had knowledge of the affairs of Rome long before I had any of those of my own house; I knew the Capitol and its plan before I knew the Louvre, and the Tiber before I knew the Seine. The qualities and fortunes of Lucullus, Metellus, and Scipio have ever run more in my head than those of any of my own country; they are all dead; so is my father as absolutely dead as they, and is removed as far from me and life in eighteen years as they are in sixteen hundred: whose memory, nevertheless, friendship and society, I do not cease to embrace and utilise with a perfect and lively union. Nay, of my own inclination, I pay more service to the dead; they can no longer help themselves, and therefore, methinks, the more require my assistance: it is there that gratitude appears in its full lustre. The benefit is not so generously bestowed, where there is retrogradation and reflection. Arcesilaus, going to visit Ctesibius, who was sick, and finding him in a very poor condition, very finely conveyed some money under his pillow, and, by concealing it from him, acquitted him, moreover, from the acknowledgment due to such a benefit. Such as have merited from me friendship and gratitude have never lost these by being no more; I have better and more carefully paid them when gone and ignorant of what I did; I speak most affectionately of my friends when they can no longer know it. I have had a hundred quarrels in defending Pompey and for the cause of Brutus; this acquaintance yet continues between us; we have no other hold even on present things but by fancy. Finding myself of no use to this age, I throw myself back upon that other, and am so enamoured of it, that the free, just, and flourishing state of that ancient Rome (for I neither love it in its birth nor its old age) interests and impassionates me; and therefore I cannot so often revisit the sites of their streets and houses, and those ruins profound even to the Antipodes, that I am not interested in them. Is it by nature, or through error of fancy, that the sight of places which we know to have been frequented and inhabited by persons whose memories are recommended in story, moves us in some sort more than to hear a recital of their – acts or to read their writings?

Tanta vis admonitionis inest in locis....Et id quidem in hac urbe infinitum; quacumque enim ingredimur, in aliquam historiam vestigium ponimus.

CHAPTER 9

[So great a power of reminiscence resides in places; and that truly in this city infinite, for which way soever we go, we find the traces of some story.

—Cicero, *De Finibus*, v. I, 2.]

It pleases me to consider their face, bearing, and vestments: I pronounce those great names between my teeth, and make them ring in my ears:

Ego illos veneror, et tantis nominibus semper assurgo.

[I reverence them, and always rise to so great names.
—Seneca, *Epistles*, 64.]

Of things that are in some part great and admirable, I admire even the common parts: I could wish to see them in familiar relations, walk, and sup. It were ingratitude to condemn the relics and images of so many worthy and valiant men as I have seen live and die, and who, by their example, give us so many good instructions, knew we how to follow them.

And, moreover, this very Rome that we now see, deserves to be beloved, so long and by so many titles allied to our crown; the only common and universal city; the sovereign magistrate that commands there is equally acknowledged elsewhere it is the metropolitan city of all the Christian nations the Spaniard and Frenchman is there at home: to be a prince of that state, there needs no more but to be of Christendom wheresoever. There is no place upon earth that heaven has embraced with such an influence and constancy of favour; her very ruins are grand and glorious,

Laudandis pretiosior ruinis.

[More precious from her glorious ruins.
—Sidonius Apollinaris, *Carmina*, xxiii.; *Narba*, v. 62.]

535

she yet in her very tomb retains the marks and images of empire:

Ut palam sit, uno in loco gaudentis opus esse naturæ.

[That it may be manifest that there is in one place the work of rejoicing nature.

—Pliny, *Natural History*, iii. 5.]

Some would blame and be angry at themselves to perceive themselves tickled with so vain a pleasure our humours are never too vain that are pleasant let them be what they may, if they constantly content a man of common understanding, I could not have the heart to blame him.

I am very much obliged to Fortune, in that, to this very hour, she has offered me no outrage beyond what I was well able to bear. Is it not her custom to let those live in quiet by whom she is not importuned?

> *Quanto quisque sibi plum negaverit,*
> *A diis plum feret: nil cupientium*
> *Nudus castra peto ... .*
> *Multa petentibus*
> *Desunt multa.*

[The more each man denies himself, the more the gods give him. Poor as I am, I seek the company of those who ask nothing; they who desire much will be deficient in much.

—Horace, *Odes*, iii. 16,21,42.]

If she continue her favour, she will dismiss me very well satisfied:

> *Nihil supra*
> *Deos lacesso.*

[I trouble the gods no farther.
—Horace, *Odes*, ii. 18, 11.]

But beware a shock: there are a thousand who perish in the port. I easily comfort myself for what shall here happen when I shall be gone, present things trouble me enough:

Fortunae caetera mando.

[I leave the rest to fortune.
—Ovid, *Metamorphoses*, ii. 140.]

Besides, I have not that strong obligation that they say ties men to the future, by the issue that succeeds to their name and honour; and peradventure, ought less to covet them, if they are to be so much desired. I am but too much tied to the world, and to this life, of myself: I am content to be in Fortune's power by circumstances properly necessary to my being, without otherwise enlarging her jurisdiction over me; and have never thought that to be without children was a defect that ought to render life less complete or less contented: a sterile vocation has its conveniences too. Children are of the number of things that are not so much to be desired, especially now that it would be so hard to make them good:

Bona jam nec nasci licet, ita corrupta Bunt semina;

[Nothing good can be born now, the seed is so corrupt.
—Tertullian, *De Pudicita.*]

and yet they are justly to be lamented by such as lose them when they have them.

He who left me my house in charge, foretold that I was like to ruin it, considering my humour so little inclined to look after household affairs. But he was mistaken; for I am in the same condition now as when I first entered into it, or rather somewhat better; and yet without office or any place of profit.

As to the rest, if Fortune has never done me any violent or extraordinary injury, neither has she done me any particular favour; whatever we derive from her bounty, was there above a hundred years before my time: I have, as to my own particular, no essential and solid good, that I stand indebted for to her liberality. She has, indeed, done me some airy favours, honorary and titular favours, without substance, and those in truth she has not granted, but offered me, who, God knows, am all material, and who take nothing but what is real, and indeed massive too, for current pay: and who, if I durst confess so much, should not think avarice much less excusable than ambition: nor pain less to be avoided than shame; nor health less to be coveted than learning, or riches than nobility.

Amongst those empty favours of hers, there is none that so much pleases vain humour natural to my country, as an authentic bull of a Roman burgess-ship, that was granted me when I was last there, glorious in seals and gilded letters, and granted with all gracious liberality. And because it is couched in a mixt style, more or less favourable, and that I could have been glad to have seen a copy of it before it had passed the seal.

Being before burgess of no city at all, I am glad to be created one of the most noble that ever was or ever shall be. If other men would consider themselves at the rate I do, they would, as I do, discover themselves to be full of inanity and foppery; to rid myself of it, I cannot, without making myself away. We are all steeped in it, as well one as another; but they who are not aware on't, have somewhat the better bargain; and yet I know not whether they have or no.

This opinion and common usage to observe others more than ourselves has very much relieved us that way: it is a very displeasing object: we can there see nothing but misery and vanity: nature, that we may not be dejected with the sight of our own deformities, has wisely thrust the action of seeing outward. We go forward with

CHAPTER 9

the current, but to turn back towards ourselves is a painful motion; so is the sea moved and troubled when the waves rush against one another. Observe, says everyone, the motions of the heavens, of public affairs; observe the quarrel of such a person, take notice of such a one's pulse, of such another's last will and testament; in sum, be always looking high or low, on one side, before or behind you. It was a paradoxical command anciently given us by that god of Delphos: "Look into yourself; discover yourself; keep close to yourself; call back your mind and will, that elsewhere consume themselves into yourself; you run out, you spill yourself; carry a more steady hand: men betray you, men spill you, men steal you from yourself. Do thou not see that this world we live in keeps all its sight confined within, and its eyes open to contemplate itself? It is always vanity for thee, both within and without; but It is less vanity when less extended. Excepting thee, O man, said that god, everything studies itself first, and has bounds to its labours and desires, according to its need. There is nothing so empty and necessitous as thou, who embracest the universe; thou art the investigator without knowledge, the magistrate without jurisdiction, and, after all, the fool of the farce."

13

ON EXPERIENCE

There is no desire more natural than that of knowledge. We try all ways that can lead us to it; where reason is wanting, we therein employ experience,

> *Per varios usus Artem experiential fecit,*
> *Exemplo monstrante viam,*

[By various trials experience created art, example showing the way.

—Manilius, i. 59.]

which is a means much more weak and cheap; but truth is so great a thing that we ought not to disdain any mediation that will guide us to it. Reason has so many forms that we know not to which to take; experience has no fewer; the consequence we would draw from the comparison of events is unsure, by reason they are always unlike. There is no quality so universal in this image of things as diversity and variety. Both the Greeks and the Latins and we, for the most express example of similitude, employ that of eggs; and yet there have been men, particularly one at Delphos, who could distinguish marks of difference amongst eggs so well that he never mistook one for another, and having many hens, could tell which had laid it.

Dissimilitude intrudes itself of itself in our works; no art can arrive at perfect similitude: neither Perrozet nor any other can so carefully polish and blanch the backs of his cards that some gamesters will not distinguish them by seeing them only shuffled by another. Resemblance does not so much make one as difference makes another. Nature has obliged herself to make nothing other that was not unlike.

And yet I am not much pleased with his opinion, who thought by the multitude of laws to curb the authority of judges in cutting out for them their several parcels; he was not aware that there is as much liberty and latitude in the interpretation of laws as in their form; and they but fool themselves, who think to lessen and stop our disputes by recalling us to the express words of the Bible: forasmuch as our mind does not find the field less spacious wherein to controvert the sense of another than to deliver his own; and as if there were less animosity and tartness in commentary than in invention. We see how much he was mistaken, for we have more laws in France than all the rest of the world put together, and more than would be necessary for the government of all the worlds of Epicurus:

Ut olim flagitiis, sic nunc legibus, laboramus.

[As we were formerly by crimes, so we are now overburdened by laws.

—Tacitus, *Annals*, iii. 25.]

and yet we have left so much to the opinions and decisions of our judges that there never was so full a liberty or so full a license. What have our legislators gained by culling out a hundred thousand particular cases, and by applying to these a hundred thousand laws? This number holds no manner of proportion with the infinite diversity of human actions; the multiplication of our inventions will never arrive at the variety of examples; add to these a hundred times as many more, it will still not happen that, of events to come, there shall one be found that, in this vast number of millions of events so chosen and recorded, shall so tally with any other one, and be so exactly coupled and matched with it that there will not remain some circumstance and diversity which will require a diverse judgment. There is little relation between our actions, which are in perpetual mutation, and fixed and immutable laws; the most to be desired are those that are the most rare, the most simple and general; and I am even of opinion that we had better have none at all than to have them in so prodigious a number as we have.

Nature always gives them better and happier than those we make ourselves; witness the picture of the Golden Age of the Poets and the state wherein we see nations live who have no other. Some there are, who for their only judge take the first passer-by that travels along their mountains, to determine their cause; and others who, on their market day, choose out someone amongst them upon the spot to decide their controversies. What danger would there be that the wisest amongst us should so determine ours, according to occurrences and at sight, without obligation of example and consequence? For every foot its own shoe. King Ferdinand, sending colonies to the Indies, wisely provided that they should not carry along with them any students of jurisprudence, for fear lest suits should get footing in that new world, as being a science in its own nature, breeder of altercation and division; judging with Plato, "that lawyers and physicians are bad institutions of a country."

Whence does it come to pass that our common language, so easy for all other uses, becomes obscure and unintelligible in wills and contracts? and that he who so clearly expresses himself in whatever else he speaks or writes, cannot find in these any way of declaring himself that does not fall into doubt and contradiction? if it be not that the princes of that art, applying themselves with a peculiar attention to cull out portentous words and to contrive artificial sentences, have so weighed every syllable, and so thoroughly sifted every sort of quirking connection that they are now confounded and entangled in the infinity of figures and minute divisions, and can no more fall within any rule or prescription, nor any certain intelligence:

> *Confusum est, quidquid usque in pulverem sectum est.*

[Whatever is beaten into powder is undistinguishable (confused).

—Seneca, *Epistles*, 89.]

As you see children trying to bring a mass of quicksilver to a certain number of parts, the more they press and work it and endeavour to reduce it to their own will, the more they irritate the liberty of this generous metal; it evades their endeavour and sprinkles itself into so many separate bodies as frustrate all reckoning; so is it here, for in subdividing these subtilties we teach men to increase their doubts; they put us into a way of extending and diversifying difficulties, and lengthen and disperse them. In sowing and retailing questions they make the world fructify and increase in uncertainties and disputes, as the earth is made fertile by being crumbled and dug deep.

> *Difficultatem faci tdoctrina.*

[Learning (Doctrine) begets difficulty.
—Quintilian, *Institutio Oratio*, x. 3.]

We doubted of Ulpian, and are still now more perplexed with Bartolus and Baldus. We should efface the trace of this innumerable diversity of opinions; not adorn ourselves with it, and fill posterity with crotchets. I know not what to say to it; but experience makes it manifest, that so many interpretations dissipate truth and break it. Aristotle wrote to be understood; if he could not do this, much less will another that is not so good at it; and a third than he, who expressed his own thoughts. We open the matter, and spill it in pouring out: of one subject we make a thousand, and in multiplying and subdividing them, fall again into the infinity of atoms of Epicurus. Never did two men make the same judgment of the same thing; and it is impossible to find two opinions exactly alike, not only in several men, but in the same man, at diverse hours. I often find matter of doubt in things of which the commentary has disdained to take notice; I am most apt to stumble in an even country, like some horses that I have known, that make most trips in the smoothest way.

Who will not say that glosses augment doubts and ignorance, since there's no book to be found, either human or divine, which the world busies itself about, whereof the difficulties are cleared by interpretation. The hundredth commentator passes it on to the next, still more knotty and perplexed than he found it. When were we ever agreed amongst ourselves: "This book has enough; there is now no more to be said about it"? This is most apparent in the law; we give the authority of law to infinite doctors, infinite decrees, and as many interpretations; yet do we find any end of the need of interpretating? is there, for all that, any progress or advancement towards peace, or do we stand in need of any fewer advocates and judges than when this great mass of law was yet in its first infancy? On the contrary, we darken and bury intelligence; we can no longer discover it, but at the mercy of so many fences and barriers. Men do not know the natural disease of the mind; it does nothing but ferret and inquire, and is eternally wheeling, juggling, and perplexing itself like silkworms, and then suffocates itself in its work; "Mus in pice." ["A mouse in a pitch barrel."] It thinks it discovers at a great distance, I know not what glimpses of light and imaginary truth: but whilst running to it, so many difficulties, hindrances, and new inquisitions cross it, that it loses its way, and is made drunk with the motion: not much unlike Aesop's dogs, that seeing something like a dead body floating in the sea, and not being able to approach it, set to work to drink the water and lay the passage dry, and so choked themselves. To which what one Crates' said of the writings of Heraclitus falls pat enough, "that they required a reader who could swim well," so that the depth and weight of his learning might not overwhelm and stifle him. It is nothing but particular weakness that makes us content with what others or ourselves have found out in this chase after knowledge: one of better understanding will not rest so content; there is always room for one to follow, nay, even for ourselves; and another road; there is no end of our inquisitions; our end is in the other world. It is a sign either that the mind has grown shortsighted when it is satisfied, or that it has got weary. No generous mind can stop in itself; it will still tend further and beyond its power; it has sallies beyond its effects; if it do not advance and press forward, and retire, and rush and wheel about, it is but half alive; its pursuits are without bound or method; its aliment is admiration, the chase, ambiguity, which Apollo sufficiently declared in always speaking to us in a double, obscure, and oblique sense: not feeding, but amusing and puzzling us. It is an irregular and perpetual motion, without model and without aim; its inventions heat, pursue, and interproduce one another:

Estienne de la Boetie:

> *So in a running stream one wave we see*
> *After another roll incessantly,*
> *And as they glide, each does successively*
> *Pursue the other, each the other fly*
> *By this that's evermore pushed on, and this*
> *By that continually preceded is:*
> *The water still does into water swill,*
> *Still the same brook, but different water still.*

There is more ado to interpret interpretations than to interpret things, and more books upon books than upon any other subject; we do nothing but comment upon one another. Every place swarms with commentaries; of authors there is great scarcity. Is it not the principal and most reputed knowledge of our later ages to understand the learned? Is it not the common and final end of all studies? Our opinions are grafted upon one another; the first serves as a stock to the second, the second to the third, and so forth; thus step

Chapter 13

by step we climb the ladder; whence it comes to pass that he who is mounted highest has often more honour than merit, for he is got up but an inch upon the shoulders of the last, but one.

How often, and, peradventure, how foolishly, have I extended my book to make it speak of itself; foolishly, if for no other reason but this, that it should remind me of what I say of others who do the same: that the frequent amorous glances they cast upon their work witness that their hearts pant with self-love, and that even the disdainful severity wherewith they scourge them are but the dandlings and caressings of maternal love; as Aristotle, whose valuing and undervaluing himself often spring from the same air of arrogance. My own excuse is, that I ought in this to have more liberty than others, forasmuch as I write specifically of myself and of my writings, as I do of my other actions; that my theme turns upon itself; but I know not whether others will accept this excuse.

I observed in Germany that Luther has left as many divisions and disputes about the doubt of his opinions, and more, than he himself raised upon the Holy Scriptures. Our contest is verbal: I ask what nature is, what pleasure, circle, and substitution are? the question is about words, and is answered accordingly. A stone is a body; but if a man should further urge: "And what is a body?" – "Substance"; "And what is substance?" and so on, he would drive the respondent to the end of his Calepin. [Calepin (Ambrogio da Calepio), a famous lexicographer of the fifteenth century. His Polyglot Dictionary became so famous, that Calepin became a common appellation for a lexicon.]

We exchange one word for another, and often for one less understood. I better know what man is than I know what Animal is, or Mortal, or Rational. To satisfy one doubt, they give me three; it is the Hydra's head. Socrates asked Menon, "What virtue was." "There is," says Menon, "the virtue of a man and of a woman, of a magistrate and of a private person, of an old man and of a child." "Very fine," cried Socrates, "we were in quest of one virtue, and thou hast brought us a whole swarm." We put one question, and they return us a whole hive. As no event, no face, entirely resembles another, so do they not entirely differ: an ingenious mixture of nature. If our faces were not alike, we could not distinguish man from beast; if they were not unlike, we could not distinguish one man from another; all things hold by some similitude; every example halts, and the relation which is drawn from experience is always faulty and imperfect. Comparisons are ever-coupled at one end or other: so do the laws serve, and are fitted to everyone of our affairs, by some wrested, biased, and forced interpretation.

Since the ethic laws, that concern the particular duty of everyone in himself, are so hard to be framed, as we see they are, it is no wonder if those which govern so many particulars are much more so. Do but consider the form of this justice that governs us; it is a true testimony of human weakness, so full is it of error and contradiction. What we find to be favour and severity in justice – and we find so much of them both, that I know not whether the medium is a—s often met with are sickly and unjust members of the very body and essence of justice. Some country people have just brought me news in great haste, that they presently left in a forest of mine a man with a hundred wounds upon him, who was yet breathing, and begged of them water for pity's sake, and help to carry him to some place of relief; they tell me they durst not go near him, but have run away, lest the officers of justice should catch them there; and as happens to those who are found near a murdered person, they should be called in question about this accident, to their utter ruin, having neither money nor friends to defend their innocence. What could I have said to these people? It is certain that this office of humanity would have brought them into trouble.

How many innocent people have we known that have been punished, and this without the judge's fault; and how many that have not arrived at our knowledge? This happened in my time: certain men were condemned to die for a murder committed; their sentence, if not pronounced, at least determined and concluded on. The judges, just in the nick, are informed by the officers of an inferior court hard

Chapter 13

by, that they have some men in custody, who have directly confessed the murder, and made an indubitable discovery of all the particulars of the fact. Yet it was gravely deliberated whether or not they ought to suspend the execution of the sentence already passed upon the first accused: they considered the novelty of the example judicially, and the consequence of reversing judgments; that the sentence was passed, and the judges deprived of repentance; and in the result, these poor devils were sacrificed by the forms of justice. Philip, or some other, provided against a like inconvenience after this manner. He had condemned a man in a great fine towards another by an absolute judgment. The truth some time after being discovered, he found that he had passed an unjust sentence. On one side was the reason of the cause; on the other side, the reason of the judicial forms: he in some sort satisfied both, leaving the sentence in the state it was, and out of his own purse recompensing the condemned party. But he had to do with a reparable affair; my men were irreparably hanged. How many condemnations have I seen more criminal than the crimes themselves?

All which makes me remember the ancient opinions, "That it is of necessity a man must do wrong by retail who will do right in gross; and injustice in little things, who would come to do justice in great: that human justice is formed after the model of physic, according to which, all that is useful is also just and honest: and of what is held by the Stoics, that Nature herself proceeds contrary to justice in most of her works: and of what is received by the Cyrenaics, that there is nothing just of itself, but that customs and laws make justice: and what the Theodorians held that theft, sacrilege, and all sorts of uncleanness, are just in a sage, if he knows them to be profitable to him." There is no remedy: I am in the same case that Alcibiades was, that I will never, if I can help it, put myself into the hands of a man who may determine as to my head, where my life and honour shall more depend upon the skill and diligence of my attorney than on my own innocence. I would venture myself with such justice as would take notice of my good deeds, as well as my ill; where I had as much to hope as to fear: indemnity is not sufficient pay to a man who does better than not to do amiss. Our justice presents to us but one hand, and that the left hand, too; let him be who he may, he shall be sure to come off with loss.

In China, of which kingdom the government and arts, without commerce with or knowledge of ours, surpass our examples in several excellent features, and of which the history teaches me how much greater and more various the world is than either the ancients or we have been able to penetrate, the officers deputed by the prince to visit the state of his provinces, as they punish those who behave themselves ill in their charge, so do they liberally reward those who have conducted themselves better than the common sort, and beyond the necessity of their duty; these there present themselves, not only to be approved but to get; not simply to be paid, but to have a present made to them.

No judge, thank God, has ever yet spoken to me in the quality of a judge, upon any account whatever, whether my own or that of a third party, whether criminal or civil; nor no prison has ever received me, not even to walk there. Imagination renders the very outside of a jail displeasing to me; I am so enamoured of liberty, that should I be interdicted the access to some corner of the Indies, I should live a little less at my ease; and whilst I can find earth or air open elsewhere, I shall never lurk in any place where I must hide myself. My God! how ill should I endure the condition wherein I see so many people, nailed to a corner of the kingdom, deprived of the right to enter the principal cities and courts, and the liberty of the public roads, for having quarrelled with our laws. If those under which I live should shake a finger at me by way of menace, I would immediately go seek out others, let them be where they would. All my little prudence in the civil wars wherein we are now engaged is employed that they may not hinder my liberty of going and coming.

Now, the laws keep up their credit, not for being just, but because they are laws; it is the mystic foundation of their authority; they have no other, and it well answers their purpose. They are often made by fools, still oftener by men who, out of hatred to equality, fail in equity, but always by men, vain and irresolute authors. There is nothing so much, nor so grossly, nor so ordinarily faulty, as the laws. Whoever obeys them because they are just, does not justly obey them as he ought. Our French laws, by their irregularity and deformity, lend, in some sort, a helping hand to the disorder and corruption that all manifest in their dispensation and execution: the command is so perplexed and inconstant, that it in some sort excuses alike disobedience and defect in the interpretation, the administration and the observation of it. What fruit then soever we may extract from experience, that will little advantage our institution, which we draw from foreign examples, if we make so little profit of that we have of our own, which is more familiar to us, and, doubtless, sufficient to instruct us in that whereof we have need. I study myself more than any other subject; it is my metaphysic, my physic:

> *Quis deu shanc mundi temperet art edomum:*
> *Qua venit exoriens, qua deficit: unde coactis*
> *Cornibus in plenum menstrua lunar edit*
> *Unde salo superant venti, quid flamine captet*
> *Eurus, et in nubes unde perennis aqua;*
> *Sit ventura dies mundi quae subruat arces....*

[What god may govern with skill this dwelling of the world? whence rises the monthly moon, whither wanes she? how is it that her horns are contracted and reopen? whence do winds prevail on the main? what does the east wind court with its blasts? and whence are the clouds perpetually supplied with water? is a day to come which may undermine the world?

—Propertius, iii. 5, 26.]

Quaerite, quos agitat mundi labor.

[Ask whom the cares of the world trouble

—Lucan, i. 417.]

In this universality, I suffer myself to be ignorantly and negligently led by the general law of the world: I shall know it well enough when I feel it; my learning cannot make it alter its course; it will not change itself for me; it is folly to hope it, and a greater folly to concern one's self about it, seeing it is necessarily alike public and common. The goodness and capacity of the governor ought absolutely to discharge us of all care of the government: philosophical inquisitions and contemplations serve for no other use but to increase our curiosity. The philosophers; with great reason, send us back to the rules of nature; but they have nothing to do with so sublime a knowledge; they falsify them, and present us her face painted with too high and too adulterate a complexion, whence spring so many different pictures of so uniform a subject. As she has given us feet to walk with, so has she given us prudence to guide us in life: not so ingenious, robust, and pompous a prudence as that of their invention; but yet one that is easy, quiet, and salutary, and that very well performs what the other promises, in him who has the good luck to know how to employ it sincerely and regularly, that is to say, according to nature. The most simply to commit one's self to nature is to do it most wisely. Oh, what a soft, easy, and wholesome pillow is ignorance and incuriosity, whereon to repose a well-ordered head!

I had rather understand myself well in myself, than in Cicero. Of the experience I have of myself, I find enough to make me wise, if I were but a good scholar: whoever will call to mind the excess of his past anger, and to what a degree that fever transported him, will see the deformity of this passion better than in Aristotle, and conceive a more just hatred against it; whoever will remember the ills he has undergone, those that have threatened him, and the light occasions that have removed him from one state to another, will by that prepare himself for future changes, and the knowledge of his condition. The life of Caesar has no greater example for us than our own: though popular and of command, it is still a life subject to all human accidents. Let us but listen to it; we apply to ourselves all whereof we have principal need; whoever shall call to memory how many and many times he has been mistaken in his own judgment, is he not a great fool if he does not ever after suspect it? When I find myself convinced, by the reason of another, of a false opinion, I do not so much learn what he has said to me that is new and the particular ignorance – that would be no great acquisition – as, in general, I learn my own debility and the treachery of my understanding, whence I extract the reformation of the whole mass. In all my other errors I do the same, and find from this rule great utility to life; I regard not the species and individual as a stone that I have stumbled at; I learn to suspect my steps throughout, and am careful to place them right. To learn that a man has said or done a foolish thing is nothing: a man must learn that he is nothing but a fool, a much more ample, and important instruction. The false steps that my memory has so often made, even then when it was most secure and confident of itself, are not idly thrown away; it vainly swears and assures me I shake my ears; the first opposition that is made to its testimony puts me into suspense, and I durst not rely upon it in anything of moment, nor warrant it in another person's concerns: and were it not that what I do for want of memory, others do more often for want of good faith, I should always, in matter of fact, rather choose to take the truth from another's mouth than from my own. If everyone would pry into the effects and circumstances of the passions that sway him, as I have done into those which I am most subject to, he would see them coming, and would a little break their impetuosity and career; they do not always seize us on a sudden; there is threatening and degrees

Fluctus uti primo coepit cum albescere vento,
Paulatim sese tollit mare, et altius undas

Erigit, inde imo consurgit ad aether afundo.

[As with the first wind the sea begins to foam, and swells, thence higher swells, and higher raises the waves, till the ocean rises from its depths to the sky.

—*Aeneid,* vii. 528.]

Judgment holds in me a magisterial seat; at least it carefully endeavours to make it so: it leaves my appetites to take their own course, hatred and friendship, nay, even that I bear to myself, without change or corruption; if it cannot reform the other parts according to its own model, at least it suffers not itself to be corrupted by them, but plays its game apart.

The advice to everyone, "to know themselves," should be of important effect, since that god of wisdom and light' caused it to be written on the front of his temple, [At Delphi] as comprehending all he had to advise us. Plato says also, that prudence is no other thing than the execution of this ordinance; and Socrates minutely verifies it in Xenophon. The difficulties and obscurity are not discerned in any science but by those who are got into it; for a certain degree of intelligence is required to be able to know that a man knows not, and we must push against a door to know whether it be bolted against us or no: whence this Platonic subtlety springs, that "neither they who know are to enquire, forasmuch as they know; nor they who do not know, forasmuch as to inquire they must know what they inquire of." So in this, "of knowing a man's self," that every man is seen so resolved and satisfied with himself, that every man thinks himself sufficiently intelligent, signifies that everyone knows nothing about the matter; as Socrates gives Euthydemus to understand. I, who profess nothing else, therein find so infinite a depth and variety, that all the fruit I have reaped from my learning serves only to make me sensible how much I have to learn. To my weakness, so often confessed, I owe the propension I have to modesty, to the obedience of belief prescribed me, to a constant coldness and moderation of opinions, and a hatred of that troublesome and wrangling arrogance, wholly believing and trusting in itself, the capital enemy of discipline and truth. Do but hear them domineer; the first fopperies they utter, it is in the style wherewith men establish religions and laws:

Nihil est turpius, quam cognitioni et perceptions
assertionem approbationemque praecurrere.

[Nothing is worse than that assertion and decision should precede knowledge and perception.

—Cicero, *Academica*, i. 13.]

Aristarchus said that anciently there were scarce seven sages to be found in the world, and in his time scarce so many fools: have not we more reason than he to say so in this age of ours? Affirmation and obstinacy are express signs of want of wit. This fellow may have knocked his nose against the ground a hundred times in a day, yet he will be at his Ergo's as resolute and sturdy as before. You would say he had had some new soul and vigour of understanding infused into him since, and that it happened to him, as to that ancient son of the earth, who took fresh courage and vigour by his fall;

Cui cum tetigere parentem,
jam defecta vigent renovate robore membra:

[Whose broken limbs, when they touched his mother earth, immediately new force acquired.

—Lucan, iv. 599.]

does not this incorrigible coxcomb think that he assumes a new understanding by undertaking a new dispute? It is by my own experience that I accuse human ignorance, which is, in my opinion, the surest part of the world's school. Such as will not conclude it in themselves, by so vain an example as mine, or their own, let them believe it from Socrates, the master of masters; for the philosopher Antisthenes said to his disciples, "Let us go and hear Socrates; there I will be a pupil with you"; and, maintaining this doctrine of the Stoic sect, "that virtue was sufficient to make a life completely happy, having no need of any other thing whatever"; except of the force of Socrates, added he.

That long attention that I employ in considering myself, also fits rile to judge tolerably enough of others; and there are few things whereof I speak better and with better excuse. I happen very often more exactly to see and distinguish the qualities of my friends than they do themselves: I have astonished some with the pertinence of my description, and have given them warning of themselves. By having from my infancy been accustomed to contemplate my own life in those of others, I have acquired a complexion studious in that particular; and when I am once interit upon it, I let few things about me, whether countenances, humours, or discourses, that serve to that purpose, escape me. I study all, both what I am to avoid and what I am to follow. Also in my friends, I discover by their productions their inward inclinations; not by arranging this infinite variety of so diverse and unconnected actions into certain species and chapters, and distinctly distributing my parcels and divisions under known heads and classes;

> *Sed neque quam multae species, nec nomina quae sint,*
> *Est numerus.*

[But neither can we enumerate how many kinds there what are their names.

—Virgil, *Georgics*, ii. 103.]

The wise speak and deliver their fancies more specifically, and piece by piece; I, who see no further into things than as use informs me, present mine generally without rule and experimentally:

CHAPTER 13

I pronounce my opinion by disjointed articles, as a thing that cannot be spoken at once and in gross; relation and conformity are not to be found in such low and common souls as ours. Wisdom is a solid and entire building, of which every piece keeps its place and bears its mark:

Sola sapientia in se tota conversa est.

[Wisdom only is wholly within itself.
—Cicero, *De Finibus*, iii. 7.]

I leave it to artists, and I know not whether or not they will be able to bring it about, in so perplexed, minute, and fortuitous a thing, to marshal into distinct bodies this infinite diversity of faces, to settle our inconstancy, and set it in order. I do not only find it hard to piece our actions to one another, but I moreover find it hard properly to design each by itself by any principal quality, so ambiguous and variform they are with diverse lights. That which is remarked for rare in Perseus, king of Macedon, "that his mind, fixing itself to no one condition, wandered in all sorts of living, and represented manners so wild and erratic that it was neither known to himself or any other what kind of man he was," seems almost to fit all the world; and, especially, I have seen another of his make, to whom I think this conclusion might more properly be applied; no moderate settledness, still running headlong from one extreme to another, upon occasions not to be guessed at; no line of path without traverse and wonderful contrariety: no one quality simple and unmixed; so that the best guess men can one day make will be, that he affected and studied to make himself known by being not to be known. A man had need have sound ears to hear himself frankly criticised; and as there are few who can endure to hear it without being nettled, those who hazard the undertaking it to us manifest a singular effect of friendship; for it is to love sincerely indeed, to venture to wound and offend us, for our own good. I think it harsh to judge a man whose ill qualities are more than his good ones: Plato requires three things in him who will examine the soul of another: knowledge, benevolence, boldness.

I was sometimes asked, what I should have thought myself fit for, had any one designed to make use of me, while I was of suitable years:

> *Dum melior vires sanguis dabat, aemula necdum*
> *Temporibus geminis canebat sparsa senectus:*

[Whilst better blood gave me vigour, and before envious old age whitened and thinned my temples.

—*Aeneid*, V. 415.]

"for nothing," said I; and I willingly excuse myself from knowing anything which enslaves me to others. But I had told the truth to my master, and had regulated his manners, if he had so pleased, not in gross, by scholastic lessons, which I understand not, and from which I see no true reformation spring in those that do; but by observing them by leisure, at all opportunities, and simply and naturally judging them as an eye-witness, distinctly one by one; giving him to understand upon what terms he was in the common opinion, in opposition to his flatterers. There is none of us who would not be worse than kings, if so continually corrupted as they are with that sort of canaille. How, if Alexander, that great king and philosopher, cannot defend himself from them!

I should have had fidelity, judgment, and freedom enough for that purpose. It would be a nameless office, otherwise it would lose its grace and its effect; and it is a part that is not indifferently fit for all men; for truth itself has not the privilege to be spoken at all times and indiscriminately; its use, noble as it is, has its circumspections and limits. It often falls out, as the world goes, that a man lets it slip into the ear of a prince, not only to no purpose, but moreover injuriously and unjustly; and no man shall make me believe that a virtuous remonstrance may not be viciously applied, and that the interest of the substance is not often to give way to that of the form.

For such a purpose, I would have a man who is content with his own fortune:

Quod sit, esse velit, nihilque malit,

[Who is pleased with what he is and desires nothing further.
—Martial, x. ii, 18.]

and of moderate station; forasmuch as, on the one hand, he would not be afraid to touch his master's heart to the quick, for fear by that means of losing his preferment: and, on the other hand, being of no high quality, he would have more easy communication with all sorts of people. I would have this office limited to only one person; for to allow the privilege of his liberty and privacy to many, would beget an inconvenient irreverence; and of that one, I would above all things require the fidelity of silence.

A king is not to be believed when he brags of his constancy in standing the shock of the enemy for his glory, if for his profit and amendment he cannot stand the liberty of a friend's advice, which has no other power but to pinch his ear, the remainder of its effect being still in his own hands. Now, there is no condition of men whatever who stand in so great need of true and free advice and warning, as they do: they sustain a public life, and have to satisfy the opinion of so many spectators, that, as those about them conceal from them whatever should divert them from their own way, they insensibly find themselves involved in the hatred and detestation of their people, often upon occasions which they might have avoided without any prejudice even of their pleasures themselves, had they been advised and set right in time. Their favourites commonly have more regard to themselves than to their master; and indeed it answers with them, forasmuch as, in truth, most offices of real friendship, when applied

559

to the sovereign, are under a rude and dangerous hazard, so that therein there is great need, not only of very great affection and freedom, but of courage too.

In fine, all this hodge-podge which I scribble here, is nothing but a register of the essays of my own life, which, for the internal soundness, is exemplary enough to take instruction against the grain; but as to bodily health, no man can furnish out more profitable experience than I, who present it pure, and no way corrupted and changed by art or opinion. Experience is properly upon its own dunghill in the subject of physic, where reason wholly gives it place: Tiberius said that whoever had lived twenty years ought to be responsible to himself for all things that were hurtful or wholesome to him, and know how to order himself without physic; and he might have learned it of Socrates, who, advising his disciples to be solicitous of their health as a chief study, added that it was hard if a man of sense, having a care to his exercise and diet, did not better know than any physician what was good or ill for him. And physic itself professes always to have experience for the test of its operations: so Plato had reason to say that, to be a right physician, it would be necessary that he who would become such, should first himself have passed through all the diseases he pretends to cure, and through all the accidents and circumstances whereof he is to judge. It is but reason they should get the pox, if they will know how to cure it; for my part, I should put myself into such hands; the others but guide us, like him who paints seas and rocks and ports sitting at table, and there makes the model of a ship sailing in all security; but put him to the work itself, he knows not at which end to begin. They make such a description of our maladies as a town crier does of a lost horse or dog – such a color, such a height, such an ear – but bring it to him and he knows it not, for all that. If physic should one day give me some good and visible relief, then truly I will cry out in good earnest:

Tandem effcaci do manus scientiae.

Chapter 13

[Show me an efficacious science, and I will take it by the hand.
—Horace, xvii. I.]

The arts that promise to keep our bodies and souls in health promise a great deal; but, withal, there are none that less keep their promise. And, in our time, those who make profession of these arts amongst us, less manifest the effects than any other sort of men; one may say of them, at the most, that they sell medicinal drugs; but that they are physicians, a man cannot say.

I have lived long enough to be able to give an account of the custom that has carried me so far; for him who has a mind to try it, as his taster, I have made the experiment. Here are some of the articles, as my memory shall supply me with them; I have no custom that has not varied according to circumstances; but I only record those that I have been best acquainted with, and that hitherto have had the greatest possession of me.

My form of life is the same in sickness as in health; the same bed, the same hours, the same meat, and even the same drink, serve me in both conditions alike; I add nothing to them but the moderation of more or less, according to my strength and appetite. My health is to maintain my wonted state without disturbance. I see that sickness puts me off it on one side, and if I will be ruled by the physicians, they will put me off on the other; so that by fortune and by art I am out of my way. I believe nothing more certainly than this, that I cannot be hurt by the use of things to which I have been so long accustomed. It is for custom to give a form to a man's life, such as it pleases him; she is all in all in that: it is the potion of Circe, that varies our nature as she best pleases. How many nations, and but three steps from us, think the fear of the night-dew, that so manifestly is hurtful to us, a ridiculous fancy; and our own watermen and peasants laugh at it. You make a German sick if you lay him upon a mattress, as you do an Italian if you lay him on a feather-bed, and a Frenchman, if without curtains or fire. A Spanish stomach cannot hold out to eat as we can, nor ours to drink like the Swiss. A German made me very merry at Augsburg, by finding fault with our hearths, by the same arguments which we commonly make use of in decrying their stoves: for, to say the truth, the smothered heat, and then the smell of that heated matter of which the fire is composed, very much offend such as are not used to them; not me; and, indeed, the heat being always equal, constant, and universal, without flame, without smoke, and without the wind that comes down our chimneys, they may many ways sustain comparison with ours. Why do we not imitate the Roman architecture? For they say that anciently fires were not made in the houses, but on the outside, and at the foot of them, whence the heat was conveyed to the whole fabric by pipes contrived in the wall, which were drawn twining about the rooms that were to be warmed: which I have seen plainly described somewhere in Seneca. This German hearing me commend the conveniences and beauties of his city, which truly deserves it, began to compassionate me that I had to leave it; and the first inconvenience he alleged to me was, the heaviness of head that the chimneys elsewhere would bring upon me. He had heard someone make this complaint, and fixed it upon us, being by custom deprived of the means of perceiving it at home. All heat that comes from the fire weakens and dulls me. Evenus said that fire was the best condiment of life: I rather choose any other way of making myself warm.

We are afraid to drink our wines, when toward the bottom of the cask; in Portugal those fumes are reputed delicious, and it is the beverage of princes. In short, every nation has many customs and usages that are not only unknown to other nations, but savage and miraculous in their sight. What should we do with those people who admit of no evidence that is not in print, who believe not men if they are not in a book, nor truth if it be not of competent age? We dignify our fopperies when we commit them to the press: it is of a great deal more weight to say, "I have read such a thing," than if you only say, "I have heard such a thing." But I, who no more disbelieve a man's mouth than his pen, and who know that men write as indiscreetly as

Chapter 13

they speak, and who look upon this age as one that is past, as soon quote a friend as Aulus Gelliusor Macrobius; and what I have seen, as what they have written. And, as it is held of virtue, that it is not greater for having continued longer, so do I hold of truth, that for being older it is none the wiser. I often say, that it is mere folly that makes us run after foreign and scholastic examples; their fertility is the same now that it was in the time of Homer and Plato. But is it not that we seek more honour from the quotation, than from the truth of the matter in hand? As if it were more to the purpose to borrow our proofs from the shops of Vascosan or Plantin, than from what is to be seen in our own village; or else, indeed, that we have not the wit to cull out and make useful what we see before us, and to judge of it clearly enough to draw it into example: for if we say that we want authority to give faith to our testimony, we speak from the purpose; forasmuch as, in my opinion, of the most ordinary, common, and known things, could we but find out their light, the greatest miracles of nature might be formed, and the most wonderful examples, especially upon the subject of human actions.

Now, upon this subject, setting aside the examples I have gathered from books, and what Aristotle says of Andron the Argian, that he travelled over the arid sands of Lybia without drinking: a gentleman, who has very well behaved himself in several employments, said, in a place where I was, that he had ridden from Madrid to Lisbon, in the heat of summer, without any drink at all. He is very healthful and vigorous for his age, and has nothing extraordinary in the use of his life, but this, to live sometimes two or three months, nay, a whole year, as he has told me, without drinking. He is sometimes thirsty, but he lets it pass over, and he holds that it is an appetite which easily goes off of itself; and he drinks more out of caprice than either for need or pleasure.

Here is another example: it is not long ago that I found one of the most learned men in France, among those of not inconsiderable fortune, studying in a corner of a hall that they had separated for him with tapestry, and about him a rabble of his servants full of licence. He told me, and Seneca almost says the same of himself, he made an advantage of this hubbub; that, beaten with this noise, he so much the more collected and retired himself into himself for contemplation, and that this tempest of voices drove back his thoughts within himself. Being a student at Padua, he had his study so long situated amid the rattle of coaches and the tumult of the square, that he not only formed himself to the contempt, but even to the use of noise, for the service of his studies. Socrates answered Alcibiades, who was astonished how he could endure the perpetual scolding of his wife, "Why," said he, "as those do who are accustomed to the ordinary noise of wheels drawing water." I am quite otherwise; I have a tender head and easily discomposed; when it is bent upon anything, the least buzzing of a fly murders it.

Seneca in his youth having warmly espoused the example of Sextius, of eating nothing that had died, for a whole year dispensed with such food, and, as he said, with pleasure, and discontinued it that he might not be suspected of taking up this rule from some new religion by which it was prescribed: he adopted, in like manner, from the precepts of Attalus a custom not to lie upon any sort of bedding that gave way under his weight, and, even to his old age, made use of such as would not yield to any pressure. What the usage of his time made him account roughness, that of ours makes us look upon as effeminacy.

Do but observe the difference between the way of living of my labourers and my own; the Scythians and Indians have nothing more remote both from my capacity and my form. I have picked up charity boys to serve me: who soon after have quitted both my kitchen and livery, only that they might return to their former course of life; and I found one afterwards, picking mussels out of the sewer for his dinner, whom I could neither by entreaties nor threats reclaim from the sweetness he found in indigence. Beggars have their magnificences and delights, as well as the rich, and, it is said, their dignities and polities. These are the effects of custom;

she can mould us, not only into what form she pleases (the sages say we ought to apply ourselves to the best, which she will soon make easy to us), but also to change and variation, which is the most noble and most useful instruction of all she teaches us. The best of my bodily conditions is that I am flexible and not very obstinate: I have inclinations more my own and ordinary, and more agreeable than others; but I am diverted from them with very little ado, and easily slip into a contrary course. A young man ought to cross his own rules, to awaken his vigour and to keep it from growing faint and rusty; and there is no course of life so weak and sottish as that which is carried on by rule and discipline;

> *Ad primum lapidem vectari quum placet, hora*
> *Sumitur ex libro; si prurit frictus ocelli*
> *Angulus, inspecta genesi, collyria quaerit;*

[When he is pleased to have himself carried to the first milestone, the hour is chosen from the almanac; if he but rub the corner of his eye, his horoscope having been examined, he seeks the aid of salves.

—Juvenal, vi. 576.]

he shall often throw himself even into excesses, if he will take my advice; otherwise the least debauch will destroy him, and render him troublesome and disagreeable in company. The worst quality in a well-bred man is over-fastidiousness, and an obligation to a certain particular way; and it is particular, if not pliable and supple. It is a kind of reproach, not to be able, or not to dare, to do what we see those about us do; let such as these stop at home. It is in every man unbecoming, but in a soldier vicious and intolerable: who, as Philopcemen said, ought to accustom himself to every variety and inequality of life.

Though I have been brought up, as much as was possible, to liberty and independence, yet so it is that, growing old, and having by indifference more settled upon certain forms (my age is now past instruction, and has henceforward nothing to do but to keep itself up as well as it can), custom has already, ere I was aware, so imprinted its character in me in certain things, that I look upon it as a kind of excess to leave them off; and, without a force upon myself, cannot sleep in the daytime, nor eat between meals, nor breakfast, nor go to bed, without a great interval between eating and sleeping,as of three hours after supper; nor get children but before I sleep, nor get them standing; nor endure my own sweat; nor quench my thirst either with pure water or pure wine; nor keep my head long bare, nor cut my hair after dinner; and I should be as uneasy without my gloves as without my shirt, or without washing when I rise from table or out of my bed; and I could not lie without a canopy and curtains, as if they were essential things. I could dine without a tablecloth, but without a clean napkin, after the German fashion, very incommodiously; I foul them more than the Germans or Italians do, and make but little use either of spoon or fork. I complain that they did not keep up the fashion, begun after the example of kings, to change our napkin at every service, as they do our plate. We are told of that laborious soldier Marius that, growing old, he became nice in his drink, and never drank but out of a particular cup of his own I, in like manner, have suffered myself to fancy a certain form of glasses, and not willingly to drink in common glasses, no more than from a strange common hand: all metal offends me in comparison of a clear and transparent matter: let my eyes taste, too, according to their capacity. I owe several other such niceties to custom. Nature has also, on the other side, helped me to some of hers: as not to be able to endure more than two full meals in one day, without overcharging my stomach, nor a total abstinence from one of those meals without filling myself with wind, drying up my mouth, and dulling my appetite; the finding great inconvenience from overmuch evening air; for of late years, in night marches, which often happen to be all night long, after five or six hours my stomach begins to be queasy, with a violent pain in my head, so that I always vomit before the day can break. When the others go to breakfast, I go to sleep; and when I rise, I am as brisk and gay as before. I had always been told that the night dew never rises but in the beginning of the night; but for some years past, long and familiar intercourse with a lord, possessed with the opinion that the night dew is more sharp and dangerous about the declining of the sun, an hour or two before it sets, which he carefully avoids, and despises that of the night, he almost impressed upon me, not so much his reasoning as his experiences. What, shall mere doubt and inquiry strike our imagination, so as to change us? Such as absolutely and on a sudden give way to these propensions, draw total destruction upon themselves. I am sorry for several gentlemen who, through the folly of their physicians, have in their youth and health wholly shut themselves up: it were better to endure a cough, than, by disuse, for ever to lose the commerce of common life in things of so great utility. Malignant science, to interdict us the most pleasant hours of the day! Let us keep our possession to the last; for the most part, a man hardens himself by being obstinate, and corrects his constitution, as Caesar did the falling sickness, by dint of contempt. A man should addict himself to the best rules, but not enslave himself to them, except to such, if there be any such, where obligation and servitude are of profit.

Both kings and philosophers go to stool, and ladies too; public lives are bound to ceremony; mine, that is obscure and private, enjoys all natural dispensation; soldier and Gascon are also qualities a little subject to indiscretion; wherefore I shall say of this act of relieving nature, that it is desirable to refer it to certain prescribed and nocturnal hours, and compel one's self to this by custom, as I have done; but not to subject one's self, as I have done in my declining years, to a particular convenience of place and seat for that purpose, and make it troublesome by long sitting; and yet, in the fouler offices, is it not in some measure excusable to require more care and cleanliness?

> *Naturt homo mundum et elegans animal est.*

[Man is by nature a clean and delicate creature.
> —Seneca, *Epistles*, 92.]

Of all the actions of nature, I am the most impatient of being interrupted in that. I have seen many soldiers troubled with the unruliness of their bellies; whereas mine and I never fail of our punctual assignation, which is at leaping out of bed, if some indispensable business or sickness does not molest us.

I think then, as I said before, that sick men cannot better place themselves anywhere in more safety, than in sitting still in that course of life wherein they have been bred and trained up; change, be it what it will, distempers and puts one out. Do you believe that chestnuts can hurt a Perigordin or a Lucchese, or milk and cheese the mountain people? We enjoin them not only a new, but a contrary, method of life; a change that the healthful cannot endure. Prescribe water to a Breton of threescore and ten; shut a seaman up in a stove; forbid a Basque footman to walk: you will deprive them of motion, and in the end of air and light:

> *An vivere tanti est?*
> *Cogimur a suetis animum suspendere rebus,*
> *Atque, ut vivamus, vivere desinimus.*
> *Hos superesse reor, quibus et spirabilis aer*
> *Et lux, qua regimur, redditur ipsa gravis.*

[Is life worth so much? We are compelled to withhold the mind from things to which we are accustomed; and, that we may live, we cease to live... Do I conceive that they still live, to whom the

Chapter 13

respirable air, and the light itself, by which we are governed, is
rendered oppressive?

—Pseudo-Gallus, *Eclogues*, i. 155, 247.]

If they do no other good, they do this at least, that they prepare
patients betimes for death, by little and little undermining and cutting off the use of life.

Both well and sick, I have ever willingly suffered myself to obey
the appetites that pressed upon me. I give great rein to my desires
and propensities; I do not love to cure one disease by another; I hate
remedies that are more troublesome than the disease itself. To be
subject to the colic and subject to abstain from eating oysters are two
evils instead of one; the disease torments us on the one side, and the
remedy on the other. Since we are ever in danger of mistaking, let us
rather run the hazard of a mistake, after we have had the pleasure.
The world proceeds quite the other way, and thinks nothing profitable that is not painful; it has great suspicion of facility. My appetite,
in various things, has of its own accord happily enough accommodated itself to the health of my stomach. Relish and pungency in
sauces were pleasant to me when young; my stomach disliking them
since, my taste incontinently followed. Wine is hurtful to sick people,
and it is the first thing that my mouth then finds distasteful, and
with an invincible dislike. Whatever I take against my liking does me
harm; and nothing hurts me that I eat with appetite and delight. I
never received harm by any action that was very pleasant to me; and
accordingly have made all medicinal conclusions largely give way to
my pleasure; and I have, when I was young,

Quem circumcursans huc atque huc saepe Cupido
Fulgebat crocink splendidus in tunic.

[When Cupid, fluttering round me here and there, shone in
his rich purple mantle.

—Catullus, lxvi. 133.]

given myself the rein as licentiously and inconsiderately to the desire that was predominant in me, as any other whomsoever:

> *Et militavi non sine gloria;*

[And I have played the soldier not ingloriously.
> —Horace, *Odes*, iii. 26, 2.]

yet more in continuation and holding out, than in sally:

> *Sex me vix memini sustinuisse vices.*

[I can scarcely remember six bouts in one night
> —Ovid, *Amores*, iii. 7, 26.]

It is certainly a misfortune and a miracle at once to confess at what a tender age I first came under the subjection of love: it was, indeed, by chance; for it was long before the years of choice or knowledge; I do not remember myself so far back; and my fortune may well be coupled with that of Quartilla, who could not remember when she was a maid:

> *Inde tragus, celeresque pili, mirandaque matri*
> *Barba meae.*

[The odour of the arm-pits, the precocious hair, and the beard which astonished my mother.
> —Martial, xi. 22, 7.]

Physicians modify their rules according to the violent longings that happen to sick persons, ordinarily with good success; this great desire cannot be imagined so strange and vicious, but that nature must have a hand in it. And then how easy a thing is it to satisfy the fancy? In my opinion; this part wholly carries it, at least, above all the rest. The most grievous and ordinary evils are those that fancy loads us with; this Spanish saying pleases me in several aspects:

Defenda me Dios de me.

[God defend me from myself.]

I am sorry when I am sick, that I have not some longing that might give me the pleasure of satisfying it; all the rules of physic would hardly be able to divert me from it. I do the same when I am well; I can see very little more to be hoped or wished for. It were pity a man should be so weak and languishing, as not to have even wishing left to him.

The art of physic is not so fixed, that we need be without authority for whatever we do; it changes according to climates and moons, according to Fernel and to Scaliger. [Physicians to Henry II.] If your physician does not think it good for you to sleep, to drink wine, or to eat such and such meats, never trouble yourself; I will find you another that shall not be of his opinion; the diversity of medical arguments and opinions embraces all sorts and forms. I saw a miserable sick person panting and burning for thirst, that he might be cured, who was afterwards laughed at for his pains by another physician, who condemned that advice as prejudicial to him: had he not tormented himself to good purpose? There lately died of the stone a man of that profession, who had made use of extreme abstinence to contend with his disease: his fellow-physicians say that, on the contrary, this abstinence had dried him up and baked the gravel in his kidneys.

I have observed, that both in wounds and sicknesses, speaking discomposes and hurts me, as much as any irregularity I can commit. My voice pains and tires me, for it is loud and forced; so that when I have gone to a whisper some great persons about affairs of consequence, they have often desired me to moderate my voice.

This story is worth a diversion. Someone in a certain Greek school speaking loud as I do, the master of the ceremonies sent to him to speak softly: "Tell him, then, he must send me," replied the other, "the tone he would have me speak in." To which the other replied, "That he should take the tone from the ears of him to whom he spake." It was well said, if it is to be understood: "Speak according to the affair you are speaking about to your auditor," for if it mean, "it is sufficient that he hear you, or govern yourself by him," I do not find it to be reason. The tone and motion of my voice carries with it a great deal of the expression and signification of my meaning, and it is I who am to govern it, to make myself understood: there is a voice to instruct, a voice to flatter, and a voice to reprehend. I will not only that my voice reach him, but, peradventure, that it strike and pierce him. When I rate my valet with sharp and bitter language, it would be very pretty for him to say; "Pray, master, speak lower; I hear you very well":

> *Est quaedam vox ad auditum accommodata,*
> *non magnitudine, sed proprietate.*

[There is a certain voice accommodated to the hearing, not by its loudness, but by its propriety.

—Quintilian, xi. 3.]

Speaking is half his who speaks, and half his who hears; the latter ought to prepare himself to receive it, according to its bias; as with tennis-players, he who receives the ball, shifts and prepares, according as he sees him move who strikes the stroke, and according to the stroke itself.

Experience has, moreover, taught me this, that we ruin ourselves by impatience. Evils have their life and limits, their diseases and their recovery.

The constitution of maladies is formed by the pattern of the constitution of animals; they have their fortune and their days limited from their birth; he who attempts imperiously to cut them short by force in the middle of their course, lengthens and multiplies them, and incenses instead of appeasing them. I am of Crantor's opinion, that we are neither obstinately and deafly to oppose evils, nor succumb to them from want of courage; but that we are naturally to give way to them, according to their condition and our own. We ought to grant free passage to diseases; I find they stay less with me, who let them alone; and I have lost some, reputed the most tenacious and obstinate, by their own decay, without help and without art, and contrary to its rules. Let us a little permit Nature to take her own way; she better understands her own affairs than we. But such an one died of it; and so shall you: if not of that disease, of another. And how many have not escaped dying, who have had three physicians at their tails? Example is a vague and universal mirror, and of various reflections. If it be a delicious medicine, take it: it is always so much present good. I will never stick at the name nor the colour, if it be pleasant and grateful to the palate: pleasure is one of the chiefest kinds of profit. I have suffered colds, gouty defluxions, relaxations, palpitations of the heart, megrims, and other accidents, to grow old and die in time a natural death. I have so lost them when I was half fit to keep them: they are sooner prevailed upon by courtesy than huffing. We must patiently suffer the laws of our condition; we are born to grow old, to grow weak, and to be sick, in despite of all medicine. It is the first lesson the Mexicans teach their children; so soon as ever they are born they thus salute them: "Thou art come into the world, child, to endure: endure, suffer, and say nothing." It is injustice to lament that which has befallen any one which may befall everyone:

Indignare, si quid in to inique proprio constitutum est.

[Then be angry, when there is anything unjustly decreed against thee alone.

—Seneca, *Epistles*, 91.]

See an old man who begs of God that he will maintain his health vigorous and entire; that is to say, that he restore him to youth:

Stulte, quid haec frustra votis puerilibus optas?

[Fool! why do you vainly form these puerile wishes?
—Ovid, *Tristia*, 111. 8, II.]

is it not folly? his condition is not capable of it. The gout, the stone, and indigestion are symptoms of long years; as heat, rains, and winds are of long journeys. Plato does not believe that Aesculapius troubled himself to provide by regimen to prolong life in a weak and wasted body, useless to his country and to his profession, or to beget healthful and robust children; and does not think this care suitable to the Divine justice and prudence, which is to direct all things to utility. My good friend, your business is done; nobody can restore you; they can, at the most, but patch you up, and prop you a little, and by that means prolong your misery an hour or two:

Non secus instantem cupiens fulcire ruinam,
Diversis contra nititur obiicibus;
Donec certa dies, omni compage soluta,
Ipsum cum rebus subruat auxilium.

[Like one who, desiring to stay an impending ruin, places various props against it, till, in a short time, the house, the props, and all, giving way, fall together.
—Pseudo-Gallus, i. 171.]

We must learn to suffer what we cannot evade; our life, like the harmony of the world, is composed of contrary things – of diverse tones, sweet and harsh, sharp and flat, sprightly and solemn: the musician who should only affect some of these, what would he be able to do? he must know how to make use of them all, and to mix them; and so we should mingle the goods and evils which are consubstantial with our life; our being cannot subsist without this mixture, and the one part is no less necessary to it than the other. To attempt to combat natural necessity, is to represent the folly of Ctesiphon, who undertook to kick with his mule. [Plutarch, How to Restrain Anger, c. 8.]

I consult little about the alterations I feel: for these doctors take advantage; when they have you at their mercy, they surfeit your ears with their prognostics; and formerly surprising me, weakened with sickness, injuriously handled me with their dogmas and magisterial fopperies – one while menacing me with great pains, and another with approaching death. Hereby I was indeed moved and shaken, but not subdued nor jostled from my place; and though my judgment was neither altered nor distracted, yet it was at least disturbed: it is always agitation and combat.

Now, I use my imagination as gently as I can, and would discharge it, if I could, of all trouble and contest; a man must assist, flatter, and deceive it, if he can; my mind is fit for that office; it needs no appearances throughout: could it persuade as it preaches, it would successfully relieve me. Will you have an example? It tells me: "that it is for my good to have the stone: that the structure of my age must naturally suffer some decay, and it is now time it should begin to disjoin and to confess a breach; it is a common necessity, and there is nothing in it either miraculous or new; I therein pay what is due to old age, and I cannot expect a better bargain; that society ought to comfort me, being fallen into the most common infirmity of my age; I see everywhere men tormented with the same disease, and am honoured by the fellowship, forasmuch as men of the best quality are most frequently afflicted with it: it is a noble and dignified disease: that of such as are struck with it, few have it to a less degree of pain; that these are put to the trouble of a strict diet and the daily taking of nauseous potions, whereas I owe my better state purely to my good fortune; for some ordinary broths of eringo or burst-wort that I have twice or thrice taken to oblige the ladies, who, with greater kindness than my pain was sharp, would needs present me half of theirs, seemed to me equally easy to take and fruitless in operation, the others have to pay a thousand vows to Aesculapius, and as many crowns to their physicians, for the voiding a little gravel, which I often do by the aid of nature: even the decorum of my countenance is not disturbed in company; and I can hold my water ten hours, and as long as any man in health. The fear of this disease," says my mind, "formerly affrighted thee, when it was unknown to thee; the cries and despairing groans of those who make it worse by their impatience, begot a horror in thee. It is an infirmity that punishes the members by which thou hast most offended. Thou art a conscientious fellow;"

Quae venit indigne poena, dolenda venit:

[We are entitled to complain of a punishment that we have not deserved.

—Ovid, Heroides., v. 8.]

"consider this chastisement: it is very easy in comparison of others, and inflicted with a paternal tenderness: do but observe how late it comes; it only seizes on and incommodes that part of thy life which is, one way and another, sterile and lost; having, as it were by composition, given time for the licence and pleasures of thy youth. The fear and the compassion that the people have of this disease serve thee for matter of glory; a quality whereof if thou bast thy judgment purified, and that thy reason has somewhat cured it, thy friends notwithstanding, discern some tincture in thy complexion. It is a pleasure to hear it said of oneself what strength of mind, what patience! Thou art seen to sweat with pain, to turn pale and red, to tremble, to vomit blood, to suffer strange contractions and convulsions, at times to let great tears drop from thine eyes, to urine thick, black, and dreadful water, or to have it suppressed by some sharp and craggy stone, that cruelly pricks and tears the neck of the bladder, whilst all the while thou entertainest the company with an ordinary countenance;

576

droning by fits with thy people; making one in a continuous discourse, now and then making excuse for thy pain, and representing thy suffering less than it is. Do thou call to mind the men of past times, who so greedily sought diseases to keep their virtue in breath and exercise? Put the case that nature sets thee on and impels thee to this glorious school, into which thou wouldst never have entered of thy own free will. If thou tellest me that it is a dangerous and mortal disease, what others are not so? for it is a physical cheat to expect any that they say do not go direct to death: what matters if they go thither by accident, or if they easily slide and slip into the path that leads us to it? But thou do not die because thou art sick; thou diest because thou art living: death kills thee without the help of sickness: and sickness has deferred death in some, who have lived longer by reason that they thought themselves always dying; to which may be added, that as in wounds, so in diseases, some are medicinal and wholesome. The stone is often no less long-lived than you; we see men with whom it has continued from their infancy even to their extreme old age; and if they had not broken company, it would have been with them longer still; you more often kill it than it kills you. And though it should present to you the image of approaching death, were it not a good office to a man of such an age, to put him in mind of his end? And, which is worse, thou hast no longer anything that should make thee desire to be cured. Whether or no, common necessity will soon call thee away. Do but consider how skilfully and gently she puts thee out of concern with life, and weans thee from the world; not forcing thee with a tyrannical subjection, like so many other infirmities which thou seest old men afflicted withal, that hold them in continual torment, and keep them in perpetual and unintermitted weakness and pains, but by warnings and instructions at intervals, intermixing long pauses of repose, as it were to give thee opportunity to meditate and ruminate upon thy lesson, at thy own ease and leisure. To give thee means to judge aright, and to assume the resolution of a man of courage, it presents to thee the state of thy entire condition, both in good and evil; and one while a very cheerful and another an insupportable life, in one and the same day. If thou embracest not death, at least thou shakest hands with it once a month; whence thou hast more cause to hope that it will one day surprise thee without menace; and that being so often conducted to the water-side, but still thinking thyself to be upon the accustomed terms, thou and thy confidence will at one time or another be unexpectedly wafted over. A man cannot reasonably complain of diseases that fairly divide the time with health."

I am obliged to Fortune for having so often assaulted me with the same sort of weapons: she forms and fashions me by use, hardens and habituates me, so that I can know within a little for how much I shall be quit. For want of natural memory, I make one of paper; and as any new symptom happens in my disease, I set it down, whence it falls out that, having now almost passed through all sorts of examples, if anything striking threatens me, turning over these little loose notes, as the Sybilline leaves, I never fail of finding matter of consolation from some favourable prognostic in my past experience. Custom also makes me hope better for the time to come; for, the conduct of this clearing out having so long continued, it is to be believed that nature will not alter her course, and that no other worse accident will happen than what I already feel. And besides, the condition of this disease is not unsuitable to my prompt and sudden complexion: when it assaults me gently, I am afraid, for it is then for a great while; but it has, naturally, brisk and vigorous excesses; it claws me to purpose for a day or two. My kidneys held out an age without alteration; and I have almost now lived another, since they changed their state; evils have their periods, as well as benefits: peradventure, the infirmity draws towards an end. Age weakens the heat of my stomach, and, its digestion being less perfect, sends this crude matter to my kidneys; why, at a certain revolution, may not the heat of my kidneys be also abated, so that they can no more petrify my phlegm, and nature find out some other way of purgation. Years have evidently helped me to drain certain rheums; and why not these excrements which furnish matter for gravel? But is there anything delightful in comparison of this sudden change, when from an excessive pain, I come, by the voiding of a stone, to recover, as by a flash of lightning, the beautiful light of health, so free and full, as it happens in our sudden and sharpest colics? Is there anything in the pain suffered, that one can counterpoise to the pleasure of so sudden an amendment? Oh, how much does health seem the more pleasant to me, after a sickness so near and so contiguous, that I can distinguish them in the presence of one another, in their greatest show; when they appear in emulation, as if to make head against and dispute it with one another! As the Stoics say that vices are profitably introduced to give value to and to set off virtue, we can, with better reason and less temerity of conjecture, say that nature has given us pain for the honour and service of pleasure and indolence. When Socrates, after his fetters were knocked off, felt the pleasure of that itching which the weight of them had caused in his legs, he rejoiced to consider the strict alliance between pain and pleasure; how they are linked together by a necessary connection, so that by turns they follow and mutually beget one another; and cried out to good Aesop, that he ought out of this consideration to have taken matter for a fine fable.

The worst that I see in other diseases is, that they are not so grievous in their effect as they are in their issue: a man is a whole year in recovering, and all the while full of weakness and fear. There is so much hazard, and so many steps to arrive at safety, that there is no end on it before they have unmuffled you of a kerchief, and then of a cap, before they allow you to walk abroad and take the air, to drink wine, to lie with your wife, to eat melons, it is odds you relapse into some new distemper. The stone has this privilege, that it carries itself clean off: whereas the other maladies always leave behind them some impression and alteration that render the body subject to a new disease, and lend a hand to one another. Those are excusable that content themselves with possessing us, without extending farther and introducing their followers; but courteous and kind are those whose passage brings us any profitable issue. Since I have been troubled with the stone, I find myself freed from all other accidents, much more, methinks, than I was before, and have never had any fever since; I argue that the extreme and frequent vomitings that I am subject to purge me: and, on the other hand, my distastes for this and that, and the strange fasts I am forced to keep, digest my peccant humours, and nature, with those stones, voids whatever there is in me superfluous and hurtful. Let them never tell me that it is a medicine too dear bought: for what avail so many stinking draughts, so many caustics, incisions, sweats, setons, diets, and so many other methods of cure, which often, by reason we are not able to undergo their violence and importunity, bring us to our graves? So that when I have the stone, I look upon it as physic; when free from it, as an absolute deliverance.

And here is another particular benefit of my disease; which is, that it almost plays its game by itself, and lets me play mine, if I have only courage to do it; for, in its greatest fury, I have endured it ten hours together on horseback. Do but endure only; you need no other regimen play, run, dine, do this and the other, if you can; your debauch will do you more good than harm; say as much to one that has the pox, the gout, or hernia! The other diseases have more universal obligations; rack our actions after another kind of manner, disturb our whole order, and to their consideration engage the whole state of life: this only pinches the skin; it leaves the understanding and the will wholly at our own disposal, and the tongue, the hands, and the feet; it rather awakens than stupefies you. The soul is struck with the ardour of a fever, overwhelmed with an epilepsy, and displaced by a sharp megrim, and, in short, astounded by all the diseases that hurt the whole mass and the most noble parts; this never meddles with the soul; if anything goes amiss with her, it is her own fault; she betrays, dismounts, and abandons herself. There are none but fools who suffer themselves to be persuaded that this hard and massive body which is baked in our kidneys is to be dissolved by drinks; wherefore, when it is once stirred, there is nothing to be done but to give it passage; and, for that matter, it will itself make one.

I moreover observe this particular convenience in it, that it is a disease wherein we have little to guess at: we are dispensed from the trouble into which other diseases throw us by the uncertainty of their causes, conditions, and progress; a trouble that is infinitely painful: we have no need of consultations and doctoral interpretations; the senses well enough inform us both what it is and where it is.

By suchlike arguments, weak and strong, as Cicero with the disease of his old age, I try to rock asleep and amuse my imagination, and to dress its wounds. If I find them worse tomorrow, I will provide new stratagems. That this is true: I am come to that pass of late, that the least motion forces pure blood out of my kidneys: what of that? I move about, nevertheless, as before, and ride after my hounds with a juvenile and insolent ardour; and hold that I have very good satisfaction for an accident of that importance, when it costs me no more but a dull heaviness and uneasiness in that part; it is some great stone that wastes and consumes the substance of my kidneys and my life, which I by little and little evacuate, not without some natural pleasure, as an excrement henceforward superfluous and troublesome. Now if I feel anything stirring, do not fancy that I trouble myself to consult my pulse or my urine, thereby to put myself upon some annoying prevention; I shall soon enough feel the pain, without making it more and longer by the disease of fear. He who fears he shall suffer, already suffers what he fears. To which may be added that the doubts and ignorance of those who take upon them to expound the designs of nature and her internal progressions, and the many false prognostics of their art, ought to give us to understand that her ways are inscrutable and utterly unknown; there is great uncertainty, variety, and obscurity in what she either promises or threatens. Old age excepted, which is an indubitable sign of the approach of death, in all other accidents I see few signs of the future, whereon we may ground our divination. I only judge of myself by actual sensation, not by reasoning: to what end, since I am resolved to bring nothing to it but expectation and patience? Will you know how much I get by this? Observe those who do otherwise, and who rely upon so many diverse persuasions and counsels; how often the imagination presses upon them without any bodily pain. I have many times amused myself, being well and in safety, and quite free from these dangerous attacks in communicating them to the physicians as then beginning to discover themselves in me; I underwent the decree of their dreadful conclusions, being all the while quite at my ease, and so much the more obliged to the favour of God and better satisfied of the vanity of this art.

There is nothing that ought so much to be recommended to youth as activity and vigilance our life is nothing but movement. I bestir myself with great difficulty, and am slow in everything, whether in rising, going to bed, or eating: seven of the clock in the morning is early for me, and where I rule, I never dine before eleven, nor sup till after six. I formerly attributed the cause of the fevers and other diseases I fell into to the heaviness that long sleeping had brought upon me, and have ever repented going to sleep again in the morning. Plato is more angry at excess of sleeping than at excess of drinking. I love to lie hard and alone, even without my wife, as kings do; pretty well covered with clothes. They never warm my bed, but since I have grown old they give me at need cloths to lay to my feet and stomach. They found fault with the great Scipio that he was a great sleeper; not, in my opinion, for any other reason than that men were displeased that he alone should have nothing in him to be found fault with. If I am anything fastidious in my way of living it is rather in my lying than anything else; but generally I give way and accommodate myself as well as any one to necessity. Sleeping has taken up a great part of my life, and I yet continue, at the age I now am, to sleep eight or nine hours at one breath. I wean myself with utility from this proneness to sloth, and am evidently the better for so doing. I find the change a little hard indeed, but in three days it is over; and I see but few who live with less sleep, when need requires, and who more constantly exercise themselves, or to whom long journeys are less troublesome. My body is capable of a firm, but not of a violent or sudden agitation. I escape of late from violent exercises, and such as make me sweat: my limbs grow weary before they are warm. I can stand a whole day together, and am never weary of walking; but from my youth I have ever preferred to ride upon paved roads; on foot, I get up to the haunches in dirt, and little fellows as I am are subject in the streets to be elbowed and jostled for want of presence; I have ever loved to repose myself, whether sitting or lying, with my heels as high or higher than my seat.

There is no profession as pleasant as the military, a profession both noble in its execution (for valour is the stoutest, proudest, and most generous of all virtues), and noble in its cause: there is no utility either more universal or more just than the protection of the peace and greatness of one's country. The company of so many noble, young, and active men delights you; the ordinary sight of so many tragic spectacles; the freedom of the conversation, without art; a masculine and unceremonious way of living, please you; the variety of a thousand several actions; the encouraging harmony of martial music that ravishes and inflames both your ears and souls; the honour of this occupation, nay, even its hardships and difficulties, which Plato holds so light that in his Republic he makes women and children share in them, are delightful to you. You put yourself voluntarily upon particular exploits and hazards, according as you judge of their lustre and importance; and, a volunteer, find even life itself excusably employed:

Pulchrumque mori succurrit in armis.

[It is fine to die sword in hand. (And he remembers that it is honourable to die in arms.)

—*Aeneid,* ii. 317.]

To fear common dangers that concern so great a multitude of men; not to dare to do what so many sorts of souls, what a whole people dare, is for a heart that is poor and mean beyond all measure: company encourages even children. If others excel you in knowledge, in gracefulness, in strength, or fortune, you have alternative resources at your disposal; but to give place to them in stability of mind, you can blame no one for that but yourself. Death is more abject, more languishing and troublesome, in bed than in a fight: fevers and catarrhs as painful and mortal as a musket-shot. Whoever has fortified himself valiantly to bear the accidents of common life need not raise his courage to be a soldier:

> *Vivere, mi Lucili, militare est.*

[To live, my Lucilius, is (to make war) to be a soldier.
—Seneca, *Epistles*, 96.]

I do not remember that I ever had the itch, and yet scratching is one of nature's sweetest gratifications, and so much at hand; but repentance follows too near. I use it most in my ears, which are at intervals apt to itch.

I came into the world with all my senses entire, even to perfection. My stomach is commodiously good, as also is my head and my breath; and, for the most part, uphold themselves so in the height of fevers. I have passed the age to which some nations, not without reason, have prescribed so just a term of life that they would not suffer men to exceed it; and yet I have some intermissions, though short and inconstant, so clean and sound as to be little inferior to the health and pleasantness of my youth. I do not speak of vigour and sprightliness; It is not reason they should follow me beyond their limits:

> *Non hoc amplius est liminis, aut aquae*
> *Coelestis, patiens latus.*

[I am no longer able to stand waiting at a door in the rain.
—Horace, *Odes*, iii. 10, 9.]

584

CHAPTER 13

My face and eyes presently discover my condition; all my alterations begin there, and appear somewhat worse than they really are; my friends often pity me before I feel the cause in myself. My looking-glass does not frighten me; for even in my youth it has befallen me more than once to have a scurvy complexion and of ill augury, without any great consequence, so that the physicians, not finding any cause within answerable to that outward alteration, attributed it to the mind and to some secret passion that tormented me within; but they were deceived. If my body would govern itself as well, according to my rule, as my mind does, we should move a little more at our ease. My mind was then not only free from trouble, but, moreover, full of joy and satisfaction, as it commonly is, half by its complexion, half by its design:

Nec vitiant artus aegrae contagia mentis.

[Nor do the troubles of the body ever affect my mind.
—Ovid, *Tristia*, iii. 8, 25.]

I am of the opinion that this temperature of my soul has often raised my body from its lapses; this is often depressed; if the other be not brisk and gay, it is at least tranquil and at rest. I had a quartan ague four or five months, that made me look miserably ill; my mind was always, if not calm, yet pleasant. If the pain be without me, the weakness and languor do not much afflict me; I see various corporal faintings, that beget a horror in me but to name, which yet I should less fear than a thousand passions and agitations of the mind that I see about me. I make up my mind no more to run; it is enough that I can crawl along; nor do I more complain of the natural decadence that I feel in myself:

Quis tumidum guttur miratur in Alpibus?

[Who is surprised to see a swollen goitre in the Alps?
—Juvenal, xiii. 162.]

585

than I regret that my duration shall not be as long and entire as that of an oak.

I have no reason to complain of my imagination; I have had few thoughts in my life that have so much as broken my sleep, except those of desire, which have awakened without afflicting me. I dream but seldom, and then of chimaeras and fantastic things, commonly produced from pleasant thoughts, and rather ridiculous than sad; and I believe it to be true that dreams are faithful interpreters of our inclinations; but there is art required to sort and understand them

Res, quae in vita usurpant homines, cogitant, curant, vident,
Quaeque agunt vigilantes, agitantque, easi cui in somno accidunt,
Minus mirandum est.

[It is less wonder, what men practise, think, care for, see, and do when waking, (should also run in their heads and disturb them when they are asleep) and which affect their feelings, if they happen to any in sleep.
—Attius, cited in Cicero, *De Divinatione*, i. 22.]

Plato, moreover, says, that it is the office of prudence to draw instructions of divination of future things from dreams: I don't know about this, but there are wonderful instances of it that Socrates, Xenophon, and Aristotle, men of irreproachable authority, relate. Historians say that the Atlantes never dream; who also never eat any animal food, which I add, forasmuch as it is, peradventure, the reason why they never dream, for Pythagoras ordered a certain preparation of diet to beget appropriate dreams. Mine are very gentle, without any agitation of body or expression of voice. I have seen several of my time wonderfully disturbed by them. Theon the philosopher walked in his sleep, and so did Pericles servant, and that upon the tiles and top of the house.

I hardly ever choose my dish at table, but take the next at hand, and unwillingly change it for another. A confusion of meats and a clatter of dishes displease me as much as any other confusion: I am easily satisfied with few dishes: and am an enemy to the opinion of Favorinus, that in a feast they should snatch from you the meat you like, and set a plate of another sort before you; and that it is a pitiful supper, if you do not sate your guests with the rumps of various fowls, the beccafico only deserving to be all eaten. I usually eat salt meats, yet I prefer bread that has no salt in it; and my baker never sends up other to my table, contrary to the custom of the country. In my infancy, what they had most to correct in me was the refusal of things that children commonly best love, as sugar, sweetmeats, and march-panes. My tutor contended with this aversion to delicate things, as a kind of over-nicety; and indeed it is nothing else but a difficulty of taste, in anything it applies itself to. Whoever cures a child of an obstinate liking for brown bread, bacon, or garlic, cures him also of pampering his palate. There are some who affect temperance and plainness by wishing for beef and ham amongst the partridges; it is all very fine; this is the delicacy of the delicate; it is the taste of an effeminate fortune that disrelishes ordinary and accustomed things.

Per qux luxuria divitiarum taedio ludit.

[By which the luxury of wealth causes tedium.
—Seneca, *Epistles*, 18.]

Not to make good cheer with what another is enjoying, and to be curious in what a man eats, is the essence of this vice:

Si modica coenare times olus omne patella.

[If you can't be content with herbs in a small dish for supper.
—Horace, *Epistles*, i. 5, 2.]

There is indeed this difference, that it is better to oblige one's appetite to things that are most easy to be had; but it is always vice to oblige one's self. I formerly said a kinsman of mine was overnice, who, by being in our galleys, had unlearned the use of beds and to undress when he went to sleep.

If I had any sons, I should willingly wish them my fortune. The good father that God gave me (who has nothing of me but the acknowledgment of his goodness, but truly it is a very hearty one) sent me from my cradle to be brought up in a poor village of his, and there continued me all the while I was at nurse, and still longer, bringing me up to the meanest and most common way of living:

Magna pars libertatisest bene moratus venter.

[A well-governed stomach is a great part of liberty.
—Seneca, *Epistles*, 123.]

Never take upon yourselves, and much less give up to your wives, the care of their nurture; leave the formation to fortune, under popular and natural laws; leave it to custom to train them up to frugality and hardship, that they may rather descend from rigour than mount up to it. This humour of his yet aimed at another end, to make me familiar with the people and the condition of men who most need our assistance; considering that I should rather regard them who extend their arms to me, than those who turn their backs upon me; and for this reason it was that he provided to hold me at the font persons of the meanest fortune, to oblige and attach me to them.

Nor has his design succeeded altogether ill; for, whether upon the account of the more honour in such a condescension, or out of a natural compassion that has a very great power over me, I have an inclination towards the meaner sort of people. The faction which I should condemn in our wars, I should more sharply condemn, flourishing and successful; it will somewhat reconcile me to it, when I shall see it miserable and overwhelmed. How willingly do I admire the fine humour of Cheilonis, daughter and wife to kings of Sparta. Whilst her husband Cleombrotus, in the commotion of her city, had the advantage over Leonidas her father, she, like a good daughter, stuck close to her father in all his misery and exile, in opposition to the conqueror. But so soon as the chance of war turned, she changed her will with the change of fortune, and bravely turned to her husband's side, whom she accompanied throughout, where his ruin carried him: admitting, as it appears to me, no other choice than to cleave to the side that stood most in need of her, and where she could best manifest her compassion. I am naturally more apt to follow the example of Flaminius, who rather gave his assistance to those who had most need of him than to those who had power to do him good, than I do to that of Pyrrhus, who was of an humour to truckle under the great and to domineer over the poor.

Long sittings at table both trouble me and do me harm; for, be it that I was so accustomed when a child, I eat all the while I sit. Therefore it is that at my own house, though the meals there are of the shortest, I usually sit down a little while after the rest, after the manner of Augustus, but I do not imitate him in rising also before the rest; on the contrary, I love to sit still a long time after, and to hear them talk, provided I am none of the talkers: for I tire and hurt myself with speaking upon a full stomach, as much as I find it very wholesome and pleasant to argue and to strain my voice before dinner.

The ancient Greeks and Romans had more reason than we in setting apart for eating, which is a principal action of life, if they were not prevented by other extraordinary business, many hours and the greatest part of the night; eating and drinking more deliberately than we do, who perform all our actions post-haste; and in extending this natural pleasure to more leisure and better use, intermixing with profitable conversation.

They whose concern it is to have a care of me, may very easily hinder me from eating anything they think will do me harm; for in such matters I never covet nor miss anything I do not see; but withal, if it once comes in my sight, it is in vain to persuade me to forbear; so that when I design to fast I must be kept apart from the suppers, and must have only so much given me as is required for a prescribed collation; for if to table, I forget my resolution. When I order my cook to alter the manner of dressing any dish, all my family know what it means, that my stomach is out of order, and that I shall not touch it.

I love to have all meats, that will endure it, very little boiled or roasted, and prefer them very high, and even, as to several, quite gone. Nothing but hardness generally offends me (of any other quality I am as patient and indifferent as any man I have known); so that, contrary to the common humour, even in fish it often happens that I find them both too fresh and too firm; not for want of teeth, which I ever had good, even to excellence, and which age does not now begin to threaten; I have always been used every morning to rub them with a napkin, and before and after dinner. God is favourable to those whom He makes to die by degrees; it is the only benefit of old age; the last death will be so much the less painful; it will kill but a half or a quarter of a man. There is one tooth lately fallen out without drawing and without pain; it was the natural term of its duration; in that part of my being and several others, are already dead, others half dead, of those that were most active and in the first rank during my vigorous years; it is so I melt and steal away from myself. What a folly it would be in my understanding to apprehend the height of this fall, already so much advanced, as if it were from the very top! I hope I shall not. I, in truth, receive a principal consolation in meditating my death, that it will be just and natural, and that henceforward I cannot herein either require or hope from Destiny any other but unlawful favour. Men make themselves believe that we formerly had longer lives as well as greater stature. But they deceive themselves; and Solon, who was of those elder times, limits the duration of life to threescore and ten years. I, who have so much and so universally adored that "The mean is best," of the passed time, and who have concluded the most moderate measures to be the most perfect, shall I pretend to an immeasurable and prodigious old age?

Chapter 13

Whatever happens contrary to the course of nature may be troublesome; but what comes according to her should always be pleasant:

Omnia, quae secundum naturam fiunt, sunt habenda in bonis.

[All things that are done according to nature are to be accounted good.

—Cicero, *De Senectute*, c. 19.]

And so, says Plato, the death which is occasioned by wounds and diseases is violent; but that which comes upon us, old age conducting us to it, is of all others the most easy, and in some sort delicious:

Vitam adolescentibus vis aufert, senibus maturitas.

[Young men are taken away by violence, old men by maturity.
– Cicero, *ubi sup.*]

Death mixes and confounds itself throughout with life; decay anticipates its hour, and shoulders itself even into the course of our advance. I have portraits of myself taken at five-and-twenty and five-and-thirty years of age. I compare them with that lately drawn: how many times is it no longer me; how much more is my present image unlike the former, than unlike my dying one? It is too much to abuse nature, to make her trot so far that she must be forced to leave us, and abandon our conduct, our eyes, teeth, legs, and all the rest to the mercy of a foreign and haggard countenance, and to resign us into the hands of art, being weary of following us herself.

I am not excessively fond either of salads or fruits, except melons. My father hated all sorts of sauces; I love them all. Eating too much hurts me; but, as to the quality of what I eat, I do not yet certainly know that any sort of meat disagrees with me; neither have I observed that either full moon or decrease, autumn or spring, have any influence upon me. We have in us motions that are inconstant

591

and unknown; for example, I found radishes first grateful to my stomach, since that nauseous, and now again grateful. In several other things, I find my stomach and appetite vary after the same manner; I have changed again and again from white wine to claret, from claret to white wine.

I am a great lover of fish, and consequently make my fasts feasts and feasts fasts; and I believe what some people say, that it is more easy of digestion than flesh. As I make a conscience of eating flesh upon fish-days, so does my taste make a conscience of mixing fish and flesh; the difference between them seems to me too remote.

From my youth, I have sometimes kept out of the way at meals; either to sharpen my appetite against the next morning (for, as Epicurus fasted and made lean meals to accustom his pleasure to make shift without abundance, I, on the contrary, do it to prepare my pleasure to make better and more cheerful use of abundance); or else I fasted to preserve my vigour for the service of some action of body or mind: for both the one and the other of these is cruelly dulled in me by repletion; and, above all things, I hate that foolish coupling of so healthful and sprightly a goddess with that little belching god, bloated with the fumes of his liquor [Montaigne did not approve of coupling Bacchus with Venus.] or to cure my sick stomach, or for want of fit company; for I say, as the same Epicurus did, that one is not so much to regard what he eats, as with whom; and I commend Chilo, that he would not engage himself to be at Periander's feast till he was first informed who were to be the other guests; no dish is so acceptable to me, nor no sauce so appetising, as that which is extracted from society. I think it more wholesome to eat more leisurely and less, and to eat oftener; but I would have appetite and hunger attended to; I should take no pleasure to be fed with three or four pitiful and stinted repasts a day, after a medicinal manner: who will assure me that, if I have a good appetite in the morning, I shall have the same at supper? But we old fellows especially, let us take the first opportune time of eating, and leave to almanac-makers hopes and prognostics. The utmost fruit of my health is pleasure; let us take hold of the present and known. I avoid the invariable in these laws of fasting; he who would have one form serve him, let him avoid the continuing it; we harden ourselves in it; our strength is there stupefied and laid asleep; six months after, you shall find your stomach so inured to it, that all you have got is the loss of your liberty of doing otherwise but to your prejudice.

I never keep my legs and thighs warmer in winter than in summer; one simple pair of silk stockings is all. I have suffered myself, for the relief of my colds, to keep my head warmer, and my belly upon the account of my colic: my diseases in a few days habituate themselves thereto, and disdained my ordinary provisions: we soon get from a coif to a kerchief over it, from a simple cap to a quilted hat; the trimmings of the doublet must not merely serve for ornament: there must be added a hare's skin or a vulture's skin, and a cap under the hat: follow this gradation, and you will go a very fine way to work. I will do nothing of the sort, and would willingly leave off what I have begun. If you fall into any new inconvenience, all this is labour lost; you are accustomed to it; seek out some other. Thus do they destroy themselves who submit to be pestered with these enforced and superstitious rules; they must add something more, and something more after that; there is no end on't.

For what concerns our affairs and pleasures, it is much more commodious, as the ancients did, to lose one's dinner, and defer making good cheer till the hour of retirement and repose, without breaking up a day; and so was I formerly used to do. As to health, I since by experience find, on the contrary, that it is better to dine, and that the digestion is better while awake. I am not very used to be thirsty, either well or sick; my mouth is, indeed, apt to be dry, but without thirst; and commonly I never drink but with thirst that is created by eating, and far on in the meal; I drink pretty well for a man of my pitch: in summer, and at a relishing meal, I do not only exceed the limits of Augustus, who drank but thrice precisely; but not to offend Democritus rule, who forbade that men should stop at four times as an unlucky number, I proceed at need to the fifth glass, about three half-pints; for the little glasses are my favourites, and I like to drink them off, which other people avoid as an unbecoming thing. I mix my wine sometimes with half, sometimes with the third part water; and when I am at home, by an ancient custom that my father's physician prescribed both to him and himself, they mix that which is designed for me in the buttery, two or three hours before it is brought in. It is said that Cranabs, king of Attica, was the inventor of this custom of diluting wine; whether useful or no, I have heard disputed. I think it more decent and wholesome for children to drink no wine till after sixteen or eighteen years of age. The most usual and common method of living is the most becoming; all particularity, in my opinion, is to be avoided; and I should as much hate a German who mixed water with his wine, as I should a Frenchman who drank it pure. Public usage gives the law in these things.

I fear a mist, and fly from smoke as from the plague: the first repairs I fell upon in my own house were the chimneys and houses of office, the common and insupportable defects of all old buildings; and amongst the difficulties of war I reckon the choking dust they made us ride in a whole day together. I have a free and easy respiration, and my colds for the most part go off without offence to the lungs and without a cough.

The heat of summer is more an enemy to me than the cold of winter; for, besides the incommodity of heat, less remediable than cold, and besides the force of the sunbeams that strike upon the head, all glittering light offends my eyes, so that I could not now sit at dinner over against a flaming fire.

To dull the whiteness of paper, in those times when I was more wont to read, I laid a piece of glass upon my book, and found my eyes much relieved by it. I am to this hour – to the age of fifty-four – ignorant of the use of spectacles; and I can see as far as ever I did, or any other. It is true that in the evening I begin to find a little disturbance and weakness in my sight if I read, an exercise I have always found troublesome, especially by night. Here is one step back, and a very manifest one; I shall retire another: from the second to the third, and so to the fourth, so gently, that I shall be stark blind before I shall be sensible of the age and decay of my sight: so artificially do the Fatal Sisters untwist our lives. And so I doubt whether my hearing begins to grow thick; and you will see I shall have half lost it, when I shall still lay the fault on the voices of those who speak to me. A man must screw up his soul to a high pitch to make it sensible how it ebbs away.

My walking is quick and firm; and I know not which of the two, my mind or my body, I have most to do to keep in the same state. That preacher is very much my friend who can fix my attention a whole sermon through: in places of ceremony, where everyone's countenance is so starched, where I have seen the ladies keep even their eyes so fixed, I could never order it so, that some part or other of me did not lash out; so that though I was seated, I was never settled; and as to gesticulation, I am never without a switch in my hand, walking or riding. As the philosopher Chrysippus' maid said of her master, that he was only drunk in his legs, for it was his custom to be always kicking them about in what place soever he sat; and she said it when, the wine having made all his companions drunk, he found no alteration in himself at all; it may have been said of me from my infancy, that I had either folly or quicksilver in my feet, so much stirring and unsettledness there is in them, wherever they are placed.

It is indecent, besides the hurt it does to one's health, and even to the pleasure of eating, to eat greedily as I do; I often bite my tongue, and sometimes my fingers, in my haste. Diogenes, meeting a boy eating after that manner, gave his tutor a box on the ear! There were men at Rome that taught people to chew, as well as to walk, with a good grace. I lose thereby the leisure of speaking, which gives great relish to the table, provided the discourse be suitable, that is, pleasant and short.

There is jealousy and envy amongst our pleasures; they cross and hinder one another. Alcibiades, a man who well understood how to make good cheer, banished even music from the table, that it might not disturb the entertainment of discourse, for the reason, as

Plato tells us, "that it is the custom of ordinary people to call fiddlers and singing men to feasts, for want of good discourse and pleasant talk, with which men of understanding know how to entertain one another." Varro requires all this in entertainments: "Persons of graceful presence and agreeable conversation, who are neither silent nor garrulous; neatness and delicacy, both of meat and place; and fair weather." The art of dining well is no slight art, the pleasure not a slight pleasure; neither the greatest captains nor the greatest philosophers have disdained the use or science of eating well. My imagination has delivered three repasts to the custody of my memory, which fortune rendered sovereignly sweet to me, upon several occasions in my more flourishing age; my present state excludes me; for everyone, according to the good temper of body and mind wherein he then finds himself, furnishes for his own share a particular grace and savour. I, who but crawl upon the earth, hate this inhuman wisdom, that will have us despise and hate all culture of the body; I look upon it as an equal injustice to loath natural pleasures as to be too much in love with them. Xerxes was a blockhead, who, environed with all human delights, proposed a reward to him who could find out others; but he is not much less so who cuts off any of those pleasures that nature has provided for him. A man should neither pursue nor avoid them, but receive them. I receive them, I confess, a little too warmly and kindly, and easily suffer myself to follow my natural propensions. We have no need to exaggerate their inanity; they themselves will make us sufficiently sensible of it, thanks to our sick wet-blanket mind, that puts us out of taste with them as with itself; it treats both itself and all it receives, one while better, and another worse, according to its insatiable, vagabond, and versatile essence:

Sincerum est nisi vas, quodcunque infundis, acescit.

[Unless the vessel be clean, it will sour whatever you put into it.
—Horace, *Epistles*, i. 2, 54.]

CHAPTER 13

I, who boast that I so curiously and particularly embrace the conveniences of life, find them, when I most nearly consider them, very little more than wind. But what? We are all wind throughout; and, moreover, the wind itself, more discreet than we, loves to bluster and shift from corner to corner, and contents itself with its proper offices without desiring stability and solidity-qualities not its own.

The pure pleasures, as well as the pure displeasures, of the imagination, say some, are the greatest, as was expressed by the balance of Critolaiis. It is no wonder; it makes them to its own liking, and cuts them out of the whole cloth; of this I every day see notable examples, and, peradventure, to be desired. But I, who am of a mixed and heavy condition, cannot snap so soon at this one simple object, but that I negligently suffer myself to be carried away with the present pleasures of the, general human law, intellectually sensible, and sensibly intellectual. The Cyrenaic philosophers will have it that as corporal pains, so corporal pleasures are more powerful, both as double and as more just. There are some, as Aristotle says, who out of a savage kind of stupidity dislike them; and I know others who out of ambition do the same. Why do they not, moreover, forswear breathing? why do they not live of their own? why not refuse light, because it is gratuitous, and costs them neither invention nor exertion? Let Mars, Pallas, or Mercury afford them their light by which to see, instead of Venus, Ceres, and Bacchus. These boastful humours may counterfeit some content, for what will not fancy do? But as to wisdom, there is no touch of it. Will they not seek the quadrature of the circle, even when on their wives? I hate that we should be enjoined to have our minds in the clouds, when our bodies are at table; I would not have the mind nailed there, nor wallow there; I would have it take place there and sit, but not lie down. Aristippus maintained nothing but the body, as if we had no soul; Zeno comprehended only the soul, as if we had no body: both of them faultily. Pythagoras, they say, followed a philosophy that was all contemplation, Socrates one that was all conduct and action; Plato found a mean between the two; but they only say this for the sake of talking. The true temperament is found in Socrates; and, Plato is much more Socratic than Pythagoric, and it becomes him better. When I dance, I dance; when I sleep, I sleep. Nay, when I walk alone in a beautiful orchard, if my thoughts are some part of the time taken up with external occurrences, I some part of the time call them back again to my walk, to the orchard, to the sweetness of that solitude, and to myself.

Nature has mother-like observed this, that the actions she has enjoined us for our necessity should be also pleasurable to us; and she invites us to them, not only by reason, but also by appetite, and it is injustice to infringe her laws. When I see alike Caesar and Alexander, in the midst of his greatest business, so fully enjoy human and corporal pleasures, I do not say that he relaxed his mind: I say that he strengthened it, by vigour of courage subjecting those violent employments and laborious thoughts to the ordinary usage of life: wise, had he believed the last was his ordinary, the first his extraordinary, vocation. We are great fools. "He has passed his life in idleness," say we: "I have done nothing to-day." What? have you not lived? that is not only the fundamental, but the most illustrious, of your occupations. "Had I been put to the management of great affairs, I should have made it seen what I could do." "Have you known how to meditate and manage your life? you have performed the greatest work of all." In order to show and develop herself, nature needs only fortune; she equally manifests herself in all stages, and behind a curtain as well as without one. Have you known how to regulate your conduct, you have done a great deal more than he who has composed books. Have you known how to take repose, you have done more than he who has taken empires and cities.

The glorious masterpiece of man is to live to purpose; all other things: to reign, to lay up treasure, to build, are but little appendices and props. I take pleasure in seeing a general of an army, at the foot of a breach he is presently to assault, give himself up entire and free at dinner, to talk and be merry with his friends. And Brutus, when heaven and earth were conspired against him and the Roman liberty,

stealing some hour of the night from his rounds to read and scan
Polybius in all security. It is for little souls, buried under the weight
of affairs, not from them to know how clearly to disengage themselves, not to know how to lay them aside and take them up again:

> *O fortes, pejoraque passi*
> *Mecum saepeviri! nunc vino pellite curas*
> *Cras ingens iterabimus aequor.*

[O brave spirits, who have often suffered sorrow with me, drink
cares away; tomorrow we will embark once more on the vast sea.
—Horace, *Odes*, i. 7, 30.]

Whether it be in jest or earnest, that the theological and Sor-
bonnical wine, and their feasts, are turned into a proverb, I find
it reasonable they should dine so much more commodiously and
pleasantly, as they have profitably and seriously employed the morning in the exercise of their schools. The conscience of having well
spent the other hours, is the just and savoury sauce of the dinner-
table. The sages lived after that manner; and that inimitable emulation to virtue, which astonishes us both in the one and the other
Cato, that humour of theirs, so severe as even to be importunate,
gently submits itself and yields to the laws of the human condition,
of Venus and Bacchus; according to the precepts of their sect, that
require the perfect sage to be as expert and intelligent in the use of
natural pleasures as in all other duties of life:

> *Cui cor sapiat, ei et sapiat palatus.*

Relaxation and facility, methinks, wonderfully honour and best
become a strong and generous soul. Epaminondas did not think
that to take part, and that heartily, in songs and sports and dances
with the young men of his city, were things that in any way derogated
from the honour of his glorious victories and the perfect purity of

manners that was in him. And amongst so many admirable actions of Scipio the grandfather, a person worthy to be reputed of a heavenly extraction, there is nothing that gives him a greater grace than to see him carelessly and childishly trifling at gathering and selecting cockle shells, and playing at quoits, amusing and tickling himself in representing by writing in comedies the meanest and most popular actions of men. And his head full of that wonderful enterprise of Hannibal and Africa, visiting the schools in Sicily, and attending philosophical lectures, to the extent of arming the blind envy of his enemies at Rome. Nor is there anything more remarkable in Socrates than that, old as he was, he found time to make himself taught dancing and playing upon instruments, and thought it time well spent. This same man was seen in an ecstasy, standing upon his feet a whole day and a night together, in the presence of all the Grecian army, surprised and absorbed by some profound thought. He was the first, amongst so many valiant men of the army, to run to the relief of Alcibiades, oppressed with the enemy, to shield him with his own body, and disengage him from the crowd by absolute force of arms. It was he who, in the Delian battle, raised and saved Xenophon when fallen from his horse; and who, amongst all the people of Athens, enraged as he was at so unworthy a spectacle, first presented himself to rescue Theramenes, whom the thirty tyrants were leading to execution by their satellites, and desisted not from his bold enterprise but at the remonstrance of Theramenes himself, though he was only followed by two more in all. He was seen, when courted by a beauty with whom he was in love, to maintain at need a severe abstinence. He was seen ever to go to the wars, and walk upon ice, with bare feet; to wear the same robe, winter and summer; to surpass all his companions in patience of bearing hardships, and to eat no more at a feast than at his own private dinner. He was seen, for seven-and-twenty years together, to endure hunger, poverty, the indocility of his children, and the nails of his wife, with the same countenance. And, in the end, calumny, tyranny, imprisonment, fetters, and poison. But was this man obliged to drink full bumpers by any rule of civility? he was also the man of the whole army with whom the advantage in drinking, remained. And he never refused to play at noisettes, nor to ride the hobby-horse with children, and it became him well; for all actions, says philosophy, equally become and equally honour a wise man. We have enough wherewithal to do it, and we ought never to be weary of presenting the image of this great man in all the patterns and forms of perfection. There are very few examples of life, full and pure; and we wrong our teaching every day, to propose to ourselves those that are weak and imperfect, scarce good for any one service, and rather pull us back; corrupters rather than correctors of manners. The people deceive themselves; a man goes much more easily indeed by the ends, where the extremity serves for a bound, a stop, and guide, than by the middle way, large and open; and according to art, more than according to nature: but withal much less nobly and commendably.

Greatness of soul consists not so much in mounting and in pressing forward, as in knowing how to govern and circumscribe itself; it takes everything for great, that is enough, and demonstrates itself in preferring moderate to eminent things. There is nothing so fine and legitimate as well and duly to play the man; nor science so arduous as well and naturally to know how to live this life; and of all the infirmities we have, it is the most barbarous to despise our being.

Whoever has a mind to isolate his spirit, when the body is ill at ease, to preserve it from the contagion, let him by all means do it if he can: but otherwise let him on the contrary favour and assist it, and not refuse to participate of its natural pleasures with a conjugal complacency, bringing to it, if it be the wiser, moderation, lest by indiscretion they should get confounded with displeasure. Intemperance is the pest of pleasure; and temperance is not its scourge, but rather its seasoning. Euxodus, who therein established the sovereign good, and his companions, who set so high a value upon it, tasted it in its most charming sweetness, by the means of temperance, which in them was singular and exemplary.

I enjoin my soul to look upon pain and pleasure with an eye equally regulated:

> *Eodem enim vitio est effusio animi in laetitia*
> *quo in dolore contractio,*

[From the same imperfection arises the expansion of the mind in pleasure and its contraction in sorrow.
—Cicero, *Tusculum Disputations*, iv. 31.]

and equally firm; but the one gaily and the other severely, and so far as it is able, to be careful to extinguish the one as to extend the other. The judging rightly of good brings along with it the judging soundly of evil: pain has something of the inevitable in its tender beginnings, and pleasure something of the evitable in its excessive end. Plato couples them together, and wills that it should be equally the office of fortitude to fight against pain, and against the immoderate and charming blandishments of pleasure: they are two fountains, from which whoever draws, when and as much as he needs, whether city, man, or beast, is very fortunate. The first is to be taken medicinally and upon necessity, and more scantily; the other for thirst, but not to, drunkenness. Pain, pleasure, love and hatred are the first things that a child is sensible of: if, when reason comes, they apply it to themselves, that is virtue.

I have a special vocabulary of my own; I "pass away time," when it is ill and uneasy, but when it is good I do not pass it away: "I taste it over again and adhere to it"; one must run over the ill and settle upon the good. This ordinary phrase of pastime, and passing away the time, represents the usage of those wise sort of people who think they cannot do better with their lives than to let them run out and slide away, pass them over, and baulk them, and, as much as they can, ignore them and shun them as a thing of troublesome and contemptible quality: but I know it to be another kind of thing, and find it both valuable and commodious, even in its latest decay, wherein I now enjoy it; and nature has delivered it into our hands in such and so favourable circumstances that we have only ourselves to blame if it be troublesome to us, or escapes us unprofitably:

Stulti vita ingrata est, trepida est, tota in futurum fertur.

[The life of a fool is thankless, timorous, and wholly bent upon the future.

—Seneca, *Epistles*, 15.]

Nevertheless I compose myself to lose mine without regret; but withal as a thing that is perishable by its condition, not that it molests or annoys me. Nor does it properly well become any not to be displeased when they die, excepting such as are pleased to live. There is good husbandry in enjoying it: I enjoy it double to what others do; for the measure of its fruition depends upon our more or less application to it. Chiefly that I perceive mine to be so short in time, I desire to extend it in weight; I will stop the promptitude of its flight by the promptitude of my grasp; and by the vigour of using it compensate the speed of its running away. In proportion as the possession of life is more short, I must make it so much deeper and fuller.

Others feel the pleasure of content and prosperity; I feel it too, as well as they, but not as it passes and slips by; one should study, taste, and ruminate upon it to render condign thanks to Him who grants it to us. They enjoy the other pleasures as they do that of sleep, without knowing it. To the end that even sleep itself should not so stupidly escape from me, I have formerly caused myself to be disturbed in my sleep, so that I might the better and more sensibly relish and taste it. I ponder with myself of content; I do not skim over, but sound it; and I bend my reason, now grown perverse and peevish, to entertain it. Do I find myself in any calm composedness? is there any pleasure that tickles me? I do not suffer it to dally with my senses only; I associate my soul to it too: not there to engage itself, but therein to take delight; not there to lose itself, but to be

present there; and I employ it, on its part, to view itself in this prosperous state, to weigh and appreciate its happiness and to amplify it.
It reckons how much it stands indebted to God that its conscience
and the intestine passions are in repose; that it has the body in its
natural disposition, orderly and competently enjoying the soft and
soothing functions by which He, of His grace is pleased to compensate the sufferings wherewith His justice at His good pleasure chas-
tises us. It reflects how great a benefit it is to be so protected, that
which way soever it turns its eye the heavens are calm around it. No
desire, no fear, no doubt, troubles the air; no difficulty, past, present,
or to, come, that its imagination may not pass over without offence.
This consideration takes great lustre from the comparison of different conditions. So it is that I present to my thought, in a thousand
aspects, those whom fortune or their own error carries away and torments. And, again, those who, more like to me, so negligently and
incuriously receive their good fortune. Those are folks who spend
their time indeed; they pass over the present and that which they
possess, to wait on hope, and for shadows and vain images which
fancy puts before them:

> *Morte obita quales fama est volitare figuras,*
> *Aut quae sopitos deludunt somnia sensus:*

> [Such forms as those which after death are reputed to hover
> about, or dreams which delude the senses in sleep.
> —*Aeneid*, x. 641.]

which hasten and prolong their flight, according as they are pursued. The fruit and end of their pursuit is to pursue; as Alexander
said, that the end of his labour was to labour:

> *Nil actum credens, cum quid superesset agendum.*

CHAPTER 13

[Thinking nothing done, if anything remained to be done.
—Lucan, ii. 657.]

For my part then, I love life and cultivate it, such as it has pleased God to bestow it upon us. I do not desire it should be without the necessity of eating and drinking; and I should think it a not less excusable failing to wish it had been twice as long;

Sapiens divitiarum naturalium quaesitor acerrimus:

[A wise man is the keenest seeker for natural riches.
—Seneca, *Epistles*, 119.]

nor that we should support ourselves by putting only a little of that drug into our mouths, by which Epimenides took away his appetite and kept himself alive; nor that we should stupidly beget children with our fingers or heels, but rather; with reverence be it spoken, that we might voluptuously beget them with our fingers and heels; nor that the body should be without desire and without titillation. These are ungrateful and wicked complaints. I accept kindly, and with gratitude, what nature has done for me; am well pleased with it, and proud of it. A man does wrong to that great and omnipotent giver to refuse, annul, or disfigure his gift: all goodness himself, he has made everything good:

Omnia quae secundum naturam sunt, aestimatione digna sunt.

[All things that are according to nature are worthy of esteem.
—Cicero, *De Finibus*, iii. 6.]

Of philosophical opinions, I preferably embrace those that are most solid, that is to say, the most human and most our own: my discourse is, suitable to my manners, low and humble: philosophy plays the child, to my thinking, when it puts itself upon its Ergos to preach to us that it is a barbarous alliance to marry the divine with the earthly, the reasonable with the unreasonable, the severe with the indulgent, the honest with the dishonest. That pleasure is a brutish quality, unworthy to be tasted by a wise man; that the sole pleasure he extracts from the enjoyment of a fair young wife is a pleasure of his conscience to perform an action according to order, as to put on his boots for a profitable journey. Oh, that its followers had no more right, nor nerves, nor vigour in getting their wives' maidenheads than in its lesson.

This is not what Socrates says, who is its master and ours: he values, as he ought, bodily pleasure; but he prefers that of the mind as having more force, constancy, facility, variety, and dignity. This, according to him, goes by no means alone – he is not so fantastic – but only it goes first; temperance with him is the moderatrix, not the adversary of pleasure. Nature is a gentle guide, but not more sweet and gentle than prudent and just.

> *Intrandum est in rerum naturam, et penitus,*
> *quid eapostulet, pervidendum.*

[A man must search into the nature of things, and fully examine what she requires.

—Cicero, *De Finibus*, V. 16.]

I hunt after her foot throughout: we have confounded it with artificial traces; and that academic and peripatetic good, which is "to live according to it," becomes on this account hard to limit and explain; and that of the Stoics, neighbour to it, which is "to consent to nature." Is it not an error to esteem any actions less worthy, because they are necessary? And yet they will not take it out of my head, that it is not a very convenient marriage of pleasure with necessity, with which, says an ancient, the gods always conspire. To what end do we dismember by divorce a building united by so close and brotherly a correspondence? Let us, on the contrary, confirm it by mutual offices; let the mind rouse and quicken the heaviness of the body, and the body stay and fix the levity of the soul:

Qui, velut summum bonum, Laudat animac naturam, et, tanquam malum, naturam carnis accusat, profectd et animam carnatiter appetit, et carnem carnaliter fugit; quoniam id vanitate sentit humans, non veritate divina.

[He who commends the nature of the soul as the supreme good, and condemns the nature of the flesh as evil, at once both carnally desires the soul, and carnally flies the flesh, because he feels thus from human vanity, not from divine truth.

—St. Augustin, *De Civitate Dei*, xiv. 5.]

In this present that God has made us, there is nothing unworthy our care; we stand accountable for it even to a hair; and is it not a commission to man, to conduct man according to his condition; it is express, plain, and the very principal one, and the Creator has seriously and strictly prescribed it to us. Authority has power only to work in regard to matters of common judgment, and is of more weight in a foreign language; therefore let us again charge at it in this place:

Stultitiae proprium quis non dixerit, ignave et contumaciter facere, quae facienda sunt; et alio corpus impellere, alio animum; distrahique inter diversissimos motus?

[Who will not say, that it is the property of folly, slothfully and contumaciously to perform what is to be done, and to bend the body one way and the mind another, and to be distracted between wholly different motions?

—Seneca, *Epistles*, 74.]

To make this apparent, ask any one, some day, to tell you what whimsies and imaginations he put into his pate, upon the account of which he diverted his thoughts from a good meal, and regrets the time he spends in eating; you will find there is nothing so insipid in all the dishes at your table as this wise meditation of his (for the most part we had better sleep than wake to the purpose we wake); and that his discourses and notions are not worth the worst mess there. Though they were the ecstasies of Archimedes himself, what then? I do not here speak of, nor mix with the rabble of us ordinary men, and the vanity of the thoughts and desires that divert us, those venerable souls, elevated by the ardour of devotion and religion, to a constant and conscientious meditation of divine things, who, by the energy of vivid and vehement hope, prepossessing the use of the eternal nourishment, the final aim and last step of Christian desires, the sole constant, and incorruptible pleasure, disdain to apply themselves to our necessitous, fluid, and ambiguous conveniences, and easily resign to the body the care and use of sensual and temporal pasture; it is a privileged study. Between ourselves, I have ever observed supercelestial opinions and subterranean manners to be of singular accord.

Aesop, that great man, saw his master piss as he walked: "What then," said he, "must we drop as we run?" Let us manage our time; there yet remains a great deal idle and ill employed. The mind has not willingly other hours enough wherein to do its business, without disassociating itself from the body, in that little space it must have for its necessity. They would put themselves out of themselves, and escape from being men. It is folly; instead of transforming themselves into angels, they transform themselves into beasts; instead of elevating, they lay themselves lower. These transcendental humours affright me, like high and inaccessible places; and nothing is hard for me to digest in the life of Socrates but his ecstasies and communication with demons; nothing so human in Plato as that for which they say he was called divine; and of our sciences, those seem to be the most terrestrial and low that are highest mounted; and I find nothing so humble and mortal in the life of Alexander as his fancies about his immortalisation. Philotas pleasantly quipped him in his answer; he congratulated him by letter concerning the oracle of Jupiter Ammon, which had placed him amongst the gods: "Upon thy account I am glad of it, but the men are to be pitied who are to live with a man, and to obey him, who exceeds and is not contented with the measure of a man:"

Diis to minorem quod geris, imperas.

[Because thou carriest thyself lower than the gods, thou rulest.
—Horace, *Odes*, iii. 6, 5.]

The pretty inscription wherewith the Athenians honoured the entry of Pompey into their city is conformable to my sense: "By so much thou art a god, as thou confessest thee a man." It is an absolute and, as it were, a divine perfection, for a man to know how loyally to enjoy his being. We seek other conditions, by reason we do not understand the use of our own; and go out of ourselves, because we know not how there to reside. It is to much purpose to go upon stilts, for, when upon stilts, we must yet walk with our legs; and when seated upon the most elevated throne in the world, we are but seated upon our breech. The fairest lives, in my opinion, are those which regularly accommodate themselves to the common and human model without miracle, without extravagance. Old age stands a little in need of a more gentle treatment. Let us recommend that to God, the protector of health and wisdom, but let it be gay and sociable:

Frui paratis et valido mihi
Latoe, dones, et precor, integra

Cum mente; nec turpem senectam
Degere, nec Cithara carentem.

[Grant it to me, Apollo, that I may enjoy my possessions in good health; let me be sound in mind; let me not lead a dishonourable old age, nor want the cittern.

—Horace, *Odes*, i. 31, 17.]

Or:

[Grant it to me, Apollo, that I may enjoy what I have in good health; let me be sound in body and mind; let me live in honour when old, nor let music be wanting.]